Books by Herbert S. Parmet

Richard Nixon and His America (1990)
Two Hundred Years of Looking Ahead: The Bank of New York (1984)
Jack: The Struggles of John F. Kennedy (1980)
JFK: The Presidency of John F. Kennedy (1983)
The Democrats: The Years After FDR (1976)
Eisenhower and the American Crusades (1972)
Never Again: A President Runs for a Third Term (1968)
Aaron Burr: Portrait of an Ambitious Man (1967)

GEORGE BUSH

The Life of a Lone Star Yankee

❧

HERBERT S. PARMET

A LISA DREW BOOK

SCRIBNER

A LISA DREW BOOK/SCRIBNER
1230 Avenue of the Americas
New York, NY 10020

Set in New Baskerville
Designed by Colin Joh

Manufactured in the United States of America

1 3 5 7 9 10 8 6 4 2

Library of Congress Cataloging-in Publication Data

Parmet, Herbert S.
George Bush: the life of a lonestar Yankee/Herbert S. Parmet.
p.   cm.
Includes bibliographical references and index.
1. Bush, George, 1924–   . 2. Presidents—United States—Biography. I. Title.
E882.P37   1997
973.928'092—dc21   97–33616
[B]   CIP

ISBN 0-684-19452-X

*For
Anna Parmet Lanoue and Gladys Gold
and to the memory of
Minna Scharf
and my grandparents
Osias and Molly Scharf*

Acknowledgments

※

This work, six years in the making, could not have been done without the active assistance and cooperation of a small army of people who either permitted themselves to be interviewed—sometimes repeatedly—gave me access to relevant documents, or both. Others were there when I needed advice and criticism. Among those to whom I owe many thanks are: Elliott Abrams, Kenneth Adelman, Phillip Allen, Martin Anderson, David Ashbrook, Thomas Ludlow Ashley, James Addison Baker III, Catherine Barr, David Bates, Michael Beschloss, Richard Bond, Richard Burris, former President George Bush, Barbara Bush, George W. Bush, Prescott Bush Jr., Andrew Card Jr., Dick Cheney, Alexander Chodaczek Jr., James Cicconi, the Reverend William Sloane Coffin, William Colby, Barber Conable, Charles J. Cooper, Earle Craig, Frank DiClemente, Ronnie Dugger, Nancy Bush Ellis, William R. Emerson, M. Marlin Fitzwater, former president Gerald R. Ford, Craig Fuller, Robert Furhman, Mary Sheila Gall, Dan Gilchrist, Victor Gold, Roy Goodearle, C. Boyden Gray, Lanny Griffith, Linda Hansen, Marie B. Hecht, Richard L. Herman, Clyde Heron, Seymour Hersh, Bobby Holt, Fred Israel, Molly Ivins, Michael Jackson, Kathleen Hall Jamieson, Rudolph F. Juedeman, Ronald C. Kaufman, David Keene, William Kristol, Florence Lawless, Hart Day Leavitt, Burton Lee III, Hugh Liedtke, Arthur Link, Nelda Lee, George Marlin, Simon Middleton, Robert A. Mosbacher, Brian Mulroney, Daniel J. Murphy, former President Richard M. Nixon, Kirk O'Donnell, Joan K. Parmet, James P. Pfiffner, James Pinkerton, Richard Pipes, W. Robert Plumlee, Roger Porter, Colin Powell, Ray Price, Dan Quayle, Condolleeza Rice, Peter Roussel, William Rusher, Brent Scowcroft, Glenn Speer, Jack Steel, John Sununu, Peter Teeley, Chase Untermeyer, Guy Vander Jagt, Elliott Vose, Louis Walker, George U. Warren, Ralph Yarborough, and Rose Zamaria.

I was also helped by the staffs at various branches of the City University of New York, especially those at Queensborough Community College and the Graduate School. Living and working in Columbia County, it was of particular value to have the services of Simon's Rock College of Bard in Great Barrington, Massachusetts, and of my own community library in Hillsdale, New York, which never missed supplying what I needed. David Alsobrook of the

Bush Presidential Materials Project at College Station, Texas, cooperated in every way possible.

Many of the essential steps would not have been possible without the cooperation of those at the Office of George Bush, especially his wonderful chief of staff, Jean Becker. Many requests were also handled by Michael Dannenhauer, Quincy Hicks, Jim McGrath, Susie Peake, Laura Pears, Linda Poepsel, Don Rhodes, and Mary Sage, working out of both Houston and Kennebunkport.

Former President Bush himself responded by graciously granting no-strings-attached access for interviews and documentary material. My complete freedom to shape the biography is deeply appreciated. It says a great deal about the character of the man and leaves me with total responsibility for the outcome.

At Scribner, long before President Bush cooperated, the project got its start thanks to the initial confidence shown by Bill Goldstein. Lisa Drew then contributed her enormous editorial talents. I quickly learned the hazards of ignoring her suggestions. Working with her turned out to be a marvelous cure for complacency.

My long-time literary representative, Timothy Seldes, of Russell and Volkening, saw the work through its various stages, providing encouragement and essential assistance at key points.

Contents

%

GEORGE BUSH

The Life of a Lone Star Yankee

Prologue

%

Walker's Point is little more than a rock pile jutting into the Atlantic, one of those vulnerable but picturesque fingers of land along that stretch of New England shoreline. North of the beach and sheltered from the view of tourists on the roadway above the cliff that separates the Point from the rest of the world stands a solitary fisherman, tall and engagingly lean at seventy-one. He casts his reel against the stiff onshore breezes, hoping for more of those striped bass that have been replacing cunners and pollock. "There's no way to describe the excitement I feel when a bass hits the lure or when a sixteen-pound bluefish hits my surface plug," he tells a reporter.[1]

He turns away, stepping nimbly from rock to rock and back to the path, past the new sauna, the swimming pool, and the tennis courts. Time to return to his study, where a visitor awaits. He walks up the flight of steps to what he jokingly calls his "Oval Office," located right above the postpresidential staff's headquarters. He has all he needs: a telephone, laptop computer, fax machine, and a combination television and video cassette recorder. A VHS tape of the 1947 Dodger-Yankee World Series has just come in. He demonstrates the gadget by scrolling through the reel to find a still shot of that year's Yale baseball squad. Could his visitor pick him out from among those players leaning toward the camera from the dugout steps? No problem. One of the world's more familiar faces looked little different forty-eight years ago. Handsome, clean-cut, smooth as only a twenty-three-year-old's can be. He is the first baseman and captain of the team, the club that made it to the College World Series. Fast-forwarding the machine, he locates what he had really been looking for, a picture of himself with Babe Ruth. The Babe is handing him the original manuscript of his autobiography. He is donating it to the Yale library, and presenting it to the team captain, George Herbert Walker Bush.

Turning away from the VCR, he talks baseball in that little Oval Office; mostly trivia, team records, batting records, who did what, when, and where.

Bush says that one of his more memorable days in the White House was when he had both Ted Williams and Joe DiMaggio in to present them with Distinguished Service awards.

He and his visitor go out to walk along the path. Grandchildren are plainly visible, one busily buckling up catcher's shinguards. How many kids around the place? he's asked. "Four," he says, at least at that moment. A full complement of family that he likes to gather together every August totals twenty-three.

George Bush was as much at home at Kennebunkport as the bluefish that swim in the surrounding waters. Wait until you see him in Maine, said his sister, "then you'll see the real George." Off with the formal clothes, the suit, tie, and white shirt, and into cotton pants, a knit shirt, jogging shoes, and a windbreaker.[2] He and Barbara could really roam on the peninsula's ten acres.

He seemed to cling to the place almost defiantly. It was his little world wherever else he happened to be. He savored the swift-changing tides that perpetually shift the shoreline. "The New England side of him is replenished by Walker's Point," said an old friend. "It really is out of a Thomas Hardy novel, the setting and all. Nothing else could satisfy that part of him."[3] Bush himself, for all his efforts to transform himself into a Texan, never did overcome Walker's Point as the sine qua non of his existence. "We were . . . never happier," he later wrote, "than when we crammed into the station wagon each summer . . . to visit Walker's Point in Kennebunkport, Maine."[4] He never got over the days when *Tomboy*, his grandfather's lobster boat, would take them out after the small mackerel and pollock, in those days before the bluefish had returned to the coast. "For pure summertime pleasure, bringing one in, especially a green beauty, ranked right up there with eating ice cream and staying up late."[5]

Into that scene, appropriately, enters Barbara Bush. She is proud of the gardens, the entire layout, all the way from the building at the farthest point, the one where the fury of a hurricane sent waves rolling over the roof and swept much of the structure out to sea. Mrs. Bush, or Bar, as he calls her, wants the visitor to see the garden. She's proud of three things that morning: the marvelous royalty check that recently arrived for the spectacular success of her memoirs, her flower beds, and the little springer spaniel, Millie, the "author" of one of Barbara's three best-sellers. She created the garden herself; of course, over a period of time. She also shows off a handy gadget called The Claw that George bought for her seventieth birthday. He saw it advertised while watching a commercial on CNN. And it really works. She grabs the handle, straightens the shaft, and digs its four metal claws into the ground. Up comes a whole clump of earth, and in just one twist. A great buy for $19.95. She walks away toward the motorized cart, off to play golf, just as son Neil drives by with his wife and slows down enough to say hello to his parents. Then he speeds off across the grounds of the point.

The former president is clearly at home. Workers seem to be everywhere along the grounds, some obviously laborers, others in casual office getups. One can hardly distinguish relatives from staff or Secret Service personnel. Bush stops to chat as he passes by. They answer, hardly looking up from their chores. They're obviously accustomed to the camaraderie and seem unimpressed by their boss's fame.

So is he.

"Yeah," says the former president with a big smile. "I guess you can write that I *am* glad to be here instead of in the White House."

Only a joke. He assumes the visitor understands.

CHAPTER ONE

Down East

%

T he Bushes were English, which, to some, meant ipso facto aristocracy; in their case, their ancestry was arguably traceable to rulers of old. Whatever the democratic pretense, there are always those eager to tie any American president to the appropriate lineage. When Burke's Peerage Ltd., the 162-year-old directory that had made a sport out of linking American presidents to the British Crown, weighed in with the thought that George Bush was about to become the "most royal" of American presidents, it seemed entirely credible. That notion, however, could not have been more poorly timed, coming as it did at the outset of his campaign for the presidency—a potential embarrassment for a transplanted New Englander who had long since become a Texan. But Bush, insisted Burke's, came from a "typical old Yankee family."[1]

Little was more natural, according to Burke's, than for American presidents to spring from British royalty, and in George Bush they found the most authentic product. His pedigree could be traced back to at least the fourteenth century, which made him a thirteenth cousin of Queen Elizabeth II and a kin of the entire royal family. Considering the intermarriages of European royalty, that meant that he carried the genes of other current European rulers, on or off the throne.[2]

In the New World, the Bush heritage represented the mergers of well-established families. George's maternal ancestors, the Walkers, who were early arrivals in America, settled on the coast of Maine in the seventeenth century before moving on to Maryland and St. Louis, which became central to their Midwestern dry goods business. Devout Catholics, they named the man who became George Bush's maternal grandfather after a seventeenth-century poet and Anglican priest, George Herbert. Their religion also left them dissatisfied with Catholic schools in Missouri, so they sent their son to study in England, an effort at spiritual purity that, in the long run, proved inadequate.

When George returned, his eye was set on the woman the family has remembered as "the most beautiful girl in America." Lucretia Wear's attractions had already drawn the favors of Conde Nast, the developer of a magazine publishing empire, so George figured there was no time to dawdle. Winning her hand was easier than mollifying his parents. Lucretia was Presbyterian, "the biggest Christian that ever lived," remembered one of her sons. She didn't move without her Bible. The staunchly Catholic Walkers "wouldn't have anything to do with it," said a grandson, Louis. "They were really bigoted Catholics. They cut him off just like that. They left everything to the Catholic Church." George Herbert and Lucretia did not even have stock in the family business, Ely Walker & Company. One compromise was struck: two wedding ceremonies, one in each church. "So," as their granddaughter, Nancy Bush Ellis, later recalled, "my grandmother had her way with church twice a day, no cards on Sunday, no movies. We didn't have that in the summer at Walker's Point, either, while growing up. No dice on Sundays. We could play checkers, but no backgammon. We could play anagrams, but not 'twenty-one.' No chips; we couldn't play poker."[3]

Their Puritanism can be traced back to Scotland before the English Civil War and Oliver Cromwell. In America, the Bush heritage intertwined with some of the great landowning families of colonial New York and New England. One descendant, James Smith Bush, George Bush's great grandfather, came out of that stock. Smith married Harriet Fay of Boston and, after living for a time in New Jersey, settled for life as an Episcopal clergyman on New York's Staten Island. Their son, Samuel Prescott Bush, may properly be said to have been the family's modern "founding father." In Samuel can be found the seeds of much that characterized his descendants.

Samuel was gifted and energetic, an athlete as well as melodic in voice. Born in Orange, New Jersey, on October 4, 1863, he left his parents behind in Staten Island when, at the age of seventeen, he crossed the Kill Van Kull and went a few miles north to the Stevens Institute of Technology. There, taking up his residency at 427 Garden Street in Hoboken, he majored in mechanical engineering. Of Bush's prominence in the class, there seems little doubt. He held the student vice presidency during his sophomore year and was an active athlete. He was on both the baseball and tennis teams and directed the Stevens Athletic Association. He also displayed vocal talents, a trait that found its way into later generations of Bushes. Sam Bush sang baritone in the Glee Club and first bass in the Crescent Glee Club. He even joined the Stevens Whist Club.[4]

Upon his graduation in 1884, he went to work for the Pennsylvania Railroad, a position that brought him to Columbus, Ohio. It was there, in 1894, that he married a twenty-two-year-old local woman, Flora Sheldon, the daughter of a dry goods merchant and bank officer. Her dowry included some of the purist blood that enriched early American gentry. An ancestor was the first Robert R. Livingston, the Puritan dissenter who left Scotland after the Stuart restoration and made his way to America in 1673. She and

Samuel raised four children before she was run over by a car and killed in 1920 at the age of forty-eight. Bush waited five years before marrying again, this time to Martha Bell of Milwaukee. She was "Aunt Martha" to his grand-children, a nice companion for the widower, one who fitted in completely with his life, but was remembered as "kind of a drag."[5] Even if she did not have the same stature, "Aunt Martha" replaced Flora in leading a luxurious life as the wife of a prominent industrialist.

Samuel, a Democrat in Ohio politics, did well for himself, active in certain ways that, except for his partisan affiliation, anticipated his son Prescott's later activities. From Milwaukee, for two years, he worked as general superinten-dent of the Chicago, Milwaukee, and St. Paul Railroad Company. He returned to Columbus and became associated with several railroad supply companies that later became Buckeye Steel Castings, a connection that lasted some two decades. He served as its president from 1905 until he retired in 1927. The company manufactured railway car equipment, supplying, among other things, bolsters and couplers for freight cars. Samuel's credentials as an industrialist and railroad man, however, were enhanced by his numerous directorships, which included the Pennsylvania's lines west of Pittsburgh, the old Hocking Valley Railway, the Norfolk and Western Railway, and the Huntington National Bank. A mover in both the Ohio Manufacturers Asso-ciation and the Ohio Chamber of Commerce, Samuel was placed at the head of relief activities by Columbus's mayor during the disastrous flood of 1913. He has been credited with two contributions to the American war effort after the U.S. became a belligerent in 1917, the organization of the first war chest drive and, at the request of Bernard M. Baruch, service in Wash-ington with the War Industries Board, where he headed the facilities and forg-ings divisions. Later, in 1939, he began the Ohio Tax League, and so took his place at the head of a diligent group of outstanding citizens devoted to safe-guarding their property from confiscatory taxation. He became the first president of the National Association of Manufacturers, a group that became synonymous with industrial conservatism, and was also a charter member of the United States Chamber of Commerce. Grandfather Bush was, according to Nancy, "a high-minded, impressive, wonderful-looking person," who, along the way, began a golf course that became Jack Nicklaus's first training ground.[6] He also organized the first rugby football team west of the Alleghe-nies as well as the first baseball league and tennis clubs in Columbus.[7]

He built a big country house at Bexley, just outside of Columbus, which was known for its exquisite gardens. Lavish as well as large, it has since been extended to function as a nursing home. Samuel's mansion clearly gave him a great deal of pleasure. He had a love for landscaping that was not shared by his son Prescott, who "didn't know a rose from a peony."[8] The old man died on February 8, 1948, at the age of eighty-three.

Prescott, who was born to Samuel and Flora on May 15, 1895, later recounted impressions formed as a boy in Columbus. He remembered that

Douglas, his public school, was somewhat of a "melting pot." "We had a very large Negro population. We had a very large German population. In fact," he explained, "we had representatives of most every ethnic group in the public school, and I always felt that this gave me a sense of balance about those ethnic problems that was useful to me in later life, and particularly in political life."[9]

Samuel took appropriate care of his children's education, sending them all east to boarding school, the girls to Westover in Connecticut, and the boys to St. George's in Newport, Rhode Island. Summers were spent at a popular gathering place for their peers, Watch Hill. St. George's was affiliated with the Episcopal Church and had about 125 boys. It made a great impression on Prescott, and he made the most of it, doing well both in his studies and on the playing field, where he was active in such sports as basketball and football. Baseball was his major game, and he was the team's first baseman. He was, in fact, one of those all-around students, engaging in a campus debating society as well as acting and singing (which later included participation in Yale's Glee Club and the Whiffenpoof Society).[10] Long after his schooling, Prescott enjoyed singing with a choir, especially as bass with a member of such informal choral groups as the Silver Dollar Quartet and the Kensington Four. They all made the rounds with performances at various Bush homes.[11]

Prescott liked to credit St. George's with reaffirming his father's teaching "that public service would be a wonderful thing to participate in," which emphasized the sort of moral questions that held that "it was one's duty to participate in it, to the extent that one possibly could."[12] Even years later, one of George Bush's fellow prep school athletes spoke with feeling about how the boys were instilled with the lesson that, above all, "one was a good sport, winning or losing, you were supposed to do things gracefully." One was supposed to win, but "it isn't supposed to show."[13] Young Prescott, already a schoolboy golf champion in Ohio, worked as a caddy on the course at Watch Hill while at St. George's, which inadvertently stimulated his interest in the theater by bringing him into contact with one of Hollywood's leading men, Douglas Fairbanks.[14]

Amassing great wealth on his own was not one of Prescott's priorities, at least while at St. George's, where he contemplated following in the footsteps of his minister grandfather. Later, at Yale, his thoughts turned to law as preparation for politics.

Europe was caught up in the Great War of 1914 to 1918. In Washington, President Woodrow Wilson walked a fine line between aiding the Allies and preserving American neutrality, all the time taking credit in his reelection campaign for having "kept America out of war." That was true about the fighting in Europe, but Americans in 1916 were even more watchful of military activity along their border with Mexico.

A series of events that began with the overthrow of a Mexican dictator brought to the forefront peasant leader Emiliano Zapata, a revolutionary agrarian reformer. By 1916, Zapata's forces had become allied with guerrilla bandit Pancho Villa to overthrow the new government led by Venustiano Carranza, whom Wilson grudgingly endorsed after withholding recognition from the revolutionaries. With Zapata and Villa both trying to overthrow Carranza, the objective of the Mexican insurgents was to draw the Americans into the chaos as a way of achieving their goal. That March, dramatic news came from just north of the border when fifteen hundred Mexicans invaded American soil and attacked a town in New Mexico, burning buildings and killing nineteen U.S. civilians. Wilson, his hand forced, ordered General John J. Pershing to retaliate by pursuing Villa's men, a thrust that took the punitive expedition five hundred miles below the Rio Grande. The Americans, both intruders in the Mexican revolution as well as invaders, were embarrassed and bloodied when opposed by civilians and Carranza's soldiers. Humiliated, Pershing's army retreated to U.S. soil.

The students at New Haven watched all that, perhaps more keenly than the events in Europe. They even formed a "Yale Battalion" within the Connecticut National Guard. Young Bush became a private and spent three summer months taking field training at Tobyhanna, Pennsylvania. The group, which numbered some four hundred men equipped with four batteries of field artillery, never did get to Mexico. Yale's president, trying to get the students back to campus for the opening of the fall semester, intervened with the War Department, and Bush returned to New Haven for his senior year. The training paid off, however, because Bush was immediately commissioned as a captain of field artillery in the regular army when the United States entered the European war. He got to France late, over a year after Congress went along with Wilson's request for a declaration of war, and served on the front for about ten or eleven weeks, coming under fire during the Meuse-Argonne offensive. "It was quite exciting, and of course a wonderful experience," he later said, even while conceding that his record was not "particularly distinguished."[15]

Prescott's recorded reminiscences, given in 1966, presents, somewhat disingenuously, a hint of genteel poverty, undoubtedly a habit cultivated by one who had spent the bulk of his previous two decades canvassing for votes among ordinary people. To deny the realities of his background, the stature of his father as a leading industrialist of his day, was consistent with perpetuating the myth of the self-made man. Prescott had been a U.S. senator from Connecticut at the time he gave the interview and was practiced at minimizing his pedigree. He claimed that his father did not have enough money to put him through law school, a notion of financial limitations not only at variance with his career and lifestyle but one also strongly rejected by those who knew anything about him.[16] So, as he told the interviewer about Samuel Bush, "He had a modest income, but he couldn't support his adult children, and I didn't want him to anyway. So that is why I abandoned the law, and decided, I'll defer this public thing until maybe some other chance would develop."[17] Why Prescott rejected law can be attributed to a variety of reasons, but certainly none associated with impecuniousness. As Nancy later said, "I know Dad always said he never took a cent from his father after he got out of college, but I really don't think it was because Grandfather didn't have the money."[18]

Prescott then followed a classmate's recommendation and took a position with the Simmons Hardware Company of St. Louis. The company had warehouses in such places as Wichita, Minneapolis, and Philadelphia, where Prescott was assigned at various times to train for a future managerial role. One assignment in 1922 involved going to Kingsport, Tennessee, to sell "a big piece of property down there which had been built to make saddlery during the war, but which was antiquated because saddlery was going out as fast as automobiles were coming in, so this plant had to be sold." His advice to sell furthered Prescott's reputation for fiscal acumen. He lived there for about three months until the plant was bought by the Winchester Repeating Arms Company of New Haven. By then, he had already taken a wife, Dorothy, the daughter of George Herbert and Lucreta (Louly) Wear Walker.[19] They had met in St. Louis during the autumn of 1919, became engaged the next summer, and married on August 6, 1921, shortly after the death of his mother, Flora. Dorothy's response to that tragedy was to fill the vacuum left in Prescott's emotions.

Dorothy Walker was an accomplished young woman, endowed with the virtues of one of her class. "It was a simple opulent world into which Dotty Walker was born just after the turn of the century," wrote a local journalist much later.[20] Her role included serving as the family's spiritual conscience, making certain that Sunday services at the Episcopal Church were not neglected. Scriptures were freely quoted over the breakfast table.[21]

She was the young female on the pedestal, about to be showcased for society, a graduate of private schools in St. Louis and Miss Porter's back east in Farmington, Connecticut; and, appropriately, also known for her grace as an athlete. An excellent, hard-driving tennis player, she was runner-up in the Girl's National Tournament of 1918. Her athleticism was always admired, even as she grew older. The story is still told about how, at the age of thirty-nine, she was brought in by the golf pro at the Forest Hills Tennis Club to play an exhibition match at the field club against Jadwiga Jedrzejowska. The Polish star had just lost out in the U.S. Open to Anita Lizana the year the championship was won by Alice Marble. Dorothy, only recently a mother for the fifth and final time, with the birth of Bucky, actually took one set.[22] Another favorite family anecdote, considerably more embellished, involves her first pregnancy. Although in her ninth month, with Prescott Bush Jr. on the way, so the story goes, she played in one of the usual family baseball games. As her children later liked to tell it, she hit a home run on her last time at bat during a softball game, ran around the bases to score her run, and then announced she was in labor and that it was time to go to the hospital, where, on that day, her first child was born. That the game was played sometime before she actually went into labor, and that it was played within the narrow confines between the back of the Kennebunkport house and the sea where, in the words of the son who was born soon afterward, "a home run was no big deal," hardly matters.[23]

Mother was legendary. And, as with all legends, truth is often impossible to differentiate from fiction. One reason was her characteristic disdain for self-importance, a trait she worked to pass on to her children. Once, when George told her he had lost a tennis match because his game had been off, she responded with, "You don't have a game."[24] Even much later, she monitored his manners and display of ego. When he was vice president, she admonished him for bad manners when he appeared to be reading while President Reagan was giving a speech, rejecting his explanation that he was merely following the printed text. George himself told some of those around him about her complaints that he tended to "talk about himself too much."[25]

A few days before Dorothy died in 1992, Nancy explained that "Mother is not much on houses and decorating. She didn't care about all that. That was an unimportant thing to her in her life. She wouldn't be in the Social Register." But she was, as her daughter added, "a wonderful horsewoman."[26] Her education ended on the tennis courts and in the school for young women in Connecticut, for those were the days when protective parents of socially prominent girls were likely to consider higher education "unladylike." Her father, George Herbert Walker, even thought it indelicate for Dorothy to pose for pictures. She was, after all, in training as a lady, and being cultivated for presentation to society as a debutante.[27]

Grandfather Walker's fortune was built on money from his father, David, whose wholesale dry goods business, the Ely Walker Company, prospered in the Middle West. The younger Walker went to New York in 1919 to set up what became one of the country's largest investment banking firms. His name is now mainly associated with his sponsorship of the Walker Cup for golf. Along with David, Grandfather Walker built a summer home on the rocky shoreline of Maine at Kennebunkport, where, at the Church of St. Ann in the summer of 1921, his daughter married Prescott.

Prescott lived in Columbus with his bride while working for his father. Buckeye had taken over a small floor covering firm, Hupp Products. Hupp, as it turned out, was an unfortunate venture. Its management was corrupt; its founder eventually went to jail. Prescott, given the responsibility, labored to salvage the operation, but it failed within a year, then sold for whatever was left of its value to Stedman Products. That changed Prescott's life forever. The Stedman company, which pioneered the development of rubber floor tiling, was located in South Braintree, Massachusetts. That took the Bushes to the Boston area. They found a Victorian house at 173 Adams Street in nearby Milton, some nine miles south of the suburban town of Brookline. Bush, whose sojourn in Milton lasted only about two years, formally listed his occupation as a "rubber manufacturer" on his son George's birth certificate.

* * *

While they were still in Kingsport, he and Dorothy had their first child in 1922, Prescott Junior. Bush, then twenty-nine, and Dorothy at twenty-three, became parents for a second time on June 12, 1924, after relocating to Milton. They adhered to their agreement and named the child after his maternal grandfather, so he became George Herbert Walker Bush.[28] His father later had second thoughts about that name, especially since Grandfather Walker's sons had begun to call him "Little Pop" and "Poppy" because their father had been known as "Pop." So "Poppy" stuck to little George, and for longer than he cared to remember, following him all the way to adulthood.[29] Two years after George's birth, the Bushes had their only daughter, Nancy. She was followed in 1931 by Jonathan and, in 1938, the family was completed with the birth of William Trotter Bush. Bucky, as he was usually called, was named after Bucky Trotter, a Bush family friend.[30]

Pop and Poppy, together with the rest of the growing family, lasted in Milton only until George was six months old. Prescott's experience with rubber flooring made him an expert in a new industry, and inevitably enhanced his value. Those were, after all, America's years of economic expansion.

With his advancement came a move that improved his own and his family's status. He rose quickly, after briefly managing the flooring department of the U.S. Rubber Company in New York City, and finally joined the investment banking house of W. A. Harriman and Company, just off Wall Street.

The Harriman firm offered a congenial atmosphere. Its president was father-in-law George Herbert Walker. While W. Averell Harriman (as he was known then), then in his thirties, was chairman of the board, his younger brother, Roland, had been a fellow Bonesman of Prescott's at Yale, meaning that both belonged to the college's elite Skull and Bones Society. But he was also, as Bush later explained, "a very intimate friend of mine, so this was one thing. My father-in-law was interested, and he had confidence in me. . . . It was a young, new organization, really, had only been started a few years earlier, and they didn't have any real young fellows just out of college, in their twenties, as I was then."[31] Prescott became a vice-president.

The start of 1931 officially marked the creation of what had long been in the works, a merger with Brown Brothers, the imposing investment house that operated out of the stately marble building on the corner of Hanover Street, virtually a keystone of the financial district. Prescott Bush had, even before the merger, distinguished himself by turning in a formal review of the company enumerating various economies.[32] Now, with the coming of the new year, he found himself among the twelve partners of the new powerhouse firm, Brown Brothers Harriman, which later moved to a thirty-six story building at 59 Wall Street. After George Herbert Walker retired, Prescott began to work at his rolltop desk in the ornate Partner's Room, under a painting of the four original Brown Brothers, along with the two Harrimans and the rest of the gentlemen who ran the firm.[33] Another partner was Robert A. Lovett, who also went on to political prominence.

Within the next three years, Brown Brothers Harriman was able to boast of investments in forty-five different countries. As Walter Isaacson and Evan Thomas have written, the company "financed much of America's imports of metals, raw materials, and foodstuffs," pioneering "a system of letters of credit and bankers' acceptances that eventually involved more than five thousand correspondents around the world."[34]

All that was during the depth of the Great Depression, and Wall Street certainly, and appropriately, felt the reach of New Deal reforms. The Banking Act of 1934 hit Brown Brothers Harriman directly, forcing the separation of commercial banking from investment banking activities. A new firm, Harriman Ripley and Company, was set up for the investment end. Still another merger and an effort to clarify the overlapping of names ultimately forced that to become known as Drexel Harriman Ripley Company.

The administration of Franklin D. Roosevelt also enlisted W. Averell Harriman for the start of what would become a very long and distinguished individual career as a public servant. He went to Washington to work for the short-lived National Recovery Administration. The involvement somewhat embarrassed his firm in the financial district for its association with "the Red bunch of Communists or Socialists," a matter that Harriman's partners would laugh off by saying that "Averell feels he wants to devote some time to the national interest."[35]

Bush, relatively junior during those early New Deal years on Wall Street, was especially responsible for attracting new business. Getting major corporations not only tested his talents and value, but also brought him into close involvement as a member of their directorships. Such associations evolved into a highly respectable and representative segment of the business world, by no means ranking him among the mightiest of moguls, but of sufficient importance to make him a director of such corporations as the Columbia Broadcasting System, the Prudential Insurance Company of America, the Pennsylvania Water & Power Company, the Simmons Company (which made beds and bedding), the United States Guarantee Company, and the Vanadium Corporation of America. One that would become especially significant to his youngest sons was what later became known as Dresser Industries.[36]

It is intriguing to consider how much the life of Prescott Bush's second son turned on circumstances that seemed to leap right out of standard textbooks about the American success story. Solomon R. Dresser, born in a log cabin in 1842 and brought up on a pioneer farm in Michigan, became a noted entrepreneur in the American rise to industrial greatness. Dresser, who had already made money by selling and detonating explosives that had been used during the Civil War, had the instinct to decide that there was an easier way to make his fortune than through oil prospecting, one that offered a better return on his investment.

He came to the town of Bradford in northwest Pennsylvania, just below the border with New York State. Bradford, its initial growth having come from lumber, had been transformed by the region's oil boom in the wake of

Edwin Drake's original gusher. When Dresser arrived in the summer of 1878, fortune hunters were a dime a dozen, all after "black gold." Dresser realized that there was a better, surer way to make money in oil, one that minimized the hazards of prospecting: Dresser would supply the industry with its basic needs.

Dresser's company became a family enterprise with a broad range of supplies for the expanding energy and natural resources markets: pipeline couplings, compressors, drilling and mining equipment, pumps, engines, graders, cranes, hoists, gauges, valves, meters, and gasoline dispensing systems. All fell under the Dresser name by the incremental addition of other pioneering companies that offered technical devices. Known as the Solomon R. Dresser Manufacturing Company by 1905, Sol Dresser himself having become a Republican congressman from Pennsylvania until his death in 1911, it had absorbed numerous producers that specialized in allied fields.[37]

The story of Dresser is one of constant expansion, an upward movement that paralleled the nation's expanding need for energy. By 1918, the company's basic coupling held together some nine thousand miles of pipeline, and growth accelerated through the 1920s. "Dresser Couplings Dominate" was more than a mere advertising slogan. Bringing natural gas through pipelines from West Texas and Oklahoma to Dallas and Fort Worth had already established the company's prominence in an area where, together with the later addition of other units in California, it received a significant boost toward becoming a major corporate giant. By the 1940s, it was considered among the most enterprising oil drilling outfits in the world.[38]

Dresser's significance to the Bush family began in 1928, when its directors decided that further expansion required leaving behind forty-eight years as a family enterprise and raising new capital by the issuance of public stock. They turned to the W. A. Harriman firm for the conversion. The banking firm paid four million for its corporate stock and sold securities against the company. Then, as Prescott Bush later recalled, they refinanced it "so that we retained a substantial measure of control." That was in 1929.[39]

Prescott Bush was directly involved as a Harriman representative in the Dresser reorganization. That, plus his knowledge of its operations, led to his becoming a director in 1930.[40] Another part of the conversion was one suggested by Roland Harriman. H. Neil Mallon, a fellow Yale Bonesman with close family ties to the Tafts of Ohio, and, at the age of thirty-four, further experienced in business through work for the Continental Can Company in Chicago, became Dresser's president and general manager. Thus began the Bush-Mallon relationship.

The family's move to Greenwich, Connecticut, had something less than the full aristocratic flourish. While the community was entirely appropriate for an ambitious financier with a growing family, especially during the halcyon days of the twenties, Prescott and Dorothy were still making their start; and they were doing so with two young children, and Poppy only an infant. In

Greenwich, while Bush had found his home of affluent commuters, he had not settled into a millionaire's hideaway. The outlying countryside did have estates, mostly out along the northern edge. Other than those that skirted a walking distance of downtown and the railroad station, more opulent properties were closer to Long Island South. For recreation, one could hardly do better than the Indian Harbor Yacht Club, which had 345 members, a marina with ninety-six yachts, and, according to a local historian, a place where "afternoon tea was a daily attraction." "Caviar and hot hors d'oeuvres were served with cocktails, and for dinner members could order just about anything, including Scottish grouse, and expect to get it."[41]

In reality, however, the community was bisected, somewhat uncomfortably, by the busy Boston Post Road. The interstates were still many years away and had yet to give private and commercial traffic better alternates between New York City and Boston.

The New Haven Railroad was a lifeline to the great city to the south. Commuters spent years oblivious to the world along the Post Road. Still, when judged by the circumstances under which George spent his later childhood, their first Greenwich home was not imposing, yet large enough for an expanding family. They moved into a five-bedroom stucco home at 11 Stanwich Road when they first arrived.[42] It was there where Nancy was born, while the youngest, Jonathan and William (Bucky), spent their infancies on Grove Lane.

In 1931, the year of Jonathan's birth and of the nation's deepening Depression, the Grove Lane house became Bush property. The lane itself was a short, tree-lined east-west country road that connected Dearfield and Brookside Drives. The house, which was listed on a 1938 property map as belonging to Dorothy Walker Bush, was closer to the Dearfield end and on the highest point at the northern side of a plot of just over two acres.[43] From the nearly three-hundred-foot frontage along Grove Lane, there was a long approach that ended in a circular front driveway. The house, a decided step-up from the one at Stanwich Road, had five bedrooms on the second floor and three more on the third. There were also two studies on that level. Alongside the main building stood a carriage house, which has since become a separate dwelling.[44]

The two oldest children, and the two closest, Pressy and George, continued to share the same bedroom even after the family moved into its new home. "Finally, one year Mother decided," Prescott Jr. recalled, "after we'd been rooming together for several years at Grove Lane, that we ought to each have our own separate bedroom. She gave us the two rooms in the back of the house. There was a bathroom and two bedrooms. The governess had been living in one of them and the other was sort of a playroom. She made them into bedrooms for both of us. That lasted for about two or three months and Christmas came along. Mother asked us what we wanted for Christmas, and we said all we wanted was a room together. So that was that."[45]

CHAPTER TWO

Poppy as Preppy

%

Prescott Bush's way of life resembled the cultural setting one finds in the fiction of John Cheever, the atmosphere of leafy, suburban Connecticut, where "prosperous men and women gathered by the sapphire-colored waters while caterer's men in white coats passed them cold gin."[1] Bush's father would join them on their daily ride from Greenwich to Grand Central Station. "There was the club car," recalled his daughter, Nancy. "It had arm chairs and you could play bridge, but Dad always read the paper and got into a thoroughly gloomy mood." From midtown, he took the subway down to Wall Street, completing a forty-five minute trip, "years and years, all the way. He'd *die* now, with limos picking them up. He was a straphanger."[2]

However, back in Greenwich, he shared the refuge enjoyed by his financial world's colleagues. Waiting there at the station was the ever-dependable Alec, the same chauffeur who got him to the train in the morning, the same Alec who drove the children to their schools and did the "yardwork" around the rambling, brown-shingled house on a massive New England stone foundation overlooking Grove Lane, just a few blocks north of the business strip along busy Boston Road but removed from the working-class homes of the recent Irish immigrants and Italians from nearby Cos Cob. Alec, a Ukrainian who had migrated with his wife from Russian-held Polish territory and had an "impossible" last name, corrupted by the Bushes and their circle as "Chowdercheck," drove the black family sedan. He also seemed to do everything else around the place, a "jack-of-all-trades." The Bush children felt Alec's presence constantly. "We used to get scolded if our shoes were not put outside our door," remembered Nancy, "because Alec came at six-thirty in the morning." He was "wonderful Alec," who drove Pres and George to Greenwich Country Day School and Nancy to Rosemary Junior School and Mr. Bush to the station.[3]

Most of all, Alexander Chodaczek and the rest of the staff, which usually included a cook and one or two maids, took care of the world Prescott left behind when he boarded the train. Greenwich was far from the wealthiest community in America, but it was among the more privileged, and the Bushes were not all that far from the top within their community. "We never felt that Dad had any kind of wealth at all," Jonathan Bush once told a reporter. "We had a cook and a maid and a chauffeur, but other kids had a lot more."[4] They never cared where they ranked in the town's social pecking order, though Nancy pointed out that, as Midwesterners, such matters were moot to Prescott and Dorothy. Even young George's best boyhood friend, who understood its relationship to the working-class neighborhood behind the old Greenwich High School, regarded the Bush place as very large but unostentatious, dating back to turn-of-the-century "nondescript," with a broad veranda that wrapped around to the back, where it faced a brook, and a handy porte cochere for bad weather.[5]

The adult Bushes appreciated the freedom made possible by the hired hands. Nancy recalls how her father encouraged Alec to learn English. He also helped Alec's two children, Alexander Jr. and Marcella, get college educations, the son at Marquette and the daughter by attending the College of New Rochelle, which led to an elementary school teaching job in Greenwich. The Bushes were, as Alexander Chodaczek Jr. later recalled, "a very generous family."[6]

Bush supplemented his Wall Street concerns with helping to run his town. His civic involvements were reminiscent of Samuel's in Ohio. He became one of the founders of the Greenwich Taxpayers Association, which, as he explained, was designed to "protect the tax structure . . . not have it go up unnecessarily. We studied local problems with that idea." Greenwich's growth led to the replacement of the 267-year-old town meeting by a more select legislative body, the Representative Town Meeting, which held its first session on October 26, 1933. The 148 elected members were chosen from each of the town's eleven districts, with representation apportioned along the lines of one for every one hundred voters. With voting power clearly in the hands of a select group, which was entirely compatible with local desires, Greenwich thereby had converted to representative government. After the body had functioned for two years, Prescott Bush was elected moderator on the second ballot, a position he held for seventeen or eighteen years "as an active practicing Republican," resigning only after his election to the United States Senate in 1952.[7] He had, during all that time, presided over the evening sessions after his long commutation to the office in New York. Some dragged on until after midnight, not long before he would have to get up to catch his morning train. At least, unlike most moderators who followed Prescott, he managed them efficiently and with a minimum of nonsense, so relatively few meetings went on until the wee hours.

There can be no doubt that the RTM, as it came to be called, reflected the fiscally conservative attitudes of the community. In March of 1937, for example, that body, in a matter that had no direct connection with Greenwich, passed a resolution protesting the attempt by President Roosevelt to get around obstacles to New Deal legislation by enlarging the membership of the Supreme Court. Only one vote was cast in dissent in 1946, when the RTM refused to consider permitting the newly constituted United Nations to establish its headquarters in Greenwich. Right after Bush left the RTM for the U.S. Senate, the body passed an antifluoridation referendum, which pleased ultraconservatives who suspected a sinister plot with political overtones to adulterate drinking water.[8]

Someone has pointed out that Bush the investment banker was actually "a contemporary money aristocrat whom a John Cheever hero would have met at a party, but in whose pool he would not have swum."[9]

True, one hardly would have just "dropped into" Prescott's pool, as does the cross-country swimmer in Cheever's well-known story, or even have knocked on his door for a casual chat. George Warren, Poppy's "best friend," found nonexistent any social interchange between his own parents and the Bushes.[10] Others noted how little George Bush talked to outsiders about his family. "I couldn't tell you a thing about them," said one who pitched on his baseball team. "The only thing I could have gotten a little bit of a feeling about was that he was frightened of his mother. That was a feeling. If she had said 'jump,' he would have said 'how high?' "[11] But the father received comparatively little attention when George published his 1988 campaign autobiography. Prescott Bush was not just another father, and certainly not just another neighbor. He was tall, a full six feet, four inches with a full head of black hair, austere, regal, dignified, imperious, "imposing," very much the authority.[12] Mary Walker, Dorothy's aunt, later recalled that while their home was a wonderful place to bring up children, "their father wasn't crazy about that . . . so Dottie would sneak them up the back steps so they wouldn't bother him."[13] Many years later, long after Prescott's death, his oldest son told an interviewer what a break their father's business trips away from home was for them. "Well!" said Prescott Jr., or Pressy, as he was called. "It was like the Fourth of July as far as George and I were concerned. . . . He didn't come back for two or three days later, so by then the thing had diminished in impact and we got off sort of scot-free."[14]

"He was an awesome figure," said one of George's friends, a frequent visitor at the big Bush house overlooking Grove Lane. "He was just a very tall, large man"; "very handsome and very dignified," with the physique of a Hollywood leading man. One of George's closest friends in Greenwich once watched the father take a spill on the frozen pond while doing figure eights. He gave out a great screech and landed on his rump, an indignity that made him seem more human.[15] To his son Jonathan, Prescott Bush was "a man on a mission." At another time, he recalled, "I never heard him fart."[16] Others who knew him thought he was stern and commanding, a "terrifying challenge" to his children, especially his sons.[17] They knew that Father expected them to be properly attired with jackets and ties at the dinner table. His grandson, George W. Bush, remembered that in Prescott's house, "one always wore a coat and tie to dinner."[18] He was, wrote one journalist, "a leviathan of a father," whom George could never get out from under.[19] "The boys were more scared of Dad than I was," thought his sister, Nancy.[20] One of George's cousins, a psychoanalyst, said, "He always placated his father. Then, later on, he placated his bosses. That is how he relates—by never defining himself against authority."[21]

"Dad taught us about duty and service," George later wrote, while his mother taught him about "dealing with life in an old-fashioned way of bringing up a family—generous measures of both love and discipline."[22]

The key words were duty, service, and discipline, all constituting that sense of noblesse oblige as benefitting their station. Frank DiClemente, Pres Jr.'s and George's physical education teacher at Andover, found it hard to describe the parent-child relationship without using the word respect. "He was an authoritarian," said DiClemente (whom the boys knew as Deke) many years later. "Those kids didn't answer him back. They fooled around with him, though; and he loved those kids."[23]

Mr. Bush was there for family breakfasts, and on workdays, morning newspapers were spread across the table, introducing them to the state of the world as well as preparing them for the coming day. He often led his wife and children in prayer and read them Bible lessons. A favorite of both mother and father, from which they often read together, was *A Diary of Private Prayers* by John Bailey.[24] On Sunday mornings, of course, the family was always at Christ Church in Greenwich. George, later, away at Andover and Yale, was attentive to chapel services; association with the faith of his family was never far from his personal devotion.

It was a day when parental roles were well-defined. He was free to tend to the business of gentlemen, to take care of whatever had to be done downtown, either at his investment house or at one of his corporations, and, when due, to chair evening sessions of the Greenwich Taxpayers Association. Or, if need be, to go off to one of the monthly meetings of his boards, some of which rotated among different cities. There was, in all that, no sense of paternal neglect; if anything, Prescott Bush was honored and respected by his children. He has been called "the single greatest influence in George's life."[25] "We were a close, happy family," his son wrote many years later.[26]

"We had strict rules," his daughter, Nancy, later said about her childhood. "We couldn't go to the Glenn Island Casino. We couldn't go out on Sundays. He was strong." And, she could have added, he was unwavering in his standards. Money was not a suitable subject for family discussions, nor was it something to be used to take advantage of others. "Dad," she recalled, "had a theory you shouldn't make money on your home. You can make money elsewhere but, you know, you don't want to take advantage of people when you sell your home."[27] Such were Prescott's standards and, as in other areas, he was unbending. At a reception while he was on the Yale Corporation, after the master of Saybrook College told an off-color joke, he turned to his wife and said, "Dorothy, we're leaving." When his brother left his wife for Mrs. Janet Rhinelander Stewart, Prescott would not have her in his house.

He would have no part of the abandonment of a wife and children to take up with a society lady from Philadelphia. When the new marriage later ended in a divorce, Prescott had nothing to do with his brother.[28]

Such circumstances nurtured the development of George Bush, of whom a cousin once said there was a "Christian innocence." Most of everything had come to him, added Ray Walker, "without any grappling about right or wrong."[29]

The formation of Greenwich Country Day School explains, in part, what was happening to Poppy's world. Take, for example, the primary education of the Bush boys, which took place at the new school shortly after the family moved to Stanwich Lane.

Scattered around the town were some twenty public schools. In general, children followed what had long since become conventional schedules, usually involving release from classes in mid- or late afternoon, which left them time to do chores at home and play with neighborhood friends in virtually every open space.

The Bushes and their more affluent world had different requirements. Two private schools were available in Greenwich, but neither was regarded by many wealthy parents as serving their concerns. Mothers, especially in that day of large families, and particularly those whose worlds were filled with social, charitable, and athletic activities, were more likely to turn over much of the child-raising to hired help. There was also the fact that estate and country life effectively isolated growing boys and girls from their own peers. So there was need for schools that not only offered good educations but provided the sort of recreation made possible by having a sufficient number of classmates. With the need already evident, the increased prosperity of the twenties, which rebounded disproportionately to the already wealthy, made the project entirely feasible. In keeping with the period, no thought was given to making the school coeducational. That it would be exclusively for boys was evident from the outset.

In Greenwich, a plan to create such a school was undertaken by a committee of well-connected parents, including William Avery Rockefeller and his wife, Florence, in order to establish a place that would offer their children a full day's program. Unlike boarding schools, this institution would offer long school days combined with athletic recreational facilities. The concept was greeted with such enthusiasm that, by December of 1925, "news of the scheme to start a new school had circulated around the tea tables and golf courses of Greenwich . . ."[30] After a preliminary start at the Rockefeller Robin Hill estate, where an old barn was converted into a schoolhouse, what had begun as the Harvey School of Greenwich took over the eighteen acres of land and buildings of the Warner estate on Old Church Road and functioned there as the Greenwich Country Day School.[31] The carriage house became the school's first gymnasium.[32]

Teachers at Greenwich Country Day were little more than extensions of the domestic servants their students knew at home. Job applicants had to conform to disciplinary and social requirements. Wives of men who wanted to teach there found themselves interviewed by the headmaster to determine how well they would fit into the atmosphere. One master, who ultimately served Greenwich Country Day for thirty-four years as a teacher, athletic director, and middle-school leader, found that he and his wife had to cheerfully accept being assigned to a converted hayloft over the carriage house.[33]

"When I went there, there was no gymnasium even," Arthur E. Grant later said. "What we did in athletics had to be done out of doors. Soon the horse stalls down near the Ritz were taken out and a gymnasium was hooked on. And then we had inside athletic activities."[34]

For all their activities, which lasted from eight-thirty in the morning until six in the evening, at least for upper-graders, students wore uniforms, black sweaters with orange stripes on the left sleeve and, in the appropriate fashion of the day, knickers. Any thoughts that the colors were intended to emulate Princeton's seem to have been erroneous, although, insofar as is known, not officially denied. The outfit, however, served the desired purpose of setting off the Greenwich Country Day students from their less-privileged contemporaries. One who had to walk to the school in his uniform was beaten up by those kids who saw him as a "snotty little Greenwich Country Day School brat." From then on, he wore dunagrees, changing into the proper uniform "once I was in polite territory."[35]

The school's curriculum was designed around Latin, history, geography, mathematics, and English. Time was also set aside for music, nature study, and art. That still left a vital part of the program for athletics. Grant, the middle school director, was in fact brought to Greenwich by Headmaster Miner for his ability to handle the boys on the playing field. Sports activities included such games as baseball (which was encouraged for everyone), soccer, ice hockey, and swimming. In addition, there was a morning assembly period that gathered all 140 or so boys in the auditorium, which, added to the academic schedule, guaranteed a busy day for all.

Headmaster Miner was very exacting and a strong disciplinarian. His office at the top of the stairs was off-limits to anyone without a prior appointment. His aide, Miss Eve Collins, who was in charge of the lower school when the first Bush became a student, was described as very particular, as she "had to be, in order to be under Mr. Miner."[36] After Grant became ill, and the year Pressy Bush graduated, Miner was replaced by his assistant, an Englishman named George Meadows. Meadows was an old-fashioned authoritarian disciplinarian who did not even attempt to charm the parents. He is still remembered for "punishing those who talked during assembly by having them stand on their chairs for the rest of the program. He also forced gum-chewers to regret their infraction by having to 'enjoy' a whole pack of gum at one time while having to stand in the front hall." How to keep the children under control preoccupied the *Teacher's Handbook,* which had such sections as "Conduct in the Dining Room."[37] The school was, in effect, a prep school for the prep schools for which the boys were destined, such places as Choate, Hotchkiss, and Phillips Andover, and the boys were occasionally visited for pep talks by such people as Andover's headmaster, Dr. Claude M. Fuess.[38]

Pressy, at the age of five when the Harvey School first evolved into Greenwich Country Day, was the first Bush child to attend. Neither brother made much of a mark at the school, Pressy because his left eye had been blinded by a congenital cataract and Poppy because he was younger than most of the boys.[39] After his older brother's first year, according to family accounts, George complained about being lonely at home and was enrolled a year ahead of his time.[40] All three boys attended from the first through the ninth grades.[41] Nancy was driven by Alec to Rosemary Junior School. By 1942, America was at war, and Greenwich Country Day School became coeducational by joining with Rosemary.[42]

For George Bush, going "home" always meant back to Kennebunkport. There, even more than in Greenwich, was the atmosphere and nostalgia of childhood and family. "Our childhood was like a beautiful dream," Nancy once told Barry Bearak of the *Los Angeles Times*. "There was a seasonal quality to our lives,"[43] Kennebunkport every May and South to Duncannon at Christmas. Duncannon, in the uplands of northwestern South Carolina, a popular winter resort known for its polo, was where Grandfather Walker, Dorothy's father, had his shooting lodge. His joy, whenever the Bush troupe would arrive at the whistle-stop station at Snelling, was to turn the whole place over to Prescott, Dorothy, and the children. Meanwhile, he took over a house in nearby Aiken. The Bush children, with plenty of contemporaries at hand, rode after the hounds, bagged quail and doves, and went out skeet-shooting. Nancy, the most effusive and romantic of Poppy's siblings, long afterward remembered how they were waited on "by the most wonderful black servants who could come into the bedrooms early in the morning and light those crackling pine-wood fires; it used to be freezing."[44]

Kennebunkport offered more of the same, and a far greater variety over a longer period of time. There, the family really came together, vindicating Mary and Herbie's decision to take over the place after the death of George Walker's widow, Dorothy's mother. It was, Mary Walker later told an interviewer, a big undertaking. "One day," she recalled, "I walked home and saw a little cousin from the West playing with a little cousin from the East and I said, 'This is a much bigger thing than I am.' I changed my mind." Herbie then pulled down the house of one of the cousins and replaced it with a large pool. Various aunts, uncles, and cousins zeroed in on the property, some staying at cottages along the ocean highway, at either side of the road. Dorothy and Prescott were given their own bungalow on the Point, one that was described by an early biographer as "simple, unpainted," and "a hundred yards shoreward."[45] George only displaced Herbert Walker, at Herbie's suggestion, because of heightened security needs when he joined the Reagan administration. Nancy, who married an insurance executive, Alexander Ellis Jr., stayed in a house about eight-tenths of a mile away, across the road from the Atlantic Ocean. They played at the nearby Cape Arundel golf course and, on Sundays, they all went to the St. Ann's Episcopal Church.

But the Kennebunkpoint house wasn't always theirs. Nor had it always been Walker's Point. It was completed in 1904 as Rock Ledge and then evolved into Surf Ledge, and only later did it become known as Walker's Point, especially after Bush bought most of the peninsula in 1981. The shingled home with six bedrooms, not counting two for servants, was quickly hailed by *American Homes and Gardens* for its ocean-side piazzas that "afford both the view and the privacy needed in a house of this description."[46] Vastly enlarged and expanded, with storm-forced renovations and construction of additional buildings that resembled the Kennedy compound at Hyannis Port, it stood almost in the sea itself.

It brought them all together and created a cohesiveness that made them somewhat forbidding to outsiders. At Walker's Point, the Walkers and the Bushes, and, upon occasion, such cousins as the Houses and the Clements, turned inward toward one another, thoroughly devoted by a common allegiance. When they weren't singing, they were playing.

Childhood at Kennebunkport consisted of many things; mostly, it meant play, from piloting their own lobster boat to sports activities with the family from sunup until sundown. Their mother, in George's later words, "was a match for anyone in tennis, golf, basketball, baseball—for that matter, I don't recall a footrace Mother was ever in that she didn't come in first."[47] Others, decidedly less charitable, thought the Bushes "played tennis to kill." They competed at anything, it was often pointed out, that measured one person against another. None of the children, it was said, had really grown up until they had beaten their mother at tennis.[48]

Nancy, as gregarious as her brother George, dated his friend "Red Dog" Warren, who considered her among the most attractive girls in Greenwich. She never lost her exuberance and passion for the family's interests. Yet, there were hints that she alone among Poppy's siblings had strayed from the Bush political conservatism. One Bush biographer made much of her experience as a student in Mabel Newcomb's Economics 105 course at Vassar. Professor Newcomb, a veteran of the New Deal in Washington, had helped to turn young Nancy's head in a rather contrary direction.[49] She explained that, "I voted for JFK, and I voted for Lyndon Johnson. I did not vote for Goldwater. Then I did not vote for Nixon. I voted for McGovern because my son John was working for him in Flint, Michigan, and I voted to support John knowing that McGovern would get clobbered but I thought I would support him. And then I voted for Ford. And I voted always for Eisenhower. So, I was temporarily a presidential Democrat," but one who remained a registered Republican all her life. (In Washington circles, nevertheless, she was known as a Democrat, at least during the 1960s.)[50]

Poppy fit into all this as he adjusted to every kind of discipline. Even as a little guy, Pressy said, George was unusually well coordinated, with "a good pair of eyes, good hands, natural reactions, and he caught and hit the ball well. He's always been quick and bright."[51] His closest boyhood friend considered that he "had the fastest eye-hand coordination of any person I have ever known. Anything with rackets; fielding at first base, he was terrific."[52] To his admiring aunts, Poppy was not only an athlete, the star among all the children, but the most "adorable."[53] Later, during his presidency, Bush was interviewed at Walker's Point, and showed that very little had changed. "I'll play a good deal of golf here, a good deal of tennis, a good deal of horseshoes, a good deal of fishing, a good deal of running—and some reading," he added with a grin, explaining, "I have to throw that in for the intellectuals out there."[54]

That he was very self-conscious about not satisfying the intelligentsia was never far from the surface. Nor, during those days of his youth, either with the family at Kennebunkport or away at school, did political ideas—partisan or otherwise—seem to intrude into their little world. Aunt Mary, however, recalls it was not long after Poppy's marriage to Barbara Pierce that a group of women in one of the Walker's Point homes was each asked, "How would you like to be First Lady?" She never forgot how George's young wife answered. "I'd like it," she said, "because, you know, I'm going to be the First Lady some time." As Mary added afterward: "It was because she felt very secure. She felt that there wasn't anybody in the world like George, whom she worshipped."[55]

When he reached Andover in the fall of 1937, he looked most improbable as a future presidential nominee. Four years makes a great difference in a boy's life, and Poppy was no exception, developing during those years from "a little tyke" into a mature young man.

However, Andover, for all its reputation of being demanding, was a snap for Poppy and his friends from Greenwich Country Day. They even took advanced French instead of introductory classes. Elliott Vose, one of the school's outstanding athletes and a pitcher on Poppy's baseball team, recalled that his family wanted him to go to Andover because of its reputation for high standards. Andover had few rules, "but," as Vose later wrote, "if you broke them and/or if you didn't do the schoolwork, you were out."[56]

In the Northeast, Phillips Andover was a stopover along the great chain that led from the Greenwiches to Yale and Wall Street. Much, in fact, was modeled after Yale, the social clubs and fraternities and the faculty, the leadership of which was drawn from the college at New Haven. To suggest, as do some who went to Andover, that the school was a mirror image of Yale is no exaggeration. The school's motto, *Non Sibi*, "Not for Self," and the reminder, *Finis Origine Pendet*, "The End Depends on the Beginning," was appropriate for such families as the Bushes, who committed their money, their sons, and their own aspirations for immortality. "The guiding ambition of many of us, and Bush is a leading example," wrote a prominent classmate, "was to first make enough money to be comfortable, and able then to go into public service of some sort."[57] Or, as Elliott Vose put it, "You're supposed to win. Basically, it isn't supposed to show, and if you win you're a good sport; if you lose, you're just as good a sport." All that stuff about Vince Lombardi and "winning is everything," is a bunch of "crap."[58]

Only in the years after Bush's graduation would social change begin to overtake Phillips Andover. Still a conditioning field for "America's finest," its name derived from the founding Phillips brothers and dated back to 1778. The other brother was responsible for nearby Phillips Exeter, across the state line in New Hampshire. The campus took up some fifty acres on a hill over-looking Highway 28, which ran into the town of Andover, just northwest of Boston. Off-campus existed as little more than a curiosity. One hardly ventured beyond the start of the commercial strip leading into downtown. "It was," said Vose, "a very limited contact with the comings and goings of the rest of the world." Even during the Great Depression, the latter part of which coincided with Poppy's life on that campus, awareness was next to nil, and what they knew came mainly from the campus newspaper, the *Phillipian*, which was squarely against everything that that "betrayer to his class," FDR, was doing in Washington, what with his use of government to shackle business and free enterprise.[59] The Bush children actually had more exposure to hard times while in Greenwich and Kennebunkport, where they at least looked at the daily papers.

George Bush's great accomplishment at Andover had little to do with academic performance. One of his English teachers, Hart Day Leavitt, a Yale product himself, remembered with pride such students as Jack Lemmon, the future actor, and H. G. Bissinger, who later wrote a biting book about the high school football craze in Poppy's temporary adopted town of Odessa, Texas; but of Bush academically, hardly anything at all. Under school restraint about giving out specific numbers, Leavitt could only say that his "grades in my course were not very good. He was in my eleventh-grade English class, but my remaining impression is that he just sat in the class and handed in his papers." Other teachers also remembered his mediocrity as a student, one whose writing was quite inferior. Leavitt recalled having "very little respect for George's mentality. Then I have to go back and say that when he was in my class maybe he was an underdeveloped young man like a lot of them." A fellow Andover athlete, who was in Poppy's American history and English classes, states directly that "he was *not* bright. He was a medium student. If you would ask me on a scholastic basis—two hundred kids in our class—and say which were the ones who had the intellectual potential of becoming president of the United States, I could have listed about thirty people. He would *not* have been on that list.[60] For all the reservations about his scholastic performance, Bush did make his mark. It may even be said that he and the school were made for each other. Andover, in common with such other institutions, stressed conformity. Its boast that "its business was making the leaders of tomorrow" suggested obedience to institutional values, and Bush, regarded by Leavitt as "one of the mechanical types," showed no youthful rebelliousness.

Leavitt was among the faculty's dissenters, who ultimately achieved what he and his fellows believed were much-needed reforms. At the time George Bush entered, Andover was no place for weaklings, especially under Dr. Alfred Ernst Stearns, an especially tyrannical headmaster. Many complained that the place was "an academic boot camp" with a "sink or swim philosophy" and an abundance of sadists; the system of discipline was ruthless. One member of the faculty described Stearns as "a Calvinist with a lethal attitude toward boys."[61] The students were "men." Those "men" who came before the discipline committee were looked at from the point of view of "Why did he break that rule?"[62] One account recalled what happened when a little ninth grader stepped over the school boundary line to retrieve his hat after it had been blown off by the wind. The miscreant was spotted by Dr. Stearns himself and immediately told to pack his bags.

As Fitzhugh Green has written, schools like Andover, which emphasized Christian teachings and modeled themselves on British "public schools," were like military academies and "tended to graduate homogeneous boys with no more originality than the products of a cookie cutter," with having a "good attitude more valued than creativity."[63] Nothing changed when Stearns was replaced as headmaster by Dr. Claude Moore Fuess.

Fuess, already in his seventies, was a noted scholar and historian. His prep school had not been Andover but a public high school in Maine and, unlike so many others at Andover, his college pipeline was Amherst not Yale. Still, Fuess, although born in the central New York State town of Waterville and having earned both his masters degree and doctorate from Columbia University, was every inch a New Englander. He joined the Andover faculty in 1908 as an instructor in English and ultimately achieved distinction there as Elizabeth Milbank Anderson Foundation Professor of English until becoming headmaster of the academy in 1933. Detractors can easily dismiss him as a typically conservative Calvinist and Republican schoolmaster who drew from his World War I military experience to terrorize his youthful charges.

However, he had already contributed to scholarship an important biography of Daniel Webster. His career, other than as a dedicated schoolmaster, is one of astonishing productivity: biographies of Carl Schurz, Caleb Cushing, Calvin Coolidge, Rufus Choate, and Richard Henry Dana. He also celebrated New England's elite educational tradition with hagiographies of Andover and Amherst (which was published two years after he became headmaster at Andover). While at Andover, he became national president of the Alpha Delta Phi fraternity from 1937 to 1939, and the man in charge of perhaps the nation's most prestigious boarding school eventually collected honorable degrees from Yale, Princeton, Amherst, Columbia, Dartmouth, and Williams.

Locally, Fuess was even more distinguished as an authoritarian. His half a century with Andover included an earned campus nickname of "Iron." "Other schools had boys, Andover had men," Fuess liked to proclaim at assemblies.[64] (One of his books about his career at the academy was pointedly named *Men of Andover.*) As might be expected, the regimen under Fuess stressed the traditional educational distinction of men of breeding, but the climate, which a later generation found oppressive, was permeated with Christian teachings and the values of fair competition.

Under Fuess, the Yale-educated Ph.D. Arthur B. Darling was recruited with full power over the school's history department and its curriculum. Darling, Hart Day Leavitt recalled, "insisted that the way to teach at the secondary school level was through fear. You intimidated your students. You made them fearful and therefore that was the way they were motivated."[65] One Latin teacher remembered by George Warren was "quite a horror" and "rather a fascist." Almost from the first day of class, he sensed that Warren was easily intimidated. "The more he humiliated me the tighter I got and the more he seemed to enjoy it. It was true psychological sadism of the worst possible sort." He had his class depart from Latin one day of each month and spent the time instead on current events and politics. "He was a Nazi. He'd talk glowingly of Hitler. This was in 1939, 1940, the Battle of Britain had been fought and we were going into that period of the Phoney War." All this was no problem for Poppy, who "seemed to have enjoyed the teachers and accommodated himself rather easily to even the most authoritarian. Bush would never defy."[66]

"We'd have bull sessions in our room. This was in the fifth year, senior year. Although I was less bright than Bush, I was much more interested in ideas. I was sort of a funny little baby intellectual at that point, I suppose, although an athlete and hail fellow well met. But there were three or four people like me in our dormitory who would often congregate after ten in the evening when study hall was over," Warren recalled. In all their conversations, however, Poppy never showed any interest in politics. But, to all who met him, and especially to those on the faculty whom he worked to befriend, he was "charming, wonderful sense of humor, quick-witted, funny." One idea of fun was to call Warren "Red Dog," a nickname that stuck.[67]

Elliott Vose, who was top-rated by his classmates in several departments when he graduated in Bush's class in 1942, agreed that Poppy was not considered to be "one of the brains of the class by a longshot." But Vose, one of the school's star athletes and for whom the school's disciplinary standards were among its attractions, stressed that Bush "was greatly admired by all of us who ended up being his classmates," among the most popular and well liked students in the school.[68]

Nobody remembered him as a student with more affection than did Frank DiClemente, the physical education instructor and coach. In Andover, where the faculty was likely to be drawn from the same elite colleges to which its students were headed, Deke was somewhat of an anomaly. He came from a working-class family in Rochester, New York, and went to Springfield College to train as a teacher. "I came from the other side of the tracks," he said about himself. "My father said if you want to go beyond high school, you better take care of it yourself. You can imagine what this place [Andover] was to me after going to public school." He joined Andover as a biology and chemistry instructor and only later moved into the athletic department as a coach, which gave him an especially close view of the youthful George Bush.[69]

George, said Deke, "just stood out. During recess, when the kids had free time, there was this kid—just the way he impressed me, all arms and legs, having a helluva good time, laughing. Everybody liked the kid. He just had so much enthusiasm." It was obvious to him that "George came from a home where family was very important." His natural sport was soccer, and he went out for that. So, too, with baseball. He became captain of both.

"He was just a natural," Deke explained, obviously talking about one of his favorite boys. "He did well in his schoolwork. He left his impression on almost every phase of school life. We had chapel. Kids who helped out the minister, took up the collection in the church. He was head of that. He headed the annual charity drive one year. The school was broken down into four clubs: Romans, Greeks, Saxons, Gauls, and he ended up being president of the Greeks. He was captain of the junior baseball team. It seemed that in every phase of his school life he seemed to make his mark. He was a very well-liked kid. You never heard that guy say anything bad about anybody. If he had anything to say about a person, it would be in a positive sense."[70]

Most saw an outgoing, likeable kid with a gift for two of the most-prized values at most schools: athletics and the reputation for being a "regular guy," one who was also in one of the biggest of the school's AUVs, clubs that were modeled after the senior societies at Yale; sort of "a mix between a fraternity and a senior society."

He became captain of the Andover baseball team during his senior year, when they played two games a week from late April into June, about ten to fifteen games in all. Vose, one of his half dozen pitchers, remembers Bush as a "logical choice to be captain of the teams he played on. He was captain of the soccer team. . . . he was a cheerleader with a small c. I think he did what all schoolboy captains do. They all look up to the coach. The coach rallied people to get their spirit up, and I think George did that very well. Poppy had a leader's personality."[71]

Take, for example, Bush's encounter with Bruce S. Gelb. The two students had never met. Gelb, then fourteen and in his second year, was the butt of an initiation prank. When a bigger boy insisted that he move a big, overstuffed couch, Gelb huffed and puffed and gave up. The bully thereupon grabbed him and put his arms around his back. "You can break it off," protested Gelb, "I can't lift that chair anymore." To his surprise, the victimized lad heard another boy order his tormentor to "leave the kid alone," and kept right on walking. "This guy dropped me like a hot potato," Gelb explained, "picked up the couch and walked away." Only when Gelb asked for the name of his rescuer was he told by one of the witnesses to the incident, "That was Poppy Bush. He's the greatest kid in the school." Bush, then in his senior year, did not get to meet Gelb until 1978. Gelb's father was the founder of the Clairol Company, and the younger man, never forgetting that incident, became Bush's finance cochairman in New York for his 1980 presidential run, helping to collect nearly $3 million.[72]

Bush, by the time of his senior year and the Gelb incident, had caught up with classes he missed due to illness. A staph infection settled under his right arm during the spring of his junior year. Infections of that sort were especially serious in those presulfa days, and George's condition was very bad. "He came very close to losing his life before they were able to get it under control," recalls Prescott Bush Jr.[73] He spent two weeks in Massachusetts General Hospital, an interruption in his schooling that necessitated an extra term to make up for lost time. Even the most vociferous among his faculty critics, Leavitt, acknowledges that the infection may have contributed to Poppy's low grades while a student in his class.[74]

The most striking evidence of Bush's standing among his fellows at Andover appears in the Phillips Academy Yearbook Student Poll published in *Pot Pouri* for 1942. Such evaluations are, of course, subject to many variables; they do, however, offer a valid snapshot of how it appeared at the time, unaffected by hindsight. They showed that, in almost every category, Bush was right behind Elly Vose, who, unlike Poppy, had gone through Andover with the same graduating class all the way through. The poll nevertheless revealed that Bush ranked third as the "best all-around fellow," third as the "most respected," third as the "most popular," third as the "best athlete" (trailing only Vose and Bo Furman), third as the "handsomest," but when it came to the category called "most faculty drag" (influence), he placed second, although at some distance behind the front-runner, John Greenway. His name is altogether absent from any scholastic honors or, interestingly, as "most likely to succeed."[75]

CHAPTER THREE

Poppy at War

%

N othing about the outside world so touched the Andover community as the news that the Japanese had bombed Pearl Harbor. "I'll never forget it," George Bush said many years later. "I was walking across the campus there near the chapel—it was Sunday—with a friend of mine. And somebody yelled across at us, and it just made a profound impact at that very moment."[1]

In the nation's capital that night, Secretary of War Henry L. Stimson confessed to a feeling of "relief": the expected hostilities had come in a way that "would unite all our people." The secretary had met at the State Department on the morning of December 7, talking "the whole matter over" with fellow cabinet officers Frank Knox and Cordell Hull. He had finally returned to Woodley, his home, and was just finishing his dinner when the president called. "Harry," said the voice from the White House, "come down here at once. The Japs have struck." Stimson, long since prepared for some disaster, asked, "Where in Southeast Asia?" "Southeast Asia, hell," shouted the president. "Pearl Harbor!"[2]

At Andover, Dr. Fuess ordered a special student assembly in the school's George Washington Hall. His young "men" were about to have their manhoods confirmed as they neared the age of military service.

Volunteers were plentiful the next morning, forming long lines in front of recruitment booths, far longer, it was noted, than after Congress had declared war back in 1917. New York City's Mayor Fiorello La Guardia ordered security guards placed at all bridges, tunnels, and factories. Air-raid wardens were called out in full force. On the city's municipal radio station, Mayor La Guardia denounced the "Nazi thugs and gangsters," calling them the "masterminds" of the bombing of Pearl Harbor.[3]

American anger, however, was most vehement against the Japanese. They had forced America's entry into the war by bombing Pearl Harbor; dead or dying sailors were submerged under carnage that came from warlords in Tokyo. From across the nation came accounts of sporadic anti-Japanese violence. Within twenty-four hours after the attack, the president signed an executive order designating as enemy aliens all Italian, German, and Japanese noncitizens.[4]

Americans who lived on the West Coast assumed that they were to be the next victims. Air alerts spread throughout the region, several sounding in the San Francisco Bay area alone. The commanding officer of the Fourth Army and the Western Defense Command did not help matters by declaring that there was no "doubt [that] the planes came from a carrier." Meanwhile, fifteen large searchlights sent beams across the night sky over the Golden Gate and the Presidio. Not an "enemy" plane materialized. But the real hazard was on the roads, where motorists found themselves contending with blackout streets; the absence of traffic lights and anxiety resulted in cars running helter-skelter through the confused traffic. A mob of nearly one thousand gathered in downtown Seattle to "enforce" the blackout. Hysteria was reenforced a few days later when American shipping off the West Coast was attacked by Japanese submarines for nearly a week, with the loss of two tankers and one damaged freighter.[5]

Things were not much better along the Atlantic Coast. New York City's morning rush hour became chaotic on Tuesday when a radio detection unit on Long Island spotted unidentified planes while they were still 150 miles out at sea. The city emptied its public schools that afternoon, sending a million children home within twenty minutes to find shelter. Air-raid alarms sounded up the coast through New England. Wardens were heard warning that enemy planes had already hit Boston.[6]

In Connecticut, the Bushes did their part. Prescott chaired the National War Fund campaign, which was a national consortium of about 600 war relief groups. His talent for money-raising did not escape the notice of the state's Republican party, which later made him chairman of their finance committee.[7] On Grove Lane, meanwhile, Dorothy joined millions of other patriotic Americans by creating a "victory garden," which Nancy recalled, with some amusement, "she and Alec fought over daily."[8]

The coming of war also made for a different world for Poppy. CBS news reports, so significant in those early days of radio dispatches from Europe, brought ominous commentaries from those who would forever become associated with that era, Edward R. Murrow from London and William L. Shirer from Berlin. Suddenly, even the two vast oceans ceased to offer Americans their long-assumed insularity. What had been read for the last several years about the travails of Europe, especially the Battle of Britain, threatened to come close to home. All thoughts of noninvolvement in overseas affairs had vanished, with isolationist groups disappearing overnight. No other external happening had so keenly caught George Bush's attention.

This dangerous turn of events was very much on his mind when, with friends, he went to a "get-together" dance at the Round Hill Country Club in Greenwich when he was at home during the Christmas break. The holiday was the year's major social event. Boys wore tuxedos and the girls displayed their best evening dresses. All were carefully chaperoned. Many of the local prep school kids were present, boys from such institutions as Andover and the Taft School, girls from Miss Porter's and Saint Tim's.

The girl who caught his eye as she danced with a Deerfield Academy boy whom George knew was from neither. George liked the way she moved around the dance floor with vitality to the beat of Glenn Miller's music, her reddish-brown hair topping her tall, slender body, which was covered by an off-the-shoulder red and green dress. The Deerfield boy was one of his tennis friends, Jack Wozencraft of Rye, a New York town just below the state line. George, an uncertain dancer at best, waited until the end of the dance and asked Jack for an introduction.[9]

She was Barbara Pierce, home for the holidays from Ashley Hall in Charleston, South Carolina. She had attended the Milton School and the Rye Country Day School and was involved with "some faceless fellow" but, for the sixteen-year-old, the matter was hardly serious. Besides, at Ashley Hall, a ladies's prep school, more like a "finishing" school, she had other distractions. This new boy, however, was something else! "I could hardly breathe when he was in the room" were the words she used to describe her feelings about George Bush at the moment. He clearly wanted to ask her to dance, but the orchestra continued with music that was too intimidating. So, for the most part, they just sat and talked.

He must have made a strong impression. Later that night, she told her mother about the attractive seventeen-year-old who was 361 days her senior. Barbara's mother was Pauline Robinson Pierce, the wife of Marvin Pierce, a vice president and director of the McCall Publishing Company, which was best known for a line of women's magazines, notably *McCall's* and *Redbook*. Pauline, a former campus beauty at Oxford College, in Oxford, Ohio, near her home town of Marysville, was one of four children of an Ohio Supreme Court justice. In 1918, she had married Marvin, whose ancestral line included America's fourteenth president, Franklin Pierce.

Marvin, who was born in Sharpsville, Pennsylvania, in 1893, came into the world at just about the time the family's fortune collapsed when their iron foundry became a victim of the severe late-nineteenth-century depression. The family never recovered from that disaster. As a young man, Marvin had to delay going to college. He worked at odd jobs to help support his family. By the time Barbara met George Bush, Marvin's success with McCall had enabled them to enjoy some real affluence. Their home, in the expensive Indian Village section of Rye, was a three-story brick house with five bedrooms and several servants. Marvin Pierce, as was later discovered, was usually on Prescott Bush's commuter train from New York.[10]

The four Pierce children included two daughters, Barbara and Martha. Martha, five years older than Barbara, was the beauty of the family. She was chosen by *Vogue* magazine to appear on its cover as its "College Girl of the

Year."[11] Barbara, in fact, has described herself at age twelve as weighing in at 148 pounds, and looking, she later said, "like Porky Pig and probably should have gone to diet camp."[12] "I was a very happy fat child who spent all my life with my mother saying 'Eat up, Martha' to my older sister and 'Not you, Barbara.' "[13] She was tall for her age, five feet, eight inches. In her later teens, however, she had become an attractive girl with large, dark eyes.[14]

She was much closer to her father than her mother. Pauline was known as a woman of many "enthusiasms," none of which, Barbara felt, included her. Nevertheless, she later realized that the need to care for Barbara's sick brother interfered with Pauline Pierce's ability to pay much attention to her. Barbara also resented a little bit of neighborhood gossip in which her mother indulged after she came home with the news about her new friend. While Barbara was still asleep, Pauline asked around to learn whether her friends knew anything about the Bushes. George's parents, she discovered, even belonged to some of the same clubs; that was fine, but, as Barbara later recalled, her mother's inquiries "really burned me up."[15]

That next night, George and Barbara met again at a dance, this time at the Apawamis Club in Rye. Young as they were, the romance continued and deepened from that point on despite extended separations. He returned to Andover, she to Charleston, but their closeness was sealed by heavy letter writing back and forth. They met only on the one day their spring breaks overlapped, but she was, that spring, George's date for his senior prom.

That was also the spring of Poppy's graduation from Andover. As the young men of the academy went through their commencement exercise, who should have been more fitting to address them than Secretary of War Henry L. Stimson? Stimson, at seventy-four, was still deeply involved in his remarkable career of government service, a Republican in a Democratic administration eager to demonstrate its bipartisanship during that time of national emergency. He had served as secretary of war under William Howard Taft and secretary of state under Herbert Hoover; there was no one more qualified to be regarded as the high priest of the nation's foreign policy establishment. Stimson had appeared before the Andover graduation class just two years earlier, at the time of the British and French evacuation of 338,000 troops from Dunkerque and the start of the Battle of Britain. At that time his message was that civilization itself was under attack, the survival of Christian values at stake.[16]

This time, with Poppy Bush in his audience, he advised the young men to complete their educations before contemplating military service. The nation would in time turn to them when they were needed.[17] George long remembered Stimson's words, especially the part when the elderly patrician said that a soldier should be "brave without being brutal, self-confident without boasting, part of an irresistible might, but without losing faith in individual liberty."

Still, he ignored this advice, also disagreeing with his father who wanted him to go directly from Andover to Yale, where he had already been accepted and where brother Pressy was a student. George's older brother had tried to enlist, but was turned down for physical reasons, his condition further exacerbated by having torn up his right leg while playing baseball in his lower middle year.[18]

But George's mind was made up. He turned eighteen on the twelfth of that month and was ready to act as he saw fit. His father turned to him in a hallway outside Cochran Chapel right after the graduation ceremony and wanted to know whether Secretary Stimson's advice had made him change his mind. "No, sir," said George. "I'm going in." They shook hands. "Dad went along with everything," recalled sister Nancy.[19] But George later told a writer that it was "the first time I had ever seen my dad cry."[20]

The war "was against imperialism and against fascism, and I wanted to be on the cutting edge," he told David Frost in 1987.[21] His mind was made up within hours after he heard that the country was at war: he would enlist in naval aviation. He had become intrigued by airplanes and by the possibility of a naval career, so much so that going to Annapolis was an option to which he had given some consideration.[22]

Deke never forgot how Poppy reacted. "He came to me and said, 'What do you think I should do? Do you think I should go in the service now or should I go on to Yale?' I said, 'George, I love you for asking me and I have much faith in you, but don't you think you should talk this over with your mother and father?' The next time I saw him he told me he had enlisted. He was so damn real."[23] "College was coming up the following fall, but that would have to wait," Bush later wrote. "The sooner I could enlist, the better."[24]

In making this decision, he was beginning a pattern that came to mark his early life: volunteering to serve, in defiance of all the elders who had any possible influence—Stimson, his father, other teachers. None of his Phillips Andover classmates beat him into the service.[25]

On his eighteenth birthday, George went to Boston and was sworn into the navy. He had reached his maturity, had declared his desires, and was now a seaman second class. On the sixth of August, he reported for active duty at the navy's preflight training center at Chapel Hill, North Carolina. "I came out of a very sheltered background," he told the present author, "and woke up in Chapel Hill," where he "had a rude awakening from exposure to the rest of the world."[26]

His first assignment to the post, at the edge of town, was to the Sixth Battalion, Company K, Second Platoon. His civvies were sent home, in exchange for his new issue, an aviation cadet uniform, which consisted of two sets: khaki for working days, and whites and blues for dress. His dress code also included a new regulation short haircut. His quarters, at 317 Lewis Hall, were shared with three roommates. But what was most worthy of writing home about was the presence of another volunteer, Ted Williams, the Boston Red Sox star who had batted .406 in 1941.[27]

* * *

The timing of George's entry into the military was especially significant for another reason. The American fleet under Adm. Chester Nimitz had just surprised the Japanese with what turned out to be a decisive blow, the major development that helped turn around the Pacific war. A combination of B-17 bombers and torpedo planes launched from three carriers had destroyed four Japanese carriers and one heavy cruiser and damaged another. *The New York Times* proclaimed that the battle demonstrated "what land-based air-power can do to naval and airpower attacking from the open sea." The reality was that all 322 Marauder bombs failed to hit their targets, of which the pilots were unaware as they returned to Pearl Harbor.[28] The damage had been done by dive-bombers from the *Hornet,* the *Yorktown* and the *Enterprise.* It also cost the enemy dearly in the loss of their best pilots, which were harder to replace than the planes. While, according to a prominent historian of the Pacific war, the full implications were not understood for a long time, the battle confirmed the importance of airpower.[29] The navy needed fliers; George Bush and his peers were godsends.

Just as inevitable, given his youth and rapid change of surroundings, the next two years affected the young man profoundly, both physically and emotionally. Suddenly removed from the relatively parochial atmosphere of both Greenwich and Andover, he encountered a succession of new faces and places. All the evidence suggests that, while outstanding at such sports as basketball and soccer, and an "average" talent at swimming, boxing, wrestling, and football, the personality traits that had made Poppy so popular at Andover were invaluable at Chapel Hill, where they translated into "leadership." Before long, he was upgraded to an aviation cadet and reassigned to continue his flight training with Class IIA-42 at Wold-Chamberlain Naval Airfield in Minneapolis, Minnesota.[30]

He also grew taller and lankier, reaching his full six feet and two inches while his weight held at 160 pounds. His overall military fitness score rose to 103 from the seventy-seven points when he was inducted.[31] The very act of flying, especially in an open plane, became for him, as one biographer has put it, "a natural extension of his own being," and a sensation of complete command over his body and spirits.[32]

He spent most of the winter of 1942 to 1943 at Wold before moving on to complete his ten-month basic flight-training course at Corpus Christi, Texas, the following June. On the ninth of that month, he became a full-fledged naval pilot with ensign's bars and gold wings, in a simple ceremony that made him the youngest commissioned pilot in the naval air service.[33]

Bush reached Fort Lauderdale, Florida, in mid-June, and there became familiar with the plane that would play the central role in his most crucial exploit in the Pacific. The TBF, as it was known, stood for "Torpedo Bomber Built by Grumman," as distinguished from those produced by other manufacturers. It was, at the time, the largest single-engine carrier-based plane in the navy with a capacity of one ton of bombs, a load that made its belly look like "some aberrant barnyard fowl." The men knew it as the "Pregnant Turkey."[34] It was all part of the VT-51 squadron, the designation given to Bush's air group while stationed at Norfolk, Virginia.

In August, before moving on for more training, George Bush had some time with Barbara before his deployment to the South Pacific. His tour in flight training had earned him some leave, which he spent with his family at Walker's Point. Barbara happily accepted his invitation to join them and it was there that she really got to know him.[35] They played together, as they always did: tennis, cycled, went on picnics. Prescott and Dorothy could not have missed the seriousness of the young couple, then only eighteen and nineteen. Neither could Barbara's parents: they had just lost a struggle to prevent what they considered the premature marriage of their daughter Martha to a Yale senior. For the Pierces, there was little taste for another argument. The simplest thing was to go along and assume, with George about to go overseas and Barbara on the verge of her freshman year at Smith College, in Northhampton, Massachusetts, that the whole thing would blow over. Their children, of course, had other ideas.

Before George reported to Norfolk in September, he and Barbara considered themselves engaged. "I do remember calling my family," Barbara later recollected, "saying that George and I were engaged. The family said, 'Oh, really,' " quite in contrast to how they had reacted to Martha. "It was so obvious to them we were in love that of course they didn't have to be told. It was sort of 'How could you be so silly? We've known it all along.' "[36]

The engagement was secret, of course, but, as Bush has written, "secret to the extent that the German and Japanese high commands weren't aware of it."[37] The outside world, however, knew nothing about it until the formal announcement appeared in the society pages of New York's newspapers the following December. "Miss Barbara Pierce and Ensign Bush, Navy Flyer, to Wed," said the headline in the *New York Herald-Tribune,* December 12, 1945.[38]

George reported to Norfolk when the Kennebunkport holiday ended. He, together with such new mates as Jack O. Guy, from rural Claxton, Georgia, and Lou Grab of Sacramento, California, spent some time at the nearby Chincoteague Naval Air Station in Virginia, a peninsula bounded on one side by the Chesapeake Bay and on the other by the Atlantic Ocean. Then it was back to Norfolk for more training, but the Norfolk stay introduced Bush to an entirely new skill and wartime function, photo reconnaissance. The planning staff of Adm. Chester Nimitz had introduced something new the previous summer: groups designated to concentrate in aerial photography. All such intelligence activities, including code-breaking, translations of captive documents, and photography were under the jurisdiction of JICOA, an acronym for the Joint Intelligence Center for the Pacific Ocean Areas, which was under the command of Brig. Gen. Joseph J. Twitty.[39] Aerial photography (far from the only kind, since pictures were also taken through the periscopes of submarines) became far more important as the Pacific War advanced, a matter made more urgent by the failure to detect Japanese gun emplacements at

Tarawa. In the summer of 1944, in fact, what was known as Operator Snapshot became a highly classified activity of the entire U.S. military.[40]

Bush, therefore, in effect served in a dual capacity: pilot and squadron leader and collector of aerial surveillance. His training at Norfolk involved attending the navy's photo squadron (VD-2). Learning the intricacies of everything to do with surveillance photography, from the basics of film processing to how to operate the navy's aerial cameras for reconnaissance under combat took about a month at the Virginia post. His role was to instruct other airmen in using the hand-held K-20 aerial camera during combat flight. One of his crewmen, John Delaney, a twenty-three-year-old radioman from Rhode Island, became the most proficient, producing photographic records of the Avengers's hits. The plane itself, the Tare Two, which Bush also called "The Barbara," was the squadron's photoplane. It had special aerial gun mounts, with three cameras stored in the bomb bay area to allow for vertical, as well as port and starboard, coverage of enemy targets. Although some of the technology changed with time, the success of Bush's aerial photo group gradually became well known within the high command of Task Force Fifty-eight.[41]

By the spring of 1944, Bush's Avenger was assigned to the carrier *San Jacinto*. He joined the carrier at Pearl Harbor that May, thereby becoming part of Adm. Marc A. Mitscher's Task Force Fifty-eight, a swift carrier striking force of the Pacific Fleet. The ship headed west, along with a small convoy, to make the breakthrough to the Pacific chain standing in the way of Japan's home islands. He saw action that month with strikes by his torpedo plane, catapulted from the deck of the *San Jacinto,* against Marcus and Wake islands. Then it was onto the Marianas and an invasion of Saipan. Ahead were the Bonin Islands, just some 600 miles southeast of Tokyo. A key to the Bonins, known to the Japanese as the Ogasawara Islands, was the craggy island of Chichi Jima. Its radio transmitters made it an essential base for the Japanese.[42]

Bush had much to do. He quickly familiarized himself with his new plane, making his first solo flight on June 18 and then practicing deck landings and carrier takeoffs. He remembered the experience as "exciting, like when I soloed. There's something about the isolation, the ocean, the tiny carrier below that gets the adrenaline flowing."[43]

The choice of operating from carriers was not for the squeamish. As a left-hander, Bush had special problems. The essential controls, those for the propeller, throttle, and fuel mixture were on the left side of the cockpit to free his right hand to determine the plane's path by using the joystick. For Bush, once he was harnessed with his yellow inflatable life vest (called a Mae West) over a lightweight flight suit, with a short-barreled .38 Smith & Wesson revolver in his shoulder holster, only rigid self-discipline enabled him to switch the functions of his hands. Then the plane was hooked onto a catapult to take off from the carrier's deck.

Landing was akin to flipping a dime onto a floating water lily from a distance of some ten feet, and clearly the most demanding of all sea operations. He had to set down his TBF Avenger onto a floating and ocean-tossed area that measured no larger than 70 feet wide by about 350 feet long, an approach that could only be made by flying clockwise, starting with a wide arc that paralleled the starboard side of the flattop. Then at a precise point well forward of the bow, he had to make a left turn. At that point, as naval photographer Robert B. Stinnett has described it, he had to make "a turn left to proceed down leg [sic] parallel to the port side, then another turn left in a wide circle to line up with the stern of the bobbing flight deck." For the final 500 feet, the pilot was guided in by a landing signal officer, who was essential at that point because the pilot could not see the flight deck and could only go by the officer's hand signals.[44] Landing safely meant hooking, and hooking took "squatting" the tail of the craft to catch one of the nine cables on the deck. Failure to engage any one risked plunging into the sea unless the plane could hook on to one of three elevated cables at the end of the landing area. The only catch with that was the potential jolt, which usually risked injury to the pilot and crew and damage to the craft. Bush's skill is amply certified by his having made 116 successful landings between January 24, 1944 and November 29, 1944. All of them were recorded by the ship's photographers.[45]

He witnessed and experienced too many accidents. One poor fellow suddenly panicked while landing, and, at the last minute, tried to gain altitude for another pass. But, at that moment, he lost his air speed. The plane fell back, spun by the gun mount and smashed into the crew, "wiping them out," as Bush later wrote. There on the deck, within plain sight, was the unfortunate man's severed leg, still quivering. Bush had never seen death "that close, that suddenly. Four seamen who also had been with us seconds before were dead because of a random accident."[46]

The entire experience was a test of personal survival. In the fall of 1943, at Chincoteague, he tried to bring down an Avenger during a practice bombing session. The collapse of his landing gear forced him to crash-land. He got out safely, but his $85,000 craft was destroyed. "I'm not sure what happened," Bush explained, "but I was more embarrassed than fearful. I kept worrying that it was a bad landing and not a fatally flawed landing gear."[47] In May of 1944, when Bush's VT-51 squadron was attacking ground installations and the harbor at Wake Island, their first bombing mission over an active target, Bush's roommate, Jim Wykes, failed to return from an antisubmarine patrol. The loss reduced Bush to tears that night. But, in command, with the need to maintain the morale of his crew, he cried privately. "No one saw me," he said, "that wouldn't do."[48] On June 13, 1944, during Operation Forager, the code name for the invasion of the Japanese-held Marianas, Bush had to make three emergency landings on the *San Jacinto* deck when the planes he took aloft developed problems.[49]

* * *

June 6, 1944, better known as D-Day in Europe, had its Pacific counterpart, the greatest carrier air battle in history. By sundown on the ninth, the so-called "Great Marianas Turkey Shoot" engaged forces that Adm. Samuel Eliot Morison has estimated were three to four times the number involved in Midway. Moreover, he points out, the American victory was so complete "that Japanese naval airpower could never again engage on any other terms than suicidal."[50] At stake during that two-day battle was control of the Philippine Sea. Vice Adm. Jisaburo Ozawa attacked Task Force Fifty-eight with four massive waves of carrier-based planes, 373 in all, but fewer than one hundred made it back.[51] The second great American naval victory in the Pacific, a triumph by Task Force Fifty-eight under Admirals Spruance and Mitscher, opened the way, by air and by sea, to the enemy's home islands. For Bush, personally, it was a prelude to his most hazardous moment. He could hardly have known that during the "Turkey Shoot," where his own role was relatively insignificant. His skill, training, intelligence, and sheer courage were all illustrative of what it took to win.

The Japanese, for their part, were shaping up for the test by deploying their full strength: long-range land-based planes, which, because they lacked the armor and self-sealing fuel tanks of the American aircraft, could strike from greater distances than could those of their opponents. Furthermore, Ozawa's objective was extremely limited: he needed only to destroy the American fleet.

To Admiral Spruance was left the need to cover and protect the American invasion of Saipan. But he had his compensations. Ozawa lacked the trained manpower, having had his numbers decimated in a frustrating attempt to defend Rabaul, the port on the northeast coast of New Guinea. It was axiomatic that hardware could be replaced more easily than talented fliers and, in the months that led to the Battle of the Philippine Sea, Ozawa was only beginning to shape up new air groups.[52] In contrast, his U.S. opponents were far more prepared; and, in Admiral Spruance, the Americans had an officer who, in the words of the official naval historian, Admiral Morison, "was tried by experience and unspoiled by victory."[53]

George Bush's task group, which formed part of Task Force Fifty-eight, was relatively small: the battleships *Essex* and *Wasp*, five cruisers, and twelve destroyers. That was the base used for Bush's VT-51 squadron to strike at the ground installations and harbor at Wake Island, the mission that took the life of his friend, Wykes. For a few brief days, they had layover on the island of Majuro, where the crew relaxed playing baseball, having a beer party, and with such other amusements as boxing contests, and music.[54] Bush, then in mourning for Wykes, was notable for instilling his men with the sort of confidence that almost artificially bolsters a potentially ominous outlook.[55]

The battle was shaping up not far offshore. In early June, at about the same time Allied forces were hitting the beaches at Normandy, the Japanese had deployed a few hundred land-based naval aircraft in the Marianas and

Carolines hoping to destroy at least one-third of the American carriers. Task Force Fifty-eight was, at the same time, ready to start Operation Forager and, with the wider objective of capturing Saipan, Guam, and Tinian, ready for a direct assault on the volcanic island of Chichi Jima with its radio towers. Bush, as it happened, was not assigned with his VT-51 to the opening show, concentrating, instead, on antisubmarine patrol in the waters off the Marianas. Their best souvenir for essentially routine and boring duty was getting valuable photo surveillances that helped to keep the commanders of Operation Forager abreast of what the Japanese counter tactics were on the ground.

That responsibility was primarily Bush's. He had to coordinate aerial coverage of the Japanese targets. Invaluable, as always, was John Delaney, who added the operation of the hand-held K-2 aerial camera from his position in the belly of "The Barbara." Bush had also placed K-20 cameras with other VT pilots and air crewmen. While fixed-position cameras had been installed at Norfolk, much of the photography done from the *San Jacinto* was still hand held. All in all, their reconnaissance created some valuable documentation of exactly what the Japanese were up to. At one point, Bush piloted his Avenger through smoke and debris while, at the rear of the plane, Delaney photographed Japanese defenses along the Charan Kanoa invasion beach. One picture caught a tall tower from which the movement of U.S. Marines could be monitored.[56]

Bush, on his twentieth birthday, got his orders for the day: a bombing mission on the big Aslito air base and other facilities used to protect Saipan. Flying a load of 500-pound bombs, Bush's Avenger was to be among eight under the command of squadron skipper Donald Melvin in an attack force to knock out Japanese antiaircraft gun emplacements.

"The Barbara" was grounded for repairs, so Bush, Leo Nadeau, and Delaney flew a plane normally used by a fellow officer, Lou Grab of Sacramento. In their substitute Avenger, a thirty-minute flight carried them to Saipan, where they began bombing at 0845 hours. Bush and his team crippled armed Japanese trawlers off the coasts of Saipan and Tinian, dropping depth charges. VT-51's photos later confirmed the enemy losses. The priority given to Saipan can only be understood by realizing that it was one of the three large islands needed as advanced naval bases for American approaches to the Philippines, the Bonins, and Japan itself.[57]

On the fifteenth, two days after Bush's success against the trawlers, the invasion of Saipan began. Admiral Toyada promptly responded by activating Operation A-GO, which aimed at destroying Spruance and his force by trapping him in waters where he would be an easy target for Japanese land-based and carrier-based planes. Everything pointed to the start of a major sea and air battle.[58]

Bush, fulfilling Admiral Spruance's objective to starve the enemy of their fuel supplies, used his VT-51 group to blast Guam, hitting the Japanese radio station and blasting the former Pan American World Airways field that the Japanese were using as a military sea plane base. The stroke was brilliant: it immobilized the Japanese ability to respond. By the seventeenth, when rumors of Japanese movements reached the *San Jacinto,* Bush and his squadron were ready to meet the main body of the Japanese carrier fleet, which was all an overture for the real show.[59] The flight operations of the *San Jacinto,* and, in fact, all of Task Force Fifty-eight, played their open water hide-and-seek game with the enemy by scouting the area west of Saipan and Guam. Bush, forced by engine troubles to substitute another plane for "The Barbara" for the sixth time that month, on June 17 made his thirteenth mission of the month.

The giant battle began on the nineteenth. Spruance commanded 127,000 troops in the transports and landing craft. Admiral Mitscher, leading Task Force Fifty-eight, had begun by softening the island with over 2,400 sixteen-inch shells.[60] The four great waves of Japanese planes were about to come.

Bush, back in "The Barbara" early on that day, one in which the sun rose shortly before 0600 over a perfectly blue ocean, was ready. Several hours were spent searching for the enemy but without success. Bush and his team, responding to instructions from the carrier, dropped a full load of depth charges to thwart the submarine patrol.

At 1000 hours, the *San Jacinto* spotted enemy aircraft some 130 miles to the west. At 1016 hours came the signal for the ship to "Scramble all fighters!" Task Force Fifty-eight stood in the path of some 400 Japanese carrier planes, which swarmed "like a cloud of hornets." At least four raids were shown on the carrier's radar scopes approaching from an altitude of 20,000 feet.

Launching orders were imminent. Overcrowding of men and planes on the flight deck made the tropical sun seem even more sweltering. Then, between 1021 and 1147 hours, the crew began to maneuver the fighters around the bombers to prepare for launch position. Fighters were ordered to climb to 24,000 feet so they could form an umbrella over the task force, a position that eased the problem of coordinating an attack on the approaching Japanese carrier-based planes. Bush saw from the white vapor in the sky that American fighters were attacking the Japanese.[61]

The launch order was given for 1155, and, while the carrier's antiaircraft guns began to blast away at the enemy planes, Bush took the catapulted plane to 1,500 feet. He suddenly saw a Japanese "Judy," a name given by American intelligence to that type of dive-bomber, falling down from above, obviously hit by one of the *San Jacinto*'s guns. Meanwhile, a dogfight among fighter planes was going on at the 20,000-foot level.

A black cloud began to envelope "The Barbara." The engine of his Avenger, which was carrying four 500-pound depth charges, struck by anti-aircraft fire, sputtered and failed. Bush took to the intercom. "We're losing oil pressure," he told Nadeau and Delaney. "I think the oil lines have sucked up shrapnel." He tried to make it back to the *San Jacinto,* but the landing area was actively launching planes.

His gunner, Leo Nadeau, confirmed the presence of "a big black cloud of smoke on the starboard side." Bush, realizing that all the oil was gone, gave the command to ditch: "Prepare for a water landing." He signaled to the *San Jacinto* that he was going down, and then, in a most perilous operation, guided the craft ahead of the fleet. Not enough time was left to jettison his bombs, which increased the need to gauge the wind velocity and height of the waves exactly right for the only kind of landing possible: lowering the Avenger's tail onto the water before setting down the rest of the fuselage. Nadeau, conscious that they were riding on 2,000 pounds of TNT, thanked God for Bush's skillful landing. "We skidded along until the nose dropped," he said. "Then it was like hitting a stone wall. The water cascaded over the entire aircraft." When he finally got out, he saw Bush on the starboard wing inflating the life raft, which he rowed as rapidly as possibly away from the sinking plane. Only minutes later, they were plucked from the sea by a cargo net dropped over the side of the destroyer *C. K. Bronson.*

Bush recorded his stay on the *Bronson* in his flight book as "sack time," which was how he spent the remainder of the "Great Marianas Turkey Shoot," one of the most significant American naval battles of all time.[62]

Bush and his two crewmen were transferred back to the *San Jacinto* on the twenty-first, after the Battle of the Philippine Sea. That vital phase over and the Japanese resistance severely diminished, the way was much clearer toward the Japanese home islands. Bush, back in action, helped prepare for the invasion of Guam during ten successive days of bombings. The island fell on the seventeenth of July, capping off a month for which Bush's personal flight log showed that he had flown more than forty-six hours and taken part in thirteen strikes against the enemy. Once Guam was secured, the next objective was the island of Peleliu located at the southern end of the Chichi Jima defensive barrier. Peleliu, part of the Paulau Island group, was north of New Guinea and east of the Philippines. Admiral Nimitz held them essential as staging points for aircraft and ships to Leyte at the center of the Philippines.[63] Peleliu was targeted to be taken by the First Marine Corps Division in mid September.[64]

Bush's aerial reconnaissance function now went into full effect. Admiral Nimitz had ordered photographic coverage of the island together with off-shore reefs. Under the code name of Operation Snapshot, Bush and his crew flew a new Tare Two replacement bomber that they called "The Barbara Two." In two days of aerial photography, at a time when Admiral Nimitz wanted coverage of all Japanese military installations in case the marines wanted to target someplace other than Peleliu, Operation Snapshot produced 1,017 different photographs of the island's jagged landscape. At the end of July, Bush wrote to his parents that "last week has been one of sadness and sorrow. We lost another one of our pilots. Four of us went out and three of us had to return without him. . . . There is still a chance that he will be rescued and that's what we're all hoping . . . ."[65]

The push was on toward Iwo Jima. The army air force in the Pacific was modified in August under the command of Lt. Gen. Millard F. Harmon, an event that coincided with the first B-24s that were based on Saipan to bomb Iwo Jima. In August alone, there were ten raids on the island, then twenty-two more in September. Their dual purpose was to decimate the airfields and also destroy ships in the harbors of Chichi Jima and Haha Jima. The Japanese regarded the radio tower on Chichi Jima as their link to the Palaus.[66]

Not surprisingly, then, the Nipponese had converted Chichi Jima into what Stinnett has called "a strategic military center for one of the most fanatical defenses of modern times." The Bonins had been discovered by Spanish explorers in 1543, although they were not settled until 1830 by a contingent from Honolulu led by two New Englanders, an Italian and twenty-five Hawaiians. Their livelihoods came from selling provisions to passing whalers. An investment of a plot on the harbor for fifty dollars was made by Comm. Matthew Perry in 1853. Perry, whose famous voyage to Japan was made that year, stocked the Bonins with cattle, created a provisional government, and hoped to make the place a base for the U.S. Navy and mail steamers. Ironically, it was Marvin Pierce's ancestor, President Franklin Pierce, who rejected the idea. That left it open to Japanese annexation, which took place unopposed in 1861.[67]

The Japanese, fully aware of their strategic importance, fortified them with Korean and Formosan labor. The military listening post at the core of the island of Chichi Jima drew its strength from the commanding position of Mt. Yoake on its east coast. Stinnett, the naval photographer, has described the seven radio antennae towers that rose from that volcanic mass as "tripod masts which stood two hundred feet tall piercing the Pacific sky like masts of tall sailing ships," all protected by antiaircraft guns and radar.[68] Japanese personnel strength on the island has been estimated as some 15,000. There were also 166 "suicide" boats. Even before Pearl Harbor, the Japanese began the construction of three underground bunkers, containing an elaborate network of chambers, separated by bank-type vault doors. Their construction, according to Maj. Yoshitaka Horie, chief of staff to Gen. Yoshio Tachibana, attested to the assumption "that Chichi Jima was one of the final strongholds of the Nipponese Island Empire."[69] The American attempt to knock out the radio tower and four outbuildings on September 1 was a disaster. One plane never returned.[70]

The job had to be done the next day. Chichi Jima's facilities had to be destroyed before the go-ahead for Iwo Jima, the Palaus, and Leyte. Task Force Fifty-eight, preparing for scaling "up the ladder," was due to head south for the linkup with Adm. William F. (Bull) Halsey, where it would become Task Force Thirty-eight. The VT-51 squadron, and Bush's Tare Two, heading out with a complement of twenty-six F6F Hellcats and nine TBM Avengers, aimed at knocking out that bastion. Bush, who had by then reached the rank of lieutenant junior grade, led the crew. Delaney, the radioman turned photographer, manned his usual position.

But also flying with them on that day was Lt.(jg) William Gardner "Ted" White, a squadron ordnance officer. White's father had been a Yale classmate of Prescott Bush, and Ted White had studied there and was a member of the secret Skull and Bones Society. He and George, however, had not met until they were on the *San Jacinto* together.[71] He wanted to check out the Avenger's weapons systems and asked to substitute for the regular gunner, Leo Nadeau.

They were not aware of the full magnitude of the dangers that were especially serious around the Bonins. There had been grim accounts of Japanese atrocities against American prisoners of war which, as it turned out, included gruesome practices at Chichi Jima under its commanding officer, Maj. Sueo Matoba. Mitscher had, accordingly, deployed American submarines as "lifeguards" to protect his pilots during such raids. The safest option for those who had to abort their missions was to attempt to guide their planes to a water landing. If they had to bail out, they could only hope that one of the "lifeguards" would reach them before the Japanese. A crash-landing into the sea guaranteed instant death.

The morning of September 2 was like all others in the South Pacific. The air was warm and humid. A few clouds marred the otherwise clear sky but, as Bush noted, they were not enough to provide cover for an incoming flight.

Bush and the others were briefed at about 0600 hours. Takeoff time was set for 0715. He settled into the cockpit and secured himself in his harness, the usual .38 in its holster. Strapped to his knee was a map of the target, made of fabric to make it resistant to water. At the takeoff hour, he was ready. He could see the takeoffs from the *San Jacinto*'s deck, first the TBMs and then the fighters. Some got into the air without using the catapult, which was not the case with Bush's Tare Two. With Delaney and White secure in their positions, his plane was hooked onto the catapult. He ran the throttle up full, signaled his readiness to the catapult officer, and the Avenger flew skyward.[72]

The flight to Chichi Jima lasted about an hour. Bush's Avenger, behind bombers led by Don Melvin and his wing man, Doug West, climbed to the 12,000-foot attack level. They flew in a V formation, then shifted and formed more of a diamond. As they closed in toward the radio communications center on the island, its masts described as a "forest" that sprouted from Mt. Yoake, they were joined by planes from other carriers.[73]

"The Japanese were ready and waiting," Bush later wrote; "their antiaircraft guns were set up to nail us as we pushed into our dives."[74] Melvin was first through the firing from the Japanese shore batteries. He and Doug West then unloaded their eight bombs on the radio station and the buildings nearby, hitting the installation squarely. Bush could do no less. Preparing to dive, he went down at a thirty-five-degree angle, taking aim at what was left of the tower without any evasive maneuvers, and keeping his Avenger right on target. Smoke from the bursts of Japanese guns increasingly obscured his vision. The plane, as it descended, was surrounded by flaming tracer fire. Through it all, he spotted the target area.

He honed in. "Suddenly," he wrote, "there was a jolt, as if a massive fist had crunched into the belly of the plane. Smoke poured into the cockpit, and I could see flames ripping across the crease of the wing, edging toward the fuel tanks."[75] He later recalled to writer Joe Hyams that the "plane was lifted forward, and we were enveloped in flames, getting closer and closer to those fuel tanks. The thickness of the smoke made the instrument panel unreadable." He continued to dive, once over the target unloading his 500-pound bombs, and then pulled away toward the open sea, his Avenger obviously doomed.

He shouted to White and Delaney through the intercom, "Hit the silk!" Their presence was hidden by the shield of armor plate at the back of the cockpit between him and the crew, but there was also no response to his command. Meanwhile, hearing nothing from White or Delaney, Bush leveled his plane, removed his headset and, getting rid of the restraining safety belt and harness, pushed himself out. His altitude at that point was only 2,500 feet, 500 less than was required to enable him to get out and jump clear of the fuselage. Once on the wing, however, there was nothing else he could do. At just little over 2,000 feet over the water, with the fierce wind tearing at his body and his vision blurred, he jumped prematurely and pulled the ripcord. His head hit the horizontal stabilizer at the rear of the plane, his parachute ripping in the process as it became snagged on the tail. With a bleeding forehead from the gash, he went down toward one of the deepest parts of the Pacific, where it was 3,500 feet to the ocean bottom, known as Bonin Trench.[76]

The hole in the chute weakened its resistance to air, and he fell quickly; instinctively, he unbuckled his harness during that downward plunge and had shed it by the time he hit the water. The Japanese at that moment, 0825 hours, confirmed the downing of one enemy plane in the sea, noting, at the same time, the descent of two men in their parachutes.[77] Bush was the second. The first had to be White or Delaney. Doug West saw one man parachute into the sea.[78]

Japanese boats were, at that moment, already aiming to pick him up. "I swam like hell," he later said. "I got to my sea pack and unleashed the inflatable raft and got in, and then I started paddling out to sea."[79] While he forced his way toward the raft with his hands, bleeding and stung by jellyfish, supporting fighter planes drove off the eager enemy. Bush finally managed to inflate the raft and climbed aboard. He paddled to an emergency medical kit dropped by one of the fighters and splashed the cut with Mercurochrome.*

"My head still ached," wrote Bush. He was also nauseous from swallowing brackish water and kept vomiting into the sea. "Those three hours, from the

---

*Over fifty years later, on March 25, 1997, George Bush jumped again. This time, at age seventy-two, he stepped out of a Skyman dive plane 12,500 feet over the Arizona desert at Yuma with members of the Golden Knights parachute team, fulfilling a vow to make a clean leap. He did, and landed on both feet. But, once again, he bumped his head against the fuselage on the way out. "Perhaps only his family really understood how deeply his bailout from a burning Avenger torpedo bomber in World War II had shaped him," reported Hugh Sidey (*Time,* April 7, 1997, p. 56).

combustion of his airplane to the moment when he crawled into the hatch of the submarine, were probably George Bush's first contact with big-league reality," Roy Reed has written.[80]

Thanks to Don Melvin, the U.S. *Finback,* which was on "lifeguard" duty, picked him up about a half hour later, a time lapse later confirmed by Japanese records. On the *Finback,* Ens. Bill Edwards, a large bearded man, aimed a small motion-picture camera at him. Five sailors from the submarine threw him a line, and he pulled himself and the raft onto the ship. Everything was done within a matter of seconds, salutes and praises. The submarine had to resubmerge and get the hell out of there.[81]

Nothing was ever seen of Delaney and White. One was undoubtedly the first parachutist, but it never opened up and streamed into the ocean. The other apparently crashed into the Pacific while still in his plane. Halsey's task force then moved on, and American amphibious troops landed on Peleliu in the Palaus on the fifteenth.[82]

Bush's rescue was described officially in the log of the *Finback:* "1156. Picked up Lt.(jg) George H. W. Bush, File No. 173464, USNR, pilot of plane T-3 of VT-51, U.S.S. *San Jacinto,* who stated that he failed to see his crew's parachutes and believed that they had jumped when the plane was still over Chichi Jima, or they had gone down with the plane. Commenced search of area on chance they had jumped over water."[83]

Such matters rarely get put to rest forever, especially when they involve those who later become prominent political figures. In the midst of the 1988 presidential campaign, the *New York Post,* a sensational tabloid newspaper, clearly attempted to impugn the heroics of Distinguished Flying Cross winner Bush. Chester Mierzejewski, a turret gunner in Melvin's bomber, explained that he was breaking his forty-four-year silence because he was incensed by what he considered were false claims made by the media on Bush's behalf. Mierzejewski, who contended that he was the only man in a position to see what happened, faulted Bush for jumping without knowing whether his crewmen had left the plane. "I think he could have saved those lives, if they were alive. I don't know that they were," he told reporters, "but at least they had a chance if he had attempted a water landing." Mierzejewski stuck to his story, which involved the loss of one of his buddies, in repeated interviews with reporters and this author.

Among the most serious of his claims was the denial that the Avenger actually was on fire, which would have made possible the kind of water landing Bush had accomplished in the past. Gunner Lawrence Mueller, who flew on the Chichi Jima mission, said that his logbook made no mention of fire. Another Avenger pilot, Thomas R. Keene, was also quoted as being surprised to hear Bush say that his plane had been on fire. The *Post* included the claim that none of "the dozens of present and former navy personnel" interviewed by the paper, other than Mierzejewski "claims to have seen Bush's plane get hit and go down." Journalist Sidney Blumenthal, writing during the 1992 presidential campaign amid charges about Bill Clinton's

Vietnam War deferment had discovered nothing conclusive but tried to reinforce Mierzekewski's doubts. Blumenthal argued that Bush had blurred the
story by giving varying accounts of what happened.[84]

Exact details are often murky in crisis situations. Mierzejewski, when
interviewed for this book about his long-delayed allegation, was clearly
reluctant to submit himself to any further questioning, preferring to rest his
case on the original newspaper revelation. Moreover, Robert Stinnett, the
photographer, has reported that the charges against Bush "were discounted
completely by four of the six surviving air crewmen who were on the mission" and were interviewed by him during 1989 and 1990. "I saw Bush get
hit," Turret Gunner Joe Foshee told Stinnett. "Immediately a blackish brown
smoke began trailing from the tail of the plane. . . . Of course I didn't know
who it was at the time. Just that the plane was one of ours. I did not see any
fire, just smoke. He kept going down, kinda like we were, then as we got out
over the water he leveled off. Then he turned the nose down again trying to
keep up flying speed. I assumed the flak hit his engine, but I wasn't sure." A
radioman, Richard Gorman, recalled that "Bush's plane was smoking like a
two-alarm fire, then I saw a chute blossom out." At just the moment he "hit
the drink," Gorman saw a "huge ball of fire," Bush's plane exploding. Moreover, the official Japanese chronology of that day confirms that Bush was not
the only man who bailed out.[85]

The Japanese themselves also confirmed the chamber of horrors that
awaited any captive Americans on Chichi Jima. The transcript of the Tokyo War
Crimes Trial reveals that Major Matoba admitted that eight American fliers who
were carrying out bombing missions on Chichi Jima were taken prisoner by
Japanese troops. When a Colonel Kato found that they were lacking enough
food to go with their sake Matoba said, "the general asked me about the execution and about getting more meat. Therefore, I telephoned personally to my
headquarters that meat and ten *sho* of sugarcane rum be delivered to the 307th
Battalion Headquarters. I do not recall now if the sugarcane rum was delivered
or not, but I know the meat was. The meat was cooked in Colonel Kato's room
and everyone present had a taste of it. Of course, nobody relished the taste."
They all knew it was human flesh, he added.[86]

Not until the war had ended and he was at Yale did George Bush find out
about the cannibalism. And not until much later did he appreciate how
much his wartime experience added to his education. The military segre-
gated officers in a manner that somewhat resembled the larger society. They
ate, slept, and for the most part, played separately. Enlisted men were
required to salute and say "sir," to respect rank. Reminders about the hierar-
chy of the military table of organization were constant. But their leadership
responsibilities did, in fact, move officers closer to an awareness of lives that
would have otherwise remained alien. Bush, for example, pulled duty in the
mail center, which required him to read the letters of enlisted men because,
as he recalled, "some guy might give away our location, what the ship was
doing, and what it was going to be doing. So we'd sit there and read these

damn things. They could hardly write. And it gave you a real feel for people and what they cared about. It was very helpful in understanding the truth about private lives."[87]

The war went on, and Bush with it. American submarines took their highest monthly toll of Japanese shipping that October. One-third of the enemy loss of 320,906 tons consisted of tankers. Saipan, on the twelfth, was the site of the first B-29 that landed from the United States, and that force became sufficient by November for the first strike against Japan itself.[88] Although eligible for rotation back to the States, Bush flew eight more missions in the Luzon area, and his VT-51 struck enemy shipping in Manila Bay.[89]

He also got official confirmation that either White or Delaney had gone into the sea with the plane and that one of them had been the victim of a parachute that had failed to open. Bush wrote to the families of both men. White's sister had married one of his friends and was giving birth to her first child when she learned about her brother's death. Mary Jane Delaney, responding to Bush's letter, urged him "to stop thinking you are in any way responsible for your plane accident and what has happened to your men. I might have thought you were if my brother Jack had not always spoken of you as the best pilot in the squadron."[90] Prescott and Dorothy Bush received a letter from him that was postmarked on October 2, which was one month after he had been shot down, but knowledge of how long the mail would take, and not wanting her to worry, kept him from writing to Barbara. He would, instead, call her as soon as he could, which he did from Pearl Harbor, saying he would be back in time for the Christmas holiday.[91]

But, from the *San Jacinto* on November 9, he wrote to his kid brother, Jonathan: "Whip out your top hat and tails, 'cause I want you to be one of the featured ushers at my wedding—when it will be I do not know, but get hot on shining your shoes, cause the day is not far off. Also get pants that are plenty big, because we're going to fill you so full of champagne it'll be coming out of your ears . . . It's nice to be flying again after my so-called vacation."[92]

Just before Christmas, on the twenty-second of December, his squadron reached San Diego. Then it was on to Pittsburgh by way of a commercial plane, and a sleeper train destined for Boston from New York reached the Rye railroad station on Christmas Eve. Barbara was waiting.

There were, Bush later wrote, "tears, laughs, hugs, joy, the love and warmth of family in a holiday setting," a description that ignores how anticlimactic that whole period was for Barbara.[93] Only a few days earlier, the possibility of her never seeing George again seemed very strong. Their original plan to get married on the nineteenth of December, to have the Christmas holidays to themselves as a honeymoon, was doomed—and so, she feared, was her beau himself. Rumors that he was missing in action were in the air. His parents had, in fact, heard that he had been shot down, but there was no reason to worry Barbara when nothing had been confirmed, when the only information had come from one of their son's friends. Not until just a few days before he reached her from Hawaii did she know he was safe, and by then their hoped-for wedding date had passed. They quickly rushed out invitations for a January eighth marriage, but that date, too, had to be scrubbed. Pressy's wedding had already been scheduled for New Year's Eve. Holding over all his relatives and those of his bride, Elizabeth "Beth" Kauffman, for more than a week was far less practical than having George and Barbara move up their date to the sixth. So it was, then, on a cold day with frozen snow making roads hazardous, that the two young people were united at the First Presbyterian Church in Rye.

Pressy, interrupting his own honeymoon, served as best man. The bride wore Dorothy Bush's veil and a long-sleeved white satin gown, and she had eight attendants, all dressed in emerald green satin gowns with matching green ostrich feathers in their hair and held bouquets of red and white carnations. For the groom, the choice of clothes was a lot easier: he wore his dress navy blues. That night, the newlyweds celebrated at a reception for over 250 guests at the Apawamis Club, where they had had their first date. George, awkward as usual on the dance floor, nevertheless left no doubt about his joy. Barbara, when she recalled that day to a newspaper interviewer years later, said, "I married the first man I ever kissed. When I tell this to my children, they just about throw up."[94]

Then they slipped out, spending the first night in New York City and taking in a Radio City Music Hall film, *Meet Me in St. Louis,* before a train took them south to spend the rest of George's leave honeymooning at The Cloisters, a five-star hotel on Sea Island, Georgia. "Married life," George wrote to his sister, Nancy, "exceeds all expectations. Barbara is a fine wife!"[95]

CHAPTER FOUR

In Search of Black Gold

%

It was a typical wartime marriage, with all the usual hazards, the endless relocations, the day-to-day uncertainties, the living on budgeted time, but by early 1945, they were confident the war would end reasonably soon.

Despite fierce resistance at the Battle of the Bulge, Nazi lines had been pierced and the march toward the Rhine begun. On the eastern front, the Red Army stepped-up the westward retreat of the *Wehrmacht*. The Pacific War was in its final stage. GIs landed on Luzon that January and, within a few weeks, Manila was back in American hands. Gen. Jimmy Doolittle's B-29s scorched Tokyo and the American flag went up on Iwo Jima's Mt. Suribachi—at the devastating cost of almost 20,000 marine casualties. Island-hopping toward the Nipponese homeland was the bloodiest experience of all. Japanese troops routinely preferred death to surrender. Roosevelt, at the same time, flew to the Black Sea resort at Yalta for what turned out to be his diplomatic finale. He got Joe Stalin to reaffirm Soviet promises to enter the Pacific War after the defeat of Germany, and to attack the Japanese home islands from the north and west. In those early months of the war's final year, with the atomic bomb still unproven and top secret, the timing for the final invasion was projected for November.

Bush's assignments were keyed to the planning for that attack. After his honeymoon, he reported back to Norfolk for the formation of a new torpedo plane group, VT-153. Plans called for them to ship out to the Pacific from Virginia. Bush, in going through the various stages of preparation, meanwhile moved around to Florida, Michigan, and Maine.

Barbara, as a war bride, found some solace initially by staying mostly with her folks; she even managed to see quite a bit of George's.[1] But none of that made sense. Time was too precious, the future too uncertain. They were, as she later put it, "eye-opening" months, a nerve-wracking period that forced her to follow him from base to base. Their lives at that stage could be recounted as from apartment to apartment.[2]

In Michigan, with Barbara at his side, George paid $350 for a 1941 Plymouth two-door sedan Grand Coupe. "It is a grand car," he wrote to friends that March, "if only the paint weren't flaking off."[3] They left behind their single room and drove across Ontario to his new squadron at Lewiston, Maine. They had hardly settled down in another tiny apartment, this time in nearby Auburn, when a news flash from Warm Springs, Georgia, announced FDR's death on April 12. "His politics had drawn my dad's fire," Bush told an interviewer, "but the day FDR died we wept for our commander in chief. He was the symbol of our determination—good over evil."[4] Only a few weeks later, they were in another apartment, this time in Virginia Beach, Virginia, where George was stationed at the Oceana Naval Air Station. That was where they heard President Truman make his radio announcement at seven P.M. on the evening of August 14. The Japanese had surrendered. The country erupted with an unprecedented release of joy, which was especially evident in a military community like Virginia Beach. George and Barbara joined the others in the streets, then gave thanks at a nearby church.[5]

One month later, on the eighteenth of September, the point system that was used to expedite separations from active military duty worked in Bush's favor, and he was discharged from the navy. His credits included 1,228 hours of flying time, 126 carrier landings, and 58 missions.[6] He had done his share.

The young couple lost little time before moving to New Haven, where they took a small apartment on Chapel Street, the first of their three residences in the Yale community. Barbara's pregnancy, however, was not welcomed by the landlord, who, as she later wrote, "liked dogs, but not babies," so they were forced to move to a place on Edwards Street, where the bias was more favorable. Their dog, Turbo, had to be sent to George's parents. They were at the Edwards Street apartment when, on July 6, 1946, Barbara gave birth to their first child, whom they named George Walker Bush. The young family of three then found another apartment, this one at 37 Hillhouse Avenue, formerly a single-family dwelling next to the one inhabited by Yale president Charles Seymour. The Bush's new home had been subdivided into thirteen separate apartments, which left too few toilets and cooking facilities. Another family had to use their bathroom, and the kitchen was shared with two others, necessitating specific eating schedules for each group.[7]

The students and their families were part of the great rush to campus that fall, a surge of over 8,000 newcomers—the school's largest freshman class ever—that placed a great strain on the number that could be accommodated by the community. At Yale, as well as at every major college in America, students assisted by government benefits under the GI Bill for veterans changed the traditional campus scene. More mature, often battle-hardened, many students had wives and children. They constituted better than 60 percent of Yale's large freshman class. The institution responded to their needs, in part, by devising a special program that enabled veterans to graduate in a year and a half.

George Bush's choice of Yale was a natural extension of his upbringing. Brother Pressy was already there; and, of course, before that there had been his father (who later became a member of the board of trustees) and Uncle Herbie, to say nothing of other relatives and friends, such as H. Neil Mallon. In fact, in George's insular world, those who really mattered were Yale graduates. Even people like Stimson himself, who had graduated in 1888 and later confessed that when he went on from there to Harvard Law School he found that even undergraduates at Cambridge were more focused on the outside world than at his alma mater.[8] The only real surprise is George's confession even to have considered going anywhere else, as he did in a 1989 interview when he admitted to a youthful flirtation with the idea of pursuing his romance with the navy by enrolling in the military academy at Annapolis.[9]

Early postwar Yale still belonged to the vintage of his father and uncle. It still had its trolley cars, and the Dutch elms that towered over the campus walks and lined the nearby streets. Yale was a school for men only; the quest for feminine companionship led Yalies to such "sister" institutions as Vassar and Smith.[10]

To George and his friends, it was still the school of *Dink Stover,* that early-twentieth-century novel by Owen Johnson of a time when Yale drew its freshman class from such prep schools as Hotchkiss, Groton, St. Mark's, and Andover. For young Stover, it was the enshrinement of his place within the proper order. The first step was making Skull and Bones, and life was lived for the coming of Tap Day. Fifteen graduating members of that exclusive secret society, its name unmentionable before outsiders, would be replaced by an equal number of inductees.

Admission to Skull and Bones was for George Bush and his friends a world separate not only from the apartment on Hillhouse Avenue, but also from the mainstream of Yale college life. Skull and Bones, the most secretive society on campus, was an inner sanctum where the truly elite could separate themselves from the merely privileged. The campus hoi polloi could conceivably matriculate for four years without knowing that it even existed.

One Bonesman interviewed over four decades after his graduation said he preferred not to discuss it and was especially uncomfortable when asked about the selection process, saying only that the names of candidates were not tapped for membership; therefore, they were not informed in advance. "There were several of us who knew each other going into Skull and Bones," he explained, "and there were half a dozen whom we didn't know. It was just the way it worked. We certainly got to know each other better that way."[11] When, at last, Tap Day came for Dink Stover, a "great sensation spread everywhere," and when he made it, there was "a shout of electrifying drama, the voice of his society speaking to the college." "God bless you, old man," said Dink's friend. "It's great, great—they rose to it. It's the finest ever!"[12]

Twice a week after six, on Thursday and Sunday nights, Bonesmen, having arranged study schedules to free them at those hours, met in the society's windowless headquarters on High Street to do their real business: Skull and Bones was dedicated to the celebration of one's brief life on earth. Much like the members of California's Bohemian Club (to which George Bush later belonged), they conducted their rituals in exclusive solitude. New members were initiated into the society's secret rituals in a triple-padlocked crypt. George paid his price by holding the others in a state of CB, or connubial bliss, as he dutifully revealed his innermost thoughts and described the highlights of his sex life.[13]

Skull and Bones was, for Bush, a stepping-stone. Lifelong friends were made in that inner sanctum, which, along with the base that had already been built as early as Andover, formed the core of a network for his future career. (Particularly helpful as fund-raisers, or fat cats, one *New York Times* reporter found that they "sounded more impressed with Mr. Bush's academic honors and records in school sports than his long resumé of public service."[14]) Several Bonesmen later invested their money in Bush's oil venture in Texas. One, Thomas Ludlow (Lud) Ashley, went on to become a Democratic congressman from Ohio and remained among Bush's closest friends. Others retained their ties as Bush rose through his political career. After their fellow Bonesman had become Ronald Reagan's vice president, Ashley hosted a large reunion dinner in his Washington home. "The dinner turned into a traditional Skull and Bones session of personal discussion and cross-examination," Walter Pincus and Bob Woodward later wrote, adding that the occasion gave Bush an opportunity for a long-sought chance to "unburden himself."[15]

As a Yale student, Ashley has acknowledged that Bush was "not among Yale's young activists or its intellectuals." He did not particularly have a probing or reflective mind. Nor was he "terribly well-informed," certainly not the kind of student who devoted himself either to the humanities or the sciences. He, instead, concentrated on business and economics, his undergraduate major. The closest he came to betraying any sort of ideology involved conservative economic orthodoxy, while reflecting his background in a broad, liberal outlook toward society, especially those of minority races. The student veterans were all too eager to "put politics behind us," as Ashley recalled. "Service was something we had done and we wanted now to pick up our lives and get married and have families and then support families."[16]

For the most part, George balanced his personal and academic lives while also pursuing other interests, especially baseball. He succeeded in winning the Gordon Brown Prize for "all around student leadership" and membership in the Torch Honor Society, and was sufficiently studious and capable of making Phi Beta Kappa, an achievement that perplexed some friends and teachers who remembered him from Andover.[17]

The likeable and affable young man was very much in the Bush mold when, in his senior year at Yale, he led the campus fund-raising drive for the United Negro College Fund. Black charities were, for the Bushes and many others of established wealth, among the leading recipients of philanthropic interests. George's father later served as his state's chairman of the UNCF. When Prescott Bush became a senator, he joined with liberal Republican colleagues in sponsoring a group of civil rights bills, which included giving the attorney general authority to bring key suits for the protection of civil rights and waiving literacy tests as a requirement for voting. George's brother, Jonathan, as an Upper East Side financier in New York City, devoted considerable time and money to the UNCF. The family's eagerness to be regarded as possessing "responsible" wealth was perhaps best illustrated by sister Nancy, who was later quoted as saying, "I think George would be marvelous with the poor, don't you think?"[18] What remains somewhat surprising, however, especially in the life of one who went on to the presidency, was the lack of any other social and political involvement, even during college years as a mature war veteran.

Baseball was another matter. Retrospectives of his student days focused on that one aspect almost to the exclusion of any other. With baseball as a leading varsity sport, the presence of so many war veterans gave Yale's teams an abundance of talent. The sport was, in a way, a natural undertaking for one whose uncle, Louis Walker (Uncle Herbie's youngest brother and only twelve years George's senior) had preceded him at Yale as a pitcher. Walker belonged to the squad that made a memorable overseas trip in 1935 to play against Japanese teams.[19] Eleven years later, when his nephew George joined the team, they were coached by Ethan Allen.

The Allen-Bush relationship was grounded in Bush's rise to national leadership as much as for his leadership abilities. As at Andover, his reputation came from his personality as much as from his talent. Another Allen, Phillip K. Allen, who helped coach him at baseball at Andover, recalled him as a "charmer" who was bright and eager and with a good sense of humor.[20] He was, above all, a friendly, personable teammate, a leader in the locker-room joshing and, on the field, one whose constant chatter sparked the pitcher and the Yale defense. "He was a real leader and fine athlete when we played together," remembered the squad's third baseman. Little wonder then that, as at Andover, his teammates chose him as their captain during his senior year.[21]

His reputation for popularity should not minimize the caliber of his talent. George's fielding around first base was outstanding. Although he batted right-handed, he threw with his left, which, combined with his height and physical grace made him ideal for that position. "The thing about Poppy," one of his teammates later told George Plimpton, "was that he was so sure-gloved. All the infielders knew that if they threw the ball anywhere near him, he was going to pull it in." In 1948, the year he homered in a game against Connecticut, the classy fielder also showed some uncharacteristic batting power against North Carolina with three hits, including a double and a triple. That helped draw the brief attention of some big-league scouts, who were shortly discouraged by Poppy's batting average. In those two full seasons at Yale, he hit only .239 and .264.[22]

His teams won the Eastern NCCA championships those years and went on to the national championships at Kalamazoo, Michigan. Each year, the finals came down to a best of three game playoffs, first against the University of California at Los Angeles and then Southern California University. Each year, Yale was the loser. In the 1948 finals, Bush scored Yale's only run in the first game and then drove home two runs in the second, although his batting average for the series was an anemic .167. On the field, he was as flawless as usual. That last championship was lost when Coach Allen ordered an intentional walk to get at the opposing pitcher. The batter, Jackie Jensen, later became an outfielder who hit 199 home runs in an eleven-year major-league career. Sparky Anderson, whose own major-league playing stay was brief but who went on to distinction as a manager with several teams, was the USC batboy that year.[23]

While he was outstanding at soccer and adept at basketball, baseball remained George Bush's game. The pride it brought cannot be minimized. George's major-league idol was Lou Gehrig, the famed New York Yankee first baseman, but it was Babe Ruth whom he met face-to-face. As Yale's team captain, George accepted from The Bambino the original manuscript of his autobiography that the home-run slugger publicly presented to the college's library shortly before his death.[24]

Yale's commencement exercises were held before the championship series in Kalamazoo. Bush returned home, said good-bye to baby George and Barbara, and pointed his red 1947 Studebaker coupe toward Odessa, Texas. Barbara and the baby would follow as soon as he found a decent place to live.[25]

The opportunities for a Yale graduate, especially for one with George Bush's personal credentials, were fortunately plentiful, even at a time when the nation's postwar economy, having recovered from a record high wave of inflation, was getting tighter. He even considered putting off a career for a year of study of Oxford, but, with a young family and already older than most college graduates, he decided to get a job. Joining his father's firm was, however, out of the question. George agreed with his brothers that "we didn't want to ride on our father's coattails."[26] He applied unsuccessfully for an opening at Procter & Gamble, but other opportunities remained.

The outlook was somewhat more limited for brother Prescott, who had graduated from Yale ahead of George. He had hoped to become a surgeon but, given his vision and the leg muscle damage from playing baseball, that dream was fanciful.[27] His career began with the help of a friend, a fellow Greenwich resident and local Republican activist, Samuel Pryor Jr. Pryor, whose estate abutted Long Island Sound on the other side of town, was an executive with Pan American World Airways. Their father was on the airline's board, and he had a working relationship with Pryor. He offered young Pres a job helping his company develop airports in Brazil.[28]

As previously mentioned, another close associate of Prescott Bush, one that dated back some eighteen years, was Neil Mallon, the president and general director of Dresser Industries. Bush served as the Mallon's "chief advisor and consultant in connection with every move."[29] Bush also held stock in Dresser, 1,900 shares as of March 1941. He served on its board and had been instrumental in transforming the company from a private to a public firm.[30]

Mallon and he were only four months apart in age and had been classmates and fellow Bonesmen at Yale. Mallon, well connected and described as a man of "uninhibited ambition," was regarded as a thoughtful and serious businessman. He was a bachelor, and remained single until age sixty-nine. To the Bushes, he had become a de facto member of the family.[31] George Bush, in his autobiography, later noted that Mallon was a "surrogate uncle and father confessor to all the Bush children while we were growing up."[32]

Turning to Mallon was easy. George Bush wanted more than merely to strike out on his own. After his military service, youthful but mature, ambitious and ready, he was not about to step into the monotonous routine of daily commutation into New York for eight hours of incarceration on Wall Street. The key to freedom, he and Barbara thought briefly, lay in Louis Bromfield's currently popular book, *The Farm*, which inspired them with the bold notion of taking up farming.[33] But reality won out. Running a farm required the investment of labor and capital in a totally unfamiliar enterprise. Moreover, Bush later wrote, "it wasn't the sort of business proposition to take up with our families." George thereby acknowledged the limits of the "independence" he offered as the reason he and Barbara wanted to make "it on our own." For Prescott Bush's sons, not following in their father's footsteps hardly meant breaking away.

Still, it was romantic as well as politic, to later rhapsodize about it. "We were young, still in our early twenties, and we wanted to make our way, our own mistakes, and shape our own future," he wrote in a campaign autobiography.[34]

All that was true, but the reasons went deeper. Barbara later confessed to writer Peggy Noonan that "George's mother was a formidable and strong woman, and so was my mother, and we wanted to get out from under the parental gaze, be on our own!"[35] That "parental gaze," of course, most emphatically included George's father, an intimidating figure for a son eager to test his own wings.[36]

Unstated but more important was the magnetic pull of George Bush and hundreds of kindred young men to the adventure and potential fortunes that awaited those with the money to play the game. Pressy remembered that his brother "met a bunch of fellows in the navy from the West and the Southwest, and they talked a lot about the oil industry and the opportunities there and everything else, and that's what made up his mind that he wanted to go out there and see what he could do in the oil industry."[37] And flock to the source they did, steered by what another Yalie oil explorer, Earle Craig Jr., called "the romance in the oil business."[38] Not surprisingly, George landed on the same soil with others who were mirror images of himself: well educated, from upper-class homes, off to duplicate on their own the success of their fathers, all mid-twentieth-century prospectors. "There were many of us Easterners in our twenties at that time," remembered Craig, "and we quickly got to meet each other."[39]

For all the cost involved in oil exploration, such wealthy young men knew that they had little to lose. At a time of confiscatory taxation of upper-income levels, they benefited from statutory inducements to invest. As long as abundant discretionary funds remained idle, they were vulnerable to taxation at the rate of 80 or 90 percent. A successful oil strike as the result of their "gamble" would leave the revenue yield partly tax free, thanks to the existing 27.5 percent oil depletion allowance. Even more favorable was the fact that the law considered as much as 70 percent of the development cost of bringing in production wells as "intangible" and applicable against taxable income for the year when the costs were incurred. A taxable income of $100,000 could be reduced to $10,000 by reinvesting in new drilling ventures.[40] The "romance" in oil was thereby encouraged by the same federal revenue laws that had come out of the New Deal and World War II. Little wonder that the California gold rush of the 1840s and the great Oklahoma land boom of the 1880s had their counterpart in the great West Texas oil craze of the 1950s.

Such federal laws brought riches to Texas as a whole. Not since the Spindletop strike, when that black fountain of oil shot up from 3,600 feet under a salt dome south of Beaumont in early 1901—soon pouring out some 25,000 to 100,000 barrels a day—had the state's economy been the same. Cattle fortunes, together with timber, cotton, and rice wealth, yielded to the growing nation's insatiable demand for oil. Spindletop itself was only a start, a national sensation at the outset but short-lived, its production quickly dwindling to a trickle.

What petered out prematurely was followed in 1930 by the development of the East Texas field, a boom that remained unequaled until Alaska's North Slope strike of the 1960s.[41] An oil strike west of Midland soon produced one hundred million barrels.[42] Venture capitalists, mostly from the East, rushed into the state. "Oil proved to be a prodigious economic multiplier for Texas," wrote a local historian, as the black gold drew more money and created a rich new class that formed "a distinctive kind of community, related in people, economy, and society more to others of its type than to older towns of its region untouched by oil."[43]

Nowhere else was the boom quite as dramatic as on the Permian Basin. Out of the prairie with its isolated cattle ranches and backwater railroad stops rose such centers as Odessa and Midland. The former was a town of oilfield laborers involved in working the wells, drilling and construction in the nearby countryside that was dotted with derricks and pumping jacks with their slow, repetitive movement to the rhythm of "Thank you very much, thank you very much, thank you very much," over and over and over again. The latter was the home of the adventurous Ivy League, managerial, investment classes, mainly independent producers, preceded by just one major company, Humble Oil, which completed the first productive well in the city in November of 1945.[44]

Midland became a petroleum headquarters on the Permian Basin. It even had the moxie to portray itself as a virtual Athens on the prairie. The First National Bank of Midland boasted about its art collections, book and music shops, community theater, and symphony orchestra. More visible was the fact that the town, once the gathering place of cowboys and itinerant oilmen, had become more notable for the incongruous skyline created by the office towers of banks and headquarters of petroleum corporations.[45] If not exactly an Athens, it was unarguably the oil capitol of West Texas, the money center of the Permian Basin, even equipped with a men's shop, Albert S. Kelley's, that Midlandians called the Brooks Brothers of the oil patch.[46]

The basin, once the home of a great salt lake of some 240,000 square miles that stretches from western Kansas to western Texas, is a vast geological region between Dallas and El Paso. Its name came from the explorations of three Russian geologists from the province of Perm, so "Permian Age" got to be a widely accepted geological designation that describes the origin of the oil from the rocks of western Texas and southern New Mexico.[47]

Today's Permian Basin was once the Permian Sea. About 500 million years ago, water advanced from the southeast, depositing limestone, sand, and shale during the following 4,000 years. (This part became the Midland Basin as distinguished from the Delaware Basin to the west.) Afterward, over a span of some 5,000 years, the water filled with gypsum, limestone, and sand. Red clay then poured in and was deposited, with one last wash, until the sea departed.

Oil first came to the Permian Basin in the early 1920s, but not as a serious flow until late in the decade. Odessa was then, in the words of two local historians, "a small, straggling, dusty, little village sprawling on the desert," to which the oil was trucked because it was the nearest shipping point on the railroad.[48] Odessa itself had a railroad history, its name taken from the Black Sea city by Russians who labored along the Texas and Pacific Railroad line. The railroad then attracted cattlemen who contended with the elements of that forbidding place, until finally, the coming of oil. Suddenly, Odessa prospered. Incorporation followed. The town's population went from 4,000 in 1935 to 30,000 in 1945, and ranked as the world's most active oil field trucking center.[49]

As with Odessa, oil did not create Midland. Early development anticipated its later character. A center of ranchers, it already had an attraction for the oil prospectors, the upscale Scharbauer Hotel, built in the late 1920s, together with office space. Already available for the newcomers of the 1940s and 1950s was the foundation for an administrative center. Although the Humble Oil and Refining Company produced its first well in 1945, large-scale production did not start until later in the decade, with the yield from a thick bed of fine-grained Permian sandstone called Spraberry Trend. Midland, first mainly via independents and then major companies, experienced its oil-boom growth. Not only wildcatters, but their geologists, geophysicists, engineers, attorneys, accountants, and other support personnel populated the center in one decade of swift upward movement. Before the 1950s were over, Midland had over 500 business firms and a population that had tripled to 70,000.[50]

Midland and Odessa have become, in effect, twin cities, each complementing the other, their rivalry played out on high school football fields and as outposts of two different worlds bound together through oil.

Neil Mallon was the perfect man to help ease George's way. The International Derrick & Equipment Company, known as Ideco, had been in Dresser's hands for only four years, its acquisition a major addition. Ideco was already a name on the oil fields of the Southwest, especially Texas, with its chain of sixteen equipment stores that catered to the needs of the drilling industry and, in 1948, was well on its way to becoming the leading manufacturer of portable rigs.[51] Mallon offered, and George accepted, an opportunity to go to Odessa.

His move was part of that postwar rush for adventure on the oil patches, booming thanks to the need for petrochemicals, which were so essential for the growing defense industry. Texas was, in fact, emerging as the nation's prime state for government defense contracts after California.[52] George Bush, with Neil Mallon and his father behind him and Uncle Herbie willing to take a flier on black gold, made his entrepreneurial debut by supplying drillers. His debut as a businessman could hardly have been better timed.

For Bush, it became the foundation for his entire career, whether in Texas or in Washington. The interests of producers and the importance of the "black gold" to modern economies remained a personal concern even as he accommodated virtually everything else to the complexities of political life.

CHAPTER FIVE

On the Permian Basin

%

W hen I was told of my assignment to Odessa," Bush explained to the sister of a local political leader some four decades later, "I had never heard of the town and didn't know what part of Texas it was in."[1] Odessa still seems isolated, still apart from today's metropolitan Texas, set off, along with Midland and Lubbock, from the rest of the state.

It is a working-class community, not the headquarters of the giant companies. Grant Avenue parallels Dixie Boulevard and is lined with symbols of Odessa's character: a videotape theater instead of a conventional movie house; laundromats, pawnshops, and tiny shotgun houses. With their lack of a central corridor, a bullet fired through the back door would theoretically go through each unit and emerge at the front.

Few buildings have ornamental facades or fresh paint. Many yards, both front and back, have low brick walls for privacy and protection when clouds of sand come out of the sky and drive the storms of dirt through the town. But there is no protection from the stench of oil, which fouls the drinking water and pollutes the atmosphere.

The Odessa of 1948 presented a stark contrast to what the Bushes had left behind. Numbers alone cannot gauge Odessa's population, so swift was its increase through that decade. Between the end of World War II and 1960, it had risen from thirty to eighty thousand.[2] When Barbara and baby George joined Bush a few weeks after his first arrival, they found themselves in a frontier outpost of post-World War II American expansion.

The differences between Odessa and Greenwich were great enough to be exotic, even adventurous. The two-room apartment that George first rented was in a house at 1319 East Seventh Street. The place was of the shotgun variety, little more than a frame building with bare boards nailed together. There was no insulation. But Bush's apartment had something that could not be found in any other house on the street: a bathroom instead of a rear-yard outhouse. George later wrote that "we had one bedroom, a small kitchen, and a shared bathroom. An old water-drip window unit that cranked up like a West Texas dust storm drew cool air into the bedroom on hot summer nights."[3] The other half of the house, across the center divide, was shared by a mother-daughter team of hookers who used to entertain their customers.[4] A single toilet was a bit of an inconvenience.

Little wonder that the Bushes moved twice in the few months they lived in Odessa, first to 1523 East Seventh Street and then to 916 East Seventeenth Street (where they finally had their own bathroom), before they left in April of 1949. The Odessa experience had evidently gone on long enough. Bush, Neil Mallon's protégé, was there only to learn the business "from the bottom up," a lot different from "working one's way to the top." As an equipment clerk for Ideco, he was paid $375 a month, which was not a bad entry rate. The hours were long and the labor mostly menial. Aside from helping out as a salesman in Odessa's Ideco store, he swept out warehouses and painted oil drilling machinery, doing, in other words, whatever odd jobs needed to be done. There were many twelve-hour days and working Sundays.[5]

Clearly, George and Barbara were strangers in a strange place. At one point, he got a sober view of the environment when he casually invited a black NAACP worker into his home. The man never did visit, but word got around quickly, and Bush was warned that such hospitality could lead to tarring and feathering. An artist, Clyde Heron, who had "watched transitions of people, having worked in the oil patch for years," remembered the young Bush as "friendly, affable," and adding approvingly, "he's got a good handshake. We believe in that out here."[6] Fortunately, Odessa was but temporary duty. Dorothy Bush later remembered that her son said, "Mother, I just hope I would have had the guts to go through with this even if it meant that Barbara, George, and I would have had to have been on the railroad train the next day."[7]

Mallon, again to the rescue, got Bush out of there soon enough. He first transferred him to California, where he represented a Dresser subsidiary called Pacific Pumps. Another move took him to Bakersfield, where, one biographer has written, he practiced "his natural talent as a salesman" peddling drill bits.[8] He also became a member of the United Steelworkers Union and went to meetings of the Bakersfield local. Then came a succession of other Dresser locations in California, Whittier, Ventura, and Compton, all involving selling Ideco products and putting heavy mileage on his car. They were living in Compton in 1949 when they received the tragic news that Marvin Pierce had lost control of his car and slammed into a stone wall in New York's Westchester County, instantly killing Barbara's mother, Pauline. Shortly thereafter, the Bushes had a second child, a girl, on December 20, 1949, whom they named Pauline Robinson Bush; they called her Robin. The baby had blue eyes and blond hair. Finally, some two-and-a-half years after George had first joined Ideco, the parent company reassigned him to Midland, which had more and more become headquarters for independent oilmen in Texas.

* * *

Few significant political careers start in middle age, but Prescott Bush, active in Greenwich government for so long, found an opening and seized it. His state was represented by two Democrats in the U.S. Senate, Brien McMahon, highly partisan and at the forefront in the battle for civilian rather than military control of the emerging arms race, and William Benton. Benton, a fifty-year-old Yalie from the class of 1921, considered "independent, outspoken, and liberal," was truly not run-of-the-mill. His fortune secured through his success in advertising with partner Chester Bowles, Benton went on to work under University of Chicago President Robert Maynard Hutchins and then to the chairmanship of the Encyclopedia Britannica before being appointed in 1945 as assistant secretary of state for Public Affairs. When Senator Raymond Baldwin, a Republican, resigned his seat in frustration in 1949, Benton's old partner, Bowles, by then Connecticut's governor, appointed him to complete the remainder of the term.[9]

Benton's seat was eyed by publisher Henry Luce. Others in Connecticut, including Prescott Bush, were ready to close ranks behind him to defeat the Democrat in his race for reelection. Luce, however, reluctant to separate himself from *Time* magazine, backed out. That April, just as he reached his fifty-fifth birthday, Bush declared his own candidacy.[10]

Nineteen-fifty was a good year for a Republican to make a first run for Washington, but it was also, in many ways, one of the more tumultuous times of the early cold war era. The Truman administration faced the crack-up of bipartisanship in its resistance to Communist hegemony, and Democrats were on the defensive. The political fallout that surrounded the recent ouster of Chiang Kai-shek's nationalists from the Chinese mainland, coupled with Soviet acquisition of nuclear capability and growing fear of internal subversion, was raised to a shriller, uglier level by Republican Senator Joseph Raymond McCarthy.

The Wisconsin freshman's rise to national prominence had already begun. In February 1950, speaking at Wheeling, West Virginia, his sensational allegation about 205 Communists employed by the State Department launched one of the more divisive and controversial brief careers in all of American history. After broadening his charges and naming names during hearings chaired by Senator Millard Tydings, a Maryland conservative, McCarthy's rampage denounced former Secretary of State George Marshall as "completely unfit" and "completely incompetent," and suggested that his handling of the situation in China had been influenced by Communist sympathizers.[11] However outrageous the senator's charges, he had the advantage of good timing. That June, North Korean Communists crossed the thirty-eighth parallel in force. American soldiers fighting on that distant peninsula in their first military action of the cold war provided a dramatic background for that fall's elections and seemed to vindicate McCarthy's alarms about Communist subversion.

McCarthy was clear about three of his own domestic political enemies, Millard Tydings, Brien McMahon, and Bill Benton. McCarthy demonstrated his power by going after Tydings because the Delaware senator's investigative committee had condemned what it called his "nefarious campaign of half-truths and untruths." In Connecticut, voters were asked to defeat McMahon and Benton. McMahon was McCarthy's antagonist as a Democratic member of the Tydings Committee. Benton, one of only twelve Democrats to attack him publicly, had called his colleague a propagandist "of the Soviet type." He "doesn't argue, he doesn't answer, he doesn't reason. He hits and runs."[12]

McCarthy's existence threatened to overshadow the election. With Benton involved in a special election to confirm his interim appointment, Connecticut was the only state in the union with two senators on the record as openly opposed to his tactics, and both were now fighting to retain their seats. The state, moreover, was supposedly fertile territory for the Wisconsonian. New England's Catholics, especially the Irish, were among McCarthy's strongest enthusiasts. And while the true believers probably did not constitute an actual majority of the potential vote, there was ample reason to fear his attraction to conservative Democrats. McCarthy was still in the early stage of his crusade, so that his excesses were yet to become obvious. Bush, in the campaign to win, undoubtedly agreed with his friend and fellow Yalie, Robert A. Taft, that he was a useful instrument for getting out the vote. But overt identification with the man was also risky, especially for its potential effect on the state's sizable number of moderates. In Maryland, meanwhile, McCarthy's people were plotting Tydings's downfall by circulating a fake photo that purported to show their senator in a friendly encounter with former U.S. Communist Party leader Earl Browder. It did have its intended effect.

McCarthy's designs on Connecticut involved three campaign visits. Invitations came from such ad hoc groups as one called Connecticut Volunteers, which brought the senator before a crowd of about one thousand just before election day.[13] The sparse crowds that awaited him in New Haven and Bridgeport hardly constituted evidence that his appearances were boosted by efficient work by Republican regulars.[14] After their joint appearance at Memorial Hall in Bridgeport, where he shared a platform with McCarthy for the first time, Bush recalled that his "very presence at a rally was enough to start a riot. . . . I never saw such a wild bunch of monkeys in any meeting I've ever attended. I went out on the stage with my knees shaking."[15] That was the closest he got to McCarthy as he made no moves to welcome the controversial visitor. Benton worked at making an issue of the McCarthy presence by repeatedly challenging Bush to repudiate the Red hunter. Bush held his tongue.[16] At the same time, he refused McCarthy's offer of a large campaign gift.[17]

The Bush campaign was well-financed and well-fought. A light touch came from televised appearances on his behalf from Yale's Whiffenpoofs. Benton managed to cut into some of his support from businessmen, nationally as well as in Connecticut. He even took a cue from Lyndon Johnson's 1948 campaign in Texas by renting a helicopter, then a novelty that attracted considerable attention, to fly to political rallies (although it once descended into the midst of a Republican picnic!). At a time when President Truman had made a system of national health insurance a vital part of his Fair Deal program, Bush benefited from a massive effort by Connecticut's antinational health insurance physicians to bombard their patients with letters warning about how supporting the Democratic candidate would jeopardize their health care.[18] Bush, accordingly, opposed "socialized medicine" together with deficit spending and extravagance in government. Such fiscal irresponsibility, he charged, brought "sly hidden taxes, confiscatory taxes." He also denounced the Truman administration for trying "to take credit for civil rights legislation when a Congress of his own party fails to act year after year." He favored federal and state grants to help poorer areas but opposed federal control as "a long step toward a police state." He called for labor laws "to protect the rights of union members and the public" and in opposition to "labor bosses, whether in union or management ranks."

In its broad view of the world, Bush echoed Republican orthodoxy, together with the party's postwar emergence from isolationism, a position that separated him from such conservative traditionalists as his friend Bob Taft. He called for the creation of a standing United Nations army, but left no doubt of his own aversion toward the Communist menace. He advocated strict control of domestic Communists and a "firm, steady, clear policy opposing Communist aggression anywhere, whether political or military." In a list of eleven items he enumerated as being opposed to, he included "confused bungling of our defense" and "Communists and softness toward Communists." The issues of 1950, he added, can be summarized in the words "Korea, communism, confusion, and corruption," thus handing Republicans a slogan they used with only a slight variation during the subsequent presidential campaign in 1952.[19]

Few words so well caught the national political mood, or explained the collapse of the bipartisanship that had supported Truman's foreign policy initiatives through the early cold war years. The Republicans were rebounding from their shocking loss in the presidential election in 1948 and nationally. Connecticut was no exception. John Davis Lodge upset incumbent Democrat Chester Bowles to win the first four-year term for Connecticut's governorship. Brien McMahon, for all his visibility and partisanship as a Democrat, held his seat with a relatively slender 52.6 percent of the vote against weak opposition. Bush, meanwhile, with a boost from the conservative resurgence and opposing an interim Democratic senator who had yet to be elected on his own, was engaged in an obviously tight race.[20]

Benton's ability to hang on was clearly in doubt by that final weekend before the voting. The outcome may well have been decided by an incident involving the state's large number of Roman Catholic worshipers that occurred so late and seemed so innocuous that it went unnoticed by the press. That Sunday, as Dorothy Bush later recalled, "cards were handed out at noon in church saying, 'Listen to the broadcast tonight at six.' It was Sunday night. . . . and Lodge's campaign manager called me up and said, 'Mrs.

Bush, have you heard this broadcast?' I said, 'No,' and he said, 'Well, Bush has been connected with the Birth Control League.' He's never been on the Birth Control League at all. But you see, this was the night before Monday [election eve], when everything stopped."[21]

The association of Bush with birth control, made that Sunday evening on the weekly radio report by Walter Winchell, was devastating. Not only was the distribution of contraceptive devices still illegal in Connecticut, but the subject itself was taboo. Even if it were possible to rebut the allegation, and it was not, it certainly could not have been done on election eve. Connecticut Republican Leader John Alsop later wrote to the president of the state's Planned Parenthood League that the word in party circles was that Bush "was beaten on account of his activities" and that "it will probably have a frightening effect on other Republican politicians." George Bush later explained that the incident was his first awareness of "birth control as a public policy issue," and it was not a happy one.[22]

Morning papers went to press late that night unable to report the winner. In Washington, President Truman authorized U.S. marshals in Connecticut to impound all ballot boxes to prevent tampering. Not until four in the morning was the final statewide tabulation completed. Benton had won with 431,413 votes to Bush's 430,311, a 1,102 vote majority. How much the outcome was influenced by the Winchell broadcast can only remain speculative, but it was something the loser's son never forgot.

His setback, however, was temporary. Brien McMahon died in the summer of 1952 and Republicans scrambled to nominate their own candidate to complete the four years remaining of the senator's six-year term. As Prescott Bush vacationed on Fisher's Island, just off the Connecticut coast south of Mystic, he received a little delegation of Republican leaders. They assured him that if he would only agree to become a candidate, he could win the party's nomination for the vacant senate seat. With their support in hand, he beat out such other hopefuls as antitax activist Vivian Kellums and Clare Booth Luce, becoming the Republican senatorial candidate in what they had promised would be a good year. And they were right, especially with Eisenhower heading their national ticket. But, first, Prescott had to make certain he would not again be bedeviled by "Birth Control League" charges. With the issue having become hotter, and the Catholic Church fighting hard to resist efforts by reformers to overturn the state's 1879 anticontraception law, Bush's campaign manager made several well-placed telephone calls urging Planned Parenthood leaders to withhold court tests until after the election, which they did.[23] The tide that swept in Ike then helped to place Prescott Bush in Washington by giving him 51.3 percent of the vote against Abraham Ribicoff. Only after his father's election did anyone ever hear George Bush raise the possibility of a political career for himself.[24]

Although it was clear from the start that they had had enough of Odessa, George and Barbara were happy to return to Texas. This time, although his reassignment placed him at the Dresser warehouse in Odessa, he relocated his family to Midland.

That community in 1950 was far more congenial than anything they had seen since leaving Greenwich. They were newcomers, but so was just about everybody else. They started out in Midland by renting a motel room on Main Street in a place called, coincidentally, George's Court. At least, from there, Bush could commute the twenty miles along Route 80 to his Odessa job, an arrangement, he knew, he would not have to put up with for long. "California was fine," he wrote in his autobiography, "but the oil boom was on in Texas. And Midland, the heart of the Permian Basin, had come into its own as the biggest boomtown of them all."[25]

Bush himself later wrote that the rising city on the plains could be called "Yuppieland West."[26] Newly laid-out streets were named after Ivy League colleges. Millionaires lived along Harvard and Princeton Streets. They drove along Country Club Drive to socialize with others who were equally deep in the business of oil. The Country Club and the Petroleum Club were the "only two nice places to go to," but they were not the only clubs in town. Just a few years later, after a decade of spectacular growth, writer John Bainbridge presented Midland to the world outside West Texas as possibly "the richest city per capita in the country."[27] In Midland, Sally Helgesen has written, "the optimistic rhetoric of advertisement takes over, and the depiction of the dream eases reality."[28] Bush later quoted *Midland Reporter-Telegram* editor Bill Collins as saying about the place: "People said we were overbuilding, but that wasn't the case. Almost every building made money for the investors. It was hard to go wrong in Midland."[29]

Finally, seizing their first opportunity, they bought into the first mass housing development to go up in the town. Built on East Maple Street, far from the most posh section, and with only 847 square feet, including a carport and a small, paved-over square that passed for a "patio," the bright blue house came with the right price tag, $7,500. George financed the purchase with a Federal Housing Administration mortgage.

However modest, the surroundings were a sharp contrast with what they had seen in Odessa. Their area became known as Easter Egg Row because all the houses were painted with vivid colors. How else could they be distinguished from one another?

Relief from West Texas extremes—the dry, parched heat of summers on the Permian Basin plains and the chill, bleak winters, to say nothing about the periodic sandstorms—came for George and Barbara during summer visits to Kennebunkport, especially for family get-togethers in August, and trips to join Prescott and Dorothy at their Hobe Sound place in Florida. They also began to spend the month of July at Camp Longhorn in the Texas hill country west of Austin.

In Texas, they lived very much the lifestyle of their contemporaries. They made new friends, drank late-afternoon martinis, and spent evenings at the Petroleum Club. They "avoided the high jinks" that attracted some of the young couples, assured one sympathetic biographer, although they "weren't prudes; they simply followed a different set of personal rules," which led them to avoid "activities that would drain their health and vigor."[30] Barbara, her hair still quite dark, was a likeable member of the social set.[31]

She and George participated in more than their share of community activities. Both taught Sunday school for awhile at the First Presbyterian Church, where they worshiped while in Midland, and Barbara was active in a group that eventually became the socially upscale Junior League of Midland.[32] A former president of the Chamber of Commerce remembered that Bush "was very deeply involved in Midland and in its growth and progress, whether it was the YMCA, the theater, or the church."[33] He was one of the organizers of the Commercial Bank and Trust Company and became chairman of the Midland County Cancer Unit and director of the Chamber of Commerce. It was also there when, in 1952, the year his father was elected to the U.S. Senate, he got his start in partisan politics. He drew the job of arranging for an airport reception for campaigning vice presidential candidate Richard Nixon, which sparked an incident that provided an example of the young Bush's toughness. Nixon had hardly begun to speak before a couple of protesters began to yell and wave signs. "Bush took one look at them," recalled his business partner, John Overbey, "and tore over there. He ripped up their signs and told them to get the hell out of there."[34] Bush worked mostly on the precinct level and became financial chairman for the local Republican effort, a job he continued through the Eisenhower-Nixon reelection campaign four years later.[35]

His family grew quickly during those Midland years. Young George, (who was called "Junior" for the sake of convenience, even though that was not strictly accurate) and Robin were joined by three brothers, John Ellis Bush (Jeb) in 1953, Neil Mallon Bush in 1955, and Marvin Pierce Bush in 1956.

Jeb had just been born, when early in the spring of 1953, three-year-old Robin woke up pale and lethargic. The small bruises on her legs had gone unnoticed, but the child's listlessness told Barbara that something was wrong. She took her to the pediatrician, Dr. Dorothy Wyvell. After testing Robin's blood, the doctor asked Barbara to return that afternoon with her husband. Bush, who was doing some work at the courthouse over in the next county, rushed back. Dr. Wyvell explained that Robin had advanced leukemia. It had probably developed while they were still in California. The doctor had never seen a white bloodcell count that high. The Bushes had many friends by then, and although Dr. Wyvell had advised that nobody be told since Robin had only about three weeks to live, word got around quickly. "I recall very vividly that we were at the Midland Country Club," said their good friend Earle Craig Jr., "and we got word of Robin's illness. We were discussing it there among ourselves with my father-in-law, who was a well-known surgeon in New York City. I remember him saying that, in all probability, it was terminal."[36]

George and Barbara ignored Dr. Wyvell's opinion that Robin's case was hopeless. They flew her to New York the next morning. Dr. John Walker, president of New York's Sloan-Kettering Memorial Hospital, was also George's uncle. He suggested that she be examined by Sloan-Kettering Foundation specialists. They gave the child a new cancer drug, which seemed to work, but not fully.

Robin held on for seven months. When she seemed well, they spent the time in Midland, but there were long days in New York. They moved into a relative's Sutton Place apartment so that Barbara could be at Robin's bedside every day. George had to return to work but flew back to New York on weekends. He left his two boys with neighbors until his mother sent a nurse to Texas to help. He drew whatever comfort he could from daily prayers in his church and by immersing himself in his work. The immediate burden of caring for Robin fell to Barbara, who was then only twenty-eight. It was at that time that her hair began to turn gray.[37]

In October, while George was on his way back to her bedside, Robin began to hemorrhage. The Sloan-Kettering doctors decided to operate, but she didn't survive the surgery, and died before her father could get there. He returned to the hospital the next day to show his appreciation to those who had helped care for her. "We gave Robin's body to Sloan-Kettering and said do with it what you will," Barbara told Donnie Radcliffe in 1988. "About three months after her death they let me know her liver had died. Sort of insensitive, except we were into research."[38] George set up what they called the Bright Star Foundation and he and Barbara also signed a document to donate their own organs posthumously.

"We need a girl," George later wrote to his mother. "We had one once— she'd fight and cry and play and make her way just like the rest. But there was about her a certain softness. . . . Her peace made me feel strong, and so very important . . . but she is still with us. We need her and yet we have her. We can't touch her, and yet we can feel her."[39]

By the time they lost Robin, George Bush had long since been able to abandon the Odessa run. In 1950, he had become an independent oil man, having joined with one who knew how to track down potential strikes, John Overbey. Given the cost of drilling holes in the plains only to find them dry, good money could be made by trading leases. Overbey's business was to scout out lands. Then, whenever prospects were hopeful, he would make a deal with the owner for a share of the mineral rights. Overbey and Bush complemented each other perfectly. Each had what the other needed: Overbey had the know-how; the Connecticut Yankee had the financial resources, plus the ability to make and keep friends, which made him an excellent salesman.

All that became clear the more they talked, often over cold martinis on George's patio in the cool of the evening after he returned from his daily commutation to Odessa. Bush's days with Ideco were no match for Overbey's accounts of his prospecting adventures. A partnership was inevitable.

Bush flew east and laid it all out for Uncle Herbie. George was his favorite nephew anyway, so that made it easier. Walker's extensive connections, especially on Wall Street, made his enthusiasm for the young man's venture easy to support, and he pitched into the process by ultimately helping to tap investors for at least $350,000. George's father kicked in $50,000.[40] Bush sought out others, including traveling to Washington to enlist one of his father's Brown Brother Harriman clients, publisher Eugene Meyer. Meyer, publisher of the *Washington Post,* agreed to put up $50,000, and then added an additional amount in the name of his son-in-law, Phil Graham.[41]

One other person needed to know: Neil Mallon. A mere phone call was obviously inappropriate. So Bush flew to the Dresser's corporate headquarters in Dallas. Mallon heard what the young man had to say, delayed responding while he cleaned his glasses, and went to the next office for a legal-size yellow pad. He began to write, as he said, "I really hate to see you go, George, but if I were your age, I'd be doing the same thing—and here's how I'd go about it." George remembered how the next half hour was spent getting "a crash course not only in how to structure but how to finance an independent oil company." That was in late 1950. By the new year, he and his neighbor were in business as the Bush-Overbey Oil Development Company.

Bush, said one observer of the Midland scene to *Los Angeles Times* correspondent Barry Bearak in 1987, "would've been just another carpetbagger if he hadn't rode [*sic*] in on a silk carpet."[42] Given the cost and inherent risks involved in oil exploration, of course, the statement can never be tested for accuracy. Capital *was* the essential first step. The annals are full of potentially effective entrepreneurs who fell short because of inadequate resources. But Bush, to be fair, had the ability to put it all together, including the initial confidence in him from his uncle, who continued to exert a role commensurate with his investment, in both raising additional funds and overseeing operations. Such backing enabled George to buy up mineral rights and arrange for oil exploration on behalf of his customers. Walker, who continued to tap investors, must have been pleased that Bush-Overbey got off to a decent start as the company that represented the "Eastern elites of Uncle Herbie's investment firm."[43]

Bush-Overbey managed to remain in the black, but not very comfortably. More precisely, as John Overbey put it in a 1986 letter, the company "rocked along and made a few good deals and a few bad ones." The close-knit, relatively intimate environment of Midland inevitably led George into a new partnership, this time with Overbey and him teaming up with brothers J. Hugh Liedtke and William C. Liedtke. Hugh was two years older than his brother and, unlike William, became a major figure in the American petroleum industry. Sons of the chief counsel for Gulf Oil and from Tulsa, by way of Amherst College and the University of Texas Law School (Hugh also had an M.B.A. degree from Harvard Business School), their law practice under the name of Liedtke & Liedtke was located across the street from Bush-Overbey. Instead of practicing general law, however, they were drawn overwhelmingly to oil. They spent most of their time forming partnerships. Proximity inevitably drew the Liedtkes to the Bushes; after all, as Hugh later explained, "there wasn't a damn thing to do out there except be friends."[44]

Friendship with the Liedtkes led to a new venture, which moved George from trading leases to contract drilling for major suppliers. The lawyers invited him to form a new oil company, which they named the Zapata Petroleum Corporation, a name drawn from a Mexican revolutionary leader.

A more inappropriate choice for capitalist free enterprisers would be hard to imagine. The curious selection, it seems, was made for no better reason than the coincidental showing in downtown Midland of the Marlon Brando film, *Viva Zapata!*, a biography of Emiliano Zapata, who fought for land redistribution on behalf of peasants, which should have made him anathema to capitalists everywhere. But in the case of Bush's new venture, Zapata seemed an appropriate symbol, as Bush and his fellow independents were in the vanguard around Midland. "We couldn't afford a public-relations counsel," Bush later acknowledged, "but if we had one he would have told us that was exactly the corporate image we were looking for."[45]

Hugh Liedtke, called by one writer the "boy genius of West Texas oil," became president and Bush vice president. So, by March 1953, Zapata was launched. Liedtke knew exactly what he wanted to do. He invested everything the new company had and then some to gamble—although he clearly did not consider it a "gamble"—on a single oilfield in Coke County. And he came up triumphant: under a series of six wells at the Jameson field, a "patch of sandy prairie," were rich deposits of oil. Bush and the Liedtkes were convinced that the wells, which were widely dispersed, were connected. They played where other investors hesitated. By the end of 1954, there were seventy-one new wells, which produced an average daily yield of 1,250 barrels. Their drilling never struck a dry hole, Liedtke later recalled.[46] The field ultimately accommodated 130 successful wells, which gave both Bush and Overbey enough money to leave Easter Egg Row.

And it was, for George and Barbara, their dream house, together with a swimming pool in an upscale Midland subdivision at 1412 West Ohio Street, off Golf Course Road. The low-slung ranch-style home was near the Cowden Park athletic field, where the Bush boys played soccer and baseball.[47]

Those years were also good to Midland. The city's growth in 1953 was hailed by the *Reporter-Telegram* as among the "biggest stories of the year." There was money to be made everywhere. Deposits in Midland banks reflecting the oil upswing registered a $3,271,617.45 gain within one year, reaching the highest level in history, and the industry celebrated Petroleum Week with the publication by the paper of a ninety-page Petroleum Progress edition. Construction gains reached a new high in 1953, $12,163,810, which included new churches, a new public safety building, the Union Oil Company building, a transmitting tower for the Midessa Television Company, and the modernization of existing buildings. "The City of Midland, headquarters for the vast Permian Basin Empire, the United States's most prolific oil producing area," exulted the *Reporter-Telegram*, "witnessed another record breaking oil exploration year in 1954."[48] But the next year was even better, although as usual, a succession of sandstorms, each given a male name, Eli, Farouk, Gus, Hubert, McDaniels (named in honor of "the terrific Midland High School football player"), Kinsey, and Leo, swept through the city.[49]

Progress had its bumps. The speculative rush helped set off a chain of unsettling incidents. Three men were arrested for stealing and selling oil field exploration maps. At the height of a nighttime sandstorm in March, a "sportily" dressed bandit held up Bert's Drive-in and escaped with $500 in cash. A Seminole oil field worker was arrested the next day, only to be later acquitted; but the city, fearing the worst, appropriated over $5,000 to hire private investigators to determine whether they were in the grip of organized crime.[50]

Prescott Bush, relinquishing his directorship from seven corporations (but not all that he held) before taking his Senate seat, went on to position himself as an Eisenhower middle-of-the-roader. He favored modifying the antilabor Taft-Hartley Act, easing the harsher antiimmigration provisions of the McCarran Act, joined the administration in opposing the Bricker Amendment and in calling for stand-by price controls, introduced a "code of fair procedures" in direct response to the abuse of witnesses by Senator McCarthy's investigating committee while refusing to attend a Lincoln Day dinner with the senator from Wisconsin in Bridgeport, all positions that outraged ultraconservative Republicans. In February of 1955, Senator Bush appeared on CBS's *Face the Nation* television program and agreed that Eisenhower Republicans were true to the party of Lincoln because they have taken "the best out of the traditional positions of the Democrat and Republican party, and put them together in what the president calls the moderate progressivism of our new Republican party . . ."

The freshman from Connecticut began his senatorial career in 1953 by taking an important pro-Eisenhower position, one that closely paralleled his son's ambitions in Texas. While George was venturing into offshore oil explorations, setting up the Zapata Off-Shore Company, Prescott Bush actively fought alongside the Republican majority to preserve such mineral deposits that were outside the three-mile limit but within the twelve-mile limit in the hands of the states. He denounced the effort by Senator Lister Hill of Alabama to federalize such natural resources in order to fund federal support for education. The two matters, Bush vigorously declared, the "so-called 'tidelands' legislation" and federal aid for education, could not and should not be linked. Placing submerged lands under such ownership, he wrote in response to an appeal from Hartford's mayor to tap that source as potentially beneficial for the schools of Connecticut's capital city, "should be an entirely separate question from that of submerged lands and warrants careful study because of the danger of federal control of education." He then voted with the majority to table the Hill Amendment.[51]

Venturing offshore was precisely George's objective. Overbey stepped aside as Bush joined with the Liedtkes and moved into the risky business of offshore drilling. By 1955, at the height of the boom of the oil fields and in the nation, he and his partners were ready to offer $1.5 million worth of stock in a subsidiary called the Zapata Off-Shore Company to drill wells on a contract basis for major distributors. They contracted with a Vicksburg, Mississippi, industrialist-engineer, R. B. LeTourneau, for the construction of rigs capable of drilling in coastal waters. The first of the three electrically self-elevating platforms that stood in the seas as on a giant tripod was commissioned in March of 1956. LeTourneau's design, which had first been accomplished in Vicksburg, was unique; for Zapata it was an important innovation. "We decided that offshore drilling was going to be a growing and major factor in the oil industry," Bush explained. "To get into that business you had to take a risk. There were other companies that had built rigs that tipped over or just cratered on the first well, and that was the end of the company."[52] Their second rig withstood the hundred-mile-an-hour winds of hurricane Audrey. Not until much later, when Bush had become involved in Texas politics, did a storm, hurricane Betsy, destroy a rig when it hit the Gulf Coast in September 1965. Rigs operated by Zapata and its affiliate, Seacat Zapata, had by then been operating all over the world, not only in the Gulf of Mexico but in the Persian Gulf for the Kuwait Shell Petroleum Development Company, off the northern coast of Borneo, and off the coast of Trinidad. Zapata Off-Shore briefly became a dummy partner with a businessman from below the border to get around laws favoring Mexican investors in running a drilling operation named Perforaciones Marinas del Golfo (Permargo). By 1959, Bush's personal holdings in Zapata Off-Shore, which became a publicly owned stock that was listed on the American Stock Exchange, consisted of about 15 percent of the company's shares and was worth about $600,000.[53]

That included the effects of hard times that had hit the industry. Much of the great Eisenhower boom exhausted itself after the first few heady years of Zapata Off-Shore. The oil boom's luster dissipated along with the rest of the great period of expansion. Bush, whose own negotiating skills had kept the company's stock in the hands of Zapata Petroleum even when arranging for the additional financing, now faced problems inherent in paring down. Methodically, with precision and yet tact, he reduced the offshore company's overhead by reducing personnel, even slicing off some with whom he had had personal relationships. "I've seen Bush let people go, terminate them," commented Hugh Liedtke later, "even though they were his personal friends. But he did it because it had to be done. And the remarkable thing was, he did it in such a way that he was still friends with them later."[54]

Hard times revealed other stresses. Uncle Herbie's presence as an "angel" for the oil ventures, whether with his or with other people's money, had, of course, been a blessing. But Uncle Herbie's largesse came with a price tag; he was a meddler, one who had no compunctions about giving the impression that he was trying to run the business from Wall Street. The Liedtkes suffered the annoyance mostly in silence.[55] In the later fifties, however, it strained their relationship. Hugh, for one, wondered why he had to put up with George's uncle any longer. In addition, he had strong reservations about continuing to stake so much in offshore drilling. Also, he now wanted to compete with the majors by heading his own company.

Once the split became inevitable, negotiations began. In their showdown, Liedtke also found Bush no pushover. His partner was tough and shrewd, and the separation process produced a series of complex swaps of stock. When the exchanges finally ended, Liedtke held control over the original Zapata Petroleum Corporation. Bush, together with Herbert Walker, commanded the $4.5 million-a-year Zapata Off-Shore Company. As Henry Hurt III has written, "he wasn't yet a full-fledged self-made millionaire, but for a thirty-five-year-old Yalie who had learned the oil business from scratch, he was doing very well."[56] Liedtke, the president of Zapata Petroleum, retained a toehold in George's company as director and secretary-treasurer. Later, in 1963, he merged Zapata Petroleum with the Penn Oil Company and became president and chief executive officer of Pennzoil.

The Bush-Liedtke relationship, and long-lasting friendship, turned out to be mutually useful. It became a cornerstone of the circle that ultimately facilitated Bush's political career and, for Liedtke, his success as one of the major powers in the nation's oil industry. He built Pennzoil by using a tactic known until then mainly in Great Britain, the hostile takeover, which shortly enabled him to gain control of a company then five times the size of Pennzoil, the United Gas Pipeline Company, one of the largest in the industry. His original Pennzoil stock value, meanwhile, multiplied by 10,000 percent by 1986, or at about the time the company won a $10.53 billion judgment against Texaco.[57]

Facilitating the Liedtke rise (younger brother William left later to join another company) from that Permian launching pad was made possible not only via Bush and Zapata but also through the legal assistance of one of Houston's most prominent and most powerful law firms, Baker & Botts. Pennzoil became one of the most valued accounts of a legal power that was foremost in the state. The two companies, with offices in each of the twin towers of Houston's landmark Pennzoil Center, did not merely do business with each other. Baine Kerr of Baker & Botts, for example, became Pennzoil's chief legal counsel before rising to the firm's presidency. "For twenty-five years," writes *Wall Street Journal* business journalist Thomas Petzinger, "the internal legal department at Pennzoil had been almost indistinguishable from Baker & Botts . . ."[58] Liedtke, having touched bases with Bush and, by then, James Baker, headed the first company to gain oil drilling rights in China after U.S. recognition. Bush, acting as a private citizen and shortly after leaving his diplomatic post at the U.S. liaison office in Beijing, traveled to the Chinese capital with Liedtke to help arrange the oil concession.[59]

"George was one of the first two of our associates from the East to be worth one million dollars [*sic*], and I was green with envy. In those days, that was a great deal of money, by a factor of five or six," said his Midland friend, Earle Craig Jr. Craig never could understand how someone so successful in the oil business could "waste" his talent by going into politics. He himself had had "no premonition whatsoever"about George's objective once he left Midland. Bush had, in fact, lost little time in moving the Zapata operation to Houston in 1959, when Barbara was pregnant for the sixth time.[60]

Their last child was named Dorothy, but she grew up answering to "Dordie" and later "Doro." "Dorothy is enchanting," Bush wrote to Yale classmate Lud Ashley. "She is a wild dark version of Robin. They look so much alike that Mom and Dad both called Dorothy 'Robin' all last week when Bar went to visit at Hobe Sound."[61]

CHAPTER SIX

Harris County

%

If not actually a millionaire—and he was certainly far from superwealthy by Texas oil standards—Bush was clearly secure. He had also reached the age of thirty-five, a crucial time when ambitious men must reconcile the often conflicting needs of family life and careers. He was ready for something other than making money. He had, after all, lived up to his father's advice: provide for your family's financial security before undertaking your own indulgences.[1]

And, like his father, George chose politics. Press accounts invariably called him charismatic. A young University of Houston graduate who signed on with him early, Peter Roussel, described the youthful Bush as similar to Jefferson Smith of *Mr. Smith Goes to Washington* fame.[2] He was universally regarded as a certain bet for future success. He was an "up-and-coming" young businessman, as the cliché goes, the well-bred son of a U.S. senator, a member of St. Martin's Episcopal Church, home of one of Houston's wealthiest congregations, and the head of a large, attractive family. Zapata remained central to his business interests, but his involvement in the corporate world had grown to include an array of directorships in the petroleum industry. His name appeared on the letterheads of such organizations as an oil equipment field company named Camco, Inc.; the Independent Petroleum Association of America; the American Association of Oilwell Drilling Contractors; and the Texas Mid-Continent Oil and Gas Association.[3] He even had another certifiable mark of ambition, a bleeding ulcer, which was diagnosed by Dr. Lillo Crain at the Texas Medical Center in Houston after George complained about dizziness while on a 1960 business trip to London.[4]

His status as a family man was emphasized after Barbara gave birth to Dorothy, an event that also reflected the age span among the Bush children; little George, who had graduated from Midland's Sam Houston Elementary School, went off to the Andover class of 1964. It was at that point that George Bush and his family settled into their comfortable two-story brick house at 5525 Briar Drive, a neighborhood in Houston's southwestern corner that was upscale, without being truly exclusive. Built on an oversized plot, one large enough later to accommodate three houses, it looked deceptively modest, ideal for a Yankee patrician starting a political career in a place like Houston.

The Yankee part, especially that "preppy Yale image," as some called it, was not yet out of George's system. He went through the motions, affected a Texas drawl, saturated himself in country music and learned all about grits and pork rinds, all in an effort to be credible as a quintessential heartlander. But his Eastern sentiments were still strong: Greenwich, Walker's Point, Washington, where his parents spent so much time, and New York, where he traveled on business and which also was a place to have fun.

Broadway was in its golden age, producing such elaborate, tuneful productions as *Oklahoma, South Pacific, Annie, Get Your Gun, Finian's Rainbow,* and by the mid fifties, *The Pajama Game* and *Damn Yankees.* At the very time George Bush was settling into Houston, *My Fair Lady, The Music Man, Gypsy,* and the *Flower Drum Song* were current. No trip to New York was complete for George without dropping into the theater or a baseball game. The family's major contribution to big league baseball, however, was Uncle Herbie's putting up money to help Joan Payson give the city the New York Mets. But George channeled his money to musicals and even convinced friends like Lud Ashley, who also invested in Zapata, to go along.[5] Later, when he was president, he and Barbara became so enamored of a musical revue called *Forever Plaid,* a spoof of the pop groups of the fifties, that after having seen the show in Washington, they had the cast perform at the White House a few weeks later and then at Kennebunkport as part of a reception for British Prime Minister John Major.[6]

One of George's theatrical investments, a comedy called *Come, Blow Your Horn,* had a road company that passed through Texas in 1961. He urged Ashley to "fly down for the evening" to see it, then adding for the enticement of his bachelor friend the information that "there is an attractive girl out there I would like you to meet. . . . She may be accompanied by an Austrian ski instructor," he then warned, "but I think *we* can probably flush him at the local dance hall. This will only set you back several hundred dollars and I think it might prove interesting."[7] They liked to tease each other, the far-afield Texas oilman from Connecticut, and the congressman from Ohio, the member of an established Democratic family. "He needled me about being a liberal," Ashley said.[8]

Ashley was only one of the many friends in Bush's expanding world. His access later became especially profitable when, after he retired from Congress, he served as a leading Washington lobbyist for the banking industry. But, as with Ashley, friends were retained over the years, including those who dated back to Skull and Bones, West Texas, and Houston, such as George Phau, Bobby Holt, Jim Allison, Harry Treleaven, Jack Steel, Nancy Thawley, C. Fred Chambers, and then, of course, there were the Liedtkes. Another member of this Texas milieu, of course, was James A. Baker III.

* * *

Poppy, as old friends still called him, also kept in close touch with his father. The temptation in later years was to look back upon the career of the elder Bush as that of an Eisenhower Republican, but that characterization, useful as it may be, is somewhat too amorphous. Prescott's Senate history showed that he was closer to the party's northeastern version, the most progressive wing of "modern Republicanism," which was less conservative than the administration in Washington. He really belonged to the Rockefeller wing, especially in its support for reforms. On April 4, 1957, he ventured the view that people in need of assistance from public welfare programs "should not be made the victims of reckless economizing."[9]

After Eisenhower had left office, Bush continued to press the cause of racial justice. Early in the Kennedy years, he sponsored a package of reforms with New Yorkers Jacob Javits and Kenneth Keating. He then tried but failed to bar federal aid to education for those states that had not shown "good faith" in complying with the Supreme Court's desegregation order.[10] He even welcomed President John F. Kennedy's first State of the Union message, especially its "proposals for the relief of the unemployed and steps to stimulate the economy within the framework of a federal budget as nearly in balance as possible."[11] A significant departure from Kennedy's program, one especially interesting in view of how much federal expenditures for the space program did to boost Houston's economy (which could not have been foreseen at the time), was Prescott's dissent from the young president's call to land a man on the moon. Eisenhower himself, once out of office, expressed his own reservations about flights to outer space. But Senator Bush was more explicit. He suggested that "money could be better spent on improving conditions on our own planet . . . to find a cure for cancer, for example, or heart disease, or to relieve poverty and distress . . ."[12]

That George himself was privy to such thoughts is beyond doubt. He had, nevertheless, clearly ventured off on his own, to a different place, a different culture, and to his own kind of economic success. Zapata Off-Shore had its big-city headquarters at 1701 Houston Club Building. Bush's financial independence was solid. Distance from Greenwich and respect for his father, as differentiated from childhood awe, may have strengthened instead of weakened familial bonds. The Bushes of the East and the Bushes of the Southwest remained close via long-distance telephone calls and periodic visits, especially during Augusts at Kennebunkport. The son was in close touch with his father's political career.

Prescott's days in Washington, however, came to a premature end. He had been reelected to a full term in 1956 but, by 1962, was feeling the effects of poor health and decided that he could not go on, a decision he began to regret almost immediately. "I feel very saddened since the election," he wrote to Arthur Krock, "and wonder if I made a correct decision last spring when I was run-down, exhausted, crippled with arthritis, etc. I feel much better now than I did six months ago, physically, but still lack the drive and vigor upon which I was so accustomed to draw heavily." With Washington out of the picture, he and Dottie were able to winter in Hobe Sound. On July 8, 1968, she underwent hip surgery in Boston and was hospitalized for six weeks. She hobbled about on crutches when they went to Florida the following winter, but that did not stop her from swimming twice a day and taking three turns on her Exercycle.[13]

A lot of things were changing for George. His political career got under way just as his father's ended. The city of Houston was still burgeoning. It had gone from the twentieth largest in the nation just two decades earlier to sixth. Texas was producing nearly 40 percent of all oil in the United States, and the city was hailed as the "oil and chemical capital of the world." The population that fed into the new center, both from the surrounding countryside and the rest of the country, was comprised of a new generation of young professionals, technicians, and industrial managers who were "turning the swamps into scrubbed suburbias."[14] "This younger element of conservatives," declared a Texas historian, "had broken with their parents' conservative Democrat politics. They believed a clean break was needed with a strong Republican party controlled, beyond a shadow of a doubt, by conservatives. To them, it was a cause. They were highly motivated, ready to work."[15] Houston, moreover, was, like Bush himself, a city of newcomers. The Republican party he found was first getting started, and if it had resisted other outlanders, it could hardly have grown.[16]

Houston, located along the East Texas Gulf Coast and much closer to the cotton kingdom of the Old Confederacy than was most of the state, did not have a Republican tradition to speak of. A local GOP had hardly ever existed. Those Republicans from the North and West who filtered into Texas after the Civil War settled mainly in the northern and western sections. Their descendants remained more Northern than Southern. Small in number, they nevertheless constituted a strong affluent minority, controlling local judgeships and, during the first half of the twentieth century, serving as "patronage dispensers" for the national party. Under the long-term leadership of R. B. Creager of Brownsville, they found their advantages in the status quo, although, during that entire period, they managed to send only one representative to Washington and held a single seat in the state legislature at Austin.[17] Not until after World War II, in the wake of the detested New Deal and amid such issues as race and control of offshore oil, and especially as Governor Allan Shivers took Texas politics into the Eisenhower camp, did Republicanism become a viable alternative for the state's discontented conservatives. Their first major breakthrough, one that rocked the state more than could have been registered by "a political Richter scale," according to a local historian, was the election to the U.S. Senate of a college professor from Wichita Falls, John Tower, a man whose modest means served as a perfect foil for the big-money interests behind his candidacy.[18]

More distinctive perhaps than any partisan affiliation, any movement from Southern Democratic "solid South" politics, was the vigorous ultranationalism that permeated Houston's culture. The city that Bush found was not only one of the major strongholds of Robert Welch's extremist John Birch Society, but it attracted all sorts of fanatical "anti-Communist" hucksterism. Every extreme manifestation of contemporary hysteria became reenergized by Houston's corps of avid loyalists. Southern writer Willie Morris noted that "the fearsome evangelical Texas Bible Belt . . . funnels into metropolitan Houston" and that a "Houston anti-Communist rally is much like a religious tent revival."[19] Historian George Norris Green quoted an East Texan as follows: "There are two things that every genuine, true American should have at his fingertips at all times: a gun and a Bible."[20]

Nothing shaped the younger Bush's political career as much as that rightward movement, and nothing shaped his course on the national scene as did the maturation of the same thrust. By the time he reached Houston, the state had broken with the Solid South tradition by twice choosing Republican electors behind Eisenhower. Bush himself was too involved in relocating his business and private life to play any role in the 1960 presidential election, but that was the year when only Lyndon Johnson's presence on the Democratic national ticket kept Texas in the Kennedy column. The partisan shift was most marked in such major cities as Houston and Dallas. Where the opposite tended to be true for Northern cities, where politics were shaped by urban ethnic machines that drew from successive waves of European immigrants, growing Sun Belt cities became major havens for a new breed of postwar entrepreneurs. All of them, the whole gamut of establishment commercial powers—finance, insurance, oil, construction, the defense industry, real estate, electronics, or through their agents in the major law firms of Houston and Dallas—found refuge in a climate where they, in effect, made and controlled the rules of the game. Texas, and the South generally, offered not only cheap electrical power but tractable, low-cost labor innocent of unionization. The ruling groups made certain that state governments were friendly. Texas, for example, was among the first to take advantage of the newly enacted federal labor legislation in 1947 by creating a "right-to-work" law. Taxation and regulatory zeal were both minimal. Market forces were tipped to favor producers over consumers. The special conditions that surrounded the petroleum environment only exacerbated that thrust. The faster the growth, the more virulent the right-wing politics.[21] "The state was a committee of the ruling class—and the ruling class was Big Oil," wrote journalist Theodore H. White.[22]

The search for black gold, with the heavy risks and costs involved in speculation, appealed to the derring-do mentality that had little patience with a Democratic party ruled by New Dealers and their sycophants. Superimposed over it all was the region's traditional social conservatism, which rested on a base of religious fundamentalism. Religion, nationalism, and economic laissez-faire went hand in hand. In such a region, investors and preachers were kings, the dollar sign and the flag their icons. The alleged Negro–New Deal–labor union–Communist conspiracy obsessed the Texas political establishment. The press encouraged the lunacy. One survey of 381 labor editorials run by Texas newspapers in 1945 showed that 295 were antiunion. Helping to protect the proestablishment point of view were the state's big-city newspapers, especially such dailies as the *Houston Chronicle,* the *Fort Worth Star-Telegram,* and the *Dallas Morning News.* The most notable, and lonely, voice of dissent was *The Texas Observer,* which began life in 1950 as a four-page liberal-populist weekly largely funded by Frankie Randolph, a one-time debutante from one of Houston's first families, wife of a blue-blood descendant of the Randolphs of Virginia, and future Democratic committee-woman.[23]

The *Observer* prospered and grew, attracting national attention, and such talented writers as Ronnie Dugger, Willie Morris, and Molly Ivins, but it was precisely that contrast with the dailies that gave it its prominence. The state was, after all, served by media that reflected the kind of conservatism that had once inveighed against the New Deal. One of Texas's most colorful politicians, W. Lee (Pappy) O'Daniel, who served successively as governor and then senator, once told a radio audience that FDR was a greater danger than Hitler and then went on to charge the New Deal with regimenting the people into an almost complete state of communism. When George Bush got his start in Houston politics, the Kennedys in Washington lowered the boiling point even further by leading a new drive toward liberalism. Relatively mild, but still noteworthy, especially in view of later events, was the uproar caused by Ted Dealey, publisher of the *Dallas News.* Dealey, at a White House luncheon for about twenty-five newspaper executives in October of 1961, at which the president was the featured speaker, responded to a call for questions by declaring that Mr. Kennedy had monopolized the discussion long enough. Thereupon, Dealey reached into his pocket and pulled out a statement that said, "We need a man on horseback to lead this nation and many people in Texas and the Southwest think that you are riding Caroline's tricycle. The general opinion of grassroots thinking in this country," Dealey added, "is that you and your administration are weak sisters."[24]

Just a slight ripple of applause followed Dealey's words. Most were too embarrassed to react. Dealey's comments were clearly rude, disrespectful, not only of the president but of his family. Yet, as Kennedy well knew, they were symptomatic of the hostility on the far right, and nowhere was that more intense than in Texas. The victory by John Tower, only a few months earlier, had produced the largest Republican turnout in the state's history. Democrats were in a quandary, divided among themselves, especially between left and right, and experiencing continuing defections to a GOP that was rapidly gaining respectability in areas where the Civil War was not forgotten.

When, in the following months, John Connally, fresh from service as Kennedy's secretary of the navy, returned to Texas and won the governorship, he was still a Democrat. But his victory put him in direct contention with Senator Ralph Yarborough, an impassioned, outspoken, even florid liberal, an anomaly given the state's oil-sodden establishment, all of which made the feisty lawyer a maverick who was anathema to his own party's leadership. Yarborough's tenure was anything but secure. Democrats, even the party's conservatives, were fighting to hold on. Never before had Texas Republicans been handed such an opportunity to take over, especially in the wake of the Tower opening. A place like Dallas was a natural GOP power base. Houston was another matter.

On the verge of success, Houston Republicans were apprehensive about the rampaging Birchers, a movement that was one of those curiosities that periodically bedevil American politics. Their agenda, in the name of defeating "Communist subversion," a definition that often seemed more xenophobic than ideological, included pressing for so-called Liberty Amendments that were designed to, among other things, repeal federal income taxes, abolish the Federal Reserve System, and take the United States out of the United Nations. Coming as it did from outside the mainstream, those who played the conventional political game neither understood the group nor were clear about how to handle it. Most politicos were more interested in power than ideology, but Robert Welch began his organization in 1958 as a protest against what he was convinced was the reluctance of politics-as-usual to appreciate the menace of international communism.

It was easy to ridicule Bircher paranoia. But, to Welch, the Belmont, Massachusetts, candy manufacturer, and his untold number of followers, the risks seemed very real. Political pros, in his view, were hypocritically exploiting the dangers of subversion without either understanding the depths of the menace or being willing to act. When, of all things, a Republican and supposedly anti-Communist administration took over power in Washington and showed timidity about waging a holy crusade against the infidels from Moscow, the danger seemed that much clearer. Conspiracy buffs took that as proof of the insidiousness of a force that poisoned by infiltration and infection. Eisenhower, Welch decided in his boldest charge, was himself "a dedicated conscious agent of the Communist conspiracy."[25] In his book, *The Politician,* through the organization's periodical, *American Opinion,* and its chain of anti-Communist bookstores that opened throughout the country, Welch spread his gospel and enlisted his followers. The organization, named for a twenty-six-year-old soldier who had been "the first American casualty in World War III" when he was murdered by Chinese Communists after the war, kept its membership lists secret while, at the same time, it sought to infiltrate the Republican party.[26] Democrats had been regarded by even some regular Republican politicians as Communist allies. The movement caught on most easily among those who, for religious, political, and cultural reasons, felt so threatened that they were receptive to the pinpointing of sinister forces. Having emerged from the Eisenhower era, the presidencies of such Democrats as Kennedy and Johnson only fueled Bircher strength. By 1961, Welch himself named Los Angeles and Houston as his two strongest cities, which was not surprising given that the volatile climate of the latter also made it home to such other fringe groups as the Christian Crusade, the Christian Anti-Communist Crusade, Freedom-in-Action, and such extremists also controlled the Committee for Sound American Education, which dominated Houston's school board throughout the decade. The city's Birch chapter claimed only fifteen members, according to its chairman, Garland B. Rowland, a businessman who owned a small cleaning and laundry company. Yet, irrespective of actual numbers, the Birchers were another intimidation from the right. Their single-minded obsession with communism, which often resembled more fantasy than reality, negated any rational dialogue. They and their immediate competitors helped drive the new Texas Republican party to the right.[27]

That right-wing presence gave George Bush his first political opening. Ironically, there never was any evidence that such zealots as the Birchers actually controlled Houston's Harris County Republican party. Such groups seemed to prefer concentrating on their own objectives and, when given the opportunity, usually responded with disinterest toward partisan political activities.[28]

Establishment Republicans, in their desire to thwart a Birch takeover, turned to Bush as the best available man. What had especially made him suitable was when, in his first substantial dose of Harris County politics that year, he cochaired the finance committee with Jack Cox. Cox, a forty-one-year-old Houston oilman, described as a "staunch conservative . . . with a populist appeal," was a strong supporter of the Republican party's rising right-wing star, Barry Goldwater. Cox weighed in heavily by opposing the New Frontier in Washington. He championed "the free enterprise system unfettered by government controls, and a strong national defense to deter Communist aggression," as well as opposition to federal aid to education, government programs to combat poverty, and the loss of U.S. sovereignty to the UN. He was also thought to enjoy funding from the Hunt oil fortune of Dallas.[29]

Bush's activities, especially his work with Cox, had made him well known to the Republican county organization. Its chairman, James A. Bertron, had also met George's father at a Washington fund-raiser, at least sufficiently for Prescott Bush to ask, "Jimmy, when are you going to get George involved?"

"Senator," replied the Harris County chairman, "I'm trying. We're all trying."[30]

Bush, in fact, had been approached to go for the chairmanship. He took time to weigh the politicial implications inherent in a county-wide position, realizing, while assessing his situation, that the opportunity could not be bypassed. He was acceptable to the Birchers because of his association with Cox, but was still able to bridge the party's various factions. He was also seen as an establishment man himself, but, at the same time, one who could defuse the threat from the radical right.

George and Barbara hosted a Republican luncheon meeting at their Briar Drive home one Saturday in the spring of 1962. The heart of the Harris County GOP was there—Roy Goodearle, who had headed the local Nixon-

Lodge campaign in 1960, together with Nancy Thawley, Goodearle's volunteer assistant that year and a future aide to Bush when he chaired the Republican National Committee. Others were Nancy's husband, Tom, a gas company
employee, and Jack Steel, who worked for Prudential Insurance and who later
became one of Bush's key political advisers and closest friends.[31]

Their immediate cause of concern was the pending resignation of Bertron,
a moderate, who was moving to Florida. In the last county-wide election, the
Birchers had been stopped only by a small margin, a situation which troubled
Goodearle a great deal. He himself was under attack as a left-winger, and had,
in fact, come close to losing. The society, certainly encouraged by such signs
of progress, was supposedly going to endorse Gen. Edwin Walker, the fiery
rightist who had been drummed out of the U.S. Army. Without a strong
opponent, they would surely carry the county.[32]

Before it was all over, Goodearle had urged them to get behind Bush for
chairman as their best hope, and Bush responded in kind, going on about
the virtues of the two-party system and the importance of a viable Republican alternative to the entrenched Houston establishment.[33] "This was the
challenge I'd been waiting for," Bush later wrote, "an opening into politics at
the ground level, where it all starts."[34] No need for prolonged contemplation. He was in. Nor was it much of a gamble.

But he was unknown in Texas politics, and had to demonstrate that he was
not an aloof Yankee with a "foreign" accent. So he and Barbara spent nights
making the rounds of precincts throughout the county, no matter how large
or small the group. She learned to be patient as over and over again, she
heard the same speech, finally learning to endure the monotony by teaching
herself needlepoint.[35]

"I am running," Bush wrote to his Democratic congressman friend Lud
Ashley, "—yes for chairman of the Republ. party of Harris County (22 Cong
and 8th Thomas districts)." Then, with recognition of his ultraconservative
supporters, Bush added, "Promise not to endorse me, OK.[?] Tonight I meet
a Birch oriented group. My election is for the unexpired term (1 yr) of the
resigned chairman."[36] Russell Pryor, a Goldwater man and Bush's only opponent, withdrew a few days later, and Bush was the committee's unanimous
choice at the February 1963 meeting. He promptly urged the end of fac-
tionalism.[37]

Bush was not an absentee chairman. He threw himself into his work with
enthusiasm. Organizing precincts was a major priority, in addition to raising
money. So well did he succeed, raising an unprecedented $90,000, that he
soon upgraded the party's headquarters by moving it to a more suitable
place on Waugh Drive near Allen Parkway, which also happened to be more
convenient for him to visit en route home from his Zapata office.

Conservative Republican politics in Texas had an abundance of women
volunteers. Bruce Alger's "mink squad" in Dallas was the most visible since
their involvement in an ugly demonstration against Lady Bird and Lyndon
Johnson at that city's Adolphus Hotel. Bush's Houston office was also staffed

largely by such women, whom he inspired with his enthusiasm and energy. Barbara would often be there, too, sometimes joining the ladies in stuffing envelopes, and often working at her needlepoint while her husband met with little groups from all over the county.[38]

Bush's method for dealing with the Birchers, however, raised some anxieties. He preached unity instead of opposition, even composing a memo saying, "We're not going to divide ourselves, calling anyone 'crazies,' or nuts," which led some of the more amused volunteers to substitute the word *kernels*. The conventional conservatives in the office were astonished when a Bircher was placed in charge of a precinct.[39]

Working with such people, along with the moderates, was all a matter of good politics for Bush. The divisions were deep, but as he later put it, "we all shared basic conservative views," so they could concentrate on tackling the Democrats instead of one another.[40]

Goodearle was not amused. Only one with so little grassroots experience could expect to contend with extremists as though he were dealing with just another personality conflict. "It was his nature to try to get along with everybody," recalled Goodearle, adding, "he didn't understand. He just saw it as a different issue. His actions created a good bit of concern to the people who fought vigorously and quite hard to hold those people out. They were pretty upset to see that, having fought them for a couple of years in county executive meetings and at the precinct level. They had fought tooth and nail to hold on to their jobs."[41]

One who would not be silenced at the time was Craig Peper, who chaired the party's finance committee. He was vocal in denouncing Bush and the leadership of the Houston Draft Goldwater drive as "right-wing extremists." Bush not only reiterated his support for Goldwater, but then forced Peper's resignation. Peper attempted to embarrass Bush during his campaign in 1964 by charging him with having allowed "Birchers to take an active role in the party."[42]

So Bush built his power base. Whatever the liabilities of accommodating the Birchers, he saw them as vital to maintain his image as a hard, dedicated conservative, a position that had to be secured to balance the possible perception of him as a Yankee carpetbagger.

And then there was the fact that George was the son of a senator linked to Rockefeller Republicanism. One circular, distributed in 1964 from Dallas under the organizational name of "Coalition of Conservatives to BEAT the BUSHES," made the point that Prescott Bush was on record in support of extending foreign aid, sending aid to Communist-dominated countries, civil rights laws, and federal control of the tidelands. Through his Brown Brothers Harriman relationship, the senator was connected to Averell Harriman. Averell, it was pointed out, belonged to the Council on Foreign Relations, which meant that George was probably getting money from Bush's CFR friends. The CFR, a "black-tie dinner group" and organization of "liberal Eastern kingmakers," was accused of always having been "an important part in planning the whole diabolical scheme of creating a ONE-WORLD FED-ERATION of socialist states under the United Nations."[43]

Bush, in his brief period as chairman, was clearly giving priority to what he perceived were his needs for a statewide race over listening to Goodearle and other anti-Birchers. And he did succeed. He gained by coopting, by taking them in with the force of his presence, confident that he could win them over. Bush, for his part, was enthusiastic about what he was doing. So closely was he identified with the John Birch Society, even while publicly denying any friendliness to their cause, that Ralph Yarborough always insisted that Bush not only "embraced the John Birch Society" but that he had "admitted" to him that he had also joined the organization.[44]

Bush fulfilled each of his objectives. The Harris County organization prospered and he built a network among local Republicans. Money came in from many of the 202 precincts in the county.

"My job is primarily an organizational job since the Republican party has quite a few unorganized precincts," he explained to Lud Ashley. "So far I like it a lot and although it takes a tremendous amount of time I think it is worthwhile." Ashley couldn't resist chiding his friend. "I was a little distressed to learn," he wrote in return, "that the new job will mean that your managerial abilities are to be diverted from Zapata to the Republican party but I'll hang on to the stock for a while longer anyway."[45]

Goodearle had underestimated Bush's ambition. On September 11, in the Capitol Press Room in Austin, in what was billed as "a major GOP development," George Bush, at the age of thirty-nine, announced his candidacy for the Republican senatorial nomination to oppose Ralph Yarborough in 1964. Bush came across, in the words of one writer, as "an open, refreshing personality."[46]

CHAPTER SEVEN

The Bush Circle

%

B ush paid the price in 1964 for initiation into the world of politics. He tried hard to dispel the notion that he was an intruder in his adopted state, but nothing could give him the advantages of having an East Texas farm background.

Ralph Yarborough, his opponent, had no such trouble. He had all that and more, an insider by virtue of his state-wide office but, too often, he was a flowery, irritating, and rambunctious fellow who verged on the demagogic. But he could also be a thorn to the political establishment of a state with such extremes of wealth and poverty. Texas had had its rebels, and especially its populists, but Yarborough's political life at a time of significant change made him more of an "outsider" than was George Bush.

Raff, as Yarborough was known, was drenched in the politics of protest. Henderson County wheat fields, in East Texas, had been a nineteenth-century hotbed of the farm alliance movement and populism. The heritage of wars against railroad barons and the financial/legal establishments lingered on.

Political life was inseparable from Yarborough's persona. Physically, he was a short, solidly built scrapper. His face was pleasant and open, with the air of a pugilist who has weathered hard times. He occasionally astonished traditionalists by stripping down and chucking the "dignity of his office by rolling around on the floor in a schoolboy wrestling match while colleagues and reporters watched in undisguised amazement."[1] He entered the academy at West Point, left after one year, and returned to complete his undergraduate education at Sam Houston State College. With his passion for championing the underdog, he decided he could be most effective by becoming a lawyer, so he got his degree from the University of Texas Law School in Austin. During the early thirties, at the depth of the Great Depression, Yarborough put in three years as an assistant attorney general to the district judge of Travis County, Jimmie Allred, another fighter for plain folk. Raff specialized in land and water rights, always a prime issue for Texas farmers, and after the New Deal's legislation to bring power to rural areas, he fought to supply Texas's backwoods with electricity. He enlisted at his local army recruiting office after Pearl Harbor, saw combat in the Pacific, served as a colonel under General MacArthur, and returned home to enter politics.

Resistance to change was, if anything, stronger than ever before. New Deal government, especially regulations of commerce and encouragement of unionization, were enough to provoke outrage. When Democrats in Washington, backed by Supreme Court decisions, favored federal control over offshore oil deposits, liberalism had gone too far. Southerners, despite their formidable power in Congress, were confronted with the demise of poll taxes and increased voting by blacks. Nothing embroiled the region in a mini-civil war as did the responses to the Supreme Court's 1954 school desegregation decision in the case of *Brown* v. *Board of Education.*

Texas was a one-party state, and the Democratic establishment meant to keep it that way. Corruption was rampant, made possible by unchallenged political power from the state house on down. Conflict of interest codes were rare. Lobbying, unchecked by the inquiring press, had free rein. Legislative bribery was routine. During the 1950s alone, nine state senators were tied to insurance company payoffs. One scandal netted 300 indictments and sent the state's land commissioner to the penitentiary.[2]

The Texas Democratic majority, really the regulars, differed little from conservatives elsewhere. The voices of a dissenting minority of liberal "loyalists," that is, loyal to the party in Washington, were hardly heard. Only *The Texas Observer* and such fighters as Frankie Randolph kept the majority from monopolizing everything. The rebels remained a minority in a party lead by the so-called "Shivercrats," who marched behind the Eisenhower leadership in behalf of states's rights, kept organized labor from getting enough clout to overturn the Taft-Hartley Law of 1947, and, above all, fought to retain control of submerged oil deposits. When Allan Shivers and his regulars delivered Texas's twenty-four electors to Ike, there was little opposition, either from the state's ruling-class newspapers or from within his own party. Oil had helped keep them all in line. Even John Connally, acting as an agent for his chief client, Sid Richardson, helped the Republicans carry the state.[3]

In all this, Yarborough was the outstanding troublemaker, a fire-eater by Texas standards. A local historian has described him as "the undisputable political leader of populist liberal forces" during the decade.[4] Raff was a pest; he did not belong. Had he championed the monied establishment, they would have praised his hot temper and florid speeches. But he was still the populist preacher who went to the mat for loyalists, attacked the establishment, and was careful not to go too far afield on the race issue. Commenting on the tax structure that favored the well-heeled, Yarborough liked to tell crowds while on the stump, "Put the jam on the lower shelf where the little man can reach it."[5] But for all his left-wing radicalism, he respected the power of the gas and oil industry, never challenging their 27.5 percent tax-depletion allowance.[6]

He made his way in Texas politics without adulterating the "Austin Fun

House," as Molly Ivins wrote in a 1975 article lampooning the state's legislature (which she called "the lege"), but, when Raff got elected to Washington, he was a strong supporter of Lyndon Johnson's Great Society programs, including civil rights; he was an architect of expanding federal minimum wages in 1966, and federal funding for bilingual education, and was the chief sponsor of the Office of Safety and Health Administration (OSHA).[7] He even brought federal money to his state through approval of the Padre Island National Seashore and Guadalupe National Park.[8] Not a bad record for one so many Texans considered an oddball. Who but Yarborough, for example, would have kept current copies of *The Nation* for visitors to his Austin law office? And what progressive from the North would have spiced a long explanation of his political positions with the liberal use of the word *nigger*?[9]

He entered the 1952 primary to challenge the regulars, practically going it alone, without an organization or newspaper support. All Yarborough accomplished was to establish himself as a pariah to Texas business and civic leaders. At a moment of bitter anti-New Deal and anti-Fair Deal hostility, he paid the price for being a Roosevelt and a Truman Democrat. In many parts of the state, he never did become known. He was better at countering Shivers in another primary two years later, coming out ahead in seventy-five additional counties. Even then, he made his compromises. Shivers forced him into the open about race and Yarborough agreed that he favored segregation and opposed "forced commingling" and favored separate but genuinely equal schools. But he stopped short of attacking the *Brown* decision or pledging to fight to preserve segregation. The Shivers forces, meanwhile, fed newspapers with a retouched photograph of the liberal Democrat that showed his skin darkened, his nose flattened, his cheekbones altered. Obviously, it suggested, someone so far out had to have African roots. Few papers bought the ruse.[10]

Yarborough tried again in 1956, this time by challenging the renomination of the incumbent Democratic governor, Price Daniel. The feisty Yarborough never had a chance. His ballots were fished out of trash heaps near polling places in several parts of the state.[11] Yarborough's loss gave Daniel the statehouse in Austin, leaving a vacant senate seat and forcing a special election. Entering that one, too, Yarborough had better luck, becoming, as some establishment Texans put it, an "accidental senator." In that election, which took place in 1957, two conservatives, Republican Thad Hutcheson and Democrat Martin Dies, divided the right-wing vote. Yarborough won with a substantial 55.8 percent majority.[12]

The Yarborough victory opened the field for George Bush. He now had a viable opponent, a Democratic liberal. For Bush, it marked his first significant break with his moderate background. Playing to his Texas constituency, he declared that it was better to keep poll taxes than to have the polls "swamped with a liberal bloc vote." His position hardly damaged him with the Birchers, who, in the heaviest vote for an off-year amendment in recent memory, orchestrated opposition to repealing poll taxes by a vote of 303,763 to 237,524.[13]

* * *

Vice President Johnson had accurately forecast in 1961 that his own legions "and the Republicans all will be gunning for Ralph Yarborough" in 1964.[14] It hardly took prescience to see this; Ralph Yarborough was a threat to the maintenance of the "good" order, and to the individual ambitions of those whose interests were to keep the lines open to power and big money. Unlike Raff Yarborough, their fortunes rested on the state's commercial resources. They quite naturally resisted the upsurge of small farmers, laborers, and working-class ethnic minorities, especially blacks and Mexican-Americans, who were threatening to depart from their traditional roles as suppliers of cheap labor.

Such opposing ends of Texas economic culture were personified by John Connally and Ralph Yarborough. Yarborough tried to cling to the days of Populist Party protest, when Texas was still dominated by fighters against Eastern capitalists. Yarborough was, in that sense, the premodernist, holding on to a time when the plight of the poor was arguably even worse than the present against intruders who would corrupt institutions for their selfish ends.

Connally's roots were much poorer economically than Yarborough's. His childhood around Harlandale and San Antonio was spent watching his father scramble for a living. The senior Connally, the father of seven children, went from menial job to menial job—driving school buses, clerking in a grocery, working as a tenant farmer. Eventually, he was reduced to trying to make ends meet by butchering cattle. Some of young John's early memories were of life in a slaughterhouse, hacking away at his father's steers.[15]

Connally had, like Texas itself, come a long way. His powerful figure symbolized the optimism of the surging Lone Star State, where capitalists were viewed less as imperialistic exploiters than as resident fortune hunters, eager to pave the way for the equally ambitious. What could be better than to keep such progress on that track? His personal success showed the potential of the new Texas. Connally's first big money came by managing the holdings of his wealthiest law client, oil giant Sid Richardson.[16] One fortune led to another, Richardson's to that of legendary wheeler-dealer Clint Murchison. Forever after that, the once dirt-poor Texan from Floresville was the handsome Chamber of Commerce stereotype, complete with cowboy hats, lavish cowhide boots, and tailor-made suits, and, of course, that bolo tie, which was like a Lone Star badge near his heart. Some two years before he went bankrupt, "Big Jawn," as some called him, faced outward from a panoramic window that overlooked Austin in the valley below and described his properties across the landscape, much like a medieval lord surveying his fiefdom.[17]

Connally was everything Yarborough was not, a Democrat saturated in oil and big Houston money, the quintessential master of the state's one-party establishment, a loyalist of stalwarts, a frontier capitalist. More recently, in the face of continuing defections to the once-invisible Republicans, Connally, who had begun via a political power base among largely impoverished South Texas counties, stood his ground in upholding resistance to a coalition of

Mexican-Americans, blacks, and organized labor. He duly criticized Kennedy civil rights proposals, a position that drew Yarborough's fire.[18]

The two men, Connally and Yarborough, became among the bitterest of Texas rivals. They were irrevocably split during the 1956 fight when Connally waged a losing battle to block the powerful, feisty, gruff-voiced, chain-smoking, liberal female candidate Frankie Randolph from taking a seat as a Democratic state committeewoman.[19] They didn't exchange a word for years.

It followed quite naturally, then, that Connally would target Yarborough every bit as much as would Bush, even giving rise to the suspicion that he would like to head him off in the Democratic primary with a strong conservative, someone like popular congressman Joe Kilgore of the Rio Grande Valley or Houston millionaire Lloyd Bentsen, a former congressman.[20] Moreover, from the outset of Bush's candidacy, Connally seemed destined to be pleased. Other than the challenge to one-party Democratic rule, something not calculated to make the governor happy, the Republican political newcomer was the odds-on favorite to win his party's nomination.[21]

Bush followed the announcement of his candidacy by resigning from the county chairmanship, readying himself for the GOP primary before a direct clash with Yarborough. "Bush is a Texan by choice, not by chance," claimed a flyer. And, in a subsequent press conference in Austin, he staked his ideological ground by expressing his devotion to "the finest concept of states' rights." Recognizing that such rights might be offensive to blacks and opponents of segregation, he insisted that "moral persuasion under the present law was the only correct approach to the racial problems." Then, reaching for the high ground, he added, "the question of a person's heart in the civil rights quest is going to determine the solution."[22] As for himself, he let it be known that his candidacy would be in "emphatic" opposition to such provisions of the civil rights bill that could guarantee blacks equal access to restaurants, hotels, restrooms, and other public accommodations.[23]

The Bush candidacy appealed to the Republican professional class. More important was the large segment of Democrats ready to vote GOP behind a credible candidate. Bush, in that sense, was second only to John Tower in making Texas a legitimate two-party state. Those uneasy Democrats had finally found someone they could support, so there was no surprise that when the *Houston Post* announced him as its choice for the primary it also carried an endorsement by a good portion of that city's downtown establishment. Two hundred and thirty-three lawyers and businessmen signed up.[24]

The Houston of George Bush's political baptism was one of free-flowing, everything-goes, unrestricted, pell-mell growth. Limits were practically "subversive." The city that had kept sprawling after the war could not be restrained, or even rationalized, by urban planning. Construction and investments were unchecked. Efforts at public modifications opened its authors to charges of "socialism" or even "communism." Money was king in the most uninhibited sense, and the accumulators the new emperors in a modern frontier anarchy.

They liked Bush; but, then again, everybody liked Bush. He still had with him all the oil patch, West Texas romance, the loyalties of the Earle Craigs, Bobby Holts, Rudy Judemans, and all who were proud of his Odessa and Midland days. In Houston, however, he bonded. He joined the Houston Country Club, the Bayou Club, and the Ramada Club—every social venue he could find.

He got into tennis matches with a thirty-four-year-old lawyer who, despite his youth, was not just any lawyer. He was Jim Baker, an ex-marine, graduate of the exclusive Hill School in Pennsylvania, Princeton University, and the University of Texas Law School, all in preparation for becoming an attorney. His family's firm, founded by his grandfather, was Baker & Botts, reputed to be the second oldest in the state. Among its early partners, Robert S. Lovett, had been counsel to E. H. Harriman's Union Pacific Railroad.[25] Jimmy, kept out of the family firm when he graduated from law school in 1957 because of its nepotism rule, went to work for Andrews Kurth Campbell & Jones, and did not join Baker & Botts until the end of the Bush presidency.

Baker has been described as "comfortable in country-club clothes one weekend and cowboy boots the next"; he was a Democrat, as was just about every Texan of his vintage.[26] Conservative without being a hard-edged rightist, he was the quintessential "closet moderate," or so it was assumed. Mike Deaver, who got to know him as chief of staff in the Reagan administration, said, "he's probably the most careful individual I have ever met, and a nice balance to my sometimes impulsive nature."[27] Reagan biographer Lou Cannon described Baker as a "Texas lawyer with marine discipline and Princeton polish."[28] That "polish" struck others as stuffy and consummately self-serving, an impression that was magnified by his measured, highly circumspect manner.

So different did he and George seem that it was hard to understand the "little brother/big brother" relationship. Observers suspected variable Bakers, a relaxed side most often visible at his Wyoming ranch (which he bought late in life), or with Bush on the tennis courts, when jogging together in Houston's Memorial Park, or at local country clubs. It took a George Bush to penetrate Baker's protective shell. A deeply private man who read his Bible nightly and whose religion was as personal as everything else about him, he protected himself, especially his reputation, "more assiduously than anyone I've ever known in politics." Outsiders saw a proper, dignified demeanor, the more formal James Addison Baker III, scion of Texan legal aristocracy. "He seems to carry the burden of his father's reputation for probity, for achievement and fair play that goes back a long ways," observed an old friend and veteran political associate. The Baker seen to the rest of the world was not Bush's Baker, not the relaxed, folksy Baker. He was not to strangers the man who could be equally at home hauling a pair of freshly shot turkeys out of the trunk of his car for processing or behaving "happy as a clown" in a "true greasy spoon."[29]

When Baker's first wife died in 1970, it was "big brother" who helped ease him through that devastating period. Eventually Baker remarried, and he went on to broaden his legal and financial base to include the political, eventually abandoning his hereditary Democratic Party, as did most conservative Texans, and became a reliable writer of checks for state and local GOP candidates. He even headed the state party's finance committee. When Gerald R. Ford became president, Jim Baker went to Washington as undersecretary of Commerce. He was also instrumental in securing Ford's 1976 nomination as the GOP presidential candidate (against a strong threat by Reagan), by heading the delegate-gathering machinery. Baker continued to gamble on forging a political career of his own, with Houston becoming merely a base for his 1978 candidacy for attorney general of Texas. He fell short by some six percentage points, but that loss was nothing to be ashamed of for a Republican statewide candidate at that point, especially one not at the head of the ticket.

Houston, of course, being Houston, had bigger gamblers, ever willing to raise the stakes. One of them—the "old man" of Bush's new associates—was Hugh Roy Cullen, the testy, graying, high-stakes wildcatter and Houston banker whose fortunes had helped him defeat such "foreign radicals" as Bill Benton of Connecticut and Millard Tydings, the Maryland tormentor of Joe McCarthy. Cullen even had more money than Clint Murchison.

They all became Bush's buddies. One, a banker named William Stamps Farish III, hosted Bush in 1964 at his Lazy F. Ranch at Beeville in southern Texas, thereby beginning an annual quail-hunting expedition. Farish, the founder and controller of Butler's Post Oak Bank and a board member of Gulf Resources, had two other residences, a Florida beachfront estate at Gulf Stream and a Kentucky bluegrass Thoroughbred farm. Bush vacationed at all three. Later, described as "an oilman, polo player, horse breeder," he managed President Bush's million-dollar blind trust.[30]

Robert Adam Mosbacher was another Houston acquisition among Bush's valuable connections. He had parlayed family money by making shrewd investments, finally creating the Mosbacher Energy Company of Houston. Variously described as a yachtsman and Republican fund-raiser, Mosbacher made a $200-million fortune by drilling for oil. He became one of Bush's major lifelines to wherever money could be found. When Bush took his temporary leave from politics in 1977, Mosbacher gave him some useful information that helped guide him to invest in liquified petroleum gas in an enterprise known as Hollywood LPG No. 2.[31] His contribution of at least $100,000 made him a leader of what was called Team 100. Bush later confirmed his confidence in his old Houston friend by making him secretary of Commerce.[32]

In all, putting together such support, Bush estimated a two-million-dollar outlay to beat Yarborough. Much of the money was needed for television and billboards. Most of that was handled by the Brown and Snyder Advertising Agency of Houston. The chief fund-raising was left to Bush friend and fellow oilman C. Fred Chambers, who was among the candidate's closest associates. He also became the namesake for a Bush family dog.[33]

On November 22, 1963, the *Houston Chronicle* could hardly have had more encouraging news for George. Their new statewide poll showed that Goldwater would carry Texas by about fifty thousand votes if the election were held then, and that Lyndon Johnson's popularity was at an all-time low.[34]

The conservative-liberal split among Texas Democrats represented by Connally and Yarborough, with Vice President Johnson in the middle, jeopardized the likelihood of Kennedy again winning the state's crucial twenty-four electoral votes. The Democrats, and Kennedy in particular, wanted to solicit Texas fat-cat money for the coming campaign, leading to a fateful presidential visit to a state with bitter rivalries and well-healed potential supporters.

Ugliness, yes; crazed protests, yes; signs calling the Kennedys infidels, yes. All were expected as part of the Dallas scene, but political assassinations were not yet commonplace in America. Not since the McKinley murder in 1901 had a president actually been killed. TR and FDR had come close, and so had Truman, but by 1963 those attempts were in the past, certainly too remote to preoccupy current realities. Kennedy had to nail down those twenty-four electors, important votes that could not be taken for granted. Anyone watching the turnouts during Texas's senate elections in both 1957 and 1961 could see what was happening. So many old-line, traditional Democrats, especially in affluent urban areas of the "new" South, were signaling an end to the days when the party bosses could simply call the shots. Texas was actually having Republican primaries. They were really little fires: grassroots revolts, hatred against all things liberal, all things New and Fair Deal, all things coming from the bureaucracy in Washington, denunciations of a Supreme Court that had substituted "niggers" for God in the schools. Dallas had, as William Manchester pointed out, "become the mecca for medicine-show evangelists of the National Indignation Convention, The Christian Crusaders, the Minutemen, the John Birch and Patrick Henry societies, and the headquarters of H. L. Hunt and his peculiar activities." [35] At all costs, it was perfectly obvious, Yarborough and Connally had to be brought together, especially if the Republicans were to head their national ticket in 1964 with conservative grassroots favorite, Senator Barry Goldwater of Arizona. Kennedy, in the face of all that, could hardly ignore what was left of his loyalists in the state, as radical as the liberal-labor coalition might seem.

On that November 22, a Friday, practically every warm body had his own hunch about a possible source of trouble. Those were, indeed, "heady days for Texas Republicans," but not without fear and apprehension. That morning's *Dallas News*, with its full-page, black-bordered ad "welcoming" the president to the city, calling Kennedy a "Communist tool," seemed to justify all the nervousness.[36] For Jack Ruby, who ran a downtown striptease club, the fact that someone with a Jewish name signed the ad was pretty upsetting. Jack knew that was misleading. His people loved Kennedy.

But, to many Bush supporters, demonizing the Kennedys was de rigueur.

The ad was appalling, but not exceptional. How all this would translate once the president actually came to Texas was another story. Would he be shown the dignity of respect, Bush wondered, or would the nuts have a field day?

Even those who were normally cool seemed on edge. One lady who worked in the millinery shop of Craig's Department Store in Houston overheard a foreign-sounding man (she thought he was Czechoslovakian or German, but couldn't be sure) tell his companion that "the president ought to be killed." Would-be political assassins were everywhere. A large number of Texans had friends or relatives who at least dreamed they could save America from the Kennedys, including a woman in El Campo who fired off a congratulatory telegram to her Baptist minister uncle in Dallas even before she knew that the president really was dead.

The formation of the presidential motorcade caused a contretemps in getting the state's leading Democrats together for the procession. Yarborough insisted he was going to ride with the vice president, despite Connally. The governor was determined to play his own game: humiliate Yarborough by isolating him, using his disgrace to trash Texas liberals. But the president would have none of that. The Yarborough people were Kennedy people; his liberals were the administration's loyalists. Jerry Bruno, the president's advance man, had clear orders to get Yarborough into that convertible alongside Lady Bird and Lyndon Johnson. Yarborough did slide into that seat, and denied long afterward that he needed to be "pushed" by Kennedy's man, Larry O'Brien. When the shots resounded through Dealey Plaza, their limousine was the fourth, two behind the president's. Connally, in the jump seat in front of Kennedy, was struck by a bullet that passed through his back and body and then ripped through his wrist into his thigh, just missing his heart.[37]

George Bush was among those who were not surprised by the assassination. His sensitivity to rumors, even wild ones, was all part of his understanding of the Texas political process. One story that especially caught his attention involved a young man. According to what Bush heard, he may have been a student at the University of Houston. One thing seemed sure: he was a political activist. The grapevine said he was eager to kill Kennedy as soon as he had a chance. That was in George's mind when he heard about the gunfire in Dallas. Calling the Federal Bureau of Investigation was a natural reflex. The person at the other end took the information seriously and made a careful notation: "On November 22, 1963, Mr. George H. W. Bush, 5525 Briar, Houston, Texas, telephonically advised that he wanted to relate some hear say [sic] that he had heard in recent weeks, date and source unknown. He advised that one JAMES PARROT has been talking of killing the president when he comes to Houston. PARROT is possibly a student at the University of Houston and is active in politics in the Houston area." Even after Lee Harvey Oswald was apprehended at the Texas Theater in Dallas, two agents went to Parrot's home to check it out. They cleared the young man the next day.[38]

Little was very clear at the moment of the tragedy, but Texas Republicans were hurt by Oswald's bullets. Goldwater was still a good bet to head the party's national ticket, a good statewide draw, but the equation had nevertheless changed. The death of Kennedy brought Lyndon Johnson, of all people, to the presidency, and it would be LBJ, the native Texan, who would be at the top of the Democratic ticket. Those reared in one-party state politics were not exactly attuned to sophisticated vote-splitting. Johnson's name was sure to cut into the enthusiasm for the senator from Arizona, and that, of course, was George Bush's problem. Meanwhile, in the wake of grief over Kennedy's murder, Bush suspended his own campaign activities.[39]

The primary was the easiest part. His opposition was so right wing, including a rampaging anti-Communist columnist transplant from New Jersey, Robert Morris, that for all Bush's Goldwater conservatism, editor and general manager Ronnie Dugger of *The Texas Observer* figured that backing him over the rest of the crowd "would be better for the general progression of the human race toward a kinder and gentler social arrangement," as he put it in 1992. With a field including not only Morris but Dr. Milton Davis, also a little-known rightist Dallas surgeon who had headed the "Doctors for Tower" organization, and Jack Cox, a Bush candidacy as its candidate would be healthier for the Republican power structure. Besides, said the *Observer* editorial, "Bush is pleasant to talk to, and he admits to having normal human feelings for the poor and the dispossessed, although he does not let these feelings interfere, in any way, with his steadfast convictions against the issues." The most important reason, however, was that "it seems to us that Connecticut needs a senator from Texas."[40]

Bush had no trouble winning the May primary. His lead over Cox was substantial, but the four-man field activated the Texas constitutional requirement for a runoff. The pro-Bush outcome was just as clear as he swamped Cox in the June showdown by getting 67 percent of their two-way vote, also winning, in the process, confirmation of credentials as a conservative Goldwater Republican.[41] Not that that satisfied conservative skeptics, who wanted George to prove himself by slaying Yarborough.

Bush got his most important point across. He eased many doubts about having a Council of Foreign Relations-style heritage. He promised opposition to the presidents civil rights bill that would "make the Department of Justice the most powerful police force in the nation and the attorney general the nation's most powerful police chief." Moreover, he charged, the public accommodations sections were "unconstitutional," vigorously warning audiences that, without him winning the general election, they would have to contend with Yarborough's backing for a national civil rights bill and a "socialistic Medicare program." He argued that unemployment can be countered only by "unbridled free enterprise" and told receptive and cheering businessmen at Austin's Commodore Perry Hotel of his devotion to "the right-to-work laws."[42]

He had, in other words, thoroughly established himself as a Goldwater Republican. Whatever the ultimate fate for the party's national candidate,

Bush's credentials were confirmed. Beating Yarborough, however, would be the true test of his power. Only then could he really prove his value. Only then could he become a true Texan.

He had won the first move, and his pleasure was obvious. He was euphoric. The right-wingers had eaten out of his hand. He even made them like him. He "took on General Walker" he boasted to his friend Ashley and got along with the kooks of the National Indignation Council, but he had to admit, "it got most unpleasant as you can imagine." But there was a bright side, too. Such nuts, he told Lud about his new insight, were far different from Goldwater himself. "I find him far more reasonable than one would believe from reading the newspapers about him."[43]

Bush's enthusiasm was getting excessive. Ashley saw his friend in a trap. Call it naiveté, or maybe just Bush optimism. He failed to recognize how he would be buffeted by loyalties for Johnson and passion for Goldwater, with defeating Yarborough the real objective of just about everybody in Texas who counted. George, it seemed to Lud, was obviously fooling himself, taking on a role for which he was ill-equipped. "You're just so much better than Goldwater, Tower, and that wing of the party," the Ohio Democrat wrote reassuringly, "ideologically and as an intelligent human being there's just no contest."[44] Behind Lud's observation was the fear that George was getting to like politics, whereas he should stay with something he knew—putting together and running an organization like Zapata—and not go after voters in the streets. He was, it was true, called "charismatic" by the press in those days, but that was because the crowds liked his tall, handsome, athletic frame, and his clean-cut good looks. His campaign speeches were another matter: it was bad enough that his voice was so high-pitched, but his sentences often had neither beginnings nor endings and ran into each other. While the candidate stood and tried to appeal to his audiences, in person or on television, he waved his hands, sometimes flailing them for no good purpose.[45]

He told crowds anything that would attract them. One line that grabbed them, and was used over and over again to predictable hollers and whoops, was that Congress had passed "the new civil rights act to protect fourteen percent of the people," but that he was as much concerned about "the other eighty-six percent."[46] He tried to engage those at the gates of factories, such as the day TV cameras waited for close-ups of him greeting workmen as they came out of the General Dynamics plant in Tarrant County. But, as one of Yarborough's relatives wrote approvingly, "the men came rolling out at the gate and they passed right on by him as though he weren't there. . . . I believe he got two to stop and shake hands with him."[47] He maintained that union dues, as he said to crowds, "are being used today for the promotion of extremist groups" and assured the voters that he was a "responsible conservative that opposes the left-wing policies of radical Ralph Yarborough."[48] He assured a crowd in Floydada, Texas, that conservatives are "not against poor people" but that "wildly spending money in a so-called antipoverty program is not the answer." Instead, business should be turned "loose so that it can create jobs and thus relieve the jobless, if there are such who want work."[49] Over and over again, he singled out Reuther and organized labor for ignoring the needs of common workers. Emulating Goldwater's national campaign, he was squarely against the admission of "Red China" to the United Nations and the "foolishness" of the Nuclear Test Ban Treaty.[50]

Lud, if he knew anything about George's inadequacies on the stump, heard about them secondhand; but if he understood his friend Poppy from Yale he knew how his enthusiasms could turn his head.

Predictably, George and Barbara fell right into it, she smitten every bit as much as he. She went out canvasing from door to door. She sported a name tag that left off the "Bush," all the better to be anonymous, something still possible in that time and place. She could be privy to gossip about what voters really thought of her George.[51] Her real hit that year, however, the valued contribution by the candidate's wife, was her design of handmade straw purses. Little elephants were stitched on them along with the words *Bush for Senate*. Barbara had to give lessons on how to produce enough to use as fundraisers.[52]

Bush's public relations man was a native Texan, James Leonard. Jim, familiar with Lone Star ways, went to work recasting the Yankee. He cleansed his language of highfalutin words and banned Bush public appearances that sported preppy button-down collar shirts. Leonard, while trying to hide the offensive traces of Bush's origins, nevertheless thought that he could become a "Republican Kennedy, young, dashing, articulate, rich," a contradiction all right, but a dream anyway. He also worked hard at bringing together Yarborough's various enemies for the Bush cause. Jim Leonard also gets credit for the bus caravan that went through Texas that July, the "Bandwagon for Bush."[53]

Barbara didn't miss her chance to take the ride. Neither did George W., fresh out of Andover that summer and waiting to get to New Haven. It gave them all, especially the candidate, a chance to break out of the limited region of the state where he was best known, in Houston, Midland, and Odessa. The bus tour raised his profile during the better part of the first two weeks of September. It had everything, including a country and western music band, The Black Mountain Boys and, in true contemporary style, a contingent of cheering females, the "Bush Bonnett Belles." Forty stops were made throughout the state, often just setting down in the center of courthouse squares so Bush "boys" and "girls" could sing: "The sun's going to shine in the Senate some day/George Bush is going to chase them liberals away." In case anyone missed the point, the main theme was the promise of "cleansing the liberals from Washington." At a Bush road show at Quanah and in countless other places, the candidate told all who would listen that the same Walter Reuther of the United Auto Workers, the same man who "even donated fifty dollars to the militant Dr. Martin Luther King Jr.," had been bankrolling the civil rights movement.[54]

His introduction to politics was in as factionalized a campaign as Texas had ever seen. Regulars, meaning, of course, Democrats, wanted to cling to monopoly control—behind anybody, that is, except Yarborough. Not even the entry of a right-wing Democrat, the owner of a radio network called the Liberty Broadcasting System, could derail the populist-liberal. The State Committee, meanwhile, preferred to ignore Yarborough's existence, working instead for Johnson's reelection as president. John Connally was not much more helpful. At least he had enough loyalty to the ticket to be quiet, but his friends were tipped off to come out for Bush. Allan Shivers, still trying to ride the Texas political seesaw, had it both ways by endorsing Johnson and Bush.[55] The man in the White House still had his loyalties to Connally, strained as they had become over the years, but hardly wanted to create a new Republican power in Texas. Yarborough, growing more desperate and uncertain, lashed out at Bush as a creature of the right, citing whenever he could Craig Peper's charges about how George had romanced the Birchers. The society, meanwhile, had its own worries about Bush, especially when it was pointed out that his father-in-law, Marvin Pierce of the McCall Corporation, published a popular woman's magazine called *Redbook,* which, to most listeners, sounded something like an official journal of the Communist Party.[56] Bush then tried to make something out of a fifty thousand dollar cash contribution given to Yarborough at a 1960 barbecue in Pecos arranged by the Kennedy-Johnson campaign committee. The scandalous part was that the money passed from the hands of Billy Sol Estes, the commodities swindler, who was jailed two years later. Estes, of course, gave to every politician in sight, and Yarborough had called him up in advance about needing the money to cover expenses even though he wasn't running that year. Nothing improper was ever demonstrated about the gift, so Bush's attempted smear, encouraged by some of his right-wing backers, fell flat.[57]

More important, an essential part of both Bush's primary and anti-Yarborough strategy, was to identify himself as a Goldwater man, which he did even before the senator was nominated at San Francisco's Cow Palace. Later in the campaign, however, candidate Goldwater's weakness became obvious. Bush's distance from the top of the ticket grew, which exposed him to a Yarborough taunt: "You can find everything on those billboards except the word Republican," claimed his opponent. "He's got it so small you have to . . . get out of your car and look for it with a magnifying glass."[58]

More of the same happened that summer when Bush went to Washington to make two Republican National Committee television campaign films, one with vice presidential candidate William Miller and the other with Republican senate leader Ev Dirksen. When facing reporters at a news conference in the capital, he emphasized that he was concentrating on just one race at a time and was only out for the senate votes of Texans whatever their choice for the presidency.[59] His campaign eventually acknowledged the changing emphasis when, with Jim Leonard's guidance, the Bush office in Houston altered its tactics and revamped its organization.

Bush was right. Texas was not the United States. Without President Johnson running in Kennedy's place, there can be little doubt that Goldwater would have swept the state. But to Bush, as well as to all other observers, the Goldwater run was doomed, which had to weigh down the ticket even in Texas. Nobody watched Goldwater's collapse with more feigned denial or greater self-interest than did Richard Nixon, who, when he was vice president, was a sometime golfing companion (Nixon hated the game) of Prescott Bush. Nixon met with George at the Inn of Six Flags in Arlington that fall and declared that the novice was "running so strong" that he was boosting Goldwater's election prospects.[60] Nevertheless, he later acknowledged, he knew Bush did not have a chance to win but recalled that he was "profoundly impressed by his fighting competitive spirit."[61]

Yarborough's desperation led him to attack Bush's connection to oil—oil that was being shipped in from elsewhere to lower the price of that being produced in Texas, and, to make matters worse, involving profits that evaded U.S. taxes. The senator prepared for his onslaught by having his staff produce a scholarly sounding paper, "Relationship Between Zapata Off-Shore Company and Zapata Petroleum Company and Pennsoil [*sic*] Company." It detailed the interlocking shares of stock held between Bush and the Liedtkes, the Zapata Petroleum Company and Pennzoil, which made George a "substantial stockholder" when the companies merged in 1963. Bush, then, was behind the imported oil and shielded his money through a system of foreign charters. Seacat Zapata, which was formed in 1961 to do contract drilling in the Persian Gulf for the Kuwait Shell Petroleum Development Company, was chartered in South America, enabling Bush to legally avoid American income taxes.[62]

With every barrel of imported foreign oil, Yarborough charged at a fundraiser in Dallas, Bush has been dealing "a body blow" to the "Texas independent oil producer." Bush, in response, admitted to operating three rigs in this country and three abroad but maintained that "we have nothing to do with the oil they produce," which sidestepped his association with Seacat Off-Shore Drilling Company. S.A. Yarborough pointed out that Seacat may have been chartered in South America but, in reality, operates as a British company without paying American taxes. Bush's profits from their operation, in 1963 alone, according to the senator's figures, came to $1,325,000.[63]

Campaign rhetoric aside, and political realities what they were, Ralph Yarborough was not about to let himself sink under pure populism. He had, in fact, never crusaded against Texas oil money; he had no enemies in that vital camp. His argument with Bush held that his rival was duplicitously trying to undermine that very interest, a charge hard to sustain under the most difficult of circumstances and, given the nature of corporate overlapping, impossible given his opponent's standing with the industry. Besides, the hour was too late and the issues too arcane for an intelligent political debate. And Yarborough, after all was said and done, had one thing over Bush: the power of his office. He was the incumbent and was more and more likely to remain in power, especially with President Johnson's popularity that year. So Raff quickly retreated, and by early October trumpeted his own big-money committee, a group thoroughly saturated with black gold.

Almost all were distinguished by the oil that bloated their bank accounts: Neville Penrose, a Fort Worth oilman; oilman R. E. Smith of Houston; J. Howard Marshall, president of Union Texas Petroleum; Paul Bramletter of Longview, an oilman and investment banker; Bailey Sheppard, a Longview attorney and oilman; and Oscar Wyatt Jr., chairman of the board of Coastal States Gas Producing Corporation.[64]

When it all came together, Yarborough was unbeatable. Enough Texas fat cats appreciated their access to his power. Maybe his greatest asset with the president was that most emphatic of political debts: Yarborough gave him that civil rights vote, the only senator from the Old Confederacy to do so. Lyndon Johnson was too good a politician to forget that. Nor did the president overlook Yarborough's support among organized labor and his standing with the state's large Mexican-American voting bloc. At the last minute, the president showed his independence from John Connally, changed his own schedule, and went on the hustings for Raff Yarborough.[65]

Bush had also built his financial foundation, which was less dependent on his own relatively modest means than on the circle of friends he could tap then and later. The Bush circle, based as it was in the Texas oil fields, proved reliable throughout his career. He was as attractive to the money men as they were to him. "A lot of people believed in George Bush right from the beginning," recalled Bob Mosbacher. "He was articulate. He was handsome. Had great presence, even then. He was movie-star handsome. He had that movie-star look. He had a lot of people who believed in him. That was his base. A lot of them were very successful monetarily. They were successful either politically or as far as contacts were concerned. So it worked well for him." Later, he could count on them for the vital funding that was becoming increasing important for a drive toward the White House. Some became his staff officers, if not his generals.[66]

They were there whenever he needed a boost, coming together to give him financial support during his own races or, when Nixon placed him at the head of the Republican National Committee, he had to demonstrate his fund-raising ability. Bill Liedtke came through at Bush's request for Nixon's 1972 reelection campaign. Mosbacher, who was Bush's chief money man in 1988 and 1992, was at the center of that Midland-Houston group (which supplemented the Bush-Walker Wall Street connections) that also included, in addition to the Liedtke brothers, the close Bush friend and native Texan oilmen they knew both in Midland and Houston, C. Fred Chambers, Bobby Holt, Earle Craig Jr., and, of course, Will Farish. Baker, whose Texas financial reach was even better than Bush's, later headed "big brother's" first presidential campaign. The Bush circle's economic base was indeed formidable. Its members had earned luxury of access to key political power. Their visibility lives on at the Wiess Energy Hall in the Houston Museum of Natural Science. The oil money circle remains memorialized on a plaque noting such contributors as The William Stamps Farish Foundation; The Dresser Foundation, Inc.; the Pennzoil Company; the law firm of Baker & Hostetler. Another member of the circle, Hugh Roy Cullen, helped build the museum, a local monument to the oil wealth that, along with the wonders of modern air-conditioning, helped to create a World's Fair-like "city of the future" on the Gulf coastal plain. At the Fondren Library on the campus of Rice University can be found more evidence of Cullen's assets, as well as the Baker Institute and the James A. Baker III Public Service Archive. George Bush, in leaving the East for Texas, had planted the seeds for more than his own economic security. His friend Red Dog's speculation that Poppy's political future was conceived early on by "going into the navy and becoming a pilot in the navy, then breaking away from the white-shoe set of Yale and Andover by going out and being a relative roughneck in the oil fields of Odessa, Texas," ignores one vital element, and that was provided by the Bush circle.[67]

When he first challenged Yarborough, their full potential was yet to be realized. As oil-centered as they were, they were not yet a match for the populist incumbent. As the votes came in that year, Bush's loss was predictable. Standing alongside Barbara and young George, he told his supporters that he hoped that the size of his vote "will serve as a modifying factor on [Yarborough's] political views." He did, however, get the largest Republican turnout in Texas history, 1,134,337, not bad for a state where Johnson swamped Goldwater with 63 percent of the total. But Yarborough had a 300,000 plurality over Bush. George told his supporters in the Hotel America that he planned to return to his drilling business in Houston and continue his interest in politics.[68]

"I just don't know how it happened," he told reporters afterward. "I just don't know how it happened. I guess I have a lot to learn about."[69]

Even his loss was a considerable investment for his future. He had made friends. John Tower, the state's junior senator, encountered Peter O'Donnell Jr., the GOP's Dallas chairman at the old Commodore Perry Hotel in downtown Austin a few days later. Tower suggested to O'Donnell that he might step aside and not seek reelection, giving Bush a seat he would have a good chance of holding. Tower may have been posturing. Unlike Bush, he was in deep trouble with the Birchers, but, in any event, the idea was vetoed by O'Donnell.[70]

The Bush race had gotten much national attention. Trying to stop Yarborough alone was newsworthy. Bill Buckley's *National Review,* which had become established as the voice of conservatism, invited Bush to join in a symposium that would enable him to make some additional observations. The Johnson landslide, Buckley argued, did not signify the failure of the conservative movement, he wrote. The tactics were at fault. They were guilty of overkill on the liberal welfare state. "We should repackage our philosophy," he concluded. "Emphasize the positive, eliminate the negative, warn of the dangers from the left but do so without always questioning the patriotism of those who hold liberal views. . . . Conservatism can and will survive—it needs to be practical and positive."[71] A few months later, Bush made a confession to his Episcopalian minister in Houston: "You know, John, I took some of the far right positions to get elected. I hope I never do it again. I regret it."[72]

He was learning to acknowledge his errors, but not to stop making them.

CHAPTER EIGHT

"Labels Are for Cans"

%

The campaign left Bush with very mixed feelings. On one hand, his loss had not really jeopardized his political future. The state's Republicans needed him for building a viable party. But, still, he could not go on contradicting everything he had been taught at Greenwich Country Day School, Andover, and Yale. Lose, yes, he heard over and over again, but do it with dignity, and, for heaven's sake, do not brag about your victories. Never demean your opponent. Make your point and let the issue rest on that. At least the *National Review*'s symposium had given him a chance to clear the air. Making his point among conservatives seemed even smarter. He was still thinking about that, about losing in a dirty fight, when he told the *Houston Chronicle* in May that he was still "ashamed for not speaking out about this kind of pandemonium."[1]

That was why he reassessed his situation. He knew that Johnson's candidacy had killed him. Goldwater at the head of the ticket should have made a real difference, especially in Texas, but look what the lefties did to him. An eccentric named Ralph Guinzburg circulated some wild stuff about how Goldwater was psychotic. That was not the Goldwater Bush came to know; maybe some of his followers were weird, but he admired the senator. Separating him from the lunatic fringe was another matter. And of all the talk about who was "crazy," wasn't it Johnson who was using the "wild man's" strategy in Vietnam (which Richard Nixon would later make more famous as the "madman" theory), opening Operation Rolling Thunder, just a few months after the election, carrying the war to the National Liberation Front? Yet, Bush, who had his ups and downs about the war many times before it was over, was ready to back it all the way no matter who *was* president. It had to be won.

One can see why Ronnie Dugger and his crew at the *Observer* had hopes that, if anyone could lead the Texas Republicans out of the "dark ages," it was George Bush. He had not only recanted the unseemliness of the campaign he had run against Yarborough but, at the University of Texas in June, he declared himself fully behind what Lyndon Johnson was trying to do with his Great Society program for America. After all, what was it all about? "A better life for all," said Bush, "elimination of poverty and disease, fair play in civil rights and domestic tranquility on all fronts." He had just one partisan reservation: "that a great society can or should be built solely by the federal government—or any government."[2] He was reasonable.

He even got himself involved in Harris County's Great Society push at the grassroots level. Civic leaders had put together a Houston-Harris County Economic Opportunity organization. Bush became part of a fourteen-member executive committee that was named in the fall, although what he did for it is somewhat vague. The party's national committee, trying to keep a role for their up-and-coming luminary, advised George to head a committee charged with taking "the initiative in fighting hardcore unemployment."[3]

If that placed him on Lyndon Johnson's side, so did the war in Vietnam. He had no doubt that the president was right on target. His own war experience, he later told David Frost in a national magazine, shaped his understanding of what it was all about.[4] Nor did anything do more to place him on public record than his debate with Ronnie Dugger.

On July first, the liberal writer from Austin confronted Bush before members of the Junior Bar of Texas at Fort Worth, an establishment gathering of youthful legal types. Vietnam was Topic A: Was it really worth fighting? Should it be stepped up? Dugger later remembered Bush seeming "strange, almost evanescent" that evening. But his words constituted a vigorous condemnation of the American far left. They seemed, to Bush, eager to denounce the integrity of the nation's anti-Communist foreign policies, especially over Vietnam and Cuba, while exuding righteousness about human rights at home.[5]

They were hypocrites; ragged kids, and some not such kids, hardly average Joes, many with bearded faces. They wore Keds sneakers, "slightly soiled," all in the name of freedom. And yet, for all their "love" of "democracy" and "peace," they lionized that Communist Castro. Bush told the audience how crazy those leftists were to "scream when we send troops to the Dominican Republic to protect people and guarantee against the Communist takeover." They would even have us pull out of Vietnam and let "Southeast Asia's last hope for freedom . . . go down the drain." Legitimate dissent was understandable, he suggested, but "we have to take a look at Thoreau and civil disobedience, and I recognize the risk when I get to talking to Ronnie Duggger about Thoreau and civil disobedience." Quite another matter, he thought, when you talk about a tormented individual Negro in Mississippi or Alabama; but those campus people are another thing all together.[6]

Bush's 1964 senatorial campaign had effectively prepared him for the future, which came quickly because, along with Johnson's escalation of the war and the continuation of Kennedy reforms came the logical next sequence in the drive for racial equality, the Voting Rights Act of 1965.

That may well have been the most significant advance of all. Rare, indeed, was the Southern black who was actually registered to vote. Still more rare was one who voted. And still rarer was their vote cast in a truly independent way, not as dictated by some sort of boss or authority figure of some kind. East Texas, the area around Houston, a Gulf Coast extension of the Old Confederacy, was almost as bad as the Dixie heartland. Blacks were most likely to have voting rights precisely where their ballots did not matter because their numbers were so insignificant. The extended battle over the franchise, however, including vestiges of the old poll taxes, roiled Congress in 1965, helped spark Dr. King's march on Selma, and finally, on August 6, resulted in President Johnson's theatrical signing of the new voting law. Throughout the South and its border states, such cities as Houston, Dallas, Memphis, New Orleans, and Atlanta experienced a surge of black registrants. In a real sense, the Old South was no more. Neither was the party structure. Blacks and whites played musical chairs, as blacks abandoned the party of Lincoln for FDRs, JFKs, and LBJs.[7]

District changes also affected Houston. Speedy progress involved either of two schemes. One diluted the new black vote by submerging it into predominantly white districts, guaranteeing blacks only minority voting status in them. A prime example was the Tuscaloosa, Alabama, arrangement, which decimated black representation and was ultimately thrown out by the courts. The other meant divvying up districts, those that were mainly white and those largely black. That method at least served the function of sending to Washington a record number of African-American legislators while, of course, also guaranteeing safe, white, solidly conservative seats.

What Bush encountered in Houston was a blend of the two. The newly created Seventh District was nearly 90 percent Caucasian and almost evenly divided between "silk-stocking," affluent professional white-collar people that included such neighborhoods as the River Oaks section and blue-collar workers. Blacks constituted hardly more than 10 percent. The Seventh took in about a third of Houston and comprised the city's northwestern section. A creation of the Texas "lege" in 1965, it became Houston's most rock-ribbed Republican district.[8]

The GOP's latest urban bastion, while still no Dallas, was useful. John Tower had no trouble there in his special election in 1961, so its potential for a Republican turnout was a matter of record. Moreover, Bush had a stronger appeal to the district's black minority.[9]

Bush was ready. He severed his official positions with Zapata, resigning as chairman and chief executive officer to devote himself full time to running for Congress. To make the break complete, he sold his stock in the corporation and, unfortunately, did so for $1.1 million, about $3.5 million less than if he had held out longer. "I didn't have as a goal a stacking-up of money," he told a reporter. "If you're going to build something like that, I could make a very stimulating case that would be worth doing. But the idea of just going out and making money for the sake of it doesn't interest me. If I didn't have any capital at all, I might be viewing that very differently."[10]

He also filed as the Republican candidate, running in true Texas style against the only kind of viable competition in that district, a conservative Democratic opponent, District Attorney Frank Briscoe. But, as was so common in the area, the Democrat was of a vintage sufficiently conservative to be to Bush's right, and emphasized his positions to confirm his "patriotic" credentials. He agreed with his rival in favoring Johnson's Vietnam escalation, and sided with management over labor by upholding the right-to-work law. In an obvious refutation of Johnson's Great Society program, he came out against heavy government spending, except, of course, for his district and the state of Texas. The figures for 1970 showed that the Seventh received an average annual federal outlay of $393,669,000.[11]

Houston's Seventh, together with Briscoe's opposition, gave Bush the most convenient political fight he would ever have. Never again, as it turned out, would there be so many options. He had, in 1966, that rare moment, the ability to command his own political theater, to orchestrate matters as he would have them, to play a role as a conservative in the classical Tory tradition of public responsibility. The way to mobilize Houston's northwestern district was through enlightened, intelligent leadership rather than through polemics. "Labels are for cans," he told someone who tried to pigeonhole him. Let Briscoe go for the rightists, those who were out to save the Republicans from moderates and liberals by defeating Bush.[12]

To call it ideology, however, was to evade the real issue, which for Houston, as for most of the nation in 1966, was neither left nor right, neither pro- nor anti-Vietnam. What really mattered was race. Three summers of urban disturbances, all following Supreme Court decisions and legislative actions on Capitol Hill, had already wrecked a number of black America's ghettos. To all the world, it looked as though the "politics of rising expectations" had indeed come to America. Whatever promises of change, minorities saw no escape from their own impoverishment and despair. They lived in inner-city enclaves trying to survive. The white majority, both workers on the fringe of black neighborhoods and in more comfortable suburbs, reacted through fear and resentment. Racial disturbances were, as with such situations, seen less in their sociological and historical contexts than as confirmation of traditional views about man's inability to govern himself. Black leadership, encouraged by a sympathetic federal government driven to compensate for the past and responding to the demands of the newly enfranchised victims and their white sympathizers, had given them unheard of responsibility. The fear arose that substantial, sober, hard-working whites were no longer safe. The phrase "white backlash" had entered the political language. John Kraft, who polled the Seventh for the GOP, reported that his constituents regarded the NAACP as more unpopular than the John Birch Society. Briscoe himself was one of those local politicos who prided himself on how many blacks he could send to jail. "Black people would have voted for an ox before they would have voted for Briscoe," said the pastor of the local Antioch Baptist Church.[13] Nor did Briscoe intend subtlety. He was out for votes, and race was the unambiguous issue. He forced Bush to stake out his own ground by daring him to draw the line on the most charged aspect of the whole problem, open housing.[14]

It was, perhaps, Bush's most personal campaign. He had to be both decent and effective, and he could hardly succeed by forfeiting the Seventh to the obstructionist district attorney. So 1966 became a model of sorts for Bush's career, one that forever characterized his political persona, both by supporters and critics. His own attractions had to transcend the ugliness that was just below the surface, and he did what he could do best. He waged what two historians later called "a people-to-people campaign." The whole effort came out of his headquarters at 4016 Richmond Avenue, where volunteers staffed the office after its opening on June 1.

He canvased the district with his ten or so "Blue Bonnett Belles." They toured the Seventh making house-to-house calls, giving out fliers and shaking hands along the way. With his campaign director, Jim Allison Jr., his secretary, Aleene Smith, and especially Harry Treleaven, a master of image-making with some two decades of experience with the J. Walter Thompson advertising agency, he was able to organize his media saturation team, getting TV spots, newspaper coverage, and plastering the district with posters. His own effort resulted in some one hundred formal speeches. At the start of July, he attended a conference sponsored by the Republican Congressional Committee at the Twin Bridges Motor Hotel at the edge of the Potomac across from the District of Columbia. There, Bush and other Republican candidates were cheered on by all those party loyalists who assured them that 1966 was their year; there was robust oratory from such people as former Congressman Walter Judd of Minnesota and Richard Nixon, still with his New York City law firm. The city of Houston had been one of Nixon's prizes during his own 1960 campaign, which contrasted with most urban areas, so, when Bush ran for Congress, Nixon returned to Texas to help boost the Bush cause.[15]

In Houston, meanwhile, candidate Bush became a celebrity. He was a "new" kind of candidate. Treleaven found him ideal, "highly promotable," as he later described his client, "an extremely likeable person," with a useful kind of "haziness about exactly where he stood politically." This was helpful, the adman noted in a subsequent report, "because probably more people vote for irrational, emotional reasons than professional politicians suspect." So he had George do what George did naturally, and Houstonians saw the results on their TV sets. Bush, congenial, attractive, walked his district with sleeves rolled up and coat slung over his shoulder, "grinning, gripping, sweating, letting the voter know he cared. About what was never made clear," Joe McGinniss later wrote.[16] George Bush, noted *The Wall Street Journal*, was among "the large number of new and appealing Republican personalities across the nation."[17] And it was true. His personal appeal went far to help attract enthusiastic volunteers, enabling the campaign to place in the forefront a constantly enlarging list of organization appointees, each with a good, important title. "BUSH VOLUNTEERS," urged his *Bulletin,* "IT *IS* LATER THAN YOU THINK. . . . Call or go by Headquarters today and offer your help to elect George Bush to Congress."[18]

Still missing was George's reaction to Briscoe's dare about open housing. The response that finally came from Bush was at once symbolic and also entirely consistent with his own values. Those cynics who hold that the move was political, a way of getting around the open housing issue without offending either race, are, of course, partly right. The later comment by an "old" Bush friend that his action was "personal not political" is also correct. It was, in reality, a little bit of both.

There was nothing complicated about the situation itself. Major-league baseball had been integrated for nearly two decades, beginning with Jackie Robinson of the old Brooklyn Dodgers. Localities, however, could be very different, not only because of the persistence of de jure segregation but of the de facto kind as well. Getting children of all colors into the same swimming pools and ball fields often involved overcoming not so subtle obstacles, and utilizing astute leadership. When Bush got his chance to do something about the situation, Yale's former baseball captain simply could not resist. The fact that it coincided with the middle of his political campaign, and in the face of the open housing issue, made it that much more meaningful.

Not that others had not tried. There were those who had worked on the local level, including in Houston, to come up with the means, which usually meant money, for such constructive purposes. One resident, Bobby Moore, experienced repeated failures when he tried to enlist sponsorship from black businessmen. He did know George Bush, however, and he knew that the man who lost to Yarborough in 1964 often had his luncheons at the Houston Club, a downtown gathering place for the city's leading businessmen. Moore, especially concerned about the need to get something constructive going for idle youngsters in and around Acres Homes, a development in the city's west side black community, wanted help in organizing a softball team among local girls who were under the age of eighteen. They could then enter league competition and go head-to-head with five other teams, all white, which usually competed at Hennessey Park. A final play-off among the leading squads would decide the neighborhood girls' softball championship.

Bush never hesitated, nor was he worried about any potential consequences. He marched Bobby Moore right to a sporting goods store. He arranged to fund all the equipment and uniforms right on the spot, which was how the George Bush All-Stars joined the league. The city of Houston got its integrated girls softball tournament.

Some five hundred fans turned out on the final night for the deciding game. They packed the field at Highland Park, at Acres Homes, and watched the Bush team go on to victory, an event that reached a much greater audience than those who happened to be there on July 10. The *Forward Times,* a local paper with a predominantly black readership, featured a group picture of George Bush with the two top teams. It told all about how he presented trophies to the winners and the losers. Bobby Moore, as manager, accepted the prize for the George Bush All-Stars.[19]

Bush, the novice urban politician, put together all that he needed. His was the candidacy of *The Houston Post, The Jewish Herald-Voice,* and such conservative outlets as *Human Events* and Americans for Constitutional Action, along, of course, with the *Forward Times.* Seventh District voters had a candidate of star quality, one who attracted such party luminaries as Dwight Eisenhower, Gerald Ford, John Tower, and Everett Dirksen. Not lost among his boosters was another man who made his pitch in person, Richard Nixon.[20]

The Richmond Street headquarters was the place to be on election night, and, before young George W. Bush finished posting the returns on the big board for all to see, as many as two thousand well-wishers, workers, and just enthusiasts packed the room. Even Democrat Bob Eckhardt, from the neighboring Eighth District, was there. So was the Bush family. Brother Jonathan made a flight from New York "because I couldn't stand being away from George at this time in his life," he told reporters. The younger children were all there, too, Dorothy, Marvin, Neil, and Jeb, amusing listeners by saying that they were so ready to go to Washington with their dad that they were prepared to take both family dogs, Motsy and Nicky.

Barbara got there at seven. "I was too excited to stay at home," she explained, and assured everybody that George would soon be there.

When he arrived, his animation was at a new high. He saw Junior post figures that showed his lead widening. He removed his gray suit jacket and was in his shirtsleeves. "What's the score?" he called out around nine o'clock. "How are we doing? I'm getting a wonderful feeling." Just before ten-thirty, he heard Briscoe announce his concession. Bush quickly called East three times to his parents in Greenwich, saying, "Gosh, Mother and Dad, it looks like we're ahead."

He had earned his "wonderful feeling." He swept Briscoe with 57.6 percent of the vote in a district that was at least nominally six-to-one Democratic, a reversal that mirrored how so many Texas "regulars" were going those days. Bush was more impressed that he got 35 percent of the black and Hispanic vote, up from 3 percent just four years earlier. He was headed back East. He'd join his friend Lud, but this time as a colleague, although on the other side of the aisle.[21]

Not since the Civil War had disorder so racked Washington. The crises of the later Johnson years were about to boil over and destroy his administration by the time Bush got there. Protests and demonstrations became part of the daily ambiance, at times even visible from the Bush home on Palisades Lane.

Their first Washington house was in the Spring Valley section. They bought it from Senator Milward Lee Simpson of Wyoming, the father of a future senator, Alan Simpson, who became a good Bush friend. The house was located on Hillbrook Lane in a suburban part of northwest Washington, quite far from downtown and the government area. They took a loss by selling the house to move to a better one closer in. During the massive protests of late 1969 and 1970, their proximity to the turmoil was from a three-story brick townhouse on Palisades Lane. Not only did it have a small front lawn and a patio but it was just fifteen minutes from Capitol Hill.[22]

The Bushes settled in with ease. The new location made it easier to get together with other congressional couples. Some of the men were among the large number of Republican freshmen, forty-seven in all. Their wives banded together and, marking their first congressional session, called themselves the 90th Club, after the 90th Congress. It also helped George and Barbara that their children were getting on with their own lives: Young George, three years out of Andover, was away at Yale. Jeb, who had yet to go on to prep school, was back in Houston, staying with Baine and Mildred Kerr, good family friends. At least the other three, Marvin, Doro, and Neil, were with their parents.[23]

Barbara would later recall George's social impetuousness, his almost incessant need for surrounding himself with the capital's most active figures. Aside from his old friend Lud Ashley, there were many others of his generation, including some Democrats, as were Ashley and Sonny Montgomery of Mississippi, and a batch of Republicans: Bill Steiger of Wisconsin, Tom Railsback of Illinois, John Paul Hammerschmidt of Arkansas, Jim Leach of Iowa, and Tom Kleppe from North Carolina. They played paddleball together in the gym of the sprawling Rayburn House Office Building on Independence Avenue, across the street from the Capitol and connected by the congressional subway. George's habit of inviting them and a whole raft of friends for spontaneous dinner parties was something Barbara had long been accustomed to, although his need to visit his district was another matter. Nothing indicates that Barbara was bored, however. Aside from the 90th Club, she joined the International Club II, founded by Dorothy Walker Bush among others, along with the wives of George's other colleagues. The little organization of a dozen women was equally divided along party lines; it devoted itself to trying to help key personnel of foreign embassies to "feel at home in America." And, while George had his paddleball, golf, and tennis, Barbara played tennis almost every day. It was, as she later wrote, "a strange life, but an exciting one."[24]

CHAPTER NINE

"Rubbers"

%

The Seventh District's newly seated member of the Ninetieth Congress was about as progressive as his constituency could stand. His legislative record matched his party's traditional center as he cast all the right votes for reducing spending and federal regulatory powers. *Congressional Quarterly* showed that his voting record placed him in 80-percent agreement with the Republicans and Democrats who roughly constituted a conservative coalition.[1] Insofar as foreign policy was concerned, he observed the old adage that "politics stops at the water's edge" even when Lyndon Johnson was in the White House. He came up on the conservative side often enough to earn a perfect zero rating by the AFL-CIO's Political Education Committee of organized labor. He also received a distinguished service award from the conservative Americans for Constitutional Action. He was, all in all, a well-liked popular newcomer. That first summer in Washington, he joined with other Republican moderates, including Charles Goodell, an upstate New Yorker, in embracing what they called a Neighborhood Action Crusade. Goodell, who headed the Planning and Research Committee of the House Republican Conference and shared Bush's pedigree, convinced Bush that Republicans should not merely thwart the president's programs but had to demonstrate their own responsiveness to social needs.

What emerged from Goodell's little group was an emphasis on voluntary action on the local level, a suggestion remarkably similar to the community action programs that were part of President Johnson's "war against poverty." Bush joined with Goodell, Bill Steiger, and a Kentuckian William O. Cowger, to propose the Neighborhood Action Crusade "to defuse the tensions now threatening the lives and property of urban Americans." They viewed it as a national movement of "autonomous local programs organized, developed, and directed completely by local citizens" and urged the creation of largely volunteer organizations to work for neighborhood stability. Five days later, on August 1, 1967, freshman Congressman George Bush took the House floor and explained that funds and equipment would be provided by the federal government. He said nothing about how much the Neighborhood Action Crusade would cost. Nor did the Republican plan envision creating the kind of federal bureaucracy then being built by the administration's Office of Economic Opportunity.[2] The initiative was, as journalist Jefferson Morley noted, a "spiritual forefather of Bush's Thousand Points of Light program" that he announced in 1988.[3]

Goodell's group had gone on record, but nothing much came of it. In the spring of 1968, the National Advisory Committee on Civil Disorders led by Illinois Governor Otto Kerner published its report. The committee had been created by the president in the wake of the urban disorders through the "long hot summers" of the 1960s. So altered was the political climate by then that Johnson's reception to the Kerner Report was cool in the extreme. The report, however, pointed to an approach similar to what Bush and his colleagues had proposed. In its conclusions about what could be done, it noted that the "cooperation and assistance of Negro leaders and their community residents with a common interest in the mainstream of order can be extremely valuable," and pointed out that volunteers "have assisted in restoring order by patrolling their neighborhoods and trying independently to persuade others to go home. Sometimes," the Kerner group added, "local authorities have actively recruited ghetto residents to perform these missions."[4] Bush then seized the opportunity to point out to the president that the Neighborhood Action Crusade had, in effect, been recommended in the Kerner Report. He also argued on the House floor for putting the power of the presidency behind the NAC.[5]

Nothing further came of the NAC, and there was just as little evidence of attempts at implementation other than the often rocky birth of community action programs being encouraged by the White House. The Goodell group, at least, had gone on record to show that some Republicans recognized the urgency of the situation.

A close and like-minded colleague, western New Yorker Barber Conable, remembered him in a manner strikingly reminiscent of Roy Goodearle's recollection of the Bush who first entered politics. Conable thought the young man was "pretty innocent of political ideas generally"; he lacked the "fire in the belly" to "accomplish something in particular, but, withitall, a thoroughly decent, experienced fellow who was very good in his personal relations." Bush "felt a strong *noblesse oblige*" to provide service, and so he moved up the ladder simply by virtue of his personality, not because he was following some banner.[6] "I think what Bush was trying to do was find common ground," remembered Richard Burris, then the counsel for the House Republican leadership under Minority Leader Gerald Ford of Michigan.[7]

Another reality was that no freshman stirred the Ninetieth Congress Republicans more by his mere arrival. He was, after all, the son of Senator Prescott Bush, a veteran of fifty-eight missions in the Pacific, captain of Yale's baseball team, and the same young man who had demonstrated skills in putting together an oil business. "People liked him instinctively," said Conable.[8] Honors followed. His colleagues made him president of their freshman class.[9]

He became the first newcomer in memory to win a seat on the powerful House Ways and Means Committee, then chaired by a congressional leader from Arkansas, Democrat Wilbur Mills. Few denied the importance of membership on a committee with such a decisive grip on taxation. Holding its chair gave Mills more sway over taxes than any single individual in the country. His intimate knowledge of tax law combined with fiscal conservatism and enough bipartisanship made him among the most powerful individuals on Capitol Hill. "In the old Washington power game," wrote journalist Hedrick Smith, "when Mills gave his word, he could deliver his committee and that virtually assured passage."[10] The seat was so prized that the Bush appointment in 1967 broke a sixty-three-year drought among freshmen.

Prescott Bush was in Washington for his son's swearing-in. "His father asked me to help," Mills told *Los Angeles Times* reporter Barry Bearak in 1988. The chairman later explained on camera that the ex-senator "used his influence to get George a seat on one of the most powerful committees in Congress—House Ways and Means." Prescott also made some well-targeted calls to former colleagues on the hill. House minority leader, Ford, who could have killed the idea of giving the prize to George, went along without hesitation. He had golfed with Prescott when the older Bush was a senator. Ford had even gone to Harris County to campaign for George, so he hardly needed a personal phone call, or even prodding from Mills. The Bush nomination passed the committee of Republicans convened to fill the vacancy. Mills agreed. The appointment was a real coup, one that was later cited repeatedly as evidence of his ability. As fellow committee member Conable put it, Mills was a "contentious man who believed Ways and Means should reflect the majority of the House and not just the majority of the party." And the "majority of the House," all hands agreed, implied protection for "oil preferences in taxation, the depletion allowance."[11]

The industry had suffered a temporary setback. Congressional Democrats, unlike their Republican counterparts, decided on assignments to such committees as Ways and Means by their votes, a process that dashed the hopes of Big Oil by the rejection of a "friendly" Texan, freshman Omar Burleson, for a New Yorker, Jacob Gilbert. Prescott Bush's boy became that much more logical. "George was a choice that was generally applauded," said Conable about his good colleague. "The two of us worked well together, very well, because I could keep George up with what was happening and he could give me his rather brilliant insights on business and the oil factor and all sensitive areas of taxation that I didn't know anything about."[12] Not surprisingly, he was an ardent advocate for the interests of the petroleum industry, which included fighting for the deregulation of natural gas. "I was a congressman from Texas," he later explained. "I felt that artificially low prices would inhibit the supply of natural gas," he added, recalling that he "was considered predictably pro-oil and my position was considered regionally inspired and biased."[13] Indeed, as one of his senatorial campaign managers later said, "One of the most significant entrees that George had for being accepted as a politician in Texas was the fact that he did come from the oil industry."[14]

The oil cartel naturally maintained numerous congressional supporters, but strength on Ways and Means was especially useful. In Bush, the industry had a consistent champion of its major agenda. By the time of his arrival in Washington, that consisted of preserving from increasing criticism two valued safeguards: the 27.5 percent tax depletion allowance, and the system of import quotas that had been in place since the previous decade to ensure sufficient domestic oil production in the interest of national security.

The depletion allowance was clear and easily understood. A generous tax write-off for so lucrative an industry was easily popularized as a government "giveaway" to Big Oil. But drillers especially made the argument about the high financial risks involved in exploration. Striking out the allowance altogether, or even lowering rates, they reasoned, would risk lowering oil reserves and gambling with national security.

In recent years, since the end of World War II, the industry's position had prevailed as its friends in Congress had repeatedly turned back assaults on the allowance. Harry Truman, full of indignation, had termed the tax credit "inequitable" and "excessive." Liberals, in particular, were arguing that the depletion percentage, which had been on the books since 1926, was completely out of line with the actual costs of recovery. More and more was heard about "oil millionaires" profiting from government policies. Truman himself gave the example of a producer whose tax-free income had built up to almost $5 million. Not only was the strength of the oil industry sufficient to beat back all attempts at reform, but they managed to increase the scope of their shelter. The Revenue Act of 1950 extended write-offs to cover transportation costs. The allowance became, in the words of Robert Sherrill, "a gold-plated albatross," one that became a public relations disaster. One New York congressman even charged that the "oil industry makes the Mafia look like a pushcart operation."[15]

George Bush's representation of the industry, despite his place on Ways and Means, left him far short of becoming a House version of Senator Robert S. Kerr, the Oklahoma Democrat whose death in 1963 weakened their ramparts. In an era when civil rights became the great moral issue that galvanized liberals, the targeted oil depletion allowance was not far behind. The reformist tide of the sixties, and heavy publicity given to tax inequities, placed the industry on the defensive as never before.

The industry and its concerns were important to Bush throughout his congressional years. There was enough noise about oil and tax breaks by early 1969, after George had begun his second term on the hill, for the newly inaugurated thirty-seventh president, Richard Nixon, to move into action. He was, he announced at the outset, assuming full responsibility for policy. On March 26, 1969, Nixon also revealed the formation of a cabinet-level task force to be headed by Labor Secretary George Shultz to look into the matter. In early July, Bush, in the wake of the president's initiatives, said he was "worried sick" about emotional attacks in Congress and vowed his own continued support. He found the "climate" in Washington toward oil depletion "unbelievable" and later went on to leave no doubt that, in the face of reductions then being considered as part of a new tax reform act, he was "not in any compromising position. I've been arguing vociferously that if the full depletion allowance was ever meaningful, it's meaningful now."[16]

The industry was ready for a strategic retreat. Shedding the albatross of the 27.5 percent depletion allowance was a small price to pay for mollifying critics and keeping the peace, especially when the difference would be more apparent than real. When adjusting the tax rates to consider smaller profits, the gap was relatively negligible. On the hill, both Mills and Senate Finance Committee chairman and friend of Big Oil, Hale Boggs of Louisiana, led the way toward a strategic retreat. Bush, who had already gone on record in opposition to any change, got the word. In late August, he and John Tower flew to San Clemente for a meeting with President Nixon. The president had campaigned by vowing to preserve the higher rate. At that seaside winter White House on the Pacific, where they were also joined by David Kennedy, representing the administration, they told Nixon that the industry was ready to give ground. The president was urged to limit his comments to a mere indication of his willingness to accept the wishes of Congress because the oilmen were willing to "accept some reduction of the depletion allowance."[17] On October 7, Bush acted in accordance with the politic retreat by joining the majority in a 394-30 vote to reduce the figure to 20 percent, a symbolic gesture to dispel the image of rigidity. Confidence remained that their best interests would still be upheld by both the president and Long's committee.[18] The president also held out for the higher figure, but was defeated when the Senate later rejected an attempt at restoration that was made by Long's Louisiana colleague, Allen J. Ellender.

The matter bounced around all that fall and into the early winter, the depletion figure wavering between the original 27.5 and 20 percent. Bush, meanwhile, concerned himself with holding the line on import quotas. Critics of such protection, which was obviously designed to protect price levels by limiting competition from foreign oil, were not quite as vociferous as those directed toward the depletion allowance.

Bush, keeping attuned to what was happening, warned that allowing more foreign oil would bring at least a temporary reduction in domestic prices.[19] The threat seemed genuine. Bush invited both Secretary Kennedy and a group of oilmen to his Houston home, where, on November 12, they plotted how to resist any changes and, in the presence of the secretary of the treasury, rendered the industry's position unmistakable. After the meeting, thanking Kennedy for the trip to Houston, Bush wrote, "I was also appreciative of your telling them how I bled and died for the oil industry. That might kill me off in the *Washington Post* but it darn sure helps in Houston."[20]

Nixon got the message. He struggled with what he knew was a no-win decision, especially in view of the pending announcement that the task force was recommending replacing the quota system with a sliding-scale reduction of the tariff on oil imports. If he agreed with his own cabinet members, Chief of Staff Bob Haldeman noted in his diary, the administration risked losing "at least a couple of seats, including George Bush in Texas," a good reason for trying "to figure out a way to duck the whole thing and shift it to Congress."[21]

Bush and the industry escaped with their political skins intact. Just before Christmas, the Senate and House adopted their conference committee report that set the rate at 22 percent. All along, even as a din was being made about 27.5 percent, the effective depletion allowance was really 23 percent, so the additional point downward was no great sacrifice. Peace can sometimes cost much more. And the price of leadership, Nixon demonstrated on February 20, involved using presidential authority to override the findings of his own cabinet-level task force. He ignored the Shultz group and upheld the protective quota system.[22] The second-term congressman from Houston's Seventh had done his job well.

Bush's brief career on Capitol Hill coincided with some of the most divisive moments of the Vietnamese War. Lyndon Johnson's leadership was already under heavy challenge within his own party. There were mounting calls for a way out, either through deescalation, holding on to strategic enclaves, or even in the simplest and most creative stroke of all, following the suggestion of Vermont Republican Senator George Aiken that the U.S. should simply declare a military victory and go home.[23] In late 1967, Senator Eugene McCarthy of Minnesota announced that he would oppose President Johnson by entering the New Hampshire primary in March. It was, at that point, equally obvious that Richard Nixon was outstanding among the GOP contenders, having campaigned around the country for Republican candidates throughout 1964 and 1966. In 1968, Nixon was ready to present himself as the one most likely to both resolve the war and salvage what remained of American prestige.

During his own congressional campaign in 1966, neither Bush nor his opponent questioned the importance of the commitment in Vietnam. Once elected, hardly a word of partisanship against the Democratic commander in chief came from his mouth. He both defended the president in his time of "terrible burden" and denounced the more virulent dissenters. Johnson did not deserve their obscenities and "scorn."[24]

By the time Gene McCarthy began what turned into a quixotic crusade, Bush decided to see for himself. Paying his own way across the Pacific, he left from Houston on the day after Christmas of 1967, reaching Southeast Asia just before New Year's. The sixteen-day trip also took him to Laos and Thailand, but he concentrated on the heart of the struggle in South Vietnam, visiting eleven of the country's forty-four provinces. He met with the military brass, first with Pacific area marine commander Lt. Gen. Victor Krulak in Honolulu. At a stopover in Tokyo, he visited with Ambassador Donald P. Gregg. In Saigon, he conferred with Ambassador Ellsworth Bunker as well as Robert Komer, Gen. William Westmoreland's deputy in charge of "pacification."

From his base at the Caravelle Hotel in Saigon, he "choppered" to daily inspection missions away from the capital, where he found a greater "feel for the war" than in the city. He visited military outposts and hamlets all the way from the Mekong Delta to the base up the coast at Danang. "We went out on a new patrol boat and headed up a little inlet to a village and we talked to the people," he wrote early on the morning of his departure for Danang. "Six months ago we'd have been zapped by the V.C.—there are still V.C. there, but the area is much more peaceful."[25] That night, thirty-one Soviet-made rockets hit the Danang airport. He reached a hamlet at Tan-An Xa only two days after eighteen enemy soldiers had been killed. On the morning of his arrival, mortar shells landed on the outpost. He got firsthand views of schools, hospitals, and medical centers. Usually in casual civilian clothes, but sometimes in khakis, he mingled with the troops and joined them in the trenches.

While Saigon's commercial life was almost immune to the war, he found a different picture in the rural areas. He noted that one elderly farmer pleaded that all he wanted was for somebody to "fix my road." Children somehow managed to smile as they do everywhere. He admired the beauty of the countryside—"and oh those marvelous-looking people." He kept thinking about how "those who clamor the most for humanitarian help to people" were often the "loudest against the war."[26] The American servicemen, GIs and marines, impressed him most of all. Nothing irritated him as much as those who complained about "the military mind" and about how they were "insensitive to people." "I wish you could have seen our young pilots in the carrier briefing room as they discussed their hazardous mission over the flak-ridden skies of Hanoi," he said when he returned to Houston.[27]

Bush's deepest irritation was with press coverage of what he saw. He compiled his own point-by-point rebuttal of inaccuracies that were being transmitted to the States. In a very personal letter, which he typed himself, he gave the following example of how his own experiences caught the press in their distortions:

> In this regard all I call for is balance—fairness—but no the emphasis is on our round that falls short—or the brutality of the south Vietnamese—or the civilians killed by our napalm—how grossly unfair this turned [*sic*] out to be. I thought the Arvin were all corrupt and cowards—how grossly unfair this was. When I came home I read about the shelling of Danang—front page big deal—and yet I was there that night—slept thru the whole thing—the airfield was shut down on one runway maybe for an hour—no one was killee [*sic*] and yet reading the paper I thought I might have been in the Bataan siege for heaven sakes. . . . The pacification effort was disrupted but in three weeks the people were out in the hamlets and things were going well—an [*sic*]

lastly the resolve of the people had been strengthened because they saw first hand the VC in operation. . . .

In his public statements, he advised that the war "is going to require patience, not only on the military side but in the 'other war' as well," referring, of course, to the war against the war being fought on the streets of America. He agreed, in an almost obligatory way, that the war was being won but acknowledged that "progress is uneven." "In the light of what I have seen and heard in South Vietnam," he said, dissenters were "tragically" out of touch. He remained confident about the realism of the U.S. objective and continued to be upbeat about succeeding "if we have the will."[28]

Still, for all his outward ebullience, so much of it reflecting political realities and his determination to remain completely loyal to the cause and the wartime leadership of the Johnson administration, he was touched by the Vietnam experience in ways that were obvious to only those who saw him up close. His office manager, Rose Zamaria, recalled that he met with students who were in Washington to protest against the war. Whether or not they were from his district did not matter. "But because they were the young people and the way they felt about it," she said, "he wanted to give his point of view, and kind of just banter back and forth, of what it was all about. He was very troubled but also wanting to help young people."[29] He even told a Lincoln Day dinner of Travis County Republicans in Houston that the protesters were responding for moral reasons and reminded his audience that "we in Texas certainly can't stand to be without the right to dissent."[30]

By the time he spoke those words, the war had taken a new turn. Just over two weeks after his departure from Vietnam, the Communist Tet offensive began with a coordinated series of attacks by 85,000 Communist troops against five major cities, military installations, and over 150 towns and villages. Suddenly, before they were finally forced to retreat, virtually all of the country was within the enemy's grip. Fighting moved to the outskirts of Saigon itself. Vietcong troops held control over much of the old imperial capitol of Hue and laid siege to Khe Sanh. In Washington, the president's informal group of elder advisers, his "wise men," met again to consider the course of events. A Sunday edition of *The New York Times* carried the following headline: "Westmoreland Requests 206,000 More Men, Stirring Debate in Administration."[31]

Foreign affairs were far more in the Senate's realm than the House's, and the harshest questions about the war came from the Senate Foreign Affairs Committee under J. W. Fulbright of Arkansas, and from among those members in the president's own party. One after another within that committee, Fulbright, Frank Church, Albert Gore, Joe Clark, and Robert Kennedy, had begun to question America's Vietnam objectives.

Writing in the midst of all the elevated passion, Richard G. Mack, a former Yale classmate and fellow Bonesman who had spent eighteen months in Vietnam for the State Department, told Bush that his own sympathies were with the antiwar people, the students who wanted it all to stop. "Do you know, George," he wrote, "that as a member of our governing body, the youth of our nation don't trust you, don't believe in you, and perhaps even worse, don't even give a damn about you! Do you know of any nation that can be strong without the support of its children?" He insisted on a "similarity between the Hitler-Stalin endoctrination [*sic*] camps and the U.S. pacification villages. . . ," and that it was a war being promoted by "businessmen who are hawks from the reaping of enormous war industry profits." To Mack, there was no choice; it all depended on the kind of America one wanted. "I believe I know you well enough, George, and therefore some of your ideals. I thus understand sadly that there are only a few like you in Washington, whose only 'special interest' is the welfare of the American people. We look to you, George, and your sparse militia of Statesmen as our only hope."[32]

It was the "wrong war," Bush conceded to his friend; "I think in retrospect that we should have learned from the history books," but "morality" was not the right ground to argue the point. Opposition on the basis of morality was selective. It betrayed a "blind willingness to emphasize the weaknesses of the South Vietnam government while totally overlooking the terror of the VC and the past slaughters by Ho and the boys [that] I can't buy." The Tet offensive had resulted in a psychological, not a military victory, and nothing about that proved that they had the corner on morality. How, Bush wanted to know, can the dissenters claim a higher morality; how, in the face of "the arrogance and the total lack of compassion on the part of some doves—who suggest that those who don't want to turn tail and quit really don't want the war to end?" Those arguing in the name of morality, he added with stepped-up passion, saw nothing wrong in the "suggestion that the president really doesn't care about human lives . . . I'm not going to take that mean step which strips the man of any feeling and assigns to him unthinkable motives." And then he added: "the next struggle will be in the Middle East. . . . Let us then hear from those on the campuses who say war is immoral or perhaps their selectivity will apply—time will tell." Your letter, Mack wrote back, is written proof "that you are even more idealistic than me, and this despite being a Texas oilman."[33]

What to do about Vietnam was one thing. The moral imperatives were debatable. As a congressman, however, and as a freshman in particular, Bush could hardly do more than express his doubts out loud. The proposed open-housing legislation being pushed by the White House and debated on Capitol Hill was, at least on the surface, quite another matter. Bush's personal reactions fused his empathy for the plight of black Americans along with the realization that those victims of discrimination were paying the greatest personal price for trying to win the war.

His letter to Mack and support of the war notwithstanding, he returned to his district after touring Vietnam persuaded about the nation's responsibilities to these historic victims of American society. He had opposed the Civil Rights Act of 1964, and when, in 1966, a bill calling for an end to discrimination in housing began to work its way through Congress, he remained resistant to federal action. But on April 10, just three months after his return from Southeast Asia, he shocked Seventh Congressional District supporters by voting for passage of the Civil Rights Bill of 1968 to guarantee "open housing."[34]

Barbara later wrote in her memoirs that George had been moved by the sight of "so many young black men . . . fighting in Vietnam for the cause of freedom" who were nevertheless "denied freedom when they came home."[35] How he came to that point is clear. That he did so with political misgivings, is equally clear. On a motion on a key vote that preceded the roll call on final passage, Bush remained with those who wanted the bill to be returned to a House-Senate conference. "The bill is discriminatory against *real estate agents* [emphasis supplied] and it exempts single-dwelling units financed by government funds," he explained to the press.[36]

Bush's colleagues hoped that delaying the legislation by remanding it to a conference would tear out its heart. However, the attempt failed by a thirty-four vote margin, which surely indicated strength for final passage. While thirteen of their fellow Texans held firm in their opposition by opposing final passage, Bush joined fellow Texans Jim Wright of Fort Worth and Kika De La Garza of Mission in shifting to a pro-civil rights vote.[37]

"I could not have it on my conscience that I had voted for legislation that would have prevented a Negro serviceman, who has the funds, and who upon returning from Vietnam where he had been fighting for the ideals of this country, would know that he could not buy or rent a decent home," he told the press immediately afterward.[38] Bill Archer, who later became Bush's congressional successor, recalled that "it was like the world came unglued. I can't think of an issue that's come along since then that's been as explosive emotionally." "I voted for the bill," wrote Bush to Dick Mack, "and the roof is falling in—boy does the hatred surface. I have had more mail on this subject than on Vietnam and taxes and sex all put together."[39] Bush faced the wolves when he returned to Houston, especially at a confrontation at Memorial High School.[40]

He came armed, as he often did, with a quote from his favorite conservative, Edmund Burke: "Your representative owes you not only his industry; but his judgment, and he betrays instead of serves you if he sacrifices it to your opinion." He went on to calm the gathering, talking about the fundamental decency that "a man should not have a door slammed in his face because he is a Negro or speaks with a Latin-American accent. Open housing offers a ray of hope for blacks and other minorities locked out by habit and discrimination." They respected their congressman enough to restrain themselves, and the objections quieted by the time he finished. Then, breaking out "like the drops of a summer rain," came the ripples of applause, then cheers and even a standing ovation.[41]

"He told me," remembered Zamaria, that "you couldn't tell somebody who was fighting and dying for their country that [he] couldn't buy a house. For Houston, that was really a vote of conscience for him." His mail afterward was overwhelmingly hostile, full of vehement hate. "There were death threats," she recalled.[42]

Similar sentiments led him to visit the Resurrection City of the poor people's campaign that had been created on the mall in Washington by the Rev. Ralph Abernathy after Dr. Martin Luther King Jr.'s assassination that April. He made a point of dropping by the tent city that summer and had a long meeting with the new black leader.[43]

Houston Chronicle noted that by now he had become so formidable that "nobody cares to take him on."[44] He was unopposed for reelection in 1968.

His service on Capitol Hill left its mark on the issue of population control and family planning. At least one commentator has suggested that it gave him "a vocabulary for talking about crime, children, pollution, and poverty—without the politically charged implications of race."[45]

Family planning had long been an interest of Protestant reformers, and none took it up more avidly than those of the Bush social set in New England and New York. His association with the cause had, of course, helped lead to Prescott Bush's defeat in Connecticut back in 1950, but a number of subsequent developments insured far greater interest in the entire subject. Connecticut's ban on the dissemination of birth control devices was overturned in 1965 by the Supreme Court decision in the case of *Griswold* v. *Connecticut*, when, in an opinion written by Associate Justice William O. Douglas, the legality of Planned Parenthood to offer birth control counseling to a married couple was upheld.[46] Widespread attention was also focused that year on the worldwide population "explosion" and the role, if any, that should be played by the federal government. Two ex-presidents, Truman and Eisenhower, the latter having been negative on the issue during his own presidency, became cochairmen of the honorary sponsors of Planned Parenthood. During those years that immediately followed the initial marketing of the new birth control pill, anxiety also increased about the safety of the oral contraceptive. In 1970, it took Planned Parenthood's president, Dr. Alan F. Guttmacher, to point out that the risks of pregnancy were greater than the risks of taking the pill. The entire question of child-bearing and the relationship of population to economic well-being was being given more prominence than ever before. Those were the years that immediately preceded the Supreme Court's *Roe* v. *Wade* decision upholding the legality of abortion.

Bush's role was within the context of growing interest in the entire question of population planning. Lyndon Johnson became the first American president to suggest that federal support for population control would be appropriate, and he later endorsed the concept of extending federal aid for birth control devices. Provisions that related to the issue appeared in several messages passed by the Congress the following year. A congressional authorization bill in 1968 provided for up to $50 million from overall economic aid funds to assist voluntary family planning activities internationally. Johnson also appointed an eighteen-member committee to study the government's role in birth control under the chairmanship of Health, Education, and Welfare Secretary Wilbur J. Cohen. Meanwhile, from Hawaii to Connecticut, local activists were pressing to overthrow state antiabortion laws. In early 1969, reformers created the National Abortion Rights League, which received a great deal of press attention.[47] By the time Nixon came to the White House, the push for population control had accelerated, and the first Republican since Eisenhower made the matter a significant part of the problem of contending with poverty at home and abroad. He created a Commission on Population Growth and the American Future, and, in a special message to Congress on related problems delivered on July 18, 1969, stated that "population growth is among the most important issues we face." He predicted that it would be one "of the most serious challenges to the human destiny in the last third of this century." All in all, five public statements from the White House in 1969 dealt with the question.[48]

Bush took up the matter almost as soon as he reached Washington. His commitment was so intense that Wilbur Mills soon called him "Rubbers." He first worked with a fellow Republican, Herman T. Schneebeli of Pennsylvania, and authored a series of amendments to the Social Securities Act to give priority emphasis to family planning services. He also joined with a Democrat, James Scheuer of New York, for the passage of legislation to make population control an integral part of domestic and foreign policy.[49] He cosponsored a bill to end the ban against transporting and mailing contraceptives. He sponsored another, to repeal ninety-eight-year-old federal anti-contraception statutes, which President Nixon signed into law.[50] In introducing a bill to establish a Select Joint Committee on Population and Family Planning, he stated on the House floor that "birth control, often misunderstood, is an answer to our increasingly important hunger problem."[51] He then chaired twenty-two hearings for the House Republican Task Force on Earth's Resources and Population. When, in December of 1969, Representative Shirley Chisholm of Brooklyn argued for the liberalization of abortion laws, Bush commended her and added that her suggestion "deserves wide attention." When his panel issued its final report, it called for eradicating "the number of unlicensed and unqualified practitioners who jeopardize the health and safety" of women seeking abortions. The panel expressed the widespread concern that the continued illegality of abortions only jeopardized the health and lives of those whose desperation made them turn to shoddy practitioners, the so-called "back-alley butchers." Bush shared that view.[52] The final bill, which was passed by Congress on December 10, contained the proviso that none of the funds could be used in programs where abortion was a method of *family planning*. That November, Bush explained to a constituent that whether to give birth to a child "should always remain a matter of individual choice."[53] Before the congressman gave up his seat, President Nixon signed Public Law 91-572, the Population Control and Research Act, which boosted the government's financial commitment to the entire area of population control. A Democrat, Joseph Tydings of Delaware, was the driving force for the legislation in the Senate, while George Bush was the principal author of the House version.[54]

The only elective stake he had in the 1968 presidential race revolved around suggestions that the one-term freshman had a chance of being chosen at Miami to fill the vice presidential slot on the national ticket headed by Richard Nixon. "With the call out for a new, young Republican face, and as a forty-four-year-old Republican congressman from Texas with family ties in the East, I was viewed as a possibility," Bush has acknowledged.[55]

Nixon later confirmed that Bush was on his "short list" of possible choices. Not only was the Republican presidential candidate "profoundly impressed by his fighting competitiveness," but he had been influenced by several Bush boosters. One was a former president, Dwight D. Eisenhower. In a long talk with Nixon at his Gettysburg farm in 1967 (in which he expressed some skepticism about his former vice president's ability to actually win in 1968), he assessed the potential Republican candidates. Ike's preference was for a youthful candidate. He was well acquainted with Prescott Bush. Eisenhower knew, as Nixon later explained, that George Bush "not only believed in the right conservative principles, but that he had the personality and charisma to win." Bush was also being pushed by George Champion.

Champion, the chief executive officer of the Chase Manhattan Bank, prided himself on being an economic conservative. Another Republican stalwart who went all out for Bush was Tom Dewey, the former New York governor and the party's two-time presidential candidate. Nixon respected Dewey. He was, in Nixon's view, a "conservative with a heart," not "a mushy moderate," so he took his advice seriously. Finally, however, he bypassed Bush, along with several others, in favor of Governor Spiro Agnew of Maryland. Ignoring the political reasons behind the choice of Agnew, Nixon later explained that he did not choose Bush because mere election to Congress from a safe district in Texas did not warrant a place on the national ticket. Or, as Dewey himself reported back to Prescott: "I think there was simply a feeling that he had not been in public office long enough. Everything else was favorable." George thanked Dewey for his efforts. "Though we finished out of the money it was a great big plus for me, and I am indebted to you for your interest—."[56]

Prescott's son was not out of Nixon's mind for very long, then or later. Shortly after the convention confirmed the team of Nixon and Agnew to oppose the combination of Hubert Humphrey and Ed Muskie, the presidential candidate summoned Bush to his hotel at Mission Bay, California. Bush joined Howard Baker, Clark MacGregor, and Governor John Volpe of Massachusetts to form a team of surrogates who would be ready to fill speaking engagements that could not be accomplished by the presidential candidate personally. The opportunity to meet more Republican leaders and make new friends was irresistible.[57]

As it turned out, those who remained loyal to Johnson had no choice by

November but to vote for Hubert Humphrey. The vice president had become his very uneasy successor, capping a trying four years for the liberal from Minnesota. McCarthy's unexpectedly strong showing in the March New Hampshire primary demonstrated the administration's weakness. A series of events followed rapidly: Bobby Kennedy also announced his candidacy. Johnson rejected the request of the U.S. commander in Vietnam, Gen. William Westmoreland, for an additional 206,000 troops. Then, in the biggest surprise of them all, he also told the nation that he would not run for another term as president. By late summer, both the Rev. Dr. Martin Luther King Jr. and Senator Robert Kennedy had been assassinated, the Democratic convention in Chicago had become the scene of a riotous clash between antiwar radical demonstrators and the city's police, and Humphrey had emerged as the party's presidential candidate. The only surprising thing about Richard Nixon's victory in November was that it was so close.

Other than that it was sweet. It also cemented the Nixon-Bush alliance, already strengthened by Nixon's flattering consideration of the Texan as his running mate and by their common legislative interests. Getting rid of Ralph Yarborough became their newest mutual objective, a cause that helped confirm the ever-thickening ties between Houston's Seventh District and the White House. One who personified that relationship was Harry Treleaven, the eighteen-year veteran of J. Walter Thompson, the same ad agency that produced Nixon lieutenant Bob Haldeman.[58] Headquartered at a Fifth Avenue firm in New York City by 1968, Treleaven shuttled between the Bush and Nixon camps. His prominence as the creative director of advertising in that year's campaign was immortalized by Joe McGinniss's highly popular insider account of how the new president was "sold" to the American people. Having struck gold for Nixon, Treleaven was ready for a second go-around with Bush. Another recruit was Marvin Collins. Collins, who became manager of Bush's senatorial campaign, was fresh from Linwood Holton's gubernatorial victory in Virginia. In defeating Democrat John Battle, Holton's role approximated that about to be played by Bush in Texas, the test of two-party viability in a once "solid South" state. Additionally, Collins's man, Holton, was not just another Republican; he was also a longtime personal friend of the president. Moreover, his moderation, at least in Old Dominion parlance of another day, attracted support from several black organizations as well as what existed as organized labor in the state, the American Federation of Labor and the Political Action Committee of the Congress of Industrial Organizations. All this enabled Collins to join the Bush cause against Yarborough with a "moderate" label. To make the stakes even more attractive, in going to Virginia to campaign personally for him and against Battle, Nixon's man was also interceding against a Democrat with close ties to the Kennedy brothers. Now, with Collins freed from Virginia and Treleaven ready to return, Bush sent Jim Allison back to Texas to scout the political scene at home. On the day after New Year's, he confirmed that he was giving strong consideration to running for the Senate.[59]

CHAPTER TEN

Good-bye to Texas

%

Prescott Bush always had mixed feelings about his retirement from the Senate; on those days when Prescott felt fit, he had his regrets. He spent fine summers in Kennebunkport and enjoyed the winters at Hobe Sound; at the same time, he kept close track of George and his growing family, and especially the young man's political career.[1]

George's accomplishments were admirable, and his father certainly appreciated his skills, but his talk about moving on to the Senate was another matter. Prescott had strong doubts, which he shared with his son. Why risk a sinecure only to buck the odds by running as a Texas Republican? The Lone Star State, in its long recovery from Reconstruction, had already elected a Republican senator, John Tower. But expecting them to go for *two* Republicans was a long shot, especially with an incumbent Democrat with thirteen years of seniority. The counterargument that Yarborough was more vulnerable without Johnson in the White House and that other liberals were losing their grip was only partly sensible. There was nothing wrong with staying put. "There's a great life to be had in the House. You've been there for only four years," he told his son. Look at Christian Herter. Herter never served a day in the Senate. That didn't stop him from going on to the Massachusetts governorship and right into the State Department, and then taking over after John Foster Dulles's death.[2]

Bush's decision was hardly more popular with some of his close friends, who not only did not relish prospects of a fight against Yarborough, but enjoyed the advantages of his incumbency.[3]

But his mind was made up. He had his eye on something bigger than just being the "man from Houston," a dream that was certainly not diminished by all that talk about running with Nixon. His younger brother, Jonathan, recalled George's assumption that the Senate was a better route to the White House.[4]

Other Bushes remembered one August at Kennebunkport. "We were all lying around watching the Democratic convention," his sister said. George slouched on the floor in front of the screen. He pointed to the television set and, turning to nobody in particular, said out loud, "I'm going to be up there someday."[5] He came close in 1968. Maybe if Nixon hadn't needed to kiss Strom Thurmond's behind by taking Spiro Agnew as his running mate to get those southern delegates into line to keep them from stampeding to Reagan in 1968 it could have been a different story. But that's politics. George was not about to let that get him down. He was only forty-four and had plenty of time. But he was aching to get to the presidency.

Anyone who watched how Republican Representative George Bush of Houston handled Lyndon Johnson could have known that something was up. He could hardly have been more solicitous toward the president. The reality was that the man in the White House was not just a Democrat; he was a Texan. It was also true that Bush genuinely enjoyed and respected him. But he could not realistically assume he would have Johnson's support. That would even be counterproductive with his fellow Republicans. But he might, at least, have him keep his distance, remained neutral, not scuttle him. He said as much when explaining to one of the president's congressional liaison aides that "coming from Texas, I am determined not to be a personal embarrassment to our president" and acknowledged Johnson's "tremendous burden" and promised "to be respectful in agreement and disagreement."[6] He carefully held back from being hard on him over Vietnam, even when he returned from his trip there and had plenty on his mind. He would only say that his policy was winning the battle. That January, after the president's last state of the union message, he was even complimentary.[7]

As Richard Nixon was sworn in as the thirty-seventh president, Bush went out of his way to show his respect for LBJ. When Lyndon and Lady Bird left right after the inauguration to return to Texas, the Bushes were waiting at Andrews Air Force Base to see them off. Not another Republican in sight. Johnson, touched by the courtesy as he prepared to step aboard Air Force One for the last time, said, "You come see me down at the ranch." University of Texas historian Joe B. Frantz spotted Bush and asked why he was skipping the Republican inaugural celebrations in the city to be at the airport. Bush, as Frantz reported back to Johnson three days later, explained, "He has been a fine president and invariably courteous and fair to me and my people, and I thought that I belonged here to show in a small way how much I have appreciated him. I wish I could do more." Johnson, ever grateful, informed Bush about Frantz's report and added that he was "deeply appreciative of your words as he quoted them to me. Please know," he added, "that I value your friendship, as I do your father's, and that I am glad you are one of us down here in Texas."[8]

Bush's real competitor was Johnson's longtime associate, John Connally, who shared with Bush a place in Richard Nixon's future. Connally was perfect for the new president—a conservative Democrat, one who had served with and was even shot at with Kennedy, capable, persuasive, a successful former governor, even a Southerner. Everything else that Nixon had heard about the self-made millionaire (a quality that Nixon especially admired) was positive, including from friends like Billy Graham. Reverend Graham, forever managing proximity to power, lost no time when he heard about the pending retirement from the Supreme Court of Earl Warren, whose civil libertarian decisions had made him a pariah to rightists. America's most popular religious leader promptly advised President Johnson to nominate Connally to the Supreme Court because of the need for a "strong conservative as chief justice," who, admittedly, would "not be popular with the extreme liberals and radicals who are already fighting you anyway," but "would make a great chief justice."[9]

Nixon's interest in Connally, undoubtedly furthered by sources such as Graham, was deepened when the Texan demonstrated his ability to deliver his state to Humphrey in 1968. "That Johnson and Connally, with so little money and at the last minute, could mobilize their forces so impressively fascinated Nixon," Connally's biographer has written. "He would have loved to be the beneficiary of such skill." Connally "tracks well" with the president, noted Bob Haldeman, "and would be an excellent addition if we could get him in."[10] And Nixon sucked him right in. He placed Connally on his Ash Commission to study government reorganization. The Texan, with little to lose and everything to gain by scouting out the Washington scene, went on to dominate the commission. He also took advantage of his temporary location to get close to the President, and the two men got to know each other. As Connally toyed with switching parties, Nixon, hoping to squeeze as much bipartisanship as possible out of the embrace, discouraged any premature conversion.[11] What is clear is that Connally left Washington reenforced in his determination to make a second attempt at cutting down Ralph Yarborough, who, as a recent opponent of two successive Nixon Supreme Court appointees, Clement Haynsworth and G. Harrold Carswell, was especially detested by the administration.[12] Connally turned to his good friend, Lloyd Bentsen, to do the job. Bentsen, a Distinguished Flying Cross winner and insurance executive who had made additional fortunes on cattle, had a University of Texas law degree and a reputation as a moderate conservative.[13]

While Connally, the Democrat, was flirtatious with the incumbent Republican in the White House, George Bush, a Republican, continued his dalliance with the Democratic ex-president, Lyndon B. Johnson. Bush, spurred by the assumption that he would soon oppose Yarborough, seized upon Johnson's invitation to "come see me down at the ranch." That April, he took the initiative by notifying Johnson that he would like to meet with him as soon as he returned from a trip to Mexico. When he arrived at Stonewall, he found him gracious and warm. Bush told him that he planned to oppose Yarborough. The senator was an accident who never truly represented the people of the state. He had, in fact, most recently become even more of a pariah to Texas regulars by having endorsed Eugene McCarthy's run against Johnson for the 1968 Democratic nomination.[14] Johnson needed no additional convincing and Bush got what he wanted, a green light from the ex-president. Publicly, however, LBJ would remain neutral. When, to Bush's surprise, the press got wind of their supposedly secret conference, and the feisty correspondent for a chain of Texas papers, Sarah McClendon, cornered him with the information, an embarrassed Bush was forced to admit that there had been a meeting. And at his request! Bush also added that the country's most prominent Democrat was hardly likely to embrace him openly, but said, "I have great respect for him," adding, "you will never find me saying anything of a personal nature about the president [Johnson] in a denigrating fashion and . . . I would think maybe the same would be true on the other side." He later sent Johnson the text of the news conference and enclosed a note. "I hope," it explained, "I have said nothing that might cause you any embarrassment."[15]

At that moment, Bush was virtually a bipartisan candidate. Yarborough's was one of those seats that had to be taken away from the Democrats, and the White House had high hopes that Bush was the man to do the job. Even before he got into it, Nixon had begun to work at peeling away layers of the traditional Democratic vote in the state. He named one Mexican-American, Hillary Sandoval, to head the Small Business Administration and another, Anthony Perez Farris, as U.S. attorney for the Southern District of Texas. "I think the point here," an aide warned Senator Yarborough, "is that the GOP seems to be doing everything possible to give Bush the best possible opportunity to win in 1970."[16] Paul Eggers, the Republican candidate for the Texas statehouse, was, in contrast with Bush, more dependent on local financing.[17]

Bush thereby became the main beneficiary of the so-called Townhouse Operation, surreptitious funding run by such Nixon people as his attorney, Herbert Kalmbach, Harry Dent, and Jack A. Gleason, a presidential appointee to the Commerce Department. The sub-rosa scheme, run from the basement of a Washington apartment near Du Pont Circle and further assisted by two of Bush's old Texas associates, Bob Mosbacher (who was also Bush's finance chairman for the campaign) and William Liedtke, ultimately sent his campaign $106,000. The funds earmarked for Bush and Eggers had been raised by Texas contributors. It was in some ways, as *The Wall Street Journal* later put it, "a dress rehearsal for the campaign finance abuses of Watergate, as well as for today's loophole-ridden system."[18] Bush began his drive for the senate assured that the money would be forthcoming.[19]

He finally announced his candidacy on January 13, 1970, but not before the way had been cleared by the establishment of a close alliance with the president, something that had been built the preceding year. The alliance rested on common needs and a shared political background. It had none of the elements that so attracted Nixon to Connally, that exemplar of self-made Texas stock. In July of 1969, Bush pointed out that Nixon was a "popular Republican [who] would be interested in my race."[20] One month after Bush saw Nixon at San Clemente, *The New York Times* reported that the congressman was among those being actively recruited to run for the Senate.[21]

All in all, reported the *Houston Post* on September 30, Nixon had met with him twice to encourage him to run. Bush, who pleaded that he needed more time to further analyze his polls, which looked favorable but showed a close race, also denied he had been given any assurance of a backup place with the administration.[22] Meanwhile, he worked the state energetically. He exploited every opportunity to face crowds, taking special care to target Mexican-American voters around San Antonio, where he was accompanied by Sandoval.[23] The Bushes mobilized as a family to send out a massive mailing of Christmas cards early that year. Many were surprised to find themselves included in Bush seasonal greetings.[24]

Even before it began, the character of Bush's campaign threatened to change. By New Year's Day, the Bentsen challenge to Yarborough was out in the open. Bentsen entered the Democratic primary on the ninth of January with the backing of two of Texas's most recent ex-governors, Connally and Allan Shivers. Connally circulated an open letter that February urging support for Bentsen. The moderate conservative who had served in Congress from 1948 until 1955 was now a pit bull unleashed against Yarborough. Even years later, when he had had enough time to mellow, Yarborough recalled the Bentsen of that campaign as far more "dirty" than he had experienced either against Shivers or Bush. Bentsen, conducting a "more violent" campaign than did Bush, denounced Yarborough as a radical.[25] Even for Texas, reported a *Chronicle* correspondent, Bentsen's fight was "memorable for its meanness." Yarborough was, in effect, a nonperson, an "ultraliberal," one who had the effrontery to back the Supreme Court on school prayers and support antiwar protesters. The insurance millionaire adopted Nixon's "Southern strategy" by denouncing the senator as "too liberal for Texas" and deplored his votes against Haynsworth and Carswell, as well as for failing to vote on an antischool busing bill.[26] When Bentsen defeated Yarborough in that year's May primary, the floor fell out from under Bush's plans. So did some of the White House's concern about how Texas needed to be saved.

Instead of a soft touch, an especially vulnerable candidate amid the Texas conservative tide, Bush had to contend with an opponent strikingly like himself. Bentsen was also close to his age, only two years older. Both were, as a Bush biographer has described them, "tall, comely, and aristocratic in demeanor," and even shared common backgrounds as businessmen and members of Congress.[27] They were, wrote a Texas journalist, like "two interchangeable peas in a pod," even with "many friends, business associates, and campaign donors in common." "Given a choice between Phillie Winkle and Winkle Pop," chortled *The Texas Observer,* "Texan'll take the dude with the Democratic label."[28]

"Bush never got his act together thereafter," recalled Lyndon Johnson's press secretary, George Christian. Bob Woodward and Walter Pincus later wrote that, with Yarborough out of the way, "Nixon himself seemed to lose interest . . ."[29] The record, however, shows that defections were not as much from the White House as from conservative Democrats, a group that held the bulk of the money available in Texas. That included such multimillionaires as Dallas oilman Clint Murchison, Allan Shivers, and that old benefactor of LBJ, George Brown, head of the giant Brown and Root Construction company.[30] Also less interested in helping Bush without the specter of Yarborough were conservative Wall Streeters, a group from which "money is not available in the quantities heretofore counted on," as Operation Townhouse manager, Jack Gleason, reported to Harry Dent. Insofar as the need to go on helping Bush, Gleason suggested that Bush be given "perhaps as much as a quarter of a million, and that the failure to do this in spite of our previous indications to George Bush could be harmful to his relations with the president."[31] Nixon himself, with Bush's outlook suddenly dimmed, noted in July that the Texan was among the candidates he wanted to award positions with the administration "in case they lost."[32] The Bush campaign, meanwhile, was forced to reduce its campaign budget from two million to $1.7 million.[33]

Bush, in a bind, could hardly move to Bentsen's right. The Democrat had preempted the ultraconservative spectrum. Bush was further pressed by the four-to-one Democratic registration advantage that still existed in Texas. About all that was left was the wooing of the center, even by making overtures toward liberals. In mid June, he and Barbara once again flew to the Johnson ranch. This time, in the company of his aide, Jack Steel, and a Republican congressman from Arkansas, John Hammerschmidt, they were photographed living it up at an LBJ barbecue. Johnson, then recovering from a recent heart attack, had been watching politics from a distance, even while his old teammate, John Connally, was getting himself pictured with such national Democrats as Hubert Humphrey.[34]

Bush's attractions for liberals even strengthened that summer as Bentsen attacked him for supporting gun-control legislation.[35] John Kenneth Galbraith, the prominent liberal economist from Harvard and political associate of Adlai Stevenson and Jack Kennedy, signed on to the Bush cause in the form of a letter to the *Texas Observer.* Bentsen and Bush were equally conservative, Galbraith explained, but a victory by the former would increase conservative influence within the Texas Democratic party. That would "force the rest of us to contend with them nationally, and leave the state with the worst of all choices—a choice between two conservative parties."[36]

An old Bush acquaintance and chronicler, Fitzhugh Green, came away from video pictures of his friend campaigning in the heat of the Texas sun with some distinct impressions of the candidate. "Bush's cheeks were flushed," he noted, "his coat lying beside him, his collar open and necktie pulled down, his brown hair wet from perspiration and slightly mussed. Still, he seemed at ease with the reporter, serious and attentive to his questions." Then, observing something that would become closely associated with Bush, he added, "although words flowed from Bush, his sentences were ragged, ran into each other, and tended to leave thoughts hanging and ideas incomplete. I was reminded of a younger version of General Eisenhower whom I had observed in a 1952 meeting with his campaigners at the Commodore Hotel in New York."[37]

* * *

The man Eisenhower had subjected to so much embarrassment about having him on his ticket, Richard Nixon, now created some discomfort for Bush. At a San Clemente press conference, Nixon was asked whether he planned to run again with Agnew. Not only was such speculation premature, he replied, but added that Agnew was "a great asset" to the ticket, "a very strong" vice president, and an effective representative of the administration.[38] Speculation, however, encouraged additional musings about Bush. One that especially embarrassed him came from the pen of David Broder in the *Washington Post.* For that to happen, of course, would require Bush to become a senator. The implication seemed clear: winning would give him a convenient interim stepping-stone. Texans felt that they were being manipulated. Bush promptly issued a denial.[39]

Bentsen, somewhat ironically, charged that Bush was Nixon's hand-picked candidate, a point that seemed confirmed when Agnew came into the state to campaign. Such "assistance" was part of Nixon's continuing help, as was the flow of Townhouse money. After making contributions on July 30, Jack Gleason went to Houston on October 5 and personally delivered $6,000 in cash to Bush. Bush, who later denied that he had been a direct recipient of the money, nevertheless confirmed that the $106,000 total from Operation Townhouse was correct.[40] With the Bush campaign faltering, $40,000 in emergency funds was wired in mid-October to account #0718643 at the Texas Commerce Bank in Dallas, which was under the name of Harry Treleaven's Glenn Advertising Agency. The deposit was never reported and would haunt Bush later. An additional sixty thousand came in over the next three weeks, reflecting contributions from such people as Chicago millionaire W. Clement Stone and Henry Ford II. To get around reporting requirements then governing contributions and gift tax regulations, the fragmented amounts were sent to fourteen different Bush campaign committees.[41] The Nixon fund contributed a lesser amount to the gubernatorial campaign of Paul Eggers.

The money went far to aid Treleaven's pro-Bush ads. TV spots placed heavy emphasis on promoting the candidate as active, vibrant, and youthful, a jogger, touch football player, an athlete so energetic he would rather run than walk down steps. Bush was also shown in conversation with President Nixon, who, with his appeal to Texans, received endorsements from such people as football coach Bud Wilkinson, John Tower, and Howard Baker. The basic theme of the Bush images was "he's in step with the Texas of today."[42]

For the White House, however, it was all too tame, and no way to win an election, reinforcing Nixon's view of Bush as a Connecticut Yankee, a dilettante, and preppy. White House Aide Charles Colson fed the president's bias by reminding him right after the voting that Bush had cavalierly turned away all suggestions for attack ads. "He refused to allow us to use some very derogatory information about Bentsen," and resisted any ads, "positive or negative," wrote Colson. "We probably should have forced him to do more."

For the additional benefit of Nixon's receptive ears, Colson told the president that political analyst Dick Scammon thought that Bush had weakened himself by rejecting use of conservative social issues and trying "to be more liberal than Bentsen." Bush also crossed up Colson by defiantly refusing to let the White House use the national committee circulate that he considered "a flamboyant attack on some editor." As he told about the incident later, he telephoned his refusal to use the material by saying, "Don't ever send anything of that nature up here again. Tell Mr. Colson I called and be sure he understands."[43]

Those midterm elections meant a lot to Nixon. He kept an even closer eye on what was going on in New York, where James Buckley, the brother of the conservative writer and spokesman, William F. Buckley, had made the senatorial race a three-way affair by entering as a Conservative party candidate against Democrat Richard Ottinger and the Republican incumbent, Charles Goodell. Goodell became a sharply antiwar legislator after his appointment to the late Bobby Kennedy's Senate seat in 1968. It was no secret that the White House was doing whatever it could behind the scenes to get Buckley elected by dividing the moderate to liberal vote.[44] The president also rallied White House big guns behind Bush, with such administration stalwarts as Vice President Agnew, and cabinet officers Kennedy and Walter Hickel all working to drum up conservative support in the state. Nixon himself, not shying away from Bush even with Yarborough out of the picture, did some heavy, and often strident, campaigning on his own, including appearing at a campaign rally at Longview, Texas, on October 28. Bush joined him on Air Force One, and they flew on to an appearance at the Dallas Memorial Auditorium, where Nixon also boosted the candidacy of Paul Eggers.[45]

Dottie and Prescott Bush had, meanwhile, flown into Texas to be with their son. The nationally syndicated column by Rowland Evans and Robert Novak that final weekend of the campaign described George as "a glittering exponent of the 'modern' school of southern Republicanism," a fine candidate who "appeals to affluent suburbanites with economic conservatism while simultaneously wooing minority groups and labor."[46]

On Monday, with his parents ready to help celebrate, Bush spent his last campaign day in Houston. A crowd estimated as up to two thousand strong filled a downtown parking lot and overflowed onto the adjacent sidewalks. The air was chilly, but the well-wishers were warm and encouraging. Bush, acknowledging forecasts of a Bentsen victory, defied the outlook by telling his audience that the results depended on the turnout right there in Harris County. The *Houston Post*, which described Bush's last-minute activities in detail, recommended thirteen candidates. George Bush was one of the only two Republicans chosen. The editorial termed the election "one of the most significant off-year political contests ever."[47]

Voters thought so, too. They turned out in large numbers, extraordinary for a midterm election in Texas. That the heaviest voting was in such places as San Antonio, a traditional Democratic stronghold, foretold a Bush loss, but the numbers were up in even such Republican centers as Dallas. All told, 53.8 percent of those registered actually voted, up some 6.5 percent over four years earlier. The Republican effort behind Bush and, to a lesser extent, for Paul Eggers, provoked the desired attention. But that very result probably had the counterproductive effect of bringing out the Democratic vote. "Like Custer, who said there were just too many Indians, I guess there were too many Democrats," Bush said that night.[48]

Bentsen's victory was solid, 53.4 percent out of some 2,150,000 votes cast, and an important contribution to the presidential anxieties of Richard Nixon. Faced with such disappointment, deepened by the specter of effective opposition to his own reelection hopes in 1972, the White House orchestrated the creation of the Committee to Reelect the President. For Bush, the short-term disappointment was clear. "He was just shattered by the loss," said Jack Steel, "he said it was just the end of everything." But, added Steel, "instead it turned out to be just the beginning." George's goal, nevertheless, had always been to serve in some elective capacity. Had he defeated Bentsen, he might well have aimed at the Texas governorship as a route toward the White House.[49] He had to deal with new circumstances. At the age of forty-six, he was no longer the sole architect of his political future.

But he had played an undeniable role in the creation of a two-party system in Texas, which, of course, was synonymous with having a Republican party at all. Where others, such as Allan Shivers, had dissented from the Democrats, John Tower, and then George Bush, took the additional step of actual conversion. Then came the apostasy of John Connally. After becoming Nixon's treasury secretary, he lead the nominal Democrats for Nixon committee during the 1972 election campaign and then sealed the switch by changing parties. Texas's national role, which ironically was given a boost by the assassination in Dallas, would never be secondary again.

Bush, out of a job, did not even have much time to contemplate his next move. It was out of his hands that quickly. Even before Bentsen had his victory, the Nixon-Connally-Bush follies played themselves out. Connally had left Washington with assurances of a major appointment with the administration. An outraged Peter O'Donnell, chairman of the Texas Republican party, interceded with the White House before the election to warn about the betrayal felt within the Bush camp. Romancing the Democrat, Connally, was reckless. The president, warned O'Donnell, was dealing with "an implacable enemy" of Texas Republicans.[50] If Nixon heard, he didn't listen.

Once Bush had actually lost, personal intervention to head off Connally became essential, especially when he got a tip from a well-connected Washington columnist, Charles Bartlett of the *Chattanooga Times*, whose ties included the Kennedys and Prescott Bush, about the pending resignation of Treasury Secretary Kennedy.[51]

But Connally remained at the center of Nixon's attention. Connally, not Bush, represented the essence of the president's political need. And from what better state than Texas? Nixon's plans for Connally were already clearly being hatched that November, especially with the negatives the president was getting about the desirability of retaining his vice president, Spiro Agnew. Bob Haldeman noted how big an impression Connally had made on Nixon at an Ash Commission dinner on November 19 and recorded for his diary that the president "is convinced he can be brought over for '72." On Air Force One en route back to Washington from New York, Nixon stressed to his gatekeeper/chief of staff the importance of having Connally in the cabinet and that he would be needed "for another more important position in the future."[52]

So it went for several indecisive weeks, with Nixon wavering back and forth, clear about Connally but merely obligated to Bush. Prescott's son's name surfaced within the White House for just about every conceivable job—head of the Small Business Administration, undersecretary of Commerce, congressional liaison, NASA, leadership of the Republican National Committee, heading the U.S. delegation to the United Nations—just about everything except what George had called about, the Treasury. In fact Nixon's later recollection was that Bush "surprisingly" first told him "that the position he would prefer would be to be undersecretary of the Treasury," an obviously impossible arrangement when Nixon clearly had the secretaryship itself pegged for Big John.[53] Before he even made that move, the president signaled his affection for the ex-governor of Texas by appointing him to the Foreign Intelligence Advisory Board. Once again, Bush, now joined by a somewhat agitated John Tower, who had been kept out of the process, called the White House to express his "extreme" distress.[54]

Nixon, however, continued to flip-flop about Bush while zeroing in on Connally. "I finally got Connally on the phone at about 11:00 tonight," the president's chief of staff, Bob Haldeman, noted in his diary on December 5, "and interestingly enough, he seems to be favorably inclined towards taking the job." Connally met the president over breakfast two days later and the appointment was sealed, a great stroke, noted Haldeman in recording Nixon's thinking, for "startling the media and the establishment." First, Connally reminded the president, the Bush matter had to be cleared up. How could the dramatic announcement of a Texas Democrat becoming Treasury secretary be made before George Bush had been cared for? That was thoughtful and rather gracious of Connally, said Bush twenty-five years later.[55]

That brought Bush into the White House on December 9 to meet the president. Nothing had been settled, just options floated. All George Bush could be sure about, at the moment, was an appointment as an assistant to the president with nothing better than unspecified general responsibilities. His business negotiator background, dealing with creating the succession of oil outfits and especially the arrangement over Zapata Off-Shore with the Liedtke brothers, now became valuable. He faced the president well-prepared to deal with the opportunity offered by the vacancy at the UN created by the "resignation" of Representative Charles Yost. Yost, a career diplomat and a Democrat, had fit nicely into Nixon's bipartisan vision of things, a concept that had even led him to dangle the job to such opposition figures as Hubert Humphrey and Sargent Shriver. Nixon came to regret taking Yost in, however, as his appointee grew restive over Vietnam. He tossed the Democrat out of the administration, dumping him in what Barbara Bush later recalled was "a cruel, awkward fashion."[56]

Nixon, determined to go with still another Democrat, had Daniel Patrick Moynihan in mind for the job. Moynihan's initial response was positive. Nixon sweetened the offer by saying he intended to upgrade the UN's importance to the administration. The younger man, a scholar and intellectual who had become most closely identified as the Democrat on the White House staff who had labored to work out a reform of the welfare system, one that became generally known as the Family Assistance Plan, or FAP, had long since intrigued and interested Nixon. Nixon, under increasing pressure from the Republican right and simultaneous criticism from Democratic liberals about the plan's inadequacy, had long since begun to backpeddle, leaving Moynihan to contend with disturbing political realities. By the summer of 1970, the president had reached the point where, as Bob Haldeman recorded his attitude, he "wants to be sure it's [FAP] killed by Democrats and that we make big [*sic*] play for it, but don't let it pass, can't afford it." On November 20, FAP was doomed by a key vote in the Senate Finance Committee. Nixon, ready to shed himself of the FAP, wanted to make sure the Democrats got the blame for its death.[57]

A distraught Moynihan had, at least for the moment, his fill of government. One week later, the press reported his "irrevocable" decision to forego the UN appointment.

By the time Bush walked in, Nixon was ready for him. And Bush did most of the talking. He told the president that he preferred going to New York as ambassador to the United Nations. His reasoning was clear, coherent, persuasive. Yost had obviously not really represented the administration. Nixon needed strong advocacy there, especially in New York, where he and Barbara could also become invaluable by pressing the president's case within the city's social circles. His self-proclaimed credentials for taking on the UN job came down to loyalty, personality, and the ability to mingle in the right circles.

Nixon listened to all this. Nothing in the record of the session indicates any discussion of global factors, or, for that matter, U.S. relationships with that world body. When Bush left the Oval Office he had no commitment from Nixon, who was mulling over his proposal, although still tantalized by the prospect of making another bipartisan appointment. But Bush's arguments were well taken, and the president's contemplation made them seem all that much more attractive. Finally, ending months of indecisiveness, he called in Haldeman and told him that Bush's arguments had been so impressive that he wanted to make the UN appointment and notified Bush immediately. Once again, John Tower, the first and still only Republican senator from Texas, did not get the courtesy of prior consultation. But Bush had his job.[58]

In a 1992 letter to this author, Nixon wrote that he acted on Bush's UN nomination because he thought the young man "not only had the diplomatic skills to be an effective ambassador, but also because it would be helpful to him in the future to have this significant foreign policy experience."[59] Not in any real sense, however, did Bush evoke either the personal stature or diplomatic seasoning of such earlier American representatives to the United Nations as Edward Stettinius, Warren R. Austin, Henry Cabot Lodge, Adlai Stevenson, Eleanor Roosevelt, Arthur J. Goldberg, or Charles Yost. Nor did he possess the experience commensurate with American responsibility for the success of the world organization.

And yet, there he was, given not only the post but the rank of an ambassador and recognition as a member of the cabinet. Even so stalwart a friend as Lud Ashley found the appointment incredible. Lud later recalled "bumping into Bush" just after the appointment was announced and being flabbergasted. "George," he remembered saying, "what the fuck do you know about foreign affairs?" to which Bush replied, "You ask me that in ten days." Steel, who was almost constantly at his side, was impressed how he "just threw himself into the UN thing."[60]

The administration's critics were predictable, complaining that Bush was "just a poor politician" who was "ignorant of foreign affairs," and that the move "demonstrated Nixon's contempt" by trying to "devalue the U.S. mission to the UN." About the only people who were pleased were some Texas Republicans. But Nancy Palm, a "raving right-winger from Houston," deplored the Bush appointment as a regrettable move toward the middle of the road. Two years later, *The New York Times,* even while conceding that Bush had "become widely respected and was uncommonly well-liked" in the post, still viewed the appointment as "a temporary sinecure for a defeated but still ambitious politician."[61]

The Times, of course, missed the point. By choosing Bush, the administration had, in effect, selected someone entirely congenial to the foreign policy establishment. He fit right into the consensus that was a sine qua non of the newspaper itself, respect for the American role in monitoring global order and maintaining close global commercial relationships. An outstanding threat to all this desired stability was the Soviet Union and its rapidly expanding bloc of troublesome client states, many of them, especially in Eastern Europe, products of wartime military relationships. Another constituted independence movements within former colonial holdings of Western powers. Working in any sort of concert, especially as they did under the People's Republic of China leadership at Bandung in 1955, they comprised the delicate neutral ground between East and West, the balance of power in a post-Axis world dominated by the Soviets and the Americans.

In all this, the United Nations had rapidly lost its value for American power. Designed by the major anti-Axis allies to accomplish in the new era what the League of Nations had failed to do in the old, it had begun as a most utilitarian vehicle for Western purposes. A fifty-five nation General Assembly, twelve-member Security Council and a Secretariat, controled by the war victors, especially those that flanked the Atlantic, had, in effect, been a handy organization to implement its visions and lay down its concept of order. Newly independent states quickly expanded the General Assembly between 1950 and the start of Nixon's presidency, more than doubling its original size. The Security Council, while retaining a permanent membership of five, expanded to fifteen, but, most significantly from the point of view of American interests, the international body had stopped functioning as a convenient marriage of balance of power concepts and self-determination. No longer an instrument of Great Power interests, the UN had strayed far from that time when sixteen of its members responded to a U.S. call for troops to counter North Korea's invasion of South Korea in 1950. Future rifts, including the one in Vietnam, were likely to involve issues far more peripheral to the concerns of cold war rivals. Mostly, the American effort in Southeast Asia evoked much more hostility than support within the UN. The organization's twentieth anniversary was "celebrated" by Indonesia's temporary withdrawal over the seating of Malaysia on the Security Council, while the General Assembly itself was thrown into crisis when Rhodesia declared its independence from Great Britain.

If nothing else, the American entrapment in Vietnam confirmed the irrelevance of much of the UN except as an outlet to vent international passions. Seymour Maxwell Finger, who had been at the mission for fourteen years, found Bush less determined than others to use it as a forum for anti-Communist propaganda, which still left him far from "gung-ho" and with "considerable skepticism" about the UN. In reality, Bush spent much of his time defending this country's military actions, especially the bombing of dikes in North Vietnam.[62]

Still unresolved when Bush arrived at the UN's U.S. mission in a twelve-story building at 799 UN Plaza, were such delicate matters as the Israeli refusal to yield territory taken via the Six Day War in 1967 and the living anomaly of the Republic of China, reduced to Taiwan for two decades, representing "China" in the Security Council. The government in Beijing, then still spelled as Peking, remained a giant outcast among nations.

That neither George Bush nor any other American representative to the UN, with all their titles—ambassador, cabinet member—could play a significant role was predictable. Bush never had the political clout with Nixon that Henry Cabot Lodge had under Dwight Eisenhower. A more valid similarity was with Adlai Stevenson. Privately scorned by Kennedy and no favorite of cynical New Frontiersmen, Stevenson's plight was most evident during his embarrassing isolation at the time of the Bay of Pigs misadventure. Given that recent history, one could hardly have expected that George Bush would have much input, especially in an administration where policy was centralized by President Nixon, his adviser for national security affairs, Henry Kissinger, and the nominal head of the State Department, William Rogers, whose limited consolation for having to contend with his own diminished influence was to call Bush a "lightweight."[63] Bush, however, was conscious of walking "into a very difficult situation at the UN because of the Kissinger-Rogers situation," which often produced "conflicting signals. The State Department would say one thing and Kissinger another." Not until he needed the organization years later did Kissinger have much use for the UN.[64]

Bush, in persuading Nixon to appoint him, had it exactly right. He would be the administration's point man in the international community within Manhattan society. He and Barbara would get to know all the right people, attend all the right receptions, and give all the right parties, both at the official residence and even up in the country in Greenwich. Most of all, they, as a team, would do what they did best, and that required no foreign policy experience—make friends. All the evidence suggests that the Bushes succeeded brilliantly. One of George's associates, Seymour Maxwell Finger, has marveled at how Bush's personal popularity withstood the White House's tendency to leave him out in the cold. "It is amazing that he was personally so popular among other delegates at a time when U.S. policy was so defensive and generally unsupportive; this is a tribute to his personal amiability and hard work in cultivating good relationships," Finger later wrote.[65] One writer for *The Nation* even gushed that the typical "nice American" representing his country's interests along the East River was a "mixture of Gary Cooper and John Lindsay—with money."[66] One Swedish delegate remarked that the American newcomer looked "absurdly young for forty-seven."[67]

Bush's job, as he and Barbara saw it, and as the president himself was convinced, was mainly social, and they set out to make the most of it. His style was informal, his manner casual, unconventionally so for those accustomed to traditional protocol. His Texas mannerisms breached the Bush Eastern establishment heritage, especially during one memorable General Assembly debate on the matter of seating competing Chinese delegations, when he gesticulated and supplicated, "sometimes managing to sound a bit like the evangelist Billy Graham—forgetting the telltale broad New England 'a' that kept popping out or the Texas habit of saying 'gonna' for 'going to.' "[68] Bright, candy-striped shirts were nothing unusual for the energetic American, especially when breaking social barriers by hosting delegates and their families at picnics in Connecticut. Also memorable was the time he snapped up Max Finger's idea about feting the Economic and Social Council at Shea Stadium, home of the New York Mets. Finger recalled, "It worked out beautifully."[69] Far less visible to reporters, and very much characteristic of the private George Bush, was taking time off to make an unpublicized visit to talk to blind children in Pelham, in nearby Westchester County.[70]

Barbara immediately scoured the Blue Book list of United Nation celebrities, studying their names and families. Aided by her personal assistant, Rudolph (Foxy) Carter, she familiarized herself with personal essentials, all to highlight the social aspects of their job. "Mr. Bush," reported *The New York*

Times, "intends to begin with a social splash. He has invited the chief delegates, deputies, and their wives of all delegations—Cuba excepted—to a get-acquainted party on Tuesday."[71] The ambassador himself, of course, was reputed as an "instrument of policy," even as a staunch Nixon loyalist, and as a loyal team player who was "punctilious about attending the many receptions and dinners hosted by other ambassadors."[72] "He was not the quarterback of American foreign policy," wrote Barry Bearak in the *Los Angeles Times,* "just one of the blockers."[73]

The real Bush headquarters, the official residence on the forty-second floor of the Waldorf Towers, apartment 42-A, once the quarters of Gen. Douglas MacArthur, was not the most lavish of UN official residences. Moreover, it had to double as a site for the secretary of state to meet privately with foreign dignitaries. The nine-room layout, with five bedrooms off a forty-eight-foot living room could, with a tight squeeze, accommodate thirty for dinner, and came at an annual rental of $33,000 with the hotel pressuring for an increase.[74] Paintings by Mary Cassatt, Gilbert Stuart, and John Singer Sargent adorned the walls. But Barbara later acknowledged that they were on loan from the Metropolitan Museum of Art which led her to return "two beautiful Monets" because she felt "that since we do not subsidize our artists as so many countries do, the least I could do was display American art."[75] All in all, the American mission was budgeted at $1,974,000 a year, mostly to cover the staff of 111. The ambassador received $42,500.[76]

For his official diplomatic functions, Bush hired the right people. His choice for deputy representative was a fifty-four-year-old conservative Georgian and ex-ambassador to the Dominican Republic, W. Tapley Bennett Jr.[77] Tap Bennett "was sort of chief operating officer," said Finger, which also meant running interference with the State Department, while Bush handled personal diplomacy. Nicholas L. King, who often served as Bush's spokesman, worked along with Aleene Smith and Jane Kenny, who came from his congressional staff.

Those two years Bush spent at the United Nations were, predictably, futile attempts to withstand certain international inevitabilities. A survey of the public mail received at the American mission in September and October of 1972 showed that the most common issues involved the U.S. attempt to block a Security Council seat for the Communist government in Beijing and the problem of terrorism, a concern that was especially triggered by the murder of eleven Israeli athletes by "Black September" Palestinian guerrillas at the recent Munich Olympics. Concern over the plight of Jews trying to flee from the Soviet Union was a close runner-up.[78]

For Bush, the China question turned out to be pretty much a diplomatic charade. Fulfilling his assignment, Bush led his delegation toward the goal of preserving a seat for the Republic of China, the government of Taiwan, despite having to yield its place on the Security Council to the People's Republic of China. Bush took the administration's public line faithfully, vowing that objective over and over again, promising to use whatever was required for success.[79] He huddled with such conservative opponents of the PCR as New York's freshman senator, James Buckley, lobbied the issue with fellow UN ambassadors and, in the words of James Reston, behaved "as if he were the Texas state chairman at the Republican National Convention."[80] "I know for a fact that the president wants to see the policy implemented," Bush told the *Washington Post*.[81] He put in long days of work preparing for the debates. Barbara, responding to public concerns that he was exhausting himself, acknowledged that he "actually looks tired" but denied that he looked like an "unmade bed," as a letter writer had feared.[82]

Even while Bush waged his fight, the president let slip an indiscretion at a Kansas City news conference. Mr. Nixon, facing a group of news executives, explained that it was "essential" for the administration to "take the first step toward ending the isolation of mainland China."[83] Already laboring to belie what Bush was promoting in New York, Henry Kissinger was meeting officials in Beijing, having arrived in the People's Republic of China just before the crucial UN vote, which, in Finger's recollection, "made it impossible. Bush never complained. I thought that was remarkable."[84]

None of this should imply that Ambassador Bush was an innocent. The UN was the public forum, the public stage, the showcase for Washington's political and diplomatic public relations, which then happened to require oaths of loyalty to China's nationalists even while plotting their diplomatic demise. Bush played his role brilliantly. He saw his own job as conducting himself "in a way to provide maximum flexibility for the president as he approaches his final decision."[85]

Kissinger's trip was preceded by an invitation to visit the People's Republic of China. Bush did his part by inviting team captain Jack Howard and the other players to New York for some talk and an exhibition match.[86] Bush, in other words, kept up the amenities of protocol while waging a battle that was neither his to win nor lose. Finally, on October 26, 1971, in an outcome anticipated by the White House, Bush's veto of the ouster of the Taiwan regime was overridden by a General Assembly vote of 76-35. It was, Bush said, "a moment of infamy."[87] The People's Republic of China thereby entered the top rank of nations in the UN. Democratic Congressman Roman C. Pucinski of Illinois quickly got on the House floor to call for Bush's resignation.[88] Especially upset, in contrast with the acknowledgment of the vote that marked the Nixon White House, was the governor of California, Ronald Reagan.[89]

Nowhere else was Bush's position as a White House spokesman better illustrated than in the ill-conceived administration's denunciation of the Indian government currently under Indira Gandhi. The affair, ultimately criticized by specialists in diplomacy and politics of the subcontinent and the subject of an ex post facto justification by Henry Kissinger, illustrated what was to become a hallmark of Nixon's world outlook, during and after he left the presidency: an increasing infatuation with the goals, methods, and interests of authoritarian regimes outside of the social democratic nations of Western Europe.[90] India represented detested "neutralism" between East and West.

American policy was accordingly respondent to triangular diplomacy, most based on the assumption of a hostile Indian policy that was backed by the USSR and was threatening to U.S. interests, including, as a former member of the National Security Council has written, "the U.S. opening to China and the prospects for a Soviet-American detente." Nixon detested Gandhi, anyway; and so did Kissinger, who "had been converting a regional conflict into one between the superpowers and had intentionally generated a confrontation, in the interests of establishing an equilibrium in the world balance of power through triangular diplomacy."[91] No matter what the ultimate verdict, or that Bush, acting under the president's direct orders, had labeled India the aggressor, Pakistani planes attacked first on December 3, striking at Indian bases deep into the Indian-administered areas of Kashmir. Nixon, who had already decided his famous "tilt" toward Pakistan several months earlier, got even more excited. Haldeman noted a president who went from being merely snappish at the start of the day to one who "was cranking under full steam" by midmorning. He got Ambassador Bush on the line and ordered him to, as Haldeman later recorded the day's events, "hit hard on our Indian-Pakistan position and making that very clear." Bush, following through at the UN, questioned India's further intentions and succeeded in condemning the government of New Delhi before the General Assembly.[92]

The conflict that was searing the Middle East between the Israelis and the Arabs, however, came closer to home for Bush and involved him in more personal ways. Arab insistence that the Israelis return the territory captured from them during the Six Day War of 1967, including the city of Jerusalem, unleashed a fury felt not only in the region itself, especially in the southern part of Lebanon, but in the form of ultranationalist Zionists in the United States. The most extreme leadership was provided by Rabbi Meier Kahane. His organization, the Jewish Defense League (JDL), with its slogan of "Never Again," carried out a series of militant attacks. They even fired automatic rifle shots through a window of the Soviet mission on East Sixty-seventh Street and provoked disturbances at the official compound serving as the residence of the Soviet delegation at Glen Cove, on Long Island. Bush himself engaged in a direct showdown with the JDL leader as Rabbi Kahane tried physically to block his way into the United Nations. On the campus of the American University in Washington, D.C., a seventeen-year-old high school girl disrupted a reception by pouring what appeared to be a bucket of blood over the head of a Soviet diplomat. Bush then testified before a House Judiciary subcommittee to urge criminalizing such acts. Invited, at one point, to appear on a television talk show hosted by the then-popular Dick Cavett, Bush refused. The arrangements called for his joint appearance with Rabbi Kahane, a forum Bush would not share.[93]

The escalation of terrorism that had centered in such diverse places as the Middle East and around the United Nations in New York spread with shocking swiftness in September of 1972 to the site of the summer Olympic games at Munich, Germany. There, members of a Palestinian guerrilla group later identified as an organization that called itself Black September, attacked and murdered eleven Israeli athletes. Ironically, at the same time, Bush resisted attempts to label Americans as "aggressors" and "terrorists" because of the bombings of dikes in North Vietnam, a point that had great currency among "Third World" members of the General Assembly.

Bush later savored the value of that UN experience. "It taught me a good deal about world diplomacy," he told the present author.[94]

That same September, Prescott Bush was admitted for tests at Cancer Memorial and Allied Diseases Hospital in New York, where he was diagnosed with lung cancer. The elder Bush, at the age of seventy-seven, died on October 8. George and Barbara were grateful that their presence in New York for that past year had kept them close to his side.[95] His widow, Dorothy Walker Bush, the matriarchal "Dottie" of the Bush family, composed a eulogy that was read for her by the Rev. Bradford Hastings, rector of the Christ Episcopal Church in Greenwich.[96] Dottie Bush eulogized her husband as a family man who "believed in necessary discipline when the occasion demanded, but was always loving and understanding. As the children grew older," she added, "he respected each as an individual, ready to back any decision thoughtfully reached, and giving advice only when sought." She also thanked him for giving her "the most joyous life that any woman could experience," and for his "lack of pride in material possessions."[97]

George had idolized his father. As he moved from youth to maturity, his respect for the senator had increased correspondingly. His death was a painful loss.

CHAPTER ELEVEN

Nixon and China

%

Prescott's world embodied "not the legacy of a class," as Nelson W. Aldrich Jr. has put it, "but the legacy of particular families" dedicated to a "common sense of custom and obligation." Surely, that colored Bush's reaction to the denouement of Watergate. Journalist Theodore H. White once caught that mood when he quoted Bush as saying, "I'm really glad Dad's not alive, it would have killed him to see this happen. He thought we were the party of virtue and all bosses were Democrats."[1]

That may well have been the only fortunate aspect of the scandals, at least as far as George was concerned. Prescott Bush Sr. had lived long enough to know how the changing political climate had torn apart the Democratic party, mainly, of course, how conflicts over race and war had brought a rapid retreat from the 1964 sweep by Lyndon Johnson over Barry Goldwater. "Participatory politics" led to romantic egalitarianism, reckless abandonment of order and stability, even civility, and the Democratic party's "big tent" expanded until it collapsed.

The Great Society joined FDR's glory years among the relics of great movements. Richard Nixon saw his opportunities, planned, plotted, and achieved a resurrection of his own power, but, alas, not respectability. Self-tortured after a frustrating off-year election campaign (in which their arsenal for 1972 was weakened by the loss of eleven governorships and nine House seats with just two gains in the Senate), and bedeviled by enemies real and imagined, Nixon's White House hunkered down, designed a rogue bureaucracy with a talent for retaliation, and set the stage for the Watergate scandals.

All could have been hidden from the public, and even the Washington press corps, if not for the botched break-in and entry during the night of June 17, 1972, at the Watergate office of the Democratic National Committee. Nixon's press secretary immediately called it a "third-rate burglary attempt," which set the tone, at least temporarily. Watergate hardly caught fire among those preoccupied with such matters as war and the state of the economy. The

Democrats denounced such tactics, enumerated all the sinister possibilities, and sued in the courts. But the issue remained a dud. Thanks, in part, to the ineptitude of his opponents, Nixon won the election.

The public's appetite failed to be aroused even by a $1 million damage suit brought by the Democrats on behalf of Larry O'Brien, the party chairman whose office had been broken into. Nor, for that matter, was much attention given to information developed by investigators in Florida, the operational base of "burglar" Bernard Barker, a Bay of Pigs veteran and CIA man, and by the House Banking Committee under the head of Texas Democrat Wright Patman. The Patman Report, made public after it had been obtained by columnist and investigative reporter Jack Anderson, accounted for the $114,000 in cash with Barker when he was caught. Named as principles in getting a total of $700,000 to Washington before the April 7, 1972, enactment of a new law requiring the identification of all campaign contributors, were Pennzoil president and former Bush oil partner William C. Liedtke and fat-cat contributor Dwayne O. Andreas, a Minnesota businessman and grain processor. Another contributor was Bush's close Houston friend who had been connected to the Townhouse Operation, Bob Mosbacher. Of the total, $100,000 had been gathered by Liedtke from Texas Nixon Reelection committee chairman, Robert H. Allen, the head of Gulf Resources and Chemical Company in Houston. Allen "laundered" his money through a lawyer in Mexico City, who made deposits in a local bank. Then, when needed in order to beat the new law, Allen's $100,000 was transferred back to Houston. There it was "sacked up," or stuffed in a suitcase, and placed aboard a Pennzoil corporate jet, accompanied by one of their vice presidents, and flown to Washington. Barker received his share of the distribution in time for the Watergate enterprise and deposited it in a Miami bank.[2] Nowhere, in all of this, was there any hint that the contributors knew about how the money was to be used, nor any connection made between its Texas origins and George Bush.

At least through the election, damage control worked for Nixon. Further helped by his opponent's righteous prairie populism, the president managed to convince most voters that the South Dakotan was far to the left of the respectable center.[3] Nixon's reward, of course, was the mightiest of landslides, a record popular majority of 60.8 percent. George Bush had flowed with the tide, worked with his usual dedication and loyalty, and did everything he could for the man who had helped him. Yet, ultimately, Bush also became an innocent casualty of the scandals, his honor compromised.

Nixon had continued to consolidate his control. He was *The Prince*, who obtained and kept power by understanding some basic principles. Machiavelli had cleverly advocated killing his rivals. But Nixon's timing was clumsy, even brutal. He started by sinking his most loyal crew, demanding resignations from the recent architects of his victory. His ruthlessness even stunned Herb Klein, the old Nixon sidekick from early California political wars. That act, said the veteran Orange County newspaperman, was "the most disheartening, most surprising, and most cruel of all . . . ungrateful and bitterly cold."[4] Nixon later explained himself. He was "determined during the second term to break the Eastern stranglehold on the executive branch and the federal government" by reaching out "into the West and Midwest for fresh talent." But, the way he went about it, he conceded, was a "mistake."[5] That was when George Bush came aboard.

If Nixon was *anything*, one thing was certain: he was no romantic. He used such epithets as "Ivy League bastards" right in front of Bush and others. Little wonder that Bush never felt as close to him personally as he later did, for example, to Ronald Reagan. Nixon, in contrast with Reagan, "kind of pulled back a little bit, tough and cold. He was always kind of—standoffish is the word. There certainly was no buddy-buddy approach, at least with me. There was never a totally relaxed camaraderie on any relation I had with him at all."[6]

When, only a few days after the election and just before a noon meeting at Camp David's Aspen Lodge, White House photographer Ollie Atkins was called in for a photo session, he caught the president on a couch facing the fire. Seated nearby were John Ehrlichman and University of Chicago economist George Shultz. Shultz, already a veteran of the Nixon presidency, had first headed the Department of Labor and the Office of Management and Budget. Since May, he had been serving as secretary of the Treasury. With Nixon again focusing on reorganization, and planning to replace "Charls [*sic*] Walker" as undersecretary of the Treasury, the conversation led to Bush, who had earned his respect by going out to the oil patch and building a business "on his own."[7] He was not to be confused with the usual run of Ivy Leaguers. He knew something about work and loyalty. He could be valuable, perhaps be given the number-two spot at the Treasury, "if he'd take it. He wants to be a cabinet officer," Nixon told Shultz.

"A new hat," said Shultz. "He'll *run* the department."

"A total Nixon man—first," agreed the president. "Doubt if you can do better than Bush."[8]

No, there was no way to top Bush. As Nixon repeated for Bush's benefit three days later, the administration needed "not brains but loyalty."[9] His natural appeal might even help to offset some of Nixon's own weaknesses, attributes again demonstrated when Bush served as a surrogate in both of the President's election campaigns.[10] In the words of Ohio's Nixon loyalist, Republican Representative Delbert Latta, George could make "friends in any audience."[11]

Exactly Nixon's need: friends. His personal sense of embattlement verged on the psychotic. The White House became a command headquarters to lash back at enemies. Nixon tightened the vise on the "liberal" press, distancing journalistic prima donnas from the Oval Office. Nixon's instructions for the State Department ordered "a complete freeze on the WASHINGTON POST, the NEW YORK TIMES, and CBS" for printing a leaked letter Nixon had written to South Vietnam's President Nguyen Van Thieu. "There must be total discipline on the press and this has got to be enforced," said a Haldeman Action Memo three days after the election, quickly followed by another directive that, in planning for the inaugural, the occasion "must in no way be a gathering of the old elite, or of the Washington, D.C. aristocracy."[12]

New cabinet appointees were to understand that they were invited to serve for no more than a two-year period. Their jobs were to be at his personal pleasure, nobody else's. Lines of communication from the UN mission would now go directly to the Oval Office instead of through Henry Kissinger, his adviser for National Security Affairs.[13]

Reorganizing the bureaucracy from top to bottom meant dumping dead weight, including Bob Dole, the head of the Republican National Committee. Dole was too independent, too acerbic, too irreverent. Nixon didn't like his "attitude." He told Haldeman that Dole was "sour" and a "poor-mouther." Nixon had, in the past, relied too heavily on the RNC and its chairman, which did little toward getting a decent Republican voter turnout.[14] Money-raising was lagging, too. Dole had to go.

Bush was perfect for the RNC, whistle-clean, a tonic for the GOP's public image, a nice guy to everyone, but tough. How else could he have built a career in oil and politics? A great combination: respectability and strength, able to firm up the administration's lines of control. He could be handy at the money-raising, too. Where Dole was flat, Bush was strong; he had access to the right sources. If you can't come up with funds of your own, tapping others was the next best thing.[15]

Nixon flew Bush into Camp David just before Thanksgiving. Shultz got to him first and tried to sell Bush on the Treasury. He could become a sort of "supersecretary" troubleshooter for the department. Bush waved Shultz off, wanting to hear what was on the president's mind. Foreign policy was more appealing, especially after his work with the UN. He might fit quite well into State. Nixon's mind was set.[16] The "paramount" security interests of the U.S. justified downgrading the UN, he told Bush. Too many pantywaists held down cushy jobs at its New York City headquarters. He'd like the names of those he could really count on. All right, said Bush, he'll come up with a "tough political memo."[17] Don't overlook the "New American Majority," Nixon then reminded him. "We have a chance to build a new coalition in the next four years, and you're the one who can do it." Bush was the logical guy to run the RNC, Nixon later explained, a "great" choice.[18]

It was far less than "great" for Bush, more of a political albatross, a place where he would have to duck as never before. He had left what was a congenial atmosphere at the UN, where his personal strengths were valued. He was liked and trusted, especially among the UN's Third World delegates, whose desire to spend their careers in New York City instead of at home gave them an even greater personal stake in having Bush stay on as their American friend.

Bush's own feelings were mixed. Barbara, never shy about telling him how she felt, thought that the RNC post was "the last thing in the world" he should accept. He'd be better off doing "anything but that," she told him. He countered by saying that "you can't turn a president down," and that was the end of that.[19] A pretty grim way to sign on; he was doing his duty. A good soldier.

A few days later, Nixon flew Dole up to Camp David. He could get rid of Dole only by pushing him out. Nixon, too fainthearted to swing the ax one on one, toyed with the senator from Kansas. He danced around the subject, only telling the incumbent RNC chairman that he planned to offer it to Bush. Dole had no choice. As Haldeman later noted, the chairman of the Republican National Committee simply "agreed [that] would be great." Loyally, Dole went to New York to ask Bush to take the job, only to learn about the charade. He had been "bushwhacked," Dole later said.[20]

Press Secretary Ron Ziegler, speaking for the White House, had instructions to "shoot down the nonsense that Dole was pushed out."[21] Liberal critics complained that the change was but another example of Washington's "downgrading" of the United Nations. *The New York Times*'s Tom Wicker spoke for many when he asked, "What does it say of Nixon's view of the United Nations that two years ago he appointed a defeated candidate to head the American delegation and now intends to shift the same man to the chairmanship of the Republican National Committee, as if these were equivalent posts?"[22] From the far right came the complaint that Dole was "unceremoniously booted out" of his job and suggested that the White House was seeking Bush as a reliable puppet.[23]

Moving on to take another Nixon job seemed natural to Bush. The UN had never been more than a temporary stopover, certainly not his career choice. His parting shots included misgivings about increasing polarization. Global bloc voting was becoming routine; political alignments dominated. The cold war had settled into the rut of competition for influence over the Third World. So called "neutralist" states had learned how to play off East against West, and vice versa. More and more, Bush explained, "moderate voices fear to speak out because they feel that they will appear less oriented or loyal to their group. So they keep their silence." With its loss of influence within UN councils, the United States would inevitably become more independent. "There was a time," he recalled, "when all my predecessors had to do was raise an eyebrow and we had an instant majority." Still, he remained optimistic about his own future and that of the UN. With the news of his Republican National Committee post and the naming of John Scali as his UN successor, he faced the press from his desk while seated behind a nameplate masked by a sign that proclaimed in bold letters: ESCHEW OBFUSCATION. He denied that his appointment or, by inference, that of Scali, a former television newsman who had played an important background role in helping to resolve the Cuban missile crisis, had any implications about devaluing the UN. The organization, he predicted, would become "more important as time goes by," and its "usefulness as a window on the world is worth vastly more than America's contribution to the United Nations' budget."[24] Bush later learned why Scali had been chosen. Nixon, he wrote, was on his "new majority" kick, so he opted for an Italian-American.[25]

First came George Bush's confirmation as Republican National Committee chairman, the unanimous choice of the delegates. If you really knew "our domestic political process," Prescott Bush's former Connecticut rival, Bill Benton, advised *The New York Times,* you would not consider the change of jobs a demotion.[26]

Then, on January 20, 1973, with the ex-UN ambassador in a pivotal position between his president and GOP colleagues, came the second Nixon inaugural. The Bushes sat with the cabinet. On the steps of the Capitol Building, below the giant dome, were the senators and members of Congress, sheltering themselves from the frigid air and bitter winds that swept into the city that day from across the Potomac. The flags, at half-mast since the death of Harry Truman on December 26, flapped in the gusts. At noon, Chief Justice Warren Burger administered to Richard Nixon his second presidential oath of office, the swearing-in marred by distant shouts of "murderer, murderer." Nixon, composed, delivered his address without once mentioning "Vietnam" or "Indochina," but gave his assurances that "America's longest and most difficult war" was ending. The adviser for national security affairs, Henry Kissinger, had, in fact, all but wrapped up the coming ceasefire in meetings with the North Vietnamese in Paris, and, barring any last-minute rebellion by President Nguyen Van Thieu of South Vietnam, Nixon's final announcement was about all that remained. The end was so near, in fact, that, ironically, the fighting intensified, an investment of hundreds of additional lives for more yardage before silencing the guns. Thus were the over 58,000 American and some half million North Vietnamese and South Vietnamese losses further inflated.[27]

Then came Nixon's ceasefire announcement. Nobody mentioned Watergate. The press behaved as though the issue was stillborn. Yet, as historian George Herring has noted about the connection between the war and the scandals, "the extreme measures he [Nixon] took to defend his Vietnam policy against enemies real and imagined led directly to the Watergate scandals" that chewed up his presidency.[28] Lyndon B. Johnson died just two days after the ceasefire was announced, undoubtedly the war's most prominent political victim.

So Bush could hardly have taken over party responsibility at a more critical moment. The incident at the Watergate headquarters of the Democratic National Committee had the potential to undercut Republican gains. Bush had two functions: keep the GOP's machinery afloat and the administration credible. Whatever the damage to the Nixon presidency, saving the party was crucial. Republicans would have no choice but to live with their losses and keep going.

His public mail reflected all that. Correspondence was about equally divided among those who demanded that Bush do more to help the president and those urging that fellow Republicans treat Nixon as an outcast.[29] Meanwhile, that April, key Nixon aides John Dean, Bob Haldeman, and John Ehrlichman were forced to resign. Hearings by the Senate Select Committee on Presidential Activities that began in May 1973 were led by Sam J. Ervin Jr., a North Carolina Democrat. They featured the startling revelation by Alexander Butterfield of the White House staff that Oval Office conversations had been routinely taped by electronic devices. Bush, meanwhile, mounted his own campaign. He clocked 97,000 miles and visited thirty-three states, where he gave 101 speeches, seventy-eight news conferences, and made eleven national television appearances, all in defense of the administration and especially the party.[30]

He tried to keep morale afloat by stressing, both privately and before audiences throughout the country, Nixon's assurances that it would be a nonissue. "Watergate," went Bush's standard explanation, "was the product of the actions of a few misguided, very irresponsible individuals who violated a high trust and who served neither the president nor their country well." So he had Nixon's personal word, the assurance of a man who has "said repeatedly he wasn't involved in the sordid Watergate affairs. I believe him."[31] When further revelations that spring tied the administration ever more closely to the schemes aimed at undermining the Democrats through a variety of CREEP-funded activities, Bush warned that all would be lost if the "grubby" affair were not "promptly and fully cleared away." There was "no point hiding it," he told a conference of young Republican leaders. "It is not good for the political party as a whole."[32] Publicly, he remained "confident." He defended Nixon's refusal to disclose tapes of what Bush termed his "private and highly confidential talks with some of his closest aides" and said he felt that the people would accept that decision. "The president knows the main thing the people want is to get this matter fully disclosed and put to bed," he said, while privately wondering just what *was* being held back. In July, with Watergate fever intensifying, Bush denied that the party had been hurt but admitted that he was "sickened" by the affair. He also pressed for the dismantling of the Committee for the Reelection of the President, complaining that its high profile was costing the party dearly among major contributors.[33]

Bush's main contacts were with state chairmen. His message to them was simple: the accusations were baseless and, moreover, Watergate and the party had nothing to do with each other.

Meanwhile, Nixon told Haldeman that Bush was a "worrywart." Bush confided to Barbara that he was distressed by White House pressure to offer some pretty excessive defenses of the administration's record. Explanations were becoming more strained, with the mounting allegations undercutting whatever moral leadership remained of the Nixon presidency. The nation heard about lists of those targeted for audits by the IRS, illegal sheltering of Nixon's own income taxes, use of public funds for improvements of his private residences, and, as John Dean testified, a pattern of actions against opponents through "excessive concern over the political impact of demonstrations, excessive concern over leaks, an insatiable appetite for political intelligence."[34] Thanks to a discovery by White House lawyers, they also heard about an eighteen-and-a-half-minute gap on a tape during what was later determined to have been a key Nixon conversation with Haldeman about launching a "counterattack."

Archibald Cox of Harvard Law School was called in as a special prosecutor. A contest followed between the independent and determined lawyer and the Nixon White House over releasing the potentially revealing tapes.

That battle led to a dramatic showdown in October when Nixon demanded that Cox be dumped. Attorney General Elliot Richardson and his deputy, William Ruckelshaus, preferred to quit rather than follow Nixon's order. Only the third-ranking official in the Justice Department, Solicitor General Robert H. Bork, was willing to fire the special prosecutor. Washington, Capitol Hill and the White House, were immediately inundated by protests over what the press branded the "Saturday night massacre." A Texas lawyer, Leon Jaworski, succeeded Cox as special prosecutor.

Bush's explanations were less and less credible. Hounding Nixon out of office, he warned, would not be in the nation's best interest. The ripple effects might be felt anywhere from Wall Street to the Pentagon. "I had two stacks of mail," he later recalled publicly, one of letters asking "how come you're not doing more to support the president?" and the other saying "how come you're keeping the party so close to the president?"[35]

Spiro Agnew gave up his vice presidency in October 1973, a blow to Nixon who had hoped that the controversial Marylander's incumbency in the office of immediate succession would make him impeachment-proof. Agnew's resignation came with a plea of nolo contendere in the face of bribery charges that went back to his Maryland governorship and extended to his taking illegal payments even while in the nation's second-highest office. Gerald Ford, the Republican House minority leader, became vice president when Nixon nominated him in accordance with the Twenty-fifth Amendment. Ford, the affable and experienced politician from Michigan, was popular with Republicans and Democrats alike.

Like almost everyone else on the hill, Bush was well-acquainted with Ford. Their relationship dated to the 1966 campaign, when the Michigan Republican visited Bush's Houston district. That Bush wanted the vice presidency for himself is clear, but he was in no position to compete for the Agnew opening. His preoccupation was as liaison between the White House and the national party, although his name showed up among the possible contenders, especially in the form of unofficial "favorite-son" preferences from Texas's congressional delegation. Nixon, waging his battle over the tapes, and facing the increasing likelihood of impeachment, chose the path of least resistance by tapping Ford.

Bush's old rival, John Connally, also figured in all this. Nixon, infatuated with the big Texan, had contemplated substituting him for Agnew on the

1972 ticket. Nixon's enthusiasm, Bush found, was recharged when the survey of national committeemen showed that Connally was almost as popular as their own favorite, Governor Nelson Rockefeller of New York. But warnings were sounded about Connally. He would, predictably, have stiff opposition, not only for partisan reasons but because of lingering charges of improprieties. Nixon, noticeably shying away from further controversy in making his vice presidential choice, did not entirely abandon his man. Ford made it easier by telling the president that if he remained vice president he would not run for the presidency in 1976. He would even join Nixon in backing Connally. "I don't know whether he would have changed his mind," Ford said later, speculating about what Nixon would have done had he not made that offer.[36] And so, with that promise in hand and confirmation certain, Nixon designated Ford.

But the sky continued to fall. Two special elections to fill vacated House seats were won by Democrats. Was Bush still confident that the party could weather the impact of Watergate? "Less than I was yesterday," he admitted exactly thirteen months after Nixon was sworn in for the second time. He also acknowledged the concern that in both cases the winners had made Watergate an issue, and, apparently, a winning one. Still, Bush remained steadfast. "We've got to look at the whole schmeer," he cautioned. "But don't color me anything but very confused." "I am worried about George as he does not love his work," Barbara confided to her diary. "How could he? All this scandal."[37]

Bush almost had a way out. Bypassed for the vice presidency, Connally was not about to sulk behind a facade of weakness; he would not rest. With the Agnew question out of the way, but with ever-increasing Watergate headaches looming, especially for a national chairman apprehensive about the effects of a spillover that had already cut the GOP's income by about a third, Bush was clearly caught in a dilemma. Connally, having confirmed his switch to the Republican party, pressed Bush to return to Texas and challenge the first-term incumbent Democratic governor, Dolph Briscoe. A key benefactor of Texas Democrats, most notably Lyndon Johnson, George Brown of the giant Brown and Root Construction Company, weighed in by urging Bush to return to the state, switch parties, and grab the renomination away from Briscoe. "We would all back you and you would win easily," was the way Bush remembered Brown's encouraging words, which he had little trouble rejecting.[38] He did explore the matter far enough to commission a private poll, but that showed little reason for optimism.[39] "Heavens knows," Bush wrote to Jim Baker in November. "I wish we were moving back to Houston today for many personal reasons, but I must stay here." He owed much to standing by the Republican party that was under so much fire, he then explained in a press release. His sense of responsibility ruled out any notion about leaving. Moreover, he explained to quell the rumors of an active gubernatorial candidacy, "I support the president enthusiastically. His overall record merits my strong support. I am confident that full disclosure on

Watergate will vindicate the president."[40] Bush's decision was fortunate. By the time Texans voted in 1974, Nixon had resigned. Watergate destroyed the candidacy of even so popular a Republican as Dr. John Granberry, a former mayor of Lubbock, who was swamped under Governor Briscoe's two-to-one landslide.[41]

So he clung to what he had—his responsibilities as Republican National Committee chairman with its fund-raising problems, however complicated by the incremental revelations. He had only Nixon's own denials. Whatever his misgivings, he chose to trust the president. On the twentieth of May, 1974, appearing on ABC-TV's *Issues and Answers,* Bush denied that Nixon was being plagued by a vendetta and added that Republicans rather than their opponents were the ones that were most concerned about Watergate. "We always thought the Democrats did more of that kind of thing," he said.[42] Bush also sent a "confidential and eyes-only" letter to Nixon's chief of staff, Al Haig, warning that unless Nixon proved his innocence by releasing his tapes, "each congressman and senator will have a justifiable reason to try to put distance between himself and the White House. There will be a *major* outcry," he wrote. "The press will play this Republican outcry for all it is worth."[43]

Nixon finally obeyed a court subpoena and released a selection of transcripts in formal-looking, made-for-television binders designed to mislead the public about how much was actually being made available. They were also so sanitized with the use of "expletive deleted" in place of profanities that the repetition of the phrase itself became provocative. The Oval Office had begun to sound like a gang clubhouse.

Bush had reached his limit. He could no longer go on defending the president. He had done everything possible to keep Watergate from rubbing off on the party. Now he was helpless. He could only watch the coming collapse with dismay. The House Judiciary Committee, after declining to accept Nixon's version of the tape transcripts, began to deliberate articles of impeachment. Three finally passed: obstruction of justice, abuse of power, and defiance of subpoenas. Nixon, faced with the certainty of becoming the first president since Andrew Johnson to face an impeachment trial, suddenly found himself with another dilemma. In the case of *United States* v. *Nixon,* the Supreme Court ruled by 8-0 that he had to surrender to U.S. District Court Judge John J. Sirica all tapes of sixty-four conversations essential for the trials of six former aides. Nixon thereupon released to the press the contents of the "smoking gun" tape. Recorded on June 23, 1972, just one month after the break-in, the words established Nixon's early knowledge of the affair and, most emphatically, his role in orchestrating a cover-up.

The conversation, with then-Chief of Staff Bob Haldeman, revealed Nixon's desire to get the CIA to stop the FBI's investigation of Watergate. Nixon conceded that the recording contradicted his earlier denials and accepted the inevitability of an impeachment. True believers were shattered by the revelation. Few personalized that disappointment more than George

Bush, whose veracity also was on the line. When first shown the "smoking gun" tape transcript by Dean Burch, an ex-RNC chairman and former FCC commissioner, then serving as special counselor to the president, Bush realized that the truth was actually worse than what he had imagined.[44]

He felt a sense of betrayal, that he was a victim of disloyalty. All his assurances of Nixon's innocence were a mockery. "He has a different sense than the rest of people [*sic*]," Bush wrote in his notes. "He came up the hard way. He hung tough. He hunkered down, he stonewalled. He became president of the United States and a damn good one in many ways, but now it had all caught up with him. All the people he hated—Ivy League, press, establishment, Democrats, privileged—all of this ended up biting him and bringing him down."[45]

Al Haig called Bush that night, and it became clear that the chief of staff had discussed resignation with the president. The whole week, said Haig, had been unbelievable; he wondered how Nixon managed to keep going. He would not survive, Haig predicted; but he added, assuringly, "we will look back when we are eighty and say he had been one of the great presidents of our time." Bush, in turn, confirmed that the president's support within the National Committee was eroding rapidly. Nixon, added Haig, was isolated and calling on no one from the outside for decisions. Bush admitted to feeling that he was in a "half-assed position—neither fish nor fowl." Haig wound up the late evening conversation by saying, "God bless you." Yes, agreed Bush in compiling notes of their conversation, "Watergate is a shabby, tawdry business that demeans the presidency. Am I failing to lead by not saying that?"[46]

"My temptation was to blast the president," Bush later explained, "blast the lie, and then I thought, why add to the personal tragedy and the personal grief? Events were moving so fast that it just didn't seem right to kind of 'pile on.' "[47]

On the sixth, there was one final meeting of the cabinet. For the first time anyone could recall, nobody in the room applauded when the president entered. They were all nervous. Ford noted that the tension was "unbelievable." "There was a kind of carnival atmosphere," Bush thought, "everyone expecting the president to resign." Nixon appeared to be elsewhere, submerged by unreality. He had for some time been going on as though nothing had happened, playing the charade that there was nothing else on his mind except the state of the economy. "Incredible!" recalled Treasury Secretary William Simon. "Absolutely bizarre. He could pull the curtain down and deal for hours on these ethereal subjects." Indeed, Nixon began the meeting by saying that he wanted to talk about "the most important issue confronting the nation, and confronting us internationally, too—inflation." He told of plans for an economic summit conference.

He looked at Bush, who thought he detected a faint flush on the president's face. Then, without actually uttering the word but speaking with his lips, he said, "George." Bush felt sorry for him. He thought of Nixon's daughter, Julie. She had come to him in tears begging him to "do more to help my dad."[48]

Ford, the man in the room most immediately affected by the constitutionality of the situation, insistently brought the president back to reality by reiterating the position he had taken at the previous day's cabinet meeting, that he was too obviously involved in the possibility of a presidential succession to continue to be visible in the president's defense. His comments "cast a pall over the meeting." Firing at the besieged president from another direction, Attorney General William Saxbe gave the meeting only a bare taste of his prepared four-page statement, and that was enough to shock them all. Before trying to deal with all those matters of state, said Saxbe, "Let's see if you can govern." Embarrassed silence followed.

Bush, who found the atmosphere "unreal," then interrupted to ask whether the president realized that there was no way to separate Watergate from confidence in the administration? An effect on the economy was a real danger. He feared punishment at the polls in that fall's midterm elections, which, he warned, could well be a disaster.

"Nixon brushed him aside," wrote Ford. "He seemed to want to talk only about budget cuts and economic strategy." Secretary of State Kissinger later noted that it was "impossible not to feel sorry for this tormented man. I had spent too many hours with him not to sense his panic; I knew the bravado was only skin-deep." Suddenly, out of context, Nixon mentioned "the subject on everybody's mind," but only, thought Kissinger, in a search for sympathy and absolution, neither of which he got. Then he retreated to the mundane topic of inflation, suppressing what had seemed an afterthought.

Ninety minutes after the meeting began, Nixon walked out, leaving them stunned and in limbo. Bush, after a few moments, turned to Nixon Chief of Staff Al Haig. Bush respected Haig. He was, he thought, a man of "total decency," his highest compliment. The chief of staff also knew quite well that the president was amoral. Still, Bush wrote in his notes, he "is loyal almost to a fault and yet I know that he represents to the president what is right." Bush asked Haig, "What are we going to do?" Haig's reply was unhelpful. What could he do? He had, he confided to Bush, gotten Nixon to the point of actively considering resignation. "But the family—." They were the real obstacle. They were resisting Haig's advice to step down, demanding that he stay in there and fight it out. Haig had actually brought Nixon to the "mountain top," to where he accepted resignation, but the family talked him out of it.[49]

Bush followed through. The next day, he sent a letter advising Nixon to resign. His view, he wrote, was shared "by most Republican leaders across the country. This letter is much more difficult," he added, "because of the gratitude I will always feel toward you."[50]

Nixon's fall came quickly. On the seventh, three Republican congressional leaders, Senators Barry Goldwater of Arizona and Hugh Scott of Pennsylvania, and Representative John J. Rhodes of Arizona, constituted a little delegation that brought the news to the president that his congressional support had evaporated. He could only resign or face impeachment. Bush called Barbara from Los Angeles, his scheduled RNC fund-raiser telethon now cancelled, and asked her to leave Kennebunkport and join him to be with the president the next day.

With cabinet members and other White House staffers, they stood with the First Family for the farewells in the East Room. Then Nixon unexpectedly delivered a rambling but revealing and also embarrassing monologue to the teary-eyed gathering. He opened with a sideswipe at his favorite target, the press, by noting that they were apt to report his remarks as having been prearranged despite their spontaneity. He reminded them that his father, Frank Nixon, could have been called a "sort of little man, a common man," one who had owned "the poorest lemon ranch in California." His mother, Hannah, "was a saint" who had nursed two dying sons. Defensively, then, in a not-so-subtle slap at liberal intellectuals, he added, "as you know, I like to read books. I'm not educated but I do read books."[51] Barbara, writing her memoirs while Nixon was still alive, ignored the East Room talk and reported only on how "sad a moment in our history" it was. "One of the brightest men of our time was brought down by a stupid cover-up."

At noon on August 9, Nixon, without acknowledging that he had done anything wrong, turned the presidency over to Gerry Ford. Bush saw Nixon off from the helicopter pad on the South Lawn of the White House. He was also eager to set matters straight with some newsmen. They had, somehow, gotten the impression that he was "relieved" to see Nixon go. The reality, he told them, was that he was only "sad."[52]

Gerald Ford, the thirty-eighth president, began under circumstances faintly reminiscent of those that surrounded Rutherford B. Hayes, the nineteenth, as an "administration of national reconciliation." Hayes, who sat in the White House exactly a century earlier, had to restore harmony to a post-Reconstruction nation. Ford's mission, while hardly of that magnitude, required repairing the mostly psychic damage after the divisive Vietnam and Watergate years. That meant healing not only the wounded Republican party but returning national confidence to the political process. The first Twenty-fifth Amendment vice presidential nominee, in office less than one year, was driven by little more than the desire for easy ratification by both houses of Congress. Ford's vice presidential selection could better express the party's direction, alter the distribution of political power in the quarter of a century since World War II, and determine the composition of the GOP's base.

Had circumstances given him the luxury of his personal first choice, the designation would have been preordained—Melvin Laird of Wisconsin. Laird was among the Young Turks who had helped Ford's rise in the House, which led to his minority leadership victory in 1965.[53] Laird, as Nixon's first secretary of defense, retained his close friendship with Ford. As a traditional Midwestern conservative of stature, he was in equally good standing with the party's right wing. He even drew some respect from Democrats for his somewhat dovish image in the Pentagon. Laird, for all his attractions to Ford, had found a good, comfortable, well-paying job with the *Reader's Digest.* He was not about to give that up for a return to government service. Nelson Rockefeller's selection as Ford's vice president had Laird's endorsement.[54] Ford, the political pro, knew something about the game of conciliation. Each wing of the party, each region, had its potential crack at the spot, from Edward Brooke and Elliot Richardson on the left, to Goldwater and Ronald Reagan on the right, and ample representation from the center. Laird pushed Ford toward Rockefeller.[55]

It soon became clear that Rockefeller's main competitor was George Bush. After several premature moves in that direction in past years, Bush finally was a serious candidate. That first evening of the new administration, at a dinner gathering of Nixon loyalists, talk inevitably centered around Gerald Ford's choice for vice president, and Bush's name was in the running from the outset.

Ford's selection process clearly signaled a departure from the Nixon style. An imperial presidency had yielded to one that began by heralding a new openness. The search for a vice president to be filled under the Twenty-fifth Amendment began almost immediately. Ford solicited recommendations from almost everyone on Capitol Hill, congressional leaders, cabinet members, and aides. Bush's job included surveying all committeemen. As one report put it, "Ford hopes to find someone youngish and mediagenic, politically moderate enough to balance his own conservatism, yet acceptable to the right wing of the GOP and to the Southern Democrats who make up his basic constituency in Congress."[56]

In Bush, Ford had a moderate who suited all such criteria, including acceptability to the party's conservatives. No one doubted that he would be an attractive choice, one symptomatic of a more hopeful Republican future. Pat Buchanan, Nixon's former speechwriter, backed Rockefeller but conceded if Ford desires "to move to a younger, newer man in the Republican party, then we could certainly do worse than George Bush." Dean Burch's recommendation also placed Bush within the context of offering him as a long-term party asset. Bush, noted a key adviser, Bryce Harlow, was the strongest candidate "across the board." His downside was that many of the nation's top leaders "regarded [him] as intellectually 'light' . . ." Yet, at the same time, in his rating system for ranking the candidates, Bush led the list, a full six points ahead of fifth-place Rockefeller. More telling, the Buchanan/Harlow recommendations for Rockefeller both zeroed in on the same element that each man regarded as decisive: the media. Rockefeller would be safe, Buchanan suggested, because either Governor Reagan or Senator Goldwater would "cause a mighty rupture in the liberal establishment and tear up the pea patch with the national press corps . . ." Harlow made much the same point by arguing that a "Rockefeller choice would be hailed by the media normally most hostile to Republicanism . . ."[57]

Bush and Rockefeller were clearly the front-runners, at least among Republican officeholders who were canvased informally. Senators, for example, gave Bush twelve first-, second-, or third-place votes. Only Rockefeller's four-teen topped that. But Bush beat the New Yorker in a poll of House members, who preferred him to the governor by 101 to 68. Ex-Governor William Scranton of Pennsylvania, an establishment party moderate, urged Bush. He had appeal "to all segments of the Republican party," he explained.[58]

Bush had obvious strengths. The Rockefeller name was inherently incen-diary, delineating the party's divisions and evoking reactions from enthusiasm to passionate hostility. Bush's attractions to the GOP's mainstream consensus made him the least controversial front-runner. The *Washington Post* con-firmed his popularity by reporting that he had out-polled Rockefeller by 255 to 181 in a strictly two-way contest.[59] Indeed, Bush topped the four-man list sent to President Ford by Ambassador Kenneth Rush. "His relative youth," wrote Rush, "Texas residence with a New England background, wide popu-larity in business and political circles, and unqualified integrity and ability, combined with his personal qualities of charm and tact, would make him a natural for the new presidential/vice presidential team."[60] Others noted that Bush was further strengthened by his Houston base and family connections on Wall Street.[61] Ford also liked him, respected his loyalty to both the party and to Nixon during the recent troubles. As one of Ford's friends explained very simply, "Bush has character."[62]

Bush met with the new president on each of his first two days in office. Described by *The New York Times* as an "eager" possibility even before Nixon's resignation, he told the press after the first session that they were merely con-cerned with "the future of the party and the country." After his second meet-ing, on Ford's first weekend in the White House, Bush said that "there has been no discussion of any kind that would give any indication that [the vice presidency] has been under official consideration."[63]

Where Dean Burch opted for Bush as his first choice, Pat Buchanan's sur-prisingly pushed for Nelson Rockefeller, the whipping boy of much of the party's right. Rockefeller, argued Buchanan, was "a strong and a safe choice," one who would be an asset to the ticket in 1976, but, most of all, a figure whom the nation would feel comfortable with, if not excited about. And then, in an oblique reference to how the governor had to endure Goldwaterite vehemence in 1964, he added that he was "a figure who has lost the old devil patina with the right." Rockefeller was also Harlow's first choice.

Bush's name, however, was the one accompanied by something novel, lobbying for filling the vice presidential vacancy. His candidacy, more than that of any other, was the most concerted and best organized. Back in Hous-ton, loyal Texans, led by Representative Bill Archer, led the campaign. Other Texans, as well as such out-of-staters as Barber Conable, fell into line.[64] Jim Baker went to Washington on a "spur-of-the-moment trip," and only got as close to the Oval Office as the House visitor's galley, but lobbied nonethe-less. He was, he reported afterward to a friend at the Republican National Committee, "still pulling hard for the bridesmaid to become a bride." To

Don Rhodes at the RNC, he wrote, "Everybody down here still has their fingers crossed."[65] At every opportunity to go on the air, Baker told audiences about Bush's special qualities for the vice presidency. In those post-Watergate days, he logically stressed his man's reputation for honesty and integrity.[66] Delicately, once Bush had polled national committeemen about their choices, he did the politic thing. He remained aloof from the battle by returning to Maine for a "vacation." "All I'm doing," Bush told reporters, "is sitting and waiting."[67]

Meanwhile, his supporters worked on. Some even wore Bush "campaign" buttons. Some of what happened behind the scenes reveals both what was shaping the Republican party as well as George Bush's role.

The GOP's rightward progression was then at a formative stage. Rockefeller was still attractive, one who had considerable sway with the party's liberals. Then serving his fourth term as New York's governor, the man whose name was synonymous with great American fortunes was a proven campaigner and money-raiser. Next to him, however, Bush, in spite of being suspected of only faint conservativism by rightists, loomed as the more acceptable to traditionalists. Richard L. Herman, a national committeeman from Nebraska, was sufficiently concerned about the potential liabilities, especially for the 1976 presidential election, to organize a telephone "boiler room" operation designed to convince Ford to choose the Texan. Herman worked alongside three volunteers from his Washington Hilton hotel room and enlisted others to make calls from more remote places. Bush, in Maine while all that was going on, knew about Herman's activities but, as Herman recalled, never said, "no, please don't." "Many of us had worked on the 1964 Goldwater deal," explained the committeeman, "and it was our feeling that it can cause a so-called rift in the party convention of 1976 if Rockefeller were on the ticket," especially, he added, among Southern conservatives hostile to the New Yorker.[68] Herman's efforts, however, were not without their downside. Bush's former cochairman of the RNC, Tom Evans of Washington, complained that the "active campaign" being waged for Bush did not "properly reflect Republican opinion." Evans also had his doubts about Bush's skill at "substantive matters" and argued that his support was inflated because their opinions had to pass through him.[69] There were other misgivings about the national chairman. Scranton, favorable though he was, doubted Bush's administrative ability. Still, conventional wisdom held that Bush was "everybody's second choice" after Rockefeller.[70] Nobody doubted that if the House had to take a second vote, Bush would win. He was acceptable to just about everyone who liked New York's governor.[71]

Then came word about *Newsweek*'s forthcoming issue. A story being carried by the weekly news magazine, one attributed to an unnamed White House source, targeted George Bush directly. The report, which was published in its issue dated August 26, 1974, revealed that of the $106,000 received by his faltering senatorial campaign in 1970, $40,000 had never been reported as required by the Corrupt Practices Act then in effect. Watergate poison now not only brushed past Bush but even touched him. Even Rockefeller was fingered. Investigative journalist Jack Anderson reported that the New Yorker's money was behind the hiring of hooligans to disrupt the 1972 Democratic convention. Anderson's piece, supposedly based on the contents of Watergate conspirator E. Howard Hunt's files, was shot down by a quick White House investigation. Rockefeller, they concluded, had been smeared by "hearsay evidence" planted by "a group of right-wing extremists."[72]

No such rescue helped Bush. The Townhouse Operation had long since come under the scrutiny of the office of the Watergate special prosecutor, which had been authorized to investigate all related matters, including financing. Leon Jaworski had found that Marvin Collins, who handled Bush's campaign's finances, said that no report had been made because it was not assumed that the contribution had gone directly to Bush. Only after it was pointed out that his comments had still left Bush in a gray area did Jaworski give him "full clearance" and omitted the case in his subsequent report.[73]

But that came later, after Ford had gone through the vice presidential selection process. Until Jaworski got around to it, the stigma remained. Bush's relationship to Nixon was inherently damning, even without the Liedtke-Mosbacher association, which was certainly available for dredging up by opponents. Bush had a known "past" with Nixon's discredited administration. Rockefeller, whatever the allegations, had none. For a new administration devoted to the healing process, trying to keep its distance from all things Nixon, that link made George Bush a political liability. Rockfeller and fellow contender Donald Rumsfeld, Ford's chief of staff, represented, in the president's view, the next generation of leadership. For an "accidental" president suddenly acceding to power in a world that barely knew who he was, Nelson Rockefeller represented continuity without contamination.[74]

Ford later insisted that the Townhouse matter played no role in his final choice. He explained the choice of Rockefeller as one that sought to "reach out to somebody who had a reputation of being a moderate Republican," implying that Bush was a shade more on the conservative side. Ford also recalled that he had served on a committee where he had a chance to work closely with the governor and to get to know him better. That very "extensive, very effective experience as a state governor was the prime reason I wanted him as my vice president," said Ford about the man who had been elected four times while Bush had failed in both senatorial races from Texas. "My decision was an affirmative one for Nelson."[75]

Bush got some advance inkling of what was going on. He heard that Rockefeller had already been flown to Washington for the announcement. When the president's call came through, he was his gracious self. He was "trying to relax me," quite the opposite from Bush's experience with Richard Nixon, with whom "there was never a totally relaxed camaraderie," only "some formal deal."[76]

Ford, apologetic, said, according to Bush's memory, "It was a very hard call. You had tremendous support, and I just wanted you to know that." "I think Ford was standing in the main floor of the residence and he was going into the East Room to announce the appointment . . . it didn't come as a total surprise . . . it was very nice to be considered and it was a little disappointing. But I never really thought it was going to happen."[77]

"Yesterday was a real downer," Bush wrote to his old friend, Lud Ashley. "I guess I had let my hopes zoom unrealistically, but today perspective is coming back and I realize I was lucky to be in the game at all."[78]

Ford did get his moderate. Laird, as Bush reflected with bitterness, had done his job all too well, kind of "a master's voice from behind the scenes. I've never understood this Machiavellian side of Laird," he added for his diary. "I like him, but I've never felt close to him. And I suppose I wouldn't be human if I didn't say I felt his hand on the VP situation very clearly and coolly. But I felt it on the back, not on the front."[79]

Laird had not, however, served Ford very well. For all Rockefeller's recent efforts to ingratiate himself with the right wing, heartland Republicans chaffed at the New York "liberal." Rockefeller Northeasterners were becoming the outcasts of the new GOP.

When the press reached Bush on the day the president released his Sunday morning bombshell announcing the pardon of Richard Nixon, he told them that the nation will be better off "with this behind us" and that Nixon "has paid a big price already."[80]

Bush met with Ford two weeks later, summoned to the White House to be offered a choice of diplomatic portfolios. Either London or Paris were available, but so was Beijing. Washington continued to skirt the problem of formal recognition by retaining a liaison office in the Chinese capital. Bush, if he wanted the post, would take it over from the outgoing career foreign service officer David K. E. Bruce. He would also be able to keep his title of ambassador.

Bush took about forty-five minutes to decide. He preferred China, he told the president, making a choice that a friend later attributed to George's desire "to get as far away from the stench of Watergate as possible."[81] As Barbara described the Ford-Bush meeting of September 3, 1974, "the more George talked, the more excited he got. I missed being with George—he had traveled a great deal as RNC chairman—and the thought of having him to myself sounded like the answer to my prayers." She had had enough of receptions and dinner parties at the UN, which led him to turn down "all the stylish embassies," even something as splendid as the Court of St. James's. China was remote, exotic, "where the action was," home to one-fourth of the world's people.[82] "Everybody in the United States wants to go to China. Everyone wants a visa. The professors don't know a hell of a lot more about what's going to happen in China than the politicians or the military."[83]

"Am I running away from something?" he wondered while en route to

China on a Japanese Airlines DC-8, and decided that, no, he wasn't. He *really* was looking forward to the "intrigue and fascination of China." He was eager and dismissed warnings about "isolation." Nor did he fear that he was buying into a political dead end, that he would be, as friends feared, "out of sight, out of mind." Such qualms yielded to his realization that going to Beijing, more than to either European capital, would give him a unique opportunity to enhance his foreign policy credentials, "credentials," he contemplated, "that not many Republican politicians will have."[84] To a reporter who asked, he replied that he needed a change of pace, adding, "What the hell. I'm fifty. It won't hurt anything."[85] Beside, neither he nor Barbara had ever been there.

China was also a "sabbatical," a shot at rest and rehabilitation, at the head of the U.S. mission in Beijing. History and politics had combined to prevent diplomatic recognition: the Maoist overthrow of Chiang Kai-shek, wars in Korea and Vietnam, and, most recently, the horrendous "Cultural Revolution" of the sixties. In that climate, the interests of U.S. diplomacy were restricted to the semiofficial, almost ad hoc operation of the Beijing office. Over one billion Chinese, comprising the world's most populous nation, could hardly be ignored, especially within the context of the ongoing cold war and the still unresolved situation in Southeast Asia.

Bush's credentials were enhanced by earlier contacts with high-ranking Chinese from his UN days, including such people as Deputy Foreign Minister Quiao Guanha. Bush's presence in Beijing would also continue to give the U.S. the protocol of having an "ambassador" in the Chinese capital. A high-ranking American on the spot would also be useful should his presence coincide with a transition in Beijing from the old leadership of Mao Tse-tung and Chou En-lai, then obviously in their final years.[86] In a land with seemingly endless commercial opportunities awaiting American developers, having a diplomat in the liaison office with business experience was entirely appropriate.

On another level, for the Bushes, the Chinese mission was clearly a sojourn, a time-out, a respite from Washington and political wars. Meanwhile, expecting a brief overseas stay, he and Barbara kept their Washington home at 5161 Palisades Lane. Ford's presidency had, by then, lost its early glow, diminished considerably by that Sunday-morning announcement in early September that Nixon had accepted a presidential pardon.

Kissinger warned Bush about boredom, perhaps signaling that the Chinese portfolio would be as empty as the one at the UN. Morale there was already low. Why Bush should prefer it over London or Paris puzzled the secretary of state, although he did concede that Bush might be able to "do some substantive business."[87] When the two men met in Beijing in November of 1974, Kissinger suggested that Bush was really interested in running for the presidency in 1980. It was too soon for talk about the White House, Bush told him, dropping the subject.[88] Kissinger, he learned before long, could ignore him as easily in Beijing as he had done in New York. He heard that the secretary was telling people that "George doesn't think I am spending enough time on China." As far as Bush was concerned, the real problem was Kissinger's habit of keeping all the "cards so close to his chest" that those at State were unwilling to take any initiatives. Contacts between the liaison office and Washington were so fragile that Bush even had to send a special cable to get updated information on when Kissinger was due to arrive. "It is difficult to define what our function is here," Bush noted privately. "How much leeway we think we should have. How much initiative we should take etc. [*sic*]" He had deep misgivings about Kissinger's "spectacular personal" diplomacy, whether in Asia or the Middle East, wishing that the secretary had more respect for teamwork. "I am wondering if it is good for our country to have as much individual diplomacy. Isn't the president best served if the important matters are handled by more than one person?" When Kissinger arrived to deal with the Chinese leadership, Bush was ignored.[89]

Most painful was the need to contain his pride, to turn away from the endless affronts to his sensitivity as an American. "I am already struck by the contrast in China," he noted right after he arrived. "The beauty in many ways. The courteous friendliness of the individuals with whom you do talk. The desire to please in many ways. And that is [in] contrast with the basic closed-society aspect of things. Lack of freedom. Discipline of people." Anti-Americanism flowed naturally from all Chinese media, especially the Hsin-hau News Bulletin (which Bush called the "Red news") with continuous invectives about U.S. imperialism that even came out of public speakers mounted in parks. The atmosphere was hardly more comfortable at diplomatic receptions, where Bush was treated warmly and humanely as an individual, but which also reeked of hostility and tension. "The American people do not have any concept of how others around the world view America," he realized. "We think we are good, honorable, decent, freedom loving. Others are firmly convinced that though they like the people themselves in our country, that we are embarking on policies that are anathema to them. We have a mammoth public relations job to do on all of this." Especially "heartbreaking" was their rejection of American explanations about the military role in Vietnam.[90]

Bush was, perhaps above all, tuned in to the enormous potential for developing trade relations with an open China. The Maoist nation in which he found himself was, however, not quite ready for capitalism. It was still in conflict between ideology and economic need, with a disturbing tendency to single out the American market as the home of the "imperialist enemy." Bush found an actual decline in U.S.-Sino trade, due largely to reduced sales of American agricultural products. By July 1975, the trade deficit was running as high as two to one with, as he noted, "no major sales in sight." American businessmen, he found, were handicapped by political preferences. Purchases from the U.S. were largely confined to such particularly good buys as oil field equipment. Too often, the Chinese shopped elsewhere whenever possible.[91]

That year's May Day festivities were especially distressing for Bush. In the first place, the State Department had not told him about the surrender of the Vietnamese countryside north of Saigon; he heard it at an embassy "drinking party." Then, as Saigon itself collapsed, he feared the "domino" effect of Thailand, the Philippines, and a good hunk of Southeast Asia rushing to join a new alignment.[92] That possibility loomed as an overwhelming reality as he watched and felt the momentum of a clear power surge. It was amazing to see South and North Vietnamese flags fly side by side over Hanoi's Beijing embassy. There were fireworks everywhere. City parks served as theaters for "cultural performances," with singing children outfitted "in the brightest colors of greens and reds and yellows and blues you've ever seen." Major public buildings—the Great Hall of the People, the railroad station, hotels, Tiananmen Square—were festively lit. So was every street. The next day was gorgeous, but Bush had to sit back and watch the celebrating go on and on.[93]

Upon leaving Washington in October, he figured, the China stay would give him the chance to enjoy the luxury of reading, finally catching up on two decades of lost time.[94] He treated himself to a novel, James Michener's *Centennial,* and was fascinated by William Safire's insider account of the Nixon administration, *Before the Fall,* which left him with "mixed emotions."

Overwhelmingly, however, he focused on his new assignment. He read Pearl Buck's popular work of the 1930s, *The Good Earth,* which, along with her subsequent writings, had done so much to shape American sympathy for the Chinese people. He read about the Manchu Dynasty from a biography of the Empress Cixi, and traced China's transformation from empire to republic. He read the writings of Chairman Mao and Doak Barnett's *China After Mao.* There were, Bush decided, great inconsistencies in what Mao "says now and what he used to believe. . . . But come to think of it," Bush added, "who shouldn't change his mind?" His reading also included *The Other Half of the Sky: A China Memoir* by the actress Shirley MacLaine. MacLaine, a Democrat and George McGovern activist in the last presidential election, astonished Bush by her "naiveté" and, as he wrote, by "the emotional kind of acceptance of things." Her book, he thought, was little more than a salute to Chairman Mao with "fist held high."[95]

His reading marked for Bush a break with past assumptions, a departure from the pronationalist consensus of his early adult years. Pearl Buck's exotic land, emblematic of human misery, a place earnest missionaries had tried to rescue from earthly pain, was, in American minds, a tiny, desolate orphan wailing on train tracks in Manchuria, victimized by Japanese slaughter, and bearers of unendurable suffering until Americans finally brought freedom. Only four years after V-J Day, however, Chiang and his nationalists were forced to retreat to Taiwan ahead of conquering Communist revolutionaries. Once again, a noble ancient civilization was brutalized, this time the result of failed policies by State Department visionaries who romanticized Mao and his followers as "agrarian reformers." Those "reformers" slaughtered Americans in Korea, joined the nuclear club, and instigated the vicious Cultural Revolution. But, insisted author Buck, the longing for freedom remained alive. "Nothing and no one can destroy the Chinese people," she wrote just before her death. "They are relentless survivors. They are the oldest civilized people on earth. Their civilization passes through phases but its basic characteristics remain the same. They yield, they bend to the wind, but they never break."[96] He encountered a new, far more jaundiced, view of Chiang's nationalists from the pages of Theodore H. White's *Thunder Out of China,* and Barbara Tuchman's *Stilwell and the American Experience in China.* His reading helped him "understand a great deal about mistakes that were made in the past" and alerted him to the magnitude of American naiveté about Chiang. He read *A Mortal Flower* by the pseudonymous Han Suyin, and Anthony Grey's *Hostage in Peking,* about the Cultural Revolution. Grey taught Bush that while you "can get close to these people," it was still necessary "to keep in mind that if a word comes from some unseen mysterious place, we could be cut off, isolated, and . . . vilified." He was, he noted at the same time, fortunate that he had not yet "felt any hostility on a personal basis at all."[97]

"I wish I could tell what China's real interest is," Bush confided in his diary almost a year later. "After reading *Hostage in Peking* and reliving some of the horrors of the Cultural Revolution I can't be sure. Should Soviet [*sic*] Union and China get together, it would be, in my opinion, a whole new ball game. . . . the question is what is their real heartbeat? What is their real intent? I don't think the United States has anything to fear from China. The talk about how we lost China infuriates the Chinese and *now* it infuriates me. I can see where it is very clearly wrong. China was not ours to lose and that has been part of the problem."[98]

It was almost like being exiled to a "Mongolian power plant." Secure but isolated on the other side of the globe, dependent on the Voice of America and dated newspapers from the States, the Bushes remained largely within the "embassy row" part of Beijing that looked very much, as he later wrote, like Southern Californian architecture, "Sunset Boulevard—one part Spanish, one part Oriental," guarded by People's Liberation Army soldiers in their green uniforms. Their private residence consisted of an upstairs apartment above the office, with a sitting/dining room, four bedrooms, and two large baths. A half dozen Chinese performed the domestic chores. None of the cleaning maids or cooks spoke English, and so there was no contact even there.

Bush managed passably well with his college French, but coping with Chinese was another matter. When he took Barbara to the airport for one of her stateside trips and tried to cash a few yuen, the man at the exchange window tried to be helpful. He smiled patiently and was as polite as could be. But Bush felt lost, uncomprehending. "Oh, the frustration," he recorded.[99]

Yet he was not entirely hopeless, as Tang Xiaojun ("Mrs. Tang") came over to give him lessons, often five days a week. "When you meet my wife, would you please tell her to stop laughing at me when I take my Chinese lessons," he joked at the outset.[100] By the fifth lesson, he decided that the sounds were "beginning to click," although the whole process was "extremely difficult." He finally began to get a feel for the tone, and the language itself seemed less alien. Mrs. Tang, polite and patient as were all the Chinese he met, put on paper all the expressions he would need in the course of his work. A diplomat needed to know the right lingo for playing tennis. He should be able to say "You have a good forehand," and follow proper etiquette in telling a fellow player that he lost without saying "You lose." By February, Bush felt reasonably qualified as a diplomat. He could pick up a phone and, with a certain amount of confidence, invite a Chinese official for a match. And, triumphantly, he actually kept score in the language. He reached another landmark in July when he found he could carry on a reasonable conversation with his barber.[101]

Even at church on Sundays, he was lost in a Chinese-speaking world. Protestants who wanted to worship—as he noted around him when he and Barbara attended services in a "beaten-up old house" that served as the Bible Institute—had little choice but to be interdenominational. On any given Sunday, they might be led by any one of three ministers, an Anglican, a Methodist, or a Presbyterian. The congregation numbered anywhere from a dozen to twenty. For the most part, especially since Catholics attended services at the cathedral, he and Barbara were the only ones from the liaison office. The others were mainly Africans and Europeans, including someone from the Dutch embassy and the Austrian ambassador. Everything, including Communion, was conducted in Chinese, even such traditional hymns as "Nearer My God to Thee" and "Holy, Holy, Holy," which to Bush's relief, he was able to follow from English song sheets. "It was a very moving service," he responded after their first Sunday at the Bible Institute, although, as he later noted, there was no sermon and, other than the hymns, the services consisted of three Bible readings, the Lord's Prayer, and, other than Communion, the Apostles' Creed.[102] The little church also served as the site for Doro's baptismal, which was performed in June, just two months shy of her sixteenth birthday. The ceremony, which occurred then because so many of their children were visiting them at the time, was, George noted, "a very special day, an occasion."[103] All in all, the "Bushers" were very visible outside the compound, often seen riding their bikes and sometimes, as when George went cycling in a red T-shirt and blue-checked pants, drawing long stares. They also traveled to Tientsin, Shanghai, and "tropical, humid" Canton, seeing the sights for themselves and guiding visitors. Even Neil Mallon, then eighty, came with his wife. The couple arrived only five days before Doro, Neil, and Marvin got there, looking "great, giggling, bubbling over with enthusiasm," and, hardly settling in, rushed away to play tennis and basketball. They and their entourage turned heads wherever they went, and that included C. Fred Bush, the cocker spaniel given as a gift by Marvin to his mother. Dogs in China were rarities so Fred, named for their dear friend C. Fred Chambers from Houston, became an immediate wonder. People "stared expressionless." The ever-present Red Guards looked "startled" when they had their first glimpse, especially as C. Fred ran along with Bush during an early morning jog past the Kuwait, Greek, and Chad missions. Bush suspected the disagreeable air in the city was responsible for the frequent respiratory illnesses that troubled them. Blowing sand was also annoying, although not as intense as in West Texas, and coal dust covered almost everything. "Things get gray here," Bush noted after he had been in the city only a few days. C. Fred was beginning to look "kind of gray" even after Barbara had given him two baths. By mid-November he decided that "Fred's personality has changed. Anyone that gets within twenty yards of him gets a growl." If the natives were startled by the cycling Bushes, whose style contrasted so much with the David Bruces, to say nothing of their children and the dog, they were especially taken with George's mother. Dottie, at age seventy-three, arrived in Beijing on a beautiful day, took twenty minutes or so to "shape up," then cycled with the rest of the family past the Great Hall of the People. "You should have seen the people stare at old momma on the bicycle" Bush said to his tape recorder.[104]

Evenings were spent reading or, as was especially his habit, writing notes to friends back in the States. The social life of the embassy subjected them to some of the city's cultural offerings, such as the Chinese opera. They also visited the Great Wall, saw the Yangtze River with its famous high bridge, and in Xian viewed the tomb of China's third-century B.C. Emperor Ch'in Shih Huang Ti and the thousands of terra-cotta horses and soldiers.[105]

Bush found Beijing an amazing city of contrasts and, for all the pollution, "spic and span." "We bike around with absolutely no concern for security," Bush wrote to Lud Ashley. "Our house remains unlocked," he added, as though oblivious of the ever-present guards.[106]

Bush's thirty-member USLO staff had considerable talent, headed by John Holdridge and Jim Lilly. Lilly, a career CIA officer, was the agency's station chief in Beijing. Herbert Horowitz was the mission's economist and Don Anderson its expert on Chinese political affairs. None became as well known, or the source of as much personal embarrassment for Bush, as did Jennifer Fitzgerald.

She first became his secretary during his last year with the Republican National Committee, recommended by Dean Burch. Jennifer, of English birth, had been married at the age of twenty-three and divorced within a year. She kept her married name and began her own career; she worked with Burch when he was chairman of the Federal Communications Commission. After serving Bush briefly at the RNC, she went with him to China, where he wanted her to serve as a "buffer" between him and the State Department. The arrangement, Bush hoped, might work as well for him there as Tap Bennett had done while he was at the United Nations.[107]

Fitzgerald ran a "no-nonsense" office. She complemented Bush's personality by supplying an efficiently formal operation. In Beijing, amid demands of the State Department, the other embassies, the Chinese bureaucracy, and visiting American businessmen she had to be tough. Some supplicants resembled the "hard-sell artists" that reminded Bush "of some of the brokers that poured into Midland when money was flowing around pretty freely in the fifties." They included a number with a "fast buck" approach, oilmen, a Midwestern brewer, and representatives of the city of El Paso's interest in negotiating a "tremendous deal for liquified natural gas." The investor types were often "pushy," and "insensitive" about the Chinese, lacking good sense about dealing with people who were more wary of commerce than ideology.[108]

Jennifer had the savvy to deal with them. She understood the politics involved, knew how to cope with the various situations, and had a greater degree of sophistication than any of the others in the office. Her imperiousness and special access to the boss also made it easy for her colleagues to resent her. "I hate these kinds of problems," Bush noted when Fitzgerald complained about their carping.[109]

The gossip that later dogged the Bush-Fitzgerald relationship undoubtedly began at the mission. Barbara's absence for much of the year to take care of family functions and to attend to other matters back home, helped to encourage that speculation.[110] More than a decade of probing, which became most intense during the 1992 presidential campaign, failed to uncover any evidence of a Bush-Fitzgerald romantic relationship. It is, nevertheless, clear that while in "that small, closed" diplomatic circle, their friendship was visible.[111] More than with others of his staff, Bush got together with her outside of the office, sometimes alone. They shopped together at Beijing's Marco Polo store. After Barbara returned to the States aboard Kissinger's plane, they spent an afternoon socializing at the American embassy in Tokyo before continuing on their flight to a conference in Honolulu. They returned to Beijing, after an absence of twelve days, the only passengers in the first-class section of an Iran Airlines Boeing-707. Not more than ten other passengers were on the flight. "The food was fantastic," he recorded. "Service was excellent. And we arrived very tired but well fed on the finest Iranian caviar." As his gatekeeper, Jennifer clearly had special access to her boss.[112]

His first big respite from China came right after the start of the new year. The Alfalfa Club, where Washington's political elite gathered for some satirical fun at annual January dinners, invited him to become their "President of the United States." "My father was in the Alfalfa Club," he later recalled. "I was in the Alfalfa Club. It was a big honor, so back I came."[113] He flew to Washington, was "inaugurated" and, on becoming violently ill, was admitted to Georgetown University Hospital in totally "miserable" shape. The attack reminded him of a similar experience after eating the same kind of pepper at the Pakistani embassy some time earlier. The medics thought his "pesky" infection may have been an amoeba. They put him through a barium enema test (which had to be redone) and a biopsy, but failed to see "any definite amoebae."[114] The tests did show that his old ulcer problem seemed to be healing. He was administered a dose of Diodoquin and confined to the hospital for the rest of the week. On his return to China, he stopped in at Rawalpindi for a reunion with an old United Nations acquaintance, Pakistani President Zulfihar Ali Bhutto. Once back in Beijing, Bush felt better and began to regain some of his weight. But shortly thereafter, the problem returned, this time in the middle of a meeting with the Bulgarian ambassador. Bush, "with no embarrassment whatsoever," coolly switched on the TV set to play a videotape of Nixon's arrival in China and disappeared into the bathroom.[115]

His health returned, but settling back into the compound seemed harder. He had been there about half a year and was getting antsy. Anyone who knew George Bush could appreciate that. Reaching him by phone from the States was no easy matter for friends, not at the long-distance rate of $16 for the first three minutes. "Back in Washington or at the United Nations the telephone was ringing all the time," Barbara told an interviewer from the *Washington Post*. "George would come home and say, excuse me, and pick up the phone. . . . I think he misses the phone as much as anything."[116] Barbara, thoughtful as ever, tried to compensate for the void by calling him at least once a day. They also began their days by listening to the shortwave broadcasts of the Voice of America at seven A.M. and went through the translated editorials from *People's Daily*, the six-page official Communist party organ.[117]

Once again he turned his attention to domestic politics, specifically to the Texas governorship and the 1978 election. Once Ford had won elections in 1976 for a full term, George would return to Houston, prop up his income by getting back into a business, then "shoot for the governorship." Briscoe, then in the state's first four-year gubernatorial term after having served a two-year turn, would surely be up for reelection. Beating him would have its attractions. Victory, with a Republican taking over the statehouse at Austin, would undoubtedly position Bush nicely for national politics. If nothing else, he thought, he'd finally get the bug about statewide politics out of his system.

But the downside, he realized, was also strong. Texas had yet to elect a Republican governor, at least not since Reconstruction and, as he thought about it in 1975, it was hard to figure the duration of the post-Watergate damage. Failure would give his record another losing campaign, which it didn't need. He had a different thought: 1978 was Tower's year for reelection to the Senate, another definite downside. John, he knew, had long had an eye on the governorship and, if he decided to shoot for that, how could Bush get in his way? And if Tower just wanted another term in Washington, wouldn't a Bush candidacy divert money that would be needed for another senate run? Texas Republicans had enough digging out to do, and Bush had done his best to keep himself above their intramural squabbling. Even while he was in China, some of his people, especially Jim Allison, were active in the newly formed Associated Republicans of Texas. So things were changing. He could be even more vulnerable to the previous criticism that he was fine at the national level but had no "qualifications for state government at all."[118]

Even at that moment, with a Ronald Reagan right-wing challenge to President Ford yet to materialize, did Bush want to get involved in presidential reelection politics, which such involvement would necessitate? "I am," he admitted to himself, "a little out of touch with what it all means down there," but still, that didn't rule out some "quiet work on the situation." Yes, he wrote to Lud a few days later, it was amazing how out of touch he really was.[119] Bush let the 1978 Texas matter ride, helping to pave the way for the razor-thin election of Bill Clements as the first Republican governor in the state's modern history, while Tower, fending off unsubstantiated charges about public drunkenness, withstood his most serious challenge yet.[120]

Even as he decided against the Texas race, there were other signals that his China tour was nearing an end. White House counsel Jack Marsh noted the following in a memorandum to President Ford: "George Bush has probably had enough of egg rolls and Peking by now . . . he's one hell of a presidential surrogate, and would be an outstanding spokesman for the White House between now and November 1976. Don't you think he would make an outstanding secretary of commerce or a similar post sometime during the next six months?"[121] The job went to Rogers Morton, who moved over to Commerce from Interior that March, but Morton himself suggested that Bush might want to get into the cabinet on another level. And Maurice Stans, Nixon's former super fund-raiser, wanted him to help the campaign. Bush, never comfortable with the money part of politics, wrote in his diary, "I hope it doesn't come true." Inevitably, as he went through his dated copies of *The New York Times* and *Washington Post,* his attention to matters at home only intensified. He was especially troubled by the continuing allegations of CIA involvement in domestic spying and covert activities. The whole thing was somewhat of a dilemma, he thought, between "guaranteeing freedoms which would make one want to see the excesses of the CIA controlled, but also conservative in the fact that institutions that have served to preserve freedom, or to hopefully prop it up in some places, are being dismantled."[122]

Bush's China tour coincided with the fall of the U.S.-backed Lon Nol regime in Cambodia. Lon Nol's military rule had taken over in March of 1970, ousting the neutralist regime of Prince Norodom Sihanouk, who had given up his throne as king and served as head of state during a parliamentary government. The Lon Nol victory, which came just before the American invasion of Cambodia in 1970 to thwart North Vietnamese and Vietcong military operations against the South Vietnamese, forced the prince into exile in China. But by April 1975, while Bush was in Beijing and just five years after Lon Nol had taken control, Lon Nol's power collapsed despite American assistance. Another corrupt and autocratic anti-Communist regime was about to go under, this time in the capital city of Phnom Penh. Secretary of State Kissinger directed Bush to intercede with Sihanouk to thwart the imminent enemy takeover. The contact was made by Bush's deputy, John Holdridge, who performed the delicate task of attempting to reinstall the prince under a new neutralist regime. But it was too late. Lon Nol was finished, and Sihanouk, ever eager to accommodate himself to all sides, had been in cahoots with the Communist Khmer Rouge. So he turned down the American effort. The prince then rode back into power with the Communists, only to resign a year later in protest against the brutality of Cambodian strongman Pol Pot, which ultimately cost some two to three million lives.[123] The affair marked Bush's most significant diplomatic role in China to date, although only weeks after the Communist takeovers in Cambodia and Saigon came the *Mayaguez* incident.

Bush was notified of the affair while attending a picnic, and was ordered to deliver a note of protest to the Chinese government. Conscious of the circumstances that surrounded the North Korean seizure of an American ship, the *Pueblo,* during the Johnson years, and aware that a tepid response could betray a sense of helplessness after the recent reverses, neither Ford nor Secretary Kissinger had any desire to contribute to the specter of Communists taking over the rest of Southeast Asia. The firing at the S.S. *Mayaguez,* a merchant ship, with a crew of thirty-nine, and its seizure by the Khmer Rouge was seen as a direct challenge. The vessel had been moved to a nearby island and its crew removed. The Chinese claim, hotly denied in a Bush protest conveyed in Beijing, was that the ship had trespassed in Cambodian waters. Ford, prodded by Kissinger, ordered the bombing of the mainland and the simultaneous deployment of marines to rescue the men. So vital was the need to "show the flag" that the assault and rescue mission was ordered to take place even after the Cambodians announced that the crew had been freed. The American loss totaled thirty-eight, including those killed in a collateral raid on Thailand, but the point was made without casualties among the captives. Kissinger's advice to "look ferocious" paid off. The Ford administration, its fortunes sagging, gained eleven points in approval ratings. A subsequent report showed that the release had resulted from pressure by the People's Republic of China.[124]

Bush was fully aware, as an early biographer has written, that by being there he was "playing in Kissinger's sandbox" and leaving all "the high-level, substantive dealings with the Chinese power-wielders" to the secretary of state.[125] But he could not leave that summer of 1975, one of the few times the Bushes, Walkers, and Wears, Barbara's maternal relatives, did not spend at least a few August days in Kennebunkport. At least most of the Bush children got to Beijing that year, except for Jeb, who was busy with his job at the Texas Commerce Bank. In 1974, he had married a seventeen-year-old Mexican girl, Columba, whom he had met while an exchange student in Mexico City.[126] Marvin took a break from working as an intern in the congressional office of Bush's friend, Bill Steiger of Wisconsin.

Bush lingered on at his post until December, and when he got the call to return, his prospects were not promising. Ford appeared to be blocking his way for a second time, either into the vice presidency or for a shot at the presidency itself. It became clear in mid 1975, and was confirmed toward the end of the year, that his "sabbatical" in China would not be rewarded by either a step upward, or, as he and Barbara wanted at the very least, the opportunity to return to Houston. As his old congressional friend, Barber Conable, noted, "everything George took on during that period of time added to his maturity because it was an unpleasant experience," and now he faced what appeared to be his own execution rather than a deserved reward.[127]

CHAPTER TWELVE

"Head Spook"

%

From Beijing, Bush followed developments at the CIA as closely as possible, little knowing that he would become a key player. The agency
was fighting for its very existence, its first institutional crisis in its
twenty-seven-year history. "We were fighting for our survival," recalled CIA
Director William Colby. "Politically, the president had to assert his own role
in running this thing, not just let it run out of hand."[1] Post-Vietnam, post-
Watergate public cynicism made for popular acceptance and indignation in
the face of revelations about an intelligence agency apparently out of control, unimpeded by the Congress, the presidency, or public opinion. It operated, in fact, with its "black budget" that kept it unaccountable, waging its
own clandestine cold war as it saw fit, ascribing sometimes controversial tactics to the interests of "national security." Rumblings about doings out of
CIA headquarters at Langley, Virginia, on the banks of the Potomac, had
begun to surface even before Bush went to China.

Congressional committees investigated vigorously, even as the American
commitment in Southeast Asia was being liquidated, triggered by Colby's
own exposure of the first of the CIA's "family jewels" that detailed the U.S.
role in destroying Chile's Marxist government under Salvador Allende.
Colby went for broke, thinking he would sate appetites by laying secrets out
on the table and buying a breather for the agency. He admitted that the
State Department's earlier assurances to congressional leaders were misleading. Under Kissinger's leadership of the "40 Committee," as it had
come to be known, some $8 million had been authorized to "destabilize"
Allende after the failure to prevent his election. No evidence ever confirmed
that the CIA was instrumental in bringing about Allende's death as well as
his government's fall, but Colby's startling testimony made for a conventional, if unproven, assumption.

Leaks, once sprung, came in a rapid succession.[2] Ex-CIA agent Philip
Agee named agents and detailed other operations. The predictable

response on Capitol Hill came immediately. A bill to create a Joint Committee on Intelligence Oversight won the sponsorship of eleven senators. President Ford, at his September news conference, admitted the CIA's deep involvement in covert actions.

So the story spun out during Bush's China sojourn. No comparable scrutiny of U.S. clandestine cold war activities had ever taken place. No longer kept from public view were accounts about operations against Castro in Cuba, Trujillo in the Dominican Republic, Lumumba in the Congo, as well as Allende. Instances of assassination attempts against foreign leaders were revealed in the Rockefeller Report.[3] *The New York Times* then fanned the uproar by running a series of front-page articles by investigative reporter Seymour Hersh exposing Operation Chaos, the CIA's domestic operations. Hersh's information presented a chilling picture of intelligence operations out of control, financed by the CIA's "black book" budget and unaccountable to Congress as it went after dissidents and journalists exposing questionable practices, including wiretapping and mail tampering.[4] Traditionally, observed Colby, nobody had paid any attention "because it was assumed that intelligence is all secret and therefore the Congress shouldn't get into it. We just had never resolved the question: law, constitution, and intelligence were in two separate categories of the mind."[5] Nixon's role was central to all of this, but information that developed traced abuses back to the Eisenhower, Kennedy, and Johnson years. Coming so soon after Watergate, the impact was sensational. Ford set up his own body of inquiry, the Rockefeller Commission, but Congress appointed two others, one in the Senate under Frank Church of Idaho and, in the House, another under New York's Representative Otis Pike of Long Island.

Conservatives tended to be defensive about the practices; repeatedly, they cited cold war needs as justifications. Their responses contained abundant contempt toward those like Church and Pike, who were suspected of exploiting what should have been national secrets for personal political gain.

A number of developments had already raised hackles on the right: the Southeast Asian situation, Nixon's openings to China, and explorations of detente with the Soviets, and such programs to remedy the effects of racial segregation as school busing and compensatory programs, also known as affirmative action, which often involved quotas. Now, as though there had not been enough deterioration, Nelson Rockefeller was just "a heartbeat away from the presidency."

To William Rusher, publisher of Bill Buckley's *National Review,* the unthinkable had happened, providing further evidence of the need for Ronald Reagan, then about to step down after a second term as California's governor. Rusher met with him in his Sacramento office on August 19, along with two of the governor's good friends, Ed Meese and Mike Deaver, the "gold dust twins" from the West, as Rusher remembered them. Reagan made it plain that not wanting to run for a third term did not mean he was giving up politics. His supporters had other plans for the man whose famous speech for Goldwater in 1964 had filled them with visions of the White House.

For Rusher and his ultraconservative allies, the choice of Rockefeller was a calamity, nothing short of a declaration of war against the party's hard-shell backbone. "God almighty," said Rusher years later, "almost anybody else was a more reliable conservative than Rockefeller"; even George Bush. He could "buy" him although even he was no natural "social conservative." And at least Bush came from Texas, an important factor argued Rusher, when one considered that Ford had ignored the South and the West, the greatest areas of Republican rebirth, by falling back on the Northeast for Rocky. He told *National Review* readers that the time had come for the launching "of a new and independent conservative movement in 1976, designed to carry these potentially dominant regions of a changing America."[6]

Matters only worsened, deepening Ford's morass. Pat Buchanan asked, "Has the Republican vessel been so severely damaged in the Watergate battering that it is no longer seaworthy?"[7] David Broder declared in the *Washington Post* that the "Republican right is a headless horseman."[8] Rusher, together with the conservative publicist and fund-raiser with the most extensive rightist mailing list in the country, Richard Viguerie, began a renewed push for a truly conservative Republican party. He believed that the last half of 1974 "represented the nadir of the conservative movement's long love affair with the GOP."[9]

Rusher and his fellows on the right, F. Clifton White, Richard Viguerie, Howard Phillips, John Ashbrook, M. Stanton Evens, Phyllis Schlafly, Bob Walker, and the Buckley brothers, with such groupings as had been formed as the National Conservative Political Action Committee, the American Conservative Union, the Young Americans for Freedom, H. L. Hunt's Liberty Lobby, and even the remnants of George Wallace's severely wounded Independent party, began a strong push to force Ford to the right, if not to replace him with Reagan. If they could not fashion their new majority within the GOP, to "blend two old wines in a new and bigger bottle" to "establish conservative domination of the American political scene," they might even consider forming a new party.

Their thrust, really an updating of the old Goldwater appeal, was as much a matter of class, culture, and history as simple ideology. Ancestral Democrats, Roman Catholic Democrats as well as Southern Baptists, were leading the movement and breaking away from traditional liberals and their moderate allies. Youthful Irish Catholic intellectuals were dominant at Bill Buckley's *National Review.* Their antielitist dogma reinforced the themes of a George Wallace and a Richard Nixon appealing to conservative populism. How better to sign on grandchildren of New Dealish blue-collar workers. Rusher himself was the product of a socialist grandfather and a father who railed against brutalization of workers. David Keene, an intellectual leader of the new right, was a fellow Midwesterner. His father had cochaired Stevenson's 1952 presidential campaign in Illinois, and his mother was president of the International Auxiliary of the United Auto Workers. Keene saw himself as much in revolt against "the old establishment-type Republicans—those who ran the local company, the board members, the lawyers—who had ties with similar people around the country; it was very much a class thing." You had to be "a member of the Episcopal choir" to be represented by the Elliot Richardsons and Leverett Saltonstalls. People "knew what their ancestors stood for." So it was with Nelson Rockefeller. Whatever the other virtues of George Bush, said Keene, considered from that standpoint, one had to realize that he "came from the wrong place both in terms of the party and in terms of me." Ronald Reagan brought together Keene and Rusher in a common cause, Keene as his earliest political director for a national campaign and Rusher as an ideological guide.[10]

Rusher drafted a forty-thousand word blueprint to bring together economic and social conservatives as a powerful force, what Kevin Phillips labeled the "new right." The *National Review* devoted much of its May issue to *The Making of a New Political Party* under the provocative heading, "A New Party; Eventually, Why Not Now?" Viguerie sent out 100,000 copies of Rusher's book.[11]

Reagan balked at a third party. Counseled by such benefactors as multimillionaire automobile merchant Holmes Tuttle, he resisted repeated lobbying by Rusher and others to accept the new party route. At a banquet in Washington's Mayflower Hotel, the ballroom overflowing with inspired conservatives, the Californian denounced Ford's policies, championed the rightwing thrust, but defiantly called for a GOP reshaped in the right-wing image.[12]

Reagan was well beyond Hollywood. A decade of denouncing high taxes, the "free speech movement" at Berkeley, the welfare system and big government, and timidity toward the Soviet Union had clearly established him as the best hope for leading rightists out "of the wilderness." Thus far, without actually ruling out a presidential run in 1976, his positions served to prod Ford. Chief of Staff Rumsfeld, given the green light by Ford, urged Vice President Rockefeller to surrender to political realities, which he did by facing Ford in the Oval Office to tell him he was quitting. "You can't get the nomination without the right wing," said the vice president, "so I'll take myself out."[13] In addition to his role in shaping the balance of the Ford ticket for 1976, Reagan's national visibility included opposition to a new treaty for the U.S. Canal Zone in Panama, and demanding an accounting of Americans missing in action in Vietnam and a return of survivors being held against their will.

This issue had no plausible solution. Anger over the MIA/POW matter was a handy political mantra, one "for which there is absolutely no hope of solution," as a Ford aide advised in January, although, cruelly, "the expectations of the National League of Families have been raised."[14] The president, warned Max Friedersdorf, was "stirring up the MIA issue again with inflammatory speeches, raising false hopes with MIA families."[15] Into that emotional issue plunged Reagan, with no hope of anything other than arousing passions, anger, flag-waving, and outrage against those ready to compromise with the devil.

But the CIA matter was of more immediate relevance. Piqued at Colby's openness with congressional investigators and responding to the need to demonstrate more oversight in dealing with intelligence matters, Ford relieved the director.

Barbara Bush remained protective of her husband. She tried to put the best of all possible faces on the CIA appointment—his willingness to do his duty, to serve the government however needed, and not least, to reciprocate Ford's friendship. Yet, at the same time, it was far from simple; nor did Bush regard it as a routine call to service, not even on a par with going to China. The CIA was, of course, at the most critical moment of its history, but what made it more sensitive for him, and what he appreciated right away, was the apolitical nature of the post. Most effective directors of central intelligence, or DCIs, were career people, starting with the precedent created by its World War II antecedent, the OSS under William (Wild Bill) Donovan. Allen Dulles, Richard Helms, and Bill Colby had all fit into that category. Jim Schlesinger, out of Harvard, was an anomaly, and his short term had been a disaster. Moreover the current revelations of sensitive activities made it even more essential for the director to have no political agenda. So if Bush took it, all hopes of joining the ticket with Ford in '76 would go down the drain, and who knew what it portended for his political future beyond that? What would warrant sacrificing his presidential ambitions? Rumsfeld, who took over as secretary of defense in the administration's cabinet shake-up that fall, had a motive for shunting Bush off to the CIA, in effect, farming him out. A credible conservative and key player in the Nixon White House, Rumsfeld took a backseat to no one, not even Haig or Haldeman, and steered his organizational system to "diminish the influence of all potential rivals at the White House."[16]

Rumsfeld was more than a contributor to the Bush transfer. He was a promoter. Thought had at first been given to attorney Edward Bennett Williams, but his declension turned it into a Richardson-Bush derby.[17] Bush was clearly Rumsfeld's man. Rumsfeld's mid July memo to Ford lauded Bush's qualifications. He also took pains, as did no one else, to note that Bush was blessed with friends in the intelligence community and understood their missions. And who could ask for a man with higher integrity and proven ability? The only "con" to balance the "pros" was that Bush's "RNC post lends undesirable political cast." Bush's "advantages" clearly sliced two ways. He was in a political game, and politics prevailed.[18]

Barbara's account recalls that she and George were riding their bikes home from church in Beijing in early November when they were notified. An "eyes-only" cable came asking him to return to Washington to head the CIA. Bush "was thrilled," she wrote, once more the dutiful soldier responding to his commander in chief.

But it was not that simple. He was clearly bothered. Was Ford, in effect, sidetracking him for a second time within a year? "Could that be what was happening?" he wrote in his memoir.[19] "Bury Bush at the CIA?" His ability to influence his president had failed him for the second time in just sixteen months.[20]

The immediate reaction was one of resignation. His old business partner, Hugh Liedtke, warned that CIA meant political suicide, but Bush wrote back that he had no choice. The president had so ordered it.[21] As he later said in his confirmation testimony when he got back to Washington, "I was offered the nomination kind of on a silver platter. I cannot tell you that I would not accept it and I frankly do not think in an office where you serve at the pleasure of the president that that should be a criterion for any office . . .—that is just my concept of service and I hope I am motivated in my public life by service."[22]

The committee that heard him testify had no inkling of how upset he had been at the appointment, so dispirited, in fact, that Barbara called on friends to keep him company. Maureen O'Ryan, the British wife of an Argentine diplomat then in Beijing, came over and found how depressed he was over the assignment.[23] George always did respond to people. He had to have them around. He played off them, enjoyed their give and take, kept active in their presence; above all, he was a bad loner. Good company was best for his spirits, especially at such times. Just as that was quintessential George Bush, so was acceptance of the presidential request, now made even more difficult because he and Barbara would not even be able to get back to Houston.

When it was suggested to him in 1995 that he had voluntarily removed himself from the possibility of becoming Ford's vice presidential running mate as the price of getting the CIA directorship, he said, "I told Ford I'm not going to do that, but if you want me in this job enough you will make the caveat."[24] When asked about his political future while still in Beijing, Bush expressed doubt that he had foreclosed his options. But he did concede that the CIA's directorship was "no springboard to political fortune."[25] Briefly complicating matters further, the Watergate Townhouse question surfaced again until Jaworski firmly ended it by stating that Bush had done nothing wrong.[26]

That was the least of it. Ford had placed Bush on the spot, not only handing him a dilemma about his own political future, but by tapping someone whose political background was widely thought to be inappropriate for the post. How could he reconcile the objective requirements of intelligence functions, separating analyses from the political interests of the administration, while remaining positioned as a potential Ford running mate for 1976? The question was raised over and over again, not only by Republicans but by such public interest organizations as Common Cause and fringe groups eager to fight back for having been monitored by government intelligence. As Stuart Symington, the Missouri Democrat on the Armed Services Committee, put it to Bush during the two days of hearings, "If you took this job, then shortly were tapped for vice president, by that time there is no possible way . . . that you could really get to the core of the problem of restoring morale and proper position to the Central Intelligence Agency."[27] Or, as Frank Church in his vigorous opposition to confirmation put it, "It is one thing to choose an individual who may have had political experience, say someone like Elliot Richardson or John Sherman Cooper, two men whose whole public life tended to demonstrate a proven independence as a muted partisan background, and quite another to choose someone whose principal political role has been chairman of the Republican National Committee."[28] Church, whose committee's critique of the agency's operations captured the lion's share of the headlines, first termed the Bush nomination "disturbing." He then looked into an on-air camera and declared on *Face the Nation* that "whoever is chosen should be one who has demonstrated a capacity for independence, who has shown that he can stand up to principle at the cost of public office." Church's message was plain: Bush had not demonstrated a capacity for political principle.[29] That was the sort of thing Bush had to face, politics. Politicians were playing politics by posturing against the insidiousness of politics in government. They were, if nothing else, eager to place themselves on record against the more unsavory aspects of the intelligence process.

Others, meanwhile, determined to substitute ideological integrity for political consensus and looking for leadership from among their own faithful, confronted Ronald Reagan at the Beverly Wilshire Hotel. It was probably, Martin Anderson has written, "the first time Reagan was braced directly with the supply-side tax rate reduction idea."[30] Meanwhile, New York Senator Jacob Javits, a Republican liberal worried about repeating the party's suicidal endorsement of Barry Goldwater, circulated a warning about the "need to back President Ford" to avoid making "the same mistake in 1976 we made in 1964."[31] Bush, apprised of all the currents and urged to prepare for stiff opposition, noted to Friedersdorf from Beijing that "it looks like I am walking into the midst of a real whirlwind, but all I know to do is to give it my all and be direct with the committee."[32]

Neither he nor anyone else appreciated it at the time, but, for those same political reasons, he was fortunate. At the CIA, and away from domestic politics in his Beijing limbo, he could sidestep the political wars. Had he been on the scene, had he been a player for 1976, or in the intramural politics dividing Republicans between "movement conservatives" and traditionalists, he would have been a loser, almost by default. Had he, rather than Bob Dole, become the party's choice as Ford's 1976 running mate, and had a Ford-Bush ticket lost to Jimmy Carter and Walter Mondale, George Bush would have had a reputation as a confirmed loser. Not just a 1976 loser, but a man remembered for having come up short in 1964 as well as in 1970; certainly, as he neared his fifty-first birthday, he was no longer an up-and-coming GOP boy wonder.

To begin with, as seen from within the Ford administration, the designation of Bush's role was not that simple. Not only did the CIA directorship have to be filled, but a replacement was needed at Commerce. Elliot Richardson, Nixon's highly respected former attorney general and now ambassador to Great Britain, was also in line for an appointment. One would get Commerce, the other CIA. "Bush—Has many of the same problems as Elliot," noted a memo from Jack Marsh to Friedersdorf, "but it is even more difficult to communicate with him. Set out the problems with Bush and how to address them."[33]

What did that mean? Was Bush too independent, even more "difficult" than Richardson, who had quit the Nixon cabinet rather than fire Archibald Cox? Or were they worried about the "boy scout," the good government man? He could, as he had in 1970 in the face of dirty campaign tactics suggested by such Nixon people as Charles Colson, refuse to join those who pitched political "red meat." Besides, the mere thought of Nixon's adversary getting CIA made Kissinger go "ballistic, to put it mildly," said a Ford ally.[34]

The whole process was distressing; only some hard work, and Ambassador Bush's personal standing, kept it from being a total disaster. "It's a graveyard for politics," he wrote to his children before leaving China, due to the "abuses of the past on the one hand, and an effort to weaken our capability on the other. Besides," he added about becoming the "chief spook," "it's not always a clean and lovely business."[35] From relative isolation at Beijing, he could only barely follow outlines of the brouhaha over the CIA, not "fully [realizing] the depth of the emotions," as he later told the Senate Armed Services Committee, addressing the fallout from such allegations as Hersh's account of the agency having dossiers on at least 100,000 American citizens and tampering with their civil liberties.[36]

The looming debate about his nomination emphasized the importance of his getting back from China as soon as possible. He had to read up on the CIA's problems, the reports on the various investigative committees, even the testimonies of previous directors of Central Intelligence, and also court the Capitol Hill power structure, especially the congressional leadership and the Senate Armed Services Committee under the chairmanship of John Stennis of Mississippi.

But Ford had further compounded Bush's problems. He chose that moment for a swing around the Far East that included a ceremonial visit to Beijing. It was time "to show the flag," recalled his chief of staff, "partly to keep some balance in terms of our dealings in Europe, in NATO, and with the Soviets . . . [to] develop good ties with China . . ."[37] The vast presidential entourage reached the Chinese capital on December 1 and stayed four days, delaying Bush's return to Washington. Finally, as he started the long flight around the globe, he thanked Jack Marsh for making the preconfirmation arrangements and told him that he planned a layover in Honolulu; he would arrive in the capital on the evening of December 9.[38] There were so many things to do, so much to prepare for, and Ford's staff contended with the details even while Bush was en route. They granted such mundane requests as assigning him parking space #97 on West Executive Avenue.[39]

He undertook his Capitol Hill courtesy calls, seeing thirteen of the sixteen committee members. Then, on the fifteenth and sixteenth, came his two days of sometimes testy confirmation hearings. Both Republicans and Democrats emphasized that they had no doubts about Bush himself; the real issue was that the ambassador was no ordinary politician. He was most successful and well-connected, one whose closeness to the president could become a disadvantage to the country by giving priority attention to the administration's political purposes. With this in mind, New Hampshire's Senator Thomas McIntyre posed a hypothetical question.

"You did not seek this appointment. I know you told me that you felt that if the president wanted you to take this vital position, that your sense of duty to the country and to the president was paramount and you accepted it. Now," the senator went on, "let us assume you are appointed. Let us assume we are moving three or four months down the campaign trail. You are not going to be impervious to that fact. You are going to read the papers, I know."

Then McIntyre plunged his dagger: "What if you get a call from the president next July or August saying, 'George, I would like to see you.' You go to the White House. He takes you over in the corner and he says, 'Look, things are not going too well in my campaign. This Reagan is gaining on me all the time. Now, he is a movie star of some renown and has traveled with the fast set. He was a Hollywood star. I want you to get any dirt you can on this guy because I need it.' Now, what are you going to do in that situation? What can you do and where would you go?"

Bush deflected the thrust coolly. "I do not think that is difficult, sir," he replied. "I would simply say that it gets back to character and it gets back to integrity; and furthermore, I cannot conceive of the incumbent doing that sort of thing," he added in an unmistakable reference to the near past. "But if I were put into that kind of position where you had a clear moral issue, I would simply say no, I have the advantages as everyone on this committee of twenty-twenty hindsight—that this agency must stay in the foreign intelligence business and must not harass American citizens, like in Operation Chaos, and that these things have no business in the foreign intelligence business. Under my leadership they will not have, and so that causes me no problem whatsoever because, as I have said, and I really believe, I am putting politics behind me on this."[40]

He never did convince McIntyre, who still believed George Bush was being installed "to hold the fort and smother problems" and not to make more trouble. The ambassador was, after all, as everybody understood, "a cut above the ambitious bureaucrats who had characterized Nixon's presidency."[41] McIntyre afterward joined fellow Democrats John Culver, Patrick Leahy, and Gary Hart to comprise the four-vote minority against the twelve who agreed to send the nomination to the floor.

Other than that, Bush emerged from those two days with his dignity intact. He deplored the moral lapses, the "appalling" tactics necessitated by "ruthless" and "tough" people who will themselves "resort to schemes that are not overly pleasant," but refused to yield to pressure to eschew political assassinations as a weapon of last resort. He suggested that it would be folly for the nation to be so straitjacketed when confronted with another Hitler.[42] He drew a careful line between protecting secrets and accountability, discreetly acceding to the possibility of greater congressional oversight. While he favored, and continued to do so as DCI, keeping Congress informed about "every penny of the CIA budget," he resisted public disclosure. A handy wedge could thus be given to those jeopardizing national security by opening the lid on all CIA operations. Nor would he forfeit the right to be on Ford's ticket in 1976. Forcing appointees to take such pledges as preconditions could clearly become a "very dangerous precedent," as the administration argued. Few were buying that point, however. As one witness before the committee, Common Cause's David Cohen, put it, "a CIA head who is ready to consider high elective office less than one year after his appointment will be perceived to service the short-term political needs of a sitting president rather than the duties of the agency and the best interests of the nation."[43]

Just three days later, Ford called Bush in. He had the draft of a letter to Chairman Stennis giving the committee what it wanted, the disavowal of political ambitions for 1976. Bush suggested one addition; he wanted a line saying that he had "urged" the president to accept his decision. The letter went off to Stennis on the eighteenth. That still displeased the minority Democrats, who argued in a letter to their colleagues that the public would still be suspicious "of the potential for political abuse of the agency."[44] The Bush nomination, McIntyre declared on the Senate floor, was "an insensitive affront to the American people." They went through two hours of debate on that last Wednesday of January, placing themselves on record with the same points, over and over again, before confirming Bush by a 64 to 27 vote. The Democratic majority obviously broke ranks to back him, along with all Republicans but one. Jesse Helms of North Carolina voted nay, objecting to Bush's political background.[45] Barbara, seated in the gallery along with Ford's lawyer, Jack Marsh, smiled and waved to supporters on the floor.[46]

The swearing-in that Saturday was a festive occasion. Bush, ever attentive to details involving people, invited five hundred to celebrate the event in the bubble auditorium of the CIA's Langley, Virginia, headquarters. They were all there, the ubiquitous Kissinger, Vice President Rockefeller, Secretary Rumsfeld, and CIA employees. Undercover agents, however, were explicitly kept away because of the "risk of exposure."

The auditorium was reached through the main building's foyer, which had, on the left side, a list of eighteen agents killed in action, although the name of the most recent victim, Richard Welch, shot dead in Greece only a few weeks earlier, was yet to be added. In fact, thirteen others had actually been lost, but their names were deemed too sensitive for the CIA to disclose. Along the left wall was a verse, "And Ye Shall Know the Truth and Truth Shall Make You Free," a favorite Scripture reading from one of the great legendary spooks, Allen Dulles.

The new DCI was sworn in by Justice Potter Stewart while Barbara held the Bible.[47]

Bush emerged as the agency's most popular director since Dulles. According to Bill Colby, "I would say he gave it dignity."[48]

Critics used his year at the CIA to prove their point that George Bush was a good guy but superficial. He took on as his deputy Henry Knoche, a likeable, career CIA man, who was qualified more because he was the director's mirror image than for experience in covert operations. His deputy director for Operations, William Wells, was "a jolly, attractive man, but short on the qualities needed for that severely taxing assignment."[49]

Bush worked hard, too hard in Barbara's opinion; back to twelve-hour days. Barbara, accustomed to having him around, enjoyed being back on Palisades Lane, but his frequent absence was a letdown. The period became her most trying since George's absence in the South Pacific.

Even worse was that side of him that those familiar with his affability and fondness for human contact did not really understand. Barbara did, and that complicated the life of the nation's chief spook. The same discipline that kept him going, that made for unwavering loyalty, extended to his own ability to distinguish the public from the private, to keep not only his emotions, but also his most private thoughts and activities locked up. George Bush knew how to separate the classified from the unclassified.

All of which left Barbara an outsider when it came to his work at Langley during those sensitive days at the CIA. "He was working such incredibly long hours at his job," she has recollected, "and I swore to myself I would not burden him." He'd try to comfort her, hold her in his arms, get her to talk. At fifty-one, she was menopausal, and her gloom was too deep for mere comforting, as was the "wallowing in self-pity," as she later put it. George advised professional help, but that only intensified her despair. "I almost wonder why he didn't leave me," she later confessed. "Sometimes the pain was so great, I felt the urge to drive into a tree or into an oncoming car." Fortunately, she added, she would then "pull over to the side of the road until I felt okay."[50] Her condition was common among wives of men consumed by public careers. The stresses on family life are too well known for further elaboration. Keeping the unit intact in the face of such strains becomes especially difficult, and the Bushes did just that.

George Bush plunged into his work at Langley. A story soon made the rounds describing Bush during a morning meeting with his senior staffers at the beginning of his tenure with the troubled agency. He turned to them, according to accounts that made his career at Langley almost legendary, and said, "What are they trying to do to *us*?" He was, he wanted them to know, one of them. He understood their shattered morale. "He does these things instinctively," said Colby, who witnessed both the gloom and the Bush factor. "It was his sense of leadership. It's his character."[51]

Foremost was his use of personal diplomacy. He took seriously congressional oversight responsibilities, assiduously briefing relevant committees, making fifty-one Capitol Hill appearances during his barely one year as director.[52] He invited Senator Church to dinner at Palisades Lane, and the head of the Select Committee to Study Operations became a Bush confrere. A handful of others from the Langley community were usually also on hand each time, at first those from upper echelons and then down the ranks. The sessions were "very healing both ways," reported the DCI's deputy for administration, another outgoing personality, who was also a retired four-star admiral, Daniel J. Murphy. Bush "found that Church turned out not to have horns, and the people he got to have dinner with also proved that they didn't have horns. They were all human beings trying to do the best they could."[53] He came to respect the sheer brainpower that gave the CIA a supply of Ph.D.s and specialists that rivaled any academic community. Bush "probably did more for agency morale and standing in Congress than any DCI since Dulles," concludes historian John Ranelagh's comprehensive account. Another student of the agency points out that he was "expected to sweep with a new broom at the CIA and yet be diplomatically and politically surefooted" and "he did not disappoint his supporters."[54] Bush was able to inform the president after six months on the job that ". . . as the excesses of the past investigations fade, things on the morale front improve. Our recruitment is up. Our people are willing to serve abroad and take the risks involved. The CIA is a disciplined organization—trained to support the director."[55]

The "excesses" Bush deplored were less the actions that led to the uproar than the investigations themselves. The CIA had been caught doing its dirty work, and there was no doubt that those who fought the cold war from the inside were inhibited more by popular perceptions of immorality than by immorality itself. One had to beat the "enemy at his own game." Compromising vital functions of intelligence, whatever they incurred, was no solution. Nevertheless, having appointed Bush to restore confidence while moving toward an election and still haunted by the Nixon pardon, the president had to be credible as the chief housecleaner.

Ford's dilemma illustrated Bush's predicament. The presidential effort that came in February, spurred by the forthcoming Church Committee report and only weeks after the DCI's swearing-in, only made things harder. Church's committee, in fact, suddenly reopened its public hearings, this time to center on the president's reforms. Two executive orders, 11905 and 11906, called for reorganizing the intelligence structure and limiting surveillance intrusions into the lives of private citizens. Any congressional actions to outlaw plots to assassinate foreign leaders were given assurances that presidential support would be forthcoming. Ford also followed through by requesting legislation to tighten penalties on former agents for disclosing agency operations and identifying undercover individuals.[56]

Overseeing the CIA would be a new three-member Intelligence Oversight Board. All three, Ambassador Robert Murphy, Stephen Ailes, a sixty-four-year-old lawyer and former secretary of the army, and Leo Cherne, the sixty-three-year old economist-lawyer, had long-standing ties with the government and intelligence.[57] The new board, along with the National Security Council and the Committee on Foreign Intelligence, which had evolved from Eisenhower's days and become known as the President's Foreign Intelligence Advisory Board (PFIAB) under Kennedy, was placed under direct presidential authority.

Ford's efforts were immediately met with skepticism. His "secrets law," as it was immediately called, looked all too suspiciously like a scheme to curb freedom of information and freedom of the press. Moreover, pointed out *The New York Times* editorially, the joint committee was a twenty-year-old proposal that should have been created long ago.[58] "Since most of the CIA's abuses," noted that paper's Nicholas Horrock, "were done in times of national crisis, the executive order offers little assurance that a future anti-war movement or militant civil rights activity will not prompt CIA [sic] to reopen operations to disrupt such activities."[59] Throughout the debates that followed Ford's initiatives were questions related to the gray area of the press's freedom to print and protect sources gained through illegal leaks. Bush himself, later that same week, accused CBS newsman Daniel Schorr of revealing parts of the Pike Committee's intelligence report on civil disobedience to *The Village Voice*. There were "clearly abuses, there were awful abuses" in connection with spying activities, he said on NBC's *Meet the Press*, while refusing to confirm Schorr's information. That, he said, would only "make things worse."[60] CBS promptly suspended the television journalist.

He was still dogged by the press, Bush told the president in August. He quoted one newsman as saying, "George, your problem is that our profession thinks you are all lying bastards." It would be best to "get the CIA off the front pages and at some point out of the papers altogether." That meant limiting his "national media opportunities."[61]

He had updated the agency's organization as well as its hardware. He created a two-deputy system, one under Knoche for Intelligence and the other under Admiral Murphy for Administration. Bush, characteristically receptive to new technology, introduced two satellite systems with the capacity to perform photo-reconnaissance capable of penetrating clouds. Four new ground stations were added to facilitate intercepts of foreign communications.[62] The enhancements, a $500 million expenditure, were part of what Murphy has described as the first consolidated intelligence budget in U.S. history. Murphy himself won Bush's lasting admiration for managerial skills and, even though the admiral afterward joined the Carter administration, he returned to serve Bush during the early Reagan years.[63]

Bush's operation, in effect, placed him closer to the White House and strengthened his hand over the agency's budget and intelligence operations. He became the most powerful director of Central Intelligence, heading a 15,000 member community.[64] Yet, paradoxically, it seemed, he nevertheless succumbed to the pressure that had been building under Colby.

Everybody involved in intelligence had, from the start, resisted efforts to penetrate the agency's deepest secrets. As mentioned, President Eisenhower, in an effort to protect the agency's skeletons, had created the advisory board in 1956, (later the PFIAB) and, in explaining why he spelled out as many details as he did, Colby said that there was "no use in trying to stonewall the Congress. I had to deal with them to protect the real secrets."[65]

As it was, Colby was waging a battle of passive resistance. Pressures there were building for what appeared to be a contrary reason, not because the agency was too zealous and overstating threats to national security from international communism, but for intelligence estimates being prepared for the president that were, as Colby put it, "insufficiently tough." A number of outside analysts, mostly academic, were making projections about future Soviet strategic weapon strength that were more pessimistic. The agency's own estimates indicated that Russian nuclear capability was also growing, but, as Colby has acknowledged, "it became clear that the Soviets moved on it faster than we thought. I shared these doubts. We were a little too soft on it, maybe. Maybe there was a basis for criticizing." Colby put it off as long as he could. He organized his own study, thereby implying agreement with the need for revised estimates that had been making the rounds for a few years.[66]

The Church Committee issued its report in April.[67] By then, few surprises were left. In tune with the president's reorganization recommendations two months earlier, the findings called for closer congressional involvement in intelligence activities. The Senate followed through a few weeks later by creating a permanent Select Committee on Intelligence to oversee activities of the CIA. How much matters changed henceforth would be best assessed by minimal expectations.

Calls for substantive reform, for overhauling the agency's operations in ways that would have thrown greater light on its activities, or even for abandoning it altogether as more mischievous than valuable, were countering a stronger political tide. Movement conservatives, Rusher, Buckley, Viguerie, Reagan, et al., were getting the upper hand. In Nixon's absence, especially, the initiatives of the early seventies were coming under attack. Not only Republicans, but Democrats also joined the trend, many calling themselves "neoconservatives," some joining *Commentary* editor Norman Podhoretz, the architect of his magazine's sharp rightward turn, in establishing an outlet for those disenchanted with such concepts as "peaceful coexistence" or "detente." Less confident than before that the ability to retaliate with devastating nuclear power would suffice to keep potential aggressors at bay, and skeptical about what had become known as "MAD," the acronym for "mutually assured destruction," they were less apt to assume that the Soviets would not launch a preemptive attack.[68] Joining them were many intellectual luminaries. Some, like Podhoretz, Irving Kristol, Richard Pipes, and the *New Republic*'s editor, Martin Peretz, were primarily concerned about Israel and the Middle East. Others worried about the problems of Soviet Jews. Democratic Senator Henry Jackson of Washington had become their strongest political ally. Jackson's advanced position against Moscow on the human rights question had made him the author of the Jackson-Vanik Amendment to the 1974 trade law that denied most-favored-nation (MFN) trading status to nations that kept their citizens from emigrating. Its ultimate effects were probably counterproductive, but the target was clearly the Soviet Union, and that was what really mattered.

What were the Soviets really up to? Was detente just another tactic for a power with such worldwide designs? Clearly, the hopes of the committee, as well as those of other converts to the conservative cause, were, as Raymond L. Garthoff has written, "directed toward defeating SALT II and building American military power for confrontation with the Soviet Union." Henry Kissinger became a lightning rod for such attitudes. With Nixon gone and discredited, Kissinger became the most visible exponent of attempting to deal with Soviet boss Leonid Brezhnev. Pipes later put it directly: "Having staked their political careers on detente, Richard Nixon and Henry Kissinger disliked intelligence estimates that stressed the Soviet threat to the United States and showed the USSR moving beyond deterrence."[69]

At home, too, inflation, the Arab oil boycott followed by shortages and zooming gas prices, agitation in response to court-ordered busing to relieve racial segregation, combined with the general repudiation of McGovern Democrats, promised more conservative presidential candidates in 1976. Of the prominent Democratic contenders, Jackson, who won early primaries in Massachusetts and New York, was most likely to reverse the liberal direction. Jimmy Carter of Georgia, a dark horse, seemed only slightly less inclined. President Ford himself was far from assured of his party's renomination, not even as late as June when he and Reagan split primary victories, Ford taking Ohio and New Jersey and the ex-governor winning his own state of California.

In that climate, with those political imperatives, CIA Director George Bush went along with the president and, for all his concern for championing the agency's standing, approved the demands of the PFIAB, now under Leo Cherne's chairmanship, for a "competitive analysis" of the magnitude of the Soviet threat. Bush, later seeking to relegate the effort to a more ancillary position, told a congressional hearing that it was a "competitive experiment" that was not designed to yield "an estimate in itself." It was, he explained, better to set it up than to say "we are always going to have a hard-line team checking you guys . . ."[70] Colby retrospectively believed that had he stayed on, he "might have accepted a separate team" but he could have "resisted a team as loaded as Team B was."[71] Pipes, who chaired what became known as "Team B," recalled that Bush was only slightly less "cool" to the idea than Colby. The DCI could have vetoed it. "He had a lot of doubts about it," he said. "He was worried about the political consequences." Explaining his acceptance of their role, Bush later testified in secret that "the outside people helped the insiders take a fresh look at things, and vice versa."[72]

The booby traps were everywhere, not least of which were in the form of jeopardizing agency morale. Pipe's ad hoc body, set up for only a few months, was predictably hard-line. His colleagues included Paul H. Nitze, the career arms negotiator; Gen. Daniel O. Graham, newly retired as director of the Pentagon's Defense Intelligence Agency; another recently retired general, John W. Vogt Jr., who had commanded U.S. Air Forces in Europe; Brig. Gen. Jasper A. Welch Jr., a missile specialist; ex-ambassador to Moscow Foy Kohler; arms control expert Paul Wolfowitz; Thomas Wolfe of the Rand Institute; and Seymour Weiss, currently the U.S. ambassador to the Bahamas and former director of the Bureau of Political and Military Affairs in the State Department. All names were chosen by Pipes from a list supplied by his CIA liaison. The rival groups (there were actually three B Teams, with Pipes's the one charged with analyzing Soviet strategic objectives) had access to the same data supplied by the agency. Pipes's team was set up in June. Their final report was due in December.[73]

Their work found its way to the public by year's end. Firmly, predictably, it called earlier CIA estimates wanting, even self-deceptive. Government analysts, they held, tended to see Soviet culture and intentions as "mirror images" of themselves, assuming that the enemy would respond in predictable ways. Most wanting was acceptance of MAD. Russians simply did not see things as we all too often assumed. "The emergence of a worldwide 'socialist' order is seen by the Soviet leadership," it declared in its final sections, "as a continuous process, inexorable in nature but not without its pitfalls and temporary reverses." Detente was therefore nothing but "a particular strategy vis-à-vis the United States" and bore no necessary relationship to actual Soviet behavior, especially in view of their belief in the American lack of "political will and discipline."[74]

Not since the Gaither Report of the late fifties had there been such a dark view of cold war prospects. Team-B analysts had fallen into their own trap. They rested much of their case on the fallacies of the CIA's pro-MAD analysis. At the same time, Team B (or the "B-Team," as it was often called) by rejecting the view of the Russians as a "mirror image" of ourselves, placed their emphasis on the single-mindedness of Soviet military objectives and supposed detachment from domestic economic considerations, removing from consideration even the remote possibility of both the rise of reform leadership and internal economic hazards.

It did, however, reveal Soviet efforts that could upset the strategic balance. Their movements toward improving defenses could conceivably strengthen their ability to survive a response after delivering a first-strike nuclear attack. Upgrading their civilian defenses was one step in that direction. The Soviets, Bush explained as a result of the study, "see their civil and passive defense programs as an essential element in the achievement of the capability to wage intercontinental nuclear war," and, at the same time, a program was under way to make their intercontinental ballistic missiles less vulnerable to attack by hardening underground launch sites. They had yet to make them immune from attacks, Bush said, but their efforts to sharply alter the strategic balance also included moving ahead with highly advanced technology that could, presumably, enhance defenses by employing laserlike beams to destroy incoming missiles.

"What is this weapons system?" asked Senator Jacob Javits of New York.

Seated at Bush's side, Howard Stoertz, the National Intelligence officer for Strategic Programs, explained, "It's called a particle beam weapon."

"Energized particles," volunteered Senator Hubert Humphrey of Minnesota.

"It is somewhere between light and a bullet," Stoertz said.

"It's a 'Buck Rogers' kind of thing," clarified Bush.

"A laser uses light," Stoertz instructed the senators; "a bullet uses a fairly large particle. A charged particle beam weapon would use subatomic particles, use a very large accelerator for power, uses magnets instead of mirrors or a sight to aim it, and would fire a stream of subatomic particles either through the atmosphere, or, if you could put one of these up in space, through the ionosphere or space. When the beam of particles impacted on an object, it would have such high velocity that it would have an explosive effect." Then, attempting to place it all in perspective, Stoertz added, "this is all in the minds of the scientists on the drawing boards. No such weapon yet exists."

Bush acknowledged that intelligence experts thought that there was only an outside chance that the Soviets could upset the strategic balance within the next few years. Then he quickly pointed out that the air force believed that they could "have a prototype of such a system by 1985."[75]

Concentrated particle beams, disintegrating missiles out of the skies— Buck Rogers, indeed. Technological warfare running amok, circumventing Nixon's Anti-Ballistic Missile Treaty with the Soviet Union. Security from attack, only if one believed that there was a better deterrent to nuclear holocaust than the "balance of terror" that had, thus far, characterized the atomic age. Technology would inevitably move toward designing defensive immunity by minimizing the inherently suicidal risks of a first-strike attack through a shield formed by protective missiles, which moved onto the drawing boards in the early 1980s as the Strategic Defense Initiative, or what critics called "Star Wars." For all the efforts to dismiss the Team B analysis as a bureaucratic reality check, as Bush suggested, or to deride it as something that "did not amount to a hill of beans," as did Admiral Murphy, there was no turning back. The process was later absorbed by Reaganite strategic thinking, and Team-B analysts became some of the key players.

The nation's Defense establishment and the agency's own national intelligence estimates were already moving in that direction. The arms game, devoted to the maintenance of parity as a minimum, was reflecting conservative critiques of detente. The very point made in Team B's report, that its members were deliberately selected from among those "known to take a more somber view of the Soviet strategic threat than that accepted as the intelligence community's consensus," impressed the Senate's new Select Committee on Intelligence as the view of "only one segment of the spectrum of opinion." Two members thought the PFIAB's recommendations were insufficiently critical of the A-Team, while another faulted it for swallowing too much of what Team B had to say. The exercise relieved the CIA of pressure and, in the long run, as Murphy has recalled, "strengthened the agency's feeling for George Bush."[76] The damage to CIA credibility was nil. The accommodation to Cherne and his hard-liners reinforced rather than contributed to a new national security agenda.

The whole point, Bush stressed later, "was simply to test the objectivity of intelligence. You get a bunch of right-wing guys looking at data and you get the professional analysts, bureaucrats, CIA analysts, looking at the data, and is intelligence objective? Or is a lot of it subjective? It proved that intelligence is less than objective, that there's always going to be subjectivity in it when it comes to Soviet estimates."[77]

Nothing about Bush's brief CIA career, including his efforts to restore standing to an embattled agency, had the long-range implications of his introduction to Manuel Noriega. Noriega had been well known before the two men ever met. He was the CIA's Central American "asset," the "single most powerful man in Panama," known throughout the region as "The Caribbean Prostitute."[78] He bedded down wherever the intimacy paid off, functioning variously as a single, double, or even triple agent. Lt. Col. Oliver North, no stranger to sleazy characters, has written that Noriega left him needing to take a shower.[79] The Panamanian, who later became his nation's strongman, collected money from whatever could be sold: intelligence, drugs, equipment, weapons, assassinations.

Bush did not create Noriega. The Panamanian scoundrel was the Frankenstein of conscious choices already made. The United States relationship with him began via the CIA in the late 1950s. Noriega came out ahead by some $100,000 just from that particular beneficiary. As John Dinges's detailed study shows, many paid him "but no one controlled him." American sponsorship was at the core of his fortunes, his empowerment another price for fighting the cold war.[80]

He was a good buy. He was especially useful at a time of turbulence in Central America. The United States position in Panama had essentially remained as it had been since the start of the century. A treaty granting rights to build, operate, and fortify a canal "in perpetuity" across the Isthmus of Panama had been virtually dictated by the Americans in Teddy Roosevelt's time. For various functions associated with operating the canal, including housing of personnel, the U.S. got a canal zone that flanked the waterway on each side. That ten-mile strip of land became the focus of much of the contention.

"Yanqui imperialism" had dominated the area through one means or another for over a century. Latin-American states became virtual satellites of U.S. power. Cuba, Mexico, Haiti, Santo Domingo, Guatemala, El Salvador, and Nicaragua all experienced the hand of the "colossus of the north."

Investors were backed and protected, but nothing justified interventionism more than assumptions about the need to secure the canal. By the 1960s and 1970s, the fallout from global anticolonialism raised the issue of whether American interests would be best served by insisting on maintaining the status quo or by making politic concessions to the new-age demands.

Manuel Noriega, the bastard child of an accountant and a maid, was ten years younger than Bush. Raised as an orphan by a godmother Noriega later referred to as Mamá Luisa, the man who became familiar as the pockmarked, menacing little man in khakis started his upward climb as a bookish youngster. He got the chance to attend the best public high school in Panama, the National Institute. He flirted with the idea of becoming a doctor. There was not enough money for medical school, but he did get to a Peruvian military academy on a scholarship. Manuel was smart, and the U.S. government started to pay for his information as early as the late 1950s. He was a source for the plans of leftist students and teachers.[81] Later, Pentagon money helped see him through elite training camps in the Canal Zone and at Fort Bragg, North Carolina.[82]

In 1969, a junta of military officers under the leadership of Gen. Omar Torrijos, of which Noriega was then a junior member, overthrew the democratically elected government of Panama. Torrijos was an interesting strongman, a paternalistic despot, and the Americans could get along with him. He was smart enough to see in Noriega a prop for his own power, and theirs was a very convenient arrangement, one that allowed Noriega to rise to become head of Panama's Defense Force, as it came to be called; or, in other words, the chief of the country's intelligence. Soon afterward, considerable evidence was collected by American intelligence agencies to show that Noriega was a key player in Panama's heavy drug traffic. He was, at the same time, dealing with Castro's Cuba. So powerful had Noriega become that neither Torrijos nor his American counterparts dared to touch him. Internal investigations compiled by the Justice Department team headed by Daniel DeFeo for the Nixon administration, then waging its high-profile campaign against drugs, included an option for the "total and complete immobilization" of Noriega, or assassination. No such attempt was ever made, at least according to the best evidence available, but action was taken on another one of the suggested options, sharing the file with Torrijos himself. Once shown the extensive evidence connecting his intelligence chief to the narcotics trade, Torrijos acknowledged that Noriega was dangerous but, tellingly, did nothing about it. Who would dare thwart Manuel Noriega? He had mastered the sources of control.[83]

Noriega's survivability was ensured by such incidents as the one in late 1971 and early 1972 that involved a U.S. subject, José Villa. The *Johnny Express,* a gunboat flying a Panamanian flag of convenience, was attacked by a Cuban ship off the Bahamas. The *Johnny Express* was one of two vessels used to launch speedboats carrying Cuban exiles to destinations that involved machine-gun raids on fishing villages in their homeland. The gunboat's captain, José Villa, was wounded in the exchange of fire and forced to surrender. A resident of Miami, Florida, Villa became the subject of Nixon's efforts to gain his freedom. That led to a round of secret diplomacy, which was rendered more complicated because neither the United States nor Panama had diplomatic relations with Castro. Intelligence worked its ways, however, and the well-connected and influential Noriega was handpicked by the CIA to negotiate as Torrijos's personal emissary. He played an important, possibly decisive, role in persuading Castro to cooperate. After the playing out of a prearranged charade, Villa was released and permitted to return to Florida. As late as 1987, Nixon, according to Dinges, "bragged about the incident as one of the favors for which the United States still owed him [Noriega] gratitude."[84]

If he could not be dumped, he could at least be used, and used as a force for preserving the area's ruling order by Torrijos and everyone else involved, whether for helping to squash attempts to organize labor unions or to sanitize the region from Marxist threats to the status quo. When George Bush was challenged for having a man like Noriega among his operatives, he accurately pointed out that seven administrations had had Noriega on their hands.[85]

International deal-makers out for big profits, legal or otherwise, concentrated on two equally attractive commercial ventures—drugs and weapons. Noriega could and did do business with both. Not coincidentally, he developed a strong friendship with an Israeli who had been, or perhaps still was, associated with his country's intelligence apparatus, the Mossad. Mike Harari, just before he got to know Noriega, had led the hunt for the Palestinians who had murdered Israel's athletes during the Munich Olympics of 1972. His reputation was not helped when he killed the wrong man in the process. Harari became a high-powered arms broker and moved to Panama, where he found it easy to become a friend of both Noriega and Torrijos, who had a Jewish wife. Israel was also one of the world's leading arms exporters, an export commodity that substituted for the oil that so many of its Middle Eastern neighbors shared. Harari's prominence as a Central American arms dealer continued to grow. He was ultimately credited with shipping some $500 million in Israeli arms to Panama. Also, in conjunction with the CIA, he helped to set up a network of airfields and support for Nicaraguan anti-Marxist rebels. One measure of the closeness of the Noriega-Harari relationship was the Panamanian's desire to send his daughter to Israel so she could learn Hebrew. Tactics developed by the PDF even began to resemble those of the Israeli defense forces.[86] Whatever enchanted Noriega, it seems, he had to have—especially power—and he could hardly realize that without money.[87]

Bush, taking over the CIA and encountering the prominence of Central American issues, fell into the situation. The work *was* dirty, and allowed little room for morality. And he assumed his functions without a full realization of their complexities. He was, for example, shocked to learn that racial segregation was still the norm in the Canal Zone.[88] He tried to temper excesses, but basically he had a job to do, just as he had faced the horrors of war, the stench of oil fields, and the squalidness of various political associates. Dealing with Noriega was no different. The CIA had a job to do, and the Panamanian was just one of the dirty resources, to be used for what he was worth and, above all, to be used with care. As DCI, Bush was hardly kept ignorant about the DeFeo report and Noriega's narcotics dealing.

Early on as DCI, Bush had evidence from an army inquiry that some sergeants had sold Noriega highly classified lists of electronic sources used for tapping by the National Security Agency. Bush chose not to press for prosecution. He took the position that it was up to the army, and the army gave greater priority to learning more from the men about exactly how the security had been compromised. The soldiers traded their information for getting off with mere dishonorable discharges. So ended the case of the "singing sergeants," its resolution hidden as a deep secret to preserve the CIA's means of penetrating Panamanian intelligence.[89]

It was against that background, and the considerable agitation during 1976 over the issue of a new canal treaty, that Bush got together with Noriega over a luncheon at the Panamanian embassy on December 8, 1976.[90] Jimmy Carter had defeated President Ford one month earlier and the transition to a new administration was under way. But Panama had been a hot campaign issue. Since the 1960s and Lyndon Johnson's presidency, Central American opposition to the 1901 treaty had grown, with left-wing activists calling for the departure of the gringos. Republican conservatives, led by Ronald Reagan, made negotiations over Panama what Dinges has termed "a focus for demagoguery." One of the high points of his unsuccessful campaign to deny Gerald Ford the nomination was Reagan's statement that "when it comes to the canal, we bought it, we paid for it, it's ours, and we should tell Torrijos and company that we are going to keep it."[91] Only a few moderate Republicans, joined by some dissenting conservatives, could be persuaded that modification of the original terms could actually aid long-term U.S. interests in the region. But the force of Reagan's opposition, his ability to use the issue to push the hard-line case, all but killed rational consideration, at least until after the election. Meanwhile, the agitation within Panama itself extended into the Canal Zone. In reaction to the lack of American movement toward a treaty, Noriega's people menaced the Zonians, largely consisting of U.S. servicemen and their dependents, by setting off three bombs within forty-eight hours.[92]

That was the background, the process that led Bush to the first of several face-to-face encounters with Noriega, although the only one when Bush was DCI. Much would later be made about the significance of the sessions. Lost in all this, and a casualty of presidential politics, was not only Bush's inheritance of an ongoing intelligence liaison—the sort that Gen. Colin Powell later acknowledged belonged to those circumstances where "cold war politics sometimes made for creepy bedfellows,"—but the fact that Noriega was no stranger to others in the U.S. government before he stopped being seen as an asset.[93] Because of his quests for elective offices, fewer parts of Bush's public career were more sensitive, or as personally distasteful, as the Noriega connection. Even many years later, only by his body language did he acknowledge that he and the venal Panamanian ever breathed the same air.[94]

Noriega, in effect Bush's counterpart as head of his own country's intelligence, was accompanied by both the Panamanian ambassador and the country's foreign minister, Aquilino Boyd, the man who had helped to ease his way as a youngster into the Peruvian military academy. Bush also knew Aquilino since both served at the United Nations. The 1976 luncheon, however, was requested by Boyd, clearly to rebut suspicions that the bombings were connected to anyone within the Panamanian government.[95]

Noriega, with the two other Panamanians, met with Bush on the McGill Terrace. The dialogue, with Noriega's Spanish translated by Aquilino, was a little test of which side would reveal the most about his sources, after Bush was assured about the absence of official complicity in the bombings. "Is Torrijos a Communist?" Bush wanted to know about Panama's repressive military dictator who had recently visited Cuba.

"Torrijos isn't a Communist, I'm not a Communist, and neither is the Panamanian people," was the literal translation that followed Noriega's words.

Bush said as little as possible. He wanted to know about which of our sources were yielding information to their sources without any admonition about the recent disturbances. He sat patiently and absorbed reassurances. However, he did not attempt to minimize the pervasiveness of American intelligence in their country. To Noriega, at least, that did not exactly come as a revelation. He had done his own penetration of American sources.

"I take your explanation in good spirit," Bush told Noriega. "Our only interest is that these things don't happen again." He himself never commented about the meeting afterward, but the American ambassador to Panama at the time, William Jorden, reported that "Bush listened courteously, never said what he really thought, and moved on to other matters. He was telling the Panamanians as subtly as he could: 'Let's drop this subject as long as it does not happen again.'" There was one thing, however, that they wanted Bush to convey to President Ford: their wishes to pass along word to the incoming administration to continue negotiations over the status of the Canal Zone.[96]

Bush never talked publicly about that meeting or suggested any involvement at all with Noriega while DCI. So touchy was the entire affair and so contentious and suffused with innuendos did it become as a political issue, especially during the 1988 campaign, that, as late as 1995, Murphy, discreet as ever, maintained the fiction that he did not believe that "Bush had anything to do with Noriega," certainly not until his vice presidency.[97]

Bush, in that instance and in every other way in that 1976 election year, managed political self-preservation. He rode out the season immune from political conflicts. If conservatives were mystified by anyone, it was Reagan.

Devotees of ideological purity were astonished by the Californian's announced choice of a vice presidential running mate, should he win the nomination. He was none other than Senator Richard Schweiker. Out of the party's liberal wing, the Pennsylvanian had a strong history of sympathy toward labor. Reagan, by moving toward his left, made what would turn out to be the first of two such nominations, the second coming later, in 1980. So devoted were the new breed of conservatives to their leader that they had little trouble finding a rationale and remained loyal while he went on almost to topple Ford at the convention. Reagan, regrouping his own campaign staff right after that loss, vowed to continue the conservative fight. "The cause goes on," he told them. "It's just one battle in a long war and it will go on as long as we all live." They should not be tempted by expediency.[98] Ford, handicapped by an abrasive and loose-cannon running mate, Bob Dole (whose behavior encouraged Ford insiders to feel that Rockefeller had been a crucial loss from the ticket), and by his own ineptitude during a televised debate with his Democratic opponent, never did get out from under the onus of the Nixon pardon. Democrats therefore managed to win with Carter and Walter (Fritz) Mondale.

It was, in effect, over for Bush's directorship, confirming the wisdom of institutionalizing reforms to give DCIs statutory terms irrespective of presidential administrations. In mid August, candidate Carter praised him for having done a better job in instituting reforms than had Clarence Kelley over at the FBI. Carter, on the defensive for the leak of a memorandum that accused the Nixon-Ford administrations of using federal jobs as dumping grounds for defeated Republican candidates, said, "I happen to think a lot of George Bush. I would not include George Bush among those who were appointed without qualifications."[99]

On November 19, after Carter's election as the thirty-ninth president, Bush, accompanied by Henry Knoche, went to Plains, Georgia, for his final intelligence briefing of the president-elect. He also offered to stay on as DCI for a few months until the new president could install a replacement, attempting to somewhat dilute the political character of the appointment. Carter declined. He would have a new man in place by January 20.[100] Filling Bush's vacated post left the new president in a dilemma when his own choice, Theodore C. Sorensen, became a victim of his own indiscretions and politics as usual.

Barbara and George Bush, sprung from Washington life after a decade in the capital, went house hunting in Houston. An exhausting search finally led them to a place at 5838 Indian Trail, where, only later, he discovered "that it had no garage and needed to have the kitchen gutted and completely replaced."[101] At least the house was on a dead-end street.

CHAPTER THIRTEEN

The Man in the Brooks Brothers Suit

%

ush could have retired in Houston without any loss of pride or dignity. He had enough success from business and government to ensure prestige and comfort. His oldest son, George W., had settled in Midland, and had also gone into the oil and gas business. He was, at the same time, preparing to run for a seat from Texas's nineteenth congressional district.[1] Young George was not seeking public office, he later explained, because the family had taught him that "you must be a politician to be successful." He had acted more out of a sense of "passing on of tradition, passing on legacy, passing on responsibility. "It's the inherited sense of service," he added, and the realization that "you can't win unless you run."[2]

That was the key: you can't win unless you run. Bushes had to be winners. So it was with the older Bush: tennis, golf, squash, or horseshoes, winning, or, perhaps more important, how you win.

It did not take much perception for those who knew George Bush during those postgovernment days, both in Texas and Maine, to realize that he was drawing a clear bead on the presidency, testing himself, gauging his popular appeal for that most American ordeal by democracy.[3] Even while his son aimed at a congressional seat and Jimmy Baker weighed the state's attorney general's office, George Bush focused on getting together enough money to run for bigger things. "George is looking for something to get into," an unnamed friend confided to a reporter. "He's been in [government] so long, he's getting a bit nervous," but "there's nothing available to him in Texas."[4]

After a decade of public life, he needed control over personal finances. Zapata had not really made his fortune, certainly not considering the dozen years devoted to building the company. Neither had other investments provided the sinecure he needed. "He didn't make a lot of money when lots of people did," one of his close friends told the *Washington Post.*[5] His financial disclosure form, issued just before announcing his candidacy for the presidency, revealed that income from investments in 1976 was just $34,000.[6] After holding four jobs in rapid succession, the time was ripe for planning ahead. The next step had to be his major leap.

He became a model civic-minded businessman. He chaired the American Heart Fund, joined the directorship of Baylor University, the board of trustees of both Trinity University in San Antonio and Phillips Academy, and helped to collect $370 million for Yale as cochairman of its 1978 fund-raising campaign.[7] His interests also led to a relatively new group of businessmen and policy specialists drawn from Asia, the United States, and Europe, known as the Trilateral Commission. All, it seemed, were the right associations, and at the right time.[8] They, plus his reputation, placed him where he could, at least for a time, earn fees for speaking and make further contacts as well.

Rapidly, during those early months in Houston, he parlayed both his circle and standing to strengthen his position. In April, he wrote to Lud Ashley that he missed Washington and the excitement of CIA life, but was already able to report on an active role in business. The largest bank holding company in Texas, First International Bankshares of Dallas, better known simply as Interfirst, took him on as a consultant and chairman of its executive committee. At the same time, he became a director of its affiliate, First International Bankshares, Ltd., of London. That gave him an additional $75,000 yearly income, apparently the value of lending his name.[9] Directorships in 1977 that earned him $112,000 represented payments from such other companies as Texas Gulf, Inc. and Eli Lilly and Company. Until he undertook full-time work as a candidate, he earned over $275,000 from the four companies. He enumerated his associations for Lud Ashley in April while also inviting his friend to Houston and offering to give the Democratic congressman from Ohio some speech-making opportunities. He'd have no trouble setting him up with an oil group. He could also guide him on an inspection trip of offshore rigs.[10]

Bob Mosbacher, fresh from serving President Ford, also helped out. He assembled a group of friends, including Baker, and got them to raise $750,000 in a partnership to buy petroleum products through a company called Holly LBG No. 2. Another $2.2 million came via a loan from a bank of which Mosbacher was a director. Bush put in $60,000 and received $115,373 within the next ten years, with an expected continuing annual income from that source of $30,000.

Baine Kerr, the Baker & Botts attorney who had moved on to Pennzoil and become its president just as Bush returned to Houston, led him into a deal with the Fidelity Printing Company. That venture turned $499,600 profit within three years, really a 1,900 percent yield from the purchase of 26,000 shares of the printing company's stock, which was fortunate because of his losses in a weak stock market. An old Connecticut friend who had moved to Dallas, Fred M. Zeder, induced him to invest in an apartment complex, which was described by a fellow real estate man privy to the deal as "a good tax gimmick" and "a typical Texas joint venture offering." The real estate partnership gave Bush paper losses of $225,160 through 1985, which was good for about $100,000 in tax savings while yielding straight profits of $14,062 and capital gains that totaled $217,278.[11]

Suddenly, Bush was as active in the corporate world, nationally and internationally, as he had ever been in politics, and continued the pattern of rapid movements that became characteristic of his life in and out of government. He and Barbara traveled widely, to the Far East, Australia, Israel, Denmark, and Germany, but it was business, especially oil, that led him to the Middle East, including Egypt and Jordan. In May, Jordan's King Hussein I advising Texans that the Arab Middle East and Houston "have many common interests, most of which are spelled O-I-L," also visited the Bush home on Indian Trail. "George had invited guests from all over the country whom he thought the king might enjoy seeing," Barbara wrote. The two dozen diners on the evening of May 2 included one of the most durable icons of American oil, Nelson Rockefeller.[12]

He could have gone to work managing one of Ross Perot's oil companies. The Texan, who had begun his fortune by getting federal government contracts to handle medicare payments via his Electronic Data Processing company, had expanded into oil and real estate. "We were friends," recalled Bush of a Perot visit to see him in Maine. "He made me an offer of a job running an oil company in Houston, Texas, as I was leaving the CIA." But, as a former Electronic Data Services official had learned, "you don't turn down Perot," which was exactly what Bush did. It did not make for a happy little Texan.[13]

By the end of 1978, Bush's friends Baker and Mosbacher put together two fund-raising groups, which were really political action committees. Created under the same law that enabled PACs to grow in Washington, Baker's Fund for Limited Government and Mosbacher's Congressional Leadership Committee became financial supports for Bush's precampaign travels, including his extensive liaisons with Republicans throughout the country. The CLC fell under the joint oversight of Senate minority leader Howard Baker of Tennessee and House minority leader John Rhodes of Arizona. Both groups were to fund multiple Republican candidates, ostensibly to reduce their election costs. The CLC did contribute over $10,000 each to twenty-one Republican candidates in its first year, but the FLG shared less than 20 percent of its proceeds and took in almost $99,000 in the first six months of 1978. Bush contributions came heavily from fellow Texans, including executives of Pennzoil, Haggar Slacks, McCormick Oil & Gas, Houston Oil & Minerals, and Texas Instruments. Out-of-state money also flowed from Exxon, McDonnell-Douglas Aircraft, and Clairol, which was headed by his old Andover schoolmate, Bruce S. Gelb. Also pitching in were the financial communities in New York, Connecticut, and Boston, as well as the Midwest. While fellow Texan John Connally had a similar fund-raising organization, Bush's appeal drew money from sources uncomfortable with both Connally and Reagan. Their contributions made possible his travel to forty-two states, covering some 96,000 miles in 1978 alone, airport hopping in single-engine Cessnas, until, thanks to more funding from the political action committees, he graduated to commercial airlines, which was a relief. "I'll go about anywhere and do about anything that's legal to try and win this thing," he said to Jim Baker's right-hand aide, Margaret Tutwiler, who later handled his scheduling, "but please don't put me in a single-engine aircraft anymore."[14]

In the fall of 1977, prior to all this, George and Barbara took a Pennzoil jet to China. The trip was a belated acceptance of a courtesy from the Beijing government; former diplomats were invited to tour the country with their friends. The offer was particularly attractive because of the country's aversion to foreigners. The Bushes, as was their privilege, invited a dozen others: a Houston friend and aide, Chase Untermeyer, who went to gather material for a proposed Bush campaign autobiography; the well-respected political journalist of the *Washington Post*, David Broder and his wife; Bush's good friend from Nixon days, Dean Burch, and his wife Patricia; the renowned world traveler and commentator, Lowell Thomas, then eighty-five years old, with his wife of six months, Marianna; Hugh Liedtke and his wife Betty; and two who came without wives, James R. Lilley, the CIA's China expert under Bush, and good friend Jim Baker. Untermeyer recalled the trip as a "combination of high-level diplomacy and tourism."[15]

In Beijing, Bush met with Deng Xiaoping, who had just come to power and was beginning his efforts at economic modernization. The Chinese leader's encouragement of trade with the West also eased the way for the complete normalization of U.S.-Sino relations one year later.* From the capital, the party traveled to the Forbidden City of Lhasa. They sailed through the gorges of the Yangtze (now the Chang River) and then journeyed ever upward toward the 12,800-foot-high Tibetan capital. They dined on barley beer that "looked and smelled like urine" and yak butter "with some rancid fat on the top," but it was that high altitude that began to dominate. "I had such a sick headache," Barbara Bush reported, "that I wanted to die," and recalled stepping "as though we were walking on eggshells, being given oxygen off and on" from portable canvas bags. At least their rooms were equipped with five-foot-high oxygen tanks. Even with that support system, Betty Liedtke's heart condition kept her in Beijing. Thomas, despite the concern of the Chinese, did not let himself be deterred just because he wore a pacemaker. The government officials were nervous, but Bush vouched that the old man was up to it.

James Baker was noticeably preoccupied on that trip. He had taken along a chronicle of the 1976 presidential campaign, *Marathon* by Jules Witcover. Baker zeroed in on the account of how Jimmy Carter exploited the opportunity offered by the Iowa caucuses, which preceded important state primaries,

---

*Bush, preparing for his presidential run, objected when Carter moved to extend formal recognition to the People's Republic of China.

to gain what turned out to be a decisive advantage. Baker already was a veteran of Washington's political battles. Acting on a recommendation from George Bush, President Ford had appointed him as undersecretary of Commerce. Again thanks to Bush, he was responsible for rounding up delegates for the 1976 Republican convention, no easy task granted the pressure from surging Reaganites. For him, perhaps as much as anybody else on that trip, with the possible exception of Untermeyer, the tour was a work-and-play affair.

For Hugh Liedtke, the trip was also useful. It opened contacts that later continued with the People's Republic of China, sending delegates from the Oil and Gas Ministry to Houston to learn about financing the production of natural gases. His introduction to the country and the Chinese laid the ground work for his oil-drilling contract.[16]

Meanwhile, Bush ducked political controversy. He avoided any comment about the highly publicized series of televised interviews that David Frost did with Richard Nixon. "I'm sparing myself," he told the members of the Press Club of Houston. "I've already lived through the agony of Watergate. I don't want to live through it anymore."[17]

He agreed to a series of lectures for the new Jesse H. Jones Graduate School of Administration at Rice University. The course, entitled Organization in Theory and Practice, was taught in tandem with Dr. Joseph Cooper. Bush was very popular with the students, explained the professor, "very open, very friendly," without any "airs about him, no pretensions. . . . After class, the students would hang around and talk to Bush as he was gathering up his materials . . . he talked about choosing good people and listening to people, getting people together and solving problems in a common-sense, collective fashion."[18]

All this did not mean Bush was turning his back on the past. Far from it. His chairmanship of the Republican National Committee, so difficult because of the Nixon turmoil, proved, finally, to be invaluable for the creation of a secondary base, one that naturally augmented the financial powers of the Bush circle. He was able to reach far outside Texas for support, with the help of his friend and sometime political mentor, Dean Burch, and that of ex-President Ford. An additional advantage was Baker's closeness to Ford. The troubled Carter administration, with its widely perceived leadership vacuum, made 1980 attractive to Bush and a slew of competitors. Their numbers attested to Carter's weakness: Tennessee's Senator Howard Baker, his visibility heightened during the Watergate hearings, the ubiquitous John Connally, John Anderson, and Phil Crane of Illinois, Bob Dole of Kansas, and Ronald Reagan, clustered around the party's center and right. And, as Bush waited, he gathered his resources through speaking appearances that promoted the fortunes of such new-breed Southern Republicans as Robert L. Livingston of Louisiana. He became a hot property on the GOP dinner circuit, raising more money, widening his own contacts, and reassuring that whatever misgivings people may have had about his reputation for moderation, he was a true-blue man of the right, especially on economic matters. He spoke out for the reelection of freshman Congressman J. Danforth Quayle at the Marriott Hotel, in Fort Wayne, Indiana. Quayle later remembered his words as "surprisingly conservative." He worked the 1978 congressional elections as hard as he could, stumping for every Republican he could, not only picking up chits for the future but also testing his grassroots appeal.[19]

No reporter following Bush from place to place, from business groups, campuses, industry associations, or political gatherings could have been surprised at the essential conservatism of his message. He was the businessman/politician spokesman for free markets, free trade, lower taxes, and fewer regulations, his message almost indistinguishable from the pitch of some hard-shells. He preached the gospel of political mobilization via the Republican party and business groups to create a better climate for investors. "One gets the feeling we are living in an age of ghastly, self-righteous, unresponsive bureaucracy—that threatens government control of our lives," he told students at his old school in Andover. The message remained the same throughout his appearances, whether his focus was on domestic or foreign policy. Government, if it had any role, was there to safeguard commercial relations. His words had particular scorn for the Carter administration's emphasis on human rights as the centerpiece of American foreign policy. It was wrongheaded, and risked strategic interests. Getting rid of the apartheid regime in the Union of South Africa only risked having it replaced by one that might block free access of oil shipments around the Cape of Good Hope. Carter was guilty of a "troubling double standard" by slapping Argentina and Brazil but catering to Castro, "whose outrageous disregard for human rights in Cuba and whose intolerance of any dissent is well known." At Georgetown University, Bush declared that our "current foreign policy seems to be one of splendid oscillation. . . . the hawks are at NSC; the doves at State; and as they squabble, American tail feathers are being scattered around the world." Carter, by saying that Americans were "free of the 'inordinate fear of communism,' " was toying with the perception of weakness and vacillation that forfeited the best deterrent against Soviet aggression. "We should consider our strategic interests in the world as well as the human rights questions," he told businessmen in Houston. Whether it was competitive obstructionism from communism or from policies coming out of Washington, ran Bush's central theme, there were threats to the freedom of American enterprise. It had to be encouraged, to constantly build and explore in an ever-expanding world market.[20]

One of those touched by George Bush in 1977 was twenty-six-year-old Lanny Griffith. Griffith, just out of law school at the University of Mississippi, was starting up his practice in Oxford. Hailing as he did from the "most yellow-dog Democrat" part of the state, his campus activism had nevertheless moved him into Republicanism. He had just become the party's chairman in Lafayette County when he was asked to put together a fundraiser that would feature a Bush speech on the Ole Miss campus.[21]

There were only about one hundred people in Griffith's organization. About seventy-five showed up, each paying ten dollars, and looking rather lost in the nine-hundred-seat auditorium. Bush spoke on foreign policy. It was good, but not great, Griffith recalled, but his personality was effective in that venue. "The crowd liked him a lot."

"Great crowd," Bush told Griffith afterward. "I've heard so much about you."

Bush called him the next day at his law office. He followed through with a personal note, which Griffith framed. "I was won over despite the fact that I was determined not to make a choice then. I think it was his personality more than anything. Good, outgoing, engaging person." By the time Griffith became the executive director of Mississippi's Republican party in 1979, he was securely on the side of George Bush.[22]

At a time when Ronald Reagan and, to a lesser degree, Jack Kemp, were leading the vanguard of the conservatives, Bush was thought of as a moderate. More accurately, he was flexible, without the hard rhetorical dogma of the group that was becoming so strong within the party's right-wing. Bush was selective, differing from most of them by accepting the idea of the Equal Rights Amendment that had been promoted for the better part of the decade by equality-conscious women. But he favored capital punishment to counter the "epidemic of crime [that] continues to plague our citizens." He had run against Lloyd Bentsen as a supporter of gun control, but had since come around to clear opposition to requirements for federal legislation. "Disarming the law-abiding will do nothing to reduce crime," said his issues positions paper.

Abortion had also risen to join the list of contentious issues, despite the Supreme Court's 1973 decision in the case of *Roe* v. *Wade,* which struck down laws prohibiting the procedure during the first six months of pregnancy. Bush stated that he was personally opposed to abortions but upheld the right of women to choose to have one *if approved by state law.*

His position failed to recognize the heightening furor over the issue, among both antiabortionists and those who proclaimed "freedom of choice," who were increasingly being placed on the defensive. Bush tried to strike a middle ground that was not only evaporating but could easily be viewed as regressive. *Roe* v. *Wade* was decided as state after state was veering toward more liberal positions. Fourteen had done so between 1967 and 1971. Among the others, one, Pennsylvania, had offered no choices whatsoever. The rest imposed various restrictions, requiring waiting periods or approvals. All, by the very nature of their prohibitions, gave the advantages of freedom to women of greater financial means. To say, as did Bush, that the matter should be left to the states, threatened to create a class of unfortunates, deprived because of residence, something completely contrary to the Supreme Court's intent in underscoring the right to privacy of Americans. Yet, by opposing a constitutional amendment banning abortions altogether,

Bush took a position that was anathema to the growing "right-to-life" tide that was surging among Catholics and fundamentalists of various stripes. As more women took advantage of their newly acquired freedom, and as abortion moved toward becoming the most widely performed medical procedure in the country, taking a middle position became even more untenable. He actually compounded his problems by his "on-the-other-hand" position, namely, that abortions in "exceptional cases—rape, incest, or to save the life of the mother" should qualify for federal funding.[23]

All his life, there was that problem, suspicion that Bush was a closet "moderate," a closet "liberal." How little they understood that someone like George Bush reflected "personality more than ideology," as Untermeyer put it. "Who would want someone who saw everything as black and white?" countered Barbara Bush when pressed about possible contradictions. Or as David Keene, who had worked for Spiro Agnew, Bob Dole, and Ronald Reagan before George Bush, put it, "one of my operating theories is that to some extent ideology is bullshit. In our system, other things are cloaked in ideology because other things are not as acceptable."[24]

That also exposed a vulnerability to the Reagan juggernaut that was enchanting the far right. As Bush watched all this and began to turn his First Interbank office into a makeshift campaign headquarters, his own traditional conservatism was becoming less and less relevant; 1978 was the year—the landmark year, in fact—for the great tax revolt that began in California and threatened to sweep all before it.

Proposition 13, a referendum on the state's ballot, was the manifestation of a firestorm of antitax fervor, the response to voters choking on property assessments. Led in California by the seventy-five-year old Howard Jarvis and Paul Gann, its enactment placed a cap on taxable property values. Jarvis's influence would continue to grow. The rebel activist talked about taking "control of the government again" in apocalyptic terms that energized his rhetoric. The whole thing represented nothing less than a "revolution against government," pollster Pat Cadell advised President Carter.[25]

Reagan, the principal political beneficiary, had embraced the issue much as he had coopted POW/MIA, welfare, and the Panama Canal treaty. He was still governor in 1973 when he supported the forerunner of Prop 13, then known as Prop 1, but without success. Yet, when Prop 13 passed after his governorship, Joe Coors, the leader of Colorado's right-wing revolt, praised Reagan as the "father" of the taxpayer revolt, and said he was the "man who should be in the White House in 1980."[26]

The far right agreed. Goldwater and earlier heroes belonged to the past. A new generation of activists had found a new messiah. Then, too, even as the Californian was rising, Bushites had two setbacks. George W., after defeating an outspoken rightist in the primary for the congressional seat and then surviving a three-way runoff, finally lost to a shrewd, well-entrenched Democrat, Lubbock State Senator Kent Hance.[27]

James Baker meanwhile, having established his credentials with the Ford administration, returned to Texas to pursue his own political ambitions. Attracted to politics ever since the Bush senatorial campaign of 1970, he had been positioning himself for statewide office. He had contributed to virtually all prominent Texas Republicans's coffers. In 1978, when statehouse Speaker Price Daniel Jr., the product of a well-established political lineage, appeared on the verge of becoming the Democratic candidate for the office of attorney general, Baker prepared to enter elective politics. Daniel was liberal for Texas and, in Baker's view, beatable. But Baker, while working behind the scenes for a one-candidate Republican primary, watched with some dismay as a more conservative Democrat, Mark White, took away the nomination from Daniel. Baker, handicapped at that time as a Republican on a relatively lower rung of his party's statewide ticket, also had to deal with an ideological division. One legacy of the bitter 1976 fight for the presidential nomination was a split between local Bush-Ford and Reaganite factions. With his own ties to the Bush-Ford faction secure, he had to reach out to the far right. He brought in as the head of his campaign Frank Donatelli, Reagan's regional coordinator for the area two years earlier and ex-chairman of the National Conservative Political Action Committee. Baker then left little to chance. His own image as a moderate notwithstanding, he "ran a very conservative, tough campaign oriented toward dealing with crime." He was able to get fund-raising assistance from the ex-president as well as from Reagan. Both men came to the state to speak for him.[28] But it was not enough. His one attempt at elective politics exposed an aristocratic detachment that hindered efforts to "bring it down to the average American citizen."[29] He came up short, with 47 percent of the vote. He had, in the process, established credentials that were far more conservative than seemed likely from his relationship with Bush.

Two Bushites down in one year. There was, moreover, no lack of press reminders that George Bush himself had lost two statewide races and how his absence from elective politics had dimmed his political glamour. He enlisted a young friend of Jeb's, a twenty-five-year-old Houstonian, David Bates, just out of law school and able to take a leave from his firm. Bates became his personal aide, his traveling companion, and his tennis partner as he went from speech to speech, picked up his IOUs and tested reactions, never ignoring a contact made along the way. Bates later remembered that the incipient candidate was tireless, his vibrant and dynamic personal appearances able to spark crowds. A contact made was a contact kept. "He wrote note after note," his aide recalled with some wonder. "He just carried those notes with him. Somebody would come up and say 'I want to help you,' and he'd make sure we'd write that name and make sure to get him on the campaign list." Once back on the plane, even after a long day, he'd first get "that briefcase open and do four or five, six or seven notes that he had to do. Then he'd finally put the briefcase away, but not till he was finished with everything. Then he kind of laid back and had a beer, but not until he did everything and stayed current." "Batesy" would stay on with Bush off and on, well into the White House days.[30]

As with most wonders, the Reagan phenomenon was best understood in retrospect. Common to those who vied with him for the nomination in 1980 were comments about the futility of their quests. In looking back after six years, John Connally thought that he and Nixon regarded Reagan's victory as "automatic."[31] The Reagan passion they were seeing was truly deep but much less wide, disproportionately strong among conservatives of both parties and far weaker in the vast mainstream of American politics. That great reluctance to move toward an ideological fringe accounted for the appeal of Republican Congressman John Anderson. A fiscal conservative who was so moderate and independent on other issues that some colleagues considered him a traitor to his party, he drew the support of 21 percent of all registered voters against 40 percent for President Carter and 34 percent for Reagan in a Gallup Poll released by an unintentional coincidence on April Fool's Day.[32]

That was the real dilemma in 1980—the course to be taken by the Republican party. Only later did it all come into better focus, less because of any sudden, overnight social and economic change that swept the country than because the Reagan "revolution" *was* a revolution; it reshaped the GOP. He, more than any leader since Roosevelt, moved the public to where they were not quite ready to go. As *The New York Times*'s Tom Wicker pointed out in 1978, when California's Proposition 13 was still being debated and its meaning not fully comprehended, the middle of the road seemed to be the best place for politicians to be. The primary need for Republicans, it appeared to Wicker, "is not for ideological commitment but for broad and inclusive appeals to Americans on issues that concern them all." By some two to one, people insisted they were conservative, not liberal. Yet when they indicated their preferences, they called "for government to do more and better, not less, about a long list of social issues such as education and health." Hadn't the party's chairman, Bill Brock, been eager to broaden their base by attracting more minority support, even going so far as to invite the Rev. Jesse Jackson to address the Republican National Committee? Senate minority leader Howard Baker was making his pitch for the nomination as a middle-of-the-roader, "not like a candidate bent on appeasing the right wing."[33]

Bush was further handicapped by the danger of having primary votes spread among four moderates: Bob Dole, coming off his disastrous run as Ford's running mate in 1976 and widely considered a weak challenger for 1980; Senate minority leader Howard Baker; maverick Congressman John Anderson of Illinois; and the relatively unknown George Bush. The irony of his situation, certainly in view of his political future, was illustrated by the efforts of his campaign to reinforce his moderation, not his conservatism; the battle was for leadership of the middle of the road. Texas journalist Harris Worcester, noting that Bush was about to start his candidacy with the former president's blessing, pointed out as early as 1978 that he was cultivating the "support of the moderate Gerald Ford wing of the party . . ."[34]

Take popular positions on the issues, for example. Gallup's pollsters found that inflation brought across-the-board backing for wage and price controls. And even the ill-fated Equal Rights Amendment had strong approval. At the start of 1980, President Carter still enjoyed two-to-one support for his handling of the hostage situation in Iran. He led 60 to 31 percent in a presidential "trial heat" taken in February later that pitted him head-to-head against Reagan.[35]

Bush's public announcement of his presidential candidacy, on May 1, 1979, hardly surprised those who knew him. Months of hard work and virtually round-the-clock travel and speechmaking had laid the groundwork. He followed his formal declaration by undertaking a four-day swing through New England, Florida, and Alabama. Nationally, however, despite more than a decade in government service, he was still a stranger to most Americans, even Republicans, at least in part a consequence of his long absence from elective politics. A survey released by Reagan's man, Dick Wirthlin, at the end of the year, taken among party faithful, showed Bush far behind Reagan, 13 to 57 percent.[36]

Jim Baker, his political skills honed under Ford and further by his own election loss, threw his intelligence and energy behind Bush. "He was bitten by the bug of politics," explained Dave Keene, "[he] didn't want to practice law or do whatever Texans do."[37] Behind Baker in the Bush circle was Bob Mosbacher. Having raised funds for Ford, he now headed Bush's financial team. Other old Bush hands included Midland pal Fred Chambers, Ben Love of the Texas Commerce Bank, and he reached out to embrace people like Fitzgerald (Gerry) Bemis of Virginia and William H. Draper III, the eighty-six-year-old establishment pillar. Serving as the committee's cochairman, with Mosbacher, was George's brother, Jonathan, an effective fundraiser in New York State and the head of the New York City investment banking firm of J. Bush & Company, then located on Beaver Street, just a few blocks down from Wall Street. Nearby, with an office at 95 Wall, was Prescott Jr., who chaired a finance committee in Connecticut. Other Bushes were not far removed. Brother William (Bucky) Bush of St. Louis ran the Bush finance committee in Missouri, and Prescott Jr. also raised money in Connecticut. Nancy was a coordinator in Massachusetts. Neil was also heavily involved, taking time off, as did the rest of the family, for his wedding on July 5, 1980 just before the convention. Jeb and Columba's fluent Spanish became handy for winning Puerto Rico's fourteen delegates to the Bush side. Their appeal targeted Cuban expatriates in Miami's "Little Havana" section. Even Marvin and Dorothy, the least political of the children, became part of the family enterprise. Only young George, the oldest son and normally among the most political, missed that battle. After having lost his own fight for a congressional seat he had to concentrate on his business.[38]

Baker turned to Reagan's former adviser, Dave Keene. Keene's knowledge of Bush dated to the RNC chairmanship. Now, summoned by Baker to help jump-start the Texan's campaign, he met with him in Houston but came away with little enthusiasm. Bush was "a good guy," all right, but Keene, who later became head of the American Conservative Union, found no "real depth in the way he looked at things." He was "smart" and very serious about being president. Keene, during that first real meeting with Bush, was certain of but one thing: "My advice is get the hell out of Houston," he told him. "Get out fast." Houston, he knew, was an arena dominated by John Connally. Bush and his friend Baker, who at that stage seemed more committed because of loyalty to his friend George than through belief he really would become president, "hated John Connally."

"You know," Keene told Bush, "the problem with you is that you're pissed because John got the tennis court and you want it."

Bush looked at the political consultant and said, "You really don't understand me, do you?"

"What do you mean by that?"

"None of the clubs that I belong to would accept John Connally," said the ambassador.

Keene, ever conscious of his own working-class background, decided that his notions had been confirmed. "Texas is made up of different kinds of people, and George Bush was part of the Easterners that moved it. They were the country-club social set. You had the same thing in the Republican party as it grew in Texas, where 'Do we want any of these people? They're tacky.' They're not the kind of people you'd want around the house because they might steal the silverware. That's the way they viewed John Connally, and they were also scared to death because he was bigger than they were. Bush wanted to be president and he was willing to work his ass off to get it. Other people supported him because he was the representative of their Yale class or their social grouping. Then there were the people who saw it as a crusade to prevent their enemy John Connally from getting anywhere. They were so obsessed with Connally at that point they had no realistic sense of what the race was likely to be about and considered Reagan not relevant to the race."[39]

Keene took a flier and signed on; predictably, he hardly survived the Bush primaries and later settled in with, for him, a much more congenial partner, Bob Dole.

Barbara talked up George Bush as often as she could, in groups sometimes tiny, in living rooms, garages, anywhere she could get a hearing; sometimes with just the hostess and a few other guests over coffee and tea. "I didn't speak at all," she recalled, meaning speechmaking from platforms. Still she had yet to develop the confidence to make pitches to perfect groups of strangers. "My knees shook. I felt sick," she recalled. "Not a good speaker, but a big speaker. But that's because I talked so much," she laughed. But Barbara was a lady, and truly political wives avoid politics. Her good friend, Janet

Steiger, whose husband Bill was one of George's congressional friends, gave her a useful idea. She had put together a slide program for herself, one that could be shown in living rooms. Barbara jumped at the tip. Evenings could then focus on the family and she could tell what the Bushes were doing rather than what they were thinking, and have it all illustrated by pictures. The slide shows went great with church and garden club tours, and she even showed them to some schoolchildren. Her little show, complete with impromptu commentaries, played before chambers of commerce and Rotary Clubs, raising thousands of dollars in the process. They proved to be a wonderful device for handling situations that could easily deteriorate under such pesky questions as George's involvement with David Rockefeller and those "secret" international bankers "plotting" to run the world through something called the Trilateral Commission, or even the "one-worlders" at the Council for Foreign Relations.[40] Barbara found reminders in her grass-roots campaigning, of old Texas encounters with the Birchite "weirdos," as she remembered them, and their crazy literature. Weren't those rich Easterners trying to sell out the U.S. to the UN, and even hiding behind the sinister power of the Federal Reserve System?

Dave Keene had been the ideal man to help Bush and Baker wade through all this. He certainly had his own ideological groundings, but political consultants could also be coldly professional, and Keene's contribution was less dogmatic than pragmatic. Fighting political wars reminiscent of generals serving commanders in chief, they moved easily through their roles. Pollsters, analysts, managers, and sometimes in various combinations, they were the impresarios of modern politics. They were the pros who were to the pols what publicists and spin masters were to the media. John Sears moved from Nixon to Reagan, before becoming a $360,000-a-year lobbyist for South Africa's apartheid rule. Dave Gergen became a teammate for a succession of clients that included Nixon, Ford, Reagan, Bush, and Clinton. Edward J. Rollins moved from Reagan to a $250,000-a-year job with the Republican National Committee and, in an inexplicable turnabout unforgivable to George Bush, had a brief fling with Ross Perot before embarrassing himself with tales about having used "walking-around money" to help Christine Todd Whitman win New Jersey's governorship. Dick Wirthlin, a true-blue conservative, drew his checks from Reagan, Margaret Thatcher of Great Britain, Dole, Bush, right-to-lifers, and the Republican National Committee. Robert M. Teeter, the Michigan-based analyst for Nixon and Ford, signed up to become pollster for Bush's 1980 primary campaign.

That post-1976 flow, from Ford to Bush, became a natural route for those identifying themselves with the moderate heart of the party. Baker, Mosbacher, and Teeter were joined by three others. Robert P. Visser, counsel to the Ford campaign, became treasurer for the George Bush for President Committee. Peter Teeley, who became Bush's press secretary, had done that job with both Jacob Javits and Robert Griffen before becoming deputy head of

President Ford's press office. Bush's candidacy stopped just short of absorbing the entire Ford apparatus.

Also moving over to Bush from London, where she had worked for Ambassador Kingman Brewster after leaving the CIA, was Jennifer Fitzgerald. By then regarded as a long-term Bush staffer, she was, at the age of forty-seven, effectively his chief of staff, either with or without that title, scheduling his appointments and, as the *Washington Post* said, serving him in "a variety of positions."[41]

For the campaign's media needs, Bush took on the Robert Goodman Agency of Baltimore, advisers to Republican candidates. Goodman, who was known as a provocative figure in the field, sometimes sounded as though he were trying to sell the candidate to himself. "The American Eagle," as he promptly nicknamed Bush, appeared to him, as he said later, as "that new face people were hungering for." Goodman, playing to the hilt both the candidate's anonymity and experience, turned out television commercials that promised "this time there will be no repeating past mistakes. This time there can be George Bush: a president we won't have to train." As two reporters then described what happened, "Bush came out of Iowa as the first hot media candidate of 1980, the Texas Yankee with the energy and resumé that wouldn't quit."[42]

The perception of Bush as more moderate than Reagan, as more in tune with the party's center, had even more to do with tone than ideology. George Bush was a Burkean conservative with the heart and soul of a moderate, a conservative moderate rather than a moderate conservative. Or as *Times* reporter Adam Clymer put it, he was a "conservative Republican who talks moderately."[43] For instance, Bush, like Reagan, opposed President Carter's efforts to abrogate the old Panama Canal treaty. Their difference, however, was less one of substance than tone. As Roy Reed pointed out in 1980, Reagan's position on the canal was unequivocal: "We built it. We paid for it. It's ours. We're going to keep it." Bush's was far more measured: "I understand trying to break out of colonialism in this hemisphere. I understand that you don't go and cut a swath through another guy's country to build a canal. But I think it's of overriding importance that the United States keep its commitments, and that's the reason I opposed the treaty."[44] Two writers for *Rolling Stone* came away with the view that "George Bush is promising to be the most appealing conservative candidate in this election," less threatening than either Reagan or Connally and imbuing "his message with the infectious optimism of a patrician entrepreneur."[45] Keene, convinced that "Bush was more conservative than his image and background would lead one to believe," recalled that however much he tried to stay to the right during the primaries, he was "not very good at it."[46] He needed to keep in mind that the party's heart and soul now belonged to Reagan. "If you attack him," Keene advised Bush, "they'll hate you. You can't do that. What you have to do is position yourself so that these other candidates are further away from him and you're there. And if he fails, then you can get it."[47]

Bush did have attractions for some on the right. Keene was right; he was a backup in case Reagan faltered because of age. Others liked Bush's knowledge of foreign policy. A *New York Times/CBS News* survey, completed just before their Nashua, New Hampshire, debate, showed that Bush backers tended to be even more antiunion and antinational health insurance than Reaganites.[48] Hugh Gregg, the former New Hampshire governor and the 1976 Reagan state chairman, also had no trouble switching to Bush four years later.

Former CIA personnel constituted another source of Bush enthusiasts. Andrew Falkiewicz, an ex-intelligence spokesman, served as a foreign-policy specialist during the campaign. Stefan A. Halper, a policy director for the campaign, was also a son-in-law of Ray Cline, the ex-CIA official and contributor to the Team-B strategic analysis. Robert Gambino quit the CIA just before joining the Bush team, creating consternation within the Carter administration because of his access to files of those given high security clearance. Bill Colby noted that he "had a flood of people from the CIA who joined his supporters. They were retirees devoted to him for what he had done." One estimate placed the number of intelligence officials who worked for him during the campaign as at least twenty-five. "The CIA guys came in droves to work for George Bush because they understood that he understood how the world works," recalled Mary Sheila Gall. So many agents worked for Bush, in fact, Keene recalled, that when Bush made his announcement of candidacy, "half the audience was wearing raincoats."[49]

A minor problem, but one of potential embarrassment, was experienced by Bush friend Barber Conable, who handled the candidate's scheduling. "We had a terrible time keeping the UN ambassadors from forming a club for George Bush, or keeping the CIA people from organizing support for him. That would not have been very helpful."[50]

Bush staffers were virtually indistinguishable from those who aligned themselves with other members of the new right, also known as "movement conservatives." There were, of course, the confirmed Bushites who went to work at the Houston headquarters housed in a suite at 710 North Post Oak Road and at the Washington-area nerve center located in a four-story brick building in Alexandria's Old Town, at 732 North Washington Street, just across the river from Washington, D.C. Connie Horner, who would head the White House personnel office for President Bush and later join the Civil Rights Commission, was an English teacher and, like her husband, a Democrat. Along with many other conservatives of her vintage, she broke with the party of the New/Fair Deal and Great Society. Horner joined the Bush campaign by way of the conservative Heritage Foundation, where she teamed up with Cathy Barr. Barr, whose first political experience came from working for the candidacy of supply-side purist Jeffrey Bell in New Jersey and had written a pro-Bush article for the *National Catholic Register,* understood that the Bush inner circle was generally more conservative than its facade of moderation. Bush, she learned, was closer to Reagan's ideologically than she realized without ever being "a conservative-movement person." His conservative instincts were visceral rather than intellectual. "When he goes with his gut reaction," she added, "he tends to be a fairly conservative guy. Bush was the nonembarrassing Republican for Democrats who were turning into Republicans."

Mary Sheila Gall, a young graduate of a Catholic school in Buffalo, New York, who first went to work for James Buckley and Jack Kemp, reflected on her move to Bush saying that she "really had to give it some thought because Ronald Reagan was running as well" and "I'm a conservative Republican," but it turned out to be "the perfect job," long hours and all. "He gets more out of people," she said about Bush. "He's able to draw people in, find out more about issues or personal situations or whatever because he has that ability to make people comfortable. I felt, well, here's a man who might not win, who comes across as a moderate Republican, who doesn't have the greatest speaking style in the world, not as compared with Ronald Reagan. While Reagan's point of view was well known to conservatives, Bush's wasn't." Watching Bush from the inside, Gall "saw how the debate was shaping up within the staff and his reaction to it" and her "comfort level increased a lot because I saw when the liberal component of the campaign would give him something, he would say, 'Oh, no. This isn't right. I disagree with this.'"[51]

So it was with Ford people who found themselves almost equally at home with George Bush. More than simply in the middle of the road, Bush's campaign was managing to draw across-the-board support among Republicans. They certainly wanted to keep things that way.

There was, though, as Alan Crawford called his 1980 book, *Thunder on the Right.* Opponents of the Panama Canal treaty were taking aim at such supporters as Democratic Senators Frank Church and John Culver, both of whom were defeated in November. Two-thirds of Americans declared themselves in favor of a constitutional amendment to legalize prayer in public schools.[52] Suggesting any interference with "the right to bear arms," despite majority approval, was unthinkable for the overwhelming number of politicians who wanted to keep their jobs.

"Their following is immense," wrote Crawford about the religious right, the proliferation of television evangelists and ultraconservative publicists. Drawing heavily from the ranks of born-again Christians, finding political compatibility with conservative Roman Catholics, and taking heavy advantage of new technology, militant fundamentalists were poised to drive national politics as never before. The most prominent individual driving forces were Rev. Jerry Falwell, the Baptist preacher from Lynchburg, Virginia, whose "Old Time Gospel Hour" aired each week on 325 television stations and 300 radio stations to help drive home the teachings of his Moral Majority, and Rev. Pat Robertson, who warned listeners to his "700 Club" over the Christian Broadcasting Network about the "humanistic/atheistic/hedonistic influence on American government" coming from such deviltry as the Trilateral Commission and the Council on Foreign Relations. The Rev. James Robison steered his Religious

Roundtable as a homophobic crusade. The Christian Voice offered a voting guide with its "report card" on Congress. Richard Viguerie, already the chief money-raiser on the right, worked the secular side of the ideological passion.[53]

Always a powerful force in American culture—"the first of their political institutions," wrote Alexis de Tocqueville in 1835—where the religiosity has consistently been found to be more intense than in any developed nation, religious fundamentalism had increased remarkably since the 1960s, with so-called "baby boomers" showing significant increases in church attendance. Spurred by various Supreme Court decisions over a period of two decades, the return-to-God movement drew additional momentum from the same changes in American society that inspired the more conservative political reactions. The trend continued for the balance of the century. "The culture of belief," noted *The Economist* of London in 1995, "is thriving in America, without the help of school prayer."[54] Not surprisingly, in a nation where culture and religion can be as strong, if not stronger, than economics as a political dividing force, more secular Democrats were steadily being abandoned by the movement of more fundamentalist religious groups toward the Republican party. As their numbers increased through the 1970s, their devotion became ever more concentrated on the political personality of Ronald Reagan. The Christian Voice, a new conservative lobby launching a million-dollar media campaign, also threw its weight behind Reagan as the true "born-again Christian" running for president.[55]

John Connally learned that the hard way when he challenged the former California governor in the South Carolina primary. With considerable bitterness, Connally, one of Bush's preconvention rivals, recalled how he had been forced to end his political career. The state was key to demonstrating that Reagan could be stopped in the South. "But I saw who nominated people in '76," said the big Texan seven years before his death,

> and seventy-five percent of them were going to be back in '80. And seventy-five percent of those in '80 would be back in '84, and so on. And it's the same group. I've worked with them. I've seen them at the precinct level. They're a different breed of people. They are people who are just committed. We did our best in South Carolina, the only state where we really met him [Reagan] head to toe. I had Strom Thurmond traveling with me on the bus, the most popular man in the history of South Carolina politics. I had the only former Republican governor of the state. I had the principal mayors of the cities and the newspapers. I had more support in South Carolina than Reagan by a considerable margin. And we worked it. We worked hard. We went on a bus, day after day, twelve, fourteen hours a day. . . . But when it was all said and done, he got fifty-five percent of the vote. I got thirty percent, and Bush got fifteen. Within a week after that, I withdrew. I said there's no point in going on with this. . . . My wife met a guy at a little airport over there. She told him who she was and asked him to support her

husband. He just looked at her. He said, "I'm for Ronald Reagan." He said, "I've always been for Ronald Reagan. I'll always be for Ronald Reagan from my head to my toes."

That's what it was; religious fervor, pure and simple. "Reagan had the same people for him," added Connally, "as Carter had for him. That's what made Carter survive against thirteen opponents in the primaries in '76. Carter was a born-again Christian. What sustained him from primary to primary was basically the evangelical Christians. Nobody knew what it was in '76. Since '80, you hear it; but in '76 nobody recognized it for what it was. And Reagan actually had penetrated that very group. And he took most of them away from Carter in 1980 because they were disappointed in Carter." Connally's campaign outlay of $12 million bought him just one delegate.[56]

Reagan's cooption of the religious right seemed complete. One of his more experienced political aides, the irreverent consultant Lyn Nofziger, noting that the former movie actor was a very religious man who always seemed to wonder what God wanted him to do, planted a disturbing thought in his head. God, Nofziger pointed out, could not be overly interested in the United States. How, if He were, could he give us the presidents we have had?[57]

First came the Iowa campaign. The state was a special objective for George Bush. Local precinct groups caucused early in the political season. Victory there, while not significant in terms of delegates, offered a big psychological boost for the primaries to follow. In 1976, Jimmy Carter scored his first coup there; little wonder that Carter's game plan was lesson one for Bush and Jim Baker. They worked the state for months before Bush announced his candidacy. Already assembled behind him were the state's leading moderates, most prominently Governor Robert D. Ray. He also had both Iowa's national committeemen on his side, Mary Louise Smith and John McDonald, who met in a Dallas Center, Iowa, living room on February 28 to develop plans for mobilizing the state's GOP structure.[58]

Rich Bond, a twenty-nine-year-old lawyer from New York's Long Island, followed, taking up residence in Ames with his young family and working to organize each of Iowa's ninety-nine counties. He and local organizers set up "Bush Brigades" that became the nucleus of support in the state. All in all, Bond made some 300 personal appearances. Bush himself campaigned in that center of the Middle West farm belt with a flair rarely surpassed.[59]

"I have covered a lot of political candidates during the last twenty-five years," wrote Roy Reed in *The New York Times*, "but I have never known one—not even Hubert Humphrey—who ran with more zeal and determination." His energy was infectious, as was his boyish enthusiasm; yet, the flow from his mouth seemed at times oddly incoherent, subjects without predicates, words pouring out at audiences without letting up for applause lines. He "speaks like a promising amateur still struggling to learn the art. He will never be a spellbinder," wrote the correspondent. "They say I'm a patrician," he said to folks in Iowa. "I don't even know what the word means. I'll have to look it up," vowed the man who wondered why, just because he came from a privileged background, he *could not* like country music and pitching horseshoes.[60] Most of all, he seemed misplaced, a "tall poised figure in a Brooks Brothers suit who sips beer out of a pilsner glass and chats easily." Tom Wicker reported that voters saw Bush as a " 'Connecticut Yankee' or 'a Yalie in a vest' in a party that is heavily Midwestern, Western, and Sun Belt in its outlook." Yet, his message was anything but clear, leaving some wondering whether he was "a moderate in conservative clothing, or a conservative with a moderate manner?"[61]

The Reagan campaign, meanwhile, became a model of overconfidence. Iowa was, in effect, Reagan's home state, next door to his birthplace, where, long before he portrayed George Gipp in *Knute Rockne,* his radio broadcast of Chicago Cubs baseball games had familiarized folks with "Dutch" Reagan. He had, moreover, entered the heartland state's caucuses in 1976 and won its delegates by two-to-one over Ford, a sitting president! Early on, three years later, polls convinced Reagan's man, John Sears, that the state was his. It made sense to conserve money and stamina by minimizing a campaign where delegates were obviously in his corner. Money was tight. The new system of matching federal funds failed to anticipate the proliferation of primaries. So Sears prevailed. Reagan became a virtual shadow candidate, visiting the state only twice to Bush's seventeen trips. Reagan also sat out the precaucuses debate.

The thirty hours before Bush participated in a candidates's debate sponsored by the *Des Moines Register and Tribune* constituted a furious whirlwind of campaign activity. A recent poll by the paper showed him a full thirty-six points behind Reagan. Reagan's own pollster, Wirthlin, calculated a much closer spread, his man ahead by nineteen points.[62]

The debate, televised across the country, did nothing for Bush beyond publicity. John Anderson got national renown for the first time, especially when he asked rhetorically, "How do you balance the budget, cut taxes, and increase defense spending at the same time?" and answered his own question with, "It's very simple. You do it with mirrors." William Safire gave Howard Baker the prize for the strongest showing.[63] But Bush, who sat at the far left of the stage in the 2,600 seat auditorium, looked all too "morticianlike" in his black suit. Robert Goodman thought he appeared "tired, taut, nervous," and seated there along with the others, Dole, Crane, and Connally, "the Eagle" was obscured instead of dominant, a far cry from being featured alone on television ads.[64] His biggest gain came from the absence of Reagan, who watched the debate via TV from his California home.

Reagan's dominance began to weaken, but slowly. Wirthlin's postdebate survey showed him with 26 percent, with 18 for Baker and 17 for Bush. Even in the wake of his intensive campaigning, the "recognition factor" as reported by Gallup showed that Bush's name was known to barely over half of registered Republican voters in the country. Ford led and Reagan was next.[65]

Bush finally did get his boost. Other indicators were more positive. He placed first in a string of straw-vote preliminaries in the state and won a poll among Republicans at a convention in Maine. A new *Des Moines Register* survey showed Reagan losing half his Iowa Republican support within the past six weeks with Bush making gains.[66] The Reagan camp was also caught unawares when Bond managed to flood the state with "millions" of pieces of Bush literature during the final week before the caucuses balloted.[67]

When they voted on the twenty-first, the turnout exceeded expectations, about 20 percent of enrolled Republicans. Bush's 33,530 total edged Reagan by 2,182, with the others far behind. The Bush victory, resulting in a *Newsweek* cover, had all the appearances of a bandwagon. Bush hailed the new-found momentum as the "Big Mo," a term derided by some as preppy and juvenile. The Bush triumph, certainly the product of hard work and organization, still needed a substantive foundation. Or, as his campaign manager, Jim Baker, later said, "We did not answer the question of 'George Why?' "[68]

But Bush's "Big Mo" was, in effect, the "Big Slow" for Reagan. Iowa had indeed given Bush his lift. The Reagan camp saw little beyond that reality. Wirthlin's new surveys showed Bush pushing ahead, moving from a 19 percentage-point deficit to a six-point lead as they went into New Hampshire.[69] The lineup had seemingly changed, from Reagan against the entire field to Reagan against Bush.

A primary there was welcome to Bush in other ways. Kennebunkport was but a short distance from New Hampshire's center of population. Bush based himself at the seaside residence and mixed family time with politics.[70] He had, in effect, returned to his northeastern origins and to presumed natural advantages.

Bets were hedged on a faltering Reagan. If New Hampshire's ultraconservatives were holding back, and at that stage it seemed that they were, they were doing so less for fear of Reagan extremism than through uncertainty about his age and physical fitness. The state, unlike adjacent Vermont, was fiercely conservative, antitaxation, and one of the few without a state income tax. Automobile license plates bore the slogan "Live Free or Die." William Loeb, publisher of the unremittingly right-wing newspaper, the *Manchester Union-Leader*, was perhaps a bit too way-out for prevailing tastes, but not by much. His paper greeted the Bush campaign by reviving the old charges about the alleged illegality of Nixon's Townhouse funds.[71] Many of Loeb's readers labored in the leather, textile, and electronics industries of New Hampshire. Mostly Democrats, they were conservative, small-state Roman Catholics largely removed from the old coalition that still dominated older urban centers. Reagan was one of their own, not at all like Bush, whom Loeb described in his *Union-Leader* as a "spoon-fed little rich kid," only "an incompetent liberal masquerading as a conservative."[72]

But the reality of the Bush campaign was that the perception of his moderation, largely because it was so amorphous, enabled him to nibble at both Reagan and Ford sources.[73] Another ex-governor, Hugh Gregg, who had led the Californian's campaign there four years earlier, now chaired the Bush forces. Nevertheless, Ford loyalists formed the nucleus of Bush's New Hampshire organization.[74]

Iowa, as Bush later conceded, made him too cocky. The "Big Mo" meant "there'll be absolutely no stopping me," thereby clearly underestimating the ability of other centrists to divide the moderate vote.[75] For Reagan, however, the test was essential. Iowa had raised too many questions about his viability. As Dave Keene explained, "if you were a New Hampshire Republican, you loved Reagan; Reagan lost Iowa," but now "Reagan was reported to be an old man who couldn't handle it."[76]

Manchester, the old textile city on the Merrimack with its large working-class population, became the site of a crucial debate. The League of Women Voters had a large television audience. Reagan was nervous. Some gasped when he said it was okay for American corporations to bribe foreign governments if that was what it took to do business there. The encounter was clearly Reagan's to lose, to confirm that he was past his prime. He picked up ground, however, and began to revive his followers with a strong closing statement about his "vision of America." Then, just near the end, he clinched success when asked by someone in the audience whether he had really told an ethnic joke that sounded anti-Italian. Reagan, clearly in full control of the situation, quickly said, "I don't tell them." Then he added, "I'm going to look over both shoulders from now on and I'm only going to tell stories about Irishmen because I'm Irish."[77]

What the audience had heard was the Reagan they had come to hear, the Reagan some feared was "over the hill and out of it." But there he was, with his marvelously modulated and reassuringly rich voice, the same delivery that had had Republicans agog since his pro-Goldwater speech in 1964. Still, the mass appeal, Reagan's ability to persuade, his raw patriotic heartland pitch, remained underestimated to the more sophisticated, even to such seasoned political people like Baker and Keene. They walked out that night satisfied. Bush had done well. Reagan had not set the world on fire. "But what we forgot," Keene said later, "was he didn't have to." There was plenty of confirmation in Wirthlin's findings. Thirty-seven percent of the potential Republican primary voters looked on, and his survey showed that fully one-third agreed that Reagan was the winner, with just 17 percent choosing Bush.[78]

Reagan's Manchester success was crucial and, indirectly, prepared the ground for the knockout of Bush in New Hampshire. A second debate, one planned for the 1,700-seat Nashua High School gymnasium on the evening of Saturday, February 23, carried the sponsorship of the *Nashua Telegraph*. The paper was ready to pick up the $3,500 in expenses because, as executive editor Jon L. Breen wrote to Gregg, it conceived of the meeting as a "one-on-one encounter given the prevalent wisdom that Mr. Reagan and Mr. Bush are the front-runners in the campaign for the Republican nomination."[79] Bush and his people could hardly have been more delighted. The arrangement would implicitly neutralize all the others, Crane, Dole, Anderson, and Howard Baker. Connally was out of Nashua in any event, busily campaigning in South Carolina. Both camps believed that excluding the others was a fine idea. "We thought it was the best thing since sliced bread," said Baker.[80]

Unfortunately, as things turned out, if Reagan came out of Manchester revived, Nashua left Bush better known for "wimpishness" and for complaining about having been "sandbagged" by Reagan. "I fear he used you to set me up," Bush wrote to Dole afterward, referring to the Kansan and three other candidates, adding that "Governor Reagan had definitely not played fair with me."[81]

Bush was right; Reagan had set him up. But Bush had also fallen right into the trap, choked, blown a chance to use his wits, and later had to admit that the whole affair was "rather devastating." The incident would almost cost him the vice presidential nomination. At that moment, too, amid new rumors that Gerald Ford's own ambitions might fill the post-New Hampshire vacuum, some of Bush's closest loyalists were tempted by the idea of teaming up once more with the ex-president. As consultant Keene noted, "Bush always believes his friends are his friends when they're not."[82]

It was also true that, as he pointed out to Dole in a confession of at least partial responsibility, that "confusion reigned until debate time." It was not until Jim Baker got a view of those other four candidates, the "Nashua Four," just before debate time that he realized that Bush was about to experience an "ambush" rather than a one-on-one with Reagan. The Federal Communications Commission, by ruling that sponsorship by the newspaper would constitute an illegal corporate campaign contribution, had opened the way for maneuvering to pick up the $3,500 tab. Reagan's men approached Bush with the idea of splitting the cost. Bush refused, so Reagan picked up the entire bill and changed the ground rules. John Sears's instinct led to the realization that it might be safer to include the other candidates rather than risk potential opprobrium as the plotters of their exclusion.

Invitations went out to the other four. Jon Breen, who was a Bush man and good friend of Hugh Gregg, had agreed to the defensive tactic of responding to a possible ambush by openly telling the audience that it was Reagan who was changing the rules in the middle of the game and that Bush was the honorable one abiding by the original commitment. On the night of the debate, with no live television cameras but plenty of news photographers and an overflow crowd, uncertainty forced a delay of almost a half hour. Bush, told that the "Nashua Four" were present, refused to meet with them, unlike Reagan, who was clearly using them for his own purpose. The commotion in a side room, off the gymnasium, was so intense that for a moment it seemed that only his wife Nancy's urging that he go on kept Reagan himself from refusing to go ahead with the whole thing.[83]

Breen, as moderator, was also determined to adhere to the original plan.

Indeed, there were just two chairs on the stage. Breen was eager to get started, and Bush got the signal to go up front. As he started forward, he was stopped by Senator Gordon Humphrey. The New Hampshire Republican had been campaigning statewide for Reagan. He urged Bush to first meet with all the others: "If you don't come right now," he told him, "you're doing a disservice to party unity."

Bush, angered, ignoring the prominence of the others as current Republican officeholders, and being signaled by *Telegraph* publisher J. Herman Pouliot to go on stage, snapped back: "Don't tell me about unifying the Republican party! I've done more for this party than you'll ever do! I've worked too hard for this and they're not going to take it away from me."[84]

Clearly upset and frustrated, and more than a touch self-righteous, Bush rushed to the stage. The crowd, furiously behind Reagan, erupted at the sight of him walking down the aisle followed by the other four candidates.

"This is getting to sound more like a boxing match," shouted Pouliot from the stage, explaining that the others had not been invited by the *Telegraph*, which only brought a wave of boos. One woman shouted, "Get them chairs!" and some two thousand people cheered. Bush, virtually isolated in his discontent, stared straight ahead as though oblivious of the turmoil.

That was fine with him, Reagan said, with the "Nashua Four" standing in a row behind him; open the debate and bring in more chairs. Moderator Breen, on the defensive, overreacted and said to the sound technician, "Turn Mr. Reagan's microphone off."

Reagan grabbed the mic, then, his theatrical instincts igniting, he delivered what became one of his most famous, game-saving one-liners: "I'm paying for this microphone, Mr. Green," he said, which effectively ended the debate. That he had butchered the moderator's name hardly mattered. The crowd went wild.

Bush slumped, looking "like a small boy who had been dropped off at the wrong birthday party," as publisher Loeb wrote afterward.[85]

Breen had clearly overreacted. "It was shocking to see it happen," commented Bush's press secretary, Teeley. "It almost took your breath away." Reagan, after all, was the ex-governor of California and running for the presidency. He did have the right to speak.[86]

All but Bush were heroes, Reagan their benefactor. They waved to the crowd. Bush kept silent, out of it, as the other four stormed off to their own press conferences. Dole, for one, was so livid when he came off the stage that "he wasn't a pleasant sight."

Bush took on Reagan after a while in a minidebate, but without much stomach; again, Reagan was triumphant. Bush later got the following assessment from Teeley: "The good news is that nobody paid any attention to the debate. The bad news is that you lost that, too."[87]

The entire episode, however, was not lost on New Hampshire's voters, even without live television. TV newscasts, both local and national, played it to the hilt for the next two days, capturing, as Jack Germond and Jules Witcover have written, "a rare moment in a political campaign—an instant of genuine drama that no media consultant could have plotted."[88] Bush then took Gregg's advice to leave the state and return to Houston while his supporters tried to publicize his side of the story. New Hampshire's television audience soon saw pictures of Bush jogging in Texas, while Reagan, seemingly oblivious to the frosty air, happily shook hands with local voters.[89]

Whatever support remained for Bush collapsed. The ground just gave way. He lost to Reagan that February 25, and lost badly, 49 percent to 23 percent of all votes cast. The five other major candidates, however, divided a total of 71,534, which indicated a distinct preference among the state's issue-conscious Republicans for moderates, even when discounting ballots cast for Connally and Crane. Bush had, at least in New Hampshire, staked out his ideological differences with the front-runner, especially on such issues as a liberalized abortion law and support for the Equal Rights Amendment.[90] The split at the center revived the Reagan campaign coffers and effectively expedited his march to the convention at Detroit. Bush still had enough power, at least in key industrial states, winning in Massachusetts, Connecticut, Pennsylvania, and Michigan. His loss to Reagan in the Texas home-state showdown on May 3, really hurt. Ultraconservative Lone Star Republicans gave the Californian only a slim popular vote edge but fifty out of the eighty delegates were chosen. Not much of an additional fight was possible.[91] Except for Anderson who then chose to run as an independent, the other candidates dropped out. Bush, the only obstacle to a Reagan victory by acclamation, faced the nine primaries scheduled for June 3, including California, with a campaign deficit of $400,000. The heavy number of primaries, up from thirteen twenty years earlier to thirty-four, had devastated budgets. The events in the tiny, atypical state of New Hampshire made the "Reagan revolution" inevitable.

One other candidate remained, undeclared, unstated, somewhere in the background, but never completely off-scene and reacting to the events in New Hampshire. As his party continued rightward, Gerald Ford became more of the centrist-moderate. As Bush and Baker stumbled, resurrecting Ford became a more attractive possibility. He believed that he could reverse his course, take back turning down the chance to enter primaries or create some campaign apparatus. Bush's New Hampshire blowout had set off the alarms.

Moderates behind Ford feared Reagan and his ideological obsessions. They feared repetition of the 1964 Goldwater disaster.[92] Reagan's base remained narrow because of all that fear about him. More and more, those guiding his foreign policy ideas were the CIA's Bush-era Team-B hard-liners bent on boosting military spending and scuttling strategic arms limitation talks, firm believers that only greater strength could bring peace.[93] Reagan would be putty in their hands. How in a cold war world forever on the brink of a nuclear holocaust could the nation pick a Hollywood movie actor turned right-winger, surrounded by self-made reactionary millionaires and digesting daily doses of polemics from such publications as *Facts Forum* and the *Conservative Digest?* "Would President Reagan be a threat to blow up the world?" went the joke. "Only between the hours of nine and five."[94] Of the entire field of declared and nondeclared candidates, nobody seemed capable of stopping the one man who charged up GOP delegates, who seemed more eager to nominate their man than to defeat Carter. Larry Speakes, Ford's former deputy press secretary, was fielding a Draft Ford Committee and GOP governors were huddling over what to do. Ford, sounding more and more eager to get into the center of the ring, spoke out from his retirement at Rancho Mirage, California, saying that "with the right kind of campaign I could be nominated." He would, he also said, have a "hard time saying no" to a draft committee and described himself, rather pointedly, as the "most electable Republican."[95]

Suddenly, both Reagan and Bush moved in the shadow of a shadow candidacy. A mid March *NYT/CBS News* poll, clearly inspired by the post-Nashua turn, showed Ford rated as a better candidate than anyone in the race. He addressed a Republican congressional dinner in Washington, seeming to edge closer to candidacy even while acknowledging that such activity would produce a Reagan victory by dividing the promoderate vote. It did, even then, seem clear that, as political scientist William Crotty later wrote, ex-President Ford would have to overcome much, especially at that late date, with, as one political scientist put it, "no organization, no established funding, campaign apparatus or a developed media campaign."[96] Bush, campaigning in Florida and trying to regain his "Big Mo," told reporters it was too late for Ford to play the spoiler's role. Finally, a few days later, Ford took the advice of those who counseled that Reagan's lead was too large, and announced he would not run.[97] Bush was relieved, but it was not the last of Gerald Ford.

He tried as hard as he could to hang on. The others, notably Dole, were less successful. The Kansas veteran of Ford's 1976 campaign suspended further activity after Nashua and soon dropped out altogether. His rivals peeled away one at a time. Sears, who had given Reagan bad advice about Iowa, was dumped even before the New Hampshire votes came in.

Reagan's people were undoubtedly correct in denying that the change had anything to do with ideology. But his rightward turn was unmistakable. He even suggested putting the country back on the gold standard, from which it had been removed at the twilight of the New Deal. Howard Baker, left in the center with Bush and Anderson, was proving himself a better senator than campaigner. Dead last in South Carolina, with 1 percent of the vote, he, too, pulled out. Anderson chose the "independent" route, while Connally banked on that showdown in South Carolina where the general pattern prevailed. The blue-collar, ex-Democratic shift was Reagan-bound.[98] Bush remained the candidate of old-line GOP blue bloods, his rhetoric a nuanced conservatism. As in Florida, in particular, reported Howell Raines, "the wealthy aristocrats who fled here from Havana are siding with Mr. Bush, while working-class Cuban Republicans, many of whom still dream of overthrowing Castro, are loyal to Mr. Reagan."[99]

In Pennsylvania, Bush did little to recover his standing with the front-runner by characterizing Reagan's fiscal supply-side ideas as "voodoo economics," a phrase suggested by Pete Teeley to clarify the differences between them.[100] Slow to be picked up by the news media, the contemptuous characterization probably damaged Bush more than Reagan in the long run. Bush also promised to deliver plans for a balanced budget within one hundred days of taking office. Reagan's tax cuts, he declared, were out of place at a time of inflation. In Florida and South Carolina, the Reagan campaign, frustrating both Bush and Connally, succeeded in its rightward move in tapping voters once drawn to Nixon and George Wallace by exploiting the fundamental conservatism of so many registered Democrats. Bush, his hostility toward Connally already deepened after being warned that his fellow Texan would use his former support for gun-control legislation against him in Alabama, got into a clash with the Connally camp over its use of some $70,000 in "walking-around money" for black ministers to give the candidate access to parishioners and get them to the polls.[101]

In Florida, a rightist named Mike Thompson sparked a campaign by his Florida Conservative Union to incite fellow sympathizers about Bush's membership in the Trilateral Commission. Bush had, in fact, prudently resigned from the group at the start of the primary season; that and its actual function were obviously irrelevant as they were charged with being insufficiently anti-Communist "hungry power brokers." Were they, Thompson buzzed the state's voters, serving the Rockefellers and banking interests who had no real passion for taking on communism? Were they scheming for "one-worlders"? The Bush campaign, on the defensive in Florida, considered a round of ads countering the anti-Trilateralist conspiratorialists, but scrapped the plan. Clearly, it would place them in the position of having to explain what Bush's Florida campaign director, Tom Kieppe, called a "nonissue." Bush, complaining to reporters about such tactics, said, "I despise it. It's terrible the way I've been abused. You'd think the national press would have been more indignant over this sort of thing. It's—well, it's antiintellectual, that's what it is. It's worse than the Birch stuff. And Reagan acquiesces—like he did when his people used it against my son George."[102]

The antiabortion forces also gunned for him in the state. Newsletters deplored his "liberalism" because of his willingness, while opposing abortion, to permit federal funding for victims of rape and incest. The harassment became so intense, with allegations that he was not really a conservative, that the issue continually confronted him on the stump. Finally, he lost his patience when a Fort Lauderdale physician kept pressing him about his position. "Go fuck yourself," Bush whispered into the man's ear. Right-wing newsletters had a field day trumpeting a new anti-Bush charge: vulgarity.[103]

Bush did poorly in Florida and, further demonstrating weakness against Reagan below the Mason-Dixon line, ran a poor third in South Carolina, a state where the Reaganites were captained by a youthful political strategist, Lee Atwater. Bush did pick up the endorsement of the first organized group of Southern black Republicans and drew support from three South Carolina papers, including *The State* of Columbia, which hailed his political philosophy as a cross between Goldwater and Rockefeller and, therefore, solidly in the "middle of the American road." Atwater reflected the growing anticipation about a Bush showing in the state by predicting that he would finish second, but he clocked in with just 15 percent, half Connally's share, and a full 39 percent behind Reagan.[104]

South Carolina, however, cost Bush Dave Keene. He had, earlier, right after New Hampshire, cut himself off from Bob Mosbacher by suggesting that Bush's fund-raiser was flirting with the idea of going back to Ford. Keene, who always felt a cultural gulf between himself and the candidate, now stood accused, this time by Bush himself. Bush suspected that the South Carolina campaign had been hedged at least partly out of a deal Keene had supposedly made with Reagan about not going head-to-head with him in the primary and leaving Connally as the sole opponent.

"It's my understanding that you went behind my back and made a deal with the Reagan people," Bush said.

"George," replied an already alienated Keene, "you can do any fucking thing you want," and walked out of the room.[105]

Keene, it would turn out, was just one in an array of consultants who passed through Bush's political career. To a large degree representatives of cultures that were inimicable to his own, they were an increasingly indispensable part of winning elections. His own distaste for the process of soliciting votes made such aides increasingly essential. In South Carolina, and more recently from the Reagan camp, Bush found such an asset in the person of young Lee Atwater.

Atwater, who had been born as recently as 1951, was a hard-driving consultant who would later be credited with updating the ancient art of attack politics. The young man was called by a *New York Times* correspondent the practitioner of "politics as a sort of nonlethal but still intense warfare" and capable of provoking the hyperbolic denunciation by a Democratic congresswoman as "the most evil man in America." But Atwater, undisciplined as an undergraduate student and limited to undistinguished Newberry College, near his Columbia, South Carolina, home, had a special gift of mastering what makes American voters tick. "When I got into politics in South Carolina," he once explained, "the establishment was all Democrats and I was antiestablishment. The young Democrats were all the guys running around in three-piece suits, smoking cigars, and cutting deals, so I said, 'Hell, I'm a Republican.'" Atwater, who received his bachelor's degree in history and earned a master's in communications, later worked on a Ph.D. dissertation about presidential campaigns. His major tutors, however, were Richard Nixon, to whose skill at exploiting the politics of anxiety he was completely devoted, J. Strom Thurmond, and Ronald Reagan. By the age of twenty-seven, his background included a reputation for using anti-Semitism to help Carroll Campbell win a congressional seat, and, two years later, for what he himself described as "guerrilla tactics." As did his mentors, he well understood the use of such wedge issues as race and class to pry apart the old Democratic coalition.[106]

Bush still headed the Republican National Committee when he first encountered Atwater. Shrewder than most people realized, with a keen understanding of personal relationships, Atwater attracted the attention of Bush, an older man sensing the potential value of one so many years his junior. In a move that the fun-loving Atwater never forgot, Bush helped him woo the girlfriend who later became his wife by lending him his boat so he could romance her on a weekend Potomac cruise.[107] Before the 1980 political season came to an end, Lee had graduated from statewide maneuvering against Connally and Bush to become Southern regional coordinator for the Reagan-Bush ticket.

It was that single-minded passion for winning, perhaps even more than the astute intelligence, that distinguished Lee. His tactics spared no opponent. Where there were no vulnerabilities, he invented them. For instance, the most insidious anti-Bush tactic in a state deemed vital for proving one's viability in the South was concocted by the innovative Lee Atwater. Atwater used radio to play the voice of William Buckley's brother, Reid. The speaker, identified only as "Mr. Buckley" with the vocal intonations associated with his brother, encouraged listeners to believe that the *National Review* editor himself had taken to the airwaves to deplore Bush's heretical contravention of their right to bear arms, although Bush's advocacy of restrictions was ten years in the past. Atwater, just as he denied responsibility for the anti-Semitic campaign in 1978, separated himself from that one. The tactic nevertheless had its effect. Whether it made the difference between a second or third place finish for Bush, the damage was done. That he had long since moved away from advocating federal controls made no difference. Atwater promoted the Reagan campaign by portraying Bush as an enemy of the "right to bear arms."[108]

The South Carolina experience did, of course, confirm that Bush had fallen a long way since his Iowa "Big Mo." The numbers were no longer there. Reagan got five times his vote in Illinois, and he even trailed John Anderson by a wide margin. In Pennsylvania, without Anderson in the race because he was in the process of converting to an independent candidacy, Bush became the favorite of the moderates with a heavy draw among upper-class Main Line Republicans just outside of Philadelphia. He finished with a solid 54 percent, but, even there, Reagan won more delegates and moved closer to the 998 needed to clinch the nomination.[109] Michigan, however, became what has been called his "most impressive" showing since Iowa. He topped Reagan by 57 to 32 percent.

But the victory was hollow. Reagan took Oregon that same day, and media calculations showed Reagan with enough projected delegates to win. Equally worrisome, with the big and costly California primary looming just ahead, the Michigan success failed to attract additional funding. Money, which had plagued both the Reagan and Bush campaigns throughout the primaries, with the New Hampshire victory making it possible for the former to go on, had become the formidable and, it seemed in all logic, decisive obstacle. The campaign's deficit included money owed to paid staffers forced to take salary cuts. With Bush cancelling further campaign stops to enable him to get to Houston for the Memorial Day weekend and contemplate what lay ahead, Jim Baker met the press.[110]

His words were only for background purposes, Baker told them, not for attribution. He had, as he faced the reporters, little idea how to manage a California campaign on a shoestring. Rich Bond and others had gone there to set up an operation to at least give the impression of a serious fight, but the entire thing was a scam to dupe the press into believing that they were running a serious operation. He hardly had the money to invest in getting the delegates he didn't have, especially with Reagan just about over the top. In that backgrounder, confronted by the press with the starkness of the situation, Baker acknowledged the dilemma. He never quite said that Bush was abandoning the fight, but to those who heard him, there was only one conclusion, and they hurried to reveal that Bush was dropping out.[111]

The only problem was the candidate, who had yet to reach that decision himself. Back in Houston that Saturday morning, Barbara was interviewed at home by a local reporter, Monica Reeves. She rejected the notion of quitting. George Bush should stay and fight, she said. Jeb agreed. So did brother Jonathan. That was clearly the sense of the family. As a close friend pointed out, "there's a strong tradition in the Bush family that you fight." They were not, however, privy to the financial and delegate realities.[112]

The candidate was. He and Jeb, defying Houston's heat and humidity, went for a three-mile jog in Memorial Park. Despite the oppressive weather, Bush ran on, outpacing his son and a fellow from the Secret Service. After about two miles, Jeb and the security man had had enough. They fell by the wayside, as the candidate went on, completing the course. Later, after showering and changing, he spent the rest of the afternoon relaxing with friends in the Houston Country Club, his decision still unmade.

Baker arrived that evening along with Vic Gold. Gold, a former deputy press secretary for Barry Goldwater and speechwriter for Vice President Spiro Agnew, was pretty savvy. He had no great love for Ronald Reagan, and certainly was pushing for a Bush nomination. He later helped Bush write his 1988 campaign autobiography. But Gold, in that situation, agreed with Baker that George had no choice but to drop out. Persistence could only lead to self-destruction. Angering the front-runner, the man who had virtually clinched the nomination, would destroy whatever chance he had to be tapped for the vice presidency. Both men, Baker and Gold, were in complete agreement. Their friend, George, had to see the logic. Baker, at a loss, had turned to Keene and asked, "What are you going to do if he decides to stay in?" The consultant could only shrug his shoulder and say, "There ain't anything I can do."[113]

Gold, who had been assisting in the campaign, was persuaded by Baker to travel to Houston with him. "I want you to go," Baker told Gold, "because I need you to talk him into it."

Baker knew, and what he was trying to say to Gold was that he was too close to Bush to try to persuade him. George was stubborn; everyone knew that. But that was only one thing. The other thing related to the dynamics of their long, close friendship. Even a good friend, Baker knew, loses credibility when wrong too often. The opposite pole, being right just too often, can be as counterproductive among two instinctive competitors. Little brother/big brother constituted an excellent example, where success could be a greater obstacle to friendship than failure. Gold recalls thinking that "it was some sort of charade."

He walked into Bush's Houston home with Baker that Saturday night and found out that "sure enough, George says he's going to run. He's going to continue. It took me about ten minutes to figure out that he means it. He feels he's made a commitment and he has to go ahead. I didn't understand this aspect of George Bush."[114]

Baker, of course, had anticipated all this. He was prepared for exactly what followed. The candidate spoke to both men, going on about the people who had been working for him in Ohio and New Jersey. They had gone out, put themselves on the line for a year or more. How could he let them down now? Dole, Gold was thinking, would not waste his time with such thoughts. He'd do what he had to do and that would be that. But Bush was different. He went on about how long all those campaign workers had been at it. And some were owed money. They'd accepted pay cuts and still stayed on board. How could he leave them stranded? "I can't do that," he said that evening, which was exactly why Baker had brought Gold along.

And Gold pressed his point. Bush would only anger Reagan. It'll be just like '64. "You'll go to the convention like Nelson Rockefeller. Only then you'd have divided the party." The yahoos on the far right, the rampaging radical "true believers" had hooted and howled, in Frisco's Cow Palace, almost verging on storming the stage and turning around and waving fists toward the "leftist" media people. Then, after the damage, and most of all to your chances, "you'll have to bite the bullet and get out."

Bush didn't reply. He just sat there, thinking. He had no answer, except, finally, "all right." He went to tell Barbara, and walked back into the room and said to Baker and Gold, "Let's go out and have dinner tonight at a Mexican restaurant."[115]

That Monday morning, he stood in the ballroom of the Marriott West

Loop Hotel, the same spot where John Connally had made his recent announcement of withdrawal. Only, Bush was not withdrawing. Not quite. Withdrawal would mean the end of federal matching funds. Too much was owed to stop that income. He would just stop campaigning, stop competing against Reagan. Against a backdrop of "George Bush for President" posters, he stood alongside Barbara. She hugged her young grandson, George, and watched her husband closely, holding back tears. Jeb stood behind them, together with Columba and their daughter, Noelle. The place looked like a George Bush rally, flanked by family and Secret Service agents. "You gotta know when to fold 'em," he said, and pledged to work for a united party effort to defeat Jimmy Carter in the fall. Baker, meanwhile, had left nothing to chance. He worked out assurances with the Reaganites not to shout Bush out of the convention, not to duplicate the 1964 San Francisco fiasco. Bush, after all, was doing his part. He was proving to be a good competitor. There should be some consideration for ending the bloodletting. All hands agreed that Gold had done his job well.[116]

Bush's work was not done. He still owed that money and the debt, for all the cost cutting in ads and travel expenses, stood at $400,000, not outlandish for a campaign but there were also those salaries. Workers had taken cuts; some stayed on as volunteers. So Bush followed that Houston announcement by appearing at a series of dinners and other fund-raisers. In August, true to his determination, salaried campaign people got their checks. As Jeb wrote in his cover letters, "Through Dad's hard work, the campaign deficit was eliminated prior to the convention because he thought that the people who had their salaries cut during the campaign should be reimbursed." Indeed, "every person from the campaign who had gone on half pay got his money," recalled Ron Kaufman, a young New Englander who went from running supermarkets—"wrapping lettuce," he liked to say—along the Massachusetts North Shore to becoming a $12,000-a-year political organizer. "It left an impression on me forever. He felt that it was a debt owed. He made a commitment to himself that, before the convention, he'd pay off his debt." Kaufman, who described himself as "a little bit of a vigilante," became a lieutenant in the Bush army.[117]

CHAPTER FOURTEEN

The Rise of the Lone Star Yankee

%

B ush had outlasted all competitors except Reagan, whose choice of a running mate would determine whether, after all those years, his only future was in Houston and the oil business.

The primaries had left their usual scars. The Nashua incident was especially costly, but Bush and his friends continued to insist that he had only tried to fulfill his commitment. Not fully understood at that moment, however, was how the perception that he was a "wimp" had filtered into the language about a man with a heroic past. Even years later, key Reagan aide Lyn Nofziger told the press that his boss shared that view.[1] More easily overlooked by Reagan, perhaps, was the "voodoo economics" jab that really cut to the economic heart of movement conservatism, but his admirers were bound to be less charitable. It brought effective ridicule to their fundamental economic assumptions.

Bush's priority was to reduce inflation. His primary campaign had opened by denouncing "tax-and-spend" Democrats. Along with Reagan, his foreign policy assumptions emphasized "credible military strength." No one could miss how that jabbed at Carter's embarrassments, especially the hostage standoff in Iran. So the firmest line between Reagan and himself was accomplished by denouncing "phony promises" and tying the creation of economic stability to wiping out the deficit and focusing on the broader dimensions of foreign policy.[2]

Four months after declaring his candidacy, he returned to the National Press Club in Washington and described his "nightmare" as the "great thunderclap that will transform the world" with the "unraveling of the international order," as the Russians were forced to scramble to replenish their own oil resources. No nation, he argued, could be secure without abundant energy. He warned that the "rushing together" of such forces could create an "open window" and vulnerability to a Soviet first strike. In that kind of situation, oil-seeking Russians would invariably go for the Persian Gulf. There could be, he suggested, a second Cuban missile crisis.

Only eleven days later, his words seemed especially prescient. A coup in Afghanistan brought to power Hafizullah Amin, who proclaimed the beginning of a "better Socialist order" with strong ties to the Soviet Union. Hafizullah himself lasted little more than three months. But what happened was no better. Soviet troops invaded the country in December and installed their own puppet as president. Jimmy Carter then insisted that the Soviets were aiming at the gulf.[3]

Bush's words seemed lost. They failed to delineate the issues in ways that could compete with Reagan's colorful rhetoric, and so nobody seemed to be paying attention. But he believed they were true and needed to be explained.

It was during that primary season when the "Jennifer problem" resurfaced. Bush, perhaps, did not believe that he had a problem. Others, including Jim Baker, were very upset, although most managed to mute their discontent. "There's just something about her that makes him feel good," said one Bush confidant. "I don't think it's sexual. I don't know what it is. But if Bush ever runs for president again, I think he's going to have to make a change on that score."[4]

She clearly was an anomaly. Bush staffers worked in a casual, informal atmosphere. He was everybody's friend, a "nice guy." Even low-echelon people could shoot the breeze with him. He thought nothing of picking up a phone and calling anyone with whatever was on his mind. Dan Gilchrist, who teamed up with him as early as 1968 and became a longtime supplier of funny stories for his speeches, remembered him as "a very, very humorous guy, aside from just telling jokes." Having a good sense of humor, or, at least, a pleasant, light-hearted personality, practically became a prerequisite for working in his world.[5] He was "a classy guy," stressed Mary Sheila Gall, touching on her introduction to Bush in 1979, "funny and charming and very relaxed." He was one of those people "with warmth and kindness" who had the ability to make others comfortable.[6] Jennifer seemed a stranger to all this, misplaced, more like a first sergeant needing to shape up the troops and getting them to respect lines of command and tables of organization, even as they relished their chummy relationships.

She became the ogre of the camp. Dave Keene thought she was "a massive pain in the ass to everyone," a barrier "between the campaign and the candidate. It's been my experience that if you're looking for the power in some of these offices, you find that person. That's the role she fulfilled."[7]

Fitzgerald had some significant predecessors. Eisenhower and Nixon had Sherman Adams and Bob Haldeman. She was Bush's "gatekeeper," the interloper who stood in the way. Her control of his schedule gave her the keys to his office. Some thought that was "what her real clout was." They suspected that "you got on or didn't get on that schedule based on how she felt." She was brusque and formal, the "ice lady" who froze out everybody else, a "bitch on wheels," who lost her temper all too easily. Once, when she scheduled

Bush to join clubby downtown businessmen at a luncheon instead of showing his face and shaking hands with factory workers, there was an ugly scene when such wisdom was challenged. Colleagues began to assume that her power must have come from the "strange hold" she had on the boss.[8]

He had "a total blind spot about it," said one coworker. She was either a martinet or a mistress. How else to account for it? Everything about her was out of sync with the known world of George Bush. "The sad thing is that he doesn't see what it's doing to him," said still another who did not want to be identified. "People who have been with him a long time are losing respect."[9] Much of the "cocktail circuit," wrote Philip Nobile and Eric Nadler in a comprehensive piece on the situation, "has held Fitzgerald guilty by intimate association."[10]

It was said that either Bush was simply unable to disappoint those who were friendly and loyal to him or he was "playing around." Buzzes about scandal were inevitable. The more his power grew, the more reckless became the tabloids. They found "Ms. Xs" and any number of fantasy dalliances to feed a gossip-hungry capital in the post-JFK world of national politics that eventually entrapped Senator Gary Hart of Colorado. As some of Bush's aides had anticipated, however, talk centered around the "Jennifer problem" and continued to haunt the rest of his political career.

Such stories were spread throughout the decade, with sleaze-seeking "new journalism" eagerly playing the game. Reporters began to fish around for clues. Included were such organs as the *New York Post, The Village Voice, Time, Newsweek,* the *L.A. Weekly,* and, during his presidency, *Spy* magazine. Even the *Washington Post*'s respectable team of Bob Woodward and Walter Pincus, in a six-part series just before the 1988 election, fueled matters by noting unexplained absences during the years when he was preparing for the 1980 primaries. His "excuse," they stated, was having to fly to Washington for secret meetings of former CIA directors, which placed him out of reach. They even quoted ex-CIA Director Stansfield Turner as saying he "never knew former directors had meetings and there were none when I was there." Had they checked more closely and been less eager to be suggestive, they would have found that Bush joined ex-Director Bill Colby and his own former deputy, E. Henry Knoche, in Washington on April 5, 1978. All three testified that day before the Senate Select Committee on Intelligence on protecting foreign and domestic secrets. Not even the Bush spokesman they interviewed later could recall the event, but he did remember that Bush took off "personal time in Washington" for "tennis, visits with friends, and dinners."[11]

The woman at the center of it all kept away from the press, which made things even more enticing. If there was substance to all the talk, she was not the one playing the game, or, for that matter, stirring excitement. The lady was not given to blackmail or peddling her story.[12] She did tell a congressional friend, Robert Dornan of California, that "these stories are sickening . . . they're vicious."[13]

Whatever may or may not have actually happened, Jennifer Fitzgerald was, in part, paying the price of being a successful female with a powerful job. How could she exercise such authority without actually having slept with the boss, went the speculation. Could anything other than sex explain how she fit into the picture? "Everyone keeps painting me as the old ogre," she once said in a rare interview. "I really don't worry about it. All these bizarre things simply aren't true."[14] Another woman, a Houston native, Shirley Green, then serving as Bush's deputy press secretary, explained that Jennifer was doing exactly what her boss wanted her to do. She had long since become his right-hand assistant, regarded by some as a "walking memory bank," always ready to tap her "computer warehouse of knowledge" with the precise piece of information he needed. Her instinct for politics was sound, enabling her to be understanding of tight spots encountered by some members of the staff; at such moments, she could even be pleasant and gracious. She used her English connections to introduce Bush to visiting Tory members of Parliament.[15]

"I'm not saying she's Miss Popularity," said Bush in 1982. "She's doing what I want done. When you have to say no, particularly to friends, there's bound to be some level of frustration."[16] Politicians live in a world where their success depends on ingratiating themselves. When hatchets have to be used, the job is left to others. Bush, one of the "kindest-hearted people," needed her to put his foot down for him. There is no shortage of Jennifers to do the dirty work.[17]

Sure, recalled Keene, who later was accused by Lee Atwater of spreading the rumors after he went to work for Bob Dole, women like Jennifer are all over Washington. "Maybe they don't all ride a broomstick," but "it's very rarely any kind of sexual thing. It's just that there's somebody they rely on and [that] they're more loyal to than anybody else."[18] Nancy Bush Ellis ridiculed the gossip. "Dumpy little Jennifer," she laughed, was "like the most reliable, good person you know. We've all known her forever. She just absolutely adores George, as do all the other people."[19] The whole thing went far enough for another close Bush relative, his son George, to tell Howard Fineman of *Newsweek* that he had asked his father whether there was any truth to the adultery allegations. "The answer to the 'Big A' question is N-O," reported George W.[20] Even among those less susceptible to being accused of self-serving, and with knowledge of the Bush-Fitzgerald relationship that dated back to as early as the 1980 campaign, some admit that there were "reasons to cast doubt on Jennifer as the long-standing mistress."[21]

It may have been that problem; it may have been jealousy about her influence or simple differences over what the candidate should do; possibly a combination of all forced Jim Baker to intervene. She had to go, he told big brother. The less visible the better. Big brother listened, removed her from the staff, shifted her to his campaign office in New York. But he did soften the blow, at least to her exchequer. He kept her on the payroll out of his own pocket. Thus was the "Jennifer problem" disposed of, at least for awhile.[22]

* * *

With Bush out of the primaries, Ford quickly got behind the man about to be selected as the party's presidential candidate. He met with Reagan for an hour and a half at the Ford desert retreat. Facing the press immediately afterward, he forgot his earlier dim assessment of the former governor's electability. His own support, he made clear, was strong. A week later, all other contenders, including Bush, fell into line at a $500-a-plate "unity dinner" at the Beverly Hills Hotel.[23]

The convention opened on the fourteenth of July at Joe Louis Arena, a hall chosen at least in part through the determination of national chairman Bill Brock to have Detroit serve the symbolic purpose of reaching out to blacks and blue-collar workers, two groups that other Republicans had been skillfully playing off against each other. Brock, who had taken over the party's post despite strong right-wing opposition, had promoted that objective from the start. The calculation contradicted the reality of appealing to low-income white workers. But Reagan was Reagan and only he on the Republican right could do the impossible. Only he could bail the party out of the Herbert Hoover trap. Only he could convince American labor that conservatives really understood. Liberals had been too caught up in their social justice designs to recognize working-class aspirations. The sixties had demonstrated their irresponsibility, if not their stupidity. As Reagan's California governorship had shown, he did not have to be convinced of the importance of a broader base even while pushing economic and social conservatism. His uncomplicated anticommunism, clear, unambiguous, evil versus virtue, took care of other weaknesses. Lack of unified opposition in the primaries had been instrumental in his drive toward the nomination.[24] Gallup surveys released in early July had, in fact, shown the rank and file less firmly ideological than delegates who had been chosen to do the actual nominating. Ford and Bush were far ahead of anyone else for the second-place spot on the ticket, with the ex-president enjoying a clear 31 to 20 percent lead.[25] Ford, meanwhile, said he would not run under any circumstance and gave his support to Bush and Howard Baker. Baker, at least, was easily disposable. He had backed Carter over the Panama Canal treaty, and that damned him with most of the party. He had no chance, especially the way matters stood by 1980.

Veteran and savvy Ford adviser, Bryce Harlow, had other ideas. Republicans had no potential candidate with greater personal popularity than Ford. His followers had remained mostly mute when the ex-president had made noises about running earlier in the year, but as a running mate for Reagan, why not? Republicans and the country would be in good hands. No more trustworthy or likeable ticket could be invented. Harlow began to push the idea of a "dream team" combination.[26] Having been floated that way, even among the very people who had so recently been cool toward Ford running again, the proposal took on a life of its own, fanned still further by enthusiastic television reporting that threatened to take it out of the hands of the politicians. The media seemed close to getting him nominated.[27]

Bush arrived in Detroit hopeful and tense. He and Barbara checked into the Ponchartrain Hotel ready to fulfill his basic convention function, which was to open the presidential nominating process by addressing the delegates early on the third evening. Dean Burch dropped by with details about how Ford's people were meeting with Reagan's to accomplish the "dream team." The rumor was presented as fact when delegates arrived for the evening session. "It's Reagan and Ford," reported one headline, the *Chicago Sun-Times*.

That was understandable. Reagan preferred to stay away from Bush. Had he wanted him, he could have said so. There could at least have been a hint when he lunched with Bush and Jack Kemp at a Polish-American club. The two junior men looked like two "bookends of anxiety" as they attempted to finesse their way through the meal without looking too eager.[28]

"I want to be very frank with you," Reagan told a friend. "I have strong reservations about George Bush. I'm concerned about turning the country over to him." All his actions during those weeks before the ticket was finally put together at Detroit in July confirmed his determination to keep Bush at a distance.[29] Much as the party's new leader needed to reach out to the center, as one of those who negotiated during the situation said off the record, Reagan "would have done anything in the world not to pick George Bush." The primary campaign had made the Texas Yankee anathema.[30] Taking the advice of his circle of advisers, which now included New York lawyer William Casey, Reagan finally offered the vice presidency to Ford, who seemed to forget that he had just taken himself out of it.

Bush, meanwhile, released his delegates and pledged to back Reagan regardless of his running mate. Other delegates flirted with the idea of turning toward Kemp, the ex-quarterback and attractive conservative congressman from upstate New York. But Ford was hooked. Spurred by his own coterie, headed by Brock, Henry Kissinger, Jack Marsh, and Alan Greenspan, he countered with the strength that came from understanding that Reagan was willing to pay a high price to avoid Bush.[31]

Bush was out jogging while Ford and Reagan negotiators at the Detroit Plaza Hotel explored how such a combination might work. Ford, as a former president, could not be a Mr. Throttlebottom. His responsibilities had to clearly separate him from innocuous vice presidents of the past. He wanted serious input in such major areas as foreign and defense policy. The president would remain preeminent in domestic politics and economic matters. It was all interesting, even possible, but the talks were inconclusive.

In 1976, Ford's blunders had hurt his own reelection chances. Now, just four years later, he blundered again by agreeing to a premature interview with *CBS News* anchorman Walter Cronkite. Cronkite, no novice, got him to talk about negotiations that were still in progress. Ford outlined the arrangement his own advisers were trying to sell to Reagan so they could achieve their "dream ticket." Seizing on the essence of what he was saying, Cronkite observed that it sounded "something like a copresidency." No disagreement from Ford. In key hotel rooms in Detroit, watchers were amazed. Ford, in effect, was insinuating himself into the chief executive's office, far from the Twelfth Amendment's provision for "distinct ballots" to designate the candidate for the vice presidency.

Bush watching in his room, was stunned, not having anticipated, as he put it, that "Ford would go public with the news." With that in mind, and nothing else, Bush left for the convention hall. "It was an important speech," he later wrote, "the most important speech I'd ever been called on to make," one capable of becoming decisive in the vice presidential choice.[32]

Delegate exuberance was at its highest since 1964. American flags, candidate placards, colorful hats, and state signs filled the Joe Louis Arena. Countless buttons pictured Nancy and Ronald Reagan. Some delegates, notably Kansans, flashed their own buttons with Reagan wearing a cowboy hat.

Adding to the hoopla that had long since characterized American nominating conventions was the emergence of the religious right, their agenda, as Haynes Johnson wrote, dominating "the public political discourse from opening session to final fundamentalist benediction" on such issues as school prayer, abortion, and godless communism.[33] Reagan, it was clear, was more than just a political leader. He spoke their language. He was an American messiah, one who would deliver the world from atheistic communism and the United States from the grip of big government Washington secularists. The convention gave Reagan 1,939 of the 1,994 delegate votes, making him the party's presidential nominee.

Bush, appearing before the convention afterward, told them what they wanted to hear, and praised the selection process that had given them Reagan. New leadership, he vowed, would unite "a coalition of all Americans from all religions, from all groups and age, and every race and heritage."[34]

Even as he spoke, such people as Ed Meese, Casey, and Dick Wirthlin were telling Reagan that Ford's conditions were not only embarrassing, they were impossible, and of dubious constitutionality. As a veteran of the Ford White House joshed him later, "Mr. President, what did you tell them you wanted to be called, Mr. President Vice President or Mr. Vice President President?" Reagan, faced with that dilemma, backed away from Ford. He didn't much care for him, anyway; he hadn't yet gotten over thinking that Ford had stolen the 1976 nomination from him. Most of all, he was a former president, someone who by definition would diminish Nancy's Ronnie. "I guess I would have done almost anything to prevent Ronnie from picking a former president," she later wrote.[35] Reagan had to move on. He would have liked to ask his good conservative friend from Nevada, Senator Paul Laxalt. The ex-governor and current national committee chairman was an ideological clone. Articulate, courtly, good-looking, he was a favorite, and Nancy wanted him badly. But what did Laxalt offer, aside from his own desire? From another western state, he would bring nothing to the ticket, neither geography nor ideological balance. And there was always the risk when dealing with a major politico from the nation's gambling capital that the guy's financial ties couldn't stand close scrutiny. So Reagan's people talked the nominee out of it.

That left him with either Howard Baker or Bush, and the governor was cool to both. "Reagan didn't like either one of them," recalled Lyn Nofziger, who was with him at the time. "He thought Bush was a wimp and he was mad at Baker because of the Panama Canal." As for Bush, that hangover from the Nashua debate, and "voodoo economics" still "rankled" Nancy, which did not make his positions on ERA and abortion any easier to swallow. When it came right down to it, however, Reagan preferred Bush to Baker. Martin Anderson, one of Reagan's key advisers, recalled later that "there was frankly no other choice that Reagan could have made, given the polls, given everything that was going on. And he just said, 'Yeah, it's Bush.' "[36]

Anderson, delegated by Reagan to get to Bush headquarters with the news, found the place a disaster area. "They have obviously come to the conclusion that they were done, beaten, defeated; they were out of it. It looked like the aftermath of a fraternity party. People were sitting around, shirtsleeves rolled up, half drunk, half-drunk bottles of beer, with blissfully happy looks on their faces. They had been having a wake."[37]

Beer also flowed in Bush's room, where George and Barbara, with Jim Baker, Vic Gold, Dean Burch, and Nick Brady discussed the latest twists and turns of an "incredible convention." Baker answered the phone. "Somebody's having second thoughts," he said to Bush. Then came another call, this time from the Secret Service. Official protection was about to begin, and they were ready to occupy a room two floors below. Their rapid deployment astonished those in Bush's room; they constituted an instant occupation force. His privacy was over. Next on the line was Reagan himself, from "out of the blue sky," as Bush later put it to waiting reporters.[38] The Bushes went into the bedroom to take the call.

"George," said the presidential nominee, "it seems to me that the fellow who came the closest and got the next most votes for president ought to be the logical choice for vice president. Will you take it?" He also told him that he was about to go to the convention "and announce that you're my choice for vice president . . . if that's all right with you." As Bush recalled the scene: "I thanked him, then slowly rushed across the room and we exchanged hugs. Jim Baker and Dean Burch shook my hand. Someone turned up the TV set. *'Not Ford!'* the network reporter was shouting from the convention floor. 'It's *Bush!'* "[39] "Why a total surprise, ambassador?" a reporter asked Bush in his room. "Well," said the designee, "you people were circulating a lot of rumors out there. . . . So, it was a surprise—it surprised me that you didn't know about it."[40]

Reagan then broke with precedent and went to the arena to explain that Ford had declined. He told the boisterously happy delegates that the other man would be of more value as an ex-president "campaigning his heart out" and not as a member of the ticket. Bush, Reagan explained, was his choice, and he had pledged to fully back the party's platform. Still, it was too much for Nancy to bear. Reagan's wife, standing next to him at the podium, fought to hold back tears. Laxalt tried to comfort her by placing his arms around her shoulders. But, noted a *Washington Post* reporter, "she looked like a little girl who had just lost her favorite Raggedy Ann doll; sad, disappointed, almost crushed."[41]

One point designed to mollify Nancy stood out among all others: "If you're on my ticket," Reagan had told Bush, "I expect you to support me on the issue of abortion." That pledge, to back the entire Republican platform, including the plank on abortion with its "pro-life" position and support for a constitutional amendment that would negate the Supreme Court's *Roe* v. *Wade* decision, was a watershed change in the life of the modern Republican party. It also, as Bush remembers, was the one substantive pledge Reagan asked him to take as a prerequisite to being on the ticket.[42] For Bush, whose previous position on the issue was so carefully nuanced as to constitute a straddle, the accommodation was a small step. Henry IV of France said it first, but, as applied to the American realm, the vice presidency was "well worth a mass." It was also, as Prime Minister Margaret Thatcher of England advised Republican conservatives, not a suitable issue for presidential politics. But her field of play was far removed from the realities of America in the Reagan era.[43]

For Bush, it was "getting right" on constitutional amendments. Accommodating himself to the party's increasingly conservative amendment proposals, and the clear preferences of the convention, meant abandoning his support for the one designed to protect equal rights for women and endorsing a constitutional ban on abortion.

Diehards still resisted. Nowhere was hostility stronger, even after Reagan's endorsement, than within the Texas delegation, where an "anybody but Bush" impulse overwhelmed any kind of "favorite son" concept. Some flirted with the idea of getting Kemp on the ticket. The delegation, strongly Reaganite as a result of the May primary and passionately conservative and attractive to many traditionally Democratic Texans, was on the Connally side of the Bush-Connally feud. "I have personally heard the governor say on at least two occasions," said a close Connally ally, "that he would never work for any ticket that George Bush was on." Only after some hard work by Senator John Tower did Bush emerge from his own state's ultraconservative band of Connally loyalists with as many as seventy-three of its eighty votes.[44]

Hours after addressing them with every expectation that Ford would be Reagan's man, Bush faced a delegate-filled Joe Louis Arena and blessed the party's platform "enthusiastically," promising his "total dedication and energies" in the battle to install Reagan because "a bright new era will begin for an America in this decade of the eighties. We need change." To excited new-age Republicans waiting to hear from Ronald Reagan later that evening, Bush recalled Dwight D. Eisenhower's mission "to restore the faith of the American people in their government."[45]

The long-haul equation had already changed. The process began back in 1970 when he had lost voters and independence to Bentsen, and, along the way, the support of Texans who surged past his more nuanced moderate stances. Signing on as Reagan's running mate took George's political identity to another level, one which meant, at least by implication, acceptance of the major tenets of the new right. None was more essential than dedication to supply-side economics—faith in the value of capital formation and greater freedom from government mandates. The new Reagan revolution vowed to liberate capital by sweeping away the forces inimical to the new order. Their team left little room for challenges. Reaganite economists called for "a new America."

Bush's acceptance speech was slated to be the first salvo of the good soldier. Politically, he had edged toward that position since 1970. He now had little choice but to be subsumed by the Reagan forces. The Californians, the Pacific Rim people, Ed Meese, Mike Deaver, Bill Clark, Martin Anderson, and on and on, were the lieutenants of the new palace guard. They were the lieutenants helping to supply the dreams for a new America envisioned by the Holmes Tuttles, Justin Darts, Charles Zwicks, and other millionaire businessmen now behind the throne.[46]

They faced the press at Cobo Hall the next morning, he and Reagan, teaming up for the first time. He dismissed an annoying question about "widespread perception" that he was the second choice for the vice presidency. Talk about a Ford courtship was "irrelevant." He intended to emphasize his "common ground" with Reagan.[47] How, then, did he differ with the governor, they wanted to know? That was all in the past. The emphasis now was on harmony. When reporters later asked about his adjustment to becoming a vice presidential candidate after fighting for the presidency, he said that there was no problem at all. Things had changed. He had a job to do, and he would do it.

His friend Jim Baker also got on Reagan's team; Bill Casey asked him to become a senior campaign advisor. His major assignment was to prepare the Republican candidate to debate against his two rivals, Anderson and the president.[48]

For their renomination of Carter and Vice President Walter Mondale, the Democrats returned to New York City's Madison Square Garden, where the ticket had been created in 1976. Not unlike their resignation to a Truman renomination three decades earlier, Democrats faced the prospect of a serious uphill battle. Ted Kennedy had stumbled badly en route to challenging the incumbent. Carter was further embarrassed by questionable dealings of his brother, Billy. But the nation was considerably less tolerant toward the stewardship that had presided over serious inflation and unemployment, interest rates that exceeded 20 percent; even worse, underscoring impotence, fifty-three Americans remained hostage in Tehran, imprisoned at the U.S. embassy since November, and Soviet troops had dug in to stay in Afghanistan. The last pre-Democratic convention *New York Times/CBS News* poll showed the president a full twenty points behind Reagan. Anderson, heading his "national unity" coalition of independents, had 13 percent. Even more distressing was the preference for Anderson over Carter in some states. Close to 30 percent of those polled cited the president's indecisiveness and incompetence.[49]

Democrats played their strongest suit by exploiting fear of reckless Republican reactionaries. Everything about Reagan came within their sights, his age, his background as a Hollywood actor, endlessly depicted as bumbling and out of touch, if not somewhat stupid, a pawn in the hands of villainous millionaire businessmen. If it wasn't senility and greed, it was surely the warmongering truculence that had helped destroy Goldwater's candidacy twelve years earlier. Striking the theme that was the convention's great hope—their only real hope—Carter's acceptance speech warned of "risk," "the risk," he added, "of international confrontation; the risk of an uncontrollable, unaffordable, and unwinnable nuclear arms race."[50] Another "lesser of two evils" dilemma faced the voters. Carter, not surprisingly, got at least a feeble post-convention boost in his public opinion standings as Gallup showed him edging Reagan by just one point in a trial heat while, at the same time, registering a 55 percent level of disapproval.[51]

Bush, having vowed to help Reagan wage "a positive campaign" and go after the Carter-Mondale ticket by concentrating on the moderate, well-educated Anderson constituency, was already carrying out his first significant mission as a vice presidential candidate.[52] Who better than Bush, the man who had fought the battle at the UN over the two-China seating plan and had headed the U.S. liaison office at Beijing, to go to China to ease Communist apprehensions about a possible Reagan presidency?

Even as Bush flew to the People's Republic capital for his diplomatic, hurried rounds with Chinese leaders, including an hour and forty-five minute session with Deng Xiaoping, Reagan did yeoman work with the religious right. Clearly, not only far right organizer Paul Weyrich, who then headed a group called the Committee for the Survival of a Free Congress, was unhappy over Reagan's choice of Bush. Such groups once considered on the "fringe" were becoming less peripheral. Ideological superconservatives broke bread with the Rev. Jerry Falwell's Moral Majority and hunted for support among the growing numbers of born-again Christians.

Religious rightists, fed by an increasing reception for televised exhortations and extremist, often hyperbolic publications, were at the heart of a significant social shift. Not since earlier gospel movements had God and politics become so closely intertwined. At the top of them all stood Falwell and his followers in a new age of electronic ministries able to reach every part of the country. No area was more fertile than the old "Bible Belt," which largely corresponded with the region of the most dramatic post-World War II expansion, the Sun Belt. As a Texas historian, John Knaggs, wrote, they produced "dedicated pro-Reagan workers throughout the South, taking their antiabortion and pro-school prayer stands before voters in the precincts."[53] Reagan hopped on the movement at precisely the right time.

And, with a perfect pitch directed to their passions, he wooed them at every turn. At a huge "seminar" in Dallas sponsored by the Religious Roundtable, he met with Weyrich and appeared with one wounded secularist, John Connally. Most embarrassing was when a scheduling blunder left him seated on the platform alone with the fiery, outspoken television evangelist, the Reverend Robison. The evangelist preached that he was "sick and tired of hearing about all of the radicals and the perverts and the liberals and the leftists and the Communists coming out of the closet" and urged that the government be led by those who shared his religious views. Reagan could do nothing but applaud. Robison decried the federal government as "public enemy Number One." Reagan then faced the church leaders and gave his own hell-and-damnation speech. He denied that the First Amendment was written "to protect the people and their laws from religious values," an apt interpretation, but he also descended into travesty by agreeing that evolution was but one of several theories recognized by the scientific community.[54]

The Republican presidential candidate compounded matters by appearing to play right into the hands of those Madison Square Garden Democrats who accused him of warmongering. He urged peace through strength wherever he went, astonishing reporters with messianic, jingoistic saber-rattling. At a Veterans of Foreign Wars convention in Chicago on August 16, he had personally amended his prepared speech to call the Vietnam War "a noble cause," which brought the old soldiers to their feet. With especially clumsy timing, given the purpose of Bush's China trip, scheduled for only a week later, he told a news conference on August 16 that he would consider making the American liaison office on Taiwan, which was being run by a private foundation, an office of the United States government. That, he explained, would be a way to have an "official relationship" with Taiwan.[55]

The notion was not bad. Hadn't Bush led one in Beijing before normalization with China? Unfortunately, Reagan's remarks stirred a brouhaha and embarrassed his running mate. He appeared unaware that Congress had capitulated to Beijing's sensitivities by granting them assurances, via a Taiwan Relations Act, that another liaison office would not be opened in Taipei. Bush, moreover, had been sent to reassure Deng Xiaoping that he and his government would be able to live comfortably with a Reagan presidency.[56] The victim of end runs on the China issue by Nixon and Kissinger now had to tolerate one from Reagan, this one unintentional.

Once more caught between his credibility and his loyalty, and with enough time to ponder the matter during his return flight before the awaiting press at Los Angeles, Bush nevertheless parried the inevitable question. His "no comment" still left reporters with a hint of disavowal. At a joint news conference the next day at Los Angeles, Reagan retreated, but effectively. He conceded that the Chinese desire had become the "law of the land" but laid the blame at Carter for making "concessions that Presidents Nixon and Ford had steadfastly refused to make."[57]

Once he became Reagan's man, Bush performed as expected. Campaigning around the country, he explained to reporters, he had a three-fold responsibility: to spread and explain the head of the ticket's positions, to attack Carter's record, and to defend Reagan from Democratic attacks. He should not be expected to play the "hatchet man" role best exemplified by Nixon under Eisenhower and Agnew under Nixon. He preferred not to make waves or distract from the importance of getting Reagan to the White House.[58]

That role, the very avoidance of extremism, was also most appropriate for cutting into the Anderson vote, which seemed to be drawing about equally from Carter and Reagan. Anderson, not surprisingly, reserved some of his sharper thrusts for Bush. Speaking on ABC-TV's *Issues and Answers* right after the Republican convention, Anderson wondered aloud about how "issue-conscious voters" were going to accept a candidate who had "totally reversed his position" on the ERA and "freedom of choice" for women.[59] As the campaign progressed, Carter's southern base began to defect toward Reagan while the president picked up from among the previously undecided and Anderson. As late as mid October, Peter Hart, a Democratic pollster, analyzed support for both leading candidates as soft.[60] Carter, however, appeared to be gaining on the so-called "war or peace" issue with fear of a nuclear-button happy Reagan continuing to bother many voters. It soon became doubtful that Anderson would come in with as much as 10 percent. With fewer than two weeks left, Carter scoffed at the notion that Reagan had a "secret plan" to free the hostages in Tehran.[61]

The potentially scandalous allegation was not that Republicans had a "secret plan" to free the hostages, but quite the opposite, a plan to have their release delayed until *after* the election. That kind of plotting made sense to those who recalled the efforts of Nixon and his people to undermine Lyndon Johnson's desire to get preelection peace talks started in Paris. It made additional sense, although ex post facto, when they were actually freed on the day of Reagan's inauguration. Additional circumstantial "evidence" came with the exposure of the arms for Iran deal six years later. Logic seemed to be on the side of those who were willing to grant duplicity. The involvement of William Casey further stimulated imaginations.

But while the campaign was still in progress, the Reagan-Bush camp kept close vigil for signs of an *early* release, which would certainly give Carter a considerable boost. At Detroit, during their convention, Casey told reporters that he was setting up an "intelligence operation" to watch the Carter campaign, which was later confirmed by others to mean that a group of retired military officers kept an eye on domestic bases for signs of an impending airlift that might indicate shipment of supplies to Iran.[62] The real surprise would have been lack of such concern. Stef Halper, having moved on to the Reagan presidential campaign after working for Bush in the primaries, directed a group of other former CIA employees at the Reagan-Bush Alexandria headquarters in keeping an around-the-clock watch over possible developments in the hostage crisis.[63] From his office on Wall

Street, Prescott Bush Jr. kept in touch with a Carter administration contact for possible "hot information for us on the hostages."[64] A strategy meeting, attended by Casey, Wirthlin, Burch, and Baker was convened on the first Saturday in October. Two weeks later, with still no movement on the hostage situation, Halper put together a "confidential" memorandum that synthesized the views of campaign insiders and such outside consultants as Cline and Brent Scowcroft on how to respond to a possible "October surprise."[65]

Iranians, as they had claimed publicly, were ready for a deal on the hostages. The *Washington Post* ran a story by Michael Getler on October 15 revealing that "some senior U.S. officials . . . now say privately . . . that they would not be surprised if a break in the U.S. embassy hostage crisis comes in the next two or three weeks."[66] The Iranians knew that Carter, as Halper summarized the views of Reagan's team, "will be susceptible to pressure in the next two weeks, perhaps now more so than in the past month." Carter's diplomatic troubleshooter, Warren Christopher, was negotiating with three of Iranian President Boni-Sadr's aides and had had contacts with Prime Minister Raja'i. There were reports Iranians were being prepared for the release by being given misleading information that the Americans had already apologized for their sponsorship of the shah. Further indications of good faith by the U.S. were about to be tested by the Iranian parliament's conditions that would include the removal of AWAC systems from Saudi Arabia. Meanwhile, Halper advised, Carter's Treasury Department was already working out procedures for freeing Iranian assets in the United States.

Reagan, as a potential incoming president, had already cooperated with Carter by giving his consent. He hinted as much eleven years later when he admitted to the press that he "did some things to try . . . to get them [the hostages] home."[67] Both American leaders agreed to grant two other conditions: the cancellation of all claims against Iran and a promise of nonintervention in Iran's internal affairs. With the Iranian military needing spare parts for their war against Iraq, a possible shipment from the United States was already on a stand-by basis at McGuire Air Force Base in New Jersey.

While doing everything possible to give the president public diplomatic cooperation, Reagan should prepare his "posture" in case of a pending release to soften the political impact. That would be accomplished by a cautious but favorable recognition that freedom may be imminent. He should "express his hopes and prayers that the hostages will be coming home soon," even if it is the day before the election. But he must also insist on no "deals or trades until all our people are home" and express concern about any possible long-range consequences. Such a "prerelease posture" would not only dilute any surprise if they *were* released but would "dull somewhat the outpouring of enthusiasm." If they are not released, it would intensify Carter's credibility problem. Most of all, cautioned the Reagan advisers, "we must be prepared for Carter to use the line 'I've got a deal all set. If Reagan comes in, it's off.' "[68] Meanwhile, during that period of careful monitoring to detect in advance any signs pointing to an early release, an emergency budget of $200,000 was set aside for a media blitz to counter the effects of any "October surprise."[69]

Out of that same intelligence work, aided in no small way by cooperation obtained from rebellious Carter people, came the filching of a briefing book that had been prepared to help Carter in his debate with Reagan. Information about the theft did not become general knowledge until three years later, with the publication of Laurance Barrett's *Gambling With History.* Casey was quickly fingered as the natural instrument of the deed, which, pure and simple, was a crime. Easily the best bet to explain the purloined briefing book was that Casey got it from a source within the Carter camp and turned it over to Baker. Joseph Persico, Casey's biographer, has put it very neatly: "Given a choice of whom to believe, that crafty old conniver William J. Casey or the universally liked James Baker, the answer was obvious."[70]

The briefing book held over five hundred pages of information, including preparation for a possible vice presidential debate between Mondale and Bush. One witness told a subsequent congressional investigating committee "something about someone coming over from the Carter campaign in a taxi bringing Carter campaign materials related to the debate preparation."[71]

Whether there would even be a debate at the presidential level was still up in the air. Reagan thought he would win the election without having to debate. That idea, which was favored by Nancy, began to unravel as Carter picked up. Dick Wirthlin's data showed him even pulling slightly ahead. Not surprisingly when dealing with a "third party" candidate, there was evidence that Anderson supporters were having second thoughts, succumbing to traditional last-minute reluctance to "waste" votes on someone with no chance of winning. A new Gallup poll showed the Illinois moderate slipping to only 8 percent, and the League of Women Voters announced that they would review his "significance."

Calculations about the possible "October surprise" also softened resistance within the Reagan camp. A possible release of the hostages, it was assumed, would be especially damaging to the governor's chances if it came two or three weeks before Election Day. Deciding in favor of debating then acquired the function of damage control.[72] That it could work in their favor became that much more apparent when Reagan and the president both appeared at the annual Alfred E. Smith dinner at New York's Waldorf Astoria. Reagan, the actor with forty years of experience, made Carter look lame. He brought down the house with the one-liner that some thought he was looking younger "because I keep riding older and older horses." Stuart Spencer, whose position in favor of a debate included the argument that Reagan "rises to the occasion," had his point confirmed. Carter, fearful of the appearance of dodging, had little choice. And Anderson was out.[73]

The debate was set for the twenty-eighth of October in Cleveland. With only a single such encounter agreed upon, Reagan had to convince the American public that he was no Dr. Strangelove about to blow up the world.

Baker's preparations for Reagan constituted what one rehearsal participant, Martin Anderson, described as "the most elaborate and detailed preparation in the history of the U.S. presidential debates." They created a mock debate auditorium in a large, empty garage. Outfitted with all the paraphernalia of a television theater, lights, cameras, and everything in exact scale, it included surrogates to play the roles of President Carter and reporters who would ask the questions. Carter, meanwhile, prepared at Camp David.[74]

Once again, the old actor's instincts came through. He strode onto the stage looking relaxed and fit, quite in contrast with Carter's stiffness, which was evident even before the cameras came on. Quickly, Reagan set the tone by deflecting a question about his militaristic tendencies with assurances that world peace was "our first priority." He was, in other words, all that he really needed to be, confident, genial, warm, and reassuring about peace as the overriding objective.[75] Assuming the pose of innocence wronged, he countered a Carter thrust at his opposition to Medicare with the deft delivery of what landed as another effective one-liner: "There you go again." Then, facing the camera squarely, he delivered his coup de grâce: "Are you better off than you were four years ago?" he asked his national audience. "Is it easier for you to go and buy things in the stores than it was four years ago? Is there more or less unemployment in the country than there was four years ago? Is America as respected throughout the world as it was? Do you feel that our security is as safe, that we're as strong as we were four years ago?"[76]

His words could hardly have touched more fertile soil. To a nation reeling from double-digit inflation, sky-high interest rates, and humiliation abroad, and when even strangers engaged in casual conversation could find common ground by bemoaning the lack of leadership, Reagan's words proved that he understood what the American malaise (which Carter had attempted to preach about with disastrous results) was all about. Carter, inexplicably, perhaps out of desire to strike a popular tone and again underscore his opponent's perceived weakness, mentioned arms control in terms that quickly brought ridicule. He said he had had a "discussion with my daughter Amy the other day." What, he explained, did you think was the most important issue? he said he asked her. To unbelieving viewers, he reported, "She said she thought nuclear weaponry and the control of nuclear arms."[77]

A clear winner of that debate was hard to determine by reading the early press accounts. But, as Wirthlin and Teeter studied their data, positive reactions to Reagan as a leader were clearly moving upward. He had made significant gains among those who had feared that his ideas would lead to war.[78]

On his final campaign swings, Bush emphasized Reagan's moderation. Leaving the far West to the presidential candidate, he delivered his message throughout the rest of the country. Late polling, other than showing Reagan as the beneficiary of the debate, was inconclusive except for showing Anderson trailing off with just 7 percent.[79] Bush raced through Illinois and Texas in one final day after two-and-a-half years of campaigning. In Houston on election night, the first anniversary of the taking of the hostages in Tehran, he learned that he was vice president elect.

Reagan's victory was complete. He won forty-four states with 489 electors and a popular majority of 51 percent, a figure that was lower than it would otherwise have been because Anderson drew 7 percent. Carter could do no better than take six states, good for only forty-nine electors. That election also gave Republicans control of the Senate for the first time since 1952. The House, where Democrats kept their partisan majority, nevertheless remained in conservative hands.

Voters had confirmed two shifts. Once the backbone of the old New Deal coalition, lower-middle-class workers were becoming more conservative. Reagan's persona, projection of strength and dedicated anticommunism also helped reduce resistance to pulling Republican voting levers. Breaking even more sharply within this category of voters were white males, further put off by social and economic tensions traceable and better understood in later years as the loss of real income in a time of inflation and reduced expansion of the job market, which was exacerbated by fear of competition from newly assertive women and minorities. Another old Democratic reliable, the once "solid South," confirmed its long-simmering partisan transformation. Reagan completed a process that first became evident with the states' rights Democrats of 1948, and the even stronger appeals of Eisenhower, Goldwater, and Nixon. Carter's victory in 1976, the one Democratic exception, was a case of a native Georgian interrupting the trend. Carter had also benefited from the newly energized politics of born-again Christians; but now, in 1980, the Reagan-Bush ticket captured that as a largely Republican vote. To whatever extent it would prove to be a realigning election, it made the political culture more hostile to a Yankee from Connecticut.

CHAPTER FIFTEEN

The Haunting of the
Vice Presidency

%

How, Bush was asked, are you going to reconcile your differences with Ronald Reagan? How will you accommodate to such conservative leaders as Paul Weyrich? The reporter was the *Houston Post*'s Arthur Wiese, who covered the political beat and had watched Bush carefully over the years. At best, Bush knew he could count on a fair shake from Wiese, unlike the Washington press corps. If even a man like Wiese was skeptical, the problem was clear. Vice presidential history was full of incumbents whose political roots posed potential conflicts for their administrations; most, in the past, had allowed themselves and their offices to be properly submerged. They were mere supernumeraries betting on the odds of life and death.

Bush was all that, but his predicament was something more: the modern vice presidency had matured since Harry Truman's accidental rise. Modern assumptions about the office became an integral part of every presidential administration. In the absence of extraordinary developments, such as the resignations of John C. Calhoun under Andrew Jackson and Spiro Agnew under Nixon, and accidental elevations to the presidency, they were almost invisible bumps in the American political process. Only slowly did the vice presidency become ancillary to the White House.

Bush's position went beyond that. Reagan was not merely head of state. He was the ideological purist whom the new right believed could do no wrong. He could hike tax rates for individuals and still be praised for opposing taxes. He could increase deficits while calling for budget balancing and win praise for fiscal responsibility. He could ignore export laws by making covert shipments of arms. He could do almost anything without jeopardizing assumptions about his patriotism and good sense, a significant test of leadership. For all the qualms and questions about how his detached style obscured his personal hand, little doubt remains that "it was Reagan, not his staff, who set the agenda and established the priorities for the major accomplishments and debacles of his presidency."[1]

The vice president was expected to show total loyalty. Lyndon Johnson was rebuffed when, early in the Kennedy administration, he reached for some independent power. After Johnson himself became president, Hubert Humphrey was relegated to a "doghouse" early in the administration by suggesting opposition to the bombing of North Vietnam. Walter Mondale was scrupulously loyal to Carter.

Bush, of course, *was* different. He was Bush, the intruder from somewhere out in Rockefeller Republican land, a stranger to the new right, a Johnny-come-lately to their conservative cause. They thought he was, as Barry Bearak of the *Los Angeles Times* once put it, "an establishment opportunist—and a weak-kneed one at that."[2] As Chase Untermeyer has recalled, "In the Reagan White House in 1981, a lot of true Reaganites could never forget that George Bush had run against their man in the primaries."[3]

He would have no problem, Bush told Wiese; he and Reagan had developed "a warm, cordial, and respectful" relationship. Their recent rivalry was behind them. All those comments about his ideological incompatability, especially as posed most pointedly by Weyrich, were really moot, pointless. It was easy, when they were alone, to get close to Reagan; he didn't keep "pulling back." They could enjoy each other, nothing like with Nixon at all. The probability for potential conflicts was greatly exaggerated by those looking for stories.[4]

The Bushes had established an anchor for themselves in Houston before moving to Washington. Maintaining their legal residence in Texas made financial sense since the state had neither an income nor a capital gains tax. Once the Bushes sold their home at 5838 Indian Trail for $843,273 before moving to Washington, they simultaneously rented suite 271 in the elegant Houstonian Hotel on the city's west side as their legal residence and bought a conventional city-size plot of land in the Tanglewood section. The lot, as he told Wiese, could even become the site for a future townhouse. In Washington, the new Second Family moved into the old Admiral's House that had been built in 1893 on the seventy-three acres of the U.S. Naval Observatory off Massachusetts Avenue in the city's northwestern section. Previously occupied only by Nelson Rockefeller (who used it mainly for entertainment as well as official purposes) and Walter Mondale (who combined both functions, even ceremoniously devoting a portion of the Admiral's House bookcases to works on the vice presidency), it had been the vice president's official residence only since 1974.[5]

George also bought more of Walker's Point. After Uncle Herbie's recent death, it made good sense to keep the property in the family. For the relatively modest sum of $250,000, Bush bought 8.7 of the ten acres from his Aunt Mary Walker. The sprawling six-bedroom, six-bath home also had a dormitory that could sleep six. The transfer, which was made on January 19,

George Bush at the age of one and a half, 1925.

Barbara Pierce Bush on the beach near Rye.

The Andover soccer captain with his team, ca. 1939.

The Navy's youngest pilot received his wings at Corpus Christi, Texas, 1941.

Wedding day, at the First Presbyterian Church in Rye, New York, on January 6, 1945.

In the cockpit of the Barbara III.

Radioman Joe Reichert, George Bush, and tailgunner Lee Nadeau, standing in front of their Avenger with the code name X-2, 1944.

Bush rescued at sea by the crew of the *USS Finback*, September 2, 1942.

The young family in New Haven: Barbara, little George, and the Yale student, ca. 1947.

Captain of Yale's baseball team: "good field, no hit"

Baseball Captain Bush receiving the original manuscript of Babe Ruth's autobiography from the Bambino for the Yale Library, 1948.

Prescott and Dorothy Bush after his election to the Senate in 1952.

George Bush with young George W. at the christening of the Zapata Offshore Oil rig, ca. 1954.

Senatorial candidate George Bush with Barbara at his 1964 campaign headquarters in Houston.

George Bush with President Nixon, whom
he served as Ambassador to the United Nations
and chairman of the Republican National
Committee, ca. 1970.

The Bushes and their bicycles were a special
sight in Beijing in 1975.

A Saturday morning family "conference" with
the vice president in his Kennebunkport
bedroom, August 22, 1987.

Lee Atwater, seen jogging with the vice president on September 12, 1987, served as a valued political consultant during his short life.

The Reagans and the Bushes at the President's Dinner, May 11, 1988.

The vice president meeting with a delegation of Nicaraguan contras on July 16, 1988. Their leader, Adolfo Calero, is third from the left, and the Assistant Secretary for Inter-American Affairs, Elliott Abrams, can be seen at the right rear seated under a portrait.

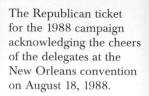

The Republican ticket for the 1988 campaign acknowledging the cheers of the delegates at the New Orleans convention on August 18, 1988.

George Bush being sworn in as the forty-first president of the United States on January 20, 1989, as Barbara Bush holds the Bible and Chief Justice Rhenquist administers the oath of office.

The President with Dr. Burton Lee III, his personal physician and head of the White House medical staff, March 14, 1989.

George Bush with French President Francois Mitterand at Walker's Point, May 20, 1989.

The President on his European swing, May 21, 1989, with Secretary of State James A. Baker III and German Chancellor Helmut Kohl, in West Germany.

The president with two key aides, Chief of Staff John Sununu, and Director of the Office of Management and Budget, Richard Darman, in the Oval Office on June 23, 1989.

The president at his first summit with Soviet President Mikhail Gorbachev on the island of Malta, December 3, 1989.

The president with his mother, Dorothy Walker Bush, at Kennebunkport, June 30, 1989.

Facing the camera at the table from left to right, surrounding the president on May 15, 1990, are congressional leaders Leon Panetta, Robert Michel, Tom Foley, George Mitchell, and Bob Dole. Marlin Fitzwater is at the rear.

James A. Baker III and Brent Scrowcroft in an animated discussion behind the president at a G-6 economic summit at Houston on July 10, 1990.

At a key moment after the Iraqi invasion of Kuwait, the president and Prime Minister Thatcher of England faced the press at Aspen, Colorado, on August 2, 1990, and expressed their agreement about the need for a firm response.

August 8, 1990: President Bush meets with Defense Secretary Cheney right after his vital trip to Saudi Arabia prior to the launching of Operation Desert Shield. Also present, clockwise, are Chief of Staff Sununu, General Scrowcroft, and Secretary Baker. Secretary Cheney is at the lower right

The president and First Lady on the cigarette boat, *Fidelity,* off Walker's Point on August 14, 1990, shortly after the outbreak of the crisis in the Persian Gulf.

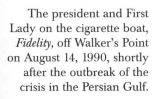

Continuing his stay in Maine to emphasize his deliberative handling of what was happening in the Middle East, the president met the press on August 22, 1990.

The president meets at Walker's Point with National Security Advisers concerning U.S. troop deployment to Saudi Arabia. Visible, clockwise, are Dick Cheney, Lawrence Eagleburger, Brent Scrowcroft, Robert Gates, Colin Powell, President Bush, and John Sununu, August 22, 1990.

The president meets with the Emir of Kuwait, Jaber al-Ahmed al-Sabah, in the White House on September 23, 1990.

President Bush and King Fahd participate in an arrival ceremony in the Royal Pavillion in Saudi Arabia and discuss the situation in Iraq, on November 21, 1990.

The president and the First Lady walking on the sands of Saudi Arabia during their Thanksgiving Day visit to the troops on November 22, 1990. General Norman Schwarzkopf is at the right.

General Schwarzkopf and the president during the Thanksgiving visit to Saudi Arabia.

Press Secretary Marlin Fitzwater with President Bush on December 6, 1990.

January 9, 1991: A grim President Bush at a press conference after the failure of Secretary Baker's Geneva meeting with Iraqi Foreign Minister Tariq Aziz to resolve the situation in the Gulf.

The gravity of the crisis with the impending start of Desert Storm are evident on the faces of the First Family as they attend church services at Camp Davis on January 13, 1991.

President Bush participates in a briefing on Operation Desert Storm at the Pentagon, January 18, 1991.

President Bush writes notes during his telephone call in the Oval Office with Soviet President Gorbachev regarding the Soviet peace proposal to Iraq and the U.S. response, on February 22, 1991.

President Bush addressing a joint session of Congress on March 6, 1991, regarding the end of the war with Iraq

President Bush with Russian President Boris Yeltsin on July 30, 1991, only a few days before they joined forces to save Mikhail Gorbachev from a coup.

The president at Walker's Point showing four of his grandchildren the fine art of pitching horseshoes, August 8, 1991.

The president with German Chancellor Helmut Kohl at the White House, September 6, 1991.

The First Family with Associate Justice Clarence Thomas at the White House on October 18, 1991, three days after the confirmation of the controversial nominee's appointment to a seat on the Supreme Court.

The president reading to his grandchildren on Christmas Eve, 1991

The end of a presidency: George and Barbara Bush about to board the helicopter after the inauguration of President Clinton.

1981, left the rest of the property in the hands of cousin Bert Walker.[6] One house, the Bungalow, remained in the hands of Bush's mother; Uncle Lou Walker lived on the other side of Ocean Avenue with his wife Grace. Unfortunately, the severe winter storm of 1977, the first in a series of "storms of the century," had left the main house in need of extensive remodeling.

With the new year, Barbara, fifty-five, her hair whitened, but, as one *Chronicle* reporter put it, "trimmer, prettier, softer, and younger than her photographs always reflect," and George, still months away from his fifty-seventh birthday, moved to Washington and a temporary residence at 4429 Lowell Street, NW.

In the capital on the eve of the "Reagan revolution," or as the *Washington Post*'s Haynes Johnson put it, the "marriage of the new right with the new rich," Bush prepared to become the forty-third vice president. In a private interview with political scientist A. James Reichley, he denied having used the term "voodoo economics" and lauded the president-elect for his "realistic assumptions about the Soviet Union's intentions." The United States, he agreed, must be clear about its willingness to maintain a strong defense and, according to the interview notes, said that such policy "would relate to efforts to subvert Saudi Arabia or the efforts by Castro to export revolution in the Western Hemisphere." Adhering to his consistency with the thinking of the incoming Reagan administration, he deflected an attempt to get him to dissent from Jeane Kirkpatrick's recent article that compared authoritarian and totalitarian governments and found the former at least benign. He failed to understand the difference, Bush said. He would need a dictionary. But it seemed logical that foreign policy had to consider human rights along with other concerns. Inevitably, there would be no escape from that question for George Bush.[7]

He was, as his friend Baker said years later, a "model vice president."[8] He was dedicated, energetic, and loyal; the subordinate who left no doubt about his selfless devotion to the cause. No longer was the office worth "a pitcher of warm spit," in John Nance Garner's inelegant phrase; it had muscle, political and statutory. They combined to make the vice presidency a part of presidential administrations in ways the Founding Fathers had not envisioned. "I am not going to be totally invisible," Bush recorded for his diary at the outset. "But I am not going to be building my own constituency or doing things like background conferences to show that I am doing a good job." Later, closer to the time to make his own run for the presidency, he said, "I think that the president must know that he can have the vice president for him and he must not think that he has to look over his shoulder."[9]

As to their staffs, mutual suspicions were only relieved, never fully overcome, and bad blood remained. The length of the preconvention season, with the vastly larger number of primaries, had deepened wounds and resentments. Burying old grievances was easier for the lieutenants than the troops.[10] The Bush people were "Bushies," a distinct breed of arrivistes, tolerated only through necessity. "People who worked for Ronald Reagan still resented the attacks that were made on Reagan," recalled Chase Untermeyer, who went to work for the new vice president. Bush himself stood apart from that, impeccably correct, just as during the campaign, jokes about Reagan's age were taboo in his presence. With his chief of staff, Bush undertook a "mission to make sure that there never was any bickering between our staff and the White House staff."[11]

Bush's notion of loyalty meant complete acceptance of Reagan's authority, of his leadership, his ideas. No bitching or second-guessing from Bush people was the order of the day. "They were to try not to make any waves," said political director Kaufman, "to do the bidding as the Reagan folks wanted them to do, to stay out of the way politically, in particular, and never, never be the subject of any story or ever, ever second-guess the president's staff or be sources for the Washington press corps."[12] That applied to the entire staff, to such Bush veterans as Chief of Staff Dan Murphy, Pete Teeley, and Jennifer Fitzgerald, who practically "fell on her sword" for the vice president, continuing to stand between his needs and everybody else. "She liked being the funnel," said a colleague. When, shortly after the administration got under way, Reagan Press Secretary Jim Brady was severely crippled by a bullet from John Hinckley's gun, another Bush veteran, Pete Roussel, was dispatched to work under Brady's successor, Larry Speakes. They were a firm, competent team, tailor-made for the mission at hand.[13]

Mutual suspicions remained. Such behavior had to be expected from "Reaganauts," déclassé fanatics, ideologues, crude, even vicious and bigoted. They were, George and Barbara had found during the long primary season, extremists who were intolerant of opposition, a culture to be suffered and, if possible, to be overcome.

The last place to learn about the Bush-Reagan relationship would be by listening to George Bush. His reflexive commitment and loyalty to friends can be deceptive. Those who knew Bush over many years talk at length about his devotion to those around him. How he tolerated certain personalities and eccentricities was always a mystery.

But he had to adjust to Reagan and the Reaganites. Differences in class were obvious, as were their educational and regional origins. The business types who surrounded Reagan—the Darts, Alfred and Betsy Bloomingdale, the Earle Jorgensens—from estates in Bel Air and all along the western slope, were a different breed. Their wealth was immense, and their indulgence in material delights left them alien to New Deal concepts of public interest economics, politics, or to ideas about mitigating the excesses of capitalism. Theirs was, in effect, the culture writers have associated with the frontier, masculine, fiercely independent, even primitive. America represented, for them, social Darwinism at its purest. One disciple, multimillionaire filmmaker Charles Z. Wick, voiced their common credo when he said, "the preponderance of these people are self-made." Not only did they "follow the American dream," but they were the living fantasies of the masses who "loved those glamour pictures showing the people driving beautiful cars and women in beautiful gowns, showing that people [really] were living the glamorous good life."[14] How different the Bush circle from Reagan's Pacific Rimmers.

Fortunately, cultural compatibility was a Bush social strength. Reagan's sense of humor was not that different, they shared similar jokes. Bush, further conditioned on athletic fields and by the military, as Reagan was not, was by his mature years as much a Lone Star Texan as a Connecticut Yankee. If New England aristocracy and Episcopalianism was his natural bent, the frontier was his acquired taste. Such qualities enabled George Bush to relate to the fortieth president, if not to some of the professed guardians of Reagan's interests. Nor could Bush distance himself from the thought that, no matter what the reasons, Reagan was the one who had placed him in his present position. He also held the key to his higher political ambitions.

In a relationship that anticipated the coolness between Raisa Gorbachev and Nancy Reagan, however, their wives were far less affable. To Mrs. Reagan, Barbara was too much "the silver-haired aristocrat who was so sure of her place in the world." Barbara remained polite and gracious. But, added Barbara for the record, "Nancy Reagan and I are friends. We were never great friends. We have zero in common. I'm very family-oriented. I'm also very George Bush-oriented. She is very much focused on Ronald Reagan, which is great. That's what she chose to do."[15]

Nancy, troublesome to George Bush earlier, continued to annoy. Not since Edith Galt Wilson served as a caretaker of her husband's White House after his debilitating stroke had a First Lady been as dominant as Mrs. Reagan. Joseph Persico has written that "the private Nancy Reagan was a Metternich in Adolfo dresses, willing to make the hard decisions that her husband let drift."[16] Her dinner talk was "so captivating," recalled Haig after an evening spent with the Reagans before the inauguration, that he failed to notice until afterward that he "had hardly exchanged a word" with the man who was about to become the fortieth president.[17] Administration insiders, indeed, experienced her influence over everything, even presidential scheduling, which was sometimes determined with "guidance" from a San Francisco astrologist. She also continued to exercise her influence in the matter of hiring and firing, including the eventual dumping of the second presidential chief of staff, Donald Regan. Fellow actor Jimmy Stewart once remarked that "if Ronald Reagan had married Nancy the first time, she would've got him an Academy Award."[18]

Among those remaining largely untouched by Nancy, however, was Jim Baker. At one point, he even got away with admonishing her for not declaring as gifts the many thousands of dollars worth of dresses she received from designers.[19] Still, Baker's appointment as chief of staff, however improbable considering his closeness to Bush and preconvention role during the primaries, carried her approval even though the move shocked "true-blue

Reaganauts," as David Stockman has put it.[20] But Baker had made his contributions. The first, of course, was by persuading Bush to curtail his own primary campaign, and the second was in helping to prepare Reagan for the November election against Carter. His standing was sufficient to merit consideration as adviser for National Security Affairs. Bill Casey, however, who had enlisted Baker for the Reagan presidential campaign, agreed with fellow conservatives that he was too much of a moderate, too much of an accommodationist, even though he was, in reality, burdened with few visible ideological passions. More effective in cutting down a potential appointment was Baker's growing reputation as a "leaker" to the press, the embodiment of the insider joke that "the ship of state is the only ship that leaks from the top." He did it a lot for her husband, Nancy Reagan later acknowledged, but added that "I always felt his main interest was Jim Baker." His relationship with the press corps was, in any event, regarded as too cozy for a high-security job.[21] It took Mike Deaver, whom the Reagans regarded as a virtual son, and one who, in the words of Lyn Nofziger, "tends to fall in love with people," to discover Baker "as the greatest thing since sliced bread."[22] Nancy was finally convinced to go along with Baker. Her natural preference was the Reagan friend from California, Ed Meese. But Deaver joined Stu Spencer in Reagan's office right after the election to sell the president-elect on Baker. "Ron was listening to his wife and to his chief advisers," explained Nofziger. "There was nobody else in the room to make the opposite point. That's the way you do it with Reagan. You sneak up to him and catch him unawares." Meese had to accept appointment as counselor to the president.[23]

There had never been such tacky ostentation before Reagan. The formerly dispossessed returned to Washington with jewels, furs, and private jets. How sweet it was! Let no one doubt, rang their collective theme, that raging free enterprise was back in charge. Unabashed opulence was okay and, for once, unapologetic. Greed itself would be, during that decade, specifically upheld as a virtue by such people as Richard Nixon and Ivan Boesky.

Washington had never seen such riches. Corporate jets and private planes clogged the runways at National Airport. One group of Indiana Republicans reached the capital in J. P. Morgan's former railroad car. Leased limousines with special corporate inaugural nameplates "discharged women in designer dresses and diamonds and men in formal wear." One reporter, noted the comments of critics who viewed the takeover by the flush new right as "a bacchanalia of the haves."[24] Their round of balls on inauguration night was the most luxurious series of them all. Designer gowns were everywhere, by Blass, Galanos, and Oscar de la Renta. They were "glittery Hollywood celebrities and wealthy Western oilmen," moving to the sentimental swing music-makers of another era, Tommy Dorsey, Les Brown, Peter Duchin, Harry James, and the crooning of Tony Bennett.[25]

To concentrate on the glitter, however, to scoff at the "Reagan revolution" as the return of the "haves" to Washington would not only be facile but inaccurate; it also misses the essence of the culture behind their coup. They were plebeians, and they were parvenus. They had come together by striking a responsive chord, the restoration of an ethos believed torn asunder by a world not recognizable to those with mythical notions of nationalism, patriotism, and laissez-faire.

Their alarm resonated most insistently among middle and working classes who saw immigrants surging toward the mainstream more as social and economic competitors than as a welcome source of labor. Working-class Republican primary voters, in fact, tended to identify more with Reagan than with Bush.[26] The steady flow of newcomers, this time black, brown, and Asian, evoked resistance that was reminiscent of late-nineteenth-century nativism in response to immigrants from southern and eastern Europe. Worse still, according to virtually every analyst who studied what had been happening for the past few decades, was the upheaval of African-Americans. Torn from their agrarian roots in the South by the mechanization of agriculture and upheld as the equals of all who had risen before, their impact was greatest in the urban centers north and west of Dixie. Democrats, in particular, had embraced their claims for restitution.

How better to create a protective barrier than by fortifying the Republican party? Rhetoric was unnecessary; the spirit was there, including before Reagan's inaugural, when some fifteen thousand celebrants gathered at the Lincoln Memorial. Standing before an immense eagle-shaped blue-and-white podium were the incoming president and the new First Lady. The voices of the Mormon Tabernacle Choir sang "God Bless America" and "The Battle Hymn of the Republic," and the cheering and chanting crowd brought forward their new leader. Reagan waved, smiling broadly, appreciating their enthusiasm, but said nothing. They kept cheering.[27]

Bush slept well that inauguration evening, about to become, in his own words, a "generalist," doing no one thing but everything; exactly what would depend on the level of "respect and confidence" that could be developed from the president. Even while Bush was getting his rest, Mondale, Carter's faithful number-two man, was monitoring the steps that led to the freeing of the hostages in Iran.[28]

Bush's phone rang at eight A.M. Mondale was on the line. Good news. All the preliminaries, the complex series of international transfers, had been worked out. The hostages were about to be transferred to American soil via North Africa, ending their ordeal after 444 days. Iranian assets in the United States, frozen in retaliation at the time of the takeover, were ready to be returned. As Reagan was being sworn in, the men would be on their way to freedom.[29]

That burden removed, the new administration could start with a clean slate, deferring other problems in the region, including the war between Iraq and Iran. So the Bushes prepared for their big day, although Barbara was still handicapped by a bandaged leg following fourteen stitches required after she tripped and got a nasty cut at the Texas Ball a few days earlier.

Ignoring her discomfort, and wearing a new white dress and blue coat, she joined her husband and the Reagans at St. John's Episcopal Church across Lafayette Park from the White House for services by the Rev. John Harper, an old friend. They shared George Washington's pew. A limousine then took the Bushes to the North Portico entrance of the White House, where they were greeted warmly by the Mondales. The Reagans entered afterward, Barbara later wrote, "and it was a long, tense forty-five minutes," the mutual tension between the wives of the incoming leaders adding considerably to the discomfort. So, in Mrs. Bush's words, they "hung around" until finally they were driven to the other end of Pennsylvania Avenue.[30] At the suggestion of Senator Mark Hatfield of Oregon, the inaugural ceremony was set for the West Front of the Capitol to provide a panoramic view of the city's monuments and landmarks.

The setting was enough to inspire the most cynical. In the brightness of the springlike day, the view sparkled from the Capitol steps of the Tidal Basin and the Potomac to the Jefferson Memorial and the hills of Arlington Cemetery. Straight ahead, beyond the reflecting pool, was the Washington Monument and the Lincoln Memorial. The Marine Corps band played "Yankee Doodle" and "The Battle Hymn of the Republic."

Taking her place on the Capitol steps, among the official guests and the rest of the Bush family, was the new vice president's seventy-nine-year-old mother, Dorothy. Following them, coming out in procession, were the justices of the Supreme Court, the retiring president and vice president, and then George Bush. Reagan waited inside the building. As Barbara held a Bible that was a gift from the Rev. Billy Graham, Associate Justice Potter Stewart swore in the forty-third vice president of the United States of America. Moments later, precisely at high noon, Chief Justice Warren Burger administered the oath to the fortieth president.

Reagan, evoking the appropriate inspirational theme for the occasion, urged a renewal of "our faith and hope," adding, "we have every right to dream heroic dreams." For decades, he had also pointed out, "we have piled deficit upon deficit, mortgaging our future and our children's future for the temporary convenience of the president," and then suggested that "government is not the solution to our problem; government is the problem." Finally, with the inspirational optimism that became his hallmark, he concluded by urging that the "crisis we are facing today" requires "our willingness to believe in ourselves and to believe in our capacity to perform great deeds; to believe that together with God's help we can and will resolve the problems which now confront us. And after all, why shouldn't we believe that? We are Americans."[31]

The Bushes napped that afternoon, and awoke to see fireworks over the illuminated facades of the Capitol and Washington Monument. They left for the round of nine inaugural balls, he in his tuxedo and she wearing a bright blue silk gown with puffy long sleeves. At the Washington Hilton Hotel, the new president had an announcement: "You might like to have a little news bulletin," he told the crowd. "I have just learned the planes have landed in Algiers. The hostages—no, I won't call them hostages, they were prisoners of war—are all hale and hearty."[32]

The vice president was the "nice man" around the White House. One writer even suggested that he replaced ideology with a "cult of courtesy."[33] He kept his views largely to himself, only rarely speaking out in front of others when differing with the president. Later, when he did, it was so noteworthy, it was front-page news. More characteristically, he held his fire until private sessions. He learned to view Reagan fondly, "as a friend, a trusted and admired friend."[34]

Neither were their Thursday lunches (or Wednesdays or Fridays, if necessary) for serious business. For Bush, as well as the president, they were times for personal exchanges, not anything official. Once in a while, Bush arrived with something on paper, but that was rare. "I never burdened him," he said of Reagan. "I wanted it to be so we could just talk about how things were going, and what did you think of this stupid story in the paper today. We joked and had fun. It was a respite. I think he looked forward to them." Later, remembering how his own presidential style contrasted with Reagan's, he said the older man "did a lot of delegating, but he'd always kind of come down in the right place and he just didn't pay that much attention to the detail behind policies. He just kind of knew in a broad sense where he wanted to be, or how he wanted to get there. It was very different. I kept getting amazed at that."[35]

Bush, as Nick Brady recalled, "kept himself out of the White House gear works."[36] He tried to blend into the crowd of Reaganites. "Not only would he never be seen or heard disagreeing with Ronald Reagan on any matter," wrote Randall Rothenberg, "but he also would never publicly offer any substantive opinions of his own."[37] Some of the president's men were eventually mollified but many remained uneasy about having him as vice president, especially with Baker so close to the Oval Office. Visions of a moderate "coup" haunted some of the most fervent true believers, who seemed more preoccupied with preserving the "Reagan revolution" from such infidels than did the president himself.

For the most part, policy differences between the president and his vice president were innocuous. Reagan's respect for the authority of Bush's office, and his confidence in the man himself, was implicit in his first major move. A cardinal faith among business conservatives was that the mounting governmental bureaucracy had bred an enormous web of regulations that choked economic growth. Nixon, even while expanding the federal apparatus with the addition of such agencies as the Environment Protection Administration (EPA), did start the pruning process, most notably when he wiped away the Office of Equal Economic Opportunity and liquidated others during his Watergate-marred final days. The impetus toward the reexamination of regulatory powers even made some headway during the Democratic Carter administration. All in all, that function, getting rid of intrusive and restrictive government regulations, especially those seen hindering the economy, was one that Bush relished as much, if not more, than did the president. It was Bush, for example, who lobbied Reagan out of dropping a slew of tax preferences for the oil industry.[38] Nevertheless, a general consensus that pruning was long overdue had begun to dilute the partisanship of deregulation. More than a matter of letting some air out of an admittedly over-bloated bureaucracy was the question of priorities and values.

Reagan left no doubt about where he stood. He went to the White House briefing room on his first day in office and announced the appointment of a President's Task Force. As though that designation was not enough to emphasize its importance, he also added that Vice President Bush would chair the group.[39] Designed to operate in conjunction with the Office of Management and Budget (OMB), and under the operational leadership of James C. Miller III, a conservative economist who had also just been appointed as director of the OMB's Office of Information and Regulatory Affairs, the need for regulatory reform took its place at the top of the administration's agenda. The vice president lent his prestige and guidance. The day-to-day work was carried out by the team under an executive staff that drew legal advice from C. Boyden Gray, the son of Gordon Gray who had served as special assistant for National Security Affairs under Eisenhower and was Bush's chief counsel.[40]

"Our goal is regulatory reform and relief," Bush later explained, adding that "we must get the country back to work," stressing the need to relieve regulatory restraints as a means of promoting competition abroad.[41]

Restrictions long deemed burdensome were discarded wholesale, resulting in a claimed savings of some $100 billion in regulatory costs and 600 million man hours. A veteran of the task force, Martin Anderson, has also written that "the task force has not merely blown a lot of hot air, it has quickly produced recommendations to end dozens of pending federal regulations. Only three months after we began, the task force had taken action on 181 federal regulations in thirteen departments and agencies. The estimated savings were as much as $18 billion the first year, with annual savings thereafter of $6 billion." More important than that, added one of Reagan's original economic advisers, bureaucratic resistance to any overhaul "seemed to take up so much of their time that they didn't have any time left over to dream up many new regulations," and none ever came up during that period "because none were ever proposed."[42]

For Bush, however, the task force was a mixed blessing. Neither defenders of regulatory restrictions nor advocates of reform got what they wanted. Some called it merely a "reporting mechanism" on the costs of regulation. William Greider, who had shaken up a lot of people with his account of David Stockman's candid view of Reaganomics*, now wrote about how the vice president

---

*Stockman was Reagan's Director of the Office of Management and Budget.

had "converted that high office into a convenient back door for corporate lob-byists and the environment." The taint of scandal that erupted over EPA administrator Anne Gorsuch, when she ran athwart the continuing high support for environmental restraints at the service of polluters, evaded Bush personally. He and his counsel, Gray, however, had at first encouraged efforts, heavily lobbied by trade associations for both large and small refiners, to ease or knock out altogether federal rules seeking to phase-down leaded gasoline. The vice president backed away when scientific evidence showed the medical and industrial costs of lead. Gorsuch's chumminess with oil interests became sufficiently public, however, for the whole thing to backfire. Bush called upon his old associate, William D. Ruckelshaus, to salvage the EPA from scandal.[43] The vice president came out of the affair, according to Greider, as a "secret 'good guy,' arguing against those who wanted to gut the federal commitment" in such areas as civil rights enforcement and aid to the handicapped—which, if true, would certainly confirm the belief of Reagan loyalists that the vice president was, as *The Economist* of London put it later, a "closet liberal" in a nation where "the L-word" "has become a term of abuse."[44]

Bush also chaired, starting in 1982, a South Florida Task Force that attempted to cope with the proliferation of drugs being smuggled into the state from Latin America. Bush, although successfully creating a coalition of governmental agencies to combat the flow, found that even that effort was inadequate for dealing with the problem. His claim of sharp cuts in south Florida drug trafficking was soon contradicted by ever greater flows of cocaine.[45]

Reagan gave Bush one job he would later rue, handing him an antiterrorist function that the administration itself would completely undo. Bush dutifully came up with a policy on the increasingly vexing problem of international terrorism. His report made a number of routine, sometimes platitudinous recommendations that were derided as examples of his "toothless war." Far worse than merely inconsequential, in the light of future events, was the following statement: "The U.S. government will make no concessions to terrorists. It will not pay ransoms, release prisoners, change its policies, or agree to other acts which might encourage additional terrorism."[46]

Not all his assignments were formal. In June, Atlanta police arrested a twenty-three-year-old suspect, Wayne B. Williams, a black freelance photographer, and charged him with murdering twenty-eight black children and two adults, whose bodies were discovered over a twenty-two-month period. Williams drew two life sentences, but as he insisted on his innocence, the case aggravated tensions between the police and Atlanta's large black community. Attorney William Kunstler, who took up the case, argued that another man had admitted to the killings and that the murders were part of a Ku Klux Klan plot. As disturbing details about the Atlanta racial crisis filtered into the White House, Reagan and his vice president "kind of agreed that I would follow up and report to him."

Bush enlisted the efforts of his staff, including Admiral Murphy, as well as

Thaddeus A. Garrett Jr., a black veteran of the federal establishment and Bush's domestic affairs adviser. Together, they helped Bush come up with over $2.3 million in aid for the city's police investigation and problems related to the crimes and resulting hostilities.[47]

Far better publicized, and the subject of an official White House action, was a matter that worsened Reagan's relations with his secretary of state. Contrary to Alexander Haig's claims about assurances given to him by Reagan, Bush was designated to head the crisis management team, a job formerly headed by presidential national security advisers. The unit, later known as the Special Situation Group, was charged with coordinating foreign policy in emergencies. Haig, who thought it should be led by the secretary of state, treated the move as an abrogation of a previous understanding, and accused Reagan of misleading him. A close Reagan friend, Bill Clark, who also happened to be Haig's deputy, had to talk him out of resigning. According to one historian of the Reagan presidency, Haig had a "tantrum." A White House aide who did not want to be quoted, explained that "the president simply feels more comfortable with George because he doesn't let his ego and ambition show and he doesn't come off as strong as Al Haig."[48]

Barely three weeks into the presidency, on March 30, Bush was tested in a crisis which brought out the best in some people and the worst in others. Al Haig, so recently disappointed in the crisis management affair, struck out once again. And the vice president, following his natural bent, comported himself in a manner that did much to consolidate the level of trust and confidence he was gaining within the administration.

Bush was traveling and, together with local Texas dignitaries, was in his limousine en route to Carswell Air Force Base outside of Fort Worth, his morning round of visits completed. Everything had gone on schedule. He had unveiled a plaque at the new Hyatt Regency Hotel and had just left his second stop, a luncheon speech at the Tarrant County Convention Center. He was due for a 1:45 P.M., Central Daylight Time, takeoff from Carswell for two appearances in Austin, a meeting with Governor Bill Clements and a speech before a joint session of the Texas state legislature.

Bush's traveling companions included some notable Texans, Democratic Majority Leader Jim Wright and a pair of Republican congressmen, Jim Collins of Dallas and Bill Archer, from Bush's old Houston district. Bush was also accompanied by an officially designated doctor, an air force military aide, Lt. Col. John Matheny, Ed Pollard at the head of the Secret Service detail, Deputy Press Secretary Shirley Green who kept contact with the White House system that enabled her to monitor communications from the passenger cabin, where she also served as a buffer between the vice president and a dozen reporters and news photographers.

There were, in his Texas visit, some largely unnoticed coincidences. His plane, a Boeing 727, was not just any 727, but Aircraft #86970, designated as Air Force Two because it was being used by the vice president. It had made many Texas runs, including carrying Vice President Johnson to Texas when he had visited with President Kennedy on November 21, 1963. Moreover, Bush's Hyatt Regency ceremonial stopover was at the same building formerly known as the Old Texas Hotel. JFK had spent his last night there.

As Bush prepared to take off from Carswell, half a continent away, John M. Dodson, a Pinkerton Agency computer specialist in Washington, D.C., looked down from his seventh floor window and saw a strange, fidgety figure on T Street, just off Connecticut Avenue, NW. The man's location and behavior attracted stares from a nearby police lieutenant, but no interference. He had, inexplicably, penetrated the press line and gone unchallenged. He kept turning his body from side to side, all the time edging toward the hotel exit and the waiting newsmen. Walter Rodgers of the Associated Press noticed that he had blond hair and heard him say something like "Who does the press think it is?" Nearby, *ABC News* reporter Sam Donaldson had a prepared question to call out to the president about a possible Soviet invasion of Poland. Inside Hilton's Grand Ballroom, 3,500 members of the AFL-CIO affiliated Building and Construction Workers of America union remained cool as President Reagan completed his remarks.

The young man, twenty-six-year-old John Hinckley Jr., stunned by the suddenness of the president's emergence from the hotel's side exit, was almost too startled to go through with his mission. But he couldn't botch this as he had with President Carter in October. Recovering and watching his target approach the Lincoln parked at the curb, Hinckley dropped to a firing crouch. No more than ten feet from his target, he placed both hands on the .22-caliber pistol and squeezed the trigger. The first round smashed into the head of Jim Brady, the president's press secretary. The second hit Washington Police Officer Thomas Delahanty. The third passed over Reagan's head and lodged in a building across the street. The fourth hit Secret Service Agent Tim McCarthy. The fifth skidded on the car's right rear panel, the hollow nose "Devastator" bullet flattening out in its split second of flight as it glanced off the metal and entered the space between the car's body and the open door, penetrating Reagan under his raised left arm and striking the top of his seventh rib, finally coming to rest in spongy lung tissue no more than an inch from the president's heart.[49]

None of this was clear at that moment of confusion. Meanwhile in Texas, word got to Air Force Two just as it left the runway at Carswell for the forty-five minute flight to Austin. Bush, seated in the front cabin, heard from Agent Pollard about a shooting. Two Secret Service men were hit, he told the vice president.

"Where did it happen?" asked Bush.

"Outside the Washington Hilton," replied the agent. "I'll let you know when we get more information."

Technologically updated as it was, communications on Air Force Two, even while flying over the heart of Texas, proved most erratic. The high altitude scrambled reception on the little black-and-white television set behind a couch on the starboard side of the staff cabin. Vital information was cut off at midpoint, compounding the uncertainty. Telephone calls from the White House to the Boeing were similarly hedged and incomplete because the messages were not secure; they went out as radio signals that could easily be intercepted. Alexander Haig, uncertain about whether that particular plane in the presidential fleet was equipped with secure voice channels, dictated a telex with the recommendation that Bush return as soon as possible. He then made his direct call. The voice was so faint that all Haig could hear was something about the vice president saying he would return.[50] Moreover, the confusion at the actual site compounded the problem, so that the sporadic information reaching Bush's plane was often erroneous. One report announced the death of Jim Brady. The president himself, according to another early piece of misinformation, had not been hit. Shirley Green, juggling all this, had to maintain contact from within the passenger cabin while keeping the reporters at a distance from the vice president. Bush then heard from Don Regan who, as treasury secretary was responsible for the Secret Service, and Attorney General Ed Meese. After further word to the plane from Meese, all Austin appointments were cancelled. Bush then huddled with about a dozen people, including Colonel Matheny and Agent Pollard, and prepared for the two-and-a-half hour flight to Andrews Air Force Base outside Washington by reviewing the logistics of their arrival.[51]

At the shooting scene, only the quick, on-the-spot action of Agent Jerry Parr saved the president. Parr noticed blood coming from Reagan's mouth and immediately pushed him into the waiting limousine, protecting him with his own body. He then diverted the Lincoln and the rest of the motorcade to George Washington University Hospital. The bullet's entry wound was almost invisible, even to the emergency room personnel who cut away the president's clothes. "Doctors believe [sic] bleeding to death," Larry Speakes jotted down on his pad while in the emergency room. "Can't find a wound." He also noted a doctor's fear that "we're going to lose him." The loss of about two pints of blood threatened to send the patient into shock. Finally, after transfusions had replaced almost all of his blood and he had been given intravenous fluids, he was stabilized. Not until a .22-caliber slug was discovered in Agent McCarthy's body were the doctors certain that the president's system had no extraneous lead from a larger bullet.[52]

"Even as we started our descent to the Robert Mueller Airport in Austin," Bush has written, "he was undergoing surgery at George Washington University Hospital in Washington." The only thing to do in Austin, it was clear by then, was to refuel before flying on to Washington. Jim Wright later told reporters that Bush remained calm and "demonstrated a complete command of his emotions." He then left the others and went into his private cabin and said prayers for the president. When the plane reached Austin, Bush said he thought he should go out to "say something to the people good enough to come out to the airport," but the Secret Service talked him out of it.[53]

Bush was in the air again headed toward Andrews, when a little drama played itself out in the White House. Totally unresolved at the moment amidst the confusion about Reagan's condition was the question of governmental authority. Section Four of the Twenty-fifth Amendment provided for temporary relinquishment of powers to the vice president, setting him up as, in effect, an "acting president" in cases of temporary presidential incapacity. Meanwhile, in the existing void with Bush nearly two-and-a-half hours away from Washington, and not knowing whether Hinckley had acted alone or was part of a wider conspiracy, Haig, as the ranking cabinet member, passed word via Richard Allen, the adviser for national security affairs, to convene all senior officials on hand.

The situation room, which was actually two rooms, was located in the White House basement below the West Wing. Windowless and ventilated by an air conditioner, it served as a secure crisis hideaway. The bigger room, with its presidential seal at one end, was about fifteen by twenty, and was furnished with a conference table at the center and straight chairs against paneled walls, which contained map cases and a television screen. Together with the smaller, L-shaped adjoining room, it was used as part of the National Security Council Staff suite. Caspar Weinberger, as secretary of defense, contacted the Pentagon's command center from there to confirm that no conspiracy was involved.[54]

About twenty men were present, double the usual number, by the time Haig appeared. Amid the commotion, with such people as Bill Casey of the CIA, Baker aides Dave Gergen and Dick Darman, Craig L. Fuller, the assistant for cabinet affairs, Regan, Allen, and Cap Weinberger going in and out, not even the noisy air conditioner could keep the room from becoming oppressive. At 3:15, word did arrive that Bush's plane would land at Andrews Air Force Base in two-and-a-half hours.

The momentary vacuum of leadership was obvious. Weinberger told Haig that he had "raised the alert status of our forces."

Haig, obviously miffed, said, "Cap, what do you mean? Have you changed the Defcon [defense condition] of our forces?" Weinberger, the secretary of state was quick to note with an air of authority, did not quite know what he was talking about. His action had merely informed field commanders of the alert status in Washington without changing the normal defense condition of U.S. strategic forces.[55]

Upstairs in the press room, meanwhile, reporters and television cameras were focused on a briefing being given by Gergen. Bush was en route, he explained. Larry Speakes, deputy White House press officer to the wounded Jim Brady, then came on. Haig, seated with his back to the screen on the wall, turned around to watch.

"Who's running the government right now?" asked one reporter. Before Speakes could reply, another shouted, "If the president goes into surgery and goes under anesthesia, would vice president Bush become the acting president at the moment?"

"I cannot answer that question at this time," said Speakes.

"The room was hushed," Haig has reported. "It was oppressively hot. It appeared that Speakes had been waylaid by the press as he returned to the White House from the hospital. Reporters hurled hard questions at him."[56]

Haig and Allen, watching Speakes's dilemma, dashed out of the situation room and ran up the steps to the press room. There, with Allen at his side, the secretary of state grabbed the microphone. What followed was remarkable, a performance that, according to Speakes, became "a source of gallows humor." Haig's sense of drama got out of hand.[57] Lou Cannon, in his biography of Reagan, describes the former general and Nixon chief of staff as taking over the situation "in a quavery voice."[58] Haig later admitted to "a poor choice of words" and to having made the unfortunate claim that he was acting "constitutionally" rather than "traditionally" or "administratively."[59] Jim Baker, who was in the hospital at the time with Reagan, appeared on the Ted Koppel television news show afterward and confirmed that they had agreed that Haig "would be our point of contact here in the situation room at the White House as he quite properly should have been as the senior cabinet officer."[60]

Baker was his guarded self. Haig's nationally televised claim was neither constitutionally correct nor politic. He was, as Baker put it, "our point of contact," but that was all. Nothing authorized him to respond, as he did, to a reporter's question about who was making the decisions in the absence of the president as he did: "Constitutionally, gentlemen, you have the president, the vice president, and the secretary of state, in that order, and should the president decide he wants to transfer the helm, he will do so. He has not done that. As of now, I am in control here, in the White House, pending the return of the vice president and in close touch with him. If something came up, I would check with him, of course."[61]

His claim and demeanor were both alarming, raising the specter of a "general on horseback." The signal that went out to the country and the world was negative in every way. The president was only temporarily in surgery. A decision not to invoke the Twenty-fifth Amendment had already been made by Baker and Meese just before the operation, and, in any case, the trigger mechanism to implement Section Four required the consent of the vice president and a majority of department heads to give their "written declaration that the president is unable to discharge the powers and duties of his office," which, in any case, would have given temporary power to the vice president. Moreover, the existing presidential succession act, which had been passed by Congress over three decades earlier, stipulated the remaining sequence as the speaker of the house, the president pro tempore of the senate, and then the secretary of state.[62]

Haig's demeanor stood in direct contrast to that of the vice president, who was careful to avoid disturbing either protocol or the symbols. As Air Force Two headed east, Colonel Matheny advised that he board a helicopter at Andrews to take him directly to the South Lawn of the White House. This would expedite his getting to the situation room without the additional nuisance of rush-hour traffic on Massachusetts Avenue. Bush, however, saw another image. It was of "Marine Two dropping out of the sky, blades whirring, the vice president stepping off the helicopter to take charge," precisely what he did not want to convey to an anxious country. He chose to go directly to the vice president's house, then by limo to Pennsylvania Avenue. "John," said Bush to his military aide, "only the president lands on the South Lawn."[63]

Meanwhile, Baker entered the situation room at 6:15 P.M. and reported that the president was in good condition. The nation had, in fact, been cheered by a reported one-liner he had delivered to his wife, Nancy: "Honey, I forgot to duck." "There would be many more jokes that day and night," Laurence Barrett has written, "some of them scribbled when the mouthpiece of a breathing device prevented speech." Among them was a comment made to his surgeons when they were about to start the operation, "Please tell me you're Republicans."[64]

Bush's plane reached Andrews at 6:30. Admiral Murphy, prepared to brief him upon his arrival, joined him on the helicopter and updated him on the president's condition as well as the legal and constitutional problems and the press reaction. At one minute to seven, Bush walked into the situation room and took his seat at the head of the table. "I have never been so impressed with Bush as I was that night, the way he instantly took command," wrote Speakes in his memoirs. The vice president announced that he would meet with the cabinet and congressional leadership the following day. "The more normal things are," he said, "the better. If reports about the president's condition are encouraging, we want to make the government function as normally as possible. Everybody has to do his job."[65]

The next morning, Bush met with the cabinet and the National Security Council. At his suggestion, they moved out of the situation room and went upstairs to meet in the cabinet room. Bush took care to assume his usual seat and not the president's. Al Haig later recorded that "the president had reason to be proud of his vice president and of the men he had chosen to serve on his cabinet and staff."[66]

Few ever heard Bush complain about his vice presidency. He had a job to do, a role to preserve, and a career to further; and he did all that, working almost as much from his facilities on Air Force Two as he did elsewhere. Little illustrates the role of the modern vice presidency as much as the realization that, when in Washington, he had seven government offices, one in the West Wing of the White House near the Oval Office and another in an impressive suite of rooms at the Old Executive Office Building across from the White House. For his constitutional function as president of the Senate, he had an office in the Capitol Building. For legislative lobbying and furthering the administration's interests on the hill, he had a place in a Dirksen Senate Office Building. Then, of course, there was the office in his official residence at the Naval Observatory. A sixth, in Houston, handled matters in Texas. At Walker's

Point, he also worked out of a building some two hundred yards from the main house, which was also used for his security personnel. Later, the government constructed a house for his physician and military aide.[67]

The seaside home continued to be Bush's other "White House," much as Warm Springs served that purpose for FDR, Hyannis Port for Kennedy, and San Clemente for Nixon. George and Barbara entertained a number of visitors, including journalists, staff members, and a wide variety of politicians. One of the noteworthy occasions was a clambake in the summer of 1983, when the Bushes hosted governors and their families. The guests included Bill and Hillary Clinton of Arkansas and Alabama's George Wallace.

The compound functioned mainly during the summer. Only three of its rooms were heated, although the family used it for Thanksgiving weekend getaways. Prominently located at a seaside tourist area and surrounded by water on three sides, the property was a challenge for the Secret Service. Keeping pace with his cigarette boat taxed both skill and equipment. Not only did agents require special training for navigating speedboats in such rocky, offshore waters, but the power of Bush's own craft, which he bought for $18,000 and had an estimated value of somewhere between $100,000 and $200,000 in 1981 (allowing for the recent inflation and optional add-ons), outsped their own. The problem was solved by having the agents use a powerful Mirage 36 speedboat with twin 400-horsepower Mercury engines.

In and out of the water, agents guarded them on family outings and while Bush navigated the *Fidelity* through breaking waves. One so upended the craft that NBC newsman Tom Pettit crashed to the deck, injuring himself enough to lose ten days' work. A story that made the rounds told of the neighbor who pulled his own boat up to the Bush dock to drop off daughter Dorothy, and was immediately startled by three frogmen who suddenly popped out of the water to inspect the unannounced intruder.[68]

Even on foot, not every agent was fit enough to keep up with Bush. Adding to the surveillance problem was the need to provide rearview security, to guard against an attack from behind. That meant that, in addition to the two protective joggers flanking him on his outings, one poor fellow had to monitor what was behind him by jogging ahead of him—backward.[69]

The real logistical nightmare, and challenge to the budget, involved his official overseas trips. Foreigners have often noted the retinues that accompany traveling American presidents, comparing them to medieval kings. Less realized, and not as interesting to the press, is what goes into vice presidential overseas travel. Bush, who made an enormous number of trips during his Reagan years, including visits to all fifty states, four territories, and sixty-eight foreign countries, dropped in to seven European capitals in the early summer of 1985. His press secretary, Marlin Fitzwater, by acknowledging that there was no way to estimate the cost, underscored the magnitude of the expedition. It involved not only Air Force Two but three other planes. Included in the fleet were a backup jet and two cargo aircraft, each carrying a bullet-proof limousine. Accompanying Bush was a twenty-member staff, journalists, Secret Service agents, and communications personnel, and more of the latter riding in the backup plane. The planning for all this, begun almost two months earlier, involved detailed scheduling worked out by members of the Bush staff in concert with personnel from U.S. embassies in Rome, Bonn, Brussels, The Hague, Geneva, Paris, and London. Then, leaving nothing to chance, teams scouted out the routes involved at each stop of the daily schedule, carefully timing each move, so that the Second Family could be handed a minute-by-minute schedule upon their arrival at each airport.[70]

The vice presidency requires a good deal of self-discipline, a problem that is compounded by both the nature of the office and the nature of its occupant. Almost by definition, and in varying degrees, with Harry Truman the possible exception, they are people with ambitions. Accidental promotions to the presidency via the second highest office, while not common, have become more possible in recent years for a variety of reasons. Truman, Johnson, Nixon, and Ford eventually rose to the top, and, among those that did not actually get there, Vice Presidents Humphrey and Mondale, for example became their party's presidential candidates. The modern vice president is expected to become an advocate for the administration. All accumulated instincts for self-assertion, so essential for the political drive, become suppressed. The expected loyalty to the man in the Oval Office, regardless of early feelings, exposes them to suspicion at the least hint that the vice president, who has expended so much political capital to rate the job in the first place, actually has thoughts about his own presidency.

Bush learned to overcome his original reservations about Reagan and even, as those who talked to him privately learned, became "genuinely fond" of him. While difficulties with the Reagan staff never stopped being a thorn, the president himself was very "cordial" and supportive.

Far less tolerant of the number-two man was Nancy Reagan. She viewed him most clearly as a rival, and one with his own ambitions. She was, according to one understatement, "not the greatest pro-Bush person," fearing at times that the vice president was trying to overshadow her husband. Told afterward that it was she who had spread false Washington gossip as early as that first March about an alleged Bush affair with the widow of a former congressman, Bush noted for his diary, "I always knew that Nancy didn't like me very much, but there is nothing we can do about all of that. I feel sorry for her, but the main thing is, I feel sorry for President Reagan."[71] Bush, already surrounded by wary ideological Reaganites, and ever conscious that others, especially more liberal journalists, considered his position somewhat anomalous, had little choice but to navigate around the hazards of his position.

No incident illustrated the vice president's quandary as well as that which occurred in the middle of the administration's first term. It never gained more than slight attention, but it showed what sort of sacrifices were expected of him. It demonstrated a price of political ambition he had not anticipated nor even considered.

His older brother, Prescott, had spent a career on Wall Street but also, like his father, was involved in Connecticut politics. He had contributed to his brother's 1980 campaign through chairing his state's Republican Finance Committee. Service on the local GOP, as a traditional conservative, also included holding positions as Greenwich town chairman and district leader, and eight years of membership on the State Committee. Prescott's activism in Connecticut politics also made him a delegate to several state and national conventions. By 1982, with party traditionalists having had to endure maverick, independent Lowell P. Weicker Jr., Prescott Bush decided that he should run for the Senate. The Bush game plan was to rally together party regulars, and then appeal to conservative Democrats to defeat a liberal candidate in November.

But first he had to beat Weicker; he needed the necessary finances and political skill to win in a primary. Prescott Bush, unfortunately, could muster only one of the necessities, the money; he "proved to be an embarrassing candidate, given to embarrassing statements."[72]

For the White House, the problem was not having brother Prescott lose the primary. Weicker was vulnerable and Bush had a reasonable chance to win, which was what Republican Senate Majority Leader Howard Baker thought. Bush might get rid of Weicker, but there was little confidence that he could actually keep the seat in Republican hands. The Democrats were ready with a liberal for November, Toby Moffett. Worry about the outcome reached from the Senate chambers to the Oval Office and, as Prescott later acknowledged, he knew his brother "wasn't enthusiastic about it." When their younger brother, Jonathan, approached him just before the primary and suggested that he withdraw, Prescott knew "that there was pressure from the White House for me to get out of that race." Staying in and causing a party embarrassment, he feared, would "jeopardize George's future," so he stepped aside.

"You're always subject to cracks from all kinds of sources about being ineffectual as a vice president," he said in his brother's defense; "things like that, needling you and partisan stuff, trying to downplay any strength you might build up for a run for the presidency."[73]

His younger brother, characteristically, kept all this to himself, except in rare situations. One occurred at a reunion of Yale Bonesmen. They had reconvened before, at the vice presidential residence shortly after his inauguration. They met again in 1985, this time at Lud Ashley's Washington home. Bush retreated into the "inner sanctum" of his youth, as he had done with his fraternity mates at Yale. One of them, Thomas Wilder Mosely, yearning for a return to the old magic, suddenly stood up and said, "Let's repair to the inner sanctum."

Bush was eager. "Why not?" he asked.

Bush, recalled Ashley, "rejoiced. He was almost the first one to go into the den, the library I have here. He welcomed the questions. . . . He was aware of the dilemma of being Ronald Reagan's vice president."

They went on for an hour, taking turns at unburdening themselves as though in a confessional, by responding to the request that they explain how well they were doing. Bush, however, drew the most attention. He told them, according to Ashley's recollection, that he was surprised at "the tone and substance of attacks on him" in the press. He felt himself trapped in the office; in a "gridlock" was the way Ashley remembered it. Being vice president, he explained, you "feel the foot in your back." Complicating it all, of course, was his intent to prepare for his own run at the presidency.[74]

That reunion at Ashley's place came after the 1984 reelection of the Reagan-Bush ticket. Bush had become more aware of his own inadequacies. They were all the more exposed when he was subjected to the inevitable comparisons with Ronald Reagan, "the great communicator." He had to both launch his campaign apparatus and to condition himself to become a more effective candidate.

Jim Baker shared Bush's problems. Not always understood, and certainly beyond the recognition of many of the president's most devoted followers, was the extent to which President Reagan's ideological "firmness" managed to accommodate compromise. The polite explanation holds that it was pragmatism over stubborn obedience to principle, something that also characterized his governorship. Some who served with him in California in appointed positions, such as Bob Haldeman, joked behind his back about his intellectual limitations.[75] Others, to use a term coined by Clark Clifford, thought Reagan was an "amiable dunce."[76] Reagan biographer Lou Cannon acknowledges his flexibility while in the Sacramento statehouse and describes him as a president who could not be trusted without handlers.[77] Budget director David Stockman, a supply-side purist, quickly learned that Reagan was really a consensus politician and "had no business trying to make a revolution because it wasn't in his bones."[78] Stockman's devastating account of how "Reaganomics" succumbed to conventional politics portrays the president as a dolt whose metier was delivering highly nationalistic speeches and recounting anecdotes. Those who still expected the consistency of an ideologue should have been alerted by his choice of liberal Republican Senator Richard Schweiker of Pennsylvania as a potential running mate in 1976; or, for that matter, moderate George Bush in 1980. One of the quaintest aspects of his political career, in fact, was the extent to which Reaganites were willing to ignore the ways in which their hero failed the test of ideological purity. It became easier to explain that he had been ill-served by his staff. So the fact that he took Stu Spencer's advice to give James Baker the chief of staff job made perfect sense.

While Baker, in his role, did not have Bush's legal and constitutional standing, his position demanded constant evidence of personal loyalty. Unlike his friend, he had no authority other than Reagan's personal endorsement and Mrs. Reagan's patience. It took courage for Baker to support Stockman when others denounced him for sharing so much inside information about the administration's number-crunching with journalist Bill Greider. Not forgotten as a Ford man and the manager of Bush's campaign against Reagan, with that "voodoo economics" charge, Baker's standing remained shaky. It mattered less that Reagan himself authorized him (as he did Bush) to team up with a group of those designated to negotiate with congressional leaders—the so-called "Gang of seventeen"—than the fact that their sessions ended with agreement for cuts in some defense spending and additional taxes. Such "lapses" inevitably exposed Baker as a betrayer of the "revolution" and as an "utter shock to true-blue Reaganauts," including Treasury Secretary Donald Regan (who wrote that Baker and Stockman got "what they wanted all along") and such faithful acolytes as Ed Meese III.[79] Meese had been the odds-on favorite among the Reaganites to become chief of staff; giving the job to the pragmatic Baker lent credence to their anxiety that their "revolution" had been short-circuited.

Not only that, but Baker's deputy was the brilliant bureaucratic in-fighter Richard Darman, who had served him back when Baker was undersecretary of Commerce under Ford. Darman, who would later be called "Bush's Rasputin," was also a suspect character among extremists because of his close relationship with moderate Republican, Elliot Richardson.[80] Often impatient with intellectual inferiors, he was not only alone among senior White House staff members who had no role in Reagan's election, but, in the words of Martin Anderson, was "one of many difficult personalities" in the administration's upper echelon.[81]

By any account, the invisibility of any sort of "revolution" by the end of the first year frustrated dedicated new-breed conservative believers in a supply-side miracle. Their faith in cutting corporate and individual taxes to stimulate investments and thereby spur the economy had yet to be tested. To the dismay of people like Stockman, interest-group politics ruled the day as usual. Republican legislators were just as eager as Democrats to feed their constituents from the Big Government trough of what Stockman called the "Second Republic" brainchild of the New Deal. "They decided when all was said and done to ratify the American welfare state as it had evolved by 1980," wrote Stockman. "They decided not to roll back the tide of history."[82]

Even more frustrating was the source of the inspirational rhetoric about the revolution, the president himself. His inattentiveness became famous as his mind wandered to shopworn anecdotes about Hollywood and his governorship. With a feeble grasp of long-range budgetary problems, he was unshakable in his faith that the deficits being created by the administration's economic program would be wiped out by the coming prosperity. He remained adamant about endorsing Defense Secretary Caspar Weinberger's rocketing increases in Pentagon spending and opposing new taxes to relieve the damage. In the long run, through the 1980s, the inflation left by the Carter years did disappear and, thanks to a combination of tightening interest rates imposed by the Federal Reserve, reduced fuel costs after the oil crisis of the seventies, and staggering deficit spending, Americans lived happily with the illusion of a healthy economy.[83]

At the moment, however, by the fall of 1981, as Reagan's first year neared its close, the nation fell into its deepest recession since the 1930s. Although the immediate slump could not be attributed to their policies, the supply-side faithful were left with economic disappointment and the surrender to politics of any hope of reversing the welfare state. Before it was all over, the contradictions would be enormous. The administration's fiscal mishandling had led to some half dozen moves to raise revenues, but Reagan, protected by his right wing, remained immune. Nevertheless, writing only in the middle of the Reagan years, Stockman despaired that the "tax revenue giveaway implemented by the Reagan administration has amounted to *four times more* than the spending takeaway."[84] The ultimate legacy would be smaller than Stockman feared it could have been, but those eight years compiled more debt than the total previous deficit accumulation in American history. Maybe Bush had been right all along, Stockman wrote. They really *were* practicing voodoo economics.[85]

There could be no winners: either be blamed for fiscal recklessness or for trying to go head-to-head with the president on tax and spending policies. Under such circumstances, the "aliens" were most vulnerable. Darman's independence made him an easy target, and he became a surrogate; easier to whip him than Baker.

Among those not shy about challenging the chief of staff was a "Young Turk" congressman, the intellectually audacious right-wing Republican from Georgia's Sixth Congressional District, just outside Atlanta. A transplanted Pennsylvanian, Newt Gingrich, the holder of a doctorate in American history and a former liberal college professor, was elected in 1978 on his third try. In 1982, he was just thirty-eight and in his second term. From early on, his confrontational style characterized his departure from traditional and more sedate Republicanism. "His goal is not to cooperate with Democrats," Michael Barone and Grant Ujifusa noted in the mid eighties, "but to demoralize them until their majority crumbles."[86]

In February of 1982, he erupted at the chief of staff. His tone left little doubt that it was provoked as much by his view of Baker as an infidel as by what the chief of staff had done or said. Baker, reading the six-page missive that contained Gingrich's charges, contemptuously added the following marginal note: "I don't need a lecture from this twit."[87]

Gingrich's anger was triggered by Baker's appearance on both *Face the Nation* and at a briefing session with congressional Republicans. Baker was at his most cautious self. Midterm elections, he well knew, often turned out negatively for the party holding the White House. The economic slump further marred the outlook. Without an early upturn, there would be no choice except to settle for modest losses. Baker was also conscious of the pitfalls of predicting popular support in the 1982 off-year elections. His mission, then, before the national television audience and in the briefing session, was to lower expectations without seeming defeatist. "We are not claiming that we're going to take control of the House of Representatives," he said. "We're not making major claims of victory. It's going to be very tough and all we're saying is we'd like to keep the losses below what they have historically been."

His position was prudent, a rational analysis designed to forestall embarrassment. To Gingrich, however, Baker had, in effect, surrendered, sacrificing the revolutionary cause. He pulled no punches. He charged Baker with dealing in "politics as trivia," of favoring a "materialist analysis" in citing the importance of the economy to national elections rather than emphasizing "the fundamental values by which a free people decides its future." By conceding the possibility of losses, Baker was encouraging their opponents and slowing "the flow of money and energy to the Republican party and [increasing] the flow of money and energy to the Democratic party." Instead of rallying Republicans, instead of emphasizing the importance of building and confirming the Reagan revolution, Baker was engaging in a "tweedle-dum, tweedle-dee campaign." A proper response would have been to confront the Democrats and Speaker Thomas P. (Tip) O'Neill about their "obstructing the American people on the budget, defense, and on the New Federalism . . ." Baker, instead, had launched a virtual "declaration of war against the Republican party," reflecting the weakness of a presidential appointee with "little faith in his program and tactics." Lest Baker think Gingrich was speaking only for himself, the congressman gave him his "word" that "the anger is phenomenal" among his colleagues. Baker, he went on to charge, was evidently more concerned with retaining and building his "personal credibility with the press corps the day after the elections." He should, instead, "work once again with us as part of a team" to "building the America President Reagan promised and we all favor."[88]

Gingrich's backpedaling began five days later. He realized, he wrote, "that some parts are too strong and too personal" and added, "I apologize. If anything I have done has embarrassed you, please accept my apologies." Four weeks later, after the chief of staff had moved to patch things up, Gingrich wrote, "I am glad you are letting me back into the tent. I look forward to our being a winning team. Your friend, Newt."[89]

Baker, as it turned out, was the more prudent of the two. He had pointed out that, on average, the party in power loses thirty-eight seats. Republicans that year dropped by twenty-six in the House and also lost seven governorships, not exactly a firm endorsement of the "revolution" but not bad; and certainly not a disaster.

Whatever the differences that pitted supply-side purists against orthodox fiscal conservatives, the president remained above such battles. He was the political "rainmaker," the outside man who brought in the business, who appealed across class and partisan lines to provide the vital popular foundation. The administration thereby empowered was unabashedly probusiness. With Reagan's ability to win a mass following and create a new majority, conservatives worked to take advantage of the opportunity to reverse federal restraints on the free market.

Much more was made, especially in later years, of Bush's continued association with Manuel Noriega. It all came back as somewhat of a Bush albatross because the Reagan administration, and especially the new CIA director, Bill Casey, had few compunctions about moving mountains, if necessary, to ensure that neither El Salvador nor Nicaragua became another Cuba. Noriega's services were worth putting up with all "his gunrunning, money laundering, and drug smuggling." As an NSC paper on "Interest and Objectives" in Central America explained in 1983, the U.S. concern in the region should be keeping it "free from outside interference" and countering "the proliferation of Cuban-model states which would provide platforms for subversion, compromising vital sea lanes and pose a direct military threat at or near our borders."[90] Throughout the region, of course, it was Castro's gang that fomented much of the trouble. And Castro's lifeline was in Moscow.

The seizure of power in San Salvador, El Salvador's capital, ignited a vicious civil war with government resistance led by a man described by the CIA as the "principal henchman for wealthy landowners and a coordinator of the right-wing death squads that have murdered several thousand suspected leftists and leftist sympathizers during the last year," Roberto d'Aubuisson.[91] D'Aubisson's responsibility for the rape of three nuns and murder of San Salvador's dissenting archbishop, Oscar Anulfo Romero, killed by a sniper as he celebrated the Mass in San Salvador, was undoubted. The peasants of the remote village of El Mozote and in nearby La Joya, over four hundred in all, were wiped out in one day by soldiers of the Atlacati Batallion sent out to cleanse the countryside of Marxist guerrillas or potential sympathizers. The Reagan administration, so ready to pounce upon every allegation of human rights violations by Communists, practiced studied denial that it could have happened. Such soldiers could not possibly have been trained by the U.S., said the State Department.[92] There was, at the same time, abundant evidence to show that the Reds, while Carter was still in the White House, kept the Salvadoran rebels at the end of a pipeline of supplies that funneled through the radical Sandinista regime in Nicaragua after coming from such sources as the Soviet Union, Cuba, North Vietnam, and Eastern Europe.[93] Carter did sign on to a top-secret finding authorizing CIA political support to the *contrarevolucionarios,* or contras as they came to be called. And, in a manner fully consistent with the cold war policy toward Noriega followed by Ford and later by Reagan, Carter's administration valued the Noriega asset enough to keep federal prosecutors from bringing drug-trafficking and arms-smuggling charges against him.[94]

An interim job was being done by an Argentine force of some one thousand, which had undertaken the sole responsibility of propping up the battlers against the successors of the Somoza dictatorship. The Somocistas had come to power under Luis Somoza via a coup in 1937, but the long regime ended with the overthrow of his younger brother, the authoritarian Anastasio Somoza, who at least was a friend of the United States. The contras, constituted under the fiction that they were anti-Somocista as well as anti-Communist, found themselves with a new sponsor as Reagan took over from the Argentine government. CIA Director Casey, who was quickly won over to the cause, also reinstated Noriega, this time at an annual salary of $200,000.[95] On November 16, the new president approved a plan to provide $20 million in covert American aid to the contras, who were then still forming in Honduras. The operation, which would involve several agencies, State, Defense, the CIA, and the NSC, was approved by the president at a meeting of the National Security Planning Group on the first of December. Vice President Bush went along, giving his characteristic silent acquiescence to a plan that would involve several departments and agencies, State, Defense, the National Security Council, and the Central Intelligence Agency.[96]

In the aftermath of the 1970s exposures of CIA activities, let alone the workings of the "Vietnam syndrome," congressional vigilance, especially from the Democratic opposition, was to be expected. The CIA, insofar as liberals were concerned, was up to its old tricks. Concealed funding supported continuing covert operations. Little had changed, after all, despite the Rockefeller, Church, and Pike investigations, and the dramatic revelations that had preceded Bush as DCI. Information that the agency was not only trying to kill the flow of arms to the rebels in El Salvador but also backing a counterrevolution in Nicaragua led to calls for action. That there already was a congressional requirement for a presidential "finding" that any covert activity was "important to the national security of the United States" in the form of the Hughes-Ryan Amendment of 1974 was not sufficient. A Democrat from Springfield in western Massachusetts, Edward P. Boland, attached an amendment to a CIA budget measure that specifically forbade either that agency or the Defense Department from spending appropriated money to overthrow the Sandinistas. The measure, attached to the Defense Appropriations Act of 1983, was no obstacle for those who really wanted to do the job. Reagan, coolly signing the law, agreed to comply. In April, he told the Congress that the purpose was not to overthrow the Nicaraguan government. Sandinista arms simply could not be allowed to flow toward her neighbors. More explicit was his finding of September 19, 1983, which stated the goal of providing "support, equipment, and training assistance to Nicaraguan paramilitary resistance groups" to end leftist insurgencies.[97] Nothing, moreover, kept the CIA from handing off the project to another agency. Nor was Congress the only source of money. Solicitations from whatever the source—drugs, weapons, private American citizens, the king of Saudi Arabia, the Taiwanese—made its way to the contra base in Honduras and into private bank accounts. Later, a "bridge loan" of $10 million from the sultan of Brunei to tide over the rebels until promised congressional funding arrived went into the wrong bank account in Geneva and never reached them.[98]

For Bush, the vice president eager to become a Reagan insider, going along seemed logical. His anti-Communist position certainly was no weaker than Reagan's or Casey's, and, in some ways, it was stronger. He had the advantage of bringing special expertise to the job, a spell with the CIA and prior knowledge of Noriega. He was no stranger to the kind of action, which, as Al Haig explained, would at least allow the "White House people to go to bed at night saying we did something, something tough, against those terrible Marxists."[99]

Casey, of all people, could really appreciate that. Bush needed little convincing to go along: use his adviser for national security affairs, a veteran of both Vietnam and the CIA. Pleased as he was at the initiation of paramilitary capability, Bush's silent consent had placed him in a position that later proved embarrassing, becoming an "ally" of Noriega's, however reluctant, however much a matter of expediency in the interests of intelligence. Such covert operations, principally directing the fight to preserve the government in San Salvador from rebels and keep alive Nicaragua's contra movement, were left to the capable hands of Donald Gregg, the former CIA station chief in Saigon. It was Gregg who was clearly fingered a decade later by the statement in the *Final Report of the Independent Counsel for Iran/Contra Matters:* "From in [*sic*] or about December 1981 until on or about October 11, 1984, the United States government, acting principally through the CIA, pursuant to written presidential findings, had provided the contras with financial support, arms, and military equipment, as well as with supervision and instruction, tactical and other advice, coordination, intelligence, and direction."[100]

Don Gregg was Bush's man. A ten-year veteran of the CIA and a graduate of Williams College, he was a six-foot, white-shoe, tennis-playing, well-connected Easterner. Most recently, until he joined Bush, he headed the NSC's Intelligence Directorate. Under Gregg, the fieldwork with the contras was first in the hands of the chief of the Latin-American Division of the CIA, Duane (Dewey) Clarridge, and then those of a Bay of Pigs veteran and helicopter expert, Felix Rodriguez (known in the field as Max Gomez). "It was Bush's office that put Rodriguez down there and kept him there," recalled Elliott Abrams. Rodriguez went to work helping to direct the contra resupply program out of Ilopango airfield in San Salvador. Before any U.S. funding could come through, and during the period of the Boland Amendment, the operation had to rest on outside donations. How much of this money would ever actually reach its target remained worrisome to such people as contra field leaders and Lt. Col. Oliver North, who helped run the guerrilla war from his National Security Council office. From the start of the Gregg operation through the involvement of North and the colonel's subsequent enlistment of retired Air Force General Richard Secord to set up what became his "Enterprise" resupply effort, sufficiency of funding was a major problem. Secord himself, in a complaint made to Gregg by Rodriguez, charged that the men in his entourage were "ripping off the contras."[101] A combination of corruption and sheer greed threatened to starve out the project before Washington had the political will to act.

Beyond that, it was something that Bush, in retrospect, would not have wanted to get in to. Whatever personal benefit he could derive was at best minor, and then in the form of grudging credits from the more zealous anti-Communists in the party's right wing. Of the entire Nicaraguan action, in the words of Elliott Abrams's assistant at the State Department's Inter-American Affairs desk, Robert Kagan, "the actual benefit to the contras of the secret efforts to arm and supply them" never offered "any more than marginal benefit from the exertions of Reagan officials and private individuals on their behalf." As with Noriega himself, what started out under Gregg and was led by North and Secord was an association best forgotten. How much Bush actually knew about each projected far into his future career, once more raising concerns about credible deniability of such questions as, for example, "Did Don Gregg tell the vice president?" which Abrams, who had recently been pardoned by the outgoing President Bush, asked rhetorically in 1993. Abrams also stated, "Don Gregg has said no and the vice president [Bush] has said no, *and* Walsh did not invite Don Gregg [to testify]. I don't know anyone who served in the Reagan-Bush administration that actually believes that." Or, as Secord has written, "Any subsequent claims by Gregg, and presumably George Bush, that they were uninformed about the interim resupply airlift should be viewed very skeptically."[102] Independent Counsel Lawrence Walsh, unable to put several key questions to then-President Bush, including querying his knowledge "of or involvement in any quid-pro-quo arrangements with Central American or other countries in exchange for their support of the contras," was forced to make the following conclusion: "There was no credible evidence obtained that the vice president or any member of his staff directed or actively participated in the contra resupply effort that existed during the Boland Amendment prohibition on military aid to the contras, which, in any event, was due to expire on December 19, 1985. To the contrary, the vice president's staff was largely excluded from RIG [Restricted Interagency Group] meetings where contra matters were discussed and during which, particularly in the summer of 1986, [Oliver] North openly discussed operational details of his contra efforts." No number of face-to-face encounters between Bush and Clarridge or Rodriguez proved the contrary.

Rodriguez, for all his skills and derring-do, compounded the Bush embarrassment. He couldn't stop boasting about his closeness to the vice president. He did get in to see him in the Old Executive Office Building on January 22, 1985, thanks to Gregg, and they reminisced about old CIA exploits. The pilot's mission, however, was to tell Bush that he wanted to work in El Salvador to squash the guerrillas.[103] Bush had other meetings with him. A Bush office scheduling memorandum for May 1, 1986, did show that the vice president met Rodriguez on that date to be briefed "on the status of the war in El Salvador and resupply."[104] Bush, in a later interview, readily acknowledged that he knew Rodriguez.[105]

Just as he still wore Che Guevara's wristwatch and carried his photograph as tokens of having interrogated him for American intelligence just before his death, Rodriguez liked to boast that he had a personal relationship with the vice president, and not always in discrete venues. As Abrams reported to Secretary of State George Shultz, "he goes around to bars saying he is buddy [*sic*] of Bush." Just as Admiral John Poindexter did for President Reagan, Donald Gregg did for his boss, providing him the cover of "plausible deniability," which did not relieve Bush of later being haunted by the goings on in Central America involving Noriega, El Salvador, and Nicaragua.[106]

For a variety of reasons, legitimate attention to national security and cold war rivalry, domestic politics, and American commercial interests, the CIA had long since undertaken covert operations in Central America and the Caribbean. By the 1980s, such activities focused on El Salvador and Nicaragua, where they took the form of sustained programs of assistance to a little band of jungle warriors. These opponents of the leftists who controlled the capital city of Managua came to be called anti-Marxist "freedom fighters." On one level, a war of peasants and small farmers against large landholders and the military establishment, and on another, a battle between Moscow-oriented collectivists and bourgeois democrats, it became a focal point of the so-called Reagan Doctrine that proclaimed devoted support for freedom fighters.[107] In the case of Central America, that meant mobilizing support from within the region and from wherever help was available.

That helped clearly and emphatically in the case of Grenada, a 133-square mile volcanic island in the southeastern Caribbean. Its fewer than 100,000 people, mainly English-speaking Roman Catholic blacks, had known independence and membership in the British Commonwealth of Nations only since 1974. All that collapsed five years later when the new nation's first prime minister, Eric M. Gairy, was replaced by Maurice Bishop in a coup. Bishop, a Marxist, was implicitly opposed to U.S. interests, with friendly ties to Castro's Cuba. Reagan, eager to secure the decapitation of communism wherever its head reared in the region, had long since watched the island with obsessive interest, linking its leftward descent with the "dark future" wrought by the totalitarian left in Nicaragua.[108] He made his point about regional subversion in a TV appearance on March 23, 1993. Reagan's pictures showed that Cuban workers had been increasing the capacity of the airport by constructing a ten-thousand-foot runway, which was suitable for jets. His desire to act escalated dramatically when a second coup d'etat removed Bishop and brought to power New Jewel movement militants led by Gen. Hudson Austin. Never doubting the need for action, he paved the way by creating a Special Situation Group under Vice President Bush to consider the options. Various contingencies contemplated by Bush in concert with National Security Adviser Robert (Bud) McFarlane and Secretary of State George Shultz became moot once Austin's people murdered Bishop. A twenty-four-hour curfew was declared, and the entire country was imprisoned. Reagan, also convinced that Castro could move almost 300,000 troops onto the island on short notice, had his excuse.[109] "He couldn't wait," recalled McFarlane, who, along with Chairman of the Joint Chiefs of Staff Gen. John W. Vessey, was not convinced about intervening. But the momentum was there, with or without the British, who were not consulted; with or without Congress, which was also ignored. "Fuck it," said Casey, not overly bothered about technicalities, "let's dump these bastards." Weren't a thousand American lives at risk, especially those of the 595 students at Grenada's St. George's School of Medicine? Nor was there anything like a legitimate government running the place. What Reagan needed was an urgent call for help, and he got it from a group then meeting in Barbados, the Organization of Eastern Caribbean States (the OECS). Its leader was Prime Minister Eugenia Charles of Dominica. Her country's $10 million road-building project was being funded by U.S. dollars, and the CIA was the donor of another $100,000 for a secret support operation. When the OECS, at the prime minister's behest, requested Washington to intervene, they were asked to put it in writing, which they did. The request was further reinforced by an urgent and secret appeal from the British governor general of Grenada, Sir Paul Scoon.[110] Nothing else stood in the way. Via a speakerphone from where Reagan was then visiting, at the Augusta National Golf Club, to a National Security Council meeting convened by the vice president, the go-ahead was given. The news that same day of the terrorist act that took the lives of 241 sleeping marines in their barracks at Beirut, Lebanon, followed the planning for the Grenada intervention and only solidified the determination to invade. Bush, never as hesitant as other senior officials, then telephoned Noriega to ask Castro to abandon any idea of countering by sending in Cuban troops. The 1,900 marine "rescue mission," as Reagan called it, then overwhelmed Grenadian resistance. It was over quickly and Americans' most lasting image was the television pictures of returning medical students kissing the tarmac when they landed in the U.S.[111]

The Grenada operation epitomized what an earlier secretary of state, John Hay, once called a "splendid little war." Most of all, unlike Vietnam, it was a return to war as designed by Pentagon planners. Postwar revelations showed that very clearly. Cuban warriors on the island, a major justification for intervention, were, in reality, scarce, not dominant. Instead of the over 1,000 troops claimed by the Pentagon to have met the American invaders, their total hardly reached 200. Nor were Castro's airport construction workers soldiers in disguise, ready to defend the socialist homeland with AK-47s. On October 27, Reagan told the American people that Grenada "was a Soviet Cuban colony being readied as a major military bastion to export terror and undermine democracy." U.S. forces had arrived "just in time," he said, to thwart Cuban occupation. The 4,341 additional "Cuban troops" cited in a postinvasion briefing by Adm. Wesley L. McDonald, commander of U.S. forces in the Atlantic region, were Grenadians. Nor, agreed both Democratic and Republican senators after closed-door intelligence briefings, did the information warrant the public alarm that justified the invasion. The medical students were divided among themselves about the extent of the "danger" to their lives. Moreover, not only had the airport not been closed to those who wanted to leave, Press Secretary Larry Speakes later acknowledged, but both Grenadian and Cuban officials had given repeated assurances that they could depart and would not be harmed. We just didn't believe them, Speakes explained. The fighting had taken the lives of eighteen American marines and wounded eighty-nine others, mostly during the first day of the operation. Several fell as the result of what the Pentagon described as typical combat condition mishaps. The Cuban loss was placed at six by spokesmen in Washington and at thirty-eight by an official in Grenada.[112]

All that was moot. The administration had won as much on the home front as on the island itself. The "rescue mission" was clean, quick, and clearly popular. A press blackout, accomplished by barring reporters from the area for at least the first forty-eight hours and giving them only limited access for days afterward, limited information to official releases.

Nearly two months after the fighting, following the disclosure of more factual details, 59 percent of those polled by Gallup still approved of the president's handling of the invasion. There would, agreed the American people, be no additional Castros, Allendes, or even Sandinistas in Latin America.[113]

Bush did not exactly "orchestrate" the invasion, as at least one political scientist has concluded, but he certainly was at the heart of the planning operation. He has also been credited with helping to convince the president to ultimately withdraw American marines from Lebanon.[114] More significant for Bush in the long run was his ringside seat at the creation of the first significant combat deployment since Vietnam. And the government avoided open press coverage, a leading obstacle in the military's view to the successful termination of that war. Manipulating public information, as World War II had demonstrated, was as essential at home as on the battlefields. The age of television and recording devices, however, had made censorship far trickier.

If, as has been claimed, including by Manuel Noriega's subsequent legal defense, Grenada continued Bush's involvement with the Panamanian strongman, it was not their last encounter.[115] They met only three months later, during a refueling stop at Panama City's airport in December 1983. Bush, with his National Security Adviser, Gregg, sat down together with the latest puppet of the chief of the PDF, President Ricardo de la Espriella. The visit embodied several functions of the vice president: the man who mourns on behalf of his country at foreign funerals, attends boring ceremonies for heads of state, and sees to diplomatic dirty work. The latest assignment was his presence at the inauguration of Argentina's new president, Raul Alfonsín. He flew down in the company of Gregg and North, who helped to arrange the mission. Then, in North's account, Bush had to fulfill the "unenviable job" he was given of delivering the personal reminder to Noriega that the United States objected to the Salvadoran death squads, which Noriega was aiding. Bush told Noriega he wanted a transition to something like the sort of democracy he had just seen possible in Argentina. The Panamanian strongman, however, "sat there like a sphinx," North has recorded. "In retrospect, it was clear that he didn't get the message." Blunt reminders that the U.S. knew about Noriega's drug-trafficking were tuned out, but Gregg later recalled Bush's surprise at hearing from de la Espriella about stories pegging Panama as a money-laundering center. The president denied their accuracy, and Bush said he was unaware of them. There was indeed, despite all the plausible suggestions, no hard evidence that he knew about Noriega's drug activities. Gregg agreed. The downplaying by Bush's people of what the vice president knew included Murphy, who portrayed Noriega as a veritable wallflower at the airport session, leaving Bush to do his business solely with de la Espriella. "Bush," said the admiral, "didn't pay any attention" to the guy.[116]

Bush then carried his message about death squads directly to the source, flying on to tropically hot and humid San Salvador. In a private session with the country's vice president over refreshing glasses of Coca-Cola and lemon, Bush asked if he would carry President Reagan's assurances on human rights to his own field commanders. North, who first got to know Bush during this period, later wrote that "he had a knack for developing a personal, effective working relationship with foreign leaders. . . . The vice president spoke bluntly, without notes and without any diplomatic cushioning. He made it clear that if El Salvador had any interest in receiving additional American aid, the death squads had to stop and the murders of American nuns and labor leaders had to be solved." Confirming the observations of those who had seen Bush in such situations before, North added that "he came across as calm, strong, and determined." He remained undeterred even when an armed Salvadoran Secret Service detail came running in brandishing their weapons. When Murphy reminded him that they had guns, Bush said, "This meeting is absolutely necessary." Later, when hearing campaign rhetoric, North thought about that session and wrote, "When George Bush was called a wimp, I would look back upon this moment. I know a wimp when I see one, and George Bush was no wimp." The mission failed to end the death squad problem, but it was not entirely useless.[117]

For one with political ambitions, perceptions of guilt by association could be as devastating as actually having acted as an accomplice. But the reality is that Bush's personal contacts with Noriega were limited and hardly unique. The Panamanian met with several Americans at various times, both in Washington and at home: Caspar Weinberger, Oliver North, and especially Bill Casey.[118] One meeting at Langley with the CIA director followed the gruesome murder of a chief political rival, Hugo Spadafora, and punitive actions by the State Department. Nevertheless, he returned to Panama with promises from Casey of additional support as if nothing had happened. Insofar as Noriega was concerned, the U.S. government spoke with several voices.[119]

Their relationship belonged to the larger picture of realpolitik that governed so much of America's cold war policy, remaining classified and beyond discussion as late as 1996. Responding to the present author, Bush rested his case with the flat statement that whatever he did was in the service of the Reagan administration.[120] Conservatives especially, but by no means exclusively, welcomed the rejection of President Carter's somewhat awkward and often contradictory emphasis on "human rights." The U.S. could deal with those that were oppressive as long as they remained friendly to American interests and securely anti-Soviet. Those guidelines made it easy to live with Pinochet's Chile, the murderous oppressors in Guatemala, the apartheid government of the Republic of South Africa, and other egregious violators of human rights. Richard Nixon's "opening to China," for example, had underscored the subservience of humanitarian to geopolitical considerations.

Closer to home, especially when delegated to help carry out President Reagan's Caribbean Basin initiative, applying the principle was especially important. In a Latin-American tour during his first October as vice president, Bush made much the same point wherever he spoke, before a joint session of the Dominican congress in Santo Domingo, at dinner remarks in Bogotá, Colombia, and in Brazil's interior capital city. His words stressed the importance of stability to create a climate conducive to commerce and investments. High interest rates at home, he acknowledged, at least temporarily inhibited American businessmen from becoming active investors in the region. The reduction of Yankee dollars had depressed prices Latinos were getting for such staples as sugar and coffee. But such initiatives could not be implemented, Bush added, even with the availability of more capital, as long as Marxists, principally from Cuba, discourage "foreign investors [who] look for political stability." In Bogatá, he delivered a cogent rationale of the Reagan Doctrine: "The United States believes in the self-determination of peoples," he said. "It also believes in nonintervention. But it cannot and will not sit by while foreign powers—hostile to the principles we in the Americas have struggled so long for—intervene brutally in the international affairs of one of our neighbors."[121] Much to the dismay of some within his administration, including his secretary of state, Reagan remained stubbornly devoted to the immensely corrupt, authoritarian rule of Ferdinand Marcos in the Philippines. Bush, well-acquainted with such cold war exigencies while he served as DCI, got carried away by his penchant for friendliness in 1981 when, as Reagan's representative in Manila for the president's inauguration, he told Marcos that "we love your adherence to democratic principle and to the democratic process," a bit of hyperbole that he later found embarrassing.[122]

So it was with Noriega. Initially an instrument of convenience and, finally, a relationship with the Reagan administration, and secondarily with Bush himself, the whole association was a glaring contradiction. Through the Panamanian strongman, who controlled his country's nominal presidents as head of the PDF and was easily traced to the murder and decapitation of Spadafora, flowed drugs from Pablo Escobar's Medellín cartel, especially with the growth of the Colombian narcotics operation in the early 1980s. But he remained an invaluable intelligence mechanism, and the United States was not about to give that up.[123] For the contras, too, the shipment of cocaine became a profitable way to raise money for ammunition and weapons.

Thus, the Reagan administration, despite its public vow to crack down on drugs and its expenditure of more antidrug resources than ever before, was also, ironically, pursuing a policy in Central America that stimulated the flow of marijuana and cocaine. Informed estimates indicated that 70 to 80 percent of refined cocaine that reached the U.S. market during the 1980s came from Colombia. Nor did the cartel limit its business dealings to the contras; they made money from the Sandinistas as well. An undercover photograph that showed Sandinista involvement with the Medellín drug trade was later used by Reagan himself as a "photo-op" for a different purpose—to appeal for contra aid. "The lesson was clear," Kevin Buckley has written. "Contras matter; drugs aren't a factor."[124] Officials within the Reagan administration, with or without the president's knowledge, winked at the situation even at a time of growing public outrage about drugs.[125] Money was shared by many, especially Noriega and such arms suppliers as Herari and Albert Hakim. Abrams, who had served as assistant secretary of state for Inter-American Affairs and who repeatedly urged cracking down on Noriega, advised during a 1993 interview: to really find out what happened, follow the money.[126] Noriega, having taken a break from narcotics activities after the early 1970s, was once more a major player.

His income from the cartel far exceeded what he got from government payrolls. It continued to rise, finally reaching, as one source suggested, an improbable $10 million per month, although the later U.S. indictment charged him with receiving at least $4 million to protect the cartel.[127] Noriega served, in effect, as a broker or agent for a system that enabled the narcotics trade to market cocaine for contra purchases of arms. Set up by the CIA and carried out by Nicaraguans, including ex-dictator Somoza's liaison to the U.S. Army, Col. Enrique Bermudez, the scheme helped to pay for the weapons. Noriega earned his cut of the profits because he controlled a string of airfields that made it hard to detect flights that dumped the cargoes onto the U.S. market. One contract pilot for such missions, Richard Brenneke, later explained how he flew his payload into Amarillo, Texas. Another, W. Robert (Tosh) Plumlee, whose radio code name was "Zapata," flew his DC-3 loaded with weapons from Panama to the secret American airfield at Santa Elena, on the Costa Rican coast near Nicaragua. Flights with drugs went northward; those with arms, back to the south. Contra leader Federico Vaughan, wrote Ollie North in his notes, "wanted aircraft to go to Bolivia to pick up paste, want [sic] aircraft to pick up 1,500 kilos," and added, the following month, that the "DC-6 which is being used for runs (to supply the Contras) out of New Orleans is probably being used for drug runs into the U.S."[128] Sen. Gary Hart of Colorado, introducing Plumlee to his Massachusetts senate colleague, John Kerry, chairman of the Foreign Relations's Subcommittee on Terrorism, Narcotics, and International Relations, explained that "Plumlee raised several issues including that of covert smuggling and distribution of drugs to raise funds for covert military operations against the government of Nicaragua." His staff, Hart added, was provided with "detailed maps and names of alleged covert landing strips in Mexico, Costa Rica, Louisiana, Arizona, Florida, and California where the alleged aircraft cargoes of drugs were off-loaded and replaced with contra military supplies." The trade was, in fact, so rampant that when Oliver North was shown to have knowledge about what was going on, despite his denials to a congressional committee, the best thing that could be said about him was that he "wasn't the only high public official involved with drug-running into the U.S. during the mid 1980s." Cocaine, for one, so flooded the American market in the 1980s that an inexpensive variant known as "crack" became a street favorite in middecade, helping, as did no other single narcotic, to bloat the rate of urban crime. Plumlee, who got his signals from Gregg, as did Brenneke, contended that the shipments were not CIA operations but rather "under the direction of the White House, Pentagon, and NSC personnel."[129]

Noriega included the vice president on his list of "friends," even boasting that "I've got Bush by the balls." As the Panamanian told Lally Weymouth of the *Washington Post* in 1983, "Bush is my friend. I hope he becomes president." Noriega, argued his defense attorney later, kept the CIA in touch about his regular meetings with Fidel Castro and followed through when the U.S. told him to ask the Cuban leader to withdraw.[130]

Nevertheless, however utilitarian they may have been, those were names that later haunted Bush: Noriega, Gregg, Clarridge, Rodriguez, North, contras; and, in the end, ironically, when it counted most, Lawrence Walsh. Indeed, Bush had served Reagan all too well.

CHAPTER SIXTEEN

Casey's Kind of Guy

%

George Bush was not exactly Bill Casey's kind of guy. Casey's working-class parochial school background in the borough of Queens, New York, made him impatient with people like George Bush. The vice president was too passive, "the consummate pragmatist" unmoved by strong convictions, more like his friend Jim Baker, cautious, tight-lipped.[1] Hardly anything was too daunting for Casey, and the folks at Langley could not have been happier than under his unrestrained derring-do. Nor could Casey have been more at home than working for Ronald Reagan, who gave him all the latitude he needed without much fussing about details.

Bush's accessibility surprised Casey, who soon told friends that the vice president could deliver, all right. He was ready for whatever needed doing. He was also easy to get along with, probably more flexible than anybody Casey had met in government. Most of all, and what he found especially appealing, was that Bush was no sieve. Casey, remembered a former high-level CIA official friend of both men, "knew that Bush was someone who could keep his confidences and be trusted. Bush had the same capacity as Casey to receive a briefing and give no hint that he was in the know." As Reagan's DCI told Bill Safire in 1983 about Bush, "He plays his cards close to his vest, but he's not the wimp we thought he was."[2]

It was on Carter's watch that the Russians went into Afghanistan, which left the new administration facing a threat to Middle Eastern oil lines. The actual danger may have been remote, but Casey took no chances. The Reds had to be stopped. War between Iraq and Iran had brought additional uncertainties, at least as Washington saw it. For Israel, the fighting that broke out in 1980 after rebelling Iranian Kurds spilled over into Saddam Hussein's Iraq was even more worrisome. Iraq had attempted to strangle Israel from the start. During the Yom Kippur War of 1973, Syria was reinforced by Iraqi troops and supplies. But for the United States, at least at the moment, Hussein's power was preferable to Khomeini's, especially in the wake of the very recent 444-day hostage crisis. That was not the way the government in Tel

Aviv viewed matters. Recent Iraqi territorial conquests not only helped lead to a situation where both sides were able to menace Persian Gulf shipping, but Saddam Hussein had nuclear ambitions that had to be taken seriously. The Reagan administration, overlooking such matters, had yet to restore with Iraq the diplomatic relations that had been broken off back in 1967, but had no compunctions about tilting toward Hussein.[3] In their analysis, moreover, Iraq was no match for Iran. Having both powers fight to a standoff would be the best possible outcome for Washington.

In 1981, Israel suddenly made a dramatic, preemptive strike against Saddam's nuclear reactor at Osirak. Baghdad's nuclear future was side-tracked, but not, at that moment, with the thanks of the Reagan administration. Weinberger was especially vehement and favored punitive action against Israel. Bush and Jim Baker were not much happier, but favored a slap on the wrist rather than a spanking. Their responses seemed wrong-headed to Al Haig, but the secretary of state, at least as he told it afterward, found himself outvoted. He later recalled, "I said we should be grateful and thank the Israelis for taking care of a potential nuclear problem down the road. My position was thank God they did it."[4]

The Iranians took advantage of the Israeli strike with a counteroffensive that threw back recent Iraqi gains and threatened to upset any delicate balance of power. Forgotten in later years was the simple fact that siding with Iraq "was popular at the time," as Maxwell Rabb has recalled. "It was popular to be with Iraq. We were suspicious of Saddam, but we didn't hate him."[5]

Middle Eastern arms trading began to resemble the Nicaraguan supply effort. A memorandum to Under-Secretary of State Lawrence Eagleburger from one of his assistants made the point. "It is uncertain how long the status quo can be maintained by Iraq in its confrontation with a much more populous Iran as long as Iran exports three times as much oil as Iraq," wrote Richard Murphy.[6] Quietly, disregarding prohibitions under the Arms Control Act, and ignoring Hussein's use of chemical weapons against his own people, Reagan's men tried to keep Iraq viable by expediting a flow of arms to Baghdad.[7]

The president himself, meanwhile, continued to wage the good fight in the cold war. The CIA mined three Nicaraguan harbors in early 1984. The Democratic majority, especially within the Senate Select Committee on Intelligence, complained about the lack of advance notification. The Boland Amendment was obviously impotent, not surprising given the support for the contras from within the administration and among conservatives. In any case, whether merely via supply operations or with the specific goal of overthrowing the Nicaraguan government, their cause was being advanced. Weapons were piling up for sale at the "warehouse" in neighboring Honduras. The congressional "restraints" themselves had a reverse effect. Instead of thwarting the program, a new level of covert operations was created. To help direct the guerrilla fighting, Don Gregg brought in Felix Rodriguez to firm up the supply line operation at Ilopango airfield in El Salvador.[8]

Meanwhile, Al Haig, having resigned within a year as secretary of state, was replaced by George Shultz. That veteran of the Nixon years joined Weinberger in favor of helping to arm Iraq. Assistance also included a plan to help Saddam Hussein build a pipeline to the Jordanian port of Aqaba to get around Iran's blockade of Persian Gulf ports. Bush, according to the agenda of the National Security Planning Group (NSPG), participated in early 1984 meetings and agreed to the pro-Iraq tilt.[9]

Then came his chance to play two important roles in the process of bolstering Iraq against Iran. The first was through his connection to Bill Draper, chairman of the Export-Import Bank. Draper, a Yale classmate, had served as a member of the Bush Financial Committee for the 1980 presidential campaign. The logic, as suggested in a memorandum by Shultz's executive secretary, was to have Bush call Draper to get the bank to reverse its refusal to finance the pipeline. Bush's instructions were to advise Draper that the U.S. position in the Iran-Iraq situation required bringing it to a negotiated end without having either side dominant. Completion of the Aqaba pipeline would help move toward that goal.

Bush made the call, and Draper got the bank to agree. Insurance problems kept the pipeline from ever being realized, but the vice president's participation in the "tilt" was initiated.[10]

Bush, in all of this, in the words of NSC Middle East expert Howard Teicher, was "good at conducting diplomatic dialogue. He knew the style, the diction. He was good at having a diplomatic discussion. . . . Bush's goals were contradictory because our policy was full of contradictions. He thought rapprochement with Iran was good. He thought talking to both sides was good." His very vagueness was then reported as serving "a long-standing ambition to play a prominent role in foreign policy." The Middle East was, in that view, another opportunity.[11]

The contra supply effort went on, more creatively after the Boland Amendment deprived the operation of U.S. funds. Noriega remained an obscure ally in the cause of avoiding a second Cuba-like Soviet base in the Caribbean, but all that was in the background. Steven R. Weisman wrote in *The New York Times* in early 1983 that even administration aides have acknowledged "that Mr. Reagan is in political trouble because of a widespread perception that he is not grappling with high unemployment and other problems." The president's passivity seemed all too likely to tolerate letting matters slide. "He likes to lie dormant and then spring to life," explained one of his aides.[12]

This behavior was attributed to aging as it had become abundantly clear that the Reagan of 1984 was not the Reagan of 1980. He was, in the words of a *Newsweek* team that scrutinized the 1984 election campaign, "as detached from the management of his campaign as he was from the workaday administration of his government; he preferred to trust in his fellas and his luck, or, as some of his associate guessed, his destiny."[13]

Not that winning a second term was guaranteed. David Stockman's inside view of Reaganomics had not helped, and the economy was faltering. Presidential pollster Richard Wirthlin's "Overview of Campaign Action Plan" prepared for Reagan on November 1, 1983, which acknowledged that "it is my belief that it [your election] is both possible and imperative," cautioned that "your reelection will not be easy."[14]

Before a March convention of the National Association of Evangelicals at Epcot Center, Orlando, Florida, Reagan continued his long-term overtures to the Christian right. Invoking C. S. Lewis, Tom Paine, Whittaker Chambers, and the Declaration of Independence, the president asked for prayers "for the salvation of all those who live in totalitarian darkness, pray they will discover the joy of knowing God"; and, he added, "let us be aware that while they preach the supremacy of the state, declare its omnipotence over individual man, and predict its eventual domination of all peoples of the earth— they are the focus of evil in the modern world." The "evil empire" speech, as it was remembered, came, as Lou Cannon has observed, "to epitomize Reagan's view of the Soviet Union."[15] Liberals were hard on the president for his statement, but so was Richard Nixon, who volunteered the off-the-record suggestion that the comment was diplomatically impolitic. "You don't humiliate your opponent in public like that," he said.[16]

Nixon's qualms were not only with Reagan. His misgivings about Bush were equally evident. As early as June of 1984, before the Reagan team stood for its reelection, the exiled ex-president, then beginning his orchestrated return to respectability, had reservations about George Bush as the presumptive heir to the presidency. "I want the Republican party to be one that brought peace," he told this writer on June 4, but added that "we also have our road to domestic progress." Negativism, he prophesied, "will not build up the party." He also suggested that Jack Kemp, not Bush or Dole, was the best hope for the GOP in 1988.[17] Not fully understood at the time, except for Nixon's obvious eagerness to set the GOP on a more moderate course, was his bold assertion that Kemp would actually emerge as the legatee of the Reagan years, about which he had many misgivings, both socially and diplomatically. Not generally known at the time were his efforts, as early as 1982, to undermine Bush's continuation as the vice president. Bush, in Nixon's view—even as he stressed the need to reject negativism—was not the "nutcutter" who was equipped to play the hardball politics Nixon envisioned as necessary to take the offensive against the Democrats. He was, Nixon argued, a poor campaigner and inadequate for playing the "bad cop" role as Nixon had done for Eisenhower in 1954 and Agnew for Nixon in 1970. Not eager to press a serious "Dump Bush" campaign, Nixon, mindful of Bush's genteel approach toward Bentsen in 1970 and gentlemanly handling of the Republican National Committee even in the face of Watergate, advised trying to remake Bush to fit the role of an attack vice president. He would, in fact, he told Rollins, create a kind of competition. The man "who campaigned hardest for Reagan and the party in 1982 would be the president's choice to succeed

Bush on the ticket in 1984," whether that might be Kemp, Bob Dole, or any one of a number of Republican governors. "Make George a little paranoid," Nixon advised Rollins with a chuckle. "Rev up his competitive juices."[18] Frighten him, Nixon was really saying. Bush was too nice. He had no killer instinct. Goad the Ivy Leaguer into becoming a slashing street politician. Rollins, on the receiving end of all this unutilized advice, thought that he was in the presence "of Machiavellian genius." He also appreciated that George Bush was "one of the genuine nice guys in American politics . . ."[19]

Certainly, as election day neared, a second term for Reagan and Bush began to seem inevitable. Americans were not ready for the Democratic ticket of Walter Mondale with his promise of a tax increase, and Geraldine Ferraro, the first woman ever to appear on a national presidential slate of either major political party.

The ineptitude of Reagan's opponents only became apparent at the campaign's later stages, displacing an earlier burst of hopeful Democratic enthusiasm that they could defeat the president. The Reagan "revolution" only seemed to bring hard times. Not since the Great Depression had there been a recession as severe as the one that slowed the economy in 1982. Unemployment was at a recent high. The effort to mitigate a possible depletion of the Social Security Trust Fund resulted in an additional burden in the form of a Social Security tax, which, by definition, cut disproportionately into the pockets of the middle and lower classes. Indeed, as early as 1983, *The Wall Street Journal* noted that, for a variety of reasons, wealth was flowing upward. "The rich are getting richer and the poor are getting poorer," said a front-page story.[20] It was hard at that point to argue that Reaganomics was working. The tax cut proposed by Reagan and passed by the Congress, with the backing of conservative Democrats, the so-called "Boll Weevils," gave the president a smashing victory. Skeptics, however, failed to see how it would boost the economy. Bush's earlier ridicule of "voodoo economics" seemed right on the mark. Reagan's celebrated popularity was well short of its glory. Two years after his inaugural, a Gallup survey showed him ahead of Walter Mondale by just one point.[21]

Reagan's biggest boost came from the combination of sympathy after his shooting and admiration for his own courageous and sunny response to it. Other than that, his disengagement from the actual operation of the Executive Office was bizarre. More and more, his aides, and especially the White House media staff, manipulated and fine-tuned his images. The "man inside the packaging" was handled with care; they stuffed him "in excelsior, wrapping him in the flag, and keeping the press at shouting distance or beyond."[22] His remoteness from the real world became a daily fact of life around the White House. Stu Spencer's "consulting firm had done the coaching and the packaging, marketing him brilliantly to the most media-oriented state in the country and, later, to the most media-oriented nation in the world."[23] He nodded off during cabinet meetings, even dozed in the presence of Pope John Paul II. Especially embarrassing was the whispered voice of Nancy Reagan telling him how to respond to a reporter's question.[24] Some staffers even talked about the president as "Dummy Number One."[25] When his media group gave him a White House screening of a campaign film that was "a symphony in celebration of Reagan's America," the simplicity of the president's emotions was alarming. "My, I didn't do this myself, all alone," he said, and then, after further thought, asked, "Am I really that good?"[26] He had, so far, disproved Teddy White's 1982 warning: "The political system today lives under the terror of television—television overexposes presidents. They burn out their popularity in four years."[27]

How much of Reagan's befuddled state, even that early in his presidency, anticipated the later diagnosis of Alzheimer's disease may never be known. The postpresidency memoirs of his aides often recall the trouble they had in getting and holding his attention, and perhaps only in the light of the later diagnosis can that fact be explained. There was, for example, an incident that perplexed a group of scholars who were invited to dinner at the White House in 1983. The president, who often dwelled on Hollywood movie scenes and his acting days, gave a characteristic performance that evening.

He told them that he had enjoyed watching the television miniseries of Herman Wouk's best-selling novel, *The Winds of War.* Then, inexplicably, he wondered out loud, "What would the world be like if the Second World War had actually taken place?" His guests at the table were stunned, their awe at being in his presence muting their gasps. Reagan went on. He then mused about how he and Nancy started each Wednesday morning—breakfast in bed and a pile of newspapers, then mounted horses for a ride in Rock Creek Park. By four, they were back in the White House for the president's midafternoon nap.[28]

A small hint of this became visible to the public when Reagan debated with Mondale during the campaign. Paul Laxalt, who greeted the president just before he went onstage, noticed that his eyes "were just flat." Mondale thought he was disoriented at their opening handshake. Reagan, at that Louisville debate, lapsed into confusion at several points, then delivered an incoherent jumble of statistics as his closing statement. "God, I was awful," he said after the cameras were turned off. As Mondale left the stage, he said to a friend, "This guy is gone. It's scary. He's really not up to it." Suddenly, once again, the "age issue" reemerged, most tellingly in the form of a previously prepared major article in *The Wall Street Journal.* The apparent "senility" became a major concern, and *Newsweek* reported that Mondale was the debate's clear winner, 54 to 35 percent.[29]

The televised performance undermined confidence that Reagan was fit to remain on the job. But, before his next test at Kansas City, postdebate damage control did its job. His lead over Mondale recovered.[30] The situation was a virtual replay of the circumstances that preceded his Manchester, New Hampshire, debate in the 1980 primaries. Again, Reagan's mission was simple: he had to convince the public that he did not *seem* too old. He always rose to the challenge, managing not to sound rehearsed and conveying a deep sense of conviction and an authority that the public found compelling.

His self-confidence and optimism were often noted for giving the impression that he, more than anybody who had sat in the office in recent years, could make the presidency work.[31] Little wonder, then, that he was widely called the "Teflon" president: whatever went wrong did not seem to stick to him, and his fondest supporters usually ignored what conflicted with what they wanted to believe about him. With the firm support of his party's ultra-conservatives, he was almost immune—but not quite—from carping by the Republican right wing. That he appeared distant from the details of governance only helped to distinguish him from his hands-on predecessor, Jimmy Carter.[32]

Yet that, precisely, was the point. Americans view their presidents as icons. George Washington's symbolic strength blessed the office from the moment of his inauguration. Constitutional realities about presidential power become subordinated to transcendent leadership qualities. For a nation shattered by the inspirational vacuum left by the Kennedy assassination and torn apart by the controversies engendered by Johnson and Nixon, only to then endure the boredom of such uninspiring presidents as Ford and Carter, Reagan came as a deliverance. The timbre of his voice, the conviction in his words, and obvious patriotism that conveyed the welcome message of unrestricted, free-market capitalism, became the reality of a presidency that had recovered its respectability.

Such qualities did not come easily to George Bush. His earlier public appeal seemed to have evaporated by 1984, his persona subsumed by single-minded loyalty. His apostasy had to be pure, credible to every dedicated Reaganite, a devotion strongly colored by his own debt to the man who had placed him in the vice presidency. All this combined with his continuing need to dispel his public image, which ironically, was the precise opposite of Reagan's. The "wimp" label had not gone away.

By the time negotiators agreed to a series of debates, both sides accepted one face-off between the vice presidential candidates. Whatever suspense there was about Reagan's ability to be reelected wore off as the campaign went on. Mondale, clearly, was no match for the president, even when he tried to sound bold by saying in his acceptance speech that he would raise taxes if necessary to counter mounting deficits. It backfired. By early October, Gallup's figures showed the Reagan-Bush advantage at sixteen points.[33] The only novelty left was having the first woman candidate for vice president in a debate that fell between the two main-round events.[34]

Bush went into that encounter recognizing the potential of a no-win situation. His opponent was unique, a novelty; few doubted that Ferraro had been chosen for any reason other than her sex. A sentimental favorite from the outset, she was cheered on by much of the press. "What I discovered after the fact," Ron Kaufman said later, "was the reason it was a tough press was the yardstick they used to measure how George Bush was doing. It wasn't the same yardstick. The press measure of us in '84 was Reagan running for president, Mondale running for president, and George Bush *as a candidate for president*. On that yardstick, we didn't do well. But we weren't trying to. We never, ever, ever got into synch with the media."[35] Ferraro herself noted afterward that Bush "had to stand up to me yet not be so aggressive he'd end up looking like a bully. At the same time, he could not be patronizing or condescending, either. He had to defend Ronald Reagan's policies. And he also had to present himself as not only a loyal follower but a potential leader as well."[36] To the Reagan camp, the vice president was but ancillary, another campaign prop. Wirthlin's thirty-page memorandum laying out what had to be done to win reelection contains not a single reference to Bush.[37]

Bush, of course, cared little about Wirthlin's projections. The campaign was Reagan's to be reelected, but *his* was to end the vice presidential trap. He lashed out, starting with his acceptance address at the convention in Dallas, about as fiery as anyone had ever seen him. He slashed at the Democrats on taxes. They were the party of "spend, tax, and spend." Their convention, which could do no better than produce Walter Mondale (at least, for a change, someone else was getting to be called "wimp"!) and Geraldine Ferraro, was a "temple of doom." What else to expect from the party of "tax raisers, the free-spenders, the excess regulators, the government-knows-best handwringers, those who would promise every special-interest group everything"?[38]

He went on hectoring through much of the campaign, so stridently, at times, that the normally mild Bush began to be put down as a "cheerleader" and a "whiner," another vice president playing hatchet man, à la Nixon and Agnew. But it seemed unnatural for George Bush. Some moderates even became uneasy about his fitness to lead them in 1988.[39]

The numbers that came out of his televised debate with Ferraro on October 11 said otherwise, by a healthy 47 to 31 percent, according to a *New York Times/CBS News* poll right after their head-on encounter. His confidence, his obvious demonstration of experience, impressed them even more.[40]

But not those who raced along with him from one campaign stop to another, and especially those who had chatted with him; they were clearly put off at seeing a different Bush. The "nice guy" was trying to be a killer. He referred over and over again to the "Carter-Mondale" administration and did his best to shift wimpishness to the man at the head of the Democratic ticket. "Do we move forward with strength and with prosperity," Bush asked, "or do we go back to weakness, despair, disrespect?" When Ferraro tried to score points on the administration handling of terrorism in the Middle East, he turned on her and said, "Let me help you with the difference, Mrs. Ferraro, between Iran and the embassy in Lebanon."

"I almost resent, Vice President Bush," she glared back, "your patronizing attitude that you have to teach me about foreign policy."

She stood up to him. Her relative inexperience seemed inconsequential. His style, on the other hand, looked phoney, even unrecognizable. Visiting with some longshoremen while campaigning in Elizabeth, New Jersey, the next day he boasted that "we tried to kick a little ass last night."[41] It was not the George Bush that people knew; and the press raised his anger by harping on that and a series of flubs that gave them excuses to wonder whether he could withstand the pressure of higher office.

He was "hyperactive" on that stage, wrote John Mashek, one of the members of the panel asking questions, and he seemed, William R. Doerner added, "so wildly overcharged in his delivery that Ferraro aides watching him on television derisively demanded that he be given a saliva test." Bush not only expressed his agreement with the president, but betrayed his need to be convincing. He is, noted *The New Republic*'s "TRB," "Ronald Reagan's understudy without the Reagan audience. He must constantly prove himself as a Reaganite, to appease the right wing without endearing himself to it." Bush's overenthusiastic declarations of loyalty led the writer to conclude that, "FDR had Fala, Nixon had Checkers, Reagan has George Bush."[42] Bush, inadequately thick-skinned for one so vulnerable, let his irritation show. It was his worst mistake, he later admitted. "My relations with the press suffered during the race in 1984 against Congresswoman Ferraro. I was too testy."[43]

One person not put off by "the other" Bush was Lee Atwater. Nobody used his talent to more effect for the Reagan-Bush team than that still youthful political streetfighter. "Since the age issue is sure to resurface in the aftermath of a disappointing performance on the twenty-first, the image of an active, aggressive, youthful vice president will be reassuring to the American people," said an Atwater memo written the day before the second debate. Forget about worrying about "charges of 'desperation,' " he urged. "We will need all the help we can get," because we'll "have to clobber Mondale" with everything we have: "Waltergate"; delegate committees; Ferraro; income tax discrepancies; "Patsy for the Soviets;" "Pal of Jesse Jackson, Teddy Kennedy, Bert Lance, Tip O'Neill, and George McGovern"; "Associates with known alumni of the Carter administration." Included in the Atwater strategic arsenal was a familiar Nixon concept, polarization. "We'd like to win the country, but we only have to win a little over half of it. Indeed, given the vagaries of the electoral college, we can win with a minority of the popular vote," wrote Atwater. "Therefore, we shouldn't hesitate to polarize, play the South against the North, the West against the East, and so on." He had learned a lot more about holding Southerners for the GOP during the midterm elections of 1982, Atwater pointed out in a memo. Hit them on just economic issues and they'll go liberal. So show them we're on their side on race, that the Democrats are with the blacks. Most of the "populists' chosen leaders," Atwater pointed out, "were hard-core segregationists." But the trick, he cautioned, was in "choosing those social issues that do not alienate the country clubbers since, again, we need their votes and the populists' to win in the South."[44]

Atwater almost needed to reach again into his grassroots well. During the second presidential debate, in Kansas City, Reagan fumbled again. When wind-down time came, the president went into the text of his prepared statement but lost his way. He began soliloquizing to an audience of millions about driving somewhere along the coastal highway in California. He was, ostensibly, describing a letter he had prepared to be placed in a time capsule. To his audience, he was on a fantasy ride, transported to another time and place, with "the Pacific out there on one side of the highway, shining in the sunlight, the mountains of the coast range rising on the other side," wondering whether others would someday encounter the same sights on "our rendezvous with destiny." Inexplicably, he was a lonely figure lost in a coastal fog, words going on and on until he was apologetically cut off.

"His answers in the second debate were in many ways worse than the first debate," said Mondale later.[45] But, even before his hypothetical drive, he had been saved by another Reagan one-liner. Asked by a *Baltimore Sun* newsman if he would be fit to respond as ably as had the youthful President Kennedy during the Cuban missile crisis, Reagan replied: "I will not make age an issue in this campaign. I am not going to exploit, for political purposes, my opponent's youth and inexperience."[46] The "great communicator" had scored again. Nothing else seemed to matter.

In the end, it came as no surprise that just about the only outcome of consequence for Bush pointed to guidelines for his political future. His second term as vice president was secured as Reagan effectively demolished his opponent. Once more, he was helped by a pithy, if hyperbolic, sound bite, saying during the closing stages of the campaign that the Democrats were the "party of April fifteenth" while the Republicans were the "party of July fourth." Once again, his ability to simplify a few fundamental themes and to associate himself with broad aspirations of "patriotic" Americans revealed the "true Reagan."

The Reagan-Bush team swept to a landslide reelection, Mondale taking only his home state of Minnesota and the District of Columbia. Almost 59 percent of the total vote went to the Republican candidates, although they failed to gain a working majority in the House and gained just one governorship. Reagan confirmed his attractions to working-class Democrats, who rejected their old party even in Ferraro's own section of Queens.[47]

Victory for the ticket, however, came close to personal defeat for George Bush. He, rather than Reagan, had been subjected to especially harsh treatment by the press. One matter involved a publicized hassle over personal income taxes resulting from the sale of his Houston house and further purchases of land around Walker's Point. He responded to an Internal Revenue Service ruling that disallowed a tax exemption from the sale of the Indian Trail home in Houston. He was forced to pay almost $200,000 in back taxes and interest and followed by publicly disclosing his 1981 IRS returns, which showed that he and his wife were worth $2.1 million; he had paid 48.6 percent of their adjusted gross income in taxes in 1981 and 24.2 percent in 1982. The IRS had rejected his contention that the Bushes should not be taxed on the capital from the sale of their Houston home because they had invested the gain in the purchase and repair of the Kennebunkport property. Since the federal government provides a home for vice presidents at the Admiral's House, the agency ruled, that was their principal residence. When, a few days later, the Geraldine Ferraro-John Zaccaro financial statements were revealed, it showed the couple was worth $3.8 million. Barbara, also campaigning and irritated by the press attention to Ferraro and Mondale's needling of Reagan about his wealthy vice president, alluded to Ferraro in the presence of reporters on her airplane as "that four-million-dollar—I can't say it, but it rhymes with rich." Geraldine had enough money to "buy George Bush any day," she added. Barbara apologized to Ferraro for her "ugly" comment, but both Bushes had obviously been nettled by the lady from New York.[48]

The discouragement but momentary, he moved on, advancing from a "good soldier" vice president whose prolonged self-subservience struck some observers less as the condition of a man dependent for his future on accommodating the constitutional and political needs of the present, than that of "a man of no discernible political passions beyond a passion to win political office." His "apparent blind faith," noted *Newsweek,* "has undermined his 'regular guy' image." Fred Barnes, commenting on Bush for *Business Month,* was much closer to the mark when he disparaged the "myth of Bush as a political Milquetoast who doesn't believe in much of anything," pointing out that he "has strong views, even stronger than when he joined the administration." Without question, he was "a supply-sider of a sort—a corporate supply-sider." He was never really interested in such questions as marginal tax rates for individuals, but "providing tax incentives for business is something else again. He loves them. They even drive him to boldness."[49] Such perceptions needed to be encouraged. And Victor Gold followed through, in the most important Reaganite venue of them all, the pages of Bill Buckley's *National Review.* The thought to be promoted, of course, was the growing willingness of the Republican right to relax, to be assured that a Bush presidency would, in effect, constitute a third Reagan term. Bush, Gold argued for conservative readers, was less a moderate than a "perfect soul mate" for Ronald Reagan.[50] Four more years could, in effect, be followed by eight, a prospect sufficiently alluring to raise hopes about the Bush fidelity to the cause.

Bush and the president took their second oath of office in the White House, on the steps of the Grand Staircase. Instead of a massive ceremony, the indoor swearing-in was limited to family and friends. The start of the new term fell on a Sunday, so the traditional inaugural was moved to the next day. But that Monday was bitter cold in Washington. The wind-chill factor was expected to be below zero, so the affair had to be moved indoors. High school marching bands, having traveled all the way to the District of Columbia for the big event, were disappointed, but, as Barbara Bush has written, "their lips would have stuck to their instruments."[51] The president and vice president went through the ceremony a second time, before about a thousand people gathered in the Capitol rotunda. Two years earlier, Barbara had made the following diary entry: "George is obviously the most qualified person for the job. Do I want him to run? Absolutely not!" But, on that Monday, she later noted, the "1988 campaign started."[52]

It was also time to get rid of the defensive squad, the key aides who served the vice president when the first priority was securing his position with the Reagan crowd. The time had now come, Jimmy Baker urged Bush, for the offensive squad, those better equipped to advance toward the goal line, while simultaneously balancing that need with continued loyalty to the administration. "He brought in brighter, younger, smarter, more aggressive people, a more political staff, that would be a better staff in getting him elected president. This is the Machiavellian Bush," explained Kaufman. "He got rid of all of them because he knew the mission he needed was different. George Bush is much smarter, much tougher than people give him credit for, much more Machiavellian."[53] Those dropped included Dan Murphy and domestic policy adviser Steve Rhodes. Donald Gregg was a holdover as his national security adviser. Another holdover, C. Boyden Gray, moved from legal counsel and deputy chief of staff to serve as counselor to the vice president. Craig Fuller, a Reagan first-term policy adviser, was brought in as the new Bush chief of staff. He promptly removed a barrier to the vice president by suggesting to Jennifer Fitzgerald that she could be more useful heading the vice president's legislative affairs office in the Senate. Bush's young friend from Houston and former travel companion, David Bates, was brought back in to work under Fuller. Nick Brady, who did yeoman work in putting together the team, also produced Roger Ailes, who had been instrumental in helping him develop as a public speaker during his brief career as a senator from New Jersey. The public relations man, with a keen mastery of television and advertising, had also been a television producer and had helped Richard Nixon. He had, more recently, produced a stunning victory for Mitch McConnell, who came from forty-four points behind to win a senate seat in Kentucky. Lee Atwater also joined the Bush team and took charge of its overall political strategy. Thus began their meetings, starting out with Fuller at the head, Atwater, Brady, Bob Teeter, and Bush's old friend Dean Burch. They eventually called themselves the "Group of Six," or "G-6," a play on the term used for international conferences of the major industrialized nations.[54]

Atwater appreciated how the party had changed. For all the recent talk about weakening of partisan affiliations, realigning loyalties had produced new coalitions. Southern states, once sure bets to choose Democratic presidential electors, were actually going for the party of Lincoln and Reconstruction. Atwater was among those who had no doubt about the durability of the realignment they were seeing. The basic root that had produced Barry Goldwater in 1964, then endorsed Richard Nixon and Ronald Reagan would continue to show that decisive strength. Bush, if he hoped to head the ticket in 1988, had to leave no doubt that his heart was not merely Republican but right-wing Republican, dedicated to keeping alive the Reagan "revolution."

It was Atwater, together with veteran Bush pollster and consultant, Robert

M. Teeter, who came up with a mirror-image version of the "Southern strategy" Clark Clifford had outlined for Truman's 1948 election. Dixie Democrats, with their power ebbing, had contrived to regain some clout by creating a gigantic primary day voting bloc, multiple states holding primary elections on the same Tuesday. Countering the influence of early contests in places like Iowa and New Hampshire seemed like a good idea. But Atwater and Teeter understood the value of that arrangement for Bush. Taking advantage of that "Super Tuesday" schedule by winning Republican Southern delegations had the potential of creating a "firewall" that could cushion Bush's preconvention drive from losses elsewhere. But it took more than just planning. It took committing money and resources for intensive fieldwork.

Atwater and Teeter laid out their plan at a Camp David meeting in April of 1985, attended by the vice president and Barbara, along with their sons.[55] This was the first comprehensive gathering of family and aides for the long haul toward 1988. Janet Mullins, who joined the team later but first knew Atwater through her ex-boss, Senator Robert Packwood of Oregon, remembered the importance of the Super Tuesday strategy. Lee was "absolutely sure" it was wise, she recalled. "We were committed to the Southern strategy."[56]

The Bushes agreed, but they were less sure of Atwater. Wary of consultants to begin with, the young man's reputation and blatant womanizing left Barbara and her sons uneasy. He could, at any moment, get into trouble. "Lee was extremely bright and effective, but he was also young," recalled Jeb's friend, "Batesy." Ron Kaufman, told by George Bush that Atwater "was too brash," was asked to do some personal overseeing. "My job was to become Atwater's buddy," said Kaufman. "I became Lee's best friend. Fascinating." Atwater's business partnership in a lobbying firm with Charlie Black, Paul Manafort, and Roger Stone was reason for further doubts, doubts about Atwater's loyalty to the Bush cause, especially when two of his business partners became part of rival Jack Kemp's campaign for the Republican nomination. "What about the gossip," William Greider asked Atwater, "that some members of the Bush family, including Mrs. Bush, were leery of you because you were a hardball player. Is this something you felt?" Atwater, implicitly acknowledging the problem, told both Greider and Eric Alterman to let him prove himself by having George W. Bush join him full time in the campaign. But George W., it was clear, while used as a senior advisor to the campaign without "a specific portfolio," served a function not unlike Kaufman's, keeping Atwater "kind of focused and on track." The oldest son, the most politically savvy of the children, took up residence in Washington in 1987, "developed a good friendship with Lee, and was a real help to Lee with giving him a sense of what Vice President Bush would want to happen."[57]

George Bush's schedule, in those months before any serious campaigning could start, emphasized shoring up his standing with fundamentalists and Southerners, often the one and the same people. He pursued such icons of the religious right as Jerry Falwell and Jim Bakker, whose wife, Tammy Faye, was received by Barbara at the vice president's house. Bush assured Bakker that he watched the PTL (Praise the Lord) Club on television "from time to time."[58] He made overtures to such other televangelists as Jimmy Swaggart and Pat Robertson, and even got himself on the cover of an evangelical monthly, *The Christian Herald*.[59] He went to the Washington Hilton on December 11, 1985, and paid homage to the memory of right-wing publisher William Loeb, whose *Manchester Union-Leader* had excoriated him in 1980.[60]

But, nonetheless, it was Robertson and his evangelist enthusiasts, many formerly nonvoters, that rattled the Bush people in the spring of 1986 and forced an early battle. Put into motion by the enthusiastic energy of Marlene Elwell, a suburban Detroit housewife, the preacher's followers registered on his behalf in such large numbers that they began what has been described as "the most hard-fought and complex sideshow of the entire 1988 presidential election cycle."[61] At stake was control of Michigan's delegation, a matter to be decided just before the Iowa caucuses were due to vote. The Bush forces, unprepared for Elwell's citizen army behind Robertson and more worried by Jack Kemp, went for Ron Kaufman's idea to start a legal artifice to get around federal fund-raising restrictions, the Fund for America's Future. First run by Kaufman and then by Janet Mullins, the fund began with a "wink and a nod" from a cooperative Federal Election Commission that accepted its mission as nothing more than a party-builder designed to educate the state's Republican voters to boost their turnout in precinct elections. Bush dropped that pretense before long, and Robertson followed with his own political action committee, called Americans for Freedom. The Robertson PAC, which was later charged with violating federal election law, ultimately drew from Kemp's failure to survive the first round of the primaries that August. Their "anybody but Bush" conservative coalition gained at least temporary control of the state's Republican central committee.[62] Helped by Bush statewide manager, John Engler, who had gubernatorial ambitions, Rich Bond rushed into the state along with his energetic deputy, Mary Matalin. Their precinct-by-precinct war, a fight that lasted nearly two years, became, as Atwater put it, "a Vietnam for us."[63] Not until Kemp's followers were instructed to join with Bush's people in a series of credential battles in early 1988 was the threat overcome.[64] Even after the Michigan victory, the Fund for America's Future remained the contribution "center for the Bush base for a couple of years," helping to pay for the vice president's many trips to the state and for supporting fellow Republican candidates running in that year's midterm elections.[65]

Meanwhile, the sideshows that hurt most were those associated with the cold war. As early as February 1985, before the Austin Council on Foreign Affairs, Bush had tried to rally American technical and financial support for the contras to offset the "massive supplies of weapons" being received by the Sandinistas "from their friends and allies in the Soviet Union, East Germany, Bulgaria, North Korea, Vietnam, Cuba, the Palestinian Liberation Organization (PLO), Libya, and other radical states." The Marxist-Leninist "rulers in Nicaragua" were not merely benign "reformers" but revolutionaries aiding the guerrillas in El Salvador and ready to back the creation of little Cubas throughout the region. "We need your support," he urged in defense of the administration's policy, "the support of the American people, to make Congress understand that the struggle of the Nicaraguan people for freedom and democracy is not an issue that can be ignored."[66]

From Texas, Air Force Two flew on to the drought-stricken Sahel countries of Africa, where George and Barbara Bush visited refugee camps filled with dying children "covered with dirt and flies." Their one-week inspection of the Sudan, Niger, and Mali left them in awe of the humanitarian aid work done by the "dedicated nurses, doctors, missionaries, and Peace Corps volunteers who worked surrounded by filth and the dead and dying." When they reached Geneva, Bush made an impassioned appeal for help before the United Nations Famine Relief Conference.[67]

From Switzerland, Bush heard about the death of Konstantin Chernenko. The Soviet leader, who had taken over from Yuri Andropov in 1984, was in poor health throughout his few months in office. Soon afterward, even before leaving Geneva, they heard that the new chairman was fifty-two-year-old Mikhail Sergeyevich Gorbachev. In Moscow for the funeral, the vice president's party was joined by Secretary of State George Shultz. Bush was startled to see how quickly the burial procession was followed by the Orwellian "vaporization" of Chernenko; posters picturing the late leader were quickly pulled down. While in Moscow, Bush and the new Communist leader, Gorbachev, met for the first time. There, in St. Catherine's Hall, the man whom Bush came to call "Gorby," insisted to the Americans that the handling of human rights was purely an internal matter. Nevertheless, his forty-five-minute monologue expressed a desire to end further cold war confrontation and to engage in nuclear arms talks at Geneva.[68]

During those months, then, even as momentous changes were taking place within the Soviet Union, Reagan administration policies toward both Nicaragua and Iran took a new turn. The matter of persuading Honduras, unhappy over contra use of its territory to strike at the Sandinistas, had already been worked out by senior administration people. And in the Mideast, even as early as 1984, the status had begun to change. While the government in Tel Aviv was still anxious about Saddam Hussein and also worried about the plight of Jews who remained in Iran, there was increasing support within the Reagan administration in favor of strengthening Tehran in the battle against Baghdad. "Our tilt to Iraq was timely when Iraq was against the ropes and the Islamic revolution was on a roll," Graham Fuller, the CIA's national intelligence officer for the Middle East, told Casey. "The time may now have to come to tilt back."[69] Fuller then got off another memorandum. In an appeal specifically designed to exploit the president's anti-Soviet passions, he warned about the importance of strengthening Iran to interdict Russian interests in "the prize" of the Persian Gulf. "The disturbing possibility," he wrote, "is that the U.S.S.R. is far more likely than the U.S. to be first in finding opportunities to improve its ties to Iran." Reagan responded as expected.[70]

Robert C. (Bud) McFarlane's national security council staff, over the vigorous opposition of Shultz and Weinberger, turned out a directive advocating supplying Iran with selected weapons. Just two weeks later, the NSC, in the presence of both the president and the vice president, held one of its "stormiest" meetings. Few in the room realized that the suggested plan being put forth by Bill Casey was already being implemented, as a way to raise money for the contras despite the Boland Amendment. Casey, armed with the opinion of the CIA general counsel that such solicitation to help the rebels was legal, encountered sharp resistance from George Shultz. "If we go out and try to get money from third countries," he warned, "it is an impeachable offense." Reagan, reinforcing McFarlane's hope that the discussion remain secret, said, "If such a story gets out, we'll all be hanging by our thumbs in front of the White House until we find out who did it." Bush, however, took the position that he did not see "how anyone could object" to the encouragement of third-party assistance.[71]

The weapons deal seemed irresistible, or at least the way it was presented by Manucher Ghorbanifer, an Iranian exile who had served the shah, and Cyrus Hashemi, an arms dealer. Ghorbanifer, at least, should have been known for the fraud that he was. He had even failed a CIA lie detector test when he tried to sign on with the agency. He, Hashemi, and other Iranians, sensing a way to make money, hatched the idea of using the seven Americans then imprisoned by the Hizbollah in Lebanon, including the CIA station chief in that country, William A. Buckley, as trade bait. Buckley had been kidnapped, thrown into the back of a Renault, and then languished as a prisoner of the Da'wa terrorists, the most extreme of Lebanon's factions. Even before anybody knew anything about his torture, Buckley was the hostage whose capture resonated most of all with Casey and Bush, two CIA directors. His was the ordeal that most strained the no-deals-for-hostages policy. Not only were there ties of friendship and collegiality toward him, he was also a walking guide to U.S. intelligence operations in the Middle East. The instant appeal of getting him out was obvious to Casey. Moreover, it would, he was assured, open lines of connections with Iranian "moderates." The United States would, in exchange, grant permission to Israel to release American-made hardware to Tehran. Whether all seven men would be freed first was another matter.[72]

Only a few days after the NSC meeting, in early July, McFarlane met secretly at the White House with David Kimche, the director general of Israel's foreign ministry. Israel, said Kimche, had successfully established a dialogue with Iranians able to influence the Hizbollah to free the American hostages. "All the elements were present for what would become an arms-for-hostages deal," wrote Murray Waas and Craig Unger. On the eighth, President Reagan delivered a speech that charged Iran with being a member of a "confederation of terrorist states . . . a new, international version of Murder, Incorporated." His pledge that day was clear and simple: "America will never make concessions to terrorists."[73]

Four days later, the president was in the Bethesda Naval Hospital having surgery to remove intestinal polyps. Bush was vacationing in Maine when McFarlane called with the news. McFarlane assured him that the condition did not warrant his return to Washington, at least right away. Chief of Staff Donald Regan, concerned about alarming the country, also encouraged him to remain at Kennebunkport. Nevertheless, before the operation on the thirteenth, the president put into effect, for the first time ever, the provisions of Section Three of the Twenty-Fifth Amendment that provides for the temporary assumption of powers by the vice president when a president "is unable to discharge the powers and duties of his office." Bush made several additional calls, then decided to return to Washington. Meanwhile, at Bethesda, surgeons removed two small polyps and a section of large intestine, which was later found to contain a malignancy. After the president recovered from the pentathol, wrote Barbara Bush, "Don Regan went in and talked to him and decided he was in total control, no more effects of the anesthesia, thus rescinding the power after seven hours. Pop played tennis, stayed out of sight, and tried to keep a low profile. But he was president for seven hours."[74]

During the next few days, Reagan was allowed a few visitors as Nancy protectively hovered over the comings and goings. On Wednesday, George Bush walked in. The president, finally relieved of the tubes from his nose and looking "as though he'd just had a shave and a shower," greeted Bush with, "What the hell are *you* doing here?" The vice president, according to Don Regan, who saw him as he left the hospital room, wore "the smile of affectionate wonder that Americans reserve for precocious children and for the commander in chief."[75]

But the fifteen minutes Reagan spent with Bud McFarlane at his bedside on Thursday were far more momentous. Almost the first thing that President Reagan wanted to know when greeting his national security advisor was the status of the hostages.[76] Never, during the entire episode, was there much doubt about the president's intense passion over the plight of the men. Their families were kept away from him by protective aides wanting to spare him further emotional anxiety. Unfortunately, explained McFarlane, an additional obstacle had turned up in the early probings. The Iranians were eager for TOW missiles. "Arms will be essential to any ultimate effort to change the government," explained the NSC adviser, "but at this point, I don't think we know enough about the people we're dealing with to take that risk."[77]

Reagan gave the point some thought. He was clearly disappointed, and, after a few seconds, said, "We can't do it." Selling arms would be a violation of U.S. law, unless, of course, the president were to make a special "finding" that would justify a covert operation necessary for the national interest. Yet, it was clear to McFarlane, as he turned away from the bedside, that the president was keeping his options open. The next day, McFarlane told him about Shultz's "cautious support" for at least taking the next step. The president still wanted to know if there was some way "to help these guys you were talking about." Right after Reagan left the hospital on Saturday, and after hearing Shultz explain that the move had serious risks, he told McFarlane, "discreetly," as the advisor has reported the conversation, to "get the guys together to talk about that matter you mentioned at the hospital."[78]

Bush was present at most NSPG meetings, including the one on that next Monday evening when, with the possible exception of Weinberger's dissent, the mood followed the president's. Bush, more wary than Reagan about the hostage exchange, nevertheless went along with what McFarlane and Casey said could be done. He heard McFarlane's November briefing just before a shipment of HAWK missiles, and, missing only the day he spent at the army-navy football game in Philadelphia on December 7, attended NSPG meetings. While worried about Buckley, he also knew how badly the president wanted the others out of the clutches of the Hizbollah. Both the secretaries of state and defense were holding back, guarded about supporting the scheme.[79]

At their meeting of January 7, the council followed through on a point made by Adm. John Poindexter, who had only recently replaced McFarlane as national security adviser, about movement on the hostages becoming possible if the Southern Lebanese Army, which was backed by the Israelis, were to release their Shiite prisoners. Reagan seized on that point as an extension of the deal that had freed Americans trapped on a hijacked TWA airliner in June. The top-secret meeting came at an odd time for Bush. He was the only one in that room with a viable political future. He was also involved in the writing of the administration's antiterrorism report, which explicitly ruled out making any concessions to terrorists. Nor would the U.S. government, the statement went on to say, "pay ransoms, release prisoners, change its policies, or agree to other acts which might encourage additional terrorism." Little wonder, then, that when the president asked if there were any objections, all eyes turned toward him, but there was no response, which was also the way Reagan remembered it. The president followed through by signing a new "finding" that gave the green light to proceed with whatever it took to get the hostages out while keeping the whole thing secret from Congress.

McFarlane, acting as a special negotiator, went to Tehran in May with Ollie North in pursuit of what North had told him was a signal from the Iranians about a willingness to deal. The American party stopped over in Tel Aviv, where North and their Israeli contact, Amiran Nir, a counterterrorist expert who replaced David Kimche, bought a chocolate cake decorated with an ornamental skeleton key as a reminder of their earlier meeting with Ghorbanifar in Frankfurt. The *key* to unlock their disagreement! North, amused by it all, explained to a perplexed McFarlane, "We're going to show them that we found the key."[80]

But, instead of unlocking anything, there was further impasse. The promised high-level contacts never materialized. All they found was more delay and meetings with low-level functionaries at Tehran's former Hilton, now called the Independence Hotel. "I was still too close to and too fond of Ollie then to acknowledge that he had been deceiving Poindexter and the president, and now me," later wrote McFarlane, who was coming to realize that deceptions by both the Iranian, Manucher Ghorbanifer, and his own Ollie were dooming the mission. The Iranians were stringing him on, Ghorbanifer especially, holding out as bait the prospect of getting Buckley out. But it was seeming less simple. The flow of equipment, McFarlane realized, was beginning to go directly from American sources without even the cover of having the Israelis do the actual shipping. The experience resulted in several days of frustration in Khomeini's capital and growing doubts about what North was doing.[81]

"Don't worry, Bud," said North when they reached Ben Gurion Airport in Tel Aviv, "it's not a total loss. At least we're using some of the ayatollah's money in Central America."[82]

McFarlane, even while on the CIA secure transmitter relaying the grim news to Poindexter, needed only a few seconds to realize what North was saying. He did not, at that instant, have the full picture, but he had every reason to believe that the so-called deal with Iran, the original rationale for the overture, was a trap. Not a single hostage was yet freed from captivity in Lebanon, but one, Buckley, was dead. The Iranians had a good thing going, blackmailing the Americans, wanting to get their hands on spare parts before releasing any of the men. And why should they stop as long as the U.S. was desperate enough to play their game? They had already received 1,508 TOW and eighteen HAWK missiles from Israel and the United States and additional HAWK spare parts, although there were some returns because of defects. Iran had even been given briefings on how the Americans viewed the Soviet threat in the light of the war with Iraq.[83]

Reagan heard all this directly from McFarlane, who briefed him in the White House on May 29, right after his return. The conversation could only go one way because it was obvious: trying to get the hostages out by delivering arms simply was not working. "I thought it was unwise to continue anything further," McFarlane later recalled his advice for the benefit of the Tower Commission. By June 2, the CIA told the army "to put the radar transfer action on 'hold,' a status which continued until 30 July 1986."[84]

Bush's attention, during that period, to both the Iraq-Iran and Central-American situations, could not distract him from the illness of his son, Marvin, who was diagnosed as having ulcerative colitis, also known as IBD, a chronic intestinal disorder, a potentially precancerous disease. Barbara, called back to Washington by George as she was on her way to a charity fund-raiser at Santa Fe, New Mexico, found her husband at Marvin's hospital bedside. "Marvin told me later," she recounted, "that he 'knew' he was dying when two things happened: his dad spent the day by his side, and Jeb called just to pass the time of day. He ended his call with 'I love you, Marvin.' " "My boys," she added, "don't say things like that to each other. They just know it and act it. That day, Jeb said it." After several blood transfusions, Marvin was given a temporary colostomy, which later became permanent.[85]

Bush continued to build his coming candidacy. He crisscrossed the country extolling the Reagan record, rallying Republicans for the November midterm elections and also raising money for his own future presidential campaign. By October, he had made 130 stops for seventy candidates in ninety-seven cities and, while not necessarily painting the Democrats as Satans, he denounced them for obstructing the president's policies. His greatest danger, explained two Washington journalists, was that he appeared to be "a bit too much the loyal number-two man and not enough of his own to lead the country when Reagan's term ends."[86]

Even two years later, the Ferraro encounter still hurt Bush, especially among women, almost, in its own way, as seriously as the "wimp" image/anti-Bush resentments that had come out of the 1980 campaign. There was little that he could do it seemed, for all his loyalty, to allay the lingering hostility.

Journalist George Will, for example, a Reagan friend and sometime companion of the First Lady, had lunch with her in January of 1986. Nancy's "favorite topic" of their mealtime conversation was George Bush. She went on about how the "whiny" vice president was weak and spineless. Will followed through with the meanest barb of them all in his syndicated column: "The unpleasant sound Bush is emitting," he wrote, "as he traipses from one conservative gathering to another is a thin, tinny 'arf'—the sound of a lapdog. He is panting along Mondale's path to the presidency."

Such ridicule, which festered during the 1984 campaign and continued to escalate on his way to the White House, was more common than ever before in his career. So hurtful were those he had endured, especially the scoffing at the "Boy Scout" loyalty to Reagan during the Ferraro debate, that some Bush aides suspected that he even toyed with giving up thinking about the presidency altogether. There were relentless examples of press amusement, including some aimed at him from the left. Texas journalist Molly Ivins, for example, wrote afterward that "Bush's finest day back in the 1984 campaign started in Minnesota when he had to get up at 6 A.M. and milk a cow in order to demonstrate his concern for the plight of the American farmer." And he "showed up in the correct red plaid."[87]

It would be nice to get back on his own turf.

CHAPTER SEVENTEEN

"With a Wink and a Nod"

※

Bush had already gone along with Casey in providing an operations base for long-term CIA operative Donald Gregg, his adviser for national security affairs.[1] Then, as though to further the vice president's credentials as a hard, international, realpolitik fighter, the CIA director picked him as the man to accomplish the objective in the fierce war between Iraq and Iran, a holy crusade with the potential to cost a million lives. At stake was control of Middle Eastern oil through the Persian Gulf. Only three months before becoming a personal emissary in that situation, Bush had visited the region in a bid to bring competitive price relief to American producers, especially for the slumping Texas fields. This time he was going to Israel, Jordan, and Egypt.[2]

Bush left Washington with a party that included his wife, Craig Fuller, and a television crew financed by his Fund for America's Future.[3] Images of his visits with Middle Eastern leaders could only help to advance his reputation as a well-traveled world leader. Reporters, however, were advised to limit their expectations. The objective, they were told, was more "like tending a garden" than establishing new breakthroughs. "And I don't think there are a lot of weeds in that garden," said a Bush aide to a *New York Times* reporter.

The reality was that all sides, the Americans, Israelis, and Iranians, had an important stake in getting things going again, and for that he would meet with Amiran Nir in Jerusalem. As North reaffirmed to Poindexter, "one American hostage will probably be killed in order to demonstrate displeasure."[4]

"We didn't want him to discuss this with anyone else, for security reasons," the NCS's Howard Teicher has explained. "He asked us some questions, but he didn't express any opinions." Later, in the face of Bush denials, Teicher reaffirmed that arms shipments were specifically discussed.[5]

For those meetings with King Hussein of Jordan and President Hosni Mubarak of Egypt, Casey briefed Bush. He explained that the Arab leaders had to "maintain their efforts to convey our shared views to Saddam regarding Iraq's use of its air resources," as a Contingency Preplanning Group memo put it.[6] The ayatollah, Casey reaffirmed to Bush, had to be made more desperate for weapons.

Even as Bush prepared to leave, one of the Hizbollah's victims, the Rev. Lawrence Jenco, was freed in the Bakka Valley of Lebanon, then flown to Germany. His release, as Murray Waas and Craig Unger have written, "betrayed the Iranian ambivalence about the negotiations and their need for weapons, which was sufficiently great for them to want to keep alive the deal." That was despite paying a 600 percent premium for the HAWK missiles. What the Americans did not know by that summer, however, even as they were dealing to get him freed, was that Buckley was already dead.[7]

With Craig Fuller serving as note taker, Bush met with the thirty-seven-year-old Nir at his King David Hotel suite in Jerusalem early on a Tuesday morning, the twenty-ninth of July. Nir (who died in a plane crash in Mexico the following year) updated Bush on the progress of the Iranian venture. Bush learned in two meetings with Ghorbanifar that a timetable had been worked out. All the hostages were to be released and, to secure the deal, the 4,000 units of supplies were to be delivered in two stages. In attempting to close their negotiations, which dated back to the summer of 1985, Nir had "activated the channel" by his "dramatic and interesting meetings" with the opposite side. He was finally told that three hostages would be released. The captors took out Father Jenco with two hostages and had released him on Friday. Bush got Nir's assurances that Prime Minister Peres had been briefed "on all of this," and Nir then reemphasized that "we are dealing with the most radical elements" of the fundamentalist regime. "This is good because we've learned they can deliver and the moderates can't," he added, according to Fuller's notes. "We have no real choice than to proceed." Thus, the Israelis pitched hard for the Americans to abandon their all-or-nothing stipulation as a prerequisite for an exchange and to accept a sequential arrangement. What was also clear about Nir's presentation was its implicit recognition that Bush lacked an insider's familiarity with the details of the negotiations. Bush, in fact, pressed for more information, especially about the strategic aspect involved in being able to maintain contacts in the event of leadership changes in Tehran. Other than that, according to Fuller's notes, he "made no commitments nor did he give any direction to Nir. The VP expressed his appreciation for the briefing and thanked Nir for having pursued this effort despite doubts and reservations throughout the process." It was, as events played themselves out, far more than merely "tending the garden," a pivotal meeting in which George Bush played a key role in seeing to it that the arms shipments to Iran were resumed. As Nir, who also found Bush noncommittal, soon afterward told Richard Secord, "Mr. Bush was very attentive, very interested in everything—a very quick study. You know, you can't always count on a good audience with foreign politicians."[8] But what mattered most was what Ronald Reagan then heard from the vice president. In that conversation, Bush evidently moved "from note taker to advocate." The president followed through the next day by authorizing the release to Iran of the remaining twelve pallets of HAWK spare parts, which were stored in Israel.[9]

Bush had, by then, crossed into neighboring Jordan. What the press observed was a luxurious three-day visit with King Hussein. Some aides called it "a tourist event," one designed primarily for the best camera angles and most interesting backdrops for a touring vice president demonstrating his knowledge of foreign affairs. His next stop was in Egypt with Mubarak. In Amman and Cairo, both good channels to Baghdad, the message was the same: pass the word to Saddam Hussein to hit Iran harder. His air force's efforts, Bush assured them, would be reciprocated with tactical and technological assistance from Washington. Within hours, literally, of Bush's departure from Jordan, and then as he left Egypt in early August, the Iraqis stepped up their pounding of Iran as Mirages flew 359 missions during the forty-eight hours following Bush's visit. Iraqi power, reenergized, struck deeper than ever before into the heart of the enemy, bombing oil refineries and previously unharmed facilities at remote Sirri Island. From the U.S. side, the strikes were followed by the CIA's transference to Saddam Hussein of highly classified tactical intelligence information and equipment to enable him to gauge the damage done to Iran. To get around the technicalities of the Arms Export Control Act about requiring congressional notification, a White House letter to the head of the Senate's Foreign Relations Committee, Richard Lugar, asserted that the arms sales were "inadvertent" and involved the "unauthorized" transfer of only a "small quantity of unsophisticated weapons." The United States was thereby well on its way to "making Saddam one of the biggest recipients of official U.S. largesse."[10]

For Bush personally, carrying out the administration's initiative, what had been set in motion in the Middle East was quickly compounded by the unraveling of covert operations out of Ilopango in El Salvador.

Eugene Hasenfus, a buddy of Tosh Plumlee's, was also a soldier of fortune. The money was good, $3,000 a month and full expenses, all automatically deposited to his account at a bank near his home in Marinette, Wisconsin. He was a much lower echelon guy than Tosh—not a pilot, just a cargo handler, the fellow who pushed supplies out of planes. He had already made ten air deliveries to the contras out of Ilopango. As much as he was exhilarated by knowing that what he was doing was beating Communists, there were "mixed" feelings. He had signed up with a San Salvador company called Corporate Air Services, and little effort was made to hide its CIA sponsorship. The agency used many such fronts, but Hasenfus began to realize that the operation was really coming out of the White House.[11]

On the fifth of October, the burly, redheaded forty-five-year-old Hasenfus was in the air over southern Nicaragua, just above the border with Costa Rica. His C-123K air transport had left Ilopango with a good load, seventy Soviet-made AK-47 rifles, 100,000 rounds of ammunition, rocket grenades, boots, and other supplies for the contras. The plane, with its four-man crew, then dipped to 2,500 feet to release its load. Beneath them, a nineteen-year-old Sandinista soldier kept his eyes on the C-123K above, adjusted the ground-to-air missile launcher on his shoulder, and aimed. The rocket found its mark. A puff of smoke, then flames, and the popping open of a parachute that brought Hasenfus down some miles from the young man on the ground. Armed with a pistol and a knife, and, wearing only soiled blue jeans, a dark blue T-shirt and a denim overshirt, the downed solider of fortune found an abandoned shack, where searchers located him the next day.[12]

Don Gregg was the first to get the news. Congress had only recently gone along with a $100-million aid bill and it was awaiting the president's signature to be implementated. With the anti-Communist fighters increasingly desperate, Elliott Abrams had been scurrying to get that "bridge loan"—$10 million from the sultan of Brunei—only to discover after a series of "frantic phone calls" that the money had been misdirected. The news of the Hasenfus flight, with pictures of the captured flier appearing on the front pages three days after his actual downing, proved that at least four people, Hasenfus and the three who were killed, were Americans working sub rosa to aid the contras.[13]

Visions of the CIA dominated the media for the next few days. The vice chairman of the Senate Intelligence Committee, Patrick Leahy of Vermont, had little doubt that the administration was encouraging mercenaries "with a wink and a nod." President Reagan, taking issue with Leahy and saying that the rebels were indigenous freedom fighters, not mercenaries, reached into the 1930s for his parallel. He insisted that they were more like the idealists who had volunteered to fight against Francisco Franco's Fascists. "Some years ago," he said to reporters, "many of you spoke approvingly of something called the Abraham Lincoln Brigade in the Spanish Civil war." Even as he reached for that comparison, the contradiction was emerging. Evidence showed that the owner of the C-123K was Southern Air Transport, a charter airline with long-standing ties to the CIA.[14]

From that moment, Bush's hand in the affair was impossible to conceal. White House staff involvement had, in fact, been known since the second and more sweeping Boland Amendment, Boland II, had gone into force. Hasenfus presented evidence, both verbally and materially, that was hard to ignore. The flights, he said at a news conference in Managua, were directly supervised by members of the CIA in El Salvador.[15]

Very quickly the world heard about "Max Gomez" and the intriguing fact that he was connected to the vice president's adviser for national security. Hasenfus named him as one of his two superiors. The *San Francisco Examiner* rapidly weighed in with information "from an unidentified source" connecting "Gomez" to Gregg and the White House. Bush spokeswoman, Gayle Fisher, denied that anyone on his staff was "directing or coordinating an operation in Central America. Allegations to that effect are simply not true," she added. Just one day later, with additional evidence that Felix Rodriguez was doing more talking, the *Los Angeles Times* reported that "Gomez" informed Vice President Bush about his activities and had met with him "twice" (a third meeting was later reported, at a Cuban Independence Day reception in Miami on May 20, 1986). Bush, in Charleston, South Carolina, that day to campaign for the Republican candidate for lieutenant governor, was confronted by the press about "Max Gomez." Max Gomez, he said, was a "patriot," which was a lot better than he had done twice before, when he had referred to him as "Felix Gomez," thereby revealing his knowledge of the man's dual identities. Now, trying to distance himself as much as possible, Bush quickly added that "to the best of my knowledge, this man is not working for the United States government." Was running guns to the contras in the best interest of the United States? a reporter then asked. "To see the contras prevail is clearly in the best interests of the United States," replied the vice president.[16]

One could never be certain whether Bush was helped or hurt in the long run, but events that soon followed removed the contra/Hasenfus/Gregg/Bush story from the limelight.

The first the world heard about what eventually became known as the Iran-contra scandal was in an Arabic language news magazine, *Al Shiraa,* published in Lebanon on November 3, 1986. It appeared right after the release from captivity of another American hostage, David Jacobsen. On November 4, both *The New York Times* and the *Washington Post* carried allegations about the arms sales. At this point public opinion polls showed the president's approval rating at an all-time high of 70 percent. It was also the day before the midterm elections, which cost the Republicans their Senate majority. Despite that setback, the votes still showed a considerable relationship to Reagan's continued personal popularity.[17]

The thought in some minds, including Reagan's, and further encouraged by a published Nixon letter that was signed by the chief aide to the former president, was that the Iran-contra arrangement was a great diplomatic coup, another "China opening," with all the Kissingerian touches.[18] In gauging the president's responses to the affair, fantasy, wishful thinking, and/or deniable plausibility became indistinguishable. According to Lou Cannon, a biographer and longtime Reagan observer, noting his vague responses when later interviewed by the Tower Board established by Congress to investigate the affair, "the extent of Reagan forgetfulness and his tendency to change his story about two issues of such importance to him—arms sales to Iran to free the hostages and aid to the contras—are suspicious. The board was not questioning Reagan about 'details,' as White House spokesmen often described the process, but about the extracurricular assistance to the contras."[19]

Reagan's first statement to the press about the situation, made on the nineteenth of November, was similar to that Tower Board interview. Before the latter, he was briefed about the facts just before being interrogated, including by Bush. In preparation for the televised news conference, he also underwent extensive briefing. Yet he was not fully informed in part because his national security adviser, Poindexter, was still dissembling. His national appearance turned into a fiasco. Only "small amounts" of arms and "modest deliveries" of weapons had been made, he told the world, and emphasized that the contacts had been with Iranian "moderates." The shipment was so modest that it "could easily fit into a single cargo plane." The weapons were "defensive." "We did not," he maintained, "—repeat, did not—trade weapons or anything else for hostages," repeating no fewer than four times that he had not "condoned" arms shipments by any third country to Iran. Still wanting to avoid citing Israel as a key player but needing to clarify the president's comments, the White House was forced to issue a statement that admitted to the involvement of a "third country." Six days later, Reagan and Ed Meese went before the television cameras to explain that they had new information. Profits from the arms sale had been diverted to support the Nicaraguan contras.[20]

Only Reagan's personal popularity kept his presidency alive, and even then it was shaky. Just days later, in early December, a *New York Times/CBS News* poll reported that the president's approval rating had dropped from 67 to 46 percent. The Gallup organization, polling for *Newsweek,* showed a 47 percent approval level with 44 percent disapproving. As recently as September, it had reached 80 percent. Not since they had begun to measure approval back in 1936 had they recorded such a sharp one-month drop. "By November 1986," Cannon has written, "the cracks in the Reagan facade were beginning to show. The results of the 1986 elections, after a [congressional election] campaign that Reagan had made a test of his personal prestige, demonstrated that he had become politically vulnerable even in advance of the Iran-contra disclosures. And these disclosures did more damage to Reagan than the initial reports of the Watergate coverup had caused Nixon."[21]

Bush, under close pressure from Senator Gary Hart of Colorado, the front-runner for the Democratic presidential nomination, had to sidestep the Iran-contra fallout. Already vulnerable in two areas, the Middle East and Central America ends of the affair, he could not afford to be dragged down any further. Not all the harsh judgments came from critics of the administration, but even some conservatives, notably the editors of the *Washington Times,* joined in the attack.

Secretary of State George Shultz's persistent negative stance on the deal, compounded by his questions raised at a meeting of the National Security Planning Group meeting before the revelations became public, had made him a "marked man."[22] Only one day after that meeting, on November 20, industrialist Charles Z. Wick, director of the U.S. Information Agency and "a pal of the president and Nancy from way back," telephoned Shultz. He had talked to the First Lady, he told the secretary, and reported that "Nancy felt that I was not being helpful."[23] Although Wick tried to assure Shultz that Mrs. Reagan would understand that he was only trying to help the president, when Cap Weinberger met with the Saudi Ambassador, Prince Bandar bin Sultan, a few days later, he was told that Nancy "thinks Shultz should go—that he has been disloyal to the president—and said he recommended to her that I [Weinberger] be named secretary of state."[24]

Bush, at that very time, resumed keeping a diary, as he had done during his year at the U.S. liaison office in Beijing. He made his first entry the day after the Lebanese paper revealed the arms trade, which coincided with the midterm elections of 1986. Dictating notes into a small tape recorder for transcription by an aide, he set out to produce "an accurate diary, with at least five and maybe fifteen minutes a day on observations about my run for the presidency in 1988." He went on to maintain the recordings diligently, sometimes making entries as he went through the day, and recapitulating thoughts and events for periods that had been neglected.[25] In the first dictation of the new series, he revealed his disturbance about the publicized link of Don Gregg with the contra resupply operation, especially the thought that the information had been leaked to the press by his deputy chief of staff Fred Khedouri.

He was also closely attuned to George Shultz's situation. Shultz, who found the entire experience a difficult one, was upset that the vice president was spreading the word that he planned to resign from the cabinet. Shultz, recalling that in at least one meeting he could remember having been in Bush's presence during a discussion of the issue, said that Bush had "made no objection to the proposal for arms sales to Iran," and so advised Nick Brady, who had called to warn "the vice president could get drawn into a web of lies." Then, according to his memoirs, Shultz added: "If he blows his integrity, he's finished. He should be very careful how he plays the 'loyal lieutenant' role now." Bush, after an NSPG meeting on the ninth, noted that Shultz felt "cut out" on the Iran initiative and might resign. "He distrusts not only North, but he feels that I'm in jeopardy . . . myself. He thought he had heard me say something that later proved to be a lie, and his advice to me as a person interested in my future, 'don't get involved in this.' "[26] Bush did, however, join with Don Regan a few days later in pushing for "total disclosure, and not making statements that are not accurate." He knew, he recorded for his diary, that "George Shultz feels this way."[27] At a meeting on the fifteenth, with the secretary of state again the topic of conversation, Don Regan leaned over to Bush and whispered that Shultz "was not on board at all." Bush, concerned about Regan's words, called him at home that Sunday for a clarification. Shultz, Regan told Bush, really wanted to clear the air by saying that such matters ought to be handled by the State Department. With that understood, no more arms would go to Iran. That was what worried him about Shultz, Regan told Bush, because it would make the president look like he was "wrong."[28] "It does seem like the vultures are circling over George Shultz," Bush dictated for his diary three days later, noting the next day, after a private session with the president himself, the White House's "feeling that Shultz was cutting and running . . . separating himself out." At their next Thursday luncheon, President Reagan heard about Shultz's call for the ouster of Poindexter, whose withholding of information had helped lead to the gaffes at the previous day's televised announcement about the arms deal.[29]

Well, said Bush, call a meeting for Monday and get all the key NSC players together and "get them all to lay it on the table." Tell them "we're going to hammer this thing out" and ask, "What are you upset about, George? What are you upset about, Poindexter?"

Bush was right, agreed the president. They needed a meeting.

"The problem is," Bush quoted himself afterward, "and I showed him certain clippings—that Poindexter, Don Regan, and George [Shultz] are all out there with leaks and peddling their own line. Regan, for example, says, 'I'm a team player.['] Everybody at State rallies around George, and it gets him all upset. And, when Regan says, or uses the word 'negotiate' or allegedly makes some comment about Israel, everybody—State and NSC—gets upset with him." A president can't afford to tolerate ultimatums about quitting, like Shultz was making. "No president," Bush told Reagan, "can have a cabinet [member] set the terms under which he will stay. It is impossible."[30]

"On Poindexter," Bush recorded a day after the meeting, "I'm concerned because today—on Friday—[of] some new revelation that there were arms shipped in September of '85. The president having said that none were and I don't know what that's all about, but I ran into Don Regan at lunch today and he said, 'Well, there's a new bombshell,' " he noted, referring to the revelations about the TOW missile shipment of September 1985. Since both Bush and Regan had known about it, it was not a "bombshell" because it happened but because, in the words of the subsequent Walsh report, "it had been made public."[31]

They discussed that HAWK shipment at the NSPG meeting in the Situation Room on Monday afternoon, with the president saying nothing, even though "he had been briefed about the shipment by McFarlane before it occurred, approved the retroactive finding, and had been reminded of his actions five days earlier by Shultz and Regan."[32] With all that had happened, however, Casey and Poindexter wanted to continue dealings with the Iranians. The president said nothing, but left the impression that he, too, wanted them to go on. Once again, a wink and a nod said it all. Shultz, the gadfly, did not waver.[33]

Little over a half hour after the meeting had ended, Ed Meese entered the Oval Office. Only the president and his chief of staff, Don Regan, were present.

"It's a terrible mess, Mr. President," said the attorney general. "I have a few things to button up and then I'll give you a full report. But it's going to be bad news."

Ronald Reagan then heard about the diversion of funds. The Iranians paid $30 million for their equipment, Meese reported, but the U.S. government received only $12 million. There was no explanation for what happened to the remaining $18 million. He had contacted North over the weekend, Meese told them. The colonel had admitted that some of the funds had been diverted to the contras. Reagan, as Meese later described him, "blanched when he heard Meese's words. The color drained from his face, leaving his skin pasty white."

"This is a bitter blow," Regan added. The president was pale and grim.[34]

Meese made the revelation public via a televised press conference the next day. Bush, at a fund-raising dinner in Venetia, Pennsylvania, where sixty supporters had each paid $5,000, was given notes on what was being said even while he ate his dinner. Then, en route to the airport at Pittsburgh, he listened to the conference on the car's tape player. "Being the cheerleader for Ronald Reagan," wrote Kevin Phillips, "doesn't look as good when the revolutionary himself becomes a has-been. Bush has to go from being a Boy Scout trying to get merit badges from the White House and become an independent force."[35]

Bush's dilemma was second only to Shultz's. At least the secretary did not have to worry, as did the vice president, about his political future. He was, Bush realized, in a trap reminiscent of the Watergate situation. That experience had taught him, and just about everybody, about the folly of letting things drip out, drop by drop. "It is important to be level, to be honest, to be direct," Bush told himself. But, with it all, revelations were hemorrhaging, and it was clear that, thanks to the wiles of North and Poindexter, who was still withholding information, the president still had less than the full truth. Dribs and drabs were coming out with no real way to stop them, except, as he urged Reagan, through "total disclosure." Yet, through it all, he admired the president's poise. He "bears up beautifully," noted his impressed vice president. "He smiles when the press fires these tough questions. That is something that I have got to learn better. I will keep trying," he noted for his diary on the fourteenth. Insofar as his own position was concerned, he decided that he had no choice but to be loyal. "I think the president must know that he can have the vice president for him and he must not think that he has to look over his shoulder." His "basic integrity and honor will help him overcome his difficulties."[36]

The bottom line, of course, was his own predicament. Shultz was right. "George does not want this to rub off on me for the run . . . for the presidency," reads his diary for the tenth. But, feeling trapped, Bush knew he was in a bind. "The irony is that on many of these key meetings I was not there. The irony is that everyone says that the vice president has no power, and yet I am the one damaged . . . he's not in on the decisions." He indulged in despair about his position, "—and yet, having said that I have better access—I am diminished. The truth of the matter is that the president makes his decisions in very oblique ways. I am not in the decision process . . . unless I am sitting in at the time the president makes a decision, then I can speak up. These so-called findings on Iran—I'll be honest—I don't remember any of them, and I don't believe . . . I've got to see them to believe they were even signed by the president, frankly. But, sometimes, there are meeting [sic] over in the White House with Shultz, NSC guy [*sic*] Casey, and Weinberger, and they are making some decisions that the president signs off on. I am not trying to have the facts. And the facts are," he wrote on January 1, "that the vice president is not in the decision-making loop. He does not have to sign off on decisions, is sometimes overlooked, although not on purpose by the NSC bureaucracy."[37]

But the contra/Gregg/Hasenfus/Rodriguez affair continued to haunt him. Wary reporters dug up all they could about Bush, Gregg and "Max Gomez." How, wondered Bush, can he have any credibility when reporters doubt his every word? "The hardest thing of all this is to have your honor and integrity questioned. The kind of doubt and meanness that gets into the faces of the reporters when they simply don't think you are telling the truth." Nick Brady and Atwater were concerned that Gregg "is hurting me very much in a political sense. They don't like the fact that this information about the contras has kind of oozed out . . . they don't think I should have seen Felix Rodriguez. I disagree with that. There is a lot of pusillanimous worry here, but they are all trying to protect my interest."[38]

He was scheduled to talk before the American Enterprise Institute, a conservative Washington think tank, on December 3. The delicacy of the situation was obvious. Amid fear that he was in a "lose-lose" position, he prepared his comments with care. He could neither be seen as separating himself too far from the administration, and certainly not repudiating policies that he had helped to carry out, nor giving his political rivals additional ammunition. "I deliberated" about the speech, he noted. "I did not want to look like I was pulling away from the president," or even differing with him. He went over it with Reagan, who seemed to approve. At least he nodded, but, as Bush dictated, "not specifically saying so—saying that mistakes were made on the NSC level was the right thing to do."[39]

Bush's speech, his first public statement on the matter, was judicious and drew much praise. He both backed the administration's initiative for its strategic geopolitical purposes, especially as an instrument of cold war policy, and acknowledged its blunders. Iran, "all that stands between the Soviets and the gulf oil states . . . all that stands between the Soviets and a warm water port," cannot be ignored, he explained. An attempt to open a dialogue would have been tried in any event, "whether we had hostages in Lebanon or not." The administration's credibility, he conceded, "has been damaged" because of the "clandestine deals" and "clearly mistakes were made." "I was aware of our Iran initiative and I support the president's decision," he told his AEI audience. "And I was not aware of and I oppose any discussion of funds, any ransom payments, or any circumvention of the will of the Congress or the laws of the United States of America. . . . Let the chips fall where they may. We want the truth. The president wants it. I want it. And the American people have a fundamental right to it. And if the truth hurts, so be it. We gotta take our lumps and move ahead." The president, he was about to add by reading from his prepared text, "is absolutely convinced in his own mind that he did not swap arms for hostages," but at the last moment thought better about actually saying "in his own mind."[40]

H. Ross Perot, that tenacious eccentric, described by *The Economist* as "a short little man, with a yapping drawl, sticking-out ears, and a head like a bottle brush," who had earlier bedeviled the Nixon administration by carrying on, as Charles Colson later told an interviewer, "one of the most effective con jobs I ever saw in the White House," was enjoying the vice president's predicament. The billionaire had already put his investigators to work looking for a Bush scandal, any kind of scandal. The hottest possibility involved the subject of Perot's crusading zeal, the continuing belief, nurtured by the grieving families of American servicemen who were missing in action in Southeast Asia and further compounded by veterans groups and opportunists eager to turn a profit, that such soldiers were still alive. Firm denial or verification was impossible. Their potential existence, raised so tantalizingly by Reagan himself in the 1970s, had become an obsession of Perot's. He could easily imagine himself marching down Pennsylvania Avenue to cheering throngs at the head of a procession of ex-prisoners of war whom he had personally liberated. Had he not already accomplished such heroics, as recounted in Ken Follett's 1983 Tehran rescue story, *On Wings of Eagles,* written with Perot himself as chief impressario? The myth-making best-seller portrayed the Texan as a world-class combination of Horatio Alger and John Wayne, a "remarkable image-shaper" that satisfied popular cravings for reaffirmations of the virtues of capitalism and American derring-do. Perot, the hero and POW/MIA crusader, searched for conspiracies that kept the truth about missing servicemen from the public. Bush, as a former CIA director, Perot theorized, was being pressured to keep his silence about their existence by heroin traffickers and money launderers. He then began searching for a possible Bush involvement in a "mini-Teapot Dome," gathering reams of documents on Bush investments and trying to tie him to tax write-off contributions made by his old oil business partner, Hugh Liedtke of Pennzoil. Perot also tried to link two of Bush's sons to the Iran-contra scandal.[41]

Reagan's people, just like Nixon's, could not easily write off the fortune that stood behind the peculiar Texan. He had to be humored at practically any cost. When Bush learned from Craig Fuller about the possible existence of a tape allegedly showing thirty-nine POWs being forced to perform slave labor in Southeast Asia, he called Perot and asked whether he could help. Perot, who readily converted every opening into an opportunity, was then able to claim that he was "asked by our government to pursue this thing, to get the tape if it existed." Bush has confirmed that Perot "went to the Pentagon with my support," adding that "there was a great deal of hysteria about it. There were many kooks who believed people were being held against their will. They were completely irrational."[42] Perot, of course, was not discouraged when the tape turned out to be nothing more than a scam; he was, in fact, more determined than ever to follow through. He then blamed Bush, not unfairly, for the administration's refusal to reimburse him. He also held the vice president responsible for not having the strength to enable him to pursue the matter. Bush failed in an attempt to sidetrack Perot by giving him access to classified files on the POW/MIA issue. Perot interpreted the move as an assurance that action would be taken if he produced evidence of live prisoners. Offended by what he regarded as personal obstructions, Perot canceled a pledge to contribute $2.5 million to the Reagan library, a move he confirmed to Bush during a telephone conversation on March 21. He was, he told the vice president, "severing all ties with the Reagan administration." Then, with White House Chief of Staff Howard Baker continuing to handle Perot delicately, Perot went on a personal mission to Vietnam. Administration officials, aware that Perot was acting in violation of the Logan Act and fearing a negative impact on negotiations with the government in Hanoi, knew they were helpless to do anything about it. When, after his empty-handed return, Perot was rebuffed by President Reagan, he turned to Bush. This time, he suggested that he might offer to buy all of Cam Ranh Bay as a form of ransom, which Bush rejected. He also turned back Perot's alternate idea of paying $1 million for each released prisoner.

"Well, George," he told the vice president, "I am looking for prisoners, but I spend all my time discovering the government has been moving drugs around the world and is involved in illegal arms deals. . . . I can't get at the prisoners because of the corruption among our own covert people." Bush, Perot later explained, had let him down. "This world is full of lions and tigers and rabbits," he told the vice president. "And you're a rabbit." Bush acknowledges that he "was then in Perot's crosshairs." From then on, it seemed that everything was personal with him. He went around talking about Bush as "weak" and a "wimp." The administration had cut Perot down, but the vice president remained his primary target.[43]

On October 13, 1987, Bush announced his candidacy for the party's presidential nomination. The setting was the atrium of Houston's Hyatt Regency Hotel where a high school band played "The Yellow Rose of Texas." As Bush announced his intent to become "the next president of the United States," red, white, and blue balloons floated down from the ceiling. "I am not a mystic," he told them, "and I do not yearn to lead a crusade." He would not, in fact, press for going off in "radical, new directions" but would give the nation "steady and experienced leadership." The Republican party was "the party of Lincoln" and so must be "attentive to human needs and for racial justice." Going beyond the needs of humanity at home, he vowed to support the "freedom fighters of the world." The history of America, he told them, was the story of "protecting those who needed our protection and making this a kinder nation."

He assured his audience that they need not worry that the price would be too high. "There are those who say that we must balance the budget on the backs of the workers and raise taxes again," he said, alluding to the Reagan tax hike of 1982 and the increased Social Security deductions. "They are wrong. I am not going to raise your taxes—period." His themes in place, he thereby began his long journey as a formal candidate, repeating his pledge as he went along.[44]

He also continued to hold firm on Iran-contra. He was, as he had earlier noted in his diary, and later repeated to *Washington Post* correspondent David Broder, "not in the loop," thereby making a fine distinction between initiating and implementing policy. He later told congressional investigators what was already clear, that he had known what was happening. He went along, he said during an interview in 1995, because he "approved" of the deal. Then, in a reference full of recognition of the president's thinking, he added, "Reagan will go to his grave thinking he didn't trade arms for hostages." The president had convinced himself that the Israeli role was somehow detached from the American position.[45] As Bush himself explained the point to Dan Rather on national television, by "not in the loop" he meant that he did not have an "operational role."[46] His opponents, both partisan and a significant portion of the skeptical press, sought to blur that point, hammering away at him for what "he must have known" about the deal. Every instance of a Bush presence at a meeting where arms was discussed was taken as a contradiction of his position, as was the release of a White House memorandum late in 1987 that showed Bush as a supporter of the arms sale.[47] Yet, just as the deal had originated within the National Security Council—the "White House basement"—and was agreed to by the president after it had been sold to him by McFarlane, Bush was exposed to a policy that already had Reagan's blessing. No one who witnessed how he responded in meetings came away with the view that the vice president was either a vigorous advocate or strong dissenter during such sessions. Such "forcefulness was not Bush's style, at least not while he was vice president," McFarlane has written. He also noted that at the Monday-night NSPG meeting in July, Bush joined Don Regan, who had replaced Jim Baker as chief of staff, in raising "mild" doubts.[48] He also offered measured dissent by teaming up with Regan in telling the president that the American people "will never believe an explanation about the arms deal to Iran that suggested that he did not believe he was dealing with terrorists."[49] Even those instances were exceptions. More characteristically, he "avoided having to express himself on a matter where he knew the president had strong feelings."[50] Neither of the subsequent congressional Iran-contra committees, nor the investigation board headed by John Tower, found evidence to the contrary. The strongest exception to the portrait of Bush's role came from Weinberger. After reading about the vice president's "not in the loop" comment, the defense secretary telephoned Shultz with considerable pique. "He was on the other side. It's on the record!" he said. "Why did he say that?"[51]

That Shultz and Weinberger made "their case with strength" has been confirmed by Lou Cannon and Theodore Draper.[52] Neither, however, was present, and both drew their information from the two cabinet secretaries. Whatever the vigor of their dissent and at whatever meetings it was made, Bush did not hear what he did not want to hear. "If I had sat there, and heard George Shultz and Cap express it strongly," he had also said to Broder, "maybe I would have had a stronger view. But when you don't know something it's hard to react."[53] Reagan, at a press conference one day after his 1988 State of the Union Address, even drew from "lost" memory to say flatly that Bush had not been present at that critical January 7 meeting. Later, on Ted Koppel's *Nightline* television show, Reagan said that he was unaware of a battle between Shultz, Weinberger, and other top officials over the arms sales. "I never really heard them that clearly," he said. "And the reason is that the machinery broke down—it never worked as it should. The key players with the experience weren't ever called together . . . to review the decisions that were made at a lower level."[54] But three specific questions lingered on: What advice did he give the president? Was he there when Shultz objected to the deal? How much, if anything, did Donald Gregg share with Bush about the diversion of money to the contras?

The affair that "grew out of the White House basement" hurt Reagan and, through him, Bush. Strategically, the entire episode was a fiasco. As hostages were released, new ones were taken; little wonder, because those freeing them were also responsible for capturing others. Politically, one of the ironies was that the vice president had succeeded only too well in identifying himself with Reagan. The sharp drop in the president's approval ratings rubbed off on Bush. A *New York Times/CBS News* poll in early January showed him behind Dole by twelve points.[55] Another survey from the same source, released just three weeks before the Iowa caucuses, showed that Republicans who approved of the president's performance were splitting almost evenly for Bush and Dole. Among Reagan's Republican critics, who were still among the minority, Dole had the edge by better than two to one.[56] In Iowa, a state where the administration's farm policies were making the president unpopular whatever the psychological benefit of coming out ahead in that early voting (the very contest that had given Bush his "Big Mo" eight years earlier), his campaign was sinking. A straw poll at the Iowa State University campus showed Bush third, behind Pat Robertson and Bob Dole, in that order.[57] Lee Atwater's on-the-spot inspection trip convinced him that Bush would have to go into New Hampshire with the burden of a loss in Iowa.[58] That something else was needed to revive the Bush campaign was clear. Not only did he lack a clear message, but he had to get off the defensive. Nobody, it seemed, and especially the press, was ready to let him escape responsibility for the arms-for-hostages trade. That became amply clear on January 7, when the *Washington Post* ran a front-page story based on Bush's Tower Commission testimony. The article, which was picked up by the *Des Moines Register,* implicated Bush as having watched the arms deal "step by step," at "several dozen such meetings that touched on the Iran initiative" and then merely echoing the president.[59]

* * *

Iran-contra was obviously not about to disappear. Republicans increasingly began to worry that Bush was "damaged goods," that his presidential candidacy would only keep the issue alive. That the Tower Commission had cleared him seemed almost moot. Nor did Bush benefit from efforts of a Congressional Joint Investigative Committee, which had collected over 300,000 documents and gone through more than 500 interviews and depositions to conclude that there was no evidence that Reagan himself knew anything about the diversion of profits to the contras. The only way to handle the situation was to go on the attack. Hitting back at the media, as Nixon and Agnew had demonstrated, brought almost instant support. But, as E. J. Dionne Jr. noted, newspapers were not his only targets. "Sticks and Stones Are Flying As Bush-Dole Rivalry Heats," was the headline on Dionne's story. "Bush," he wrote, "in a change of tactics, was trying to answer the Iran question by pouncing on everyone in sight: On Mr. Dole, on the editor of *The Des Moines Register,* on Mr. Haig."

Bush tried to recover the next evening. During a precaucus debate sponsored by the newspaper and moderated by its editor, he lashed out at the paper and James Gannon for having raised the Iran-contra issue "as if I hadn't answered it." Then he added, to the lusty applause of an appreciative audience, "and I resent it, frankly." When one of the debate participants, Al Haig, scoffed at the Bush attack as "a little political terrorism," Bush demanded to know how *he* had advised *his* president during Watergate. "George," said Nixon's former chief of staff, "I wasn't asking the Republican party to support me as a candidate. You have an obligation."[60]

Bush's Iowa campaign manager, a small-town lawyer named George Wittgraf, who had already stirred things up by releasing under his own name a Rich Bond-penned memo that charged Bob Dole with being primarily interested in "pandering to North Carolina tobacco interests to take farm assistance away from the corn and soybean farmers of Iowa," now followed through with a Bond-written press release. Dole's talk about his poor Kansas childhood, Iowans were told, masked the $2.19 million income enjoyed by the senator and his wife from 1982 through 1986. Living in the posh Watergate complex and owning a Florida condominium were hardly signs of poverty, argued Wittgraf's paper. The Doles, now labeled as millionaires, were challenged to release their personal income taxes. Bush's staff then distributed a newspaper account of complaints on behalf of a blind trust of his wife, Elizabeth "Liddy" Hanford Dole. The press was also alerted to an old congressional inquiry into help the senator had given an ex-aide in the winning of a no-bid contract. Bush, after refusing to apologize to Dole when they met in the Senate, then said on national television that he saw nothing in the statement that was critical of Mrs. Dole. He explained that Wittgraf had put it out on his own because he was tired of hearing Bush "pounded and pounded" by the Dole campaign.[61]

Even better theater was Dan Rather's *CBS Evening News,* which, according to Atwater, gave George Bush his "best moment."[62] Their televised imbroglio took place only days after the Iowa debate. Rather was not only a fellow Texan and a local newsman when Bush was in the oil business, but he had been a guest at Bush's home and a tennis partner. The staff of the *CBS Evening News* had negotiated with the Bush people for an interview on the evening of January 25, just hours before Reagan was to deliver his State of the Union Address. Assuming it could follow its normal procedure, the show wanted to tape Bush's appearance in advance. The vice president and his staff, with Ailes especially insistent about that point, wanted a live interview, which would not make the final product subject to editing. *CBS Evening News* had to take it or leave it. They agreed to go along, expecting Rather to sandbag Bush before his vast television audience, and to eviscerate him on Iran-contra. Word about such plans reached at least three of Bush's aides, Fuller, Teeter, and Teeley. Advance promotional spots run by the network also indicated that they planned to do more than a mere "political profile."[63]

Ailes saw to it that Bush was prepared. If Rather got difficult, especially on the arms matter, he urged Bush to ask him how he'd like to have his whole career hang on the day he got so pissed off that a U.S. Open tennis match was delaying the start of his newscast that he was still on the phone complaining while, unknown to him, his program went on air and the screen was blank for seven minutes.[64]

That Tuesday evening, Bush sat at his Dirksen Office Building desk as Rather opened the program prior to the interview. Pointedly, without any subtlety, the show's setup piece was an indictment of Bush's Iran-contra role. Telling his audience that "many felt, rightly or wrongly, that he is hiding things people want to know," Rather listed the dates when Bush was present during arms-talks discussions. In trying to convince his audience that Bush could not have possibly been ignorant about the matter, he drew from Craig Fuller's notes of the meeting with Amiran Nir. "The record shows he never objected." How could he not have known what Donald Gregg knew? How could he not have known about Felix Rodriguez's activities? Gregg, on camera briefly, was quoted as saying that he never told Bush about the diversion because the information was "not vice presidential." Concluding the setup piece, Rather turned to Bush and noted that the president had fired Admiral Poindexter for withholding information. "Donald Gregg still serves as your trusted adviser. He was deeply involved in running arms to the contras and didn't inform you," said Rather to Bush before the vast television audience. "Why is Mr. Gregg still inside the White House and still a trusted adviser?"

Bush, staring straight ahead at the camera from his desk, replied, "Because I have confidence in him. And because this matter, Dan, as you well know, and your editors know, has been looked at by the ten-million-dollar study by the Senate and the House. It's been looked at by the Tower Commission." Then, getting more intense and after noting Rodriguez's sworn testimony and that he has been "totally vindicated," Bush said, "If this is a political profile for an election, I have a very different opinion as to what one should be. . . . I find this to be a rehash and a little bit, if you will excuse me, of misrepresentation on the part of CBS, which said you're doing a political profile on all the candidates, and then you come up with something that has been exhaustively looked into."

Rather, on air, looked pained. He brushed aside Bush about changing the topic, obviously eager to get on to his main point. "Let's talk about your record," he said.

Bush countered by saying that the only thing he was hiding was "what I told the president."

Then, in the closest thing to an admission of his role, and referring to the prolonged torture and death of hostage William Buckley, Bush said, "I went along with it—because you know why, Dan . . . when I saw Mr. Buckley, when I heard about Mr. Buckley being tortured to death, later admitted as a CIA chief. So if I erred, I erred on the side of trying to get those hostages out of there."[65]

Then he asked Rather, "How would you like it if I judged your whole career by those seven minutes when you walked off the set in New York?"

The newscaster virtually ignored the point and proceeded to pummel Bush, giving him no chance to respond under the persistent and vehement questioning. Then, running out of time, he had to end the interview abruptly.[66] "The bastard didn't lay a glove on me," Bush later said to his aides. "I ought to get combat pay for last night," he told a campaign crowd the next day.[67] Peggy Noonan, who had written for both Rather and Bush, recalled that "it was like being a child at the top of the stairs hearing her parents in a terrible fight."[68]

Rather later told about getting a personal taste of political power. A "very, very large phone bank assault was turned loose on CBS" by the Bush campaign, along with "political spin-doctoring" that included calling newspapers to say that station managers were demanding that CBS fire Rather.[69] The anchorman defended himself, while recognizing the criticism, both orchestrated and unsolicited, of his overbearing and even disrespectful handling of the vice president. He was just doing the job reporters must do, he explained, and was curt at the end because the clock had run out.[70]

Bush, however, had scored his points, and clearly. Hitting back at Rather was a "ten-strike" with the Republican right. No major television journalist had become so detested as an icon of the "liberal" media. Even more important, perhaps, was a performance that again sought to demolish the old "wimpish" image. Democratic political consultant David Garth said, "Bush showed courage, if the definition of courage is grace under pressure." Lee Atwater, asked by reporter Terence Smith whether Bush's performance was strategic, laughed and said, "We never talk about how we make sausage." "Who won?" Bill Safire asked rhetorically in his column. "Both did; this was no zero-sum battle in which Xerxes had to lose in order for Themistocles to win," he wrote. He then added, "And if George is a wimp or a lapdog, beware of wily wimps and ferocious lapdogs—tip your hand that you intend to run 'em the wrong way, and they'll be ready to go for your throat."[71]

Neither his success against Rather nor his fresh victory in Michigan during the crucial credentials battle over seating the state's seventy-seven delegates seemed to have much of an impact on the Iowa vote. It was Dole, not Bush, who was perceived as the more moderate of the two, so closely meshed was the vice president with Reagan's standing. Bush, along with the administration, was also on the defensive about narcotic trafficking. For the first time since the start of the cold war, Americans found an evil to substitute for communism: drugs. Heightened concerns about crime, particularly in the inner cities, centered on the problem of cocaine and the more recently introduced crack. The Reagan team, having made such a show about attacking the problem, was now especially vulnerable to charges of ineptitude. Dole, better able to stand apart from the administration, made the most of Bush's connections, including his function as head of the narcotics task force.[72] Bush's connections were too burdensome for Iowans. He lost, and lost big, coming up with 17,000 fewer votes than in 1980. But most stunning was his third-place finish, a full six percentage points behind the former evangelist, Pat Robertson, and twelve fewer than Dole, who received 37 percent of the six-way split. Bush left Iowa stripped "of his finest piece of political armor, the idea that he was Ronald Reagan's logical and legitimate if unannointed successor," wrote R. W. Apple Jr. *Boston Globe* columnist Mike Barnicle, who called Bush the nation's "First Mourner" because of his attendance at so many funerals, thought his campaign "might as well be under ice in Lake Winnipesaukee."[73]

Barnicle was premature. He failed to take into account the sheer disarray of the Dole campaign. The senator lacked either a smoothly functioning organization or shrewd financial strategies. He "never managed the art of running for president," reported E. J. Dionne Jr. "He never assembled, as Mr. Bush did, a group of aides whom he genuinely trusted. And never, beyond the use of the word *leadership,* did he develop an overarching vision to offer Republican voters." His campaign spending made no strategic sense. It laid out far too much too early, $119,733 for California's June primary as early as January 31, compared to Bush's $1,328, thereby shortchanging itself for an election that, in the end, turned out to be inconsequential. Dole was hurt even while winning in Iowa, as Robertson's second-place finish helped split the conservative vote, which crippled the candidacy of New York Congressman Jack Kemp. By separating himself from the president, much as that was helpful in Iowa, Dole blundered because he only helped to reinforce the image of George Bush as the true heir to Ronald Reagan.[74]

Lee Atwater understood how essential the support of the party's conservatives was for winning the nomination. Drawing from his own experience, nothing came more naturally to him than playing the "Southern strategy." No state was more prominent in that calculation than his own South Carolina, governed by Carroll A. Campbell Jr., a forty-seven-year-old Republican from Greenville whose victory in 1978 had helped to pave the way for Reagan's power over Capitol Hill. Atwater worked with Campbell to reinforce the state behind Bush, thereby making South Carolina central to his "firewall" strategy. A sweeping victory on "Super Tuesday," March 8, would preserve his standing in California from any damage that could be caused by losses in Iowa, New Hampshire, or other states.[75]

Only victories in New Hampshire, whose conservative governor, John Sununu, recruited by Atwater as early as 1986 to head Bush's primary campaign, and in the South, where his people also dominated state organizations, could keep his nomination alive. A loss in New Hampshire, especially coming so soon after the defeat in Iowa, could bury his candidacy. Sununu was not about to let that happen. That New England state's localized political structure made it what Sununu liked to call a "see me, touch me, feel me state," where "everybody has either run for office or their spouse has run for office, or their neighbor to the left or right has run for office." Sununu seized the small-state advantage for playing retail politics at its purist form, which, at that grassroots level, was most effective. Setting up "a series of opportunities" for Bush enabled him to shake what Sununu estimated as perhaps 50,000 hands during the year before the primary.[76] Victory in the South, with sixteen primaries due on "Super Tuesday," was a test that still lay ahead. The region was Reagan's base and Republicans were no longer unusual in its statehouses. But to go with Bush was to go against history. Not since Martin Van Buren in 1836 had a sitting vice president been elected to the presidency.

Another bugaboo, especially common to Republicans, raised speculation anew. Could establishment Republicans, with their probusiness bias and upper-class base, risk nominating a patrician? The country club boys, a political scientist once wrote, had to have a "scoundrel" as a "front." Only Democrats could get away with an FDR or a JFK. "Bob Dole is one of us," the senator's banners accordingly boasted. "Nobody handed me anything," Dole told his crowds. He had "no rich and powerful parents."

"Hey," was Bush's characteristic response, "in my family loyalty is a strength. It's not a character flaw," he added, taking a jab at his opponent's divorce and remarriage.

"The two men really don't like each other a lot," observed James M. Perry of *The Wall Street Journal.*[77]

Bush's efforts to display "everyman" touches took the form of pitching horseshoes, (at which he excelled), listening to country music (which he traced back to his father's Silver Dollar Quartet), and eating taco salads and pork rinds (an acquired taste). In Houston, he loved taking friends to a rustic Texas barbecue hangout, Otto's, on Memorial Drive. To his annoyance, they were considered affectations. He resented insistence that he really had to conform to class stereotypes, and, on the campaign stump, his most unnatural and unconvincing efforts to reach voters came when he worked at reasserting that he was both an ordinary guy and a right-winger.[78]

In New Hampshire, he was persuaded, by Ailes, Bob Teeter, and by Barbara, since he was two points down in the polls, to give the go-ahead for an attack ad charging a two-faced Dole with being unable to say "no" to taxes and straddling on the issue. It ran only once, claimed Pete Teeley, and on one station "because we couldn't buy any time," so its contribution to the outcome has "been badly overstated." But, in winning his agreement to air the "senator straddle" ad, Bush's handlers overcame their candidate's ability to "go through a campaign without saying one detrimental thing about his opponent."[79]

He was in more congenial territory. New Hampshire Democrats were among Reagan's strongest admirers, which gave Bush a great advantage. He also had other shrewd and energetic help from Governor Sununu, who used his personal control over the distribution of vanity license plates to mobilize the Bush drive.[80] Ted Williams contributed by appearing with Bush, especially in heavily Republican Carroll County up north. At the eleventh hour, conservative icon Barry Goldwater was flown in from Arizona in Bob Mosbacher's private jet. Before a group of senior citizens in Portsmouth, Bush agreed that he was "a little more taciturn than I should be," and added, "Let me tell you—don't take that private side of me for lack of passion, a lack of conviction about the United States of America."[81]

He *was* one of their own, a true New Englander, not merely a Yankee elitist. Having already created "Bushisms," such as describing being in trouble as "deep doo-doo," he delighted the press when he defended the Alaska pipeline by saying, "the caribou love it. They rub up against it and they have babies. There are more caribou in Alaska than you can shake a stick at." The press teased him long after he tried to explain his Iowa straw poll loss at Ames by saying, "A lot of the people that support me, they were off at the air show, they were at their daughters' coming-out parties, or teeing up at the golf course for that all-important last round."[82] As vice president, especially, he was the limousine and motorcade candidate. Sununu, his populist streak intact, "took the campaign staff by the nape of its neck," as Marlin Fitzwater has written, even placing Bush in the blue-collar mode of driving an 18-wheeler around the parking lot at Cuzzin Ritchie's Truck Stop in Hampstead.[83] Seeking to add more substance to his pitch, he charged Dole with failing to provide leadership in the Senate on reducing the federal deficit and declared himself in favor of an oil import fee and against higher taxes.[84]

Bush's February 16 victory was solid. He came in nine points ahead of runner-up Dole and far ahead of the trailing candidates, Jack Kemp, Pete Du Pont, Pat Robertson, and Al Haig, who had withdrawn early. "Tonight, I somehow feel that I have a lot in common with Mark Twain," Bush told his cheering supporters. "Reports of my death were greatly exaggerated."[85] He was where he thought he should have been all along, the front-runner. Democratic primary voters, meanwhile, went for Governor Michael Dukakis, of neighboring Massachusetts.

"Super Tuesday" all but locked it up for both potential nominees. Bush, while taking 57 percent of the votes cast on that day, swept all the contested states. Dole vowed to remain in the race at least through the Illinois primary. When Bush also took that state, and three-quarters of its delegates, Dole gave up. For the senator from Kansas and a good many other Republicans, Bush's viability was surprising. Many had expected him to succumb to his liabilities, especially from the Iran-contra fallout, his need to defend the administration, and the reappearance in headlines of an old Bush skeleton, Manuel Noriega, which compounded Bush's vulnerability on the drug issue. Yet, helped by the talents of Atwater and Ailes, who amazed Bush aides by his ability to compose advertising copy even as he rode in the back of a limousine, the candidate showed surprising staying power, impressing even seasoned observers as a charming gentleman, a brisk and pleasant campaigner. His obvious loyalty to Reagan made him the clear favorite among those who wanted "another four years" for The Gipper.[86] Finally, a strong victory in Pennsylvania on April 26 gave Bush 1,139 delegates, effectively clinching the nomination.[87]

He had won the fight, but many still held that he had not found his voice. Without drawing his own distinctions from the president, simple loyalty would not be enough. Whatever he said and did, he was still George Bush. A fresh *New York Times/CBS News* poll showed 60 percent of the so-called Reagan Democrats preparing to return to their traditional political home.[88] Another survey, taken for *Time* magazine, found that Dukakis could beat him whether the Democratic ticket had either Al Gore or Jesse Jackson as his running mates.[89] A Gallup poll completed just before the Pennsylvania voting showed that Bush had a sliver of a statistical edge on Dukakis.[90] At that moment, *The New York Times* quoted a bit of advice recently given to Bush by Richard Nixon. The former president had told him that "a Republican could afford neither to alienate his conservative base nor to waste time in the fall campaign courting their support." Then, according to the report, he told Bush, "You can't win the election just with these people. But you can't win the election without these people, as I learned."[91]

The imperatives of his vice presidency were threatening to backfire. A new report disclosed that Everett Briggs, while the American ambassador to Panama, had briefed Vice President Bush about Noriega's involvement in drug trafficking in 1985. When Briggs promptly confirmed the information, there were clear limits to any further evasion.[92] Nevertheless, he remained ambiguous, first telling a group of high school students in Vandalia, Ohio, that it had been the administration that had moved to seek indictments against Noriega "when it became demonstrably clear" about his involvement with drugs, and later retreating to his original point that he had never been aware of even such rumors until the indictment.[93]

Behind the scenes, however, Bush carried the fight to Reagan as he never had before. He fairly exploded over the issue. He had never taken on the president so directly.[94] The new crisis over Noriega was almost a year old, ever since the strongman announced that he was not about to honor an old commitment to step down by April 1989; no way, and nobody could touch him. The head of the Panama Defense Force controlled all the lethal force. His rivals for the succession let loose with details about his crimes. Panamanians, shaken by the revelations and suffering from a troubled economy, which was not helped when Reagan imposed economic sanctions, took to the streets of the capital with massive protests. Noriega used them as an excuse to squash further protests, even putting down a coup attempt. The U.S. Senate, sensitive to the reaction over drugs and what was being revealed about the CIA's Central-American "asset," passed a nonbinding resolution that called on Noriega to resign pending a "public accounting." Jesse Helms of North Carolina attached a memorandum to an intelligence bill requiring the CIA to disclose what the agency knew about Noriega's involvement with drugs, arms dealing, money laundering, human rights abuses, and his relationship with Cuba and the Sandinistas.[95] Noriega remained defiant, "hanging on by his fingernails," as one advocate of U.S. military intervention, Elliott Abrams, put it.[96] He rejected a "retirement" plan suggested by José Blandon, his top nonmilitary intelligence aide, and spurned a more generous proposal that was offered by Daniel J. Murphy. The retired admiral and ex-Bush chief of staff had flown to Panama City in the company of Tongsun Park, the businessman who had been associated with the Koreagate scandals of the 1970s, apparently at Noriega's invitation and unconnected with Bush at that time. Not even today is it clear whether the mission was a private matter of two businessmen scouting out "investment opportunities" or sanctioned by the U.S. government, as Blandon believed.[97] Noriega's defiance led to his formal indictment by federal prosecutors in Miami, Florida, on February 4, 1988, on thirteen counts of narcotics trafficking and racketeering.[98]

Coming just four days before the Iowa caucuses, it could not have been better timed to play a role in preconvention politics. Reagan, who had made clear his preference for the vice president, was, at the same time, hesitant about military intervention as long as there was no direct threat to the canal or other American interests, choosing instead to wage economic war, better characterized as a skirmish. He did dispatch 1,300 additional American troops in early April. But the president appeared to be searching for ways to make peaceful concessions, even agreeing to Noriega's right to remain in Panama if he retired.[99]

Bush was in a bind. As one aide said about the high price of loyalty to Reagan, "George Bush can't make a speech these days with any credibility about drugs if we're dealing with the drug kingpin of the world." Shultz, however, felt free to protest, and that he did. "The president, being the president, was surprised to discover what his own people were saying."[100]

Bush stewed. Essentially, he was in a dilemma, torn between advocating vigorous action and thwarting the president or rocking his relationship by dissenting. On the first of May, a Sunday, Colin Powell, a three-star general and Reagan security adviser, called on Bush to have him read a proposal prepared by the secretary of state. Shultz's document was succinct: sanctions and the indictments would be lifted if Noriega agreed to get out of Panama, which, according to Powell's impression, seemed quite reasonable to Bush.[101]

In Los Angeles later that week, Bush told an audience that "Drug dealers are domestic terrorists, killing kids and cops, and they should be treated as such." In the speech, which won wide attention, he also said, "I won't bargain with terrorists, and I won't bargain with drug dealers either, whether they're on U.S. or foreign soil."[102] While in the city, he also visited L.A. Police Chief Daryl Gates. He told the chief about the terms being proposed to get rid of Noriega. They were too easy, Gates told him. How could indictments be dropped after so many police officers were putting their lives on the line every day in the war against drugs?[103]

Bush had heard enough. "I have never been so sure of anything in my life," he told Powell, neatly ducking away from what he had given the general a "checkoff" on just a few days earlier, "and I will do whatever I have to do to kill this deal."[104]

He was back in Washington and with Reagan the following weekend. In the second-floor residence of the White House, Powell has written, "Bush did something none of us had ever seen him do before. He argued with the president directly in front of the rest of us. The deal was bad, bad, bad, and the president should not go through with it," but Reagan was "unmovable." On Wednesday, despite such objections, the chief executive announced that he was going along with the deal. It was, said Elliott Abrams, the only "command decision" he made on Panama while he was president.[105] Further negotiations eventually collapsed. Noriega held firm, dropping only from the headlines.

That bit of business taken care of, at least for the moment, Bush got back to the Maine coast for the Memorial Day weekend, and promptly took care of another piece of damage control. With Kennebunkport becoming a huge tourist attraction, the locals anticipated an economic bonanza from Bush's political success. His Secret Service protection, totaling more manpower than the village's entire police force, had raised the possibility of having to shut down the harbor around the Bush compound for enhanced security. Bush learned that one group, the lobstermen, feared that his success might sacrifice their livelihoods. He met that public relations problem head-on by assuring the fishermen that, if it "became a choice between whether these lobstermen could fish in this bay or I would not come to this place I love, I would not come here." The papers carried his words, and Bush was pleased that "it went over very well in Maine." On Monday, he stood with his family in a light rain and watched as the annual holiday parade wound through Dock Square at the center of "downtown." He was photographed carrying his granddaughter, Ellie LeBlond, Doro's toddler. Kennebunkport's most famous person then gave a little talk in praise of the local boy whose life was lost in the Vietnam War. That sort of thing, he pointed out, showed the importance of a strong national defense.[106]

He was always glad to get back to Kennebunkport. "I love being here," he noted that evening. "I sleep like a log. I go to bed very, very early, and it's wonderful." At that point of the 1988 campaign, Bush found himself so "lifted up" by the "majesty" of the place that he found himself wondering, "Why do we do it all? Why, why, why—" Why ever leave this place? He answered his own question: "I've got to fulfill this mission."[107]

CHAPTER EIGHTEEN

"A Flag Too Far"

%

M emorial Day weekend, 1988: President Reagan, in Moscow for his fourth and final summit meeting with Mikhail Gorbachev, was enjoying his "role of a lifetime," his charm seducing Soviet intellectuals as he never could their American counterparts. The editor of a Soviet weekly lauded the American president as a "normal man." "We want to have a normal man as the leader of our state." The performances, scripted by White House aides for both men, was like a Cecil B. DeMille Hollywood epic set in Red Square and St. Catherine's Hall, observed the American president.[1] He and Gorbachev then signed the agreement to carry out the Intermediate Nuclear Forces accord, which concluded their mutual efforts toward international cooperation. Reagan had made his mark in helping to phase out the cold war.[2]

In Maine, that same weekend, the atmosphere was far less mellow, a "low time," as those who were there remembered it. The G-6 was on hand, along with an assortment of other advisers and specialists, to lay plans for the convention to develop themes for the course of the campaign. They assumed that Bush needed far less preparation on issues relative to international matters, so they emphasized domestic policies as well as the logistics of campaign politics. Gallup's mid May figures showed Bush sixteen points under Dukakis, his all but certain Democratic rival for November. The governor's ability to keep his political distance from Jesse Jackson helped to reaffirm the image of moderation that had marked his two administrations in Massachusetts. A third of the Democrats who had voted Republican in 1984 were seen as sliding back toward their own party.[3] Never a sixties-style liberal, a personally frugal man and far more of a pragmatic functionary than an ideologue, Dukakis had been an effective governor. "It's a record that combines progressive values with a sense of fiscal responsibility," Dukakis responded to suggestions that his outlook was vague.[4] He lost after one term, and then made a successful comeback that deepened his respect for politics and strengthened his administrative skills. Dukakis was, at that point, a formidable threat to the vice president.

Bush heard Bob Teeter's warning that the deficit could even get to the 33 percent level, which was enough to give him a "semipanic feeling about being behind in the polls" and the prospects for reversing the trend. "People call all the time," he noted that Saturday, "and tell our people what's going wrong. You read the articles in the paper by [Robert] Novak and others about the campaign and disarray." It was only temporary, he told himself. There was a long way to go and everything would fall into place.[5]

Fortunately for Bush, Dukakis's record had left him with some potentially explosive baggage, stuff that was easily exploitable in the climate of backlash against the sixties. Starting with the Kennebunkport sessions, the Bush managers planned to do exactly that. All they needed was for the vice president to go along, get his campaign off the mat by going on the offensive, taking the negative, red-meat approach. Nothing was more consistent with the Reaganite thrust of the eighties than to reduce whatever could pass for liberalism to a denigrated and ridiculed symbol, the "L" word, as the president had been doing.[6]

At the moment, Dukakis—for all his years in public life—was not a familiar name to much of the American public, and the vice president couldn't work himself up enough to take the governor very seriously. In spite of the polls, Bush's key aides remained confident of ultimately beating Dukakis. The squad of researchers under James Pinkerton, working at Atwater's direction, dug into Dukakis's background. He was, for all his caution, vulnerable on several items. He was a member of the American Civil Liberties Union, the advocacy group that was so closely associated with the constitutional defense against state-ordered prayers in public schools. He had vetoed a Massachusetts death penalty bill. He had invoked the First Amendment to justify killing a legislative bill mandating that school children recite The Pledge of Allegiance. He supported gun control and had a "soft" record on national defense. He let legal technicalities delay cleaning up Boston Harbor under the provisions of the Clean Water Act; despite his pious words about the environment, he could be blamed for its continued pollution.

But it was the case of Willie Horton that placed him most at risk. "If there was a better case than Horton, fine," remembered Pinkerton, "but the Horton one was sort of obvious. We were driven by what we saw in the media. It was already out there." Asked about Willie Horton eight years later, George Bush remarked laconically, "We picked up a story that won a Pulitzer Prize."[7]

Horton, who had previously served a three-year term in South Carolina for assault with intent to kill, had been convicted in Massachusetts for the murder and dismemberment of a teenage gas station attendant. Sentenced to life for a first-degree crime, and confined to the Northeast Correctional Center in Concord, he was one of four prisoners ineligible for a parole who were given a weekend furlough during the first two terms of Dukakis's governorship. The convict made his way to Oxon Hill, Maryland, where he held a twenty-eight-year-old man captive with repeated beatings and stabbings. When the victim's fiancée returned, she was assaulted and raped.[8]

Investigative work on the case by the *Lawrence Eagle-Tribune* ultimately produced nearly two hundred articles and helped to fan local anger. The subsequent furor was predictable. Dukakis defended state furloughs in the name of "rehabilitation," an objective sought by the gradual "reintegration" of inmates back into society. Not until April of 1988 did he end the program, and then only under pressure from popular outrage and a rebellious legislature. But the damage had already been done.

Most states, along with the federal prison system, had some sort of temporary release system. But only the Bay State made it available to lifers. The exceptional nature of the incident became known nationally when an account was shown by CBS television on December 2, 1987. Senator Al Gore, the Democratic presidential candidate, became the first politician to use it by putting Dukakis on the defensive during a debate before New York State's primary election.

The Dukakis record was test-marketed before the campaign team arrived at Kennebunkport that Memorial Day weekend. Using focus groups, then coming into vogue, Bush's political consultants gauged the reactions of target voters, Reagan Democrats. Two sets of fifteen were brought together in a Paramus, New Jersey, conference room, where their reactions were monitored electronically and by observation through one-way mirrors. Both groups confirmed to the satisfaction of the Bush team how working-class voters would respond when informed about the governor's record. "I realized right then," Atwater later told reporters, ". . . that the sky was the limit on Dukakis's negatives."[9]

The Willie Horton they saw could have been supplied by "central casting." His angry-looking black face, viewed via prison mug shots, was emblematic of the national crime issue and a dramatic confirmation of what everybody had heard about poverty and urban ghettos. The focus groups verified the campaign's possession of its own "ultimate weapon," and all the risks that went with it. Having "the bomb" was one thing; using it was another. Horton's race made it both more devastating and dangerous, which Bush's aides readily pointed out. They made no attempt to minimize their worry about creating an ugly backlash. "There was no effort that I know of of anybody trying to exploit the race," said Ron Kaufman, "particularly the people who understood it best, like Lee Atwater." Atwater, agreed Jim Cicconi, worried that it could become "racist" and that it might backfire. Pinkerton, the staff's intellectual and somewhat maverick conservative, recalled that "nobody would tell Bush. He would have been upset."[10]

The findings, when seen by Bush at Kennebunkport, bolstered those who were urging an attack campaign. Atwater, recalled as the brashest of the aides, warmed to the prospect by vowing to "strip the bark off the little bastard" and "make Willie Horton his running mate." After hearing that Jesse Jackson had visited Dukakis's home in Brookline, the young strategist suggested that perhaps the governor would put "this Willie Horton on the ticket after all is said and done."[11]

Pressure on Bush also came from what those around him thought was long overdue. "It was like mobilizing an army," Rich Bond told interviewer Michael L. Gillette, "a very disciplined operation and people were thinking ahead as to what the events would be and what the opportunities would be." He could and should go forth as a loyal Reaganite, but he could and should go forth as a credible candidate on his own. He could not be seen as a mere extension of the president. Even as late as that holiday weekend, he held back. "When I'm the nominee, I'll say what I want to say, but right now I'm still vice president and I haven't won the nomination yet, and I'm waiting until I win the nomination," Bond remembered him arguing. He couldn't change just yet. He'd been loyal for seven-and-a-half years. "I'm not going to stop being loyal," he told Bates. "That is a matter of principle; it's the right thing to do." "God, you've really got to make a break and be your own man," insisted his friend and aide. Craig Fuller, Bush's chief of staff, held out the options he had for striking at Dukakis. "It was always Bush's own personal theory that he was a blank tablet by virtue of the vice presidency," pointed out Bond, "and that he would step out and do his 'declaration of being' at the convention." That's where people would really begin to focus on the issues, anyway. Meanwhile, Bush was becoming convinced that the Massachusetts governor was just "a cool little guy from the liberal fringe."[12]

Your friend George, Atwater told Bob Mosbacher, should look at himself in the mirror when he shaves in the morning and ask, "What can I do to advance the cause of George Bush today." Mosbacher, less convinced that George would actually convert to the kind of fighter it took, told the consultant to forget it. "I've known this guy over thirty years and you say this of my friend. You're going to have to campaign around the fact that the farthest George Bush is going to go in that direction is to get up and look in the mirror and say, 'What can I do for America today?' That may sound corny to you, but that's the kind of guy he is. He's always been that way. He's always been a team player. You could cut him very deep and he would say, 'I'm doing this because I believe I'm really serving my country.' "[13]

That weekend, George Bush also had his fill of what he needed: an outpouring of friends. His political sense made him anxious about how those closest to him would get along with the hard-shells who were thinking of a White House under Bush as four more years of Reagan conservatism.

The president himself, who had given off mixed signals even when saying he wanted his vice president as his successor, had to be made to recognize that; his blessing had to be passed on to his own people. Former ABC-TV president Tom Arnold told Bush he tried to get that message through to Walter and Lee Annenberg, hoping he could use that route to convince Reagan. But there were wrinkles, the petty squabbling that Bush hated so much, the gossipy minutia of politics, the backbiting, the "inside baseball." There were problems, Lee

Annenberg reminded Arnold. Just a phone call to Nancy Reagan brought out the First Lady's jealousy, her resentment that, no matter what, she could never be in a "class" with Barbara. Bush, hearing the whole thing from Arnold, was troubled once again. He had always known about the tension, but that sort of confirmation made it even harder to swallow. It had bothered him earlier in the spring, when a so-called "blessing" of his candidacy by the president was so terse and tepid that it actually backfired in the press, and he and his people understood that the wording was the product of some "reductive surgery" by Nancy.[14] Perhaps "there has been some tension that we Bushes have never understood," he dictated in his diary.[15] That sort of thing would surely restrain the president from firing up much enthusiasm among his own people for the Bush campaign. But, then again, one could see that Reagan had personal problems. Nancy and Ron's distance from their children, unlike the good fortune enjoyed by George and Barbara with theirs, was revealing. "Here's this warm, wonderful human being," thought Bush, "who's short on love and what we take for granted in our family. It's amazing."[16]

Then there was Lee. The Atwater problem continued to be worrisome, almost as though the Bush's had yet another son, but one who required careful looking after. The political director was worried about rumors that Jim Baker was about to leave Treasury to take over the campaign. Not that he feared Baker, but having the secretary also meant having his staff. His right-hand aide, Margaret Tutwiler, could become the campaign's press secretary. Atwater, Baker told Bush, hoped to kill that one off by leaking word of it to the press. The situation, Bush noted, was "driving Lee right up a wall."[17]

But the vice president's announcements from Kennebunkport also included the appointment of Sheila Tate as his campaign's press secretary, with Jim Lake as his senior communications advisor. Tate had handled the press for Nancy Reagan, and Lake worked as press secretary for both of the president's campaigns. With one stroke, Bush attempted to mollify both Atwater and the First Lady. Having Tate up front could not hurt him with what the press insisted on calling his "gender gap" problem, which really pissed him off.[18]

The vice president was quick to note that, despite everything, the Reaganites and Bushies "did beautifully" together, but the papers continued to hammer away at the downside. "We'll never satisfy the press and their incessant quest for detail upon detail," Bush decided with some despair. They expected something like a ten-point program or a fifteen-point program, something for good headlines, but, anyway, "the general themes are working."[19] He would not be "pressured" to spell everything out, he told reporters who staked out the compound all four days. Bush, they heard, had rejected all warnings to revamp his campaign. After a four-hour meeting with economic advisers Martin S. Feldstein of Harvard and Michael S. Boskin of Stanford, during which he was told that higher taxes might be necessary to reduce the federal deficit, Bush told the newsmen that "I just simply said I was not going to propose a tax increase"; nor, he added, was anybody around him supporting one. On the contrary, he explained, some advisers had prepared a freeze in spending to enable him to balance out increased funding for some programs with cuts elsewhere.[20]

No matter what he did, it seemed, the media was rough, with *Newsweek* still the bitchiest. He was so angered by a cover story called "Fighting the Wimp Factor" in October that he cut out access to reporters working on the magazine's book about the campaign. Now, *Newsweek* was out with a story that made it look like Jim Baker was about to become a hero by saving Bush from his own disaster. "It's kind of typical of *Newsweek* on me [*sic*]," he complained. "It's a terrible period getting kicked around and criticized all the time." But, at least, he could take some real comfort that the country would sober up when they heard all about Dukakis.[21]

How that would happen he kept secret. The Kennebunkport meetings laid the foundation for what became the most slashing presidential campaign attacks since Harry Truman made a whipping boy out of the "Do-nothing Eightieth Congress." The "Give 'em hell, Harry" style that did so much in later years to make a folk hero out of Truman became the Bush solution.

Campaigns themselves had become more visible since Truman's day. In an era of increased media competition, with restraints loosened by revelations about JFK's private behavior, Vietnam War reportage, and Watergate scoops, little was off limits, whether staking out Gary Hart's rendezvous with a young model in a Washington townhouse, nailing Senator Joseph Biden for using plagiarized speech material, or fashioning "dirty tricks" against Ed Muskie. Such politics were hardly new in American history, but relaxed standards combined with more advanced technology worked to encourage "taking the low road."

Bush was still haunted by his last performance as Reagan's running mate. "Craig," he turned to Fuller, "I have to become more like Ronald Reagan, but I can't go all the way." He had to become more nearly as effective as the president, but his style was different. He had to be more disciplined. He couldn't delegate as much. "I can't surrender it like to Deaver, as Reagan did." "You never should," Fuller told him. "I'm not here to say that I have to run a staff like Reagan's staff," said the vice president's chief. "But I am here to say that if you're serious about trying to achieve an objective, you've got to have a team of people. You're going to manage." If you were a professional tennis player or a professional golfer, he argued, "the most natural thing in the world would be to have a coach that would insure that when you stood up there and served the tennis balls you'd perform well eighty or ninety-five percent of the time. That's what we have to do. The issue is not remaking you, or getting you to change the way you comb your hair or wear your glasses. The issue is how do we get the performance that I've seen and others have seen ten percent of the time to be what you just do as a matter of course." He advised him to put aside Wednesday afternoons for speech coaching lessons by Roger Ailes at the vice president's house.[22]

Bush agreed. Fuller bought a videocassette recorder and a camcorder. In addition to having the training sessions on film, he tracked their weekly progress. Well over two-thirds of the sessions involved trading jokes. Laughing and getting Bush to relax was an essential part of the conditioning, almost as important as training him to avoid lapsing into a voice often described as squeaky. As for the balance of time given over to his delivery, that "was about one hundred percent more coaching than anyone else could give him to improve his game."[23] However much he worked with Ailes, he was not an actor. "I can't be as good as Ronald Reagan on conviction," he pointed out to Maureen Dowd.[24]

He could never surrender as much to handlers as did Reagan, but he began to realize that he had few options if he wanted to win. Ailes knew how to move him in that direction, to accept staging that projected strength instead of weakness. Just as it was better to be identified with horseshoes, country music, and pork rinds, so was it more useful to be pictured hitting the waves with the full power of his Mercury engines than gliding along in his sailboat. Handling his craft off the Kennebunkport coast was all right, but aerial views of Walker's Point was overdoing the portrait of affluence. If admissions of wealth were allowed, it had best be of the "self-made" variety, especially for a Republican.

To demonstrate fidelity to Reagan and the cause of his "revolution," one could hardly get too far right. Further encouraged by the president's touch, the political center had shifted away from what Dukakis was calling "progressivism." What had passed as "reactionary" had begun to be described as "conservative." The Republicanism of Bush's earlier years was changing; another generational gap he had to overcome if he was going to get anywhere. He likes the polarizing language "when he hears it now," wrote journalist Fred Barnes. "Eight years of Ronald Reagan has done that, and a lot more, to Bush."[25]

It was agreed at Kennebunkport that Ailes would be at his side for some thirty minutes of prep time before every encounter with the press or major TV appearances, all to help reinforce his masculinity and antipathy to mushy moderation.[26]

A "campaign Bush" emerged. He opened a no-holds-barred attack on Dukakis at the Texas Republican Convention on June 9, thrilling 5,000 delegates. They stomped and cheered as he lashed out at the "crimes" of Dukakis and charged that the Democrat was nothing but a standard old-style sixties liberal who was "born in Harvard Yard's boutique."

After that rousing performance, he suddenly sounded like himself again. His campaign is almost "schizophrenic" in the way he alternates between partisan verbal fisticuffs and turning the other cheek in the battle against Dukakis, noted Gerald M. Boyd, who covered him for *The New York Times*. "When will the real George Bush stand up?" asked Morton Zuckerman in *U.S. News & World Report*. He had not, Bush told a reporter, "sorted out perfectly" the political accommodations needed to counter the wimp image by blending tough dialogue with his conventional Ivy League personality. He later acknowledged to his Episcopal minister in Houston, John Stevens, that he had taken "some of the far-right positions to get elected." "He hates it," Ailes told Maureen Dowd, "but he knows we'd be getting killed if we didn't go negative."[27]

But he could not permit himself to believe that he had been manipulated by Ailes or anyone else. The anger, the outrage, the righteousness were genuinely part of his campaign mode. The more he thought about his rival, the more he saw Dukakis as a sixties-style liberal in pragmatic drag. What the American public did not know about the governor's record was precisely what would damn him. He was a stupid, soft-headed idealist, and dangerous, worth slamming. When Cardinal Bernard Law of Boston flew in by helicopter, Bush confided to the prelate that Dukakis really troubled him, particularly his stand on family issues like "gay marriage and that sort of thing."[28]

He had to toughen up against the anarchy of the left. Society couldn't live that way. And the public, decent, everyday, middle-class American citizens cared about that, too. Ever since the mid sixties, their anger had helped conservatives to turn back the liberal tide. It was still happening, and at all levels of government. He was convinced, he told himself, that "we're going to have to start getting the issues into focus." Yet, when Peggy Noonan, who had been helping him with speeches since New Hampshire, showed him a draft of what he should say to those Texas Republicans, he hesitated. It was not right for him, too extreme. Nixon had warned him to let others throw the dirt at Dukakis. But his own people were saying that he should get out and fight.[29]

He had yet to prove himself with those Republicans still skeptical about his fidelity to Reaganism. "Voters want a decisive leader who is in touch with the people and who has an idea of where he wants to take the country," argued Richard A. Viguerie. Conservative working people, who had helped to make the Reagan vote decisive, had the option of not turning out at all if Bush's best is to minimize the importance of what he calls "the vision thing," wrote the conservative activist and publicist.[30] Not only to Viguerie, but to passionate critics on the far right, Bush had to do more, more, more. "His campaign acts as if Reagan is an embarrassment from whom Bush must 'distance' himself," charged a *National Review* editorial entitled "Where is George?"[31] There was no moving such people, even when he delivered Peggy Noonan's demagogic denunciation of Dukakis at Houston. The "lapdog" had to become what Congressman Robert Dornan of California had hoped he'd become, a "pit bull."[32]

Pumped up but tired, the day not yet over, the vice president retreated with Ailes to the relaxed surroundings of Otto's. Next in line for the evening was facing cameras for Ted Koppel's *Nightline* show. Looking into a lens and hearing a faceless host, Bush had little idea of what to expect but, as with Dan Rather, he was prepared to be on the defensive. The program began with a set piece that showed his earlier confrontation with Rather. Koppel then bore down without letup, on Noriega*, explosive revelations of possible corruption that surrounded Attorney General Ed Meese, Ollie North, and, Bush recalled, "almost anything negative you can think of . . . issue after issue." Three times, Bush called the unseen interviewer "Dan," until, finally they placed a sign in front of the lens to remind him that he was talking to "Ted." He had, he later decided, succumbed to "fatigue and Freudian association."[33]

He got a dose of good news in early July. James C. McKay, the special prosecutor looking into Attorney General Meese's ties to the Wedtech Corporation, a New York City defense contractor, announced the conclusion of his fourteen-month investigation. Bush's continued embarrassment as a result of administration scandals, including Meese's activities, had led him to appeal directly to the president on June 8. They met in the Oval Office, where the vice president explained that he was "really having a problem with the Ed Meese thing, and that it was killing us out there, and killing a lot of Republicans." ". . . just shook it off," Bush noted afterward, "but I made it very clear that Meese was a terrible problem for us." It was obvious that the president intended to stand by his man until he quit on his own.[34] On July 4, McKay reported that the attorney general "probably violated the criminal law" on four occasions. Meese's subsequent resignation lifted one more burden.[35]

Those at the Kennebunkport sessions were well aware, as was Atwater, that Baker would eventually command the campaign. The treasury secretary was not crazy about the change, but he had more than just a friendly stake in a Bush victory; he would take over the State Department. Bush confirmed the arrangement on a Wyoming fishing trip with his old friend in mid July.

That outing in the Rockies conceded the spotlight to the Democrats, then convening to ratify the Dukakis nomination. In a widely praised move, which Nixon assured Bush was a master stroke by the opposition, the governor also chose Lloyd Bentsen as his running mate. As popular as that turned out to be, and as useful to the Dukakis campaign, nothing that happened within Atlanta's Omni Center roused the Democrats as much as the anti-Bush taunts by Ann Richards and Ted Kennedy. Richards, then Texas's state treasurer, belted out what became the most repeated one-liner of their convention. Bush, she told the appreciative throng, was "born with a silver foot in his mouth." Kennedy, not to be outdone, led them in a chorus that mocked Reagan's loyal vice president by repeatedly asking, "Where was

*Covertly, the Reagan administration had actually imposed economic sanctions against Noriega and even planned a coup to get rid of him, only to end up by aborting the project after the *Washington Post* ran a leaked story on July 29. Cf., Eytan Gilboa, "The Panama Invasion Revisited: Lessons for the Use of Force in the Post Cold-War Era," *Political Science Quarterly*, vol. 110, pp. 550–51.

George?" A new Gallup survey, taken at the end of the Democratic convention, showed Bush seventeen points behind Dukakis.[36]

Soon thereafter, Baker arrived at the Bush campaign's Washington headquarters in the Woodward Building on Fifteenth Street and took over. "I remember that we all got convened on the first floor in this big conference room," recalled Janet Mullins, "and Lee [Atwater] was there, looking a little green, trying to figure out whether this was really going to be okay with him or not." Baker went on to "praise the hell out of Lee" and declared that there was no need to change the operation from top to bottom. Rich Bond found Baker the "most awesome person" he had ever worked for, precise, decisive, an "overwhelming presence" who "just exudes self-confidence." Detached when he wanted to be, capable of aristocratic imperiousness, he was, nevertheless "very sensitive to Lee's ego and standing . . . " He was also signaling his authority over the operation. The days of the G-6 were over. There was "a clear number one in charge."[37]

Everything now was Bush's, or so it seemed, the party, the platform, the delegates, the convention. The polls indicated a sea change. A "presidential trial heat" taken by the Gallup organization showed the gap narrowing to 7 percent by the end of the first week in August. He noted that a preconvention *ABC News* survey actually had him in the lead. The sample was small, all right, but certainly welcome. Even some in the hard-edged press were managing "a little more pleasant view of me."[38]

The most evident change involved Bush himself, his obvious new-found independence. Janet Mullins remembered how everybody talked "about the change between George Bush preconvention and *at* the convention. It was like he threw off all the robes and here he was [as] the candidate."[39]

Bush's political latitude was greatest in choosing a running mate. "The process and manner will both be important," Bob Teeter reminded him, "because it will get a great deal of attention in the press and leave the impression with the voters of what kind of leader and decision-maker you are."[40]

Finally, after going over and over an assortment of names and scribbling them on legal pads, he was ready to share them with his group and Bob Kimmitt, Baker's man, for running background checks and FBI clearances. The most obvious possibility was Bob Dole. Dole's wife, Elizabeth Hanford Dole, Reagan's former secretary of transportation, was also named, along with the more plausible Jack Kemp. Not especially revealing for its political or geographic coloration, Bush's list also extended to include Carroll Campbell, Lamar Alexander, Peter Dominici, Alan Simpson, Jack Danforth, Richard Lugar, John McCain, Bill Armstrong, Thad Cochran, Lynn Martin, John Sununu, George Deukmejian, John Ashcroft, and Kay Orr. Another was Senator J. Danforth Quayle of Indiana, known more casually as "Dan."

The Hoosier had intrigued Bush for over a month before the convention. From the outset, he knew that he wanted "somebody different." The surprise would be sure to have an impact. Ideological compatibility was important, but he also wanted somebody young enough to reach across to a different generation.[41]

Lee Atwater couldn't have agreed more. Dole clearly would not help to bridge the generation gap. However, Dole was the assumed front-runner among the press corps. Conscious of the Kansan's own anxiety, Bush told himself, "Bob Dole would die if we picked Kemp." If you can't give us Kemp, suggesting the need for a populist who could retain those Reagan Democrats, at least go with Quayle, said a leading New Hampshire Republican.[42] Kemp never had a real chance. The ex-quarterback had a "one-track" mind; he was hard to work with. While later acknowledging that there was more than a germ of truth in the comment that Bush "went young and right" in choosing him, Quayle pointed out that Kemp would have pleased the conservatives even more.[43] Sununu would have fit that bill, too, but Ailes argued that he was "no Robert Redford" and was an "odd-looking fellow" in ill-fitting suits. Alan Simpson was witty and bright, and Bush considered him a "good" friend; he was loyal and would add "spice," but he worried about Alan on the "human life question" and feared going with one so congenial to pro-choicers. If there were any doubts about that situation, Newt Gingrich weighed in by warning Ailes that he would not only oppose Simpson, but his hostility to the Wyoming senator's abortion views would force him to lead a walkout from the convention.[44] Simpson solved the problem by withdrawing, as did Kassebaum, Deukmejian, and Dominici, which sharpened Quayle's position as the only alternative to Dole.

Roger Ailes, who had worked for Quayle's most recent reelection, seconded the wisdom of opting for the unexpected, which would fulfill the need for a "bold stroke." "Dan Quail [sic] looks like Robert Redford," he wrote in a memo to Bob Teeter on the twentieth of July, "only he is better looking. He symbolized youth in the future of the Republican party."[45]

The elimination process was full of ruts. Each name had its advantages and disadvantages, with the ever-present specter of an unanticipated disaster. Nixon, who had been lobbied by Dole, backed the senator. Ailes, weighing all this, pointed out that the senate's minority leader was a potential hazard because "he doesn't like George Bush."[46]

Even while crossing out name after name, Quayle was far from an obvious choice. None of the rankings submitted by the senate list placed him among the top three. He didn't figure on Frank Fahrenkopf's national committee list. But time was running out, and some editorials began to suggest that failure to make an announcement would make him look, as Bush put it "wishy-washy." By the morning of August 16, when he boarded his plane for the trip to Louisiana, his mind was set. Kimmitt had given him last minute medical clearances on Quayle. While, he told himself, Dole would be "instantly perceived as president," Quayle remained more "exciting and new." They would get to know him pretty quickly. After all, he reminded himself, Teddy Roosevelt was also forty-one when named to the vice presidency, and Jack Kennedy's youth was a big advantage.

There was no apparent downside to Quayle. He had a decent, if not distinguished, record in the Senate. First elected to the House in 1976, he went on to unseat an incumbent liberal senator, Birch Bayh. "Baby boomer" Quayle, with rich, right-wing newspaper publisher Eugene Pulliam's reputation behind him, made his own mark very quickly by taking command of the local political structure and by doing some deft fund-rasing. Once in the Senate, he developed a working relationship with Ted Kennedy on the Human Resources Committee, and they got mutual credit for the Job Training Partnership Act, which sought to replace the failed CETA program by putting people to work through private business investments. His voting record was solidly conservative, but even liberal rating groups managed to approve of a quarter of his actions. Most of all, Quayle was not a rigid ideologue, and that came across during personal meetings. The man was pleasant. He had a good sense of humor; he could play along and get along. All that helped to make him attractive to George Bush, who had gone to Indiana several times to speak out for him. "He is honest and a strong campaigner," Ailes further assured the vice president. That, plus loyalty, was a bottom line for Bush. Quayle's youth, diminishing the gender gap, and the fact that he was acceptable to conservatives, even the religious right, helped to settle the issue.

Any hesitations that remained were removed during the final days, even hours, before the convention. The president's veto of a $300-billion defense appropriations bill in early August had the fingerprints of Quayle's behind-the-scenes lobbying to get it killed. Too many strings were attached, giving congressional oversight the edge over local options. Bush, who liked the younger man's willingness to buck even the big heavyweights in the defense establishment, took his case to Reagan.[47] Then, on the day before the convention opened, Quayle put aside the advice of several people concerned about his best interests, including his wife Marilyn, and accepted an invitation to go on the *This Week with David Brinkley* TV show with Dole and Kemp. His two competitors, conscious of being front-runners, were cautious and mundane. Quayle came out with the assertion that "the themes, the issues, the articulation on the campaign will be George Bush's." On that Sunday, Bob Kimmitt thought Bush ought to look at the tape. He did.[48]

That clinched it. Bush had sat down without saying much, certainly nothing about his preferences, just scribbling notes on a yellow pad. "I've played a lot of poker and this guy would just sit there stone-faced," said one of the insiders.[49] The vice president then met with Baker, who avoided commenting within the earshot of others or putting names in writing. He chose to confide his views only to Bush. Still, his lack of enthusiasm for Quayle became an open secret, and one that he never chose to deny or confirm.[50] Their decision at that point, very likely encouraged by Baker, resulted in a trial balloon in the form of an article in *The New York Times* on the Saturday before the convention opened, and the day before Quayle appeared on the Brinkley show. Quayle's name appeared as one of six possibilities.[51]

Quayle had done his best to advance himself with Bush. His efforts in what his wife Marilyn called a "win-win" situation, involved working to solidify his standing among conservatives under scrutiny by Bush and Atwater. The *Washington Times,* the antidote for conservatives annoyed with the *Post,* carried a column on August 10 by Quayle's good friend, Kenneth Adelman, who had served President Reagan as head of the Arms Control and Disarmament Agency. Adelman's piece was designed to promote the senator. Terming what he and Quayle were doing as "a mini campaign to get him on the ticket," he argued that the "dark horse" was "a true conservative on abortion, school busing, prayer in the schools," and could help the Bush ticket with "Reagan Democrats, women, and young voters in the Midwest." Adelman later conceded surprise that Bush actually went for it.[52]

The vice president had made up his mind before Air Force Two left Washington on the Tuesday morning of the convention. With Quayle already primed for an important phone call, the Bushes made their actual entry to New Orleans by theatrically arriving on an old-fashioned Mississippi riverboat. Meanwhile, as Quayle tried to relieve the tension by taking a walk with his wife among the crowds on Bourbon Street, his beeper went off. When he rushed back to the hotel room to call back, Baker confirmed his selection. When Quayle then heard from Bush, he was assured that he was his first and only choice. The vice president had kept the suspense going as long as he could, and, for all the embarrassment generated by the media, the payoff was good. Evangelicals, antiabortionists and supply-siders joined in the applause.[53]

It was anything but routine. So unprepared were even the vice president's aides that they were forced to find copies of the *Congressional Quarterly* or the *Almanac of American Politics* to get biographical information about the candidate.[54] On being introduced to the press, Quayle reacted like a school kid at a prep rally, almost jumping with glee. He exuberantly grabbed Bush's arm and shoulders several times, and urged the crowd "Let's go get 'em."[55] However, he was soon on the defensive, embarrassed, unprepared for a barrage of press questions about why he had joined the Indiana National Guard instead of fighting in Vietnam. His father's newspaper, the *Huntington Herald Press,* had unremittingly attacked peace activists and draft dodgers who "enjoy all the comforts and pleasures and extravaganzas of the good, prosperous life" while soldiers were fighting "under such harsh conditions."[56] Had he used family money and influence to secure a refuge in the guard? Was he guilty of "draft dodging" or was it an honorable way to serve his country's effort in Vietnam? Even worse, was he a hypocrite who wanted others to do the fighting? Had he paid his way to get into law school? One especially nasty story had him with a party of lobbyists at a Florida golfing resort in 1980 that also included Paula Parkinson, who had posed nude for *Playboy* magazine; two congressmen had been ousted by voters after publicity about the incident. Questions kept coming; in the glare of the lights and before the cameras, he seemed befuddled. "Oh, shit," said Roger Ailes "we'd better get a hold of this thing." Ailes, who had worked with Quayle in 1986, had never before seen that "deer-in-the-headlights" look.

Baker pressed Darman and Kimmitt into a frantic search to get at the bottom of the allegations. Was, as Darman has put it, Quayle "hiding some unexplained bombshell," although as a friend and neighbor in McLean, Virginia, he remained confident. Some of the allegations were anticipated, but they had seemed less troublesome earlier. Darman and Kimmitt worked through the night, calling whatever sources they could find—Quayle's law school classmates, former Indiana National Guard officials. They woke his father at one A.M. and also talked to Marilyn Quayle. Media pressure was so intense, even at that hour, that they walked separately to evade the attention of reporters when they went to Quayle's hotel. Finally, at three A.M., Darman concluded that the charges were without substance. But the damage already done was nonetheless potentially irreversible.[57] Whatever the possible damage to the ticket by election day, the immediate liability took the form of an enormous and largely negative distraction, giving Quayle more television network attention than the presidential candidate. "The surprise dominated and basically the choice has been favorable," Bush noted in his diary a few days later.[58]

On Thursday, the ticket having been nominated by acclamation, Bush gave his acceptance speech. Once again, the Reagan shadow overwhelmed. This time it was because the president had been supportive, had come through by opening the convention that Monday with a rousing, unambiguous endorsement. He had seen Bush from "up close" for eight years; he was "someone who's not afraid to speak his mind" and "never runs away from a fight, never backs away from his beliefs, and never makes excuses." He had handed off the ball to his potential successor by recalling his movie role as Notre Dame's George Gipp. "I'll help keep the facts straight or just stand back and cheer. But, George, just one personal request: go out there and win one for The Gipper."[59] With the polls showing him pressing Dukakis, the stakes were especially high.

"I felt calm but not bashed and not hyped for the event," Bush wrote at week's end, "I knew what I had to do." The speech was mainly written by Peggy Noonan, who came to Bush from Reagan. She still identified with Reagan and worried about trying to adjust to a "voice" so different from the president's "in so short a space and do them justice." Still, having her "on loan" helped Bush. She had worked with him on the 1987 speech that first announced his candidacy, the one that vowed that he would not raise taxes.[60]

During the speech preparation, as Bush went over the television techniques with Ailes, the conflict was with Dick Darman: "Darman the inimitable," she wrote, "whom I admire and respect and would sometimes like to punch in the nose."[61] Darman raised the key objections. The deficit reduction law then in effect, the Gramm-Rudman-Hollings Act, would leave no choice but to slash entitlements in order to comply. The combination of the enormous deficit, growing massively by the hour, and built-in commitments, especially to defense, made the possibility of having to raise taxes at some point far from remote. For the vice president to remove that option, and to do so with a rhetorical flourish, like "read my lips" was locking himself in a box. "I noted the obvious," he has written. "George Bush was not Clint Eastwood," which, unfortunately, led to the contrary rationale, advanced by Ailes, which was that that was precisely why such dramatics were important. Besides, he had been making the promise since the start of his campaign for the presidency.[62]

Bush's delivery was strong, indeed; a "home run," Bob Mosbacher called it. All the old fighting shibboleths of movement conservatism were there: the burden should be on the individual, not on the government; he was opposed to gun control, abortion, backed the death penalty, and prayer in public schools. He honored the flag and followed his address in a way some aides thought he should every campaign speech, by having his audience stand for The Pledge of Allegiance. If not exactly evoking Reagan's "morning in America," Bush reached out to the imagery of a Norman Rockwell America, before "values" were corrupted by bigness: the family as the center of society, "the essential unit of closeness and of love," the "idea of community" so misunderstood by liberal Democrats. He called for a "kinder and gentler nation," but it was to be achieved by volunteerism. Citizens must not wait passively "while Washington sets the rules." It was a challenge for America's heterogenous mix. They, the potential sources for creating "a new harmony, like stars, like a thousand points of light in a broad and peaceful sky."

His words were not designed to please liberal critics. He called for the creation of thirty million jobs, but failed to say how this could be achieved. His economic advisers were not far behind in saying that they, too, did not see how; he must have meant it as an "inspiration," said one.[63] His pledge to impose no new taxes—in the long run the most unfortunate message—was an almost eerie denial of realities. "The Congress will push me to raise taxes, and I'll say no. And they'll push, and I'll say no. And they'll push again," he added, "and I'll say to them," as he theatrically pressed a finger to his mouth and with perfect timing said, "read my lips: no new taxes." Such words, incredible to critics, fell on ears that were as convinced as he of the failure of past Democratic social programs. Society, as they saw it, was no better off for them, and a lot more impoverished, both in the public and private sectors. The poor were poorer, and there were more of them. Cities were rotting and crime-infested, filled with people increasingly becoming more irresponsible about themselves and their families (wherever such traditional concepts still applied) and all too easily subordinating any personal initiative to antisocial behavior and government beneficence. His acceptance speech, so well received by the delegates within the

Superdome and by the nation at large, struck the right note between continuity and transition to a new administration.[64]

Within days of the convention, leading polls—*Newsweek, CBS News,* Gallup, *The Wall Street Journal, Washington Post/ABC News*—all showed Bush pulling ahead or in a virtual tie.[65] He was finally running toward an open field.

Dan Quayle came out of New Orleans as the easy butt of jokes, an implausible vice president. Bush, however, did everything he could to show his confidence and loyalty to the younger man, gaining, in the process, admiration for standing by him. In the privacy of his diary, however, Bush wrote at the end of that convention week that "it was my decision, and I blew it, but I'm not about to say that I blew it."[66]

Never before, *Time* later noted, had "attacks on an opponent, rather than promotion of one's own agenda, [become] the primary target of a presidential campaign."[67] One originally designed to boost Dukakis but that backfired involved footage of Dukakis circling the lot of a General Dynamics plant with a helmet on his head as he waved from the open turret of an M-1 battle tank. Reporters watching the filming laughed so much that they could be heard on the sound track. And Bush was supposed to be the wimp! The commercial became more effective in the hands of the Bush media team, as a spot ad that pointedly declared, "And now he wants to be our commander in chief."[68]

Their major objective was to counter the persistent image of their man as a wimp and attract women to his candidacy. Ailes laid out the importance of four basic types of commercials: those that worked to show the candidate as an attractive and positive strong leader; tactical positives, to associate him with specific areas of popular appeal; those that placed him in a favorable light in comparison with his opponent; and ads that attacked Dukakis on specific grounds.[69] Of the nearly three dozen that were finally made, Bush's image-makers pointed out, only Dukakis in the tank and three others were negative.[70] The more positive notes associated Bush with Reagan's presidency, with seven years of prosperity, keeping the peace, and, most of all, his laudatory character and achievements. Critics carped that Bush was the "candidate with the resumé" and not much else, but the work of Ailes and Las Vegas advertising executive Sig Rogich, who had headed Reagan's 1984 media team, concentrated on reinforcing his assets. If the negative spots, or so-called "attack" ads, got most of the attention, it was because they were more effective. The old adage that "dog bites man is not news" held true. Like the Republicans, the Democrats also got better mileage by going after their opponent. Their "Packaging of George Bush" series showed impersonators of media consultants plotting the production of Pledge of Allegiance and prison furlough spot ads.

One attack ad made by the Bush shop, filmed over a weekend in August, panned across the littered and polluted waters of Boston Harbor. The environmental point was so obvious, so unforgivable—especially for a governor being promoted as an enlightened, efficient administrator—that it became the basis for "California Environment," a spot ad designed to engage the ecological concerns of the West Coast.

From the filthy Massachusetts waters, the videographers turned westward to Utah State Prison, which served as the locale for what became Ailes's most controversial production. A specially built gate that served to make a dramatic rendition made it impossible to miss the point about "revolving door justice." The Young Republicans chapter in Salt Lake City helped fill the need for men who could be shown filing through the turning gate. When they realized that the Mormon men recruited to act the role were too clean-cut and entirely too wholesome-looking to pass for convicts, they sent a van downtown for drifters interested in earning thirty dollars for a day's work. Filmed in black and white, the "Revolving Door" spot showed a silent procession of men in regulation prison outfits moving through the gate, in and out, and right back into society. Meanwhile, viewers heard that the governor had vetoed the death penalty and given furloughs to "first-degree murderers not eligible for parole" while "many committed other crimes like kidnapping and rape."[71] The ad made no mention of Horton, using neither his name nor photograph because, as Rogich later explained, "We very carefully elected not to show him or mention his name because we knew we'd be hit with racism."[72]

They didn't have to. The convict's identity was already well known. For twenty-eight days, starting with the second week in September, he had been shown and named in an ad that ran on cable TV. Aired and discussed as a news item by *The McLaughlin Group* on public television stations, it was also picked up by the major network news shows. After "Revolving Door" began its run on October 5, distinctions between the two versions, the Bush-Quayle campaign's and the one from "Americans for Bush," became lost; the impact made by Horton's picture fused perfectly with the procession of convicts. Two-and-a-half weeks after the Bush-Quayle ad's first appearance, viewers saw a commercial that featured the fiancé of Horton's Maryland victim. Another, shortly afterward, featured the sister of Horton's teenage murder victim. In each round of those ads, paid for by yet another sponsor, this time a pro-Bush Political Action Committee, listeners heard that the crimes were caused by Dukakis's "liberal experiments." By that time, the Horton story had wide publicity through newspapers and television stations throughout the country. Even earlier, in July, the *Reader's Digest* ran its own account with the title, "Getting Away with Murder." Local Republican groups contributed their own versions. North Dakota voters were asked to "Imagine life with Jesse Jackson as secretary of state." They had not, claimed the ad's sponsors, thought of race as a factor.[73]

Bush, meanwhile, in speeches around the country, denounced his rival and the "L-word." "Liberal has become a term of abuse in America," editorialized the conservative British paper, *The Economist*, "partly as a matter of

Republican policy. President Reagan refers to it as the L-word, something too unsavory to enunciate in public. Mr. George Bush uses it to describe his opponent as though he suffered from an unmentionable disease."[74] Dukakis was hung aloft with Willie Horton, sometimes, as *The New York Times* reported, in "vivid detail" when Bush's enthusiasm overflowed.[75] "Ronald Reagan ran campaigns based on gaining the people's confidence," wrote R. W. Apple Jr., "while Mr. Bush is evidently trying to destroy any confidence that people might have in Governor Dukakis."[76]

"Issues like the National Guard issue [involving Quayle], Pledge of Allegiance issue, death penalty issue, and several others work in our favor—not his," Bush had noted at the outset. When, early in the campaign, he told a crowd that he couldn't understand why Dukakis had vetoed a bill mandating The Pledge of Allegiance, the "whole audience," he wrote, "went ooh, ooh, finding it hard to believe that he could've done such a thing. The American people do not have this kind of focus, but I will start now to spell these differences out."[77] His exhortations to flag-waving patriotism impassioned such people as Idaho's Republican Senator Steve Symms, who contributed to the cause by charging that Dukakis's wife, Kitty, had burned an American flag during a 1970 anti-Vietnam War demonstration. Mrs. Dukakis vigorously denied the allegation and the Symms charge was denounced as "false and beneath contempt." Symms never did produce any evidence, but the incident demonstrated the precarious balance between jingoism and reason.[78] Spurred by the momentum as he went along, feasting on hoopla from bands, cheerleaders, and the inspiring sight of thousands of red, white and blue flags, Bush gave "a fired-up speech" in York, Pennsylvania, as "they barely let him talk without cheering."[79] In Jefferson City, Missouri, with the state capitol as a backdrop, he said that he alone among the two candidates "believes in voluntary prayer in the schools" and "in the sanctity of human life," which also meant "adoption instead of abortion." "Let's not take away the guns from innocent citizens," he shouted. "Let's get tougher on the criminals." Unlike Dukakis, the "card-carrying member of the ACLU," he didn't think "we want to go too far to the left in this country." Nor did he "see anything wrong with having teachers lead the kids in The Pledge of Allegiance, and that's the way I feel. I have your values."[80] He visited the Annin Flag Company in New Jersey. Speaking outside the factory, amid three giant flags, he said that "the flags you make fly over an America that today is stronger and more prosperous than at any time in its proud history," evoking once again in his campaign Reaganesque appeals to patriotism. He had, finally, overdone his point. Even Ailes thought he had gone "a flag too far."[81]

But, notably, and differentiating himself from Reagan, he told those at the factory what he had been saying elsewhere, too, that his administration would steer the country in a more compassionate direction. He had, he added, been "haunted" by the thought of the children trying to grow up "amidst the violence and horror" of the inner cities; the beneficiaries of the economic prosperity must reach out and help "the little guys" and the children. Gallup's mid October presidential "trial heat" had the Bush-Quayle ticket seven points ahead of Dukakis and going up. Bush, in the process of knocking out his opponent, was strengthening his own image.[82]

In such ways, as with the Quayle designation, Bush began to separate himself from Reagan. He started to do it on the West Coast, and now continued as he moved through the country. Dukakis, by terming his humanitarian positions merely the "cynical" ploy of one from an administration noted for shortchanging the poor, inadvertently called attention to the distinction. The trend was largely unnoticed, however, buried under the imagery behind Bush's strident uses of patriotism and crime.

Most hurtful to Bush personally was the charge of racism that grew out of the Willie Horton affair. To claim, as he did, that it was a distortion perpetrated by the media seemed disingenuous. Critics thought he could have retained his integrity by a public disavowal of any racist intent. But the Nixon precedent of 1960, when, as the Republican presidential candidate that year, he said voters should not respond to John F. Kennedy on the basis of his religious faith, offered no encouragement. Cynics simply sneered at Nixon's "pious" attempt to distance himself from bigotry while actually trying to publicize Kennedy's Catholicism. Once Bush accepted and exploited the race issue, however, the outcome was inevitable. The political culture simply took over.

The trail that had led from the conference room in Paramus suggested that the campaign did whatever it could to distance itself from the more provocative Horton ad without killing it altogether. As both director of the CIA and as vice president, Bush had managed to finesse far more complex matters. His chief of staff, Jim Baker, did go on record in opposition to the commercial, and it may be argued that neither he nor Bush had the power to do much more.

The inflammatory Horton ad came from an independent group, the National Security Political Action Committee, which had established ties not only to the Republican party but to Ailes. At least three production people used for the job, Larry McCarthy, Floyd Brown, and Jesse T. Raiford, were veterans of Ailes Communications, a circumstance that obviously raised the specter of collusion. Not only would evidence of cooperation between the NSPAC establish a violation of Federal Election Commission rules, but it would confirm Bush-Quayle surreptitious designs to gain politically by dividing racially. The Ailes-Rogich designers of the antiseptic ads, then, had obvious reasons for avoiding any taint. As early as May 4, before Horton became their issue, they tried to disown connections to the group, which had been organized by Elizabeth T. Fediay, the daughter of a right-wing activist. Acting by letter, they informed the NSPAC that the Bush campaign "does not endorse nor approve of your activities." Fediay, whose interest lay in claiming credit for making an impact with their version, was not shy about alleging a tie. Jim Baker, the arbiter of all that was done by the Bush campaign committee, including passing on spot ads, had, according to Fediay, been given veto power over the run of her commercials just before they were aired. He nevertheless delayed flashing a red light until they were twenty-five days into their twenty-eight-day run. Fediay also produced a grateful letter from Dan Quayle that was sent on October 22. Baker, true to his style, kept his counsel on the matter, while Quayle, somewhat lamely, said his letter was unauthorized. He claimed that it was signed by an autopen wielded by an intern in his office. An FEC investigation to determine compliance with their regulations suggested possible cooperation, but left its findings inconclusive after an investigation that was intentionally limited by the commission's partisan members. The upshot of the affair, of course, was that nobody could definitively rule out the suspected collusion. The NSPAC was, after all, adding immensely to the election cause. As journalist Martin Schram later wrote, the Bush people protested "loudly and publicly with all the anguish of a pro wrestler pounding the mat in feigned pain." For all we know, Jim Pinkerton has pointed out, "any little group of insiders in Washington or upstate New York or someplace else could have been the link to what is generally attributed to the Bush campaign."[83]

Had Dukakis had his way, he would have debated Bush early and often. The governor was an accomplished debater, more of a professional than any previous player in one of those presidential campaign debates that had become de riqueur ever since Kennedy and Nixon in 1960. Negotiations worked out by Republican National Committeeman Frank Fahrenkopf and his Democratic counterpart, Paul Kirk, called for an early start. Bush's advance to the head of the polls, however, dictated otherwise. Ailes wished he didn't have to go head-to-head against Dukakis at all: all the prepping work done with the vice president could not lift him to the plane of Dukakis, who had spent two years as a successful debater for a public television show called *The Advocates*. Baker, undoing the Fahrenkopf-Kirk efforts, drew the line at September 20 as the earliest date they would even consider for a debate; finally, he contributed his experience at debate arrangements (a job he had done successfully for Reagan in both 1980 and 1984) by accepting two encounters for the top of the ticket, the first at Wake Forest University at Winston-Salem on September 25 and the second sixteen days later. Unfortunately, they could not keep Dan Quayle from having to confront Lloyd Bentsen, Dukakis's "smooth, unflappable" running mate, so a vice presidential debate was set for Omaha's Civic Auditorium on October 5.

How much difference it would all make was never clear. About all that seemed certain was that Bush had more to lose. At Wake Forest, Dukakis came out fighting, placing the vice president on the defensive about Noriega, Iran-contra, and for cozying up to Ferdinand Marcos of the Philippines. He met Bush's recollection that he had been "a card-carrying member of the ACLU" and scored the best points of the evening by excoriating the vice president for "questioning his patriotism." He then added, "I resent it. I resent it." He went on to reminisce—Cuomo-style—about his immigrant parents and said that "nobody's going to question my patriotism," as the vice president had been implying. Bush lapsed into some incoherent comments but worked in his defense of cutting capital gains taxes as a revenue and job-enhancer and vowed that the economy would grow because he would not raise taxes. Few thought Bush had won. Nor had Dukakis delivered a knockout. Bush had, at least, preserved his lead. He vowed to Jim Baker that "I'm going to do a heck of a lot better the next time."[84]

Dan Quayle, however, did embarrass himself, fulfilling the fear of his handlers. His replies had contained too many verbal blunders, too many juvenile ripostes. His attention span was all too often rather brief. Joe Canzeri, a public relations veteran of Nelson Rockefeller and Ronald Reagan, noted how "the camera makes love to the guy." He had never seen anyone take better pictures. But, Canzeri lamented, "He looks twelve. He got his hair cut one day and we all died. He looked ten."[85]

Then there was the managerial instinct of Marilyn Quayle, who had been pushing the Kennedy-Quayle analogy. Don't bring it up in the debate, Quayle was warned; avoid the Kennedy comparison.

Yet, he fell into it at Omaha, first by an inane response to a key question from reporter Brit Hume. What would he do, the panelist wanted to know, if he suddenly found himself president of the United States? The total thrust of Quayle's reply, which most observers considered a key to gauging his fitness to take over the Oval Office in an emergency, was: "First," he started out, "first, I'd say a prayer for myself and for the country I'm about to lead," and that was about all—nothing even vaguely recalling the institutional apparatus available in such situations. Hume's dissatisfaction was obvious, and he picked up the question again at his next turn. Nothing much better; then again. Finally, frustrated, Quayle rested his case on the litany of qualifications he had been making on the campaign trail. Age was not the only thing, he said; it was experience. "I have far more experience than many others that sought the office of vice president of this country. I have as much experience in the Congress as Jack Kennedy did when he sought the presidency . . ."

Bentsen could not resist. "Senator," he said to the younger man, "I served with Jack Kennedy. I knew Jack Kennedy. Jack Kennedy was a friend of mine. Senator, you are no Jack Kennedy."

Quayle froze, his Adam's apple, Bentsen noted, going up and down. Those in the Civic Auditorium clapped and cheered. Finally, still inert, Quayle said, "That was really uncalled for, Senator." "You are the one making the comparison," snapped Bentsen, "and I knew him well." Quayle, clearly knocked out, stood his ground, and limped through the rest of the debate. Four out of five viewers surveyed by the Cleveland Republican organization had Bentsen the winner. A CBS exit poll later found that 10.9 percent of all Dukakis voters interviewed gave the vice presidential candidate as the explanation for the vote, while only 4.3 percent of Bush voters said Quayle was their reason.[86]

Going into the second presidential debate, an ABC survey of the fifty states showed that Bush had virtually locked up the election. Bush was primed; he did much better during the debate preparations, when Dukakis was, for the second time, played by Darman, who had at one point arrived wearing a tank helmet. Dukakis was ill the night before. A fever carried over into the next day, and he slept for much of the afternoon. Bush, ready to come out swinging before a national audience of seventy million despite the country's involvement in major-league baseball's championship series, had been smothering his opponent under the furlough issue, the death penalty, and The Pledge of Allegiance.

CNN's Bernard Shaw directed the first question to Dukakis. "Governor," he asked, "if Kitty Dukakis were raped and murdered, would you favor an irrevocable death penalty for the killer?"

It wasn't even what Dukakis said; that was feeble enough. It was his automaton frigidity and studied professorial response to a hypothetical question about his wife. His response was impassive, strangely disconnected from how most viewers perceived how they would have reacted.

"I don't, Bernard," he said, confirming his opposition to the death penalty. "And I think you know I've opposed the death penalty during all of my life. I don't see any evidence that it's a deterrent, and I think there are better and more effective says to deal with violent crime. We've done so in my own state. And that's one of the reasons why we have the biggest drop in crime of any industrial state in America; why we have the lowest murder rate of any industrial state in America."

Not bad for a civil libertarian textbook; inexplicable at that moment before the shocked Pauley Pavilion audience and television viewers. "We saw the floor fall in that weekend after the second debate," said his manager, Susan Estrich, as viewers unhesitatingly rated Bush the clear winner by a large margin. The first major survey of opinion following the debates confirmed that Bush had opened up a large lead, 17 percent according to both *The New York Times* and *Washington Post/ABC News* polls. "Too good to be true," wrote Barbara in her diary. "Do we believe it? No. We are scared to death that people will stay home."[87]

About the only downside were new rumors rehashing a George Bush "romance" with Jennifer Fitzgerald, which caused stocks to plunge on Wall Street. Bush, continuing on his way and making new efforts to minimize his "silver-spoon, elite background," relaxed amid speculation about the composition of his administration as the only remaining suspense. Dukakis, lacking time to get out any message, or perhaps because of the hopelessness of his cause, mounted a last-minute appeal to liberalism; the gap narrowed and scared the Bush camp. "If this sucker [*sic*] lasted forty-eight hours longer, I'm not sure we would make it," said Lee Atwater.[88]

The Bushes, back in Houston for Election Day, voted early by paper ballots at the Ramada Inn near the Houstonian Hotel. They then made the rounds of local campaign headquarters, and the vice president went jogging.

That night, they awaited the results from the city's Brown Convention Center. By eleven o'clock, Eastern Standard Time, Governor Dukakis called Bush with his congratulations. When all the ballots were counted, the Republican ticket had taken 53.4 percent of the popular vote. Their forty-state sweep was resisted only by the District of Columbia and three states in the Northeast, New York, Massachusetts, and Rhode Island; Minnesota, Wisconsin, and Iowa in the Midwest; the congenitally Democratic "border state" of West Virginia; and the far Northwest, Washington and Oregon. On the negative side, Republicans actually lost seats in both houses of Congress, which drew Bob Dole's complaint that Bush had not done enough to bolster their Senate race, and his popular vote trailed the totals won by the winners in 379 of the nation's 435 congressional districts.[89]

Bush went jogging in Memorial Park the next morning with Lee Atwater, and then attended services at St. Martin's. Then he held his first press conference as president-elect. His opening statement praised Dukakis and Bentsen as dedicated public servants. He did not doubt that he and Dukakis "share a common interest in building a better America." After all, the election was over and the American people understand "when a campaign ends and the work of business begins," he answered in response to a question.

He had one big announcement: Jim Baker would be named to succeed George Shultz as secretary of state. His administration, in dealing with the Soviet Union, hoped for continued reduction in regional tensions and progress in the arms control process. "I would like to see my secretary of state continue that which George Shultz has done in terms of the numbers of meetings with the Soviet foreign minister."[90]

Craig Fuller went to work heading the transition team. The press, awaiting both cabinet nominees and indications of policy, monitored the president-elect's fidelity to everything associated with the eight years of Ronald Reagan. *New York Times* columnist Tom Wicker, noting the prominence of long-standing Bush circle faces amid slow movement toward major appointments and decisions, complained that the incoming president "has hit the ground limping."[91] Flying to New York City for a reception for Mikhail and Raisa Gorbachev, in the United States so the Soviet leader could address the UN, Barbara Bush realized that she was on the "biggest plane—and discovered that it was Nancy Reagan's." Such were the perks of power![92]

Power was something Ronald Reagan still had. He was president, General Powell, speaking for Bush, reminded the Soviets at an informal luncheon on Governor's Island in New York Harbor. The president-elect intended to stay in the background, a post both politic and unrealistic. At the table, Reagan, gallant as usual at such occasions, lifted his glass of Chardonnay and said to the visiting leader, "I'd like to raise a toast to what we have accomplished, what we together have accomplished, and what you and the vice president after January twentieth will accomplish together."

Gorbachev turned to Bush. "This is our first agreement," he said.[93]

CHAPTER NINETEEN

"Reagan Doesn't Work Here Anymore"

%

The "wimp factor," while not totally dead, was at least diminished. George Plimpton recounted Bush's athleticism for *Sports Illustrated* readers. A *New York Times* front-page story described his relentless pursuit of the out-of-doors, from fishing to tennis and speedboating. Midwinter vacation trips to Bill Farish's Beeville ranch and Kentucky bluegrass farm and the Florida Keys yielded pictures of Bush the hunter and fisherman. No longer a lapdog, he was a likeable, energetic sportsman who happened to be on his way into the White House. It was almost "as if Clark Kent became Superman," remarked Barbara Walters.[1]

He held press conference after press conference, more in that transitional period than had the outgoing president held in the past two years. Journalists who followed wherever he went were assured that they were about to see a president who needed no "image-maker" and was always well prepared. We must have "failed to see through the facade he put on for the Reagan administration and the campaign," noted one writer. "George Bush," decided political commentator Christopher Matthews, "is the real Ronald Reagan."[2]

The transition between the election and the inauguration virtually gave the nation a copresidency. The incumbent held the power but his successor the limelight. In Washington, Chase Untermeyer went on with the personnel selection process, a job he had begun offstage much earlier. John Sununu, rewarded as much for savvy in dealing with conservatives as for helping to engineer Bush's New Hampshire victory, became chief of staff, replacing Craig Fuller, who had held that title since 1985. Fuller, along with Bob Teeter, was appointed to head the transition team. As press secretary, he brought back Marlin Fitzwater. Fitzwater, who had begun as Reagan's deputy press secretary and joined Vice President Bush's staff in 1985 only to take over the president's press office in 1987, was installed in place of Sheila Tate. Tate's appointment in 1988 was an evident attempt to mollify Nancy Reagan, and she remained with Bush through the campaign. Once preparing for his own administration, President-elect Bush eased her out.[3] The announcement that Baker would head the State Department squashed talk about "little brother" becoming a de facto deputy president. "George Bush is not only going to be the president," James Cannon told the press, "but he is also going to be very different from Ronald Reagan—familiar with the details, profoundly engaged with a lot of issues, right in the thick of it all."[4] He really intended to become *president,* not merely a stand-in for one constitutionally unable to succeed himself.

"And I think that the word went out," was the subsequent lament of Reagan's leading economists, "that whatever we're going to do it's Bush. We are going to put our own imprint, our own style; we are not going to be a Reagan clone, brother, or whatever."[5]

After the announcement of Baker's appointment, the process bogged down, stretching out for nearly the entire length of the transition. Bush had hoped, he explained to his staff at the outset, to go beyond white males, and he did. Nineteen percent of his appointees were women, and 17 percent were identified with a racial minority.[6] They were also heavily from inside Washington's I-495 "beltway," a term increasingly used, often as a way of purely pandering to populist notions about the "elitists" of the government "establishment." In addition to Baker and Sununu, Bush's choices also fell on such old reliables from his circle as Robert Mosbacher to head Commerce, Nick Brady at Treasury, Richard Thornburgh of Pennsylvania as attorney general, Samuel Skinner of Illinois as secretary of Transportation, and, as his secretary of Labor, Elizabeth Dole, wife of the Senate minority leader. Baker's aide in the Reagan White House, Dick Darman, was named to head the Office of Management and Budget. Brent Scowcroft, who had drawn closer and become more indispensable, took over as adviser for National Security Affairs for the second time, having served Ford in that capacity. Clayton Yeutter, whom Bush had known as an adviser and tennis partner for many years and one who had worked with Darman since the Nixon years, was named to head Agriculture. Yeutter, like the budget director, was to become one of the cabinet's "genuine heavyweights."[7] The weakest link, as it turned out, somewhat ironically in view of Bush's vow to be "the education president," was a Reagan holdover and William Bennett's successor as secretary of education, Lauro Cavazos. He, too, was an old Bush friend; the vice president had, in fact, helped him get that job. A former Andover classmate, Bruce S. Gelb, who had once helped him out with a campus bully, was named to direct the United States Information Agency. Certainly the most controversial and troublesome of his appointments was the naming as secretary of defense of his political colleague from Texas, former-Senator John Tower, who had also recently headed the President's Special Review Board on Iran-contra.

Noteworthy for the ease with which he, the major appointee, got through the confirmation process was Jim Baker. His relative inexperience in foreign affairs was widely viewed as counterbalanced by his brilliance as a negotiator and political cunning. He was never more adept than when he prepared for his hearings before the Senate Foreign Relations Committee. In turn cautious and charming, choosing his words carefully, he showed obvious confidence. At the hearings, he used a carefully prepared forty-two-page paper to review the status of conflicts in Central America and arms control. In what was, not surprisingly, the incoming administration's virtual foreign policy keynote, Baker's message heralded a strong emphasis on international commercial considerations. Settlements in such areas as Latin America, Southeast Asia, and the Middle East were necessary for world economic stability.

Everything was changing. Even Communist countries were starting to dabble with market economies. In a new world, information was becoming a key commodity, and the new technology was making the "global economy" more of a reality. It was still an open question, Baker suggested, whether the international community could achieve the "cooperation which we need to cope with these changes." Lest all this become submerged under American reactions to human rights infringements, such as apartheid in South Africa, where Congress had passed trade sanctions over a Reagan veto, Baker left himself with the greatest possible latitude. "I think our standards ought to be straight and we ought to play it down the middle." He came away from his two days of testimony triumphant, instilling a sense of his own preparation and intelligence and signaling the Bush approach of the United States in a post–cold war world.[8]

One who was hardly a "Bushie," Jack Kemp, was an icon of movement conservatism. In naming the congressman from New York, Bush had placed one of Reagan's economic "founding fathers" in seemingly uncongenial territory, as secretary of Housing and Urban Affairs. To some loyal Reaganites, he was just a "token," the survivor of "purges" of "anyone with any association with the Reagan-Nixon-Goldwater wing of the party," in the manner of that other "president from the left wing of the Republican party, Ford." Bush, concluded Reagan's key economic theoretician, had "completely fooled most Republicans during the '88 campaign. They thought he was going to carry out the legacy of Ronald Reagan."[9]

When pro-lifers attacked the abortion views of his choice for Health and Human Services, Dr. Louis W. Sullivan, an African-American, Bush stood by his man, getting key congressional powers to go along. The president-elect even wrote to tell the National Right to Life Committee that Sullivan's job was the most important he would fill. When Sullivan staffed his department, however, he tempered his position by bringing in antiabortionists.[10]

Some wondered at his continued attachment to Lee Atwater, especially in the wake of the nasty campaign, but Bush was undeterred; he needed him. Atwater, John Sununu came to appreciate, "had a great sense of what politics was all about, a great understanding of the need to connect with people, that issues were only the vehicle."[11] Bush had no hesitation about naming the young man to head the party's national committee.

Yet, it was in no sense a complete makeover of the Reagan team. In addition to Lauro Cavazos, Brady stayed on at Treasury, having taken over for Baker during the latter's departure for the Bush campaign, and Thornburgh remained at Justice. William H. Webster, at the head of the CIA, was also a holdover, as was the United States Trade Representative Carla Hills, whose position the new president regarded as extremely important.

There were glimpses of insight into the fact that George Bush was not just another patrician politician moving to the top. Almost unnoticed since Willie Horton, flag pledges, and the ACLU was, as R. W. Apple Jr. pointed out, that Bush was "a man of the right-center." All in all, especially as embodied in his choice of Jim Baker as secretary of state, Dick Cheney (after Tower's defeat) as secretary of defense, Scowcroft, and Dick Darman as director of Budget and Management, the Bush choices reflected his own sense of dedication to government service, expertise, and loyalty. In other words, as a *New York Times* headline put it soon after the inauguration, "Reagan Doesn't Work Here Anymore."

Despite more realities that lay under that comment, the press focused more on the slowness of filling lower-level staff positions. Only a handful of those slots were filled by the inauguration, and the process was far from complete even months later, slowed down, in part, by FBI checks and clearances. At one agency, Health and Human Services, the word was that the top brass were being called "the thespians" because so many were merely "acting appointees."[12]

Less attention went to "horror" stories that contradicted notions of a "friendly takeover." In staffing a White House with political holdovers of the same party from a previous administration, a problem not experienced since the advent of FDR, the Reagan-to-Bush turnover was closer to the 80 percent range rather than the feared 90, a figure unsettling for those who worried about the fate of the "Reagan revolution." About a third of the Bush people, according to an estimate from the Heritage Foundation, had worked for Reagan.[13] Loyal Reaganites were quick to view "Bushies" as a counterrevolutionary occupying force eager to purge Washington. There was gossip that Reagan's secretary of defense, Frank Carlucci, was chauffered to the inaugural in his official limousine but that he had to fend for himself to get home.[14] Loyal Reagan conservatives told of being forced to make way for the newcomers, even threatened with IRS audits if they didn't step aside.[15] "People were fired when there was nobody to replace them with," recalled veteran Reagan adviser Lyn Nofziger. He personally intervened, with limited success, in placing people with the new administration; but the question always was, "Do they have any Bush credentials? It was not good enough to be Reagan people."[16] One holdover complained that the new staff was "precisely what Bush wants; nice people who will not handle him or try to, people who are technically competent and without much ideology, people who will not usurp that power that belongs to the president and the cabinet." After the traditional changing of photographs in the White House during the inauguration, it was also rumored that Bush people removed Reagan's pictures from the

West Wing even as they left those of Ford and Carter in place.[17] "You will find," Martin Anderson complained afterward, "a very systematic purge went into effect of anyone with any association with the Reagan-Nixon-Goldwater wing of the party."[18]

The press was more interested in the new administration's failure to spell out a substantive program. Whatever Bush might come up with, Reaganites were more vigilant about holding him to his tax pledge. Intimations of the need for some kind of increase were quite current. A National Economic Commission, first suggested by Governor Cuomo of New York after the stock market crash of 1987, and then created by Congress to remove the tax issue from partisan politics, was leaning in precisely that direction. Its Democratic cochairman, Robert Strauss, advised incoming Treasury Secretary Nick Brady and the new budget director, Richard Darman, that the commission's findings could serve as a fig leaf for the new administration. Bush, however, somewhat further emboldened by Federal Reserve Chairman Alan Greenspan's adroit preference for deficit reductions over tax increases when testifying before the NEC, dismissed what Strauss thought could be his "life-saver." Taking advantage of his option, as president-elect, to appoint two additional members, one from each party, he chose good friends—Reagan's pal Paul Laxalt and one of his own favorite Democrats, old reliable Lud Ashley, which gave him an effective eight-to-six majority to guard against a pro-tax recommendation.[19] Bush's economic advisers, Strauss recalled later, gave him "bum advice" by not reading the political tea leaves.[20]

At a preinaugural meeting at the vice president's residence, however, in the presence of both Bush and Quayle, not everyone was sure. Brady, backed by Teeter, seemed to be leaning toward accepting the need for new taxes. Bush, however, held the line, as did Quayle. The incident was later cited as evidence that the incoming vice president was, contrary to gossip, quite capable of "standing firm" on his own without being manipulated by Republican conservatives.[21]

Two days before the swearing-in, with the Quayles about to take over the vice president's house, the Bushes left the Naval Observatory and moved into Blair House. When Bushes "move in," they become an occupying force, complete with grandchildren (ten at the moment, with an eleventh on the way, Ashley Walker Bush, born to Sharon and Neil in February) who helped enliven the stuffy interiors of that historic building. "Blair House is bubbly," said the president-elect. "George running and playing with his computer; Jebby playing with his computer; Sam running around," he noted while continuing to revise his inaugural address. It was shaping up just fine: conciliatory but firm, high-minded and humane, open and tolerant. "A president is neither prince nor pope," it read, "and I don't seek a window on men's souls. In fact, I yearn for a greater tolerance, and easygoingness about each other's attitudes and way of life." He liked that. "I don't know if it'll live forever," he recorded, "but it seems to be good to me." It even repeated the "thousand points of light" theme. Mostly, he told himself, "it's one American helping another." "Resources are short, resources are tight, but all we can do is do our best." He put aside Peggy Noonan's antiabortion language, deciding that her words could make him look as though he preferred "family practices that lead to pregnancy—the unwed mother." His message would include no negatives that could upset the atmosphere of calm, relaxed confidence.[22]

In his first postelection news conference, he responded to a question about having ignored black neighborhoods and then having attracted few votes from such districts. A president has to use "the bully pulpit of the White House," he told them, to make very clear that "bigotry has no place in America."[23] He appeared with black leaders, mainly Republicans, at a prayer breakfast of the American Bicentennial Presidential Inaugural Afro-American Committee and told the 500 present that morning that the Rev. Martin Luther King Jr. "lived a hero's life" and "dreamed a hero's dreams." The civil rights leader was "a great gift from God," whose vision would also be his. His appearance at the Washington Hilton gathering was publicized by a picture high on *The New York Times*'s front page that showed his obvious delight at being greeted by the black-liaison director of the inaugural committee.

The contrast with the outgoing president could not have been more vivid. Just two days earlier, speaking on the last Sunday of his administration, President Reagan appeared on the CBS-TV show *60 Minutes* and accused civil rights leaders of exaggerating discrimination against blacks through a desire to increase their own "prominence." Civil rights activists, who had clashed repeatedly with his administration over racial and economic policies, were outraged but not surprised. Nor, to hear Reagan, was there an apparent awareness that he had accomplished anything to bequeath to his successor a changed international climate. There had been "no change" in his skepticism about the Soviet Union, he told reporters with just two days left in his presidency, despite the remarkable changes that had been made in relations between Washington and Moscow. He doubted the coming days would see any lessening of Russian expansionist resolve, whether in Nicaragua, Cuba, or elsewhere in Latin America, but Gorbachev, he conceded, was "quite different" than the leaders who came before.[24]

Republican conservatives, already suspecting the worst, were further discouraged. A Democrat, Arthur M. Schlesinger Jr., thought that Bush could "turn out to be more of a tribune of the people than he chose to suggest in the campaign. We may find noblesse oblige replacing greed as the White House style." Dan Quayle advised viewers of NBC's *Today* show to "watch what President George Bush is going to do for the poor and for members of minority groups."[25] Bush, however, made sure to caution a group of reporters from Texas that he was not about to make the kind of criticism of Reagan during his final hours in office that he had resisted for eight full years.[26]

That Wednesday evening, "points of light" keynoted a candlelight ceremony in front of the Lincoln Memorial. The Gatlin Brothers led with a rendition of "Houston Means I'm One Day Closer to You." Most spectacular were the fireworks, forty minutes of explosives put on by the Grucci family. Shells reached the height of the Washington Monument, then burst and fell to earth, each symbolizing a "point of light." The playing of "The Star Spangled Banner" hushed the evening crowd, which then saw navy jets from the aircraft carrier *America* flying over the memorial in a wingtip-to-wingtip formation in a "twenty-one-plane aerial salute." Parachutists from the U.S. Army Golden Knights team floated to a perfect landing next to the platform that held the Bushes and the Quayles below the steps. George Bush lit a large Olympic torch. The crowd, given little penlights, turned them on and waved them in unison. Bush talked about how individuals can do their part by helping one another. His presidency would aim "to make these thousand points of light shine brighter than ever before." Not since Hoover's day had the spirit of volunteerism been so blessed.[27]

Bush, escorting Barbara, then made the rounds of three black-tie dinner parties. Guests paid $1,500 each to dine at the newly renovated Union Station, the Corcoran Gallery of Art, and the Pension Building. Inaugural planners had originally designated two others, but had to call them off for the lack of additional contributors.[28]

The next afternoon, the president-elect went to the Jefferson Hotel on Sixteenth Street, which housed members of his extended and immediate family. His mother had just flown in from her winter home in Hobe Sound, Florida, on an ambulance plane with two physicians. As George Bush's brother wrote, "in fragile health at eighty-seven, she had disciplined herself daily to be ready for a moment which she may have viewed privately with mixed emotions—bursting pride that her second son was about to become the forty-first president of the United States, mixed perhaps with some concern for his welfare in a dangerous world."[29]

At three minutes past noon, in the cold of a clear Washington day, George Bush, in a business suit rather than the traditional waistcoat that Reagan had worn, took the oath to become the forty-first president of the United States. Barbara held two Bibles, one used by George Washington at the first inaugural two hundred years earlier, and the other a gift to Bush from the House and Senate prayer group. He repeated the vows after Chief Justice William H. Rhenquist. The U.S. Army Band followed with "Hail to the Chief," and the firing of a twenty-one-gun salute boomed from across the Mall.

The speech was Jeffersonian in its call for reconciliation. Others were reminded of Kennedy, especially in Bush's appeal to the American people to demonstrate their "goodness and courage" by helping to do what the government alone cannot do. "We are not the sum of our possessions," he declared, in a passage that some interpreted as critical of the Reagan era ethos of greed.[30] "They are not the measure of our lives." Reaching out across political divisions, he called for "the old bipartisanship" to be "made new again." Then, signaling continuity with the Reagan past while vowing to "go to the people and the programs that are the brighter points of light," he said that "for the first time in this century, for the first time in perhaps all history, man does not have to invent a system by which to live." The purpose of America "is to make kinder the face of the nation and gentler the face of the world." There were the obligatory paeans to unity and tolerance. The only specific call for domestic action urged liquidating the deficit and balancing the budget. The time had also come, he urged, to be liberated from the imprisonment of the "final lesson of Vietnam" because "no great nation can long afford to be sundered by a memory." The address drew praise for rejecting the spirit of divisiveness and callousness.[31]

"That was a very nice inaugural address George Bush gave, as nice as nice could be," was the wry comment of *The New Republic*'s current "TRB." "It was nice to the Democrats, nice to the Russians, nice to the homeless, nice to kids and old folks. It was just incredibly nice. The new president's new breeze blew in off the West Front of the Capitol in the form of a great howling gale of niceness."[32] As another journalist wrote, "His text was pre-Enlightenment, words that could have been spoken with equal impact in the seventeenth century about the restorative powers of faith and prayer and good deeds and the balm of living in a community."[33] It was, however, consistent with what has come to be considered appropriate for inaugurals and completely in tune with Bush's own thoughts, if not his language. "A thousand points of light" was Bush's ideal caught by Noonan's prose.

During those first moments of his presidency, the Bushes walked some thirty yards with the Reagans to a waiting helicopter, following the steps of the East Front of the Capitol and across a red carpet. President Bush then joined the motorcade down Pennsylvania Avenue. He got out of the limousine only for brief intervals en route to the reviewing stand. The "friendly takeover" had begun.[34]

All in all, between Wednesday the eighteenth and Sunday, the second day after the inaugural, the official celebration, funded by contributions from individuals and corporations and twice as expensive as Reagan's, involved ten luncheons, thirty-three dinners or balls, twenty-three receptions, eleven festival celebrations or salutes, six worship services, and an open house at the president's mansion. The new First Family showed up at fourteen events in all, thirteen of them balls, and managed to dance at some before going "home" at nearly one in the morning. "When we got back," the president explained for his diary, "I had that almost so tired you couldn't sleep feeling and I knew that at 8:00 this morning, we had to greet the first group of people who stayed out all night to get to be one of a handful of several thousand people to go through the White House."[35]

What he saw through the window that Saturday morning were "people all over the darn place. They'd spent the night there, literally, in the cold, some of them later coming through the receiving line with their blankets." He didn't mind it, said one young visitor, because it was "like waiting for a rock concert." They were the first of 4,002 who got in before the doors closed at eleven A.M. Not since Taft took over in 1909 had there been an open house. The president and Mrs. Bush, in an enthusiastic revival of the tradition, greeted the public at the driveway of the South Portico, welcoming them to "the people's house." Forming a group from the first fifteen on the line, the First Family took them on a private tour that led through the East Room, the Blue Room, and the Red Room.[36]

Thirty minutes later, the First Couple, accompanied by the wheelchair-bound Dottie, entered Bush's new office. Stately and opulent, the Oval Office was a blend of traditional and high tech, a museum filled with icons of Americana. The walnut and white oak floor dated only from Reagan's second year, and the oval wool rug, with its gold, brown, and green center medallion of the presidential coat of arms, only a few months old. The cove lighting around the ceiling, also new, was a state-of-the-art fluorescent lamp for a warmer and more pleasant environment.

Only since 1902, Teddy Roosevelt's first full year as president, and the construction of a new addition to the building, had the president's office been located in the West Wing instead of within the Executive Residence. Yet, when the second Roosevelt took over, it was at the center of the south end of that wing; with its subsequent expansion to the east in 1934, it was moved to the southwest corner, where it overlooked the Rose Garden. It received a fresh coat of off-white paint—with a more pristine white for the cornice and woodwork—before the addition of the new flooring and upgraded lighting. The furniture in Bush's office included two new sofas and two new white-upholstered Chippendale-style armchairs. There were also six others that had caned backs and had been redone in a rust color. Two mahogany folding tables against the west wall, with a key-motif inlay and various fancy-grained panels, dated back to early New England. A card table near the window was made in Salem, Massachusetts, in about 1810. The fireplace was flanked by a pair of more recent vintage Chippendale-style armchairs, their front legs with carved knees and ball-and-claw feet. The small bronze figure sculpted by Norman Hines of a kneeling Gen. George Washington that had been cast by the Danbury Mint was a contribution made by Bush when he was vice president. (He later added to the mantelpiece a gilt-cased clock from Switzerland by Jaeger-Le Coultre.)

The ceiling featured a plaster relief presidential seal. A stunning portrait of Andrew Jackson by Thomas Sully hung to the right of the door. A small bronze bust of Theodore Roosevelt in his Rough Rider outfit sat on the northwest card table, and in front of the right window under the east wall was Frederick Remington's *Bronco Buster.* The French sculptor Jean-Antoine Houdon, was represented by his figure of Benjamin Franklin, which was made when the American was in Paris as a diplomat in 1778. Over the mantel, which was part of the original office, was Rembrandt Peale's portrait of Washington.[37]

The desk Bush found when he first entered (which he replaced afterward with the walnut partner's desk and large leather chair from the vice president's office) had been used by presidents Kennedy, Carter, and Reagan. In the top desk drawer, the new president found the traditional note from the man who had helped to make the ongoing peace process possible, Ronald Reagan. With his customary humor, Reagan's message was handwritten under the following printed heading: "Don't let the turkeys get you down." He wrote, "Dear George, You'll have moments when you want to use this particular stationery. Well, go to it. George, I treasure the memories we share and wish you all the very best. You'll be in my prayers. God bless you and Barbara. I'll miss our Thursday lunches. Ron."[38]

The Bushes also had some 250 in for lunch that first day, "all our relatives and our children's in-laws."[39]

Then the president went on with his first full day, mainly getting himself organized and adjusted. He told reporters at an impromptu news conference that he hoped America's allies would help win the release of nine hostages still in Lebanon. He went through paperwork carefully piled up by longtime aide Patty Presock, now deputy assistant to the president. He was briefed by CIA Director Webster and discussed the state of the world with Sununu and Scowcroft in preparation for a meeting with congressional leaders. For the first time as president, he enjoyed the service of Oval Office ushers. But it was the thought of all those "people who stayed out all night . . . to go through the White House" that impressed him most. "I loved that part," he dictated. "Young people and old, so grateful that they had a chance to go through the White House, even though they had to stay out all night. . . . It's interesting in that regard how people view their country—it's wonderful indeed."[40]

He never did get over how special it was to be president of the United States.

The fortieth president had not only enjoyed Republican control of the Senate for his first six years, but his personal skills and national popularity seduced much of his Democratic opposition. Added to reminders that George Bush was no Ronald Reagan were the residual effects of his bitter campaigning. "Having been nasty," wrote Hendrick Hertzberg after the inaugural address, "Bush now has no choice but to be nice."[41] His party had, moreover, actually lost seats despite his comfortable victory.

Never before had a new president taken over after winning office with his own party still lacking a congressional majority. In the Senate, where Democrats began the 101st Congress with a 55 to 45 margin, George Mitchell of Maine was in his first year as majority leader. In the House, where they had a 259 to 174 majority, their leadership was dissipated by squabbles and accusations which concerned sexual misconduct and ethics, most notably involving questionable financial arrangements by Majority Whip Tony Coelho of California and Speaker Jim Wright of Texas. Waiting in the wings to lead the Republican minority in the lower chamber was Wright's principal accuser, Congressman Newt Gingrich. After Gingrich's elevation as the GOP's minority whip, he, too, was the target of questions about ethics.[42]

More serious long-term trouble, for both the new president and the nation, was bound to come from the deficit. No incoming president had ever faced a similar budgetary monster, a direct legacy of the Reagan years. So relentless was the Reagan administration's indifference to fiscal responsibility that Senator Daniel Patrick Moynihan of New York, usually meticulous and scholarly, charged that the "dysfunction of the political economy" was not symptomatic "of a failure of the political system" but planned by "young radicals who came to power in 1981."[43] David Stockman, Moynihan's protégé from Harvard days, later admitted that, yes, the deficits "keep the liberals from new spending programs," and he rescinded a denial he had made while the administration was still in power. "Oh, sure, that was Reagan," he added.[44] If that, indeed, was a conscious decision—and no better evidence that it was has ever emerged—its purpose was achieved. In his first national television address after coming into office, Reagan explained that "there were always those who told us that taxes couldn't be cut until spending was reduced. Well, you know, we can lecture our children about extravagance until we run out of voice and breath. Or we can cure their extravagance by simply reducing their allowance."[45]

Nevertheless, Bush, coming into office in the wake of that "riverboat gamble," was faced with an unprecedented budgetary deficit. Supply-side economics had tripled the national debt. The budget was more unbalanced than ever before, having been upset more than in all previous administrations put together. Obligations stood at nearly $2.7 trillion when Bush took over. Just servicing the debt came to $200 billion annually, leaving little for ambitious social programs.[46] As a Yale political scientist has put it in an influential scholarly volume, "The 'boom years' of the Reagan administration witnessed a decline of the nation's export industries, a flood of foreign products into the American marketplace, a ballooning trade deficit, the empowerment of foreign creditors in the high affairs of state, a savings and loan industry with insolvency, and a burgeoning consumer debt as ominous as that facing the federal government itself."[47] "Ask me what my vision is," Bush noted in his diary that first week in office. "Third World debts, politics in Central America, Soviet accountability, nuclear cleanup, budget deficit, and the savings and loan. . . . How does that grab you?"[48]

He worked at getting his administration off to an ostentatiously bipartisan start, one that had dignity, principles and, most of all, dedication to public service. On Friday the twenty-seventh of January, he stood at the lectern with the presidential seal in the East Room and, noting the anticipation of the reporters awaiting his first formal news conference since taking office, cracked the kind of comment that was familiar to those who had gotten to know him: "Harmony and peace in here," which brought some nervous chuckles.

But ethics was at the top of his mind. He had, he announced, "been talking this week about ethics and the emphasis is not, believe me, a fad or some passing fancy." He was trying to set high standards for government service: "duty, honor, personal sacrifice for the common good." He reminded them that he had already appointed a blue-ribbon commission chaired jointly by former Attorney General Griffin Bell and the current ambassador to Uruguay, a former judge on the U.S. Court of Appeals for the District of Columbia, Malcolm R. Wilkey Jr. The administration would soon also produce an ethics bill, one that would hold government servants to the same standards expected of others. "Our principles are clear," he explained at the outset to members of the Senior Executive Service, "that government service is a noble calling and a public trust. I learned that from my mom and dad at an early age, and I expect that's where many of you learned it—there or in school." There was no higher honor, he added, "than to serve free men and women, no greater privilege than to labor in government beneath the great seal of the United States and the American flag." And, sounding what he hoped would be an enduring keynote for his years in the White House, he added that was why "this administration is dedicated to ethics in government and the need for honorable men and women to serve in positions of trust."[49]

The implications of the ethics problem quickly affected his staff and, in ways that he could not have anticipated, his own family. Three prominent members of the administration, one who was intimately involved in helping to prepare an ethics standard, General Counsel C. Boyden Gray, James Baker, and Louis Sullivan, had to make immediate changes. Baker, who had gone through the Reagan years as chief of staff and treasury secretary, now had to effectuate purity: divesting himself of personal financial holdings lest they be viewed as conflict-of-interest problems. Placed in some embarrassment by Boyden Gray's reading of the ethics requirement, the new secretary of state stretched the literal need to comply by getting rid of not only his Chemical Bank stock but even holdings in the names of his late wife, Mary Stuart, and the present Mrs. Baker, Susan Garrett. Gray had to clear himself of possible conflicts because of his directorship of a family-owned cable television and radio business. He was finally forced to place his own securities in a blind trust.[50] Dr. Sullivan took up his case with federal election officials and agreed to waive his right to several hundred thousand dollars in accrued sabbatical and severance pay from the Morehouse Medical School. The concerns extended to the president's brother, Prescott Jr. A potential embarrassment for the president involved Prescott's ties as a financial consultant to the New York office of West Tsusho, an investment company regarded by Japanese police as a front for the Inagawakai crime syndicate. George's rise to power had placed Prescott in the position of cashing in by arranging American deals for Tsusho. His relationship to the president could not, for one moment, be ignored by those savoring its relevance or by an ethics-sensitive White House. His business associates also included Robert J. Thompson, who had worked for George Bush during the 1980 campaign and then become a vice presidential congressional liaison. Thompson then built on his access, further enhanced by a stint as Reagan's deputy director of Legislative Affairs, to become a lobbyist and investor whose activities converged quite naturally with Prescott Jr.'s. Of his brother's connections, Bush noted in his diary, "It has always worried me."[51]

Such dilemmas were never far from his mind. Maureen Dowd noted that "if ideology was the most important quality in the Reagan appointments, the loyalty factor shaped the Bush team," they to him and he to them. The entire question of ethics provided an opportunity for a differentiation that was hard to fault. He needed to personalize the new administration in a way that clearly defined his leadership; yet, the balance between loyalty and latitude for those around him was not always easy to locate. He had to both demonstrate continuity and still distinguish himself from Reagan. Deficits could no longer be ignored, however much the system mitigated against reform. The depth of the savings and loan scandals, that offspring of careless deregulation and uninhibited greed, had yet to be fully understood and the damage repaired.

Left hanging, too, after an administration so detached from domestic monitoring, were issues relating to the environment and education. Bush's campaign promises had made a big point about the latter, and his vice presidency was notable for trying to control drugs and narcotics. Where continuity was most needed was in global matters, where the Gorbachev policies of *glasnost* and *perestroika* were helping to relieve a half century of confrontation. Reagan, after introducing his Strategic Defense Initiative (commonly derided as "Star Wars") and making his "bizarre" suggestion at Reykjavik in 1986 (later attributed to his possible "lack of preparation") about nuclear disarmament, had seized the opportunity to become a "prince of peace" by his agreements with Gorbachev. It was bound to be Reagan's greatest legacy.

Where Bush was determined to differ, and where he thought he could and do so at a minimal expense to taxpayers, was in the area of ethics in government. Public service, he had always believed, was a responsibility best left to responsible custodians. Many had associated greed with the style and character of the Reagan administration, whose First Lady had often appeared as a queen of conspicuous consumption. And swirling around the president were scandals in the Department of Housing and Urban Development, which led to profiteering that redirected millions of dollars that were to have ameliorated the lives of the poor in city slums; Ed Meese's resignation over conflicts of interest in the Wedtech case; and Mike Deaver's questionable exploitation of his White House access so soon after leaving government. All this was apart from the mysterious money trail of Iran-contra intricacies, the sleaze that festered under the somnambulant Reagan, who, as a parting shot, had even vetoed a bill requiring outgoing government officials and their staffs to wait for a decent interval before profiting from their special access. Bush would change all that.

Eager not to let the press conference pass without a follow-up question, one reporter wondered whether spending his first week as president "dwelling as you have on ethics," turning it into, in effect, a "National Ethics Week," was not an implied criticism of "the Reagan administration's record?"[52] "Because I feel strongly about it," came the president's crisp response. The man, undeterred, asked, "Can I follow on that line, sir?" Bush quickly pointed to a woman and said, "No, she's first, and then you. Need to cool off on that one." They laughed again.[53] Business leaders also laughed the next week when Bush addressed them at an East Room luncheon. His concept of a thousand points of light, he told them, had given the nation's editorial cartoonists a field day. One drawing showed a beer guzzler exulting because the new president was "selling" kegs with a "thousand pints of Lite."[54]

The new mood carried over into Bush's first appearance before a joint session of Congress. There, on February 9, speaking also for the benefit of his television audience and while obviously lacking what some called "Reaganesque flourishes," he made some notable departures. He outlined a program to center on such urgent priorities as investment in the future, attacking the deficit, and doing it all without new taxes. His social welfare goals were so precise, together with a plea for "a more tolerant society that will stop such barriers [hindering racial equality] from ever being built again," that E. J. Dionne Jr. noted in *The New York Times* that it was "anything but an attack on the power of the state." It even had "catch phrases that the Democrats thought were their own." Still, press comments managed to hurt, especially their complaints that his spending plans were insufficiently detailed.[55]

A lot of other things were more fun. He got away to Camp David and was able to relax in that Catoctin Mountain woodland retreat—FDR's "Shangri-la" and renamed by Eisenhower for his grandson—despite the damp and penetrating cold of an early February weekend. "I love my little office there," he later wrote, "and I love Aspen Lodge where I can sit and relax and enjoy life, and there are no press anywhere. It's just friends and nobody else you have to see." That Sunday afternoon, so soon after his inaugural, he killed some time just watching a "silly" televised softball game between major-league ball players until he fell asleep. Either at Camp David or at "home," he exercised on the Schwinn stationary bike, and did his running when the weather was bad by using a treadmill near the White House's pool annex. He really loved the horseshoe pits, and was pleased to find the clay was just right at the new one that was put in for him at Camp David. On the second weekend of February, he tipped the scales at 200 pounds, a bit more than he was used to, and took his first workout in nearly two weeks. Arnold Schwarzenegger and his wife, Maria Shriver, visited at the camp on Sunday the nineteenth, and they all went to church together. The Quayles were there that night, along with the Bakers, Sununu, Marvin Bush and his wife, the former Margaret Molster, and a half dozen or so old friends.[56]

He was proud of being president, and he had fun in his job. He enjoyed talking foreign policy with those who knew their stuff, like Brent and Deputy Secretary of State Lawrence Eagleburger, and, one day in mid February at Kennebunkport, a group of Sovietologists. "It was great," he exulted after one two-hour session. "I love this kind of thing."[57] He also liked getting together with the full cabinet every couple of weeks for a review of what was going on, and they seemed to like him. His secretary of state sent him a note about how good it was not to have "those long gaps when President Reagan conducted those meetings." After a brief flight to Canada to see Prime Minister Brian Mulroney in Ottawa and hear the Progressive Conservative minister tell him to take the initiative with Gorbachev, he dropped into Kennebunkport. By the time he neared Dock Square at the heart of the village near the little bridge, word had gotten around. The place was mobbed; "tons of people" wanted to say "hello." The beat was up, the crowds more excited. He and Barbara were the local treasures. A far cry from even being vice president; "very, very different," he told his recorder. "But we can't change our life entirely."[58]

Already out front, of course, were the intricacies of the presidency, the workings of the so-called honeymoon, a period of orientation when critics were supposedly gracious about beginners' rough edges; in reality, the adoption of a not altogether comfortable lifestyle. He missed the freedom of reaching out to friends, of just picking up the phone and dialing out. He worried about getting those subcabinet jobs filled; so much paper blocked the way: personal checks, FBI checks, political criteria, questions of race and gender. How antithetical to getting "on the ground running, having things happen—vision, vision, vision. What is my vision they keep saying. It's not enough to say you want a better-educated America; that you want to whip the scourge of drugs; that you want to enhance the peace by handling the Soviet account well." He watched the Sunday talk shows. "Right wingers" like Fred Barnes came on with their cynicism. George Will was already out with an "ugly" story, about "how he's going to destroy me if he could." Will was the pits. He couldn't help "but to take shots." He'd already "prostituted himself" by becoming an accessory of Reagan's administration when he helped to brief the president, and certainly by "catering to Nancy." He'd be damned if he'd let Will "darken" the White House door. "When the budget goes up, the press was sure to jump on me saying, 'What do you mean, "kinder and gentler." ' " They made the atmosphere "ugly and hostile." If only all were as fair and friendly as were Gerry Boyd, Brit Hume, the "photo dogs." So many had been nice and pleasant, even fun, when they followed him during those exhaustive campaign travels![59]

"It's so damn ugly," the president said on February 9, about how gossip was being spilled to the press about John Tower, whose nomination as defense secretary was being considered by the Senate Armed Services Committee. "They did the same thing to Dan Quayle in *Newsweek*. I don't know what it is, why people think they have to endear to [*sic*] the press by doing this."[60]

Nothing hurt Bush as much at the outset—marring that "first one hundred days" benchmark—as the Tower nomination, a fight the president neither anticipated nor could abandon. He had been warned but not convinced that it risked souring his "honeymoon" or his "era of good feeling" approach to bipartisanship. After mulling for some five weeks over sending Tower's name to the Senate as secretary of Defense, Bush and his key congressional people, especially Sununu and Fred McClure, the assistant for Legislative Affairs, finally thought they could get him confirmed.

At least on paper, Tower was uniquely qualified. His Senate years had been capped off by chairing the Armed Services Committee. Few on the hill were more conversant on defense matters. Nobody was more of a hard-liner in national security issues, just the man best positioned to woo Senate support for an arms control agreement. Now, with Democrats in control and Tower having long since left government, his old committee was under the leadership of Sam Nunn of Georgia.

Nunn was the most astute, and perhaps the most balanced, moderate among the Democrats. He was also respected for his knowledge of military matters. His reputation for nonpartisanship made the White House more secure that Tower would get a fair hearing and that he would ultimately get confirmed. The prospect seemed reasonable, since no incoming president had ever had his choice for Defense turned aside, and not since Lewis Strauss lost out for Commerce in 1959 had any cabinet appointment been rejected. So precedent was on Bush's side. Nevertheless, there were allegations against Tower that warranted careful review. How does one interpret raw FBI files? How does one distinguish the unsubstantiated from the valid? Yet, in retrospect, it hardly seemed worth staking the prestige of the new administration, certainly not worth provoking the most bitter and rancorous personal fight in Senate memory.[61]

Among those who warned Bush about Tower was Nick Brady. Brady knew Tower from his brief turn as a senator from New Jersey and fellow member of the Armed Services Committee, which gave him a closeup view of Tower's boorish behavior and "autocratic" handling of the Democratic minority.[62] Tower, it was clear, had few friends, and his love of women and booze made for salacious gossip. Even before his name was placed before the Senate, Richard Nixon was telling people that Tower was "bedding down" with a beautiful and well-connected Chinese woman despite his third marriage. Senators who trooped off to room S-407 of the Capitol to read the FBI's report found that the gossip included the story about how Tower kept a Russian ballerina in Texas, and of the time when they both danced nude on the top of a piano. Other accounts had him staggering out of restaurants, bumping into things as he walked. "Rumor after rumor" was Bush's reaction, "insinuation after insinuation, investigation after reinvestigation. And it's damned unfair," with "one salacious bit of gossip after another." How could he, as president, respond to all those allegations? Rumors and more rumors, "some Mata Hari, a sexual liaison, first in Geneva, then in Dallas."[63]

Fidelity to Tower was a sine qua non for the political right. Reaganite conservative publications saw it as a test of Bush's need to stick to his principles. Yet, that was not enough to explain the president's determination to get Tower through. There was a political fallout to be sustained either way, just by sending the man's name up. His lifestyle clearly outraged religious conservatives. Paul Weyrich, chairman of the Coalition for America, told a public session of the committee about his personal encounters with a besotted and obviously lecherous Mr. Tower. There were clearly reasons for "grave doubts" about his "moral character."[64] Others questioned how the man's record could be reconciled with the administration's stand on ethics. In little over three years since leaving the Senate, he had earned three-quarters of a million dollars as a consultant for defense contractors. He had also clearly exploited his entre gained as a Reagan arms control negotiator. By his own acknowledgment, the prospect of questions over his confirmation led him to sever relations with seven major clients.[65]

Not a few thought that nominating Bush's colleague from the days of the Lone Star State's nascent Republican party made no sense. Defense, not ranking constitutionally as State did, was in many ways the more sensitive post. Born out of the cold war in Truman's time, a successor to the old War and Navy Departments, Defense was at the center of not only every ideologue's view of what to do about the Russians but of sheer financial clout. Nowhere else were the cold war stakes so high. Nowhere else could the federal government spend so much and have conservatives cheer for every dollar. With the growth of what Eisenhower called the military-industrial complex, any clear distinction between the priorities of national security and plain old pork-barrel spending became lost, even with the Soviet Union receding as a threat to the international order. Even so combative and experienced an industrialist as Charles Wilson of General Motors found himself chewed up by its military machine. In the early 1960s, Robert McNamara followed the path of least resistance, and went on far too long in a state of denial about the righteousness of his course in Vietnam. In a post where enemies were made at every turn, vultures were sure to attack the first potential kill.

Sam Nunn also thought so. Bush, doing his best to avoid a personal confrontation with the powerful opposition senator, exchanged thoughts with him about the charges. The man was getting shortchanged by a lot of really scurrilous stuff, Bush insisted. But Nunn was clearly leaning against confirmation and held his ground. The job was different from most, he told the president. It wasn't enough to say, as Tower tried to explain, that he sobered up by the next morning. It was too chancy, insisted Nunn; on that job, you "have to be with it" twenty-four hours a day.[66]

Bush's stress was greater when Sununu walked Tower into the Oval Office. He wanted to see the president for "thirty seconds." His face was red and his eyes were tearful. As Bush later wrote down his words, the former senator said, "I'll be a good secretary of Defense—I'll be the best secretary of Defense we've ever had. I'll strongly support you, and I can never thank you enough for standing at my side."

His only regret, replied the president, was not finding a way to defend him more vigorously. He reminded him that he had just reaffirmed his support at a press conference, denouncing the allegations and saying that they "simply have been gunned down in terms of fact" and adding that he has "never wavered" in his support for Tower.[67] The president was resting on the White

House's interpretation of the FBI files, which claimed that the Senate should go ahead with speedy confirmation because a background check had disproved all charges.[68] "No one has ever questioned his ability to run the department and his knowledge of defense matters, but he has been tested by fire and he's earned my support. And he damn sure has got it," Bush added.[69]

That was the way it stood when, on the afternoon he comforted Tower in the Oval Office, the presidential party headed toward the Far East. Attending the lavish state funeral for Emperor Hirohito was one objective. Touching base with as many people as possible was another, even with U.S. military personnel, whom he addressed from Hangar Five at Elmendorf Air Force Base during a brief stopover in Anchorage, Alaska. Another was establishing the presence of his administration, reminding them that Reagan was out and he was in. On Air Force One, the president fell into a sound sleep, waking up when they landed. He had never seen such tight security, as he followed Barbara into a waiting limousine and rode to the hotel. Nunn, while maintaining his usual nonpartisan facade, led his committee in a straight party-line vote. By eleven to nine, the nomination was turned back.

That was all the press wanted to know about, not Bush's opportunity to see François Mitterrand and other foreign leaders, not about the possibility of a joint U.S.-Japanese venture to produce the FS-X fighter plane. When he did take some questions, they were all about Tower. "Here we were seeing interesting world leaders, but they didn't want my reaction to the funeral." They didn't give a damn about the rise in interest rates; just wanted to know whether he'd admit he'd lost, whether the Democrats really were playing partisan politics. He just said they've got to do their thing and we'll fight it out on the floor, and backed away from falling into their trap about getting him to criticize Nunn for playing politics with the nomination, even though, as he later told himself, "I'm a little disappointed with Sam Nunn. Obviously, he has become a party liner—and we could lose it if it stays on this basis."[70]

He slept fitfully that night. After tossing around and getting up every three hours or so, he finally gave up. By five A.M., Beijing time, he was on his secure line, adding his own calls to those Sununu was making from another room: tapping possible Democratic soft spots, trying to eke out a vote wherever possible. The process dumped a big load on Fred McClure, trying to carry the burden for the White House on the hill. He talked to Bob Dole and found him amazing, mustering the full strength of emotions to carry the fight for Tower. One Western Democrat listened to the president's personal pitch but pleaded that he couldn't go along because of Tower's problem with the bottle. "Hypocrisy at its worst," Bush thought. Carl Levin of Michigan, at least, had a more respectable reason: Tower's coziness with contractors. "But then," Bush thought, "what about these congressmen that leave to lobby the government? What about the fact that you need to know the bureaucracy, you need to know the Defense Department in order to cut through the massive buildup of red tape and horrendous paper (?)."

It didn't take much to feel the rigidity of the partisan lines. There was, through it all, as some suspected there might be, at least a whiff of the flavor of resentment over what the recent campaign had done to the character of Governor Dukakis, hard feelings that were resisting all the recent bipartisan wooing. It didn't take much analyzing to know, after that night, that the numbers were not there. The lines were holding. Tower was lost; he'd go down before the full Senate. Bush, at least, had the satisfaction of knowing that he had been patient; he'd been understanding and held to the principle that we can't "knuckle down to the idea that allegations and rumors should bring down a man whose qualifications are unchallenged." John had done a lot of things wrong, but nothing to disqualify him from Defense. Are we going to go into the past of any senator "or any individual, to say you have to be purer than the newly driven snow in order to serve," he asked himself. "There's nothing wrong. I will adhere to my high ethics crusade, but I don't want it to go so far that good people are kept from serving." There was, at least, a potentially helpful mechanism in the Senate. Vice President Dan Quayle would be on hand to cast a tie-breaking vote, if they were that lucky.[71]

There was one piece of good news: despite all the bitching and the ugliness of the allegations about his choice, a *New York Times/CBS News* poll showed Bush's approval at 61 percent. That was higher than the 55 percent Reagan had at *his* start. Bush also had lower negatives. Yet, as he well knew, The Gipper had left office on a 68 percent high with a 90 percent approval level among Republicans. If Bush was outclassing Reagan, however, it was with a 15 percent reduction of loyalty from within his own party. Yet, in that head-to-head test, on the third of his first one hundred days, Bush was ahead. He couldn't hide his personal satisfaction.[72]

The "sentimental journey" to Beijing was simply "wonderful," back to their "second home" or their "home away from home," as the Bushes kept saying during their two-day stay; the fifth return for Bush, the sixth for Barbara. The intervening decade and a half had led to the kinds of changes they now found, changes that marked Beijing's evolution from, as one American journalist noted, "a village in everything except size" to a brisk modern metropolis that blended capitalism with Communist orthodoxy. Hard pressed for cash, even official institutions were trying to raise capital by turning out consumer goods: TV sets being manufactured by the army, schools operating shoe factories on the side, and hotels being managed by the Public Security Bureau. Private hands also controlled over 90,000 businesses. A favorite place for wedding receptions was the Kentucky Fried Chicken restaurant located within easy walking distance of Mao's tomb. Normalization of relations between the People's Republic and the United States had transformed the old twenty-four-person U.S. liaison office of Bush's time into a full-fledged embassy with a staff of 130.

The "guest house" to which they were driven had become a veritable bastion of capitalism. The Diaoyutai Guest House was once an imperial park, but now was a collection of fifteen villas that were each fetching the management as much as $20,000 a night. The least expensive rooms in some of the villas went for just $140 a night, still more than the monthly pay of many Chinese workers. Good money came from selling corporate memberships at $40,000 a clip, with such takers as AT&T, Johnson & Johnson, and Occidental Petroleum already ensconced. Another welcome feature was the pool.

Then came the protocol gift exchange with Premier and Mrs. Li Peng. The Bushes received "his" and "her" bicycles, their hosts a large box wrapped in gold paper. Peng, described as "stunned" by those who saw his face, removed a pair of expensive black cowboy boots. One had a Chinese flag on the side, the other an American.[73]

The next morning they visited an old building that now housed the Chongmenwen Christian Church for prayer services that turned into a commemoration of Doro's baptism. "It is a pleasure for Barbara and me to return to this special place of worship," said the president. They were presented with Bibles, and the congregants were asked to "remember their sister, Dorothy, a member of the church." "It was very moving," Bush noted afterward. "I felt a tear well up when the choir began singing 'What a Friend We Have in Jesus.' It wouldn't have been possible fifteen years ago to have anything like this." He remembered that he was almost the lone American at those Sunday services.[74]

At the Great Hall of the People, Bush met with Chairman Deng Xiaoping, who called the president "a good friend." A session with Li Peng, wearing a dapper Western suit, covered a wide range of issues, and Marlin Fitzwater told the accompanying American reporters that the exchange, which touched on Taiwan, the Koreas, the Middle East, trade, Afghanistan, and nuclear proliferation, was "remarkable."

A much longer time, a whole hour it seemed to Bush, was spent listening to President Yang Shangkun. He was much taken, as were all the Chinese hosts, by the impending visit of the Gorbachevs for four days in May, an occasion that held the promise of helping to thaw out three decades of Sino-Soviet frost. Yang, in a Mao suit, had his spittoon and "still smoked." He went over ground also covered by Deng: how they had to live with the realities of Soviet encirclement and infringement into Outer Mongolia, which had forced them to take territory to preserve a buffer and maintain their vigilance. Even in the face of Gorbachev's charm? Bush wanted to know. Yes, replied the president of the People's Republic; they had to educate their children; their children needed to know the history, including all about the Khrushchev days. From the meetings with Deng, Li Peng, and others, the president came away with what he thought was a great deal of substance and detail. He told reporters that he saw "nothing detrimental to the interests of the United States" in the Soviet visit.[75] But their presentations were so "vehement" that he wondered "how fast the Chinese can move with the Soviets in the spring of 1989 when Gorbachev comes to China."

He had, though, come away from the sessions with some good, informal exchanges that had managed to cover American prospects for future relations, including dealings with the subcontinent of Asia and Cambodia, where Vietnamese occupation was continuing. Bush also, finally, had a chat with Prince Norodom Sihanouk. The prince was Bush's obvious choice to head a coalition to keep Cambodia from once again falling into the hands of the murderous Khmer Rouge.[76]

For all the good talk in Beijing, the Bush administration sustained a huge public relations embarrassment. For the great state dinner barbecue to be hosted by the president and Mrs. Bush on Sunday evening for some 250 guests at the Great Wall Sheraton, Ambassador Winston Lord's invitation list had included the name of a prominent prodemocracy movement dissident. Fang Lizhi, a fifty-three-year-old astrophysicist, was an obvious enemy to the regime. A critic of Marxism, he had also denounced Chinese corruption. When five American universities invited him to visit in 1988, the Chinese government had denied him a passport, which drew a condemnatory letter to Beijing from Andrei Sakharov but not a word of protest from Washington.[77]

The problem had rankled Bush even before he left Japan, fearing that it was a "crazy incident" that could kill a visit designed to ease commercial and diplomatic relations between the two countries. Fang's name on the guest list had obviously escaped being "flagged" down by anyone at State or the NSC. Deputy Vice Premier Wu brought it up to Bush almost casually, in a rather "friendly fashion," right in the limousine that picked them up at the airport. Wu's mention was light, diplomatic, but the significance could not be missed. After expressing his diplomatic regrets, the president explained with appropriate gravity, saying that it should not have been done, but to cancel it now would be a far bigger story. It would damage China by calling attention to their human rights problem. The Americans suddenly feared that the Communist leadership, so sensitive to what they clearly regarded as an affront, would boycott the dinner. Retracting the invitation might well satisfy Beijing, explained the president, but it would "kill us at home." Ambassador Lord defended the invitation, but Bush agreed that it was just not wise, that it was a case of humiliating people just to make a point. Wu brought up the Soviets and one of their dissidents, Sakharov. The Russians, he pointed out, don't shove him in front of Gorbachev's face. It was a mistake and a fait accompli, said Bush, who worried to himself about the adequacies of his staffing.[78]

Later, sitting through a long talk by Deng that covered why it would take a long time for China to move toward a socialist democracy with human rights, Bush had to steer clear of references to Fang. Finally, there was good news at almost the last minute: the top Chinese leadership would attend the farewell banquet.

"All of our people seemed very relieved," Bush wrote. "I rushed off to do a live television interview that I was told was seen by 300 to 400 million people broadcast . . . all across China." The banquet was a "good Texas barbecue, big Texas flag, country music, checkered table cloths, bandannas around the necks of the waiters, White House china for the head table, and it was a very relaxing, friendly evening." Everything Texan was there, Lone Star beer, Cabernet from Llano County, and a group called Country Currents played "Your Cheatin' Heart."

Bush leaned over and thanked Li Peng for his understanding.

"We may need your help later on," explained the premier.

That was, thought Bush, a clear indication that the Chinese guests were worried about the price they may have to pay for attending the same banquet with the dissident. Then, looking around, the president wondered: which of the many faces in the Grand Ballroom of the Great Wall Sheraton Hotel was Fang's? He was surely there, assumed Bush, as did the other Americans, but he could hardly ask the nearby dignitaries to point him out.

He found out the next morning. Fang was not there at all. The police had run interference, preventing him from getting to the banquet. Fang was a passenger in a car with an American scholar and his wife, and the police quickly pulled it over and accused the driver of a traffic violation. When the party of three then decided to walk to the hotel, police stopped them at the entrance and told them they were not on the guest list. Then, obviously unable to penetrate the Great Wall Sheraton, they got into a taxi to take them to the American embassy, but that car was also pulled over for a traffic violation. Bus drivers were then ordered not to pick them up. So Fang, with Prof. Perry Link and Mrs. Link, headed on foot toward the residence of the American ambassador. Police on foot and in cars followed them all the way. Not until seen by two Canadian diplomats in front of the building were they able to contact American officials and reporters. Fang later told reporters that Bush "was a little weak" in his handling of human rights on his visit.[79]

"We ended up with the worst of worlds out of this, annoying as hell," wrote the president. Papers all ran stories about the abuse of human rights, forgetting, noted a vexed president, to point out that no one seemed to note that 200,000 dissidents were untouched and that China had come a long way. If the NSC had erred in making the invitation possible—as, he found out, Brent Scowcroft assumed Fang was an old friend of Bush's (he had so many) and thought he should be invited—the matter was compounded by the failure to have him taken to the banquet by an official from the embassy. But that, of course, would have been a diplomatic step too far. "In the long run," Bush confided to his diary, "it will not obscure the substance of our visit with the Chinese, but it is not a good thing and the press will have a field day. . . . This incident mars the visit."[80] Yet, all was not lost. It was clear, he said right after returning and speaking at the Woodrow Wilson International Center in Washington, that "China really continues to experiment with free market capitalism—dramatic change." It should be clear, he also cautioned the scholars, that "we're going to depend more than ever on the counsel of learned men and women in a world that is changing rapidly, a world interconnected as never before in history. New ideas, new technologies, and the diplomatic and trading relationships that they spawn, are developing at literally an outstanding pace."[81]

Unfortunately, just eight days later, there was no acceptance of his confidence in John Tower. Despite his promise to give up drinking and recognize the sensitivities involving the Defense secretaryship, the ordeal came to an end on March 9, when the Senate defeated his nomination 53 to 47. Dick Cheney, an ex–chief of staff for President Ford and the House's Republican minority whip in the new 101st Congress, became secretary of Defense. Just about everybody had good things to say about Cheney. "Tough as nails," was the way Colin Powell put it, "a lonesome Wyoming cowboy who could keep anybody under control."[82] But it was still, critics were charging, an administration adrift. More personally, it begged questions about loyalty. Was it a question of a stubborn president crippled by blind spots? Loyalty, Republicans seemed to agree, was for Bush what ideology had been for Reagan.[83]

"The vision thing," as Bush termed it with evident frustration, kept coming up. Nobody knew precisely what it meant; nor did Bush ever discover how it could be handled. It was almost, it began to appear, something unique to his presidency, as if everybody who had gone before had articulated a coherent ideological message. It was not enough for Bush to declare, as he had in his campaign kick-off speech in Houston in 1987 that he was "a practical man" who prefers "what's real," and was not one "for the airy and abstract."[84] That first speech, as well as his acceptance of the nomination in New Orleans and the inaugural address, were all crafted by Noonan, who supplied what Bush happily called the "flowery and glowing language." His own mode was more prosaic. For all his endless insistence that he favored lower taxes, reduced capital gains rates, regulatory reform, and opposed just about everything that inhibited commercial development, most essentially trade and access to foreign markets, people kept asking what he stood for. Despite it all, despite messages that were consistently conservative, probusiness, and skeptical of government programs, the political climate, led by an insistent press, described Bush as a man without "vision."

It—the "vision thing"—was another legacy of Ronald Reagan. Bush, no matter what he could do, could not become a "rhetorical" president, notwithstanding the importance of that skill to the leadership process. His eloquence was no match for the man who told the people that he dreamed of "morning in America." Did it matter if that "voice" was needed behind the aspirations of the "common man," or was it, as a liberal journalist assumed, an expression of "right-wing ideology" that helped to fill the recent declining influence of leadership? Some sort of "Bush vision will have to emerge" to differentiate him from Reagan. Even before his inaugural message had registered, an editorialist for *The Economist,* noting the problem with the "vision thing," declared that the new president "remains something of a mystery."[85]

The sequence of administrations always influences how Americans view their presidents. Reagan was rhetorical in a way that Bush never could be—

not that Bush could not be rhetorical; he could and there were occasions when he was, albeit with far less skill or theatrics than his predecessor. He lacked, to start with, the timber of voice that propelled Reagan's career, and the stage presence and timing for one-liners that was perfectly suited to the new age of sound bites. Reagan, more importantly, was rhetorical in a way that Lincoln, FDR, or Kennedy were all rhetorical. Those remembered for eloquence did not gain fame by asking for the status quo—they sent up flares for change, in each case, perceived by the newly empowered as sorely needed and eagerly awaited by much of the public. Bush's mission, in the "movement" view of things, was to keep Reaganism alive. Even so insightful and balanced a Washington political observer as David Gergen made the point at the outset of the Bush years that, "without a clear vision for his presidency," he could "wind up closer to Jimmy Carter . . . than to Ronald Reagan." Such voices were more eager for the expression of "clear goals" to sound continuity rather than for change. For Republicans, Bush could not be Reagan; for Democrats, he didn't have the liberal populism of a reformer. Signaling at the start that he would pursue matters in his own way, Bush removed the portrait of Calvin Coolidge from the Cabinet Room and replaced it with Theodore Roosevelt.[86]

He was, as the inaugural address reaffirmed, "a genuine conservative, an American Tory," a breed, explained political scientist Nelson Polsby, that cares "about the society and the government that is handed to them; they want to keep the boat afloat."[87] In that sense, Bush's speech, with its acceptance of things as they were, and most emphatically meaning the course as set by Reagan, signaled continuity as his first priority, a conservative statement in "the most profound senses of that word."[88] He had, in that best defined statement of the essence of his leadership, vowed the dedication to competence and integrity of one anointed to preserve American institutions, setting out on what came to be termed a "guardianship," "custodial," or "transitional" presidency.[89] Missing from most analyses and understanding of Bush and what his presidency meant, however, was recognition that he was the first president of the new post–cold war world. If he was a Tory, and he was, it was with a belief in a new American universalism that adapted the imperialistic and hegemonical concepts of a century that began with Teddy Roosevelt and Woodrow Wilson to a new era governed by the concepts of a global village economy. While the Reagan "revolution" aimed at freeing U.S. capitalism from legislative and budgetary constraints, Bush was determined to hold the line against having domestic restrictions become liabilities in competing in an international marketplace. Thanks to high budget deficits and the heightened value of the dollar, the Reagan period saw the furthest American retreat from free trade "than in any comparable period since World War II."[90] Foreign policy could, in Bush's view, achieve nothing more important than to preserve America's ability to play a key role in not only monitoring the operation of the process but, as Wilson had aimed, to prevent his nation from becoming an outsider. In this, the domestic economic policy was inseparable from the foreign. He made that point very succinctly when he told business-men that he had two "key priorities: to promote economic growth through low tax rates and to encourage the kind of free trade that makes all nations better off. . . . The goal of competition is not simply to disadvantage the com-petition, it's to better deploy the advantages that we have and to create new ones."[91] At the swearing-in ceremony for Carla A. Hills, the president, noting that trade issues had taken on a new prominence with the emergence of a truly global economy, quoted Lord Macauley as having said that "free trade is one of the greatest blessings which a government can confer on a people." And, in a marked difference from the imperialism of a century earlier, he added the vow to "apply firmness to help promote what is fair, but we will always remember that our major trading partners are not our enemies but, indeed, they are our allies."[92]

Half a century earlier, Truman, picking up from George Kennan and others, had staked out the formula of containment as a response to the expansion of communism. George Bush, subscribing to Henry Luce's con-cept of "an American century," became the steward for the updated vision that his country had to create to preserve a delicate balance for a new world economy.[93]

A White House Rose Garden ceremony on the fourteenth of April hailed agreement on a budget for fiscal 1990. It was remarkable in a sense; it required only nine weeks of discussion, led by Budget Director Darman in negotiations on the hill with partisan leaders. As *The Progressive* commented with just a bit of sarcasm, it was "Reaganism with a human face," an amal-gam of proposals left over from the requests made by the outgoing adminis-tration plus some Bush touches. An effort to reduce capital gains taxes was, once again, more ritual than reality; and what Bush had been talking about as a "flexible freeze," with all its ambiguities, turned out to take the form of increasing the funding for some programs, which included a cost-of-living allowance for such items as the WIC (Women, Infants, and Children) food program while reducing subsidies for mass transit and Amtrak. The process, as is often the case, contained the usual optimistic projection of increased revenues. What was perfectly clear to almost everybody, including Bush's man Darman, was that the reality of the Gramm-Rudman-Hollings deficit reduction law (known more formally as the Balanced Budget Emergency Deficit Reduction Reaffirmation Act of 1987) pointed toward the necessity of confronting increased taxes for fiscal 1991. If Bush, holding to his promise of no new taxes and trying to achieve as much bipartisanship as possible in reaching a fiscal 1990 agreement, failed to face that need at that point (as the minority members of the National Economic Commission had suggested), it would be much harder in a year when all members of the House faced reelection. Meanwhile, without indicating where they would actually make other cuts, the administration's proposal identified $30 bil-lion in outlays for such "priorities" as defense, drug enforcement, education, and environmental initiatives. The new projected deficit totaled $91.1 billion, slightly smaller than Reagan's budget. There was little question that, at some point, a concentrated effort would have to be made to cope with it once and for all. Of the agreement presented in the Rose Garden that day, a Price Waterhouse analyst said that it "doesn't do much for the budget or for the deficit," but it was sure to "do a great deal for the politicians." The budget, which was to go into effect on September 1, was adopted by the House on May 17 and by the Senate the next day. Bush had said that cutting the deficit would be his top priority for his first one hundred days.[94]

The judgments were sure to come, and the White House's public relations office cranked up the administration's visibility. Bush himself followed a hectic multistate speaking schedule, but there was not much new about that. His chief of staff, Sununu, led the public relations "blitzkrieg," which was duly noted by the press as preparation for the "judgment day." The Tower episode and the China visits had been embarrassments rather than triumphs, but the president had, they were reminded, worked out with Nick Brady a plan to finally respond to the savings and loan crisis they had inherited and even to reverse Reagan's course on handling of debts to the Third World. The budget plan, faulted for its failure to tackle the deficit issue head-on, was at least an accomplishment of conciliation over confrontation. Jim Baker had sent a clear signal about a change in responses toward Central America. Finally, after spending twenty-two days negotiating with congressional leaders and overcoming such right-wing opponents as Jesse Helms, the administration agreed to abandon all military aid to the contras in exchange for congressional approval of $50 million in assistance for goods, clothing, and medical supplies. They also signed on to a peace plan that called for Nicaraguan elections the following February. The new administration was clearly embarking on a less partisan, less confrontational course toward the region.[95] In an interview with *The New York Times*'s Bernard Weinraub, Bush joked about presidents looking better after the passage of time and noted that Teddy Roosevelt was not hurt although he had come out of "the same elitist background." He had, he added, learned from his predecessor how difficult the presidency was, "about the toughest, loneliest job in the world; how can anybody be asked to bear the burden singlehandedly?"[96]

Leading polling comparisons provided mixed results. The *Washington Post/ABC News* poll rated Bush's April level of approval at 71 percent against Reagan's 62 for the same month in 1981, which was right after the assassination attempt boosted his standing. Bush came out behind, however, according to Gallup, which had him at 58 percent to 67 for Reagan.[97] Much more clearly than polls could show, his presidency had yet to establish itself. He was still "a work in progress," whose goals and performance were mystifying. However they might complain about the president's hectic style, some journalists had to admit that after eight years of complaining about snooze and about manipulation by Mr. Michael Deaver, who produced the "television spectacular known as the Reagan years," spontaneity had to be welcomed.

"The contrast with Mr. Reagan," editorialized *The Economist* of London, "whose days were planned in advance, whose speeches and even small talk were scripted on three-by-five cards, and who knew where to stand because there was a white cross on the ground, could not be more marked."[98]

He had, of course, always preferred dealing on the world scene. Some thought the Tower fiasco helped push him further toward that direction, but global changes, especially involving the Soviet Union, the Western alliance, and Central America, made some movement inevitable. Noting the recent democratic elections in El Salvador, elections that resisted threats of disruption from guerrillas, the president told businessmen assembled in the State Department auditorium that the "historic shift in political and economic thinking now underway in Latin America is good news for us all" and called for a "new partnership for the Americas, a partnership built on mutual respect and mutual responsibilities." And that, he stressed, meant an end to Soviet intervention in the area, and a cessation of Sandinista interference with democratic processes.[99]

The major focus of change, however, involved the Soviet Union and Eastern Europe. Reagan's performance was already being lauded, applauded for advancing from truculence to detente.[100] Historian Paul Johnson hailed *perestroika* as the result of military and economic challenges that came from "an act of will—the will of one simple, single-minded man."[101] Reagan, for his part, thought that Bush was "behaving the way new presidents do when replacing someone from the opposing party with different views."[102] "The pressure was on us," Bush has recalled.

Internationalists, especially from such establishment centers of Bush's own past associations as the Council on Foreign Relations, were urging the president to continue the Reagan-Gorbachev strategic arms limitation process.[103] Almost at the precise same time, in the pages of the council's journal, *Foreign Affairs,* Richard Nixon warned against naiveté in confusing changes in rhetoric "with shifts in substance and policy." The Soviets, he reminded the incoming president, were still in control of Eastern Europe and, given their buildup of conventional and strategic weapons, should not be viewed as a stagnant society. Westerners were deluding themselves, argued the former president, by seeing the USSR as suffering from "terminal illness" rather than as a power fully capable of making the world "a more dangerous place" even while appearing to "contribute to global security."[104] From traditional conservatives, people very much part of the Reagan-Bush succession, Bob Gates, Dick Cheney, and Brent Scowcroft, came warnings that reflected Nixon and the former president's mixed signals. Bush, asked at a news conference about Scowcroft's suspicion that Gorbachev's "peace offensive" might be just another Soviet cold war ploy, chose to sidestep criticism in favor of giving some advice about the negative implications of "cold war" to describe the relationship. First, he suggested, gauge the progress of talks on strategic arms limitations and other sensitive issues, then proceed with caution, understanding that "we still have problems" and that "there still are uncertainties."[105] "My own sense," he wrote privately, "is that the Soviet challenge may be even greater than before because it is more varied."[106] What was true, and Bush found that out for himself, was that Gorbachev continued clinging to communism. More eye-opening to Western statesmen was the Soviet leader's ignorance of market capitalism. An essential point that fused with the president's own doubts about what it all meant was the reality that "if American-Soviet relations suddenly collapsed and Bush seemed too soft," he would not have "the kind of Teflon protection against right-wing criticism that Reagan had enjoyed."[107] The specter of Republican conservatives coming down hard on Reagan's successor never left their thinking. More common during that period, especially from the more liberal side, were complaints about inertia, of unresponsiveness, of the failure to formulate foreign policy initiatives capable of matching Gorbachev's.

Not long after taking office, the president "called for a thorough review of our policy toward the Soviet Union, in terms of arms control, in terms of everything." Bush got the formal finding, in the form of National Security Review-3 (NSR-3), a single-spaced, thirty-page secret analysis. In their period of transition, it advised, U.S. interests lay not with helping Gorbachev but in trying to "institutionalize" his reforms, to "move them in the direction we want." The U.S. had to control the conditions that would determine their acceptance in "the community of civilized nations."[108] The Bush administration, Moscow's former ambassador to the United States, Anatoly Dobrynin, later noted, pushed reforms "quite successfully."[109]

More immediately, politically, it was time to answer the calls for some kind of breakthrough. "We should have hit the ground running," Bush later recalled. The press was wondering whether the administration knew "what they're doing." He was determined to "start to articulate our views on the Soviet Union." The response was, in part, a response to the criticism, but one that "might very well have happened anyway. These speeches would show the country what we were thinking. That was the purpose of the speech, and to send a signal abroad: here's how we're going to deal with the Soviet Union. Here's what we see beyond containing it and the family of nations."[110]

An opportunity for a major speech was already there. Back in February, the president of Texas A & M University at College Station had invited Bush to be the commencement speaker, as he had been back in 1984 as vice president. By April, the need for a major message already clear, the White House agreed to his appearance on May 12.[111] Bush thought the time had come to "think big." Scowcroft turned to Condi Rice, of his national security staff, for something with "more bite" and a more "forward looking" expression of U.S. policy. She drafted a five-page national security directive. "Now it is time to move beyond containment—to a new doctrine—one that recognizes the changes taking place around the world and in the Soviet Union itself," she wrote. "This new doctrine will hold the Soviet Union to a higher standard of international behavior than ever before. This new doctrine will insure that the

Soviet Union keeps its pledges to institutionalizing greater openness and democratization. This new doctrine will hold the Soviet Union to its commitment to verifiable arms reduction. In sum, it is the determination of the United States that this new doctrine has as its soul the reintegration of the Soviet Union in the community of nations."[112]

The moment, a turning point in history, was inevitably compared to epochal events of World War II and the cold war. Models drawn from were Winston Churchill's broadcast from London made soon after the Nazis and the Soviets began that cataclysmic period by their invasion of Poland. The eloquent Churchill at that moment described Russia as "a riddle wrapped in a mystery inside an enigma." Bush's staff also went back to another commencement address, Secretary of State George Marshall's at Harvard in 1947, in which he introduced the European economic recovery plan that not only bore his name but became the foundation of the containment policy to resist Soviet expansionism. Bush drew from Rice's memorandum what, much to her surprise, turned out to become the key message.

Working principally with speechwriter Mark Davis and Bob Hutchings, Rice turned out draft after draft for what was hoped would be seen as a major statement. Reagan had challenged the Soviets. He was aggressive and single-minded. His SDI was perhaps the final straw in pushing to the brink the ability of their economy to keep pace with military technology. He believed that Moscow needed to be challenged not coddled, and had gone far in helping to hasten their fall. His mixture of force combined with a heartfelt fear of Armageddon had pushed the cold war until it finally reached its turning point. Reagan, whom Kissinger recalled as a man who made some associates wonder how he ever got to be a governor, let alone president of the United States, believed in both "the evil of Soviet conduct as well as the susceptibility of Soviet leaders to ideological conversion."[113] His aggressiveness and toughness were needed. "For the West," Rice reasoned, "the historical forces got arrayed in exactly the right order." It needed Ronald Reagan, "who was aggressive and tough." By the time Bush took over, however, continuing to press Moscow too forcefully as its power was disintegrating "would have produced a rehardening rather than collapse." The Soviet Union was still a nuclear superpower with 12,000 nuclear warheads pointing to the United States and 390,000 troops in East Germany. "The last thing you wanted to do as it was going like that was to challenge it." Yet, at the same time, she recalled, "We were very worried about the political right." Talk about no longer needing to contain the Soviet Union was provocative and a little bit simple: "It doesn't tell you where you are." So, to suggest a new initiative, they wrote in a new version of the "open skies" proposal Eisenhower had made at Geneva in 1955. If Bush wanted them to think big and come up with something dramatic, they had delivered, although not with exactly the message that had been intended to make a big splash.[114]

The final version was delivered in the university's G. Rollie White Coliseum. "No generation can escape history," said the president, then recalling that containment had worked but that now, "We are approaching the conclusion of an historic postwar struggle between two visions: one of tyranny and conflict and one of democracy and freedom." The time had come "to move beyond containment to a new policy for the 1990s—one that recognizes the full scope of change taking place around the world and in the Soviet Union itself." Then, in an attempt to endow the speech with that "new initiative" it recalled Dwight D. Eisenhower's Geneva address. Bush asked for the realization of "open skies" to provide thorough and verifiable scrutiny of each other's nations. "The very Soviet willingness to embrace such a concept would reveal their commitment to change," he added.

The "beyond containment" speech became the "catchphrase to describe the Bush approach toward the Soviet Union" in the next two years. The president also left the campus with an honorary degree. "Great enthusiasm!" he noted. "I gave my Soviet speech talking about reintegrating Soviets into the world order and an open-sky proposal, as well, and it was pretty good. It got fairly good reviews except from those who want us to match Gorbachev, proposal for proposal, though it's not that dramatic."[115]

Still, for all the president's excitement, the speech had not exactly sparked cheering; more of a "yawn," remembered the NSA staffers who helped put it together. Rice worried that the inclusion of the "open skies" message may have diffused its central point about the status of cold war thinking.[116]

At just that point, Baker returned from Moscow with some advice. The president of the United States, he told Bush and Scowcroft, had to be defined "as the leader of the alliance," or, if he failed, lose it to Gorbachev, who was about to grab the lead with a proposal on short-range missiles. Already, in February, their policy review had covered strategy for confronting a Soviet Union without Gorbachev. "Suppose, God forbid," asked Bush, "that his heart stops tomorrow?" Was it in America's interest to encourage the pursuit of perestroika? Bush had told the Sovietologists in February at that Kennebunkport meeting that encouraging movements for freedom in Eastern Europe was one thing, but having them lead to the kind of disaster that provoked the negative reaction in Hungary in 1956 was quite another. Dealing with the Russians might, in some ways, be more complex than before. He had to prepare for varied scenarios.[117] Now, on the eve of two trips to Europe, one to attend the fortieth anniversary session of NATO in Brussels, and the second, a nine-day journey to Poland, Hungary, France, and the Netherlands, he quickly invited a handful of advisers to another review at Kennebunkport so they could firm up arms control proposals before he left.

The Germans were nervous about the continued deployment of the Lance short-range ballistic missiles, and Bush's advocacy of installing new ones was hardly reassuring. With a range of no more than 300 miles, just about guaranteeing they would land on West German soil, their existence was intolerable for whoever headed the Bonn government. Chancellor Kohl's Christian Democrats could easily lose the next elections, and a Social Democratic succession would be inimitable to West Germany's fidelity to the

Western alliance. Bush had not endeared himself to Germans by advocating the updating of the Lances in their country.[118]

The meetings on the Maine coast that weekend brought together the president's elite foreign policy people. None were more influential with Bush than General Scowcroft and Secretary of State Baker. Bush's fondness for Scowcroft dated back to his CIA directorship. The man was serious, sound, and dedicated to hard work, a scholar in government. A retired air force officer with both a diploma from West Point and a doctorate from Columbia University, where he wrote his dissertation on Congress and foreign policy, he became known for immersion in international affairs with a predilection for analyses that dismayed more doctrinaire thinkers. The son of a wholesale grocer, he held a variety of academic and diplomatic posts before becoming Henry Kissinger's deputy national security adviser during the Nixon years. After serving as Ford's adviser for national security affairs, and helping to brief Bush when Bush went to China to head the liaison office, he worked in government in one capacity or another during the Carter and Reagan administrations, even as a member of the Tower Commission that investigated the Iran-contra affair.[119] When Kissinger left government to become a private consultant, Scowcroft became vice chairman for Kissinger Associates, foreign policy analysts very much in tune with Bush's way of thinking. His "idea of recreation," Bob Woodward has written, "was attending a seminar on arms control, a subject he loved in all its obscure detail."[120] If Bush really did spend more of his waking hours with Scowcroft than with Barbara or any other adviser and treated him "less like an aide than like a beloved older brother," it may also be said that the general was Bush's top foreign policy manager while Baker, "little brother," was his chief negotiator.[121]

Scowcroft, aided by his deputy, Robert Gates, and with such specialists as Richard Haass, his top assistant for Middle Eastern Affairs, and Robert Blackwill, his senior director, had his own impressive staff. Blackwill came into the Bush administration from a teaching post at the Kennedy School of Government at Harvard, but he was also a career foreign service officer who had worked for both Kissinger and Zbigniew Brzezinski. He, in turn, brought in Philip Zelikow, a career diplomat and lawyer, to manage European policy. Bob Hutchings headed the Southeastern Europe and Germany desk.[122] Directing the NSC's Soviet Union and East Central Europe department was Condoleezza Rice. Rice, who was born in Birmingham, Alabama, and graduated cum laude from the University of Denver at age nineteen and earned her Ph.D. from the same school seven years later, was spotted by Scowcroft. The ascetic Mormon from Utah listened to the political scientist (who had gone to school with one of the four black girls who were killed when their church was bombed in 1963) lecture on the MX missile, and that was it. He invited her to attend a strategy group at Aspen, Colorado, and then brought her in to join his staff as his Soviet specialist.[123] With Baker heading State, Lawrence Eagleburger (like Scowcroft, a Kissinger Associates man) as his deputy, the creation of a strong working relationship between Foggy Bottom and the NSC, and Dick Cheney in place at Defense, a powerful national security team was in place. Their departure from the animosities and inexperience of the recent past was striking, especially breaking from the Kissinger–William Rogers bitterness during Nixon's time, the Zbigniew Brzezinski–James Schlesinger rivalries under Carter, and the combination of truculence, ignorance, and ideological jockeying that marked the Reagan team. Bush's crew, with such players as Scowcroft and Eagleburger close to Kissinger, was arguably the best national security team since the start of the cold war. It also remained, throughout the presidency, a tight inner circle of advisers, although not quite as exclusive as a pack of Bonesmen.[124]

They all came together in Maine once again, this time joined the next day, Saturday, May 20, by President Mitterrand, who flew in by helicopter with his wife and his foreign minister from Pease Air Force Base near Portsmouth, New Hampshire. It was, for Mitterrand, a stopover on his way to Canada. The man who had risen to French leadership as a Socialist had, to Bush's relief, become more convinced about the importance of West Germany in the alliance. Their discussion, joined in at various times by Sununu and members of the White House staff, attempted to weigh how far the Soviets under Gorbachev had really come. Some remained skeptical that things had really changed that much from Leonid Brezhnev's time, when their troops rushed to repress every instance of dissent. Baker, ever the persuasive lawyer, argued successfully that a bold initiative to cement the alliance would make the differences over the Lance missiles irrelevant. "I want this thing done," the president told the skeptics in the crowd, primarily Adm. William Crowe, the chairman of the joint chiefs of staff. "Don't keep telling me why it can't be done. Tell me how it can be done."[125] The administration's flexibility hit the press that weekend, and the group in Maine, joined by Bush's sister Nancy and his daughter Doro, celebrated their work by drinking a 1986 Talbott Chardonnay and feasting on steamed Maine lobster, charcoal-broiled swordfish, broiled marinated shrimp, and cheddar cheese puffs. Their planning done, Bush was ready for the NATO summit.

He first went, that May 21, to Boston University with Mitterrand. There, paying homage to the forthcoming two-hundredth anniversary of the French Revolution and the Declaration of the Rights of Man and the State, he recalled his Texas A & M message and, while emphasizing the importance of the Western European alliance and the "ideological earthquake" taking place in the East, he stressed that Gorbachev's progress was still incomplete. At the Coast Guard Academy at nearby New London, Connecticut, three days later, he longed for the "ascendancy of the democratic idea" as the outcome of the success of containment. That idea, he told the graduates, was already beckoning "trade unionists in Warsaw, the people of Panama, rulers consulting the ruled in the Soviet Union." He welcomed *perestroika* and *glasnost* and hoped for their institutionalization within the Soviet Union. Out of that may yet come "a growing community of democracies anchoring international peace and stability, and a dynamic free-market system generating prosperity and progress on a global scale." He had the vision of a bright post–cold war world, "the triumph of a particular, peculiar, very special American ideal: freedom." "Democracy," he wound down, "isn't our creation; it is our inheritance."[126]

He used "beyond containment" freely as the new mantra. He repeated the phrase as he left Washington on May 26 en route to the NATO summit meeting at Brussels on the organization's fortieth anniversary. His purpose in undertaking the trip, he added, was also to move "beyond the traditional economic and security spheres" to achieve a truly common market and "an even more transatlantic partnership." To emphasize his concept of the importance of the Continent in forging a new relationship and to mark both Italy's economic growth and willingness to accept American cruise missiles and F-16 fighters, he flew directly to Rome, where he and Mrs. Bush were given an audience with Pope John Paul II in the Papal Library.

At the NATO summit, the president announced he would delay any decision on modernizing the Lance missiles, leaving their future disposition in the hands of negotiations. He had other initiatives to announce: similar ceilings for both the Soviet bloc Warsaw Pact nations and NATO for ground forces, including combat manpower, and an acceleration of the timetable for reaching a conventional arms forces agreement in Europe. "If the Soviet Union accepts this fair offer," he told the NATO leaders, "the results would dramatically increase stability on the continent and transform the military map of Europe. We can and must begin now to set out a new vision for Europe at the end of this century."

"Does this revolutionary plan signal the end of the cold war?" he was asked.

"I don't know what it signals," answered the president, still cautious, "except it signals a willingness on our part to really put Mr. Gorbachev to the test now."

At the same time, he explained at a Brussels news conference, any talks on short-range missiles would only lead to partial reductions, not the so-called zero solution that would remove all such weapons from NATO. "There will be no third zero," Bush said. "Partial means partial."[127]

From Belgium, after attending working sessions of NATO, the president and Barbara "dropped by" for a luncheon with Queen Elizabeth at Buckingham Palace. The biggest stir, however, came from Bush's embrace of West German Chancellor Helmut Kohl, whom he visited in Bonn. Kennedy boosted Conrad Adenauer in 1963, and Reagan had taken the heat for Chancellor Kohl by speaking at the Bitburg military cemetery in 1985; now, an American president had come to his aid again. In the chancellor's hometown of Mainz, Bush's enthusiasm was evident as he declared ringingly that "the cold war began with the division of Europe," and added that "it can only end when Europe is whole." The United States and the Federal Republic were "partners in leadership."[128] He had also signaled British Prime Minister Margaret Thatcher that he was far less likely to follow her lead than she had come to expect from Reagan. For all his Anglo-Saxon affinities, Bush was not about to reflect the "Iron Lady's" misgivings about German unification. Had Bush joined her in objecting to an end of the divisions that separated Bonn from Berlin, he could have helped feed a revival of the rapprochement resentments that had played into Hitler's hands in the 1930s, to say nothing about the inherent impediments to any kind of meaningful arms control. More importantly for the immediate future, Bush was determined to get Soviet troops out of the East and bring a unified Germany into a full partnership with the Atlantic alliance.[129]

At the start of the cold war, with East Germany occupied by Soviet troops, Western leaders overcame hesitations about rebuilding what remained of Hitler's former Third Reich. Now, with the cold war dissolving, George Bush was in the lead—ahead of a considerable segment of public opinion, especially in Europe—in urging reunification. A unified Germany, he held, would prepare the way for a new, democratic Europe, one that could heal old wounds and become less militarized. "If ancient rivals like Britain, or France and Germany, can reconcile," he pointed out at Mainz, "then why not the nations of the East and the West?" The process, he suggested, was inevitable, an unstoppable force propelled by images that enable the world "to bear witness from the shipyards of Gdansk to Tiananmen Square," and encouraged by "a single powerful idea: democracy." Having "convinced the Soviets that their arms buildup has been costly and powerless," it should now be understood that "unity and strength are the catalyst and prerequisite to arms control." He envisioned "a Berlin without barriers . . . a Europe that is free and at peace with itself." Without saying so, he was calling for the most significant reform of the legitimate order in Europe since Wilson's after World War I.[130]

After the president and Prime Minister Thatcher spent two hours at 10 Downing Street, a reporter asked him, "Is Britain America's most important ally in Europe?"

That brought a noticeable tightening from Mrs. Thatcher, who said, "I think you might put it more tactfully."

Bush laughed.

Happily, the president's diplomatic initiatives in Europe lacked a spoiler in the form of a Tower affair or a Dr. Fang incident. His presence at each point along the way made a positive impact, and the critics agreed. It was, proclaimed The New York Times, "Bush's hour." An administration that had been accused of lacking boldness and vision had pulled off a "foreign policy coup." He had contributed to a sequence of events that soon reaffirmed the reason for going "beyond containment." "Never underestimate Mr. Bush," wrote a British editorialist. "He has a habit of bouncing back, of doing best just when things look bleakest for him. . . . One effect of Mr. Bush's European success will probably be to enamor him of foreign policy and divert his mind from the tedium and intractability of domestic issues, such as the budget and the environment."[131]

Bush didn't hide his satisfaction. He joked about passing "the Milton Pitts test," a count of how much gray the White House barber finds when cutting presidential hair. He said to reporters, "I'm the same guy I was four days ago."[132]

"I feel more comfortable in the job," Bush told Maureen Dowd. "And I feel more aware of why it might age the president, because there's just an accumulation of problems. You start in and there's two or three. A month later, there's six or seven."[133]

"Once upon a time," observed *The Economist* wryly, "there was a president who was doing very badly. Everybody said he was at the mercy of events and did not have a vision thing. So he went to Europe and outmaneuvered the Germans and outbid the Russians and bypassed the British and found a vision thing. And then, all of a sudden, everybody said he was a very good president."[134]

CHAPTER TWENTY

"It's Six P.M. and We Don't Know Where Noriega Is"

※

T

hey managed a weekend in Kennebunkport after leaving London. "Do you think you will have a little more respect at home after this trip?" asked a reporter while Air Force One was over the Atlantic. "I never felt kind of—you mean," answered the president, "along with [a] Rodney Dangerfield kind of thing?" to appreciative laughter. "I've not suffered from lack of respect. These fellows have all been very pleasant. Haven't you guys?" he asked, to more laughter. Right now, he told them, he was eager to take his boat out on the water.[1]

On Sunday, he got disturbing news from Beijing. Even before the start of the European trip, the president had been following the growing confrontation between the prodemocracy movement and the government. Students, with some worker components, took over Tiananmen Square at Beijing's center, tied up other parts of the city, and provoked the authorities into proclaiming martial law. In Bush's absence, the White House had, only three days earlier, sent on to the Congress the formal certification required for renewal of China's most-favored-nation status (MFN) for trade relations. Having been in the Chinese capital so recently, Bush watched developments there with intense interest, especially as the dissidents prepared to make the most of the Gorbachev visit. Gorbachev, in dealing with the People's Republic after three decades of conflict between the two giant Communist countries, had taken the initiative in offering to negotiate outstanding differences, the continued Vietnamese occupation of Cambodia, Russian troops along the Sino-Soviet border, and the intervention in Afghanistan. As elsewhere, the attractions of *glasnost* were sparking desires for liberty within the world's major repressive society, where martial law had been declared on May 20.

While Bush was still in Kennebunkport, People's Liberation Army–supplied land carriers rolled over encampments and people in the square, crushing or shooting hundreds, perhaps thousands—the precise number is not known. But the scene was unforgettable, with their symbolic Goddess of Democracy smashed and permanently etched pictures of a lone youth defying a Communist tank. Early reports, Bush heard, told of at least sixty-eight corpses retrieved from the scene, while students were claiming that the toll was closer to five hundred. "To be an American on the square this morning was to be the object of fervent hope and inarticulate pleas for help," wrote Nicholas D. Kristof for *The New York Times.* He quoted a student's appeal for "help from abroad, especially America. There must be something that America can do."*[2] The unthinkable, though not unexpected, had happened.

Even before that dreaded news came, Secretary of State Baker told CNN's viewers that he could not say whether the administration would respond to the repression by cutting off arms sales to China. From the Maine coast, Bush issued a statement deploring the Chinese use of force and their not heeding pleas to use restraint. Fearful of an overreaction that might play into the hands of their hard-liners and jeopardize the diplomatic value of China to the U.S. for American interests in Asia, Bush limited himself to hoping for "a return to nonviolent means for dealing with the current situation." The next day, after returning to Washington, he told the press about the danger of "an emotional response" and gave them a historical sketch of Chinese history since the Cultural Revolution. He did announce the "suspension of all government-to-government sales and commercial exports of weapons, suspension of visits between U.S. and Chinese military leaders," and would view with sympathy requests by Chinese students to remain in the United States. He refused, however, to impose economic sanctions. It was precisely those commercial contacts, he explained, that had led to the popular "quest for more freedom." Their disruption would only "hurt the Chinese people." The pressures were great, the dramatic impact of TV pictures rendering "diplomacy" impotent, but, as Tom Wicker wrote, the president has "done as much as he could in the wake of the awful events in Tiananmen Square."[3]

He also dreaded the "inside baseball" that awaited his return to the White House. The Iran-contra "thing" kept bobbing up as his former aide, Don Gregg, ran into difficulty and had a hard time having the Foreign Relations Committee pass on his nomination as ambassador to South Korea. Had he misled his boss, they wanted to know, by not telling him about the contra resupply operation? He was finally confirmed, but even some of the Democrats on the committee squirmed about a line of questioning that led so closely to the president. All in all, Capitol Hill infighting was at its ugliest, haunted by financial irregularities, real or suspected, wherever one turned. Only one week earlier, Representative Tony Coelho, stung by charges of fraud in the purchase of a $100,000 "junk bond," had announced his resignation. On Wednesday came Speaker Wright's news of his own "retirement," but by then it was hardly "news." Investigations had stretched over ten months. Specific charges had piled up. They involved some sixty-nine

*Dr. Fang Lizhi took refuge in the American embassy.

House rules violations; six weeks after the ethics committee had turned in its findings, Wright's announcement was about all that was left. A newspaper headline as Bush arrived that Sunday also announced that "Gingrich, Pursuer of Democrats, Now Finds Himself the Pursued," dogged by questions about a book of his own.[4] Democrats went on to choose Representative Tom Foley of Washington and Senator Richard Gephardt of Missouri to replace Wright and Coelho, and even that was followed by a brief and nasty incident.

Foley was soon stung by a memorandum headed "Out of the Liberal Closet." If anyone missed that innuendo, especially in the aftermath of revelations about the homosexuality of Barney Frank, the liberal Massachusetts Democrat, the memo went on to compare the voting records of the two men. That it came from the Republican National Committee made the matter especially sordid. A likely suspect, of course, was Lee Atwater. Several Democrats, mainly in the House, quickly demanded his resignation. Foley himself, however, remained calm. He called for getting on with the work of the legislature.[5]

Bush was less complacent. With the Tower episode very much in his mind, he termed the document "disgusting" and said it was "against everything I have tried to stand for in political life." Atwater, Bush later explained, was called to the Oval Office "woodshed." The party chairman "looked me right in the eye and said he did not know about it," and explained that he had been out of town when it was circulated. He also promised to get rid of whoever had written it.[6]

Bush had no illusions about Atwater. He knew that Lee had long since created his own reality and had little concept of what was real. He dealt in deception, not truth, a valuable asset for those dependent on the wiles of political operatives. His "explanation" became a way of getting beyond the incident. At a party fund-raiser a few days later, the president praised Atwater as a strong "and a correct voice arguing that the Republicans need to reach out to minorities and the disadvantaged." The next day, however, brought a resignation and an apology to Foley from Mark Goodin, the Atwater aide whose posting of a crude representation of Willie Horton on his office wall had created an embarrassment during the 1988 campaign, just as other Bush people were denying that the furlough matter had anything to do with race.[7]

Foley's grace, which contrasted so sharply with what was acceptable behavior from Atwater, was not lost on the president. Of all the opposition leaders, Bush later said, Foley was the most "statesmanlike," and, for all their partisan differences, the two men enjoyed a decent personal relationship. "We could talk very frankly. I always felt he would try to give me the benefit of the doubt."[8]

The most ominous cloud left, one that grew increasingly large and frightening whenever it was examined more closely, was the savings and loan disaster. Nick Brady had just told the House Banking Committee that 722 banks and

1,037 thrifts were facing closure. Losses to the government, he predicted, could reach $98 to $132 billion. To step in and clean up the disaster by selling off confiscated properties to reimburse the government, Congress created a new agency, the Resolution Trust Corporation. On August 9, with considerable flourish suggesting a confident response to the problem, President Bush signed the Financial Institutions Reform, Recovery, and Enforcement Act. One hundred and twenty billion dollars in taxpayer bailouts were thereby authorized, but the final burden became less calculable, with projections going as high as a half trillion. After a Supreme Court decision in the case of *U.S.* v. *Winstar Corporation* placed even more of the liabilities in the hands of the government, a revised estimate, as of late 1996, approached $160 billion.[9]

The Bush administration, meanwhile, was caught up with the Congress and lobbyists representing all sorts of lending institutions in designing bailout legislation chiseled from schemes designed to hand off the burden to America's taxpayers.[10]

By far the worst dimension of the scandal would strike close to the presidency itself. Neil Bush was in trouble, seduced by a get-rich-quick crowd and by his own desire to replicate his grandfather's and father's independent means. His dad was not even president yet when the opportunities came, but operators calculated the value of hooking a vice president's son.

It was obvious that many congressmen had cozy ties to the S&Ls, sometimes referred to as "people's banks," often the Democratic financing institutions, the ones competing against commercial banking. Those major players got their first big deregulatory boost not from the Reagan administration, as is generally assumed, but from the Democratic Congress while Carter was still president in 1980. Without a cap on mortgage interest rates, it was argued, the free market would take over, which seemed fine until it got the thrifts (S&Ls) up in arms. So the "people's banks" lobbied, and Congress delivered in 1982 in the form of compensatory legislation that enabled them to lend money for commercial property as well—shopping malls, office plazas, giant complexes that could exploit frenzied and seemingly unlimited growth. Within the next five years, an especially aggressive thrift in Colorado, under the leadership of a small-town Kansas buccaneer, Michael Wise, taking advantage of investments hitherto deemed too risky for S&Ls, increased its portfolio by 800 percent.[11]

Helping to make that possible, helping to fuel the boom by gambling with "other people's money," was the new $100,000 Federal Deposit Insurance Corporation ceiling. The ground rules for the new deregulatory environment were thereby laid out in the industry. It was simple: invest, make risky investments, list the anticipated value of property in portfolios to inflate the solvency for the eyes of one's own auditors and Federal Home Loan Bank regulators, and hope to make a killing. If the venture bombed, the government would step in and reimburse depositors. It was, in the end, not surprising to find that Wright and Coelho were those on the hill with ties to the S&Ls. Such funds, pointed out *The New York Times,* "help explain why, even after monumental scandal, members lunge to be lenient to the S&Ls."[12]

In the spring of 1985, Wise, ever ambitious for his Silverado Savings, Banking, and Loan Association, recruited for his board the young man who could help the company with the right people and in the right places. Neil Bush, at age twenty-nine, eager to be on his own and determined to hit success by the time he was thirty, agreed to the good deal.[13]

Why not? All sorts of big spenders wanted to throw money his way: Wise, the head of the Greater Denver Chamber of Commerce, Bill Walters, and, among others, a high-living developer named Ken Good. Good lent Neil investment money that he could use to gamble with for free. Walters, who bought $20 million in Silverado securities in 1986, got over $200 million in loans from the thrift. He was also useful in helping young Bush and two partners get started with a personal investment of just $100 in creating a petroleum development and leasing company, JNB Explorations. Walters put up $150,000 for that venture, and his three banks extended a $1.2-million line of credit to Neil. The nice young man, handicapped for all too long by dyslexia, was, finally, on the fast track. Silverado got an additional boost, thanks to his presence, when the ending of a special tax break on commercial real estate deflected investments away from developers who were not as well connected as Walters and Good. When it all became public, and before anybody knew much about Charles Keating and the major scandal involving Lincoln Savings, Neil was even called the "poster boy of bunko banking."[14]

By the summer of 1988, fraudulent manipulations and bad loans had also killed Silverado. Just two weeks before the Republican presidential nominating convention, Neil resigned from the board and joined his father's campaign team. Right after the election, Silverado was ordered shut down. Good and Walters defaulted on their loans. Wise, the former boy wonder of Emporia, returned to Kansas. By then, it was also time to walk away from JNB Explorations. Along with his two partners, James Judd and Evans Nash, Neil gave up after thirty-one dry holes. In March, with his father in the White House for two months, he began a new business, the Apex Energy Company.[15] The president was glad to hear that his son was about to "extricate himself from the financial mess he's in on oil" and go to work in the "cable TV business" in Colorado.[16] There were definite disadvantages to being the son of a president.

Anyone who knew Barbara and how she felt about her children was convinced that she believed his dad's presidency was bad for Neil. "He's probably the most sensitive of our four boys," she once said.[17] Others called him the "most naive" and Barbara's "favorite child." Jeb, a Florida land developer, was the serious one, and George W. the "smartest." Jeb found some wariness among business people about dealing with them. There was no telling what kind of audits they would leave themselves open to, or how far the press would go. It got so bad, the president heard, that Neil told his lawyer that he wished his father would disappear. After George W. bought a sizeable share of the Texas Rangers, the American League baseball club, his father began to keep up with the team in the standings.[18] When Doro, the "shy one," filed for a divorce from Billy LeBlond and left Maine and her job with the state's tourism department, the whole world knew about it. When, on her own, she wanted to buy a house, the president complained about not being able to "go out and see it or do what a father should do."*[19] Barbara, during those first months in the White House, wrote an article that revealed how she and George helped Neil learn despite his dyslexia.[20] Marvin told *Ladies' Home Journal* readers details of his ileostomy. The handicap, he wrote to reassure others facing a similar procedure, did not keep him off the tennis courts or from his other sports. He was also able to run a Washington investment company. He and his wife enjoyed parenthood by adopting a daughter (and later a son). The article spelled it all out, how the disease was diagnosed and gave details about his surgery that created an artificial opening in his abdominal wall leading from his ileum.[21] Indeed, Marvin was "the courageous one."

That was also the period in George Bush's life when Barbara was diagnosed as having Graves' disease, that unusual affliction first discovered by a nineteenth-century Irish physician, Robert J. Graves. A breakdown in the autoimmune system, which keeps the human engine going, attacks tissues—in Barbara's case, her eyes. She first felt the puffiness, the tearing and itching, and noted the red-eye effect before George's inaugural. It was, she wrote after consulting with specialists at Walter Reed, Bethesda, and the Mayo Clinic in Rochester, Minnesota, "a thyroid gone berserk."[22] For starters, they put her on prednisone. That drug's potential side effects were too dangerous. After further tests, she underwent ten low-dosage radiation treatments, which controlled the disease. An additional bonus was a twenty-pound weight loss.[23]

George's mother's health was truly worrisome. A stroke had damaged the left side of her brain, leaving her paralyzed on one side. She didn't recognize her son when he called her. But the doctors, trying to keep her alive, were contemplating using procedures that they had never tried on an eighty-eight-year-old woman before. It was hard to move her. She "wants to die," Bush told his diary. "She wants to be with Jesus in Heaven; and yet, the doctors must give her the best attention possible." How he hoped they wouldn't use artificial tricks to keep her alive![24]

The post–cold war world dawned along with Bush's presidency. In Latin America, the Nicaraguan peace process was under way, in keeping with the accord that had been negotiated, and a cease-fire was in place. The United States was finally eager to detach itself from contra support, although Vice President Quayle, encouraged by Bush to be less passive than Bush himself

---

*He finally managed to outmaneuver the press and got a peek at the house (interview with Marlin Fitzwater, July 30, 1996).

had been under Reagan and working to shore up the administration's credentials with right-wing hard-liners, went to Central America in June and delivered some of the strongest support ever given by a U.S. official in the battles against Latin America's Marxist guerrillas.[25] Yet, as Quayle toured the camps, not even those who had guided the contra resupply effort had much of a clue about the outcome. In Eastern Europe, the first Bush year coincided with cataclysmic change: the withering away of satellite states from Moscow's control and the astonishingly rapid dissolution of the Soviet empire. Only in U.S.-Sino relations, where, as James Baker has written, the two nations "treaded water," was diplomacy essentially static.[26]

China—indeed, much of Asia—continued to be an arena particularly attractive to free-traders as a "future that works," to paraphrase Lincoln Steffens's famous comment about the Soviet Union in the 1920s. Others, often more along nationalist-internationalist lines rather than through tidy conservative-liberal classifications, including some who had doubted that the "evil empire" really was *that* evil, were highly critical of doing business with oppressive regimes elsewhere, including in the Far East.[27] With the exception of modern and highly technological postwar Japan, no nation in the region was more important than the one whose military had slaughtered Americans in Korea and helped kill them in Vietnam. China's population equalled nearly one-fourth of the world's total. The People's Republic indeed had grown as a market for American goods, especially arms and technology. Ideology appeared to count for little, often in contrast with acceptable approaches toward the Soviet Union. Ancient enemies of Mao Tse-tung, even old allies to the Kuomintang, including Anna Chenault, lined up at Oriental bazaars. Richard Nixon, in taking his initiatives, insisted that the war in Vietnam was only an incidental reason for the need to develop a working relationship. Henry Kissinger, Nixon's plenipotentiary, emerged in 1989 as a strong supporter of Bush's reaction to the massacre at Tiananmen Square. "We are dealing with a huge country that has been extremely antiforeign," said the former secretary of state. Losing sight of our long-term interests, he cautioned, could create a diplomatic "antagonism" with potential for giving the Soviet Union "a free ride" in influencing the rest of Asia.[28] Others cited the People's Republic's value for dealing with Cambodia and North Korea. Bush, recalled Brent Scowcroft, "decided that what we had to do about China was not to avert our gaze from what they had done, not to rationalize the human rights disaster that it was, but to say we have to deal with that in the context of our overall relationship with the great powers."[29]

The president acted on those principles. In the aftermath of the brutal crackdown, he tried hard to avoid being cast as friendly to the "butchers of Beijing." On June 30, weeks after the People's Liberation Army had crushed the prodemocracy movement, he dispatched Scowcroft and Larry Eagleburger on a secret visit to Beijing. So important was the avoidance of exposure that the plane left before dawn and was refueled in midair rather than risk the enterprise being spotted while on the ground. The trip was "basically to explain to the Chinese the consequences of what they had done in the United States," recalled Scowcroft, who also remembered that the Chinese leadership responded by saying something like, "It's absolutely none of your business." "What you do is your own business, but I'm here to tell you that what you do has its impact in our country, and that's our business," said the president's emissary. "They never said so directly," Eagleburger later told Baker, "but I think the smarter ones absorbed the message that we can do a lot more for them when they aren't killing their own people."[30]

Politicking over the murders never ceased in Washington. "Tiananmen" was repeated over and over in the halls of Congress when the affair became absorbed into the legislative-executive struggle. The Democratic majority, assuredly on the popular side of the issue, proposed a bill to permit Chinese students in the United States to remain for an extended period of time; they could become permanent residents without returning home first. Many had demonstrated in sympathy with their fellow students and had little enthusiasm for testing the authorities in Beijing by going back just then. The passage of sanctuary legislation, warned the Chinese government, would kill their end of the Fulbright scholarship program and other student exchanges. Bush, already charged with "kowtowing" to Beijing, argued that he had already provided protection via an executive order. Senator Dole came to his side by saying that the issue was "American politics," not "China policy." But the minority leader's best efforts were not enough to keep it from passing. Only an energetic telephone campaign, personally led by the president and Jim Baker, and further helped by some Nixonian lobbying, ensured enough Senate votes to sustain the veto.[31]

Nixon had reentered the arena on Bush's behalf in another way. On his own, and against the advice of those around him, he decided on a fifth trip to Beijing. Careful to consult with the president and Scowcroft, he left in October "to salvage the China initiative by tipping glasses with those who had ordered the Tiananmen crackdown less than five months before." In his round of meetings with China's leaders, he told Deng Xiaoping that U.S.-Sino relations had never undergone "a worse crisis." The gap, he said in a toast at one banquet, was "huge and unbridgeable" and let those around him know how the rest of the world felt about the massacre. Upon his return, Bush received Nixon at the White House for dinner; on that occasion and in a memorandum to congressional leaders, Nixon repeated all the familiar reasons why, despite their insistence that the cold war was not over, an opening to China must be kept intact.[32]

The point, of course, was one Bush believed all along. In December, half a year after the secret mission, Scowcroft and Eagleburger returned. The trip, a goodwill attempt to keep open the lines of diplomacy between the two countries and, as Scowcroft later described it, to lay out "a road map for getting back together," included an exchange of toasts in the Great Hall of the People. They succeeded, according to Baker, by persuading the Chinese that the president was serious when he had made the point that "goodwill begets goodwill." Besides, went the main explanation, it was important to keep China from becoming "isolated." Only three weeks later, martial law ended in Beijing and the square was reopened to the public. The president, reciprocating, waived a congressional ban on Export-Import Bank loans to U.S. firms doing business with them and announced that Beijing was buying three communications satellites from the United States.[33]

Bush, however, had to battle annually to renew the People's Republic's status. The U.S. had become their largest single market, but the "butchers of Beijing" were guilty of more than just Tiananmen. They sold nuclear and missile technology to some tinderboxes, especially to the Middle East, oppressed Tibet, and used forced prison labor. Bush managed to prevail, though opposed by human rights activists, and despite George Mitchell's leadership in a Senate fight against Dole, who warned that "foolishly pulling the plug on MFN" would force the U.S. to be "out there alone" and to "suffer the consequences." Getting two-thirds plus one to overcome a veto was just too much. The president was particularly irked by the antics of some fellow Republicans, especially New York's Al D'Amato, who "don't have any responsibility" but still "feel that they have to make the grandstand play instead of just saying, 'I see the president's point and I disagree.' "[34] Noting that American opposition to the extension of World Bank loans to China had also become fairly routine, Bush deplored his country's isolation among the G-7 powers in continuing to make the normalization of relations contingent on human rights. He never doubted that free enterprise would do more to achieve that goal than "this Marxist command system."*[35] Democratic capitalism would inevitably produce freedom.

On the morning of June 27, the men and the women of the press crowded the White House Briefing Room for the president's sixteenth news conference. Hanging in the air, but not preeminent among global developments, was the Supreme Court's decision of June 21. Having heard a test of one of the forty-eight state laws that banned desecration of the American flag, the justices decided in the case of *Texas* v. *Johnson* that such legislation impinged on First Amendment free-speech rights. After the overexposure of the flag in the last campaign, reactions were predictable. Bush, without a doubt, had profited by using the flag to smother Dukakis; there was no question that it had placed the Democrat on the defensive.[36] Among officeholders, of course, the message was clear. Never again would Democrats allow themselves to be overwhelmed on the gut issue, especially when, as *Newsweek* then confirmed, Americans were so overwhelmingly upset about flag desecration. Nearly three-quarters thought a constitutional amendment banning the act was in order. A plausible nightmare, in the modern world of politics, was a

---

*Bush's successor, after criticizing his policy during the 1992 campaign, eventually followed the same course, even meeting with the Chinese leadership four years later and indicating his willingness to have China join the World Trade Organization.

thirty-second TV spot that denounced one's vote against the amendment as a vote favoring burning the flag. The Senate, accordingly, with Democrats scrambling to fall into line, lost little time in passing a resolution expressing its disapproval of the Court's decision. Every member voted, and only three dissented, two of them predictable, Ted Kennedy of Massachusetts and Howard Metzenbaum of Ohio. The third, a surprise, was Gordon Humphrey, a solid man of the right from New Hampshire. Among others who agreed with the minority, who felt that desecrating the flag, however obnoxious, was a legitimate expression of free speech, were some conservatives who did not have to stand for reelection—George Will, William Safire, and Jeane Kirkpatrick.[37] When the president walked into the news conference shortly after nine that morning, he opened by saying that, while "the right to protest government" action should be preserved, the "flag of the United States should never be an object of desecration." The administration was already in consultation with the Congress about repairing this constitutional deficiency.[38]

The announcement caused little stir among the press. The first question was about U.S.-Sino relations in the aftermath of Tiananmen. Finally, ABC-TV newsman Brit Hume asked whether the president thought it seemly to make partisan use of the flag matter. Bush agreed. "Respect for the flag transcends political party," he said. His request was neither Republican nor Democratic, neither liberal nor conservative, but American. Then he added, "And perhaps I haven't been quite as emotional as I feel about it, but I want to take this opportunity to say protest should not extend to desecration of the unique symbol of America, and that is our flag." What he did against Dukakis last year, he acknowledged to the follow-up question, was political, but that was then and this is now. Finally, after covering far more ground, including gambling in baseball, he was asked why he was calling for a constitutional amendment rather than going the legislative route. "Because," he replied, lamely, "I am told that legislation cannot correct the—in my view—egregious offense: burning the American flag."

"How about the death penalty for teenagers and the retarded?" came the next question.

"I really do have to go," replied the president.[39]

After that court decision, he really needed to stay on target, to defend what he had made such a prominent symbol in 1988. The secondary point was that such issues, along with SDI, taxes, capital gains reductions, and opposition to abortion were credentials that certified his standing with the right. His positions had to remain firm, to counterbalance vulnerabilities on such things as the risks involved in finessing the Western Alliance and Gorbachev, to say nothing of arms control, possibly undermining the contra position in Central America as a result of the peace process, and moving on child care legislation. His presidency had hardly started when Ed Rollins was renewed in his fear that "George Bush was not Ronald Reagan, and there was no way his first term was going to be Reagan's third."[40] He was already copping out on gun control by defying the NRA and banning imported AK-47 assault weapons and risking other problems by proposing renewals of the Johnson-Nixon-era Clean Air Act. It was Sununu, together with Atwater, who worked to get conservatives to understand the options, especially with a Congress from hell, unlike any a newly elected Republican president had had to put up with. Mitchell, for one, would give no quarter, not an inch, no matter how much Bush insisted on the need for lowering capital gains taxes.[41]

He had met with Sununu, Scowcroft, Gates, and the CIA briefing staff on the morning of June 26. The chief of staff explained, as Fred Barnes put it, that Bush's overall political strategy consisted of "pursuing a relatively conservative agenda while maintaining credibility all the way across the center." His need was to please the right while escaping their control. He was no Reagan. They must understand that in Central America, for example, there was no choice except to embrace the peace process. The deal Baker worked out, while ending military aid to the contras, was better than disbanding the anti-Communists. Sununu made it plain, and he was backed by Gates, that the process of free elections in Nicaragua, initiated to bring stability to the region by President Oscar Arias of Costa Rica, could not take place as long as military supplies were going to the contras. If all went well—and there was at least a chance of that—Nicaraguans would come through in a free election and toss out Ortega and his Sandinistas. It was worth the gamble. What was the alternative?[42]

However, they could, and should, keep faith with the right by getting out there with a constitutional amendment to end disgraces to the flag once and for all. Bush liked that. Just watching commentators going on about the court's decision, especially liberals yakking on about how desecrations constituted nothing more than the right of free speech, infuriated him. He listened to the justifications and simmered. Besides, it wasn't a one-way decision; just 5 to 4. If Antonin Scalia and Anthony Kennedy hadn't deserted to the liberals, or even if they had divided, it would have been a different story. The president "felt strongly about it," explained Marlin Fitzwater. "He's a veteran [and] the flag's a symbol of his life; it was an important symbol of his campaign."[43] True enough; those close to him knew how thumbing one's nose at the United States and its symbols raised his blood pressure. In Portland, Oregon, one time, there to talk to a police convention, he looked out of his Hilton Hotel window and saw demonstrators "hold an American flag and light it." He watched them actually do a dance and cheer. The sight made him "more determined than ever to protect this flag. I think of those who died for it." It was just "radical outrage" and it "really burns me up."[44] Newt Gingrich, somebody reminded the staff meeting, thought the president might get out in front of the issue in a really dramatic way. He could call for a special session of Congress on the Fourth of July and challenge them, right then and there, to pass the amendment. They let that one pass.[45]

That same day, after the staff meeting, he had lunch with Lee Atwater. No, the press was told, they didn't talk about the flag amendment. It was on his list, said Atwater, but he just didn't get to it. Nor had he conducted voter interviews or focus groups.[46] It just happened that, by the next morning, Bush had his statement and strategy ready to tell the journalists about the need for a constitutional amendment.

Not long after dawn on the thirtieth, the president faced a crowd before the Iwo Jima monument in Arlington, right by the Potomac. The scene was glorious, some 4,500 people in all, just ordinary people, all out to cheer for the flag in an paroxysm of patriotism. Many wore their military uniforms. There was red-white-and-blue bunting, tiny flags waved from hands large and small, and the crowd sang "The Star-Spangled Banner." Bob Dole told them that they had gathered to warn the rabble to "keep your hands off Old Glory."[47] The president stood in the early morning sunlight, read the brief proposed amendment, and vowed that, "For the sake of the fallen, for the men behind the guns, for every American, we will defend the flag of the United States of America."[48]

The defense, Bush made clear, required an amendment. If the Congress wanted to legislate a statute banning desecration, that was their business. He would not sign it, just let it pass into law on its own, "to signal our belief that a constitutional amendment is the best way to provide lasting protection for the flag." The administration, then, was on the winning side twice—when the Supreme Court (after the solicitor general had filed a friend of the court brief) exempted states from having to use their facilities or employees to perform abortions, and when the Congress, with hardly any debate, enacted a statute providing fines, imprisonment, or both, for any individual who "knowingly mutilates, defaces, physically defiles, burns, maintains on the floor or ground, or tramples upon" any United States flag.[49]

In October, however, the flag-burning amendment missed the required two-thirds by fifteen votes. Those who viewed flag desecration as a protected form of free speech had rallied enough support, from conservatives as well as liberals, to abort what they feared was mischievous to the work of the Founding Fathers. The flag's utility as a political weapon had advanced with increasing frequency for at least two decades. "A flag in flames seems as powerful an image today as it was twenty years ago, when the nation was divided over a war and the way that war was sometimes protested," wrote Robin Toner of one significant aspect of the "Vietnam syndrome."[50] Reagan and movement conservatives had virtually made the Stars and Stripes the proprietary icon of the new right. Nobody had used it more blatantly than Bush himself in 1988. The lesson to politicians, if not to constitutional scholars or First Amendment buffs, was that there was only one side to the flag issue. The administration, by its tactics, had cleverly continued the process by forcing its opponents to duck for cover. Easy passage in the House was assured— little debate, less hype. But Bush had no need to stain constitutional history with his signature. The Senate, as conceived during the constitutional convention of 1787 and argued in the *Federalist Papers,* would be less sensitive to the whims of popular passion. Failure to win Senate ratification, then, was fine, as long as everyone knew who was outflagged. The public, polled on the issue by Gallup months later, favored an amendment by an overwhelming two-thirds.[51]

Late June in Moscow, the American ambassador, Jack F. Matlock Jr., watched the growing economic and social protests. Already, he noted, scattered outbreaks were becoming violent and were combining with ethnic hatred. In city after city, groups were defying the best efforts of police. "What then?" he asked himself. "Could they order a Tiananmen Square?" On a plane back to Washington, he began to realize that the Soviet Union was disintegrating.[52] In Budapest, the West German embassy was getting dangerously overloaded by East Germans who had made their way into Hungary. Already, the Baltic states of Lithuania and Estonia had declared their sovereignty, and Latvia was about to follow. In Warsaw, Gen. Wojciech Jaruzelski's Communists were defeated in national elections. Gorbachev, meeting with German Chancellor Kohl in mid June, stood near the Berlin Wall and agreed that "nothing is eternal in this world." In Washington on the ninth of July, President and Mrs. Bush left the White House for a nine-day tour of Europe.[53]

Their trip, every bit like a goodwill mission, took them to Warsaw, Budapest, Amsterdam, and Paris, where the president participated in a G-7 summit that coincided with bicentennial celebrations of the French Revolution. At Warsaw, they were greeted at the airport by a delegation headed by General Jaruzelski. Also present was a close adviser to Lech Walesa, whose Solidarity Party, just after being legalized, had won an overwhelming majority in Poland's newly constituted Sejm, the country's parliament. Jaruzelski, whose chairmanship of the Council of State made him Poland's leader, had only days before responded to the election by announcing that he would not be a candidate for the newly created presidency because the Communists had not won enough seats. Bush, fearing matters getting out of hand, turned to the general and immediately told him that he had not come to talk about East-West feuding. The United States, said the president, realized that Poland was in a period of transition and should stay out of it. "We want you to have good relations with Moscow." Rather than coming in "on a high horse," demanding that Poland immediately renounce her forty-five-year relationship with the Soviet Union, Bush showed his concern with avoiding further volatility. He also brought Poland a six-part program of American aid, which included $100 million "to capitalize and invigorate the Polish private sector." The level of aid fell far short of the $10 billion hoped for by Solidarity and most others, but Bush praised it as an "unprecedented opportunity" that was made possible by Poland's experiment with democracy. However disappointing the level of American assistance may have been, both Walesa and Jaruzelski got the president's message.[54] The general soon agreed to run and, with backing by the leader of Solidarity, became Poland's president. Bush completed his two-day visit by addressing the Sejm, participating in a wreath-laying ceremony at the Tomb of the Unknown Soldier, being welcomed by the

Polish Little League baseball program as "America's Ambassador of Goodwill," and greeting Jewish leaders and survivors of the Warsaw ghetto.[55] He and Barbara also capped off their visit with lunch at the Gdansk home of Lech Walesa and his wife.

Most of all, he enjoyed meeting his counterparts, especially the "unstructured part, the part where you sit with these other leaders, tell them what you think, listen carefully to what they think. And that happens sometimes in the corridors or sometimes at a meal. I would like to think that the more emphasis we've placed on that kind of interaction [*sic*]," he told reporters in Paris, "the better it would be."[56]

In Budapest's Kossuth Square, at nearly eight in the evening, he climbed out of his car under an umbrella held by a Secret Service man and faced an enormous crowd standing in what Fitzwater remembered as a "wild, crashing rain with heavy drops of blowing wind." He was so overwhelmed by the frenzied reception that "he threw his speech to the wind," a fitting metaphor for his sometimes recklessness to the impact of words. "You've been out here too long," he shouted extemporaneously at the throng of about a half million packed into the square. "Let me just speak to you from the heart, and I'll be brief—" Suddenly, seeing someone grab one of the pages, he yelled, "Tear that thing up," and then, returning to the throng of newly liberated Hungarians, "You've been standing here long enough. But Barbara and I feel the warmth of this welcome, and the rain doesn't make a darn bit of difference. We feel at home right here in this great capital." The warmth of the welcome, he told them, would be remembered long after the rain had gone. He just shouted his ad-libbed words, with no pretense at sentence structure, adjectives, verbs, just some question about whether his English was being translated at all. The appearance went swiftly. His prepared message was lost to history, but there were wonderful pictures of him standing there with the pages flying up over his head.[57]

Wherever he went, he spoke of the desirability of moving toward democracy and a market economy. At the Group of Seven summit, Bush and the other leaders covered a range of global issues: the environment, narcotics trafficking, the Third World, and technology, but mostly, of course, free-market economics. The current Uruguay round of the General Agreement on Tariffs and Trade (GATT) was reaffirmed, and they agreed to extend the system to cover additional commodities. Planning for further international commercial relationships, however, was temporarily diverted when the host, François Mitterrand, read to the G-7's executive committee a letter from Gorbachev. The Soviet leader, citing the needs of *perestroika* as "inseparable from a policy aimed at our full participation in the world economy," clearly thought his nation should be able to participate. The missive came as a surprise, diverting their conversation considerably. "There's an awful lot that has to transpire in the Soviet Union, it seems to me," Bush later told the press, "before anything of that nature would be considered. We're talking about free-market economics here." If it was, in any way, a response to his own overtures to the Soviets, Bush found it "fascinating" that it was addressed to Mitterrand. Asked whether anyone had suggested that Gorbachev was merely grandstanding, Bush was discreet. He could not say that thought "never occurred."[58]

Facing the journalists in an evening session at the American ambassador's residence, he repeated the ideal of wanting to see Europe "whole and free." An inevitable question followed. Did he think the "cold war" was over?

"I don't like to use 'cold war,'" replied Bush. "That has a connotation of worse days in terms of East-West relationship. I think things have moved forward so that the connotation that those two words conjure up is entirely different now. And yet I don't want to stand here and seem euphoric—that everything is hunky-dory between the East and the West on arms or on differences in the economy or on how we look at regional problems. We have some big differences, still. But let's encourage the change. And then I can answer your question in maybe a few more years more definitively."[59]

Even at that point, continued movement was obvious. Contacts with Moscow were being kept alive at all levels, especially the foreign ministerial one, and White House–Kremlin telephone exchanges would only increase. Gorbachev's letter to Mitterrand may have been a publicity ploy, and Bush shared that amusing thought with the press, but for all the reservations about what he was up to, Baker pointed out even while he and the president were still in Paris, the time had come to "get engaged." Scowcroft was his usual cautious self, not wanting to derail the process but trying to guard against the political and diplomatic consequences of appearing to be over-anxious. Bush kept thinking about his little talk with Scowcroft and, after taking off from Paris, put his pen to a sheet of White House letterhead while aboard Air Force One and wrote to Gorbachev suggesting that they get together. Not lost in the overture, and certainly intended to be attractive for both leaders, was the public relations utility, a propaganda advantage Gorbachev, in particular, could use at that moment. The site eventually agreed upon for the summit was Malta. This decision followed Gorbachev's countering Bush's invitation that they meet at Kennebunkport by suggesting Spain. Bush, however, having heard from his brother, Bucky, about how happily he had vacationed on Malta, had another inspiration. Why not go there, to the tranquil Mediterranean? Diplomatic protocol could be observed by alternating the meetings between ships, a thought that conjured up memories of Roosevelt and Churchill sitting side by side in 1945. Gorbachev, with the prospects of a Mediterranean sojourn in December vastly more attractive than Moscow, agreed. The public announcement on September 23 advertised the event as a "meeting" and not a summit, a semantic twist suggestive of something less formal and more intimate, the kind of setting Bush usually favored. Meanwhile, Eduard Shevardnadze flew to Wyoming for another in a round of sessions with Jim Baker, this one at the secretary's ranch near Jackson Hole, which helped to prepare the background for the meeting.[60]

But Moscow's empire just kept on imploding, a process made less bloody by Gorbachev's realization that rushing Soviet troops to counter each trouble spot could only make matters worse. On the very day that Bush left Europe, Gorbachev warned the Soviet Central Committee that people were losing faith in the party and threatened to purge those members of the government who opposed his *perestroika*. The Supreme Soviet moved quickly after that to approve a resolution in support of the efforts of two of the Baltic states to develop autonomous free-market economic systems. In Poland, Jaruzelski had little choice but to accept Walesa's suggestion that Solidarity form a governing coalition. Refugees, meanwhile, continued to flee from East Germany, nearly one thousand to Austria on one August day. Right after that, Lithuania's Supreme Court declared the Soviet annexation illegal, and on the fiftieth anniversary of the Molotov–von Ribbentrop Pact of 1939 that had handed them over to the Communists, over two million protesters participated in the biggest demonstration ever. Perhaps a million or more, with the blessings of the governments of Estonia, Latvia, and Lithuania, celebrated the "Baltic Way" by forming an unbroken human chain that linked hands going through the capital cities of Tallinn, Riga, and Vilnius. According to one estimate, the turnout constituted 40 percent of the entire Baltic population.[61] But the Hungarian government, by annulling their pact with East Germany and opening their border with Austria (which was neutral) to refugees, was the first to make a clean break.[62] By late September, after Bush was criticized by Soviet bloc newspapers for saying that residents of Gorbachev's "common European home" should be able to move from room to room, over 5,000 refugees were encamped at the West German embassy in Prague alone. Jim Baker also agreed to shelter others in the American embassy. Massive demonstrations in Leipzig, East Germany, forced the resignation of the Communist leader, Eric Honecker. In Prague, hundreds of riot police charged into crowds, beating and arresting 355 people. Margaret Thatcher, in Moscow that September to see Gorbachev, carried a message from Bush advising him that the upheavals should not be seen as threats to Soviet security. Gorbachev didn't seem relieved.[63]

The most dramatic development, one that became emblematic of the Soviet collapse, took place in Germany. In addition to the flooding of foreign embassies, street battles were fought almost daily. A demonstration attracted half a million in East Berlin on November 4. Several German Democratic Republic Politburo members gave up their seats and were replaced by leader Egon Krenz with more faithful acolytes of Moscow. On the ninth, word spread that all citizens were to be granted exit visas "immediately" so that they would be able to move across the country's borders without "special permission." A few vital details, however, were overlooked during the confused preparation of the order and in the mess that followed. The travel instructions were yet to be submitted to the legislature, as Krenz had assured Gorbachev he would do. The visas were not for random distribution but had to be applied for in advance. And, overlooked in the sloppy preparation of the order was something that no one intended: its generalized language about border crossings could easily be interpreted as including the Berlin Wall.

All this was missed by Gunter Shabowski, the reform Communist member of the Politburo who briefed the press on its contents. Quickly, eagerly, putting aside their own doubts, journalists sped the news precisely as it had been explained to them by Shabowski. It was still afternoon in Washington when Bush heard about the new travel law. His briefing officer had some idea of the confusion because he had to tear up his notes three times on the way to the White House. Meanwhile, at the wall, rumors that there were, in effect, no travel restrictions encouraged a massive crowd to press against the wall demanding egress. None of the guards knew what to do; neither did their commanders. Equally caught up in that turbulent atmosphere, they hardly wanted to, or could, shoot everybody who might attempt to storm through at that point. Finally, with the possibility of disaster, they were instructed to step aside, thereby receiving a decision that was de facto when finally ratified by the interior minister. All through that night, the wall was breached and the process of chipping it away piece by piece had begun. The world watched in astonishment as television showed celebrants climbing to the top. When the American president was asked to comment, he kept his restraint. "I'm very pleased," he admitted, but added that he would not "beat my chest and dance on the wall." The next week, when questioned by a reporter in Helena, Montana, he repeated his faith in German reunification and, thinking of the French, British, and especially Russians, acknowledged that such confidence was far from universal.[64]

Culminating the chaotic changes of the second half of 1989, which, by then, saw defection after defection sweep through what was rapidly becoming the former Communist bloc, were the events in Romania, still ruled by dedicated Stalinist Nicolae Ceauşescu. Ceauşescu was an especially strong, unreconstructed follower of the party line. His praise of the Chinese actions at Tiananmen Square was well known. The same virus that had spread elsewhere, spurred by a combination of inspiration, nationalism, and economic distress, sparked demonstrations in the cities of Timisoara and Bucharest, the capital. Soldiers fired at crowds. Then they, too, began to defect. Ceauşescu's own security force, which outnumbered the military units, were unable to impose control. TV cameras showed the ruler and his wife hooted down by crowds as they stood at their window pleading for order, and, as it turned out, their lives. After nearly a quarter century of rule, the Ceauşescus fled, but were soon captured and executed by a firing squad on Christmas Day.

In Czechoslovakia four days later, Vaclav Havel, a playwright who had been jailed for demonstrating, was chosen president of that country's restored parliamentary democracy.

How the democratization process might unfold without East-West conflict was not entirely clear. From the American perspective—and certainly that of the president and others around him—the economic and political openness implied by *perestroika* and *glasnost* were promising but hardly trustworthy. Gorbachev still clung to his Marxism and ignorance of democratic economics. If anyone doubted his potential for authoritarianism, they saw the evidence for themselves when he hounded Sakharov off the podium at the Congress of People's Deputies in mid December for attempting to make some reform proposals. When the physicist died in his sleep of a heart attack only two days later, many thought that it was no coincidence.[65]

The Soviet's military potential, however, was foremost. The world still remembered Moscow's troops squashing opposition in Budapest in 1956, Prague in 1968, the ongoing war in Afghanistan, and the covert exports of disorder elsewhere. At several points along the way, the emphasis by the Bush team, as Elizabeth Drew put it, was in trying "to anticipate every gambit Gorbachev might come up with and figuring out the appropriate response" for incalculable diplomatic and military challenges.[66] Gorbachev's warning to Western leaders on November 10 about the dangers of "political extremism" possibly resulting from the German situation led to a move by the Bush administration to organize a unified response. The strategic and political need for forceful action, if necessary, was obvious.[67] When Gorbachev countered ominously the declaration by Lithuania's Communist Party of independence from the Soviets, another alert activated Bush's national security team. Condi Rice recalled being awakened in the middle of the night by a call telling her that Shevardnadze had resigned and was warning darkly of a coup. She called Scowcroft, who called the president. "Everybody came in immediately. We really thought that that was the prelude to a real tough reaction."[68]

The imponderables were intimidating to the Bush national security team, the paradox clear. Gorbachev, however far he might eventually take his openness, his touting of reforms, could still totter, his hold tenuous in a society with fissures similar to what was going on throughout Eastern Europe. The state-dependent Soviet production system was failing to respond to demands posed by increasing economic anxiety. Hardly anything had changed, except restlessness and a populace beset by shortages of just about everything, especially consumer goods. The American ambassador, traveling to the outer provinces, found plant managers stuck in their old ways despite their supposed greater freedom from party strictures, presiding over a system of production that was breaking down even further.[69] In that "workers' paradise," with its recalcitrant bureaucracy, coal miners went on strike from Siberia to the Ukraine, protesting poor wages, housing, and working and medical conditions. The restlessness, with the specter of greater disorders to come, led the Supreme Soviet to give workers a narrowly defined "right to strike" that forbade walkouts in key sectors. A particularly unsettling response was the defiant walkout of tens of thousands of miners in the Arctic city of Vorkuta for a one-day strike that called for the implementation of concessions won earlier. With a weakening of the coercive forces that had bonded the USSR's variety of nationalities to the central government, ethnics were rebellious. Demonstrations broke out in such republics as Georgia and Soviet Uzbekistan. Gorbachev went on television to warn that such violence and nationalism posed an "enormous danger" to the country and threatened to undermine reforms. A leading conservative, Yegor T. Ligachev, denounced growing notions of multiparty democracy and called for tighter restrictions on the press. With faith in the state further eroded by such revelations as admission of guilt for the Katyn Forest massacre and the secret police's (KGB) responsibility for "mechanisms of repression," restlessness was intensifying. Even earlier, Boris Yeltsin, who himself had been under close surveillance by the KGB after his expulsion as Moscow Communist Party chief, allied himself with reform forces and espoused a populist message en route to his election—with 89 percent of the vote—to a seat in the Congress of People's Deputies. After just missing out in the balloting for a seat in the Chamber of Nationalities, his supporters called for a national strike. In September, on a lecture tour of the United States, his request to meet with Bush was handled gingerly. The Soviet visitor was invited to Scowcroft's office, where, by prior arrangement, the president dropped in to shake his hand. He also told the maverick of his esteem for Gorbachev and support for *perestroika*. What other card could the administration play? "Early on, we were thinking in terms of counterpunching—if he did this, what do we do?" said one of Bush's people. "As things unfolded in Eastern Europe, we moved from counterpunching to 'What can we offer?' " Just before leaving for Malta at the end of November, the president cautioned reporters, "If you're looking for a surprise, there won't be one."[70]

So the administration prepared for the meeting in Malta. Only days earlier, Gorbachev had signaled a redefinition of socialism in the pages of *Pravda*. Called "The Socialist Idea and Revolutionary Perestroika," it showed some advances from his Leninist-Stalinist concepts toward social democracy. Still, he was a Communist, a Russian, and, to Bush, such distinctions were not entirely impressive. He might even arrive at Malta with a surprise, as he had distracted the G-7 at Paris. Along with other speculation about what he might do and say were suggestions that the Soviet leader welcomed the diversion. But, of more moment, as Baker later wrote, was the question of whether Malta would become another Yalta.[71]

It was a good meeting, Bush's first face-to-face diplomacy with Gorbachev, a man he had first met when, as vice president, Reagan had sent him to attend Adropov's funeral in 1985; less good, however, was its Mediterranean weather. A two-day blow, with gale-force winds and twenty-foot waves that lashed Marsaxlokk Bay, kept them confined to the American guided-missile cruiser, the U.S.S. *Belknap,* instead of alternating with the *Maxim Gorky,* which had to be abandoned when the intense storm began.

Only the weather was not worked out in advance by the national security staff. When they finally got down to business in the small, blue-and-white tiled boardroom of the American cruiser, Bush was well prepared, certainly more for a summit than for a casual meeting. The NSC staff had worked up a list of twenty initiatives the president could present that would demonstrate his support for *perestroika*. One that Bush agreed to offer to Gorbachev involved suggesting that the next as yet unscheduled Olympics, in 2004, might be held in a unified Berlin. He would, Rice remembered him saying, tell his Soviet counterpart something like, "You know, Mikhail, that Berlin Olympics in 1936 was such a great one, I think we ought to do it again." Gorbachev, when he did hear the proposal, was far less moved by the unfortunate association of the Nazi treatment of Jesse Owens during that Olympics than, as somebody else said, that "Berlin glows in the dark for him." He just skipped right over it, hoping the American president had more palatable offerings. He did; it was he, in fact, not Gorbachev, who had the surprises.[72]

He had "come armed to play his game," as Baker has written. Bush's "full plate" contained earlier timetables for a Strategic Arms Limitation Treaty (START) and the reduction of conventional forces in Europe. He would "be driving our bureaucracy" on arms control, he said somewhat disingenuously, when, in fact, key decision-making rested with his own national security team. He also offered backing for Soviet observer status in GATT after the completion of the current round of trade talks. There was also, he said, along with assurances of his backing for *perestroika,* the possibility that certain trade restrictions might be lifted. "I hope you've noticed," added Bush, to strengthen the legitimacy of his overtures, "that as change has accelerated in Eastern Europe recently, we haven't responded with flamboyance or arrogance so as to make your situation more difficult. They say, 'Bush is too timid, too cautious.' I *am* cautious, but not timid. I've tried to conduct myself in a way so as not to complicate your difficulties."[73] If Gorbachev had arrived similarly armed, he failed to show his hand. He did, however, make a point that had more significance than Bush realized. He noted much of Western property was held by corporations. Corporations, moreover, were examples of collective ownership, a definition he might be able to make back home to sell the idea of privatization of large state enterprises.[74]

They left Malta signing nothing major. Yet the achievement in personal understandings and contacts, especially about the situation in the Baltics and Eastern Europe, marked the shipboard conferences as significant. Jim Baker has written that "it became obvious from his remarks following the president's presentation that we had moved from conflictual and competitive politics to a more cooperative relationship."[75]

Another cold war residual, the Noriega problem, lingered on into the Bush presidency. A combination of good luck and fumbling in Washington had kept the ruler going. Reagan had yet to leave the presidency when bureaucratic infighting led to a press leak about a covert plot to stage a coup by getting behind Panamanian Ambassador Eduardo Herrera Hassan. Once public, the plan was aborted.[76] Noriega remained in place, and emboldened. Virtually thumbing his nose at American observers who had gone to Panama City for the country's elections, which went strongly for his opponents, Noriega nullified the results. The world then saw the winning vice presidential candidate, Guillermo "Billy" Ford, bloodied in the streets of Panama City by the strongman's Dignity Battalions, an image that became "an instant symbol of the state of lawlessness and chaos in Panama."[77] Would he now back a coup? Bush was asked. There were, of course, many stories about "coups," and no lack of rumors about others. His main interest, the president cautioned, was "the protection of the life of Americans in Panama," later adding that the Panamanian people ought to do "everything they can" to get rid of Noriega and his "thuggery."[78] Meanwhile, accused of caving in to the Chinese over Tiananmen and praised for moderation in Central America, Bush continued to hedge against a genuinely local uprising against Noriega. A solid plan, together with CIA backing, might do the job. For about five hours in early October, precisely when Colin Powell took over as chairman of the joint chiefs of staff, there was the tantalizing prospect of it actually happening. The planner, or so it seemed, was one of Noriega's PDF people and even a friend, thirty-eight-year-old Maj. Moises Giroldi Vega. Only eighteen months earlier, he had helped his leader crush one coup attempt. Giroldi, however, frightened that Noriega was courting war with the United States by ordering the shooting down of American planes that happened to be near Panama City, had his wife alert the CIA station chief that he was going to confront Noriega at the point of a gun. He would give Noriega the option of keeping his pension and taking early retirement to a hacienda in the country. All Americans needed to do to make the scheme work was to block the roads to the Comandancia, the strongman's PDF headquarters. That would foil the rescuers. All Panama would then rise up in support of the coup.

Nothing about it, neither Giroldi's credentials, planning, nor motives convinced Gen. Max Thurman, who had only recently taken over as CINC SOUTHCOM (commander of American forces in the region). Powell, Cheney, and Scowcroft all tried to sort out what to do. Who was Giroldi and what was he up to? Was it something the U.S. should enter? Thurman remained skeptical. Bush, tempted to move on it, hesitated. Dinner that Tuesday at the White House with Mexico's President Carlos Salinas de Gortari gave him an earful of how Latinos would react to new *yanqui* "imperialism." Besides, his information was confused. Thurman had to first get Giroldi's agreement to hand over Noriega, but the major seemed unwilling to do that. Bush, moreover, had no way of gauging the risks involved, hardly conditions warranting sending soldiers into combat. "Here it is six P.M.," he talked into his tape recorder, "and we don't know where Noriega is; we don't know whether he is wounded or not; and we don't know whether he is dead or alive; but this is the nature of this business."[79] Unknown to Bush at that moment, just before he got news that the whole thing had collapsed, was the specter of Giroldi and some fellow rebels holding Noriega at gunpoint in the Comandancia and perplexed about what to do with him. He couldn't talk him into just giving up. He could have shot him right then and there, but he wasn't about to do that to his friend. He did, somewhere during those confusing events, get around to the idea that it might be best to turn him over to American custody, but Bush did not know that.[80] Apparently with the assumption that General Thurman had blocked the roads, he let Noriega use the phone. PDFers streamed into the place. "I'm tired of these bastards," Noriega said to his loyalists, and shot a rebel in the face. But he couldn't do it to his old friend, Giroldi, so he delegated the job.

Within forty-eight hours after starting the whole thing, the major was tortured and killed, and the plot was dead before Thurman and the NSC could act. And not much remained secret. With the word *timid* having come into vogue lately to describe him, especially among Democrats, the president heard himself excoriated on the Senate floor. Some Republicans, such as Dave McCurdy of Oklahoma, were equally unkind. "We'll be hit from the left for being involved at all," noted the president privately, "and we'll be hit harder from the right for being timid and weak; so my problem is not with failure to order the troops to do something, but my problem is now with gaps in the intelligence."[81] Jesse Helms, who had been in touch with the situation through a close, long-term aide who had contacts in Panama, went "nutty just because he's Jesse Helms," as one of Bush's aides put it, and charged the administration with being a bunch of "Keystone Kops" who had even rejected an offer to have Noriega turned over to the United States. Powell thought they were acting "as if this Brand-X plotter were the next Simón Bolívar."[82] Satisfied that he had avoided being involved in an affair that was in the hands of others, as Powell and Cheney have both agreed, Bush accepted General Thurman's analysis and noted that the plotters had merely wanted to replace Noriega with their own colonels. Their unwillingness to hand him over to Americans, he later concluded, even as the wife of the rebellious major was calling on Washington for help, indicated that the whole thing may have been a "lure" to show "a lot of force, kill a lot of Panamanians, and then 'Katy, bar the door,'" particularly if some of our soldiers had been killed."[83] That judgment has not been substantiated. It was fine for critics like George Will and David Boren "to posture," wrote Bush, but "I am not going to order kids into combat without having reasonable intelligence assessments and without knowing what's going on."[84]

On Friday, as the administration's failure to act was being denounced in the Senate, the president had to journey to Walter Reed Army Hospital for removal of a benign cyst that had been bothering him for some time on the middle finger of his right hand. The twenty-five-minute procedure, which was performed by Dr. Allen Smith, chief of hand surgery at the hospital, who was also a colonel in the Army Medical Corps, required eight stitches. A digital nerve-blocker anesthesia administered by Lt. Charles Gandy avoided any possibility of even temporary presidential disability. The operation was so simple, in fact, that the president was annoyed at being told to strip down to his shoes and socks and don a green top and bottoms. The whole thing, he thought, could have been done as he sat at a table in the White House.[85]

Asked right afterward about whether he thought he "blew" the Giroldi affair, Bush shot back by wondering what a commander in chief could have done in that situation. Moving in on that kind of information, without control or at least a clear view of what was going on was not "prudent." It certainly was not, he told them "the way I plan to conduct the military or foreign affairs of this country."[86]

Such was his first experience with the potential need to command young Americans to risk their lives. There was not, in hindsight, any regret that action had not been undertaken with the situation under their command. If anybody had "blown" anything, it was on-site intelligence and higher-level coordination. For his national security team, given the different perspectives that had separated such people as Cheney and Powell (which included the defense secretary's more sympathetic view of Oliver North), that Panamanian incident was a bonding process for the team. Their "amateur hour" was over.

Arguably the most unfortunate part of the Giroldi affair was the notoriety, which gave it a momentum of its own. In subsequent weeks, Noriega and his PDF uncovered at least two other plots, and by rebels far more credible than the unfortunate major. Neglecting the plotter was not tantamount to abandoning Hungarian freedom fighters. A more apt parallel was with the Bay of Pigs.

As in the Giroldi affair, Kennedy's Bay of Pigs misadventure was an early setback. Each situation enhanced the administration's determination to retrieve lost honor. Kennedy's Operation Mongoose was his covert response to getting rid of Fidel Castro by any means, assassination or sabotage, and it was a threat to Cuba that helped lead to the missile crisis of 1962. Bush, equally resolved not to allow his record to rest with the embarrassment, told his national security team that it was time for some serious "follow-through planning." Noriega, very much a product of the cold war, had also become irrelevant to the new international order, no longer of much value for dealing with a Soviet-backed Cuba. He was, as Bush noted in his diary, "against everything that has changed in Europe and changed everywhere."[87]

"All of us vowed never to let another such opportunity pass by," Jim Baker has written. "If an opening ever presented itself again, the United States wouldn't be caught unprepared."[88] Within the next few weeks, the Bush administration signed on to Operations Order 1=90 (BLUE SPOON), a plan for invading Panama and disposing of Noriega. The Justice Department also updated a twenty-nine-page legal opinion, first drafted in June, that claimed presidential authority for abducting a foreign fugitive from American law.[89] CIA Director Webster, with the administration's backing, argued in an open hearing for recision of the ban on U.S. participation in the assassination of foreign leaders. Noriega, Webster, pointed out, would be gone if the agency had not been bound from joining the Giroldi coup. The Senate Intelligence Committee, however, recalling heated objections to revelations about Reagan's anti-Noriega plans in 1988, held firm. Jim Baker, judiciously, stepped in and suppressed a hard-line speech prepared by Deputy National Security Adviser Bob Gates.[90]

* * *

The "outlaw Noriega regime simply must be replaced," Bush said flatly on October twenty-eighth. The president was in San José, holding a news conference in the Convention Hall at the Hotel Cariari, having made the five-hour flight from Washington with Jim Baker to be among the sixteen regional leaders celebrating Costa Rica's democracy. So nettled was he by the thought of the Panamanian strongman that he said "Noriega" a few minutes later when he clearly meant to denounce Daniel Ortega of Nicaragua.

The Sandinista leader was present with the others at San José. It was deplorable, thought Bush, that President Oscar Arias Sanchez, the host, had invited him to a gathering supposedly in celebration of democracy. "I'm not sure how certifiably free and fair it was," said Bush, "but it was under that rubric that he was invited here." The Costa Rican president, winner of the Nobel Peace Prize for 1987, was, Bush thought, seeking "his place in the sun." He held back when both Bush and Baker asked for his help in getting the Sandinistas to refrain from forcibly demobilizing the contras. The question made him squirm and he never did answer, but Bush still found him very gracious. He just should not have helped to place the spotlight on Nicaragua by inviting Ortega. Not only was the Sandinista fighter an affront to truly democratic leaders, he also defiled the spirit of the occasion by wearing a military uniform, the uniform of a Sandinista commandant, complete with red bandanna. He looked more "like a Boy Scout," thought Bush.

Once again, to Bush's annoyance, all that the press cared about was the sideshow, this time the specter of Ortega and Bush in the same room. Would they actually snap a picture of them together? Sure enough, Ortega inched over, and Bush could see the inevitable tape recorders and cameras. They got what they wanted. Bush didn't really care about that, he told himself; he didn't go to San José to pick a fight with Ortega.

That night, Ortega walked into a conference at the University of Costa Rica and, out of the blue, announced that attacks by the contras were about to kill the Nicaraguan cease-fire. Bush reacted immediately and got to Arias. He was not about to excuse any violations by the contras, he told Arias. He just thought it was damnable that the thing was being prejudged. Ortega was hardly a reliable source. After the Costa Rican president did get a softening of Ortega's threat, Bush told the press at the Hotel Cariari that breaking the cease-fire would be "sheer folly." Ortega's act had shown contempt toward every leader who had traveled to San José. The Sandinista was obviously just "this one little man who is out of whack with the rest of the hemisphere" and out to "ruin a very good meeting." The president of the United States had not "come here to have any contretemps with this little man showing [up] in his military uniform at a democracy meeting. That's not what it's all about."

Why, a reporter wanted to know, "do you keep calling him a little man?" "Because he is," replied Bush, "that's why." Ortega left the conference early, insulted. "I was not thinking of his height—actually, he's a fairly respectable height," noted the American president in his diary, wondering whether he had unintentionally insulted Ortega's manhood, "but the pettiness of trying to ruin the Costa Rican summit by going against the one deal that Oscar wants to be remembered for in the peace agreements."[91]

Manuel Noriega, however, was the "bone" in Bush's throat, and, after he returned from Costa Rica, what had become inevitable began to unfold. The elusive Panamanian, facing drug trafficking charges and having to guard his flanks as never before, stepped up the PDF's hunt for enemies. His bellicosity toward the United States only increased Bush's need to act. On Friday, December 15, Noriega said the constant American military menace had created "a state of war," and the following day, the anniversary of his taking power six years earlier, he proclaimed himself "maximum leader" of Panama. Bush, at church that Sunday at the military base at Arlington, had to face reporters' questions about the killing of an American military officer by the PDF. He withheld any comments. He was good at that. But the unleashing of Operation Blue Spoon was already inevitable. Noriega, probably without realizing much about the president's capacity, had put Bush to the test.[92]

The death of twenty-four-year-old U.S. Marine Lt. Robert Paz and the shooting of three Panamanians by the PDF at a roadblock were bad enough. A back-channel message to U.S. officials from the defense forces explained that the violence was unplanned, an accidental and isolated incident. Noriega's foreign minister accused the Americans of using the affair as a pretext for making war "against the Panamanian people." CIA wire tappers, however, overheard Noriega himself orchestrating how the blame would be shifted.[93] Only that Sunday evening did the president hear how another American officer, Adam J. Curtis, stopped for an ID check prior to the roadblock incident, was taken to the Comandancia along with his wife. The young couple had also witnessed the shootings. Lieutenant Curtis was beaten and repeatedly kicked in the groin, while Bonnie Curtis, twenty-three years old, was interrogated and groped by PDF officers who forced her against a wall until she passed out. That was the last straw, remembered one of the president's close advisers. "That's when he gave us the order to go."[94] "I guess the thing that troubles me the most," Bush recorded, "is the humiliation of the lieutenant's wife, to say nothing of abusing him physically. . . . There is something so humiliating about threatening a woman sexually and deliberately abusing rights."[95]

Starting on Sunday afternoon, the president was briefed repeatedly. He sat there, Powell has recalled, "in his pensive pose" and wearing gray slacks and a blue blazer. One sock was marked "Merry" and the other "Christmas." He listened to his national security inner circle "like a patron on a bar stool coolly observing a brawl while his advisors went hard at it," in that quiet, calm way that had become so familiar.[96] On Tuesday morning, the president was briefed once again. He probed and questioned. Was Sunday's violence and abuse the "smoking gun"? Would Blue Spoon minimize civilian casualties?

What about American lives? Would Panama finally get democracy? Was Noriega sure to fall? Noriega, Noriega, he kept thinking. What if he didn't get caught? Could the mission be called a success without him? Would he really be captured? General Powell hedged. Special operations people, he assured the president, would be on his tail. Once Bush knew that, acting at Baker's suggestion, Guillermo Endara, the legitimate victor of Panama's annulled election, had agreed to stand by for swearing-in as president, the last restraint was off.[97]

"Okay, let's go," Bush said, and then, in his understated manner, "We're going to go."

The hour was set for one o'clock on the morning of Wednesday, December 20, allowing enough time to get Blue Spoon together.[98]

On Tuesday evening, the president and the First Lady held a Christmas reception. When the guests left, Bush told her that Panama would be invaded the next morning. She went to bed.[99]

The president stayed up through most of the night, not turning in until four A.M. The "enormity of this operation really hits me," he recorded. The kids. His mind was on the kids. "Those young nineteen-year-olds who will be dropped in at night, the JSOC team, with their grenades and their rehearsal. The operation has been rehearsed, and I'm thinking about the brutality of Noriega and what's he's apt to do. I'm thinking about what happens if he gets away or flees into some embassy—hostile or friendly." It was a major decision, one sure to add to the flak he had just taken on the news about Scowcroft and Eagleburger's secret June trip to China. By four o'clock, when he went to bed, he had also made his round of calls to the heads of state, telling them about Blue Spoon, which was about to be renamed Operation Just Cause. That was General Thurman's idea. "You do not risk people's lives for blue spoons," Powell has written, "but you do for a "just cause." After all those years, Bush finally had Noriega where he wanted him.[100]

The world of television took over. Even those who never heard about Giroldi or Noriega saw aircraft and paratroopers swoop down on tiny Panama, as if in a major invasion—the final American plan to take out the strongman. Endara had already been sworn in at the Presidential Palace, well ahead of H-hour, as the starting time was designated. Fifteen minutes ahead of schedule, an observer saw "a sky full of paratroopers," Army Rangers and soldiers from the Eighty-second Airborne Division. Explosions rocked the La Siesta neighborhood. Their objective was to close in on the Comandancia, surround and capture PDF units, and knock out the landing fields, making sure to hit Noriega's Lear jet to keep him from escaping from Punta Paitilla Airport. Along Panama's Atlantic coast, at Colón, resistance was fiercer, the mission more suited for infantrymen than navy seals. The main PDF companies at the Río Hato barracks, from which Noriega's men had gone out to smash rebels, were seized. A Delta Force team rescued the CIA source.[101]

A little after nine the next morning, the president was able to tell the press that, while it was not all over, "it's pretty well wrapped up." A freely elected government was in power. America's interests and American life were secure, and Noriega was gone. The "integrity" of the Panama Canal had been preserved.

"Are you confident that you'll get him?" he was asked.

"I've been frustrated that he's been in power this long—extraordinarily frustrated." The search, he vowed, will go on "as long as it takes."[102] His desperation to catch Noriega was so great, and his need to rally the nation behind him was so strong, that Powell had to caution him about overdoing the demonization of the man.[103]

He was obviously pleased and relaxed. He began with a little joke, saying that the "brief statement" he had for them was that he had "a pain in the neck." As he talked and answered their questions, unknown to him, TV screens showed a split image. Bodies of the first American casualties were shown being unloaded from a transport plane at Dover Air Force Base. "Sensational images," Powell has noted, "but cheap-shot journalism." U.S. military losses totaled twenty-four.[104]

Throughout Panama, the hunt for Noriega went on. The White House offered a $1-million bounty for his head.[105] In a little land of fewer than 30,000 square miles, including the canal region, and no deep underground bunkers or elaborate fortresses, and with a decidedly hostile populace, he simply disappeared. The American authorities had not the slightest clue. He had slipped out early, gone to a small apartment that belonged to the sister of an acquaintance on the fringe of Panama City. There he remained, restless and uneasy, about to snap under the idiotic talk he had to put up with from his nightclub singer pal, Ulysses Rodríguez, until, finally, the papal nuncio, Monsignor Sebastian Laboa, returned from a vacation in Spain. The prelate, regarded as neutral, agreed to give him temporary asylum. On Sunday, four days after Operation Just Cause began, dressed in blue Bermuda shorts and T-shirt, and wearing a baseball cap, Manuel Noriega slipped into the nunciature, where he was as much beyond the authorities as though he were in the Vatican itself. Monsignor Laboa, who knew his man, was convinced he would finally persuade him that surrendering to the Americans would be the lesser of evils. Noriega, meanwhile, attempted to arrange for refuge in Spain, a scheme that had been considered in the past by Washington as a possible way for him to step down. It could not be done on his own, however. Spain had an extradition treaty with the U.S. Laboa, still convinced he would have no choice but to give himself up, telephoned General Thurman to tell him of Noriega's presence. The general announced that fact to the world via a press conference, and then began a campaign of psychological harassment. As the beleaguered and frightened ex-dictator hovered inside, from the heart of the little circus around the nunciature blared a steady diet of raucous rock music, featuring stuff like "Goooood morning, Panama!," "Voodoo Child," "You're No Good," and "I Fought the Law." Engines of military vehicles were gunned to intensify the racket. A field was even burned and bulldozed in the middle of the night within sight of the nunciature to prepare a helicopter landing strip. Three days into the new year, when the president and Mrs. Bush flew to San Antonio to visit wounded veterans of the fighting, the prelate succeeded in convincing Noriega to give up. That gave the signal for Panamanians, secure that he could not return to power, to dance in the streets. By dawn on January 4, he was in a cell in Miami, Florida.[106]

Sidney Blumenthal, no friend of the administration, concluded that the Panama war had "solidified" Bush's "political identity at last."[107] A *CBS News* poll demonstrated that the invasion was overwhelmingly popular among Panamanians.[108] Americans thought Panama was Bush's "greatest achievement."[109] Gone was the image of passive and weak leadership. "No one will make the mistake of taking President Bush lightly again," wrote Jack Germond and Jules Witcover.[110] Internationally, he did less well. The intervention was condemned by both the Third World–dominated United Nations and the Organization of American States. Less than two months later, news came from Nicaragua that Violetta Chamorro's democrats had won a stunning victory. Daniel Ortega and his Sandinistas could only pack up and walk away. In Washington, George Bush agreed that there was "no reason for further military action." Democracy had been restored in both Panama and Nicaragua, two long-standing problem areas for Bush.

CHAPTER TWENTY-ONE

"Kind of Drifting"

%

Noriega was finally jailed. The invasion, if it accomplished nothing else, muted some of the crazies on the right who charged that Bush's failure to act in the bungled coup betrayed an "incompetence and timidity" that bordered on "treason."[1] Bush had, at last, one-upped Reagan's triumph in Grenada. He had, in his first real test, shown that he had the guts to send kids into battle.

Democracy, insisted those who carped, had nothing to do with it. Bush was only proving his manhood. He let an "obsession" rush him into a "splendid little war." Under the guise of establishing "democracy" and smashing the drug trade, he had indulged himself in the "conquest of Panama," a fitting coda to his cryptic association with Noriega. The whole episode, *Newsweek* reminded its readers, was a "dubious relationship," sufficiently embarrassing to keep Bush "consistently" tight-lipped.[2]

No matter what he did, he couldn't get away from the press. All his years in public life didn't make them easier to stomach. They went looking for problems, and if they didn't find any, they'd just make them up. Mostly, they bad-mouthed. Bush didn't like it when it was done to others, and he hated it when he was the subject. He shouldn't let that stuff bother him, he knew, but it did; it just cut him in the gut. For the "pack," which he felt was bitchier and bitchier, he held "a deep animosity that he doesn't try to hide," his press secretary said later. He "personalized everything." The odd thing was that *they* liked him even though he hated *them,* a Bush sensitivity rooted heavily in the Watergate days and his time as chairman of the Republican National Committee. Ann Devroy was a good example. Nobody would objectively think the *Washington Post*'s reporter was especially hostile, but she irritated Bush with those inside stories announcing what he was going to do before he actually did it. Sometimes, like LBJ with the press, he was tempted to do the opposite just to show her.[3]

"There is a direct relationship between him being at 80 percent in the polls and trying to keep secrets because it doesn't give you guys a chance to skewer him in advance," explained Roger Ailes, who then smiled and said, "I've been advising him to give press conferences at three A.M."[4]

And his thin-skinned resentments weren't just directed at ideological opponents; some he despised were real right-wingers, like Bob Novak. What really bothered him about the press's own "prince of darkness" had less to do with his ultraconservatism than his cunning, which Bush saw as a self-serving trickiness, often setting him up just to make a buck. But the worst were the "character assassins." George Will headed that crowd on the right, and Garry Trudeau, the cartoonist and satirist, "the insidious Doonesbury," was not far behind on the left.[5]

If there was anything that troubled Bush more than the press, it was staffers who should have known better, aides with the bureaucratic tendency to carve out little advantages for themselves by romancing the press with droplets of information. Wherever Bush worked, his attitude toward leakers was well known. Better at it than anyone, perhaps, was Jim Baker. Barbara knew about it, and so did the boys. Baker's leaks would, at times, even one-up "big brother." A few people, not many, even heard Bush admit that he knew all about it. But Jim was just too useful, they had gone through too many things together and he owed him something, so he put up with it. There were some, however, who thought the crack negotiator changed his ways after he became secretary of state.[6]

Baker certainly didn't leak what he was doing in Europe, working for German reunification and getting some of the American boys home from the Continent and Panama. Bush's first State of the Union Message, on January 31, 1990, had been in the works since November. The administration was putting together lists of themes and accomplishments, routing them through Jim Cicconi and then passing them on to Sununu and the president before the speechwriters had to cobble them together. The strands all gradually took shape, until it was finally thrashed out with the president. By the time Bush met with them on Tuesday, January 16, it all added up. He was eager to leaven them by showing his commander-in-chief accomplishments. Clearly, that was his strong suit.

The *Congressional Quarterly* scorecard gave him failing grades for the administration's record with the first session of the 101st Congress. They said he came out ahead less than half the time and pointed out that he had lost seven of ten key votes in the House. But, as Roger Porter argued when gathering material for the speech, there surely were proud accomplishments. Bush had held the line on taxes and kept his ground on the need to lower capital gains. Real economic growth was almost 3 percent, and nearly two million additional jobs had been created. He could take credit for the first revision of the Clear Air Act in over ten years, this one calling for reducing destructive emissions that caused acid rain, urban ozone, and toxic air pollution. (Tackling problems of atmospheric poisoning, so destructive to forestry and fishing in Canada and the northeastern United States, had helped to form Bush's friendship with Prime Minister Brian Mulroney when George was still vice president.[7]) Bush, trying to make good on his vow to become the "education president," had also brought together all the governors for an "educational summit" at the University of Virginia. He was especially pleased, Porter went on, that the speech draft focused "on the state of the nation rather than the state of the government" because that "devotes attention to fundamental values and what Americans need to do in their individual capacities rather than emphasizing exclusively what changes the president would recommend in government policies."[8]

He was introduced by Speaker Foley to the usual round of applause, this time led by the Republicans, and he began his words on prime time, five minutes after nine P.M., Eastern Standard Time. He reminded them that it was his first State of the Union Address, that he came before them as a former president of the Senate and former congressman. His message was cautious, conservative, and solid. The lead items made the right headlines. Military levels in Panama were already nearly down to their preinvasion status, and, by the end of February, they would probably be back to normal. Then, confirming what had been dribbling out only from European sources, he told the country that agreements with Gorbachev and America's allies would place a 195,000 cap on Soviet and U.S. manpower in Central and Eastern Europe. Security had been won without creating insecurity. SDI, however, was still needed, as was general vigilance to guard against the unforeseen in a new era. Little was said about domestic spending. The budgetary condition hardly gave Bush an incentive to venture into the sorts of governmental activity he had never liked to begin with. He called for the "thousand points of light concept," without mentioning the phrase, especially in the area of education. We should, he said, promote quality by learning to "help our neighbor—claim the problem of our community as our own." Then, theatrically putting on his glasses, as though he had not been reading all along, he borrowed from a favorite Reagan device by sharing a letter from a young soldier that had been written just before his death in Panama. He was there, ready to give his life, Pfc. James Markwell, told his mother, so that she could "revel in the life I have died to give you."[9]

The speech was triumphant, the negatives were few, both within and outside the chamber. On ABC-TV, Ted Koppel called it "extremely effective," and Brit Hume, agreeing that it was "unquestionably effective," noted the "useful" distinction between the "state of the union" and the "state of the government" at a time when little new spending was being proposed. On CBS-TV, Bob Schieffer thought it was a "fairly low-key address, very much in keeping with the president's personality," and Sergei Plekhanov, of the Soviet Union's Institute on the United States and Canada, told Dan Rather that he thought the challenge was to "forget about the cold war . . . put our relationship on a new basis."[10]

Seven hundred and thirty-one calls were received by the White House from ordinary citizens, 94 percent of them positive. The numbers were compiled for the president's eyes, and so were the following sample reactions:

WE CAN ALL SLEEP BETTER.
HE HAS REALLY CHANGED. HE IS JUST SO STRONG NOW. HE IS WONDERFUL.
I WISH THE CONGRESS WOULD REMEMBER THAT HE IS THE PRESIDENT AND NOT THEM.
IF THE DEMOCRATS IN CONGRESS WILL WORK WITH PRESIDENT BUSH, WE'LL HAVE A COUNTRY AGAIN.[11]

The next Gallup poll, released in mid February, showed that approval of the way he was handling the presidency was shared by 73 percent of Americans.[12] Their anxieties, however, were momentarily focused on his trip to Cartagena, Colombia, to attend a conference on narcotics. The Medellín drug cartel, it was confirmed, had put out a contract on his life. Digesting, at the same time, revelations about the ties of the new Panamanian leadership to drug money, fear for their president's safety raised doubts about whether he should attend. With security tight, Bush left with Baker, Scowcroft, and Sununu for the Drug Summit, arriving at the Ernesto Cortissoz Airport in Barranquilla. In Cartagena, he joined with President Virgilio Barco Vargas of Colombia, President Jaime Paz Zamora of Bolivia, and President Alan García Perez of Peru. They put their signatures on the "Declaration of Cartagena," which acknowledged the international nature of the problem and committed them to a strategy to "implement or strengthen a comprehensive, intensified antinarcotics program" that had to "address the issues of demand reduction, consumption, and supply."[13] Back home, the next day, he also signed a State Department authorization bill that challenged congressional intervention in presidential foreign policy-making authority. As the *Congressional Almanac* put it, "While Bush had in the past challenged the constitutionality of individual leadership provisions that he insisted infringed on his powers, he had never before raised such complaints about as many items in one bill." An administration official agreed that Bush's attack on the bill was a reassertion of "dominance" over foreign affairs.[14]

All this was just another confirmation that the Bush-Baker foreign policy team was making progress in winding down the cold war in Europe. The Soviets were learning, painfully, that repression was no longer effective in the new order of things. Troops sent into Azerbaijan after control of their government was seized by the Azerbaijani National Front only sparked off wider demands for independence from other republics. Revolts were at a new crisis level. A greater, and even more intense, challenge to Moscow's authority came from Vilnius, where the Lithuanian Supreme Council voted 124 to 0 with six abstentions to declare the restoration of the nation as a democratic republic. With Moscow apparently on the verge of intervening in that Baltic country, the

Lithuanian parliament issued an "Appeal to the Nations of the World" that warned about the imminence of force. By waiting it out, Bush finessed the situation as he had done even before the collapse of the Berlin Wall. The tactic played well in Europe but annoyed those Republicans who deplored the administration's passivity. George Will, for example, speculated that the Lithuanian situation had made the Bush presidency "an embarrassment," noting in *Newsweek* that "Bushism is Reaganism minus the passion for freedom. . . . Bush's policy is to do whatever is necessary to 'save' Gorbachev."[15] More quietly, and more deliberately, James Baker was, at the same time, working out his two-plus-four proposal that recognized the sovereignty of the two Germanys and, with the aid of Chancellor Kohl, sped up the process of moving toward unification and Soviet acceptance of the Bonn government in NATO more rapidly than had ever been imagined.[16]

Bush continued to concentrate on diplomatic initiatives. His dilemma was at the crux of a presidency caught in an ungovernable vise, a two-party system in which the presidency was paralyzed in the face of opposing congressional majorities, which, of course, also meant control of all committees. The Republican president placed in office with the fewest members of his own party on Capitol Hill was the victim of gridlock. The failure of government seemed more and more the failure of whomever was in the Oval Office.

In dealing with those Democratic majorities, with the two sides holding each other responsible for precipitating the gridlock, Bush was soon described in the press as governing by "veto strategy." All in all, before the end of his presidency, Bush used his veto power forty-four times.* Ten related to the abortion issue; the other killed legislation pertaining to the achievement of a wide array of social, regulatory, and tax and spending policies. Just one, involving a bill to reregulate the cable television industry, was overridden.[17]

Bush did achieve, by the time the 101st Congress concluded, the fruition of what he had been supporting since even before becoming president, the Americans with Disabilities Act. Despite its inherent contradiction with the administration's deregulatory goals, his support remained unqualified from the start. He never doubted that prohibiting discrimination in jobs and in areas of public accommodations (patterned after the 1964 act) was "a really forward looking piece of civil rights legislation affecting the disabled." Bush's own enthusiasm reflected the public's sympathy for such goals. Backed by a coalition of AIDS and civil rights activists, as well as public health groups, it went through Congress with largely bipartisan support. Signed by the president on July 26, 1990, critics nevertheless faulted it as too productive of frivolous law suits, bureaucratic-building, and filled with mandates requiring costly structural changes to achieve such assistance. Nevertheless, in reviewing the Bush domestic record, it remained not only

---

*This total includes one pocket veto.

the major accomplishment of the 101st Congress but his clearest push toward a "kinder and gentler society."[18]

When a group of Wellesley feminists protested Barbara Bush's selection as the college's commencement speaker on the grounds that she had gained recognition through the achievements of her husband, she grandly turned her appearance into a model of dignity, poise, and strength. She was, Barbara Bush preferred to tell interviewers, "extraordinarily happy," which, she left no doubt, was synonymous with being "very family-oriented" and also "very George Bush–oriented." As a First Lady, she was a symbol of traditional virtues, the keeper of "family values," and the key practitioner of Calvinistic good works, a selfless promoter of such social benefits as literacy and education. She was, in fact, she pointed out with pride, more public service–minded than even Eleanor Roosevelt, who took money for writing a newspaper column while her husband was still in the White House. She also proudly lauded her own avoidance of policy-making roles. She could accomplish so many more positive things "by just getting out and plugging away" at promoting caring for one another.[19]

She had left the Indian Village neighborhood of Rye, New York, at a young age, and had gone directly into George Bush's constellation. In Texas, they were refugees from a patrician world, anomalies in a society that preached the virtues of egalitarianism. Nowhere was that saluted more fervently than in the American heartland, and nowhere was it more enshrined than in the Lone Star State. Try as they could, argued a devoted aide, Barbara and George did not know or understand poor people; they did not know farm people; they could not relate to a culture that was forced, no matter how strong the backbone or the ferocity of independence, to subsist on welfare. They lived *real* lives vicariously through symbols. Even that modest plot of land Bush owned in Houston's Tanglewood neighborhood, gossiped some reporters, was to prove that they really were commoners at heart; it was unthinkable that they would actually build there after leaving the White House. How extraordinary the discipline must have been to break loose from such cultural moorings to compete in an environment so different from their hereditary "Eastern establishment." "If there ever was a way," contemplated George Warren in 1992, "of breaking away from the white-shoe set of Yale and Andover, he really did it by going out and being a relative roughneck in the oil fields of Odessa." Was his childhood friend suggesting that he had anticipated the necessity of creating an artificial persona to override the establishment environment of Greenwich-Andover-Yale? How could he have had the foresight to think that far ahead? A newspaperwoman from Baltimore had once suggested that scenario to Warren. The more he reflected on George's career, the less outrageous it seemed.[20] The more Bush became understood, the clearer was the view of that young man who rode into the frontier where American individualism had its mythic origins. He had, in effect, saddled up and galloped into a land that was less a relic of the past than where the future was percolating. George Bush, a good, honorable man, proudly pragmatic, was caught up in working out his own dreams. De Toqueville never imagined him that clearly: the aristocrat not only abiding the hoi polloi but swallowing them whole. It was not easy, after all, to accommodate one's special grace to the demands of temporal life.

Along with him, Barbara fell right into that public world, her private sectors only imperfectly protected. She did, of course, lock into her own sources of security, advancing from the household of Marvin Pierce to the one of George Bush. She even referred to him as "George Bush," as though he were an icon. She needed his approval. She worked hard, jogged and dieted, trying to beat the laws of nature. She chaffed at comments about looking older than he. His success was also hers, and she was proud of what they had done together. Her social anchor virtually replicated her husband's politics. She remained the Victorian wife and mother while hinting, sometimes in devilish ways, that not far below that matronly figure was a modern woman. She wrote that he was the one with the "stability and ability to keep things on an even keel," and added with admiration that "it takes guts to be George Bush." He would not have said it about himself, nor she about herself.[21]

She was, of course, far too intelligent, too strong-minded for martyrdom. Devotion had its limits. There was, for a while, a longing to "go home to family and friends and live happily ever after." But that was back in 1970 and she adjusted. When they were in China together for that year, she managed long stretches in the States for proximity to friends and children. Whenever she could, even in the White House years when he was stuck in Washington, she got up to Maine.

Yet, behind the scenes, friends assumed that she influenced the president more than most people recognized. Not that she resembled Nancy Reagan in pulling her husband's strings. Nobody, she knew, pulls George Bush's strings. His closest aides learned what she had long since discovered. His tactical acceptance of a "pro-life" position on abortion continued to leave him exposed to skeptics who, once they got to know the savvy Barbara, thought he was, in reality, more under her influence. Her suspected "pro-choice" position certainly had helped to attract Nancy Reagan's hostility, if only because it showed less than total loyalty to Ron. Abortion, Barbara Bush told the present author in 1995, has "certainly been one of those things, along with that unmentionable gun control, that we have had a gentle past argument about. We stopped discussing both these things about fifteen, twenty years ago, thirty years. What's the point? He thinks conception is the beginning of life." In a "slip of the tongue" just before George's presidential inauguration, she told reporters that assault weapons should be illegal.[22] Her press secretary, Anna Perez, tried some damage control by saying there would be no further discussions about gun control or other controversial matters.

The signals were mixed. She was, on one level, primarily a defender of her husband, a protector of his political interests, and also sufficiently independent to temper the extremes. Journalist Marjorie Williams once wrote that "White

House aides are especially eager to suggest that she differs from him on abortion and gun control, fanning some faint hope among Republican moderates that she is fighting a good fight over morning coffee every day."[23]

She felt strongly about people. She put up with Lee Atwater and others because she accepted their usefulness to her husband. But, insiders recognized, she was the conduit for the family collective decisions. Just enough cunning showed through to reveal that nobody could push Barbara around. A Houston reporter noted how casually she responded to a question about Nancy Reagan's new book, *My Turn*; Barbara, never one to appear obsequious, would only say "maybe" when asked whether she would read it. She was busy, she pleaded; being First Lady was hard work. There were piles of clerical work and miles to be flown. Graves' disease may have affected her eyes but not impaired her mind.[24] Canadian Prime Minister Brian Mulroney, whose wife was close to Barbara, said she was a "pillar of strength."[25]

She kept the banner of cultural correctness aloft by assuring Maureen Dowd that, yes, we will go to sleep and wake up to country music. Her husband's instinctive good taste, she added, helped fill the White House residence with Brahms, Leontyne Price, and Placido Domingo. "I don't want to ruin his myth," she explained, "but we also do love to hear classical music. And we have it bellowed through the house."[26] When Bush invited her to lunch with a guest, she smiled and said she'd rather do a round of golf. Those who signed on with her husband's team found that she lost little time in throwing down her marker. An aide, who answered one of her questions only vaguely at the outset of their relationship, got a sharp reprimand in return. "When I ask you a question," she replied, "I don't want to know if you're not sure. You either tell me you know the answer [or you don't]." To have a good day, advised a White House photographer, start out by saying, "Good morning, Mrs. Bush. You look nice, Mrs. Bush. If you can get through the day without anything more, you're a success." Most of all, of course, she was not only part of the Bush circle; she was Bush's family, and outsiders only deluded themselves when they thought they could breach that divide. There were ways, not always subtle, in which she drew the line that separated peers from servants.[27]

She was proud of her personal achievements. Her campaign talks for her husband evolved into well-received lectures about China, then literacy. After George became vice president, she wrote a book that immortalized the cocker spaniel that Marvin had given her as a forty-eighth birthday gift. *C. Fred's Story: A Dog's Life* became the first of two successful fund-raising books that helped her secure her own special home page in a world dominated by George Bush. At about the time their springer spaniel, Millie, produced a litter, she wrote another volume, *Millie's Book,* an inside view of the White House through the "eyes" of the "First Dog," which raised over $1,000,000 for literacy. Pets were very important to George and Barbara.

They were both seared by Neil's ordeal. Right after the holidays closed out 1989, they confronted the public revelation that federal regulators, after shutting down Silverado and penalizing Michael Wise, had called in their son for questioning. "I've done nothing wrong," Neil had been insisting. He was only thirty-three, and, unlike the other ex–board members of Silverado, he would be damned if he'd sign an agreement to waive forever his rights to sit on a bank board or ever have anything to do with a financial institution. "His whole problem," Barbara wrote in her diary, "is that he is our son," and "just one of literally hundreds of outside directors of failed savings and loans."[28] And Neil held fast. He would not sign any pledge to never again violate savings and loan rules, he told the House Banking Committee.[29] None of his father's political advisers could dissuade him. Why should he take that kind of fall all by himself? The Federal Home Loan Bank Board, newly renamed the Office of Thrift Supervision, released 1,000 pages of documents and called young Bush guilty of "one of the worst kinds" of conflicts of interest. A *Newsweek* survey reported loss of confidence in the president's handling of the crisis and confirmed that Neil's case had damaged his father. "After simmering for five years as a financial crisis," reported its staff, "the S&L mess has exploded as a political issue." The problem, with ever-inflating bail-out numbers and the reality of the intense financial strings that tied so many of the legislators to the industry, roiled the first session of the 101st Congress.[30]

In the turmoil over Neil, the family turned to Lud Ashley. Bush's old friend had retired from the House and had become head of the Association of Bank Holding Companies. His affability, intimacy with the Congress, and proximity to the president all helped him become the top lobbyist behind the administration's efforts to deregulate the banking industry.[31] Who better to prepare Neil to face the House Banking Committee? Ashley also set up a defense fund to get contributions, as he explained, "just from family and close friends" for a battle that might cost $250,000.*

On March 5, Lee Atwater collapsed. He was at a Wednesday morning fund-raiser breakfast for Phil Gramm, having fun at the lectern bashing the Democrats. Bush's RNC chairman was already a party hero, almost legendary, his personal zest only embellishing the fascination with the young man whose stratagems had so helped the GOP to succeed. His comments had gone on for about twenty minutes, when suddenly, as he spoke, his left foot shook uncontrollably. An unbearable rush of pain followed. "Help me! Somebody help me," he shouted as he fell to the floor clutching his side.[32] At the George Washington Medical Center, he was diagnosed as having "a small nonmalignant growth on the right side of his head." Therapy to combat the

---

*Ashley's legal assistance enabled Neil to settle his conflict of interest situation by paying $50,000 in 1992. Financial writer Martin Tolchin, reporting the story, noted that it was "the lightest penalty that could have been imposed by the Office of Thrift Supervision." Bush, whose settlement was not expected to involve significant "out-of-pocket" costs, agreed to avoid any future conflicts of interest in the banking industry. (Martin Tolchin, *NYT,* May 17, 1992.)

tumor, however, was evidently futile and the original diagnosis, an olive-size nonmalignant tumor, an astrocytoma deep in his brain, left some doctors skeptical. Lee, forced to cancel a scheduled appearance to play at a rhythm-and-blues concert in Columbia, South Carolina, switched to the Montefiore Medical Center in The Bronx, New York City, where he was placed under the care of the head of neurosurgery, Dr. Paul Kornblith. His condition was not "benign" but life threatening. The highly aggressive tumor was found at the right frontal lobe of his brain near the area controlling such motor functions as speech and the use of his left arm and leg. Treatment involved drilling tiny holes in his skull and inserting thin plastic tubes with closed tips directly into the tumor, then placing a tiny radioactive 'seed' into the tip of each tube, a five-hour procedure. The thirty-nine-year-old political strategist was, however, sufficiently lucid afterward to ask at least one caller, his former public relations associate, Charlie Black, about the kind of flak Bush was getting on Lithuania from conservatives. From that point on, Atwater received out-patient treatment, mostly back at George Washington. He was left to struggle with the excruciatingly painful condition and the medication needed to make existence bearable. Public appearances became limited. Finally, after the prognosis was abundantly clear, Bill Bennett replaced him as RNC head. John Sununu moved in to take over Atwater's functions, a blatant move, wrote Mary Matalin, to "suck" political power back into the White House from the national committee.[33]

It was at that point, too, that the relative harmony that had marked the budget process the year before was beginning to unravel, just as House Ways and Means Chairman Dan Rostenkowski had warned that it would. Without much publicity, or challenge, the administration's proposals for fiscal year 1991 had already been filed, as required by law. Tucked into its schedule were not only spending reductions but some $14 billion of what were termed "user fees." In that intensifying political atmosphere, with congressional elections little more than half a year away, the Illinois Democrat told Dick Darman and John Sununu that his majority was going to act unilaterally to bring up their own deficit reduction plan. The majority leader, George Mitchell, had also clearly signaled the advent of such a confrontation. The administration, meanwhile, aimed to minimize the annual deficits, hold spending levels to necessary domestic and national security purposes, and continue to work for capital gains tax reductions. As the economic outlook stood at the moment, forecasts for fiscal 1991 projected deficits at the $120 to $160 billion level, well above the Gramm-Rudman-Hollings target of $64 billion. Pushing them even higher, worried Bush and Darman, would hike interest rates. Coupled with a shortage of credit, the economy could go into a depression. At the very least, failure to provide new appropriations before the end of the current fiscal year raised the real possibility of shutting down vital governmental functions. Even military spending could suffer. Michael Boskin, the chairman of Bush's Council of Economic Advisers, maintained from the outset that the president was "a realist" despite his antitax views.[34]

Darman, crackerjack numbers man, pulled onto his side the ideologically incompatible and less economically astute Sununu. The chief of staff was the latest of George Bush's "pit bulls," heir to a long line of those whose behavior contrasted with the "decent and honorable" man who was their boss. Jennifer Fitzgerald, Ron Kaufman, Rich Bond, Mary Matalin, Roger Ailes, and Lee Atwater had all served him well in that capacity, doing what he could not or would not do for himself. Of the current leaders about to enter into the budget negotiations with the Democrats, Darman later wrote, "Sununu had a reputation for arrogance and abrasiveness, which I welcomed for a selfish reason. I hoped his reputation might make mine less notable. Unfortunately, it didn't. Soon we were *both* said to be arrogant and abrasive."[35]

Bush admired Darman's intellect, his firm grasp of budgetary policy, and his ability to put forward the administration's proposals. Sure, Bush would agree, his budget director "had a tendency to be somewhat abrasive," but his real problem was that he was "anathema to movement conservatives."[36] As resentments grew among his colleagues, Darman's power was seen as a combination of brilliance and superb bureaucratic manipulations. Always close to Baker, however, the budget director's authority also fed on Bush's confidence that, in the key area of finance, Darman had a better grip of the situation than just about anybody else. The enemies he was making made him no less indispensable. "I must say I hate this dealing with Congress and these budget matters," Bush confided to his diary that spring. "I much prefer foreign affairs. I salute Sununu and Darman for doing it."[37]

Others were less complacent, and even bitter. One well-placed aide explained that the budget director and the chief of staff were "the class kids who were so smart they couldn't play baseball."[38] Sununu seemed to be indifferent to the victims of his power but ultrasensitive to the press. His arrogance in congressional relations was far less suitable than when he led a small one-party state. One New Hampshire House Democratic leader remembered him as "unbearable! Unmerciful! He didn't care if he embarrassed you in front of people. He would be impatient. Condescending. Arrogant. Short-tempered. Abrupt. Rude."[39] When a highly respected senator resisted his pleas during a clash over cutting capital gains taxes, the chief of staff asked, "How much do you want your pay raised?"[40] After another legislator heard a Sununu threat about the consequences of not going along on a deal, he told him that he knew George Bush and "he would never do anything like that." Sununu, unfazed, answered, "George Bush is a much nicer guy than I am."[41] Darman, volunteered a senior member of the White House staff, was a "destructive personality for any organization," one with a "fundamental misunderstanding of the American political process" and one who drove policy decisions with his "ego and arrogance." It was really something to see both of them at meetings, still another recalled, "preening" for each other.[42]

During that clash over the budget, Bush's disavowal of new taxes hindered deficit reform. The almost daily escalation of the cost of bailing out crippled thrifts only made matters worse. Bush's good friend, the secretary of the Treasury, Nick Brady, didn't have the stomach for the battle. He was definitely *not* a "pit bull." Brady, the former head of the Wall Street investment firm of Dillon Read, was an old family friend, a business partner of a Bush relative on the Walker side and had played tennis as a teenager with Jonathan Bush. Brady, an archetypical member of the Bush circle, thought of himself as a fiscal conservative and a social moderate. While his friend occupied the vice presidency, Brady served a brief interim term as a Republican senator from New Jersey. Having been drawn into the cabinet, he said, he "took very seriously Bush's admonition that this thing should work. Why can't it work?" There was, he thought, no better incentive for getting along with Darman.[43]

If Darman was the "prince of darkness" and Sununu the "bull in the china shop," Brady was the gentle, guileless accommodator, who was all too ready to agree, in the words of one very conservative critic from within, that "Ronald Reagan's decade of growth was a thinly veiled decade of greed, led by Keynesian deficit spending policies, not . . . supply-side policies . . ."[44] He was, moreover, reflective of Wall Street's concern over deficits and, given any firm commitment to the avoidance of additional taxes and an unimpressive advocate in any case, not exactly the powerhouse needed to resist Rostenkowski, Mitchell, and their Democratic majority. Nor was he shaping up as an effective Treasury head in any case. "Nick is just so affable, so laid back, such a good friend," one close associate told Bob Woodward. There was, finally, the suspicion that his real role was to keep Darman in check.[45]

How the budget talks would have worked out with a healthy Lee Atwater calling political signals remained an open question. There were many in the White House who thought there would have been a different outcome.

As complaints about the inadequacy of Darman and Sununu mounted, and the inadequacy of Brady was realized, things exploded. The common picture of a presidency easily manipulated on a wide range of domestic policy issues contrasted with Bush's decisiveness and personal interest in diplomatic matters. "I'm no freelancer," Sununu protested at one point. "I meet with the president dozens of times during the day. . . . The president knows I'm following his agenda. . . . I know enough about the president to do exactly what he wants done."[46] Even the president's use of his constitutional powers vis-à-vis the legislature, which, in the spring of 1990, he was preparing to do again, this time to thwart Democratic passage of the Family and Medical Leave Act, was coming to be seen by right-wingers within the administration itself as a "hesitant, timid, reactive" substitute for effective supply-side initiatives and by liberals as rule by "veto strategy."[47] Almost lost in all this was the recognition of the character of Bush's conservatism. For example, "family leave"—the concept that prevailed in most other industrialized nations providing for time off for working parents to tend to problems involving spouses or children—was, to Bush "an important benefit" but one that should not be mandated by the federal government.[48] Roger Porter, the architect of the "veto strategy," recalled it as an effective tool for a president disadvantaged by heavy partisan opposition on the hill.[49] Again, as he had done repeatedly with each of his vetoes, he prevailed when the House fell fifty-four votes short of overriding the president, even though, as the Gallup poll then showed, 69 percent of the public favored its passage. A victory, Bush mulled over afterward, "but barely when we had to use the veto."[50]

Similarly, the outcome of the budgetary process came to be viewed as the unhappy consequence of a situation into which the president had somehow been euchred by Darman, who had, it was true, been pressing him about it for some time. Yet, there were those who insisted that, from its inception, Bush knew that the "no new taxes" pledge would ultimately have to be compromised. Hitting Darman, in that view, was merely "a translation of their frustration with the president."[51] Finally, by early May, after his many meetings with Republican and Democratic congressional leaders, Bob Dole, Bob Michel, Newt Gingrich, Tom Foley, and George Mitchell, at Camp David and in the White House, he was ready.

On Sunday, May 6, he took advantage of an innocuous-looking opportunity to bring everybody together without having the press know what was happening. Congressional leaders were present that afternoon for the second of five in the series of presidential lectures, an event that had been inspired by the president's sister, Nancy Bush Ellis. David McCullough, the popular historian, biographer, and television narrator, gave a talk about one of his favored subjects, Theodore Roosevelt. As McCullough concluded his remarks, seven of the conferees recognized their signal to slip away without any fuss and take the elevator upstairs to a meeting with the president in the White House residence.[52]

For nearly two hours, they talked "over popcorn and shrimp with hot sauce," as Darman has described it. Darman went on at length about the budgetary cost of delay, the problem of a potential sequester, and the urgency of contending with the deficits. The Democrats agreed to a continuing series of meetings, with the number of participants varying all the way from the eight in the residence that evening to as many as twenty-six. Secrecy was essential to avoid any grandstanding or posturing, especially on a matter as sensitive as taxes in an election year. Everybody must be able to speak his mind without worrying about politics. When decisions were made, there would be no breaking of ranks. The process was a mutual commitment to a clear national need. The essence of the understanding was that neither side would try to exploit the situation for partisan advantage. Their sessions, hopefully out of view of the press, would include many additional meetings of the Group of Eight, over which the president would preside.

Taking an "all right, if you go first" tack, Mitchell asked if Bush was prepared to extend the negotiations to taxes. He was. Fine, was the response, if the White House puts out a statement making that clear, we're prepared to go along—as though they had much choice. If they couldn't get the Republicans to take the fall for new taxes, for once, they could well be left hanging, congressmen gumming up the works.[53]

The statement, the price of agreeing to a budget "summit," came via Fitzwater's announcement on Wednesday. The most basic Democratic demand was met by the deceptively simple agreement that "the special budget group would function best if there were no preconditions for negotiation and if there were no negotiations through the public." A *Washington Post* story, based on a "nonattribution" comment by Sununu that "no preconditions" meant that "Democrats could propose tax increases, but the White House would veto them," helped to poison rather than improve the atmosphere. The resulting brouhaha, however, brought quick reassurances that there were no preconditions. Any talk about a veto threat was ruled out as "crazy." Darman and others have argued that such suspicions, derived from the ugliness of the 1988 campaign and battles over capital gains the next year, revealed the flimsiness of the "reservoir of trust."[54] The question of "trust" also applied to Republicans. Nobody, in any of this, hinted about what *kind* of taxes would thereby be placed on the table. Nobody mentioned "income." Were "user fees" and higher excise rates for gasoline, alcohol, and cigarettes also taxes? His "exploitation of the tax issue" had "come full circle," declared Elizabeth Drew in *The New Yorker.*[55]

In a day when "taking the pledge" against further taxation was rapidly supplanting anticommunism as the rallying point for conservatives, the administration's initiative appeared as an incredible betrayal. Bush's making it a negotiable item, said the National Republican Congressional Committee's cochairman, Ed Rollins, was "a disaster" that could sacrifice as many as ten House seats in the midterm elections. "Keep your snorkel above the water," advised the president, however, in trying to mollify concerned Republicans, passing on old wisdom from his mother. He, too, he reminded them, knew something about taxes.[56]

Thank God he could manage to get away from the White House as often as he did. There was Farish's Texas place in December, Baker's in Wyoming, Kennebunkport in the warm weather and Thanksgiving weekends, Camp David whenever he chose, and all those trips overseas. He spent untold presidential hours in helicopters and in Air Force One's version of the Oval Office. His truly was a mobile presidency.

On Friday, the day after Fitzwater tried to undo Sununu's heavy-handedness, Bush flew off again, relieved that the budget flap stirred by his chief of staff was dying down but worried that the "intolerable" deficit was going "to be far bigger than anyone thought." If he needed to find a "presidential high," he had only to go out to the hinterlands, where patriotism lived on, where people still waved flags proudly and where they truly respected their president. "There is something marvelous about going into a small town as president," he confided to his diary about his outing to Kingsville for a commencement address at Texas A & M University. "The kids turn out, the citizens all turn out, and families stand with flags in their front yard." The Kingsville crowd was special, mostly Hispanic-American, the young ones reminding him of his own grandchildren.

"I've been doing a series of graduation speeches on Eastern Europe," he dictated, "choppered to Lynchburg, Virginia, and had an enormous turnout at Liberty University, Falwell's college. The press will probably take a shot, but it was very moving, and a mammoth turnout." He told Rev. Jerry Falwell's group about how they had shown "how a thousand points of light can become a galaxy of people working to solve problems in their own backyard." Speaking that afternoon in the university's Willard May Stadium, he said that "through the adventure of community service, we can unlock new frontiers of empowerment, joining hands and linking hearts to further the work of God and man."[57]

Back in Washington after his brief southern swing, he plunged into what turned out to be only a preliminary round of negotiations. The Democrats were clearly out to force him to take the fall for tax increases, to go out to the country with his neck on the line. He wasn't going to do that, he told Mitchell, Foley, and the Democratic whip, Dick Gephardt; whatever had to be done had to be done together. A speech by the president alone would only polarize the situation, sharpen the political knives, and kill any chance of a deal. But Mitchell kept insisting that the ball was in the White House's court, even though, Bush complained, "it's Congress that appropriates every dime and every nickel." In that situation, Bush decided, "the best thing is to shut up and let the Congress do the talking, and us try to be responsible and work something out." What else could he do? He faced the same situation with the Kennedy-Hawkins civil rights bill, battling over language that the White House could support. "Politics is rampant and guts are lacking," he complained to his diary in mid May. "We got through the weekend, but we're getting pounded, and the right-wing is the worst, and much more so than the left-wing it seems to me, or maybe it's just that when you're attacked by your own, it stings more."[58]

Reagan, of course, had never actually "raised" taxes. Lou Cannon, the distinguished early biographer of his presidency, has pointed out that the hero of the Republican right "accepted such transparent rationalizations because the competitive side of his nature demanded political victories" and this "served as a check on ideology, and his more pragmatic aides [i.e., the same Dick Darman] took advantage of this tendency whenever they could." Therefore, the fortieth president not only "tolerated stories that gave Baker and Darman and later Regan the credit for the administration's legislative accomplishments" but "reformed" the structure after the injudicious cuts of 1981 and the subsequent recession by accepting significant increases when signing the TEFRA of 1982. Raising taxes? Of course not. The acronym stood for the Tax Equity and Fiscal Responsibility Act, a series of loophole closings and corporate reforms that then constituted what Darman has called "the largest single tax increase in history."[59] In pursuit of deficit reduction, Reagan soon afterward accepted new gasoline excises. He and the Democrats did not "raise taxes" in 1983 but worked together to "rescue" the Social Security Trust Fund by enhancing "contributions." After the stock market collapsed in

1987, Republicans and Democrats worked together to "simplify the tax code" to make it "easier to understand," which explained that year's rate changes. Bush, alluding to all this during a presidential news conference on May 24, 1990, and retaining his loyalty to Reagan, recalled that the congressional Democrats bore "a greater responsibility" for the huge budget deficit. "But I'm not trying to assign blame. That's why I'm not doing it now," he added, and the White House Briefing Room filled with laughter.[60]

What with the budgetary impasse and facing mandatory spending cuts under the Gramm-Rudman-Hollings cap, which could further weaken an already uncertain economy, Bush knew he had little choice. He heard as much on the morning of June 26. He would have to do better than in his early May statement. Without an unequivocal endorsement of the possibility of new taxes, he could forget about any real progress. With the country already burdened with ever-mounting deficits, including sharply escalating pressures from the savings and loan bailout situation, with the Federal Reserve unwilling to jump-start the economy by lowering interest rates in the absence of any progress, he could not afford to preside over collapsed negotiations. Possibly, he had already been assured by all hands—Sununu, Darman, Brady, Boskin, and pollster Bob Teeter—going into a reelection campaign in 1992 as the bearer of tax hikes would be less lethal than as the architect of a recession.[61] He could, in short, no longer avoid penalties for his pledge. The new statement was unequivocal, all right, but still ambiguous: "It is clear to me that both the size of the deficit problem and the need for a package that can be enacted require all of the following: entitlement and mandatory program reform, tax revenue increases, growth incentives, discretionary spending reductions, orderly reductions in defense expenditures, and budget process reform to assure that any bipartisan agreement is enforceable and that the deficit problem is brought under responsible control. The bipartisan leadership agree with me on these points."[62]

The big word, however, was not "taxes" but "income"—and he did not use that. He didn't have to; he had already said too much. Vice President Quayle has let it be known that he was taking a shower when an aide called out that CNN was reporting Bush's agreement to raise taxes. Quayle thereby implicitly proclaimed his distance from the process. He "probably should have looked at the drain," wrote the vice president afterward, "because that's where the Republican party's best issue—the one that had gotten us elected in 1980, 1984, and 1988; the one that had, more than any other, made the Reagan revolution possible—was headed . . ."[63]

Quayle was not, it was true, very much part of the budget-making process. His role, in certain essential, if sometimes subtle ways, did not resemble the Reagan-Bush relationship. When he spoke out in terms that seemed contrary to the administration, as he did early on about support for the contras and a hard line toward the Soviet Union, it was not possible to determine whether he was serving his own interests among the conservatives by hoisting right-wing credentials or was merely a loyal "Bushie" and humoring the extremists. Within the Oval Office, however, there was little doubt that the vice president was "a pawn in the hands" of his ideologue chief of staff, William Kristol.[64]

Either way, Quayle loomed at that moment as a palliative to the unreliable Bush. "Was he lying or did he just not understand the situation?" asked a writer for the *Houston Post*.[65]

Republicans everywhere, it was noted, were beginning to scramble for ways to adjust election year strategies.[66]

The Bush administration's most soothing accomplishment that summer, perhaps, was getting David Souter onto the Supreme Court. Sununu, who certainly knew New Hampshire, agreed; as governor, he had appointed Souter to the state's supreme court. A Harvard Law School graduate and Rhodes scholar only recently named to the U.S. Court of Appeals for the First Circuit in Boston, he was neither a William Brennan "Eisenhower liberal" nor a Robert Bork. Bork's acceptance of the concept of "original intent" of the Founding Fathers, and his interpretation of how the Fourteenth Amendment should be applied, which he had since repudiated, was enough to get him turned down. Having been Reagan's choice did not give him adequate protection from outraged liberals, who were out for political blood.

But Souter had left no "paper trail," no body of opinions liberals could savage, not even a clear position on the fiery abortion question; he was a stealth candidate, but, with it all, safely conservative. At first, Bush had even toyed with naming a judge from the federal appeals court, a tested conservative, Clarence Thomas. But Thomas had served on the D.C. Circuit, Boyden Gray pointed out, for only eight months. Besides, Thurgood Marshall was still there. How could you have two black men on the Court out of the nine? Thomas wouldn't do, Bush agreed, and Sununu helped wrap it up.[67] Even then, Bush heard loads of protests from the "Vigueries and a handful of right-wingers," who "get rich only from raising money opposing someone. But they *really* upset me."[68] Before Souter's confirmation, Bush also heard from prochoice activists, who cited as "profoundly alarming" a brief submitted by Souter's office in 1976 to a federal appeals court opposing Medicaid funds for "the killing of the unborn." Once confirmed, Souter took his place at the center of the Court, more often siding with its liberals than with such conservatives as Chief Justice William Rhenquist and Antonin Scalia, both Reagan appointees, especially on First Amendment questions.[69]

More upsetting, more contentious, was the continuing battle over new civil rights legislation. Activists and a broad array of liberals, overwhelmingly antiadministration to begin with, championed restoring the ability of employees to sue if they could prove that they were the victims of discrimination in the workplace. That power had been undermined by recent Supreme Court decisions, especially in the *Wards Cove* case of 1989. Their cause, incorporated in the Kennedy-Hawkins bill and blessed by every civil rights organization in the land, was firmly contested by conservative opponents of "racial preferences" that took the form of quotas or affirmative action.

Bush's dilemma was very evident. He was, as his staff secretary saw it, "tortured" by the problem, and others could agree that, personally, it posed a dilemma, morally and politically. Former Klansman David Duke's identification with the Republican cause and his attempt to climb to political legitimacy in Louisiana was one aspect of a problem Bush wanted to avoid. Duke, who aimed at a Senate seat, merely represented the most extreme hate-mongering racists but, nevertheless, found common ground with whites who thought liberals had overreached by giving African-Americans advantages for certain jobs. Bush, much closer to the latter, was, at the same time, uncomfortable opposing black leaders and liberal Republicans who urged him to sign the bill. The issue would not go away; a veto would make it more visible. He told his people that he wanted to sign it if he could only get a satisfactory compromise. John Sununu, for example, might help. He was on good terms with Kennedy, "of all people." One powerful group, the Business Roundtable, to which Boyden Gray was close, opposed it, but as Gray later said, they "didn't mind the quota stuff because they're rich enough to train their own employees." The real problem, as Gray outlined his opposition in a memo to the president, was that it would shift to employers the burden of proving that the potential worker was not qualified for reasons other than race. To avoid costly litigation, Gray added, businesses "would concentrate on hiring by race, sex, and religion rather than by qualification." The bill had other problems, he argued, such as thwarting challenges to "quota systems approved by courts in settlement of litigation to which the new victims were not a party." After eight weeks filled with bargaining, the Senate went ahead on July 18 and passed its version, still two votes short of what they needed to override a veto.[70]

Similarly confronted by politics, this time within the context of cold war diplomacy, Bush came down on the side of the latter. Gorbachev, arriving in Washington at the end of May, was, as Bush and Baker soon appreciated, in need of help. Bush, who drew closer to Gorbachev than he had before, also sensed what Baker confirmed for him. The Soviet leader was torn between having to placate his own hard-liners, especially over the pending reunification of Germany and its possible membership in NATO, and by tensions over the Baltics.

The two presidents kept alive the arms control initiatives begun under Reagan, and that included an accord on Conventional Armed Forces in Europe. They also signed onto what Bush called a "landmark agreement," a bilateral pact to phase out the great stockpiles of chemical weapons accumulated over the years, as well as protocols on limiting nuclear testing.[71]

Gorbachev, it also became clear to the president and the secretary of state, needed to return to Moscow with evidence of some tangible achievement for his failing economy—an agreement on trade and the sale of grain to the Soviets. Bush, weighing the conflicting forces of politics and diplomacy, chose the latter, giving the visiting leader what he needed. By making the gesture, as Michael Beschloss and Strobe Talbott have noted, he not only avoided rubbing Gorbachev's nose on the outstanding issues but "managed to impose exactly the sort of linkage between U.S.-Soviet trade and the Kremlin's policies" that earlier "Soviet leaders had always found not only objectionable but unacceptable."[72]

After meeting with Gorbachev on June 2, 1990, Bush could not have been more casual when chatting with reporters. Why, a newsman wanted to know, had he made concessions despite continued differences over the Soviet handling of the situation in Lithuania? Bush's response, spoken from a golf cart, could not have been more direct.

He had made his decision, he said, in "the interest of the United States. The agreement we signed on arms, the agreement we signed on trade, maritime, Bering Straits [sic]. Why do you single out one agreement? I look at the overall relationship. If somebody wants to argue with me, fine, we'll take him on. I'm doing what I think is in the best interest of the United States of America."[73]

In Houston, where the G-7 executive committee was meeting, the president continued to be confronted by unresolved aspects of Soviet needs. With the Soviets represented by Gorbachev deputy Yevgeny Primakov, Bush was joined in Texas by Mitterrand, Thatcher, Kohl, and Brian Mulroney. It was, of course, partly festive, a nice social fling for the heads of state, with a barbecue and an indoor rodeo at the Astrodome. Hugh and Betty Liedtke threw a lavish dinner.

Unfortunately, however, money was at the top of the agenda, a request for some $15 to $20 million in aid to Gorbachev. As Bush well knew, the Soviet leader needed to be propped up to stay in power. All the others, including Mulroney, to whom Bush had become close, agreed with that essential reality. Letting Gorby be "chucked out" of office would be a "disaster." Yet, for Bush, with the thunder on the right already deafening, it was a hell of a time to be giving money to the Russians, especially right after his approval on trade. Better to send "experts to help the Soviet Union rebuild its rail and communications networks, grain storage sites, food distribution systems, and other essential services." He had nothing against putting encouragement of *perestroika* into writing while deferring action about money pending the outcome of international studies of the Soviet economy. It was, either way one looked at it, "a polite and thinly disguised rejection," as two students of the diplomacy have judged.[74]

In the days after the G-7 meeting, the S&L crisis went from bad to worse. The public, hitherto rather indifferent to the situation, had warmed up to its magnitude by that summer, helped by the administration's admission that its own estimates were off the mark, and the designation by the General Accounting Office of possibly as much as half a trillion dollars in taxpayer money to complete the bailout.[75] Common Cause released a study showing there was enough blame to go around the government. The S&Ls had blanketed the Congress, especially key committee chairmen, with some $11 million during the 1980s alone.[76] "By 1982," stated a special report by Jeff Gerth in *The New York Times,* "every dollar of capital—the real estate or cash contributions made by owners—was a license to raise $33 in federally insured deposits."[77]

Moreover, the entire scandal was falling closer to the White House doorstep. After Neil Bush appeared before the House Banking Committee on his conflict of interest charges, maintaining his innocence, federal regulators went before that body to detail his actions. Newly released documents, moreover, showed that consideration was being given to barring him from ever again serving as a savings and loan officer. In mid July, the young Bush was faced with the possibility of a $200-million suit against him and other Silverado directors. The president, at a press conference from the scene of the G-7 summit at Houston, had become emotional in defense of Neil. "I have confidence in the honor and integrity of my son," he told reporters, and added that "if the system finds he's done something wrong, he will be the first to step up and do what's right."[78] Then, gradually, emerged the story of how Bob Thompson, a high-roller identified as Vice President Bush's former legislative director, had exploited his knowledge of the inner workings of the White House and the FDIC. Thompson's expertise enabled an Arizona businessman, James M. Fail, to overcome a history of having pleaded guilty to fraud and go on to make a killing buying off RTC properties. Thompson, whose lobbying network, it also turned out, included business dealings with the president's brother, Prescott, had helped set up a dummy group for Fail and access to valuable information with the help of the top White House aide for the savings and loan cleanup, "an old friend," Richard C. Breeden. Thompson worked with key movers, including Federal Home Loan Bank Chairman M. Danny Wall (who denied that his order to delay the closing of Silverado had anything to do with the 1988 election) to get a good deal for his client, Fail. Fail, by putting up just $1,000 of his own money, was able to get $70 million in loans and an additional $1.85 billion in federal aid to relieve the RTC of a chain of fifteen thrifts in Texas and another in Oklahoma. Thompson, whose services for Fail stood to earn him $2.5 million, was also a partner with Prescott Bush Jr. in organizing an oil fund called the Thompson Exploration Company.[79]

Little helped the public comprehend it better than the prominence of Neil Bush, who continued to criticize federal regulators for acting against him "with vengeance."[80] "Jail Neil Bush" graffiti appeared in Washington. His case, wrote Andrew Rosenthal in *The New York Times,* "recalls George Bush's background of privilege and his lifetime in the old-boy network of politics and business."[81] A *Newsweek* story was headlined as "A Crisis in the First Family."[82] About half of the public, according to the magazine's own poll, thought regulators were zeroing in on Neil unfairly but, at the same time, seven out of ten agreed that his involvement was damaging the president.[83] In an Indiana congressional race, the conservative Republican incumbent, John Hiler, found himself on the defensive in a losing cause, attacked by his opponent, Tim Roemer, for the president's reneging on the tax pledge and for serving on the Banking Committee while the S&L crisis grew. In Colorado, a long-shot Democrat competing for his party's Senate nomination, rode on Bush's S&L problems to lift his candidacy out of the long-shot category.[84] As the summer wore on, 59 percent of respondents, according to a *New York Times/CBS News* survey, feared that the thrift crisis would worsen. Only 27 percent voiced approval of the administration's handling of the situation. "So far it looks like Bush is just letting the taxpayers pay for it," said one man. The poll confirmed that the president's son was handy for public personification of the crisis, especially when, during that midsummer, pessimism about the economy began to merge with news about taxes and the cost of the bailout.[85]

Then there was the matter of working out a bipartisan budget. Bush, while happy to leave most of the haggling to Darman and Sununu, presided over the Group of Eight. He hated every minute. He found them wearying and frustrating. He had not, he realized, conveyed any urgency about the situation to the country. No one gave a damn. Sequestration, shutting down the government, billions of dollars for additional interest, all counted for nothing. The leaders wanted to break, to get away from Washington on schedule. He wondered what "kind of carrots" he could offer them to defer summertime pleasures. But, in the midst of the crisis, all had different reasons for wanting to go home. They had already reserved flights out of the capital, some on discount tickets that they'd be damned if they had to forfeit. "They would just as soon go to Disneyland, or take their cruises, or whatever else it is." The "focus" should be put on them. "Where's your congressman," he confided to his diary mockingly; "—well, he's at Disneyland with his mother." Impossible, and with the S&Ls "hovering out there" as well, and the Democrats trying to blame the Republicans. "Newt and to the right of Newt—can do nothing but criticize. We've got one hell of a problem." What was it about Republicans? "Why they can't be more supportive—but the right wing is giving me a lot of fits."[86]

Gingrich, the ambitious, cocky minority whip from Georgia, "halfhearted" and playing "into the hands of critics like Novak and others who say I am undermining the conservative credentials of the Republican party," was already jumping on the Bush "betrayal" of the "new right" and pumping up his ambitions. In May, his goal to recruit "nonvoters and people who were apolitical" to achieve "Republican control of the United States House of Representatives," he began televised "American Opportunities Workshops." The AOW, the first of several Gingrich operations that eventually helped him get the speakership, reached out across the country via some 600 workshop sites.[87] The Bush "abdication" on the tax issue provided an opening. The momentum, noted Elizabeth Drew at the time, "has been building over the years, and Gingrich is only going further than some of his predecessors in both exploiting it and trying to build a new Republican base." Representative of "generational and demographic changes within the Republican party—the old Eastern wing is desiccated and about dead, while the party grows stronger, with a new type of Republican, in the South and Southwest." Bush, while trying to "reflect both," was nevertheless "surrounded in the White House by Easterners—Sununu, and Darman and other staff members from what Bush, attacking Dukakis, once called the 'Harvard Yard boutique'—who don't understand this new group and 'think of them as clods,' as representing the lower classes." There were enough behind Gingrich, "a rebel who likes to command attention" but with "a coherent set of thoughts about where the future of the Republican party lies," to believe that they could have destroyed the budget agreement even without the Georgian's revolt.[88] Gingrich, nevertheless, by breaking ranks, also signaled the Republican right's disaffection with their president and helped to pave the way for the rise of their congressional power over the White House.

On Tuesday, July 31, the FDIC's chairman, William Seidman, whom the administration had replaced as head of the RTC after his angry run-in with Sununu over the projected cost of the cleanup, said that weakening real estate markets and mounting bank failures would bring the insurance fund down to a dangerous level, "the lowest point at any time in modern history."[89]

It was the "feeling at this juncture," Bush observed, that the presidency was not at "high center" but "kind of drifting" and in "disarray," with some conservative papers urging Gingrich and his allies to rally against the "Democratic" budget.[90]

CHAPTER TWENTY-TWO

"Give Me the Strength to Do What Is Right"

※

President Saddam Hussein's invasion of Kuwait coincided with that low point, when events compounded perceptions of a downward slide since Panama. With Barbara in Maine and Millie sick, the lousy news in the morning papers only fed Bush's melancholy. Finally, when he found something upbeat, he noted it with delight. Nolan Ryan's forty-three-year-old right arm had won again, a three-hundredth career victory, and for George W.'s Rangers. Everything else was miserable, the papers full of "every lousy piece of news you can imagine": S&Ls, Bob Thompson's shenanigans, banks going broke. Even the so-called Panama "democracy" was a joke. President Endara had reconstituted Noriega's personal army and given it a different name, but the cadre looked very much like Noriega's. Again, this was accomplished with American money. In Washington, budget talks were broken off, suspended until the fall, a $50-billion gap dividing the two parties. A Republican plan "doesn't exist," complained Minority Whip Newt Gingrich; just "meandering and interesting ideas of random individuals." He could have added that this was thanks, in part, to a leak that the administration planned to fish for revenues by digging into deductions for state and local income taxes and upping rates on alcohol. The leaker, Bush heard, was none other than Republican Senator Bob Packwood of Oregon. Packwood had spilled, "and suddenly we see the Democrats pull back," probably because "they see us getting clobbered for putting a beer tax out there or something and so they don't want to move." "I have never seen such a frenzy of horrible news," the president thought.[1] Only hours later, after hearing of the Iraqi invasion, he noted with dismay that "the country at this juncture doesn't really care."[2]

With it all, and while keeping a close eye on Europe and the situation in Russia, the Persian Gulf suddenly became dominant, spinning off into a situation that would demonstrate the validity of British Laborite Tony Benn's subsequent comment that "all war represents a failure of diplomacy." Long after Saddam's aggression, there were dark suggestions that Bush himself had "lured" the dictator—or president, as his title had it—into Kuwait, and then, happily, played commander in chief. Successes, "winners, as they're called—must flow from his foreign policy," wrote *The New Yorker*'s diligent Washington correspondent.[3] The "consistent" preinvasion voice that the administration expressed "assured Saddam the U.S. would look the other way if Iraq were to attack Kuwait," explained a critic in the muckraking *Village Voice* in a story picked up by at least one mainstream paper.[4] Much was made of Ambassador April Glaspie's telling Saddam, as she did on July 25 when she was summoned with great haste, that the United States had "no opinion" about his border quarrel with Kuwait. Bush "lost Kuwait," wrote Christopher Hitchens, by playing Kissingerian realpolitik filled with "signals and nods and tilts and intrigues" that collapsed in a failure of policy to keep the "region divided and embittered, and therefore accessible to the franchisers of weaponry and the owners of black gold."[5] The very idea of mobilizing a half million in the Persian Gulf to "defend" Saudi Arabia came in the face of "considerable" evidence indicating that the kingdom of Saudi Arabia "was not in jeopardy."[6] Others questioned the president's constitutional right to move the country toward a potentially "offensive war" without congressional authorization.[7]

With all else troubling the administration, an explosion in the Middle East contained the seeds of more political risk than opportunities. Unlike Grenada and Panama, Kuwait was remote; affairs in the region, outside of those involving Israel and the remaining hostages held by Shiites in Lebanon, went unnoticed. Still, it is true that Bush's early actions in mobilizing responses did lift his standings. What made it all seem like conventional "rally around the flag" spirit was the country's clear discomfort with the savings and loan situation and the deepening of existing hints of a weakening economy. Two-thirds of Americans told pollsters that they opposed taxes to reduce the deficit and 53 percent opposed paying any more, if needed, to help Saudi Arabia resist Iraqi aggression.[8]

He reminded his aides that he knew more about the region—"about the diplomacy, the military, the economics, the oil"—than any of them, which was true.[9] Back in the 1960s, Zapata's Seacat affiliate had built Kuwait's first offshore well. Bush's activities in the oil industry and with banks inevitably crossed paths with the area's movers and shakers. He built up relationships, one of the things he did best. He was on good terms with King Hussein of Jordan and had once even taken Egypt's Mubarak to an Orioles game in Baltimore. Saudi Arabia's King Fahd was hardly a stranger, especially with the very active presence in Washington of his ambassador to the United States, the flamboyant, American-educated Prince Bandar bin Sultan.[10] He had been on personal terms with the king since his CIA days when Fahd headed Saudi intelligence. To this enumeration should be added the Chinese, Japanese, and Russians, to say nothing of Chancellor Kohl and Prime Minister Thatcher. Less than two years into the presidency, Bush's international web of friendships was reminiscent of his circle at home. He was well on his way toward becoming the foremost practitioner of "telephone diplomacy."[11]

The contrast with Israel was vivid, especially with the country's right-wing leadership, going back to Menachem Begin in the Reagan years and the current Likud prime minister, Yitzhak Shamir. U.S.-Israeli relations had become uncertain.[12] Bush, much more than had Reagan, personified the differences. Interactions had often been unpleasant, even allowing for the peculiar ugliness that marked his encounter with Rabbi Meier Kahane of the Jewish Defense League while Bush was still with the UN.[13] He had, as vice president, been one of Reagan's leading critics of the Israeli incursion into Lebanon.[14] The relationship had deteriorated since then, exacerbated by Israeli insistence about seeking a peace formula through giving up land. The suspicion, Baker has noted, was not helped by the "mythology" that the Bush-Baker Texas backgrounds automatically made them hostile toward Israel, nor, he could have added, their closeness to Arab oil sheiks.

Mutual suspicions were more intense than they had been since the 1950s. Secretary of State Baker raised stern questions about the legitimacy of Israel's position in East Jerusalem.[15] The Bush-Baker leadership, as eager as their predecessors to achieve some equilibrium in that powder-keg area, was less likely to tilt in favor of the Israelis, as such political pressures had borne upon every presidency to the consternation of a succession of State Departments. The "even-handed" approach of more recent years seemed less feasible than the more singular determination of President Dwight D. Eisenhower and Secretary of State John Foster Dulles in pressing the American economic and strategic interests in the Middle East. More relevant for the president's immediate attention was the post–cold war reduction of Israel's importance to East-West diplomacy, and the reality, as one cartoonist noted, that "the truly overriding concern is the principle we hold dear—eighteen miles per gallon."[16] Not surprisingly, then, such Bush administration initiatives as edging closer to the oil sheikdoms and Palestinian interests in the areas occupied by Israel since the Six Day War of 1967 were blamed by Israeli activists for the troubles of Shamir's government. Tensions were stretched even more when the administration granted Yasir Arafat's request for a visa to enable him to address the UN. That act alone brought Israel's American lobbyists down on the White House. "It is outrageous," the president wrote privately, "and they are pushing anything that Shamir can use in order to delay moving forward with the peace process . . . it is always some rationale of this nature."[17]

Even Iraq, despite Saddam's brutalities, had become more significant than Israel for Western geopolitical concerns. The Israelis had knocked out the Iraqi nuclear reactor at Osirak in 1981 and gotten away with it, but, for Saddam, preeminence among the Arabian states in leading the holy war against the Jewish state became a unifying goal. Their struggle against Iran, starting in 1980 and backed by antiayatollah sentiment in the United States and Western Europe, kept Baghdad well supplied. Arms, especially, flowed in abundance from France; chemicals from Germany. Altogether, Saddam laid out $14.2 billion in hard currency between 1984 and 1989 alone, which enabled him to secure the most modern technology from American suppliers. However much disturbed it was by the Iraqi use of poison gas against Iranian soldiers in 1984 and its own Kurdish people four years later, the administration in Washington retained its diplomatic reserve. Even after that war ended in 1988, the U.S.-Iraqi relationship went on, all to do some good business with Saddam and keep the power balance.

The brutal Iraqi dictator renewed historic disputes over Iraq's border with Kuwait. The emirate had been delineated by a line drawn over the sands of old Ottoman empire provinces by a British government that had no inkling of the oil under the desert. The al-Sabah family acceded to Kuwait's becoming a British protectorate after World War I and, in 1934, gave them a concession to establish the Kuwait Oil Company (actually, a partnership between Gulf Oil of the U.S. and the British Petroleum Company). Full independence came in 1961. A veritable family corporation with hereditary stockholders and managers, the nation has been described as a "tribal structure" functioning with mostly foreign labor and serving the top 40 percent very well as "an air-conditioned Eden where wealth accumulated without work."[18] The glass-sheltered utopia was a society with one of the world's richest per-capita populations.[19]

Iraq's earlier attempts to cross the line over the desert were rebuffed by British troops, but Baghdad's covetousness only intensified. His war with Iran left Saddam pleading poverty. Eager for more oil revenue, he kept pressing, although unsuccessfully, to have the oil-producing states (OPEC) cut back production to bring up the prices.[20]

The 1989 discovery of the operations by the Atlanta branch of the Italian Banco Nazionale Lavoro (BNL) revealed how agricultural credits, which were responsible for a healthy grain trade with American farmers, were diverted for weapons purchases by the Iraqi president. But that revelation only helped draw more attention to what had been going on throughout the decade, when Iraqi trade with the U.S. zoomed from around $500 million in the early 1980s to over $3.5 billion. Americans, unable to restrain their appetites for fuel despite the crisis with OPEC in the 1970s, were also top purchasers of Iraqi oil. Discomfort with the trade within the administration did not interfere with the business. Designs to trim some of the additional funds that came out of the Agriculture Department were vetoed when Baker pressed Agriculture Secretary Clayton Yeutter for a billion dollars in new agricultural-loan guarantees. The U.S., in fact, dissented when a special international conference on chemical weapons held in Paris in January 1989 named Iraq as a violator of human rights. So tied was Washington to maintaining an equilibrium in the Middle East that even acknowledging that Saddam's purchases contributed to his nuclear weapons program brought no cutoff. Only with the start of actual hostilities against Kuwait was the administration able to curtail shipments capable of reinforcing Iraq's menacing military aspirations, and, even then, the process could not be stopped abruptly.[21]

"We were trying to work with Saddam Hussein and trying to bring him along into the family of nations," Bush later said in a televised interview with Larry King.[22] It was certainly more complex than that, but he was trying to fulfill his obligation to explain the nation's goals in plain English.

On July 31, a page sixteen *Washington Post* story told of a large movement of Iraqi troops headed toward the border with Kuwait. Pete Williams, the State Department spokesman, was evasive when a reporter asked whether a force of 100,000 troops had really been deployed, but the gray area had to do with actual numbers.[23]

John Kelly, meanwhile, the assistant secretary of state for Near Eastern and South Asian Affairs, answered House Foreign Affairs Committee Chairman Lee Hamilton's question about what we would do if Iraq attacked Kuwait by saying it was "hypothetical." We had no treaty obligation to dispatch troops if that happened, he explained.[24]

On Saturday, August 4, when the president talked to King Hussein of Jordan, his optimism (as well as Hosni Mubarak's) was bolstered by assurances that "the situation will not exceed the limits of reason."

"There is no possibility for this," said the king, "and it will not reach this point," thereby encouraging the common view, shared by even the Israelis, that the Iraqi president was just blustering. If he moved at all, most assumed it would be to snatch Kuwait's Rumaila oil field and possibly the strategically located Warba and Bubiyan Islands.

On the phone again two days later, the king told the president that "the Iraqis are angry," but, he hoped, "something will take place in the interests of greater cooperation in the region."

"Without war?" asked the president.

Yes, yes, said the king. He really hoped so.

The administration quickly released a statement via a White House spokesman. "Obviously, coercion and intimidation have no function in this kind of dialogue," it declared. "We are concerned, but we do look forward to the Arab neighbors of those two countries to continue the mediation efforts and to continue urging dialogue, and we're still hopeful that a second round will take place and that some kind of amicable agreement can be reached."[25]

"We are not going to move against anybody," Iraqi Ambassador Muhammad al-Mashat told Kelly that afternoon.[26]

At just about that time, Charlie Allen, already a veteran CIA intelligence analyst at thirty-two, walked into the White House National Security Council office of Richard Haass, the NSC's top Middle East expert. He wanted to hand deliver his message to Haass. "This is your final warning," he said, alluding to reports of a dangerous buildup that his office had been passing along for nearly two weeks. Allen's latest information indicated a 70 percent chance of an Iraqi invasion of Kuwait by the end of that day. Saddam aimed to take Kuwait City and depose the al-Sabah royal family, who owned and ruled the emirate.[27] "Allen's warning on that August day," two historians of the war in the Persian Gulf have written, "was one that the White House, State Department, Defense Department, and even some of Allen's superiors in the intelligence agencies would find hard to accept. For it meant that the Bush administration's policy toward Baghdad had been an utter failure."[28] With military logistics as difficult as they were, with any substantial American forces over 7,000 miles away, there remained the hopeful assumption that Saddam, if he actually moved, aimed only to seize the expected limited objectives, sufficient to satisfy Iraq's economic need.[29] At about the same time as Allen's alert, Gen. H. Norman Schwarzkopf's intelligence people also notified Washington of the imminence of war. General Powell ordered the United States Central Command (CENTCOM) chief back from Tampa, Florida, headquarters to brief the JCS the next afternoon.[30]

Richard Haass gave Allen's warning to General Scowcroft. Bush's adviser for National Security Affairs was busy readying a statement about a revised defense budget scheduled to be announced by the president on Thursday. Congressional critics, especially Democrats, were carping that the end of the cold war had brought no reduction in Reagan-era military expenditures. Dick Cheney had made a preemptive move right after the fall of the Berlin Wall, convening the Joint Chiefs and convincing them that it would be better for them to suggest decreases rather than have cuts imposed by politicians. The revised new force structure envisioned a departure from the cold war scenario for waging an all-out global war. An updated objective had a more limited goal, one designed to secure a particular region from seizure by a potential adversary, thereby making possible a 25 percent cut in forces and an overall cost reduction of some 10 percent over five years.

Cheney, who had earlier taken a forward position by saying that the U.S. would back up its "commitment" to defend Kuwait, only to have the State Department deny the existence of any "special defense commitments," went to "the tank" that afternoon—the secure room in the Pentagon reserved for JCS meetings—for the briefing by General Schwarzkopf. The general, a tempestuous field-soldier veteran of Vietnam, had his greatest challenge.

Even if Saddam should move on the oil fields and the two islands, none of the American analysts thought he would then threaten Saudi Arabia.[31] Military deployments had been limited to two KC-135 aerial tankers and a C-141 cargo transport sent in response to a July 23 request from the United Arab Emirates, which was especially fearful of Iraq. The action, as explained at the time by a "senior administration official," was intended to "bolster a friend and lay down a marker for Saddam Hussein." Yet, so sensitive was the administration to deployments in the face of regional nervousness about non-Arab intervention, that a subsequent statement by the secretary of the navy that "our ships in the Persian Gulf were put on alert status" was quickly retracted.[32] All Scowcroft's NSC people could do was hope that, if an invasion came, it would be with limited goals. But, they agreed, some movement was probable. Bob Kimmitt, undersecretary of state for the office of Political Affairs, relayed the information to Jim Baker, who was then, fortunately, on a diplomatic mission in the Soviet Union with Eduard Shevardnadze. Baker, due to move on to Ulan Bator, Mongolia, had reached Irkutsk, Siberia, when he got the call at midnight, local time.[33]

At the Pentagon, Cheney turned the presentation over to Schwarzkopf. "What do you think they'll do?" asked the defense secretary.

"I think they're going to attack," replied the CENTCOM commander. He displayed surveillance photos of Iraqi troop dispositions together with diagrams, then detailed the kinds of retaliatory strikes that could be launched against Iraq. He had no doubt that Saddam was ready for a military offensive. The dictator would not "grab the entire country," just, possibly, the oil field and the islands, prizes slightly south of the 30th parallel. That should not be too critical.[34]

What else could be done? The president, making one last effort, informed the Iraqi dictator by cable that his administration "continues to desire better relations with Iraq." Cheney and Powell, on their way out of the tank, agreed that Bush ought to get off "a tough message" as soon as possible. He might even "call him," said the commander of the Joint Chiefs, "but try to scare him off." But, before "we could fire a diplomatic warning shot," Powell has written, "eighty thousand of Saddam's Republican Guards were across the border rolling toward Kuwait City."[35]

At about seven that evening, Bob Kimmitt, in the absence of the secretary of state, received a phone call from the American ambassador in Kuwait, Nathaniel Howell. Gunfire had broken out in Kuwait City. Kimmitt relayed the message to Scowcroft, who then went to the residence with Haass to review the situation with the president. Bush, in true form, fired off a series of questions: Would an eleventh-hour warning help? What were our options? What do the analysts think? "What's our intelligence community saying?"[36]

By 8:30 P.M., Ambassador Howell was back on the phone to Kimmitt. The emir wanted military help, but with one condition: no public announcements. Inappropriate, he was told; tell the emir that our democracy can't work that way. Not long after that, the phone rang with another Howell update. The emir and his family had changed their minds. Never mind what the neighbors think: just send help. Even as Howell completed that third call, the al-Sabahs were in their royal limousine fleeing Kuwait.[37]

By nine, going over everything with Scowcroft, the president had received scattered reports about Iraq's further movements. Bush kept in touch with UN Ambassador Thomas Pickering and followed the Security Council's after-midnight debate on a resolution seeking Iraq's withdrawal, while Scowcroft kept updating the president. At five A.M., the retired general dropped in to get signatures for executive orders to freeze Iraqi and Kuwaiti assets. The president worried that a puppet government installed in the tiny, oil-rich emirate "would try to move billions of dollars out of Western banks and out of U.S. banks illegally."[38]

At six that morning, the Security Council voted to order Iraq out of Kuwait under the threat of sanctions. The action, taken under Articles Thirty-nine and Forty of the UN Charter, passed by a vote of 14 to 0; even Cuba went along. Only an hour later, Secretary of State Baker called with the comforting news that Shevardnadze had agreed to cut off arms to Iraq and condemn the invasion, the first real breakthrough in building an alliance. Post–cold war dividends were being paid.[39]

The submission of Kuwait was essentially complete by the time Bush met with the NSC at eight A.M. on the second of August. Saddam's elite Republican Guard, decorated veterans of the Iran war and fiercely loyal to their ruler, had moved into the capital city, which was also attacked by a Special Forces commando division. Soviet-made T-72 tanks encountered only sporadic resistance while rolling along a six-lane highway across the flat terrain to secure the border with Saudi Arabia. Simultaneous paratroop jumps took over other strategic sites, including Bubiyan and Warba, at the tip of the Persian Gulf and valuable also for the protection of Umm Qasr, Iraq's only seaport. All of a country the size of New Jersey was under effective enemy control within twelve hours. No more than 100 lives were lost on both sides. Nor did the Iraqis lose any time in sending out telexes to seize Kuwaiti funds. Most failed, thanks to the emergency freezes, but Saddam did manage to get $2 billion from the Kuwait Central Bank.[40]

"Intelligence getting worse all day yesterday," Bush observed, and added that "there is little the U.S. can do in a situation like this."[41] About the only decent news was the Soviet assurance of, at the very least, noninterference with whatever the Western powers decided to do in the region. Otherwise, options for reactions, other than the U.S. and UN sanctions, already implemented during the last few hours, had yet to be clarified.

More immediately, foreign nationals, including some 2,500 Americans who lived and worked in Kuwait, as well as 600 in Baghdad, were caught in the Iraqi outreach, including fourteen oil workers who were captured.[42] Bush envisioned another hostage situation, a replay of what contributed so much to Carter's downfall. Bad enough to be bogged down in another Vietnam, as a number of people, including Jim Baker, were worried about, but he would not let himself become a Jimmy Carter, "a U.S. impotence in the eyes of the world."[43]

Such dark thoughts were first beginning to dawn as the president entered the Cabinet Room for that morning's meeting. An even more apparent realization was that the United States was facing the first significant post–cold war test of its ability to maintain global or regional stability.[44]

In reporting that morning's events, and also what happened later in the day, it was easier for the press to get attention by focusing on what could be heralded as dramatic rather than on any diplomatic or political nuances. A quick vow to intervene militarily might suggest an "imperial presidency" defying the ineffectual War Powers Act and, less than a year after Panama, putting on a display of "macho" belligerence. Inaction, however, would invariably get commentators going on about "wimpish" responses to world crises. A Bush comment to correspondent Helen Thomas, made in the Cabinet Room just before the start of the NSC meeting, that "I'm not contemplating any such action, and I again would not discuss it if I were," got passed along with emphasis on the first clause. In some accounts of the decision-making process that lingered on, the second part of that sentence was omitted altogether.[45]

It was not a niggling point. The full context of those informal remarks to the press, even before the NSC began to contend with their options, indicates a far more determined and nuanced approach. He made clear, in his opening statement, that he wanted "the immediate and unconditional withdrawal" and recision of "naked aggression." While the U.S. had taken first steps, other governments had to take similar action because "we view the situation with the utmost gravity."[46]

What about the military options? What about sending troops? Unappreciative of Bush's penchant for secrecy, little attention went to his following two sentences: "We're not discussing intervention. *I would not discuss any military options even if we'd agreed upon them.*"* Commentary about Bush's preference for working with a small group of advisers ignores precisely the point he was making. Only with a limited number of the most reliable people would the possibility of leaks be minimized. Later, for example, after a long day that did not end until 2:30 the next morning, he expressed in his diary his determination "to think through the economic impact of any military action we take." He added, "but if we're going to move unilaterally, I want it to come out the way we want it and I want it to have total secrecy—this means I want to avoid leaks—that means that some people will not be included to keep down the chance of leaks." At Camp David, he anticipated, he would have a chance "to get back into a small planning group like we had in Panama, concentrating on 'need to know.'" But it was already obvious to the president that "sanctions alone" would be inadequate, certainly without "military interdiction of tankers" cutting off key delivery points.[47]

Yet, at the same time, Bush's tendency to be careless with words, as with the "Bushisms" so often ridiculed by the press, were often self-inflicted wounds. His meaning was clear to *him* and it should have been to others. But to the more critical minded, as with the press and those interested in faulting him later, it exposed a vulnerability. During that decision-making crisis, his qualification about declaring that he had not decided about intervention was ignored when it became useful to show him as wavering.[48]

He was thinking, right from the outset, of "a temporary bridge" necessary to "energize the international community" and something he would have "if nothing else worked." He could not call for military commitment, and certainly not for actually liberating Kuwait, without showing that all other options had been tried.[49] Building that coalition was an essential first step.

*Emphasis supplied.

Meanwhile, the timing was fortunate. Jim Baker was with Foreign Minister Shevardnadze getting Soviet support for an embargo. And Bush was on his way to Aspen, Colorado, traveling with Scowcroft and Bill Webster, to address a symposium at the Aspen Institute, where he would see that other key player, Margaret Thatcher. The British prime minister, who was invited to give the closing talk to the symposium on Sunday, had decided to arrive early and turn the trip into a minivacation at the ranch home of the American ambassador to the Court of St. James, Henry Catto, and his wife Jessica, in nearby Woody Creek. Thatcher and her husband, Denis, had looked forward to a brief holiday until their arrival in Colorado coincided with the news from the Persian Gulf. Dick Cheney was also scheduled to join them, but he decided to remain at the Pentagon. Bush left the White House and walked to the helicopter with Vice President Quayle and John Sununu looking especially troubled, showing the effects of a long night and an anxious morning.[50]

All in all, over a five-day period, he made a series of some four dozen calls to other leaders. No precise total, however, can take into account all the conversations initiated and received, and from places so varied as the Oval Office, the presidential residence, Camp David, Air Force One, and from the Catto bedroom near Aspen.[51]

Several calls originated in-flight before Bush reached Colorado: to Jim Baker in Ulan Bator and to both President Mubarak and King Hussein in Alexandria, where the monarch was visiting. Brent Scowcroft also phoned Dennis Ross in Moscow. Bush's pleasure with the efficiency of their air-to-ground communications was tempered by hearing the Jordanian monarch minimize Saddam's behavior by emphasizing Kuwaiti and Western responsibility for the situation. Hussein, not particularly disturbed at the prospect that Saddam threatened Saudi Arabia, was skeptical of what the Americans could or would be willing to do about it. Very upset about Hussein's position, Bush worried about his emergence as "almost an apologist" for Saddam. Both of them, Bush thought, the king and Mubarak, were "in the hand-wringing stage and neither of them is being a constructive influence for positive action by the West, by the United States, or by the Arabs themselves." The "bottom line" was that "a lot of these Arab countries are scared to death of Saddam Hussein."[52] The Arab League would meet, the king told the president. They would find some kind of solution that would satisfy the Iraqi, who was warning about unleashing "the mother of all wars." Mubarak, although angry at Saddam for having deceived him with assurances that he had no plans to invade Kuwait, was not much more eager to break ranks with present Arab hesitation to seek outside assistance. Let them first have their own summit in Jiddah, Saudi Arabia, he advised the president, and give Saddam's opponents in the area a chance to pool their resources.[53] Significantly absent from those called by Bush personally, other than Shamir of Israel, was François Mitterrand.

As soon as Bush and Thatcher met, Iraq became Topic A. Her interactions with the president continued to be cordial but hardly in the same league as her dealings with either Reagan or, for that matter, his secretary of state, George Shultz. The "Iron Lady," Britain's "shopkeeper's daughter," prided herself on being heir to the conservative traditionalism that viewed the French Revolution as, in Bill Rusher's words, a "misbegotten child" of the Enlightenment. More important to the prime minister, and more off-putting, was the Bush-Baker emphasis on a united Europe, with its potential for augmenting "the power of a united Germany." Fearful, also, of Bush's worries about the budgetary deficit, she considered him less determined than Reagan to upholding the priority of defense spending. In such ways, including her suspicions that the new American president "felt the need to distance himself from his predecessor," she reflected the views of the considerable number of Republicans who were to Bush's right.[54] Yet, one can also accept Brian Mulroney's observation that, as with many of his own countrymen, Reagan had become an icon and the Reagan-Thatcher relationship somewhat "mythic."[55] Grateful to Reagan for his crucial help during Britain's war with Argentina over the Falklands, she nevertheless then had to watch the Americans go into Grenada over her objections. British and American interests were not always identical, as the Suez crisis had demonstrated earlier, and contemporary differences over the desirability of early German reunification were cooling that "special relationship." If the Americans could not be taken for granted, neither could the British. But, in coping with the problem of Saddam's incursion, as the two leaders did for the first time that day, Bush had every reason to believe that long-standing British interests in the region would whet her appetite for assertion. Both shared, in addition to a mutual interest in the unimpeded flow of commerce, the problem of having nationals trapped in Kuwait City.

They met at the main Catto house. Bush was glad to see her, along with "the beauty of the place." He also found the prime minister vehement about Saddam's violation of international law. The lesson of the 1930s, the failure to stop Hitler early and Neville Chamberlain's appeasement of the dictator, was very much on her mind, as it was on the president's.

Yet, there was an element of emphasis that distinguished her from an American leader with memories of Korea and Vietnam. In her view, the Security Council's call for withdrawal was all the authorization needed for collective action. Article Fifty-one of the UN's charter already recognized the right of sovereign nations to call upon others for military assistance at times of crisis. Turning to the United Nations for a special resolution, she argued (incorrectly, as she later conceded), would make them unable to use Article Fifty-one unilaterally at some later date. The point, appealing to those favoring a maximum amount of latitude in dealing with the situation as well as to Americans skeptical about the world organization to begin with, became the latest Anglo-American difference.[56]

Mrs. Thatcher, Bush also learned, had talked to Mitterrand. The French president was, as usual, a touchy matter, as were the French themselves, with their pride in their own autonomy and position in Europe, especially when it came to influences from the United Kingdom and the United States. "Mitterrand will give you trouble until the end," she advised President Bush, "but when the ship sails, [France] will be there."[57]

The Bush-Thatcher talk was interrupted because President Saleh of Yemen was on the phone for him. His was the only country to register an abstention at the UN's early morning vote. Bush, not well disposed toward him to begin with, was startled to hear him bring up Reagan and Grenada.

"Let me tell you something," Bush told him. "American lives were at stake then and [you should] make very clear to your friend Saddam Hussein that any risk to American life will have serious consequences."

Later, he talked to Turkey's President Turgot Ozal, who, along with Canada's Mulroney, recognized that no compromise with Iraq was possible. Bush thought Ozal was the "toughest" of them all, keenly opposed to any situation where "some of them would peel off and support a puppet regime." The Syrians and Iranians were also firm. The Israelis, not reached in person by Bush, condemned Iraq, with Foreign Minister Moshe Arens even comparing Saddam to Hitler.[58]

Somehow, between exchanges with Thatcher and the luncheon that preceded his symposium appearance, Bush managed to divert himself by fishing in a nearby pond, catching a brook trout. "Not a bad-sized little guy," noted the president, "fly-casting on a wet fly—it was fun."[59]

His comments, delivered as the symposium's opening talk, reported on Cheney's revised defense concept for the new budget. They stirred little interest, even though they told of the projected shift from global to regional defenses. While he promised to revamp the military rather than merely cut forces, he also assured his listeners that there would still be enough strength "to respond to threats in whatever corner of the globe they may occur."[60]

He resumed his talks with the prime minister, who gave unequivocal assurances about helping to reverse Saddam's conquest. At least Thatcher and Bush were of one mind about Iraq, if not entirely clear on how to use the UN, and they said as much when they met with the press outside the Catto house. The president would not discuss military deployments already under way by both powers, such as the movement of carriers. He repeated to reporters that all other options were open. He was, he confirmed, working at putting together a coalition. UN action under Chapter Seven was definitely being contemplated, but how was another matter. Iraq, he added, was guilty of "naked aggression" that had "gone beyond simply a regional dispute," and he also viewed the protection of American citizens in Kuwait as "a fundamental responsibility of my presidency."

The "Iron Lady's" unqualified rhetoric ("What has happened is a total violation of international law. You cannot have a situation where one country marches in and takes over another country which is a member of the United Nations.") and unspoken but strong conviction about using Article Fifty-one as cover for a unilateral response, left reporters impressed that she must have "stiffened" Bush's "backbone." Other reports, implicitly encouraged by her own memoirs, even had it that at one point during their conversations, she said, "Remember, George, this is no time to go wobbly."[61] George joked a lot about that, recalled one of his "commanders." But, as Henry Catto has pointed out, the president "needed no steel in his spine. His eyes were flashing, and he was clearly not going to put up with this kind of thing." Thatcher herself has written that she "never found any weakness" in Bush's position "from the start."[62] And Bush, unknown to Thatcher or anybody else, noted in his own diary right afterward that *he* was "trying to *stiffen** the spine of the Saudis," an objective he had in mind from the start of the crisis.[63]

The formidable Mrs. Thatcher did help to ease the way. She was "stalwart," the president noted. He also had good news about other allies backing economic sanctions. Not for a moment did anybody minimize the importance of winning over neighboring Muslim states in the gulf area or in North Africa. Keeping Israel out of the situation figured heavily in an equation that assumed the possibility of Arab solidarity against the Iraqi transgression.

Later that Thursday, President Bush returned to the magnificent Catto mountain ranch, with its great floor-to-ceiling windows offering splendid views of the Rockies. He disappeared into the bedroom for another round of calls. The longest was to Saudi Arabia's King Fahd, still reluctant to invite Western military units into the region. He preferred to maintain solidarity with the other Arab states. He even held back when Bush offered to send planes. The gulf states were so nervous about the situation that they were withholding news of the invasion from their own people.[64]

Bush was convinced that the Arabs were taking the worst possible course. Their fear of Iraq could result in Saddam keeping Kuwait. The implications were more serious than oil alone. Oil was the key to regional hegemony. "I worried from day one about the talk of an 'Arab Solution,' " Bush explained later; at the time, dictating for his diary from Air Force One, he noted that "somehow they'll [accept] . . . the status quo with guarantees and nothing will happen to Saudi Arabia. But, in the meantime, Iraqi forces are going south and, in that kind of spot halfway around the world, American options are limited." An Arab solution would thoroughly upset the balance of power in the area, and in a way that "could have the magnitude of a new world war with so many countries involved." Saddam would, as Mrs. Thatcher put it to Bush, have the power to "blackmail" just about everybody else.[65]

Bush's friend, Mulroney, who also began the deployment of Canadian military units, later emphasized that acting at that moment had enormous "geostrategic consequences."[66] Saddam, already equipped with the world's fourth-largest army, could then have used his newly acquired 20 percent control of global oil production to complete his domination. Saudi Arabia's production leadership among the OPEC oil producers, if it capitulated to Iraqi power—which, it was widely assumed, it would have had to do without U.S. help—would enable him to not only drive up oil prices on the world market but to dominate the most vital international energy lifelines. His not

*Emphasis supplied.

stopping with Rumaila and the islands began to make that seem apparent. "What you are seeing today in the gulf," said one prominent analyst, Martin Indyk, "is a battle shaping up between Iraq and the United States over Saudi Arabia."[67] In that kind of regional balance, with the Saudis in tow—for all the immediate internecine conflicts sure to be sparked among the Arab states— the long-term vulnerability of Israel would be complete, its survival prob- lematic, the diplomatic and commercial interests of much of the rest of the world thrown into deep jeopardy. With a capacity for the use of poison gas (the "poor man's A-bomb") already in place and the wealth to obtain nuclear capability, Iraq would give the West little choice but to recognize the replace- ment of the crumpling Soviet Union by a new major force.[68]

Stopping Saddam, Mulroney later pointed out, "was responsible for the peace settlement that we're seeing today in the Middle East. You can draw a straight line from that to the South Lawn of the White House. That's why George Bush's presidency has not been fully appreciated and not fully understood." Moreover, he added, Bush's decision, countering Thatcher's advice, "to go under the umbrella of the United Nations was the only way he prevented Saddam from demonizing him."

As Bush ended his marathon day by returning to the White House in the dark of Friday morning, stock prices had already seesawed on Wall Street. The Dow Jones industrial average closed down by 54.95, which was not as bad as that day's earlier 120 point loss. Bond prices also tumbled on the news from the Middle East, which jumped the interest rate on thirty-year Treasury notes to 8.55. Uncertainty about the turn of events, while a major factor in the investment climate, was not the only cause. Reactions were also tied to fresh unemployment figures showing a July rise to 5.5 percent, up three-tenths of a percent, a height not seen since early in 1986.[69] Anticipat- ing a fuel shortage, gasoline prices moved upward from between four and fourteen cents a gallon across the country within forty-eight hours of the invasion.[70]

"It's probably been the most hectic forty-eight hours since I have been president in terms of national security interest," Bush noted that weekend.[71]

The president said much the same thing on Friday morning when the NSC convened in the Cabinet Room. He reported that he had seen "eye-to-eye" with Prime Minister Thatcher. No doubts were in his mind. Now he had a right to expect political and economic cooperation in meeting the crisis.[72]

"That's George Bush," recalled Powell, "when he starts with a problem, his first reaction, I've learned, is never take it to the bank. He takes a little time to look at the problem, thinks about it. He gets counsel from people. He makes his famous phone calls. He reflects on it. He gets more counsel. He makes a judgment as to whose counsel he should have confidence in. It's not just matters of war and peace. It's matters of friendship as well, which is a strength and a weakness."[73]

By the time the president convened his staff and sat down in the Laurel

Conference Room of Aspen Lodge at Camp David on Saturday, the decision to use the military had been made. But how? The Saudis remained pivotal, and satellite reconnaissance photos showed their vulnerability. Saddam's armed brigades were lining the border and reinforcements were mounting in Kuwait, now under the control of Saddam's puppet government. Webster's CIA status report confirmed the implicit dangers. All the Iraqis had to do to grab another 20 percent of the world's oil was to move a few more miles. "We can expect the Arab states to start cutting deals," the intelligence chief had told them.[74] The Arab summit conference due to be held in Jiddah had collapsed. Differences were too great, the disarray no longer capable of being glossed over. The Israelis were right in assuming that Saddam's moves would expose regional conflicts, but it was no time for complacency. Saddam, as the emerging center of power, was attracting worrisome numbers of allies. Those led by the Palestine Liberation Organization were demonstrating the potential for future trouble.[75]

In Cheney's office on Friday as the news from the area unfolded, Prince Bandar was shown impressive photographic evidence of the buildup. Having that kind of force simply to stand still in Kuwait lacked credibility, vindicating Bandar's suspicion that "he who eats Kuwait for breakfast is likely to ask for something else for lunch."[76]

Cheney told the prince that the U.S. was "ready to help you defend yourself from Saddam."

"Like Jimmy Carter did?" he shot back.

The embarrassing allusion referred to the Saudi request for emergency stand-by assistance when the Iranian shah was overthrown. A presidential contribution of ten F-15 planes was vitiated by a public admission, which was made even before they landed, that they were unarmed. The Americans would simply have to be more credible in the future.

Bush and Cheney understood all that, along with Saudi hesitation about inviting in a foreign army. Cheney then played a strong suit by telling Bandar that 100,000 troops could be sent in "for starters."

"I see," Bandar said. "You are serious."

"We suggest you urge King Fahd to accept our offer to protect the kingdom," the defense secretary told him.[77]

Bandar rushed to update King Fahd. The monarch still hedged; he would first like to hear from the delegation Bandar had advised if they could be flown from Washington to brief him.[78]

Bush followed through with a Saturday morning call. The king would be willing to receive a low-level, nonpolicy-making delegation, one consisting mainly of tactical people. But Bush, now confident that the king really did not have much choice but to accept an American force, knew a low-echelon group would lack sufficient authority to pressure the king. Bush did not want to send them all the way to Jiddah only to be turned down after they had served Fahd's purpose.

Cheney, as the head of the delegation, would clearly be a direct emissary of the president. Nothing could make the American determination clearer than that. He would, moreover, be accompanied by key people. Fahd still wanted to think about it, but Bush remained confident.[79]

The president sat in his usual seat at the conference table in the lodge at Camp David. Powell introduced Schwarzkopf, his first meeting with Bush, and the head of CENTCOM made his presentation. Supported by black-and-white slides to show the magnitude of Saddam's military thrust, and especially the power of the Republican Guard divisions, Schwarzkopf detailed the logistical nightmare involved in countering Iraq with its million-man army from far-flung bases. Plan 1002-90, which had been kept in abeyance for such an emergency, could be implemented with an initial ground force of two to three thousand American soldiers. Within two to three weeks, that strength would go to forty thousand with two Air Force squadrons and almost fifty ships, including the carriers *Independence* and *Eisenhower,* until ultimately, if accepted by the Saudis, there would be a quarter of a million troops. Four months would be needed to reach that level of strength. Schwarzkopf, a gung-ho infantry man, gave a respectful rendition of what others in the room wanted to hear, the potential efficacy of airpower, certainly a lifesaver. "Now, if you want to eject the Iraqis *and* restore Kuwait," he emphasized, they were talking about hundreds of thousands and a buildup of some eight months to a year.[80]

At Friday's NSC meeting, Powell had questioned whether it was worth going to war to liberate Kuwait. "The question was premature," he later admitted, and, moreover, was not appropriate for a soldier whose function was to give only military advice. But, as a Vietnam veteran, he had been "appalled at the docility of the Joint Chiefs of Staff" trying to fight that war "without pressing the political leaders to lay out clear objectives . . ."[81]

After Schwarzkopf was excused from the Laurel Conference Room, Powell and Cheney agreed that defending Saudi Arabia was the bottom line, a job for ground forces, not airpower. The outlines for that deployment, then code-named Desert Shield by the Pentagon, were thus in place. President Bush listened and said little. His thoughts were his alone.[82] He had yet to hear from King Fahd, but he remained confident.

The meeting broke up. On the way to their helicopters, Richard Haass and others, walking with him, saw a golf cart headed toward the tennis courts. Chris Evert and her husband, Andy Mill, were the president's weekend guests. The president, turning to his aides, suggested that they should "figure out who to send to talk to Fahd," well knowing, of course, that Cheney had already been chosen. Meanwhile, he was going off to volley with Evert.[83]

Sunday's talks by phone and at the Aspen Lodge wrapped up the decision to send a delegation to Jiddah. The key call from Saudi Arabia, Cheney remembered, came around noon. The Saudis were ready for Cheney and his delegation. Even then, there were no guarantees that the king would agree to accept a non-Arab army. If Bush wanted to send the delegation anyway, Cheney was ready with his entire entourage, which included Schwarzkopf, Bob Gates, Undersecretary for Policy, Paul Wolfowitz, Pete Williams, the American ambassador to Saudi Arabia, Charles W. Freeman Jr., who happened to be home on leave at the time, and a CIA photographic interpretation expert.[84]

In Washington, Bush got off his helicopter. Powell, at home, watched the scene on television and heard shouted questions from reporters. On the White House lawn, Richard Haass rushed over to the grim-looking president and handed him a briefing sheet. The president glanced at it, then turned to the nest of microphones. His options, he explained, were still "wide open" and everybody should wait, "watch and learn." That said, he added, "This will not stand, this aggression against Kuwait." Powell was startled. "Had a tail-end option suddenly become the front-end option?"[85]

Others were equally surprised. Jim Baker's spokesperson, Margaret Tutwiler, wondered what had gotten into him. "It was true that Bush had said the first day after the invasion that he wanted it reversed, but it had not been set in stone," Bob Woodward reported afterward. "Now here it was, a personal and emotional declaration."[86] Bush thereby—unilaterally, claimed a historian of the war—had "set a new goal for the United States" with "one offhand comment." Eviction of Saddam, not defending Saudi Arabia, was the real objective.[87] He had, he reaffirmed after the war, regarded the invasion as intolerable from the start, but had not yet really "determined at that point that force would be required" to get Saddam out of Kuwait.[88]

Logistical considerations, daunting to begin with, still needed to be clarified in the form of King Fahd's permission to use Saudi Arabia as a base for U.S. forces. Politics, if that were the leading consideration, would have militated against Bush's statement. While he himself had worried from the start that sanctions alone could not work, they were "the necessary political precursors of war." In the variety of options, each would be "a box to check" before the president could say he had given diplomacy and sanctions a fair shot, as a Bush aide explained privately that weekend.[89]

Why that comment, then? It was, as Powell has written, "pure Bush," the product of quiet reflection and deliberation, followed by a need to release it "at his first opportunity."[90] Had the implications been weighed in advance, the remark would not have been uttered. As his press secretary had long since noticed, he was "an emotional man," to whom "words meant nothing" but "emotions meant everything."[91] He spoke his mind.

It was Monday in Jiddah by the time Cheney's mission reached the Saudi coast. The meeting was supposed to start that afternoon, but the Americans soon learned from Prince Bandar that the king did not actually start to do business until after sunset. When they were finally ushered into Fahd's marble palace, they found him with his brother Abdallah, the crown prince, and

Foreign Minister Saud a-Faisal. They joined them in drinking tea laced with cardamom.

Cheney never forgot the king's appreciative comments about the American president. At least, he said, he knew he could trust George Bush. Bush had been head of the CIA when he was in charge of Saudi intelligence. Cheney digested the receptive words without realizing how far along Fahd actually was toward accepting the military deployment. Clearly, as he thought about it afterward, the exercise in the palace was largely for the benefit of the other Saudis.

The two-hour meeting began with Schwarzkopf detailing the plans for military deployment. At the end, Cheney closed the argument, stressing that there was no time for delay; the operation was bound to take a long time. Immediate approval was essential.

When Cheney finished, the king turned away from the Americans and began speaking in Arabic. Only later, from Ambassador Freeman, the only American who spoke that language, did the defense secretary know what they said.

"We have to do this," Fahd said to the crown prince. "Look at what happened to the Kuwaitis. They waited, and today there is no Kuwait."

Abdallah, as Freeman recounted the conversation, replied, "Yes, yes, there still is a Kuwait."

"Yes," said the king. "They're all living in our hotel rooms. Who'll put us up?" Then, turning back to Cheney, Fahd said, in English again, "Okay. We'll do it."

Cheney rushed back to the guest house and called the president. It was Monday afternoon in Washington. Prime Minister Thatcher, having accepted Bush's suggestion that she stop at the White House on her way back to England from Colorado, was with him. Bush gave the go-ahead to begin the deployment of forces; Cheney passed that order on to Powell at the Pentagon. The chairman of the Joint Chiefs of Staff began notifying the commanders.[92]

That was also, Bush has reported, one of the most "traumatic days of my presidency." In midmorning, he went five blocks down Pennsylvania Avenue to George Washington University Hospital. High fever and back pains had forced Lee Atwater's readmission on Tuesday for further medical tests, bone and brain scans. "No, he's not dying," Mary Matalin told reporters. "The president just got to thinking about Lee and wanted to see him." Bush was not confident. Quietly, Sununu had already undertaken a search to replace Atwater at the RNC.[93]

Word about the troop deployment was already getting around, the president also heard that day. It was a young aide who told Barbara that troops were about to be sent into the Persian Gulf. She was in Kennebunkport and Bush had not thought she needed to know about it, fearing she would only worry ahead of time. But when she called the White House for information about a fund-raiser, one of Sununu's deputy assistants, Ed Rogers, gave her what she needed and then added what no one should have been told. "Bar is not a leaker," the president recorded, "but it's just a manifestation of this difficulty of keeping things of this nature quiet."[94]

With his wife in Maine, he relaxed that night over dinner with a few invited guests. As usual, Scowcroft came, and so did Larry Eagleburger, standing in for Baker, who was trying to maintain business-as-usual appearances by keeping his August vacation routine in Wyoming. Brian Mulroney then arrived with his chief of staff, Stanley Hart. After another long, difficult day, made harder by his visit with Atwater, Bush was relieved to be with friends. He relaxed, first, with a couple of martinis, then ate four popovers with his meal.

Mulroney long remembered that evening. Bush, he realized, deeply appreciated Scowcroft's constant companionship and advice. The general "was forever bouncing ideas" off the president, which kept the adviser for National Security Affairs up to date and Bush sharp. Clearly, over that dinner, the president remained obsessed by the crisis.

He was determined that Saddam's aggression would not stand. The Iraqi army, he was also certain, could be removed only "by a massive display of airpower."

Nobody disagreed. The Canadian prime minister, consciously countering Mrs. Thatcher's advice, argued that victory without the UN would be hollow, that going it alone was an "extraordinarily dangerous" proposition.

Mulroney, relishing his friendship and access to the president, suggested that the best route to UN cooperation lay with François Mitterrand. He well knew, having helped to forge a relationship with the Franco-Afrique states, that what was once French West Africa remained a cultural bond with Paris spanning the northern part of the continent all the way from Senegal on the west coast to Egypt, which, despite its British past, had a French-speaking elite. Nothing could get them on board faster than Mitterrand leading the way.

"George," Mulroney quoted himself as telling the president, "if this information is conveyed to François Mitterrand as having come from Margaret Thatcher, or if François Mitterrand thinks that Margaret Thatcher is aware of this before him and to his exclusion, I recommend that you call him tonight. You tell him that no one else in Europe is aware of this. He will not be offended if he knows that I was here because Mitterrand knows of our relationship. If he thinks this is a conversation you've been having with Mrs. Thatcher and he's been excluded, it will be bloody."[95]

It was good to have that kind of strength and advice from the man who had been Canada's prime minister since 1984. Savvy, articulate, and forceful, and fifteen years younger than Bush, he was energetic and athletic. His background, however, was very different. Born to English-speaking Irish-Canadian parents in the paper mill town of Baie-Comeau in eastern Quebec near the mouth of the St. Lawrence, where his father worked as an electrician, Mulroney became his country's first working-class prime minister. With a degree from the University of Laval, he practiced labor law and also became president of a mining company, Iron Ore Canada. Drawn by a mutual interest in business and the flow of international commerce, the Bush-Mulroney connection strengthened during the process of working out a free trade agreement between their two countries in 1987. The successful pact became the model for the subsequent North American Free Trade Agreement (NAFTA).[96]

Mulroney's support was certainly welcome. Yet his words only supplemented what Scowcroft had been telling Bush all along. And Eagleburger had been among the most forceful from the start. At Friday morning's NSC meeting, he had "delivered a rousing call to action," one that warned about the potential international consequences of timidity. A powerful, unchallenged Iraq, even if it did not invade Saudi Arabia, would inevitably confront Israel and draw the U.S. into a Middle Eastern war, warned the deputy secretary of state. Bush, remaining silent during that presentation, was keenly receptive.[97]

He needed no further convincing. Never far from a phone, he was able to reach from his seat to the one on the dinner table and call the White House switchboard. Although it was three in the morning in France, he asked to be put through to Mitterrand.[98]

Little over twenty-four hours after their conversation, the French president, while eager not to be seen "as slavishly following American policy," issued a strong public statement: "France has for long had friendly relations with Iraq. You know that we continued to help it during the war with Iran. That allows us to say all the more clearly that we accept neither the aggression against Kuwait nor the annexation which followed."[99]

On Tuesday, the president had dinner with Marlin Fitzwater, somewhat overdoing his delight with the cuisine prepared by a new White House chef. At the age of sixty-six, he understood about going to "excess on food or drink, particularly at night."[100]

Stress, he thought, was getting to him. Tension led to pain and headaches. After Fitzwater left that Tuesday evening, he went to Dr. Burton Lee's ground-floor office near the South Portico entrance, for the second night in a row. The facility, one of three that constituted the White House medical unit, including the main out-patient clinic in the Old Executive Office Building, became especially valuable to George Bush after the Kuwait invasion. He was "a workaholic, really," remembered the president's personal physician and old friend, "and never paid any attention to me." Dr. Lee saw to it that his nurses were trained in physical therapy. The president needed work on the muscles of his neck and shoulders. The treatments were sometimes done on the third floor, where they had another physical therapy room, and sometimes in one of the doctor's own offices, hideaways where he could rest and think.

The nurses most often in attendance, Kim, Debbie, and Art, were young. Bush enjoyed them, particularly their "sense of fun." His closemouthed tendency about his own aches and pains rendered them especially indispensable as Dr. Lee's "eyes and ears." Kim, that night, gave him a much-needed rubdown, with special attention to the arthritis in his shoulders. He then slept on the table for almost two hours. "She must be exhausted," he noted later. "She's very nice and caring. All the people in the medical unit simply remind me how spoiled I am."[101]

Cheney's plane was still in the air when a fax came in, the draft of a statement worked out by Scowcroft, Gates, and Haass prepared for delivery by the president on Wednesday morning. Twice since taking off from Jiddah, Cheney received calls from Bush, first to tell him to stop over in Alexandria to see Mubarak. He found the Egyptian president "steamed" because Saddam had lied to him, and he readily gave permission to move the nuclear warship *Eisenhower* through the Suez Canal. Responding to another presidential call, Cheney landed at Rabat, Morocco, to see King Hussan. Conscious of the presence of an interpreter and realizing that what he was about to tell the American was still classified, the king put a copy of the Koran in the man's hands and made him swear on the pain of death that he would not reveal what he was about to hear. When the king turned back to Cheney, the Defense secretary said, "I will need one of those for the Pentagon."[102]

Yes, remembered Cheney, "diplomacy was easy under those circumstances. You show up in Morocco and the king is waiting for you. His old buddy, George Bush, has talked to him and, yes, he'll send troops. The strength of his personality, his experience, the fact that he dealt with these guys over the years and they liked him and trusted him."[103]

On Wednesday morning, the president, who rarely got much sleep anyway, went over to the office at half past six. At a good hour for one still skittish about prime-time television, nine A.M., he faced cameras and the press and began to tell the world about the deployment headed for Saudi Arabia and the Persian Gulf. Elements of the Eighty-second Airborne Division and key units of the United States Air Force were arriving today, he announced, to take up key defensive positions in Saudi Arabia. "Appeasement does not work. As was the case in the 1930s," he recalled, "we see in Saddam Hussein an aggressive dictator threatening his neighbors." Not just an "American problem or a European problem or a Middle East problem," it was "the world's problem." And the UN had, for that reason, also followed through on Monday by approving mandatory sanctions under Chapter Seven of its charter.[104]

Some viewers thought that his performance, especially the Q&A session immediately afterward, was "deceptive" and "inarticulate."[105] While satisfied with his speech, he acknowledged that he was "not nearly as good as President Reagan on these situations." Reading it through beforehand, he made some additions that were not on the TelePrompTer. That went well, but critics later jumped all over him for being misleading about the purely "defensive" purpose of the mission, dissembling when asked why the press was being left behind by the military (as it had been in Grenada and Panama), for blatant distortion in saying that "we were prompt to respond" when "requested" to go to Saudi Arabia by King Fahd, and for his expression of strong confidence in the efficacy of sanctions.[106] Visibly tired during the interview, he "flubbed a couple of key questions." He concluded with the admission that he had "screwed up a couple of times here and I'm very grateful for your assistance in straightening it out. God," he added, "I'd hate to have some of those answers stand."[107]

Mrs. Thatcher soon called, all fired up about putting together a force. Did he know, she asked, that a stewardess from a British plane had been raped by the Iraqis? When the British protested, she told him, they explained that the man had been shot. That was, agreed Bush afterward, "typical [of] the way this man operates, and yet the world does not realize the brutality that has taken place in Kuwait."[108] Questions about why the administration had consorted with Saddam in the face of more massive examples of inhumanity were not long in coming, nor did the explanations differ very much from justifications for relations with Beijing. That was, in the words Jude Wanniski had used for the title of a book that became a primer for supply-siders, "the way the world works," and George Bush had his feet on the ground.

Perhaps it explains why his direction, as Dick Cheney reflected later, was about as fine an example of presidential crisis management that can be found in the twentieth century. "The finest moment of George Bush's presidency," wrote Fred Barnes in *The New Republic*. "I can't think of another president who could have pulled this off." It was easier, he added, for "the United States to throw its weight around" in the era of the Marshall Plan and the Truman Doctrine and the Korean War, but now "American clout in the world is in relative decline."[109] All in all, aided by grants of trading privileges and, as with Egypt, debt forgiveness, the presidential leadership of George Bush and the diplomacy of Jim Baker and Dick Cheney enlisted the military forces of twenty-seven other countries. Others, including Japan and Germany, pledged financial contributions. Only two days after Bush spoke, in a decisive vote, twelve of the twenty-one Arab League members meeting in Cairo went on record behind a seven-point resolution backing the Saudis against Iraq.[110]

The Gallup organization showed Bush's rating up by 14 percent almost immediately. Three out of every four questioned told pollsters that they approved of his presidency, a new high for George Bush.[111] Congressional support was even more emphatic, loud applause commending multilateralism. Senator Alan Cranston, a California Democrat, spoke for the majority when he said that he hoped "we won't be the Lone Ranger the way we were in Vietnam."[112]

Everything Bush did, every word, every nuance, each gaffe or just carelessness—and there were too many, he knew—were monitored for their potential significance. Saddam Hussein's ruthlessness and frequent blunders were all too infrequently countered by rhetorical eloquence, a deficiency compensated for largely by imagery and hyperbole.[113] Bush, as he had done during the 1988 campaign, "seemed to be at his most natural when personalizing politics."[114]

Just as Jimmy Baker had gone off to Wyoming, and resolved to make a decent show of staying there for a while, so did the president determine to keep his seasonal pleasures at Kennebunkport, arriving on that Friday afternoon after his speech. To some it seemed a peculiar time to take a vacation. How politic, aides wondered, were shots of him riding his golf cart at lovely Walker's Point? But there was no way that he'd let himself become a Carter-like prisoner of the White House. Communications could be handled from Kennebunkport almost as easily, even with the heavy media focus on the new hostages in Kuwait City and Baghdad.[115] Meanwhile, the H-word was off limits.[116] Jimmy Carter offered to help by volunteering to mediate differences with Saddam; hardly better, thought Bush, than an Arab solution. The last thing he needed was "another Tehran."[117]

More even than the invasion itself, that entrapment of some 3,000 Americans, some saw as "the critical moment in his presidency." More than on any single aspect of the Gulf crisis—the plight of Kuwait, Saudi Arabia, Israel, or oil—the inhumanity of holding innocent men, women, and children against their will shocked the American public.[118] Getting them out by whatever means, even a military strike (which was impossible because they were not concentrated in specific locations), in the event of their mistreatment or imprisonment was favored by 70 percent of those surveyed by a *Wall Street Journal/NBC News* poll.[119]

Saddam thereupon demonized himself. "You are going to receive some American bodies in bags," he warned the president in a prepared statement that suggested they would be used as human shields.[120] The dictator, overstepping once again, as he had done by overreaching into Kuwait in the first place, played clumsily into the hands of savvy public relations people. Bush, while still commuting between Kennebunkport and the White House, as he did until Labor Day, overruled Brent Scowcroft's misgivings about "emotional speeches equating Saddam with Hitler." Bush's adviser, circumspect and thoughtful as ever, worried about using hyperbole that suggested a fight to Saddam's death. Bush persisted. Americans did not want to bloody their sons for oil, or for diplomatic infatuation with "balance-of-power politics." As he knew from experience, they needed a demon. He would give one to them, although it remained doubtful that most Americans really accepted the comparison.[121] Through that entire process, there existed a risk that demonizing Saddam might only strengthen his position with Arabs showing solidarity against the hostile West.

Until the very end of the four-month ordeal, 163 Americans remained trapped by power geopolitics. Saddam ultimately realized that he could gain more by letting them go than by continuing their confinement. Gradually, strategically, hoping to weaken the coalition, he first freed the nationals of other countries. Americans and British, after some had been moved to strategic sites, potential military targets, were let go almost immediately after

Bush declared at a news conference that he was prepared to go "the extra mile for peace."[122]

The whole hostage affair was cynical and sordid, an irrelevant sideshow that caught the unwary in an international clash. Fifty-eight Englishmen, for example, fell into the web because they happened to have been in a British Airways jumbo jet en route to Kuala Lumpur when it touched down in Kuwait at the wrong time.[123] They, and all the others, became mere propaganda chips, their plight useful for focusing outrage. Saddam, of course, thought their presence would discourage retaliations against his invasion as well as demonstrate his capacity for mischief. At several points, he tried to display his "humanity." One televised image pictured a "solicitous" Saddam patting the head of an obviously frightened seven-year-old English boy brought before him. The Iraq leader shrewdly released other views that showed European and American hostages getting on more comfortably in their confinement, even in elegant hotels, than victims from the Third World. He evidently hoped that the governments of the less fortunate would respond with demands to ease the food sanctions.[124] With such mixed messages coming out of Baghdad, Jim Baker was taken aback at the skepticism from a group of congressmen who suggested that the administration was exaggerating the hostage situation to justify going to war.[125]

Meanwhile, working from Maine as the situation dominated headlines, Bush made all the calls he could to secure the alliance. The sixteenth was "an extraordinary day," Barbara Bush wrote in her diary. First, King Hussein of Jordan arrived at nearby Pease Air Force Base in Portsmouth, New Hampshire. After a fifteen-minute helicopter ride, he landed on the pad behind the house.

Worried about alienating old friends in London and Washington by appeasing Jordanian loathing of rich, arrogant Kuwaitis, Hussein was looking for a way out. He and the president sat down together in the Bungalow, Dorothy Walker Bush's summer cottage. From the large bay window in the tiny dining room, the two men had a spectacular view of the ocean. The king, as the president let him know, was backing a lost cause. Efforts at an "Arab solution" were dead. An Iraqi puppet state for Kuwait was totally unacceptable.

The king's helicopter had barely disappeared from the afternoon sky off the Maine coast when another, this one with Prince Bandar and the Saudi foreign minister, Prince al-Faisal, reached the Bush compound. What a show for the grandchildren, out "riding their bikes and playing down by the helo pad. They wanted to meet a real live king and prince," wrote their grandmother. "We had a few lessons on shaking hands firmly, looking into the eye, and speaking politely."[126]

For the president, however, it merely capped off another long and dismal day. On news of his Uncle Johnny Walker's emergency operation, he had rushed to the hospital, worried about the attention provoked by a presidential visit upsetting his mother, only to find that her brother—"a great athlete and a surgeon," noted Barbara—had already died. Dottie's angina was also acting up. Not a good day. "We've got this major national crisis going on," he noted for his diary; "conflict—family, nation, family [sic], responsibilities." Fortunately, however, he was in Maine, and in spite of it all he managed to get out on the water with George W., catch himself a nice bluefish, play a round of golf, and take a two-mile run.[127]

He had also managed to sign a "finding" that authorized the CIA to do whatever was necessary to get rid of Saddam, and, on the twenty-fifth, was euphoric when the Security Council ratified the use of force to stop ships trading with Iraq.[128]

Still, that August, Kennebunkport, for once, was not proving to be a tonic. The pace had been hectic, and he was clearly tired. "He just could not recharge his batteries," said one aide, not even with the presence of his family and the ocean air at Walker's Point. Richard Darman, in Maine to review the budget, also found him weary. "He was increasingly obsessed by the deepening conflict with Saddam Hussein."[129]

Hussein was, at the same time, obsessed by Gorbachev, clearly shocked by Bush's ability to bring the Russian along with him behind the UN resolutions. Moscow's past ties with Baghdad should have weathered the invasion of Kuwait, which, in Saddam's reasoning, merely meant reclaiming "stolen" territory. Relationships surely were changing, so much so that even within Gorbachev's realm suspicions festered about Washington's long-range intentions. Were the Americans scheming to establish a foothold in Saudi Arabia as a way of guaranteeing control of Middle Eastern oil even if German unification should force the loss of their base on the European continent? Did the U.S. intend to become a military force in the region by going into and occupying Iraq, only some 200 kilometers from Soviet territory?

In a rapidly changing order of things, not since FDR and Stalin had a president and Communist Party chairman as many grounds for common cause. Bush and Gorbachev had shared problems. Unhappy, even restless, conservatives were sniping at each, at Bush over the budget, taxes, and a foreign policy appearing to dilute the strong Reaganite military resolve by complacent responses to Beijing and Baltic anti-Soviet rebelliousness; and at Gorbachev for what was happening in Germany and its possible absorption into NATO, arms limitation treaties, and a tottering Soviet empire. Even Moscow's new thinking on foreign policy, a hallmark of the Gorbachev ascendancy, was moving toward the American capitalistic concept of stressing globalism over primarily regional concerns. His willingness to stand with Bush so firmly over Saddam Hussein compounded the growing discontent. Suspicions about where Gorbachev was heading were being confirmed.[130]

When, after that Labor Day weekend Bush and Gorbachev decided that it was time for an emergency get-together, this time in Helsinki, Saddam had a fit. He wanted Gorbachev to explain just how allied with Bush he was. Saddam lost no time in arranging for his foreign minister, Tariq Aziz, to visit Moscow. Aziz, however, could only have been shocked at meeting Gorbachev on September 5 and being told that his country was the aggressor and that a "complete withdrawal" was expected.[131]

Bush sensed the need to communicate what he was trying to do. He would, he told Scowcroft, address a joint session of Congress, get to them on prime time, and put forth to the American people the ideals that animated his orchestrated thrust against Saddam. He was, really, when all was said and done, trying to bring together civilized nations to achieve a post–cold war configuration, something along the lines of a new world order. When it was suggested there would be an inadequate amount of time for such a speech to be prepared, he said not to worry. He'd work out the details on Air Force One en route to Finland.[132]

When, four days after Aziz's trip to Moscow, Bush sat down with Gorbachev for a full seven hours, the Soviet president seemed to agree in full. He stressed that their congeniality had become so routine and their meetings so frequent that they no longer merited being newsworthy. As he explained to reporters at a joint news conference immediately afterward, if it had not been for their previous meetings, "we would now be in a difficult situation facing the crisis in the Persian Gulf." Bush, beaming as he stood with his Soviet counterpart, made the point that Gorbachev needed no prodding to stiffen his resistance to Saddam Hussein. All this should not be surprising, suggested Gorbachev, because it is "becoming a normal element of the new kind of cooperation—in trade, in technology, in human exchange. All of these elements characterize the new peaceful period upon which we are just now embarked, which we have to get used to."[133] Gorbachev's own political position, deteriorating along with the chronic Soviet internal economic and political stresses, was a major American concern. After Gorbachev, without Gorbachev, then what? His trepidations could not be ignored without, it was increasingly feared, great risk to the West. Puffing up foreign leaders to help preserve their political lives was an old story.[134]

Back in Washington on Tuesday evening, the president addressed a joint session of Congress. "A new partnership of nations has begun," he told them. "Out of these troubled times . . . a new world order can emerge: a new era, freer from the threat of terror, stronger in the pursuit of justice, and more secure in the quest for peace. An era in which the nations of the world, East and West, North and South, can prosper and live in harmony." That was the vision, he explained, that he shared with President Gorbachev. Both had the same objective: "Iraq must withdraw from Kuwait completely, immediately, and without condition."[135]

Politically, Saddam had clearly made a difference. Bush was "on a roll," as at least one writer put it. Domestic troubles, from S&Ls to breaking his tax pledge, "have been all but forgotten."[136] At the United Nations, where the president spoke in the General Assembly Hall on September 30 to open the World Summit for Children in New York City, seventy-one heads of state were assembled, the largest such gathering in history. Brian Mulroney recalled that it "turned into a meeting on Kuwait" and emphasized the potential utility of the UN in the fight against Saddam.[137]

Back in Washington just hours after his UN appearance (before immediately returning to New York again for the dinner session of the children's summit), Bush joined the bipartisan congressional leadership, Mitchell, Dole, Gephardt, and Michel, along with his own people, Brady, Darman, and Sununu, to announce what he called "a good, positive, solid" $500 billion deficit reduction budget that should "help the American economy."[138]

Achieved, also, in the face of bipartisan dissent, the "bipartisan budget" was, in effect, dead on arrival.[139] The president then appealed to the American people. While the nation was "standing together against Saddam Hussein's oppression," he declared, the "cancer" of deficits "was gnawing away at the nation's economic health." With the nation facing a potential deficit of over $300 billion for the fiscal year, he urged them to let their leaders in Washington know that they support the agreement.[140] But with Republicans in open revolt behind Gingrich, and with Democrats railing about Medicare and welfare cuts falling disproportionately on the poor and middle classes and while wealth remained protected, Bush's humiliation was plain. For every caller to the White House who backed him, six were opposed.[141] "The president who succeeded for so long at giving Americans only good news," declared Andrew Rosenthal of *The New York Times*, "is now telling them to prepare for economic pain at home and the possibility of war abroad."[142] Only two days after his appeal, and with Bush especially rankled by the Republican deserters complaining about his reneging on the no new taxes pledge, the budget resolution went down in the House by 179 to 254. He managed to get no more support than about 40 percent of each party. From the high point in August, reached just after the invasion of Kuwait despite the weakening economy, Bush was down some fifteen to twenty points as measured by various surveys.[143]

Trying to pressure the Congress, with the fiscal year having expired on the first of October, he refused to sign a congressional resolution to fund the government for an additional seven days. His veto, together with the failure of the House to muster enough votes to override, forced implementation of the Gramm-Rudman-Hollings sequestration. The partial government shutdown mostly inconvenienced tourists in Washington and at national parks around the country.[144]

The president was also caught in a contradictory dilemma between a trade-off for tax increases. The administration appeared confused and he also wavered, finally announcing that both capital gains and new taxes were "off the table." With only a month left before the midterm elections, he made several out-of-town campaign trips, especially for gubernatorial candidates in Texas and Florida. In the Lone Star State, he spoke out for rancher-oilman Clayton W. Williams's attempt to defeat Democrat Ann Richards. In Florida, where he backed the Republican incumbent against

Lawton Chiles, he was out jogging when a reporter asked whether he was ready to "throw in the towel on capital gains." Bush pointed to his rear end and said, "Read my hips."

What should Americans think "when their president pokes fun at his most solemn promise to them?" asked the *National Review.* "Is his constituency now invited to study body language?" More pointedly, William Buckley's editorial stated, "Ronald Reagan was often denounced for being divisive, but it was precisely because he was divisive that the American people saw that, in the contest between Us and Them, The Gipper was one of Us. In the last six months, the signal President Bush has sent is that he is a Them." It is no coincidence that the country has moved "from the largest peacetime expansion since World War II to the brink of recession."[145]

Much more treacherous to Bush personally were the actions of Ed Rollins. The political consultant, already developing a reputation for indiscretion, was cochairman, under Representative Guy Vander Jagt of Michigan, of the National Republican Congressional Committee. Rollins, acting without Vander Jagt's signature, sent out a memorandum on the fifteenth, three weeks before the midterm elections, advising Republican congressional candidates on how to respond to the "dramatically" changed mood of the voters as reported during the past ten days by GOP surveys. Voters, reported Rollins, by "significant numbers," were convinced that "Republicans in Washington are more interested in protecting tax breaks for the rich than in reducing taxes for average Americans." Candidates should continue to oppose taxes and "not hesitate to oppose either the president or proposals being advanced in Congress."[146]

The memo, subsequently leaked to the press, sent Bush into a rage. Fitzwater, who was with him at the moment aboard Air Force One, recalled that he had never seen the president so angry. "We were up in the nose of that 747, just the two of us on the couch," said the press secretary, "and Bush started screaming that he wanted Rollins gone; he wanted him fired." Vander Jagt, who confirmed the incident, argued with him, but the president, shouting as Fitzwater had never heard him in all the years they had been together, insisted that "either he goes or I will never sign another fundraising letter for you."[147]

"I don't know why I ever let that SOB over there," the president has been quoted by Rollins, who, "unrepentant," nevertheless finally resigned.[148] The cochairman of the NRCC, however, did not go quietly. He later offered more private advice that Neil Bush's involvement with the savings and loan situation was another reason for keeping distant from the president. Rollins ultimately sent the president an apology, which he accepted, but the matter remained so sensitive that aides shied away from discussing it for the record.[149] For Bush, that would not be the last he would hear about Rollins's disloyalty. The political consultant's apprehension about the election was, however, well placed.

So were misgivings about his presidency. On October 22, just as others believed a compromise was possible, Bush, pushed further by Boyden Gray and Attorney General Thornburgh, vetoed the civil rights bill. He needed, he had said, a bill that "he could sign"; he could not accept a "quota" bill. *The Economist* of London, noting that Lee Atwater had made noises about getting blacks into the Republican party, calculated that Bush's veto was, nevertheless, largely political. "Since the late 1960s," wrote the correspondent from "Lexington," "Republicans have been pandering to working- and middle-class voters by exploiting their resentment of liberal social policies," which meant highlighting such issues as "busing, affirmative action, and welfare reform."[150]

Finally, five days after that encounter with civil rights, the Democratic-led Omnibus Budget Reconciliation Act of 1990 cleared both houses of Congress. Unlike the original agreement announced by Bush, the new package raised income taxes. With more of the burden for deficit reduction shifted to the wealthy, the top marginal tax rate rose from 28 to 31.5 percent. While income taxes were reduced for the working poor, Medicare cuts were eased, proposed gas tax increases were cut in half, and a new tax on home heating oil was deleted entirely. Designed as a deficit reduction vehicle to cut $492 billion over five years, it effectively put Gramm-Rudman-Hollings out of business. Only one-fourth of the Republican members of each house backed the president. The Senate went along that afternoon.[151] Bush, only the third president in history to have vetoed a civil rights bill, had also separated himself from his party's right. The *Washington Post/ABC News* poll registered a 19 percent drop in his approval rating between mid September and mid October, with the free fall reaching as much as 25 percent. The month closed out with Gallup showing that disapproval of the president had more than doubled within the past month.[152]

George Bush, wrote Michael Duffy in *Time* magazine, "is a closet Democrat," a "mole who has burrowed deep behind enemy lines for the sake of the party of the working stiff. It is the only logical explanation for the president's recent political behavior."[153]

After they counted the votes cast on November 6, the story was carried under the banner of "The Great Taxpayers Revolt." Bush "suffered some painful cuts and bruises," wrote Germond and Witcover.[154] His two highly contested gubernatorial candidates both lost. Gingrich himself came close to defeat, holding his congressional seat by a mere 974-vote margin. Not since 1974, right after Watergate, had so few Americans turned out to vote. In an election that was widely reflective of taxes and regional fears of recession, in addition to the normal range of local issues, the Republicans, who had won three straight presidential elections by promising not to increase taxes, suffered a net loss of nine House seats. Rollins, unfazed, later wrote that he was convinced that his memo "and the heroic salvage operation of my staff saved fifteen incumbent seats that otherwise would have gone down the drain."[155]

The budget battle, and especially the fruitless fight against capital gains taxes, left Bush especially open to complaints that he favored the rich, but it was precisely that segment of the electorate, at the heart of his party's power, that viewed him as a Judas. At the same time, civil rights activists denounced him for being a "Reagan in sheep's clothing," which, thought significant numbers of Republicans, was exactly what he was not.

Comparisons with World War II gave the Gulf crisis a dimension fully consistent with reality, the first important international showdown of the post–cold war era. Constant shifting, hedging on the question of war or peace, hung on interpretations of what was being said at the UN, in Washington, or in the Middle East. Optimism and pessimism fluctuated along with confusion about the long-term benefits of prolonging sanctions or actually going to war; or, if fighting was truly the right thing to do, whether that made the present a time of "phoney war" not unlike Europe in the months before the Nazi invasion of the Low Countries.[156] Bush, a reader of nonfiction, especially history and biography, kept the Hitler-era analogy alive by telling a group of congressmen that Martin Gilbert's *The Second World War* had confirmed for him the fallacies of appeasement. No historian would ever be able to say that about him.[157] At a press conference in Alexandria, Virginia, two days later, he rejected the need for a pretext in order to act. "You just do what's right," he said firmly. Then, rhetorically, he asked, "And what am I going to do about it?" Then tipping his hand in a way no one there understood, added, "Let's just wait and see." Back at the White House that afternoon, he told reporters gathered on the South Lawn that there "is no compromise with this aggression." The allies stood "together on this." He was not, he said the next day in Orlando, Florida, trying to "sound the tocsin of war," but "the sand is running through the glass."[158]

His decision, made with Scowcroft, Cheney, Powell, and Schwarzkopf, was already sealed, but, prudently, held until after the elections. We "didn't want to get it wrapped up in the political climate," recalled one of them. Half a million men and women were not going to be kept "sitting on the sands of the desert waiting for sanctions to work." General Schwarzkopf had submitted his list of what was needed to launch an offensive. American units were ready at various locations, the Seventh Corps in Germany near Heidelberg, and, along with other forces, the First Infantry at Fort Riley, Kansas, all for redeployment to the Gulf. The 230,000 already in place, a task more enormous than the planners themselves had anticipated, would be augmented by 150,000. The order Bush then issued on November 8 calling for "an adequate offensive military option" to force Iraq out of Kuwait was followed by Cheney's cancellation of plans to rotate U.S. forces in the area. They would remain there for the duration of the crisis.

Bush's determination, nuanced militarily, diplomatically, and politically, became clear only afterward. His guiding focus fixed on the counterinvasion he had assumed to be all but inevitable. His tactics were necessary to sustain the fragile coalition he had put together (testing the patience of both new and old allies), cope with the ability of the American people to appreciate the limitations of sanctions, and give military weight to considerations that involved such seasonal factors as the onset of desert heat and the Muslim holiday of Ramadan, both in March.

In a bravura display of politics and diplomacy, teaming up closely with Scowcroft and Baker, he captured the initiative from his Iraqi rival. He contemplated, first, a direct challenge: either Saddam reveal himself as merely bluffing, which he doubted, or pay the consequences. Already convinced that Saddam would not get out without the use of force, Bush has recalled, he "had to know directly from me, that unless he got completely and quickly out of Kuwait, we would use our military power to force him out." Why not, thought the president, as he later said, publicly, go the "extra mile" toward peace? Why not break with the warrior mold by demonstrating anxiety to avoid the ultimate solution? Why not, Bush pondered, send a direct, personal emissary to Saddam? Let the challenge be up to him. But who should go? A few names went through his mind, most obviously Scowcroft's, the veteran of one sub-rosa mission to Beijing. As Bush talked the matter over with Scowcroft, both men realized that it had to be done openly. It was, more properly, Baker's job.[159] Going the diplomatic route, both through a personal emissary and via the United Nations was, as one of Bush's people put it, "a necessary analogue to the military strategy."[160]

With all that in place, with only the timing of its release in question, Bush flew out of Andrews on the evening of the eighteenth to do his coalition building on the other side of the ocean. He stopped in at Paris where, on the next day, Gorbachev, increasingly hungry for prestige enhancement, put his signature, along with Bush's and twenty other leaders, on what was in reality the culmination of his own announcement about arms limitations made at the UN when George Bush was still president-elect. Worked out at staff and ministerial levels first, as are all such protocols, it relieved Soviet defense burdens while, at the same time, adjusting the balance of conventional forces in Europe to the advantage of the U.S. Having signed, in the words of Ambassador Matlock, a treaty that "was one of the events that formalized the end of the cold war" by limiting conventional forces in Europe (CFE), Bush traveled on to the Middle East, stopping first in Jiddah to reaffirm matters with King Fahd and the ousted Kuwaiti emir, Sheik Jabel al-Ahmad al-Sabah.[161] With his wife at his side, in a manner reminiscent of his Christmas visit to American soldiers in Panama, the president dropped in to spend Thanksgiving with marines in Saudi Arabia.

"As I ate lunch with the troops," he spoke into his little recorder, "I kept thinking to myself, 'How young they all are.' They seemed ready to fight, ready to do the job and then go home." They reminded him of what it was like in the South Pacific half a century earlier, and, as one of Bush's tight circle recalled with admiration, the soldiers "knew how much he cared about them." "All the food looked the same and tasted the same in 1990 as it did in 1944." Barbara prompted them to talk about "hometowns and girlfriends. And I wonder," he reminisced, "what will happen if and when the battle begins? Will these guys be okay?"[162] Good talk, good visit, excellent photo opportunities for back home; the president not only caring, but truly acting the part. "Just a masterstroke, a masterstroke," marveled Bush's colleague.[163] From there, he went on to Egypt to meet with President Mubarak, then to Geneva. There he helped seal another part of the coalition vital to the region, the Syria of President Hafez Assad, who "is lined up with us with a commitment to force" in the Gulf, Bush was then able to say.

He was right. He did, and would continue to, have just enough strength to keep it together, however gingerly. Less convinced, at the moment, even less so than when the doubled deployment was announced, was the American public. Bush himself had noted, and deplored, the suggestion "that oil is the sole reason that we are involved in this enormous commitment." There were a lot of other interests, he wanted everybody to know, and they related to "security and stability." He mentioned nothing else.[164]

But, along about mid November, popular anxieties deepened. Official explanations were becoming inadequate. It was getting harder to reconcile talking about sanctions while raising the military ante so dramatically. Why rush ahead? he was hearing from the Hill. Why prepare for war? Sanctions would surely require more patience than that. Demonstrators, however, were becoming more likely to argue that there should be "no blood for oil." "Some people never get the word," Bush retorted. Even as he left for Jiddah, a *New York Times/CBS News* poll documented the increased popular anxiety, with a majority now believing that the country was headed toward war. *Why* was not clearly understood. Sympathy for the initial objectives that created Desert Shield was being distracted by concern over the weakening economy. Within the past week alone, support for sending in those extra troops had dropped by nine points. Only fear that Saddam might achieve nuclear weapons created any kind of consensus.[165]

Bush, on returning from the Middle East, began to hit harder at the nuclear issue. By doing that, as well as talking about Saddam's chemical warfare capacity, he was unilaterally upgrading the UN resolutions. How to actually eliminate Iraq's potential for mayhem, however, was a problem most conveniently left to the future, not for when there was a need, as one contemporary writer put it, for selling "a war like a breakfast cereal." But it did mark a turning point from the years of acquiescence in Saddam's nuclear preparations, to say nothing about his already demonstrated use of chemical weapons. No longer a handmaiden to his designs, U.S. policy began to focus on thwarting and destroying Iraqi's most menacing potentials for human destruction, realizing what would have happened had the dictator waited until he had achieved that kind of power before striking. Was it another Saddam blunder?[166]

At the end of the month, the administration's movement toward war got a boost from the UN. Baker, taking full advantage of the American turn to chair the Security Council in November, negotiated the strongest international challenge yet. With the secretary of state in the chair, the Security

Council voted by 12 to 2 to reaffirm not only all eleven previous UN actions since the invasion, but now Resolution 678. Saddam got a January 15 deadline for withdrawing his forces. If he refused to budge, his opponents were authorized to use "all necessary means" to get him out. The vote, said Baker, was "a watershed in the history of the United Nations" and also the result of more wheeling and dealing than may ever be known. Bush, however, was ready to move on.[167]

In a special news conference that next morning, obviously timed to follow up on the UN resolution, with reporters speculating that it was part of his overall plan for action, he tested the Iraqi dictator. He was ready, Bush explained, "to go the extra mile for peace." He was willing to send Baker to Baghdad to see Saddam Hussein "at a mutually convenient time between December 15 and January 15 of next year." Baker's Iraqi counterpart, Tariq Aziz, would be invited to the White House. "However, to be very clear about these efforts to exhaust all means for achieving a political and diplomatic solution," Bush took care to point out, "I am not suggesting discussions that will result in anything less than Iraq's complete withdrawal from Kuwait, restoration of Kuwait's legitimate government, and freedom for all hostages." He added assurances that, "should military action be required, this will not be another Vietnam."[168]

Maureen Santini of the New York *Daily News* wanted to know whether he realized that he was asking "some parents to give up the lives of their children."

"I know it," said the president.

"We all know how important your children are to you," she said as a follow-through. "Do you feel that this issue is important enough to you that you could conceive of giving up one of their lives for it?"

Only the president could make that decision, he replied. "These are worldwide principles of moral importance. I will do my level-best to bring those kids home without one single shot fired in anger."

The meeting days proposed for Saddam turned into a farce, played out in the press, leader to leader. Saddam had the nerve to say he couldn't fit Baker into his schedule. "Over a two-week period," Bush noted, he couldn't "make a couple of hours available"; of course, he wanted to "circumvent the United Nations deadline" by saying he'd see him on the twelfth of January.[169] Finally, not yet yielding on his "extra mile" vow, Bush proposed that Baker see Aziz earlier, on the seventh, eighth, or ninth, before going on to Baghdad if things warranted. Aziz agreed: the ninth in Geneva.

They met for six-and-a-half hours that day. The stakes were clear. Aziz was stoic. He wouldn't even accept a letter written by Bush to Saddam. The whole charade, Baker said later, was "a total stiff-arm, a total rebuff." Any notion of a trip to Baghdad was gone. Even UN Secretary General Javier Perez de Cuellar's last efforts to reason with Saddam were obviously futile.[170]

One option left for Bush took the form of a letter to Congress asking for a resolution of support. His request both took care of constitutional questions about complying with the War Powers Act and made good political sense. Truman's failure to consult over Korea in 1950 ultimately helped to destroy his political position, and that lesson was kept in mind by Eisenhower and Johnson. The legislature, abandoning politics as usual to a surprising degree by acting as though they had a devotion to a higher obligation, accepted the charge solemnly. A few members, including Kennedy of Massachusetts, compared it to the Gulf of Tonkin Resolution of 1964, in which Congress gave President Johnson a "blank check" to make whatever military response he deemed fit in Vietnam. The "most humbling, painful decision I can imagine," said Joseph Lieberman, a Connecticut Democrat, whose sentiments were regarded as highly representative. Despite opposition from Mitchell and Nunn, which did not surprise the president, the Senate finally voted a supporting resolution by 52 to 42, after prodding from the White House. The House, led by the prestige of two Democrats, Les Aspin of the Armed Services Committee and New York's Stephen Solarz, aided by Rostenkowski and John Dingell of Michigan, backed the president by 250 to 83. The final authorization for the use of force, passed by the Congress and signed by the president on January 14, specified the existence of "Iraq's conventional, chemical, biological, and nuclear weapons and ballistic missile programs" as "a grave threat to world peace."[171]

The week had been chaotic. Several phone exchanges with Gorbachev referred not only to the Gulf situation, although they talked at length about that, but also to Bush's distress about the Soviet leader's decision to send troops not only to quell rebellions within his own republics but into Lithuania. The deployment, Bush reminded him, was inconsistent with the recent course his country had been taking. However, the American president later told reporters, it was a happy thought that Gorbachev even wanted to call him. He also firmly rejected a suggestion that the Russians were acting because U.S. attention was being diverted by the Gulf. At Camp David after attending church services, Barbara Bush went sledding with some of the grandchildren when she slammed into a tree, leaving her bruised and with what doctors called a "nondisplaced fracture." The president, returning to the White House soon after the incident, told reporters at the South Lawn that there was nothing to report about Perez de Cuellar's initiatives. The Security Council president was making his second try, and Bush clearly did not expect any success. The next morning, after a Sunday evening NSC meeting, he signed an executive order authorizing the use of military force against Iraq, "fully consistent with UN Security Council Resolution 678."[172] Unless Saddam made some dramatic last-minute diplomatic move, Cheney was instructed to call Schwarzkopf to start the air strikes on the night of the sixteenth, the early hours of the seventeenth in Baghdad. Bush had done his job. The military had to take over. He knew when to let go. The "pause of goodwill," or whatever it was that the UN meant by giving Saddam until the fifteenth to effectuate the pullout, was over.[173]

"Oh God, give me the strength to do what is right," George Bush wrote that Tuesday. In the evening, he told Barbara that the war would start the next night.[174]

On Wednesday, he had lunch alone with Jimmy Baker at the White House. Baker was, of course, "a good friend. He calls it as he sees fit," and he shared "my nervousness." Afterward, he presided over a meeting on education, but kept thinking about bombs heading toward Baghdad. He had previously shared details about Saddam's atrocities with Bishop Edmund Browning. The cleric, the presiding bishop of the Episcopal Church, had protested in front of the White House about use of force until the president asked him to read the Amnesty International report about Saddam's use of torture and rape. His mind was full of such thoughts. He tried to nap, but just couldn't. He kept thinking about what other presidents had gone through, about the "agony of war," and what it meant to order into combat "our able pilots" with their "gung-ho spirit." He and Barbara had, at least, invited the Rev. Billy Graham to spend the night at the White House so he could lead their church services the next day. Dr. Graham, a spiritual adviser for a succession of presidents, was not, however, told when the war would start. One who was having last-minute jitters, Mikhail Gorbachev, sent a message via his new foreign minister, Alexander Bessmertnykh. Give it one last try, the Soviet leader urged. "Call it off for now." It was too late. Anxieties about Soviet Muslims, speculated Bush, must be making Gorbachev skittish.[175]

After the planes and Tomahawk missiles had gone out, Dick Cheney called to report that all fifty-six navy pilots had returned. Some 200 air force planes were also out; so far, none missing. "The skies are lit up in Baghdad at twenty of seven," the president noted, and went on national television at a minute after nine to confirm what CNN had been showing viewers for two hours. "Our objectives are clear," he said: "Saddam Hussein's forces will leave Kuwait."[176]

Billy Graham "tucked" him in that night. But he didn't sleep very well. He got up three times, visited the medical unit in the wee hours, hoping to shake off tightness in his shoulders. At five in the morning, unable to get back to sleep, he walked into the Situation Room. Gorbachev, he then heard, had made a supportive speech. Good news.

CHAPTER TWENTY-THREE

"With High Fidelity"

%

Even before Baghdad became the target during the early morning hours of January 17, there were those who thought that George Bush's statecraft had become "the most important factor shaping the post–cold war world," his "diplomatic calibrations near perfect."[1] Yet, at the same time, the concept was somewhat ambiguous, a nice tribute to patriotic pride, but, alas, a goal blocked by formal obstacles posed by post–cold war considerations. Nobody was more conscious of that sort of thing than Jim Baker, who would later call his memoirs "the politics of diplomacy."

Take, for example, the "Vietnam syndrome." Avoiding "another Vietnam" had become somewhat of a shibboleth, a residual liability of that war. Instead of giving the Vietnam commitment the authority of a declared war, as Col. Harry G. Summers Jr. has pointed out, the nettlesome question of the commander in chief's authority was sidestepped by the passage of the Gulf of Tonkin Resolution of 1964. In hindsight, the loss of 58,000 Americans became hard to justify. More than most armed conflicts, the protracted one in Vietnam gave rise to a schizophrenic form of patriotism: it was both a "mistake" and a test of one's willingness to celebrate Stephen Decatur's toast: "Our country! In her intercourse with foreign nations may she always be in the right; but our country, right or wrong!" There were, as a result of Vietnam, two kinds of miscreants: planners and dissenters. The only bit of common wisdom that ever did emerge, and even that was a gross oversimplification, was that it should be either fully fought or fully avoided. Bush, who had seen Vietnam not merely as a moral issue but within the context of the ongoing struggle between systems, representative of free societies versus those that embraced inherently undemocratic collectivism, had from the outset vowed that he would never permit the Gulf to become another Vietnam.

The reality, of course, was that no two wars are alike and the stakes in the Gulf had little in common with those in Southeast Asia. Saddam Hussein had launched a clear-cut direct invasion against a country that contained no significant body of his sympathizers. The threat to lifelines was obvious, the supply of oil and the Middle Eastern power balance clearly at risk. Then, too, when the fighting started, it was the "generals' war," left to the civilian-controlled Pentagon and their professionals in the field. Bush valued them, trusted their dedication and patriotism, and respected their decisions; they, in turn, had a level of confidence in him that had not been seen since FDR's day. Once Bush gave the signal to start the battle, orders went down the line, from Cheney to Powell and then to Schwarzkopf; and, until it once again became a matter of war or peace, remained there. For his part, the president followed every step diligently, reviewed Pentagon presentations, presided over NSC meetings, and monitored what the public was seeing and hearing. Especially pleased by Lieutenant General Thomas W. Kelly's briefings before the cameras, for example, Bush gave him a more visible public relations role. Kelly and Pete Williams, Cheney's Pentagon spokesman, became respected for the effective way they reported the official version of what was happening.[2]

Night after night, beginning with flashes over Baghdad at seven P.M., Washington time, on January 16, the attacks became a serial TV drama. The audience for Cable News Network (CNN) became enlarged dramatically with missile-by-missile accounts and by giving over the network to twenty-four-hour coverage. Helped by an eight-hour time difference between Iraq and Washington, the after-dark attacks in the Gulf became daily postpriandal events. Scud missiles from Iraqi launchers struck Israel for the first time on the seventeenth, landing at Tel Aviv and Haifa. TV viewers saw civilian casualties, emergency ambulance workers, and women and children wearing gas masks in apartments. The question of whether the Shamir government would risk fracturing the delicate Arab segment of the coalition by retaliating riveted the American public. The Israelis held off, mollified, it was reported, by promises of Patriot missiles advertised as virtually perfect insulators from incoming Scuds.* Additional financial assistance for the coalition, meanwhile, was announced by both Japanese Prime Minister Toshiki Kaifu and German Chancellor Helmut Kohl.

Saddam failed to fulfill his "mother of all wars" vow, but unleashed bizarre forms of retaliation. He threatened to disperse to "civilian, economic, education, and other targets" allied pilots who had become prisoners of war. He released 450 million gallons of oil from tankers anchored off Kuwait, creating the largest oil slick ever. In the most dramatic, and ecologically disastrous, long-lasting act of defiance, he ignited refineries and oil fields, creating images that outlasted the war itself, the Persian Gulf version of a scorched-earth policy.

Nevertheless, Pentagon news releases said it was as clean a war as war could be, fought with "smart" products of American technology that calculated non-civilian targets precisely and hit them exactly. And the managers were media

---

*One landed at the center of Riyadh, Saudi Arabia; later, during the one-hundred-hour ground war, another killed twenty-eight U.S. Marines at their barracks in Dhahran.

friendly. The CENTCOM commander, General Schwarzkopf, was generous in granting interviews—too generous, some thought. The other commanders, Powell and Cheney, also became so familiar that they emerged from Desert Storm as potential candidates for the White House.

With the first week of fighting nearly over, talk came from within the administration of more ambitious goals. The U.S., said Defense Secretary Cheney, planned to go beyond simply driving Saddam out of Kuwait, to "destroy that military capability that he's used to invade Kuwait and to threaten the other nations in the Middle East." Bush, deploring the mistreatment of allied airmen shot down during the bombing raids, accused Iraq of violating the Geneva conventions on prisoners of war. Bringing Saddam to justice would require nothing less than the conquest of Iraq and the capture of the criminals, but the president never said that. "If you're talking about a choice between the original idea of containing Saddam politically or destroying his capabilities militarily, then obviously, the military option is more of a guarantee," said one of the president's colleagues.[3] More than one member of the coalition, certainly the Soviet Union, France, and those of the anti-Iraq Arab bloc, had reasons to wonder whether the U.S. was about to overstep the UN mandates. Had the Americans merely used the UN as a cover for their own ambitions? The security council had said nothing about going beyond getting Saddam's armies out of Kuwait, nothing about his nuclear technology or chemical weapons.

Mixed messages had begun to muddy Washington's preparations for the ground war. Gorbachev, still worried by Iraq's sympathizers within the USSR and again confronted by the prospects of seeing Americans actually occupy Iraq, began a new peace initiative. He invited Tariq Aziz to the Kremlin and gave him a set of proposals. He then phoned Bush. It was clear, the American president told the Russian, that no matter how much the situation worried the French and Brits, Saddam was still not in compliance with the UN's resolutions. His soldiers were out there fighting. The missiles were still being launched, and the oil was burning. There was no way, Mr. Bush told the Soviet leader, after having publicly praised his initiative as "a serious and useful effort," that he could accept any "negotiating down" from the UN resolutions. Iraq would be left unpunished, he argued, rejecting it completely.[4] There was only one way to avoid further attack: a complete, no-strings-attached compliance with the UN by noon on Saturday.[5]

Bush feared that Saddam, by flirting with Gorbachev's proposals, was trying to manage "some kind of a half-assed victory out of the jaws of defeat." Not ambiguity but "clarity of purpose" was necessary for the outcome to "finally kick in totally the Vietnam syndrome." What worried him especially was that the goals were still distant. The fighting could end with Saddam still in Iraq, surrounded, all right, by his toughest units, the Republican Guard, still surviving and "we will not have settled anything. . . . given what has happened in Kuwait, given the death of our soldiers, given the Scud attacks, given this man's basic evil—we cannot let this decision tail off," which was exactly, he pondered, "what the Soviets now are trying to do, and trying to step in. We cannot let them do that."[6]

Then, just hours later, on word that Saddam was going to withdraw from Kuwait, Bush, strangely, felt no satisfaction. "We need a surrender—we need Saddam out [of Kuwait]. And yet, our objectives are to stop short of all that." He was grateful, at least, that the country had united so strongly in support of his handling of the situation. He had never seen anything like it, in fact. "The polls, by which we live and die, are up in astronomical heights, and the country is together."[7]

Just ousting Saddam from Kuwait and doing no more accomplished the objective of the coalition. If he was really to be overthrown as a result, it would have had to have been done by an internal rebellion, which was why Bush called for precisely that, and, indeed, launched a CIA authorization. Postwar critics who fault the U.S. for not having "finished the job" gave the mission a unilateral twist. It was not meant to be that, nor did Bush ever envision that kind of approach. As Flora Lewis wrote from London during the first week of the war, "There is no stated plan on what is to be achieved beyond forcing Iraq out of Kuwait." The Gulf emirates, she then noted, "have long supported the Hussein regime as the best way to keep the various countries in Iraq's population together in a 'stable' state and to prevent Iran from influencing Iraq's Shiite majority." Turkey, which, behind President Ozal's leadership, strongly supported the coalition, also preferred a strong regime in Baghdad to "hold down any Kurdish independence movement, which could spread to its territory."[8] Any doubts about where Gorbachev stood were amply demonstrated not only by his last-minute attempt to delay the attack but also by his later effort to halt the fighting with a proposal which, alas, because of its implications for continued Israel occupation of the West Bank, was unacceptable to the United States.

At 0400 hours on the twenty-fourth of February, local time, the ground war began. Marines crossed the border into Kuwait and the left flank of the U.S. Army invaded southern Iraq. At no point since the start of Desert Storm was the president as wary, the projections as daunting. Some analysts were calculating as many as 45,000 potential casualties. The levels of stress became that much more apparent on the president and Cheney, especially, when a CIA report showed that the mission of smashing half of Saddam's T-72 tanks before sending in marines had not been carried out. Cheney was then relieved to hear that, as he had hoped, the analysis was a botched job. Intelligence had "tripped itself up" with inadequate data. With Saddam Hussein having failed to heed an American ultimatum to withdraw, there was no reason for further delay. Bush was glad to have finally reached that point, to have made the decision, but unable to get the loss of lives off his mind. And, also, suppose Saddam should choose that moment to withdraw? What then? He was, Bush realized, weary from it all, very tired, in fact, but there was nothing "lonely in this decision." He had had good teamwork.[9] On

Saturday afternoon, after just an overnight in the Catoctins, the president left Camp David and flew back to the capital.

The next morning, he went across Lafayette Park for services at St. John's conducted by John Harper. The rector had responded to a call made by the president from Camp David the night before and had arranged an early morning Communion service. Just about the entire cabinet was there. So were Doro and Marvin. "It was a lovely service," Mrs. Bush later wrote. "John gave the best sermon, I thought. It was sincere and sweet. We have been friends for a long time and that made the service even more special."[10]

Cheney, before taking a seat in the pew behind the president's, received a report that things were going very well for the marines. He passed a note with the information to Bush. The news was "glowing." The marines had gotten through the barriers, through the barbed wire, and into Kuwait, penetrating mine fields, and accomplishing everything else Bush and the command had worried about; and yet, so far, only four men lost. He also heard more during a direct call from General Schwarzkopf. He was "choking up just as [he] did in church."[11]

For entirely logical reasons, Schwarzkopf had overestimated Iraqi fighting power. They had the largest army in the Gulf, the fourth strongest in the world. Saddam, in the past, had shown no hesitation about going to extremes. His Republican Guard operated from the rear, where they stood ready to kill those who refused to advance into enemy fire. To a degree that was not appreciated until later, however, they were being salvaged, moved to the north, even beyond Baghdad, together with some of the best T-72 tanks.[12] Half of Saddam's grunts had deserted, and others intended to give up. In all, the allies took some 8,000 prisoners during those first few hours. The desert itself was turned into a killing machine as bulldozers plowed mounds of sand over Iraqi tanks, suffocating at least 150 of Saddam's armored men.

By the second day, marines were well on their way to Kuwait City when a fresh force of enemy tanks, suddenly emerging from burning oil fields, launched a desperate counterattack, their final military thrust of consequence. Gen. Chuck Horner, who heard that the enemy was pulling out of the city, recalled that an F-15 bomber crew was ordered to hit their fleeing lines as they followed the road to Basra.[13] Each plane carried twelve 500-pound bombs. Dropped three at a time, the "turkey shoot" turned the escape route into "the highway of death." Schwarzkopf, determined to trap the Guard by blocking their escape, ordered in the Eighteenth Corps and the Seventh Corps, joining with the 101st Airborne Division. At the point where the CENTCOM commander claimed that 3,700 of the enemy's 4,000 tanks had been destroyed, the allies were but 150 miles from downtown Baghdad.[14] Seventy thousand Iraqis had surrendered by then, and Saddam, hearing that nothing stood between the Republican Guard and destruction, was on the verge of pulling out. Either way, it was obvious to the CENTCOM commander that a cease-fire was near.

At the Hyatt Regency Hotel in Riyadh at nine on the evening of the twenty-seventh in Saudi Arabia (one P.M., Washington time), Schwarzkopf displayed his battle-line charts at a press conference that was dubbed the "mother of all briefings." "We almost completely destroyed the offensive capability of the Iraqi forces in the Kuwaiti theater of operations," he announced. "The gates are closed." There were some leaks, yes, he added, civilian vehicles, unarmed Iraqis getting out, but their military machine was trapped.[15]

Powell was on the secure line to the commander several times, before and after the briefing. When he called at seven A.M. Washington time, he was clearly getting anxious. Saddam was saying he was withdrawing, but his armies were still fighting. Surely, negotiating with him to end the fighting was the last thing he or the president or Cheney wanted. Moreover, he told the commander, television was beginning to show some very "unpleasant" stuff, almost as though "we were engaged in slaughter for slaughter's sake."

"I've been thinking the same thing," said Schwarzkopf. Just one more day; only that was needed to continue the operation by driving toward the sea. "We can have a cease-fire tomorrow evening at dark and we would have completely accomplished the plan." The commander then added a thought: "Do you realize, if we stop tomorrow night, the ground campaign will have lasted five days? How does that sound, the Five Day War?"[16]

One-upping Israel's victory over the Arabs in 1967 sounded fine. "Not bad," said Powell. "I'll pass it along."

"Instead of feeling elation," Bush thought to himself on the twenty-sixth, the night *before* that decisive meeting, before Powell and the others said it was time to wind it down, "I'm feeling apprehension. I don't want to see an unhappy ending. I told these groups last night, 'Can you remember that we're in a war and there's going to be a winner and a loser in a war?' " He surprised himself, he went on, with how much he dwelt on "the end of the Vietnam syndrome. I felt the division in the country in the sixties," continuing to record, "in the seventies," and he remembered that he was in the Congress and spoke at Adelphi University and at Yale, too, when his alma mater was turning its back. "I remember the agony of the ugliness, and now it's together. We've got to find a clean end, and I keep saying, how do we end this thing? How do we end it? You can't use the word *surrender*—the Arabs don't like that. . . . How do we quit? How do we get them to lay down their arms? How do we save good civilians? How do we get on with our role with credibility, hoping to bring security to the Gulf?"[17]

After lunch that afternoon, Powell was driven over to the White House for the daily military briefing. He took his place at the U-shaped conference table in the Oval Office. The president, facing the others as he sat with his back to the fireplace, got the latest details of the Iraqi rout. "I told him we were starting to see some scenes that were unpleasant," Powell then wrote. "We were in the window of calling an end to it so that there was not an additional loss of life on the part of American and coalition forces or on the part of Iraqi youngsters."[18] We could, he also told him, lose the high moral ground by going on.

After all, they had fulfilled the UN mandate, and no one wanted to ask nineteen- and twenty-year-old American kids to engage in unnecessary bloodshed. We had liberated Kuwait; Saddam's offensive capability was gone; the power balance in the Gulf was preserved. The secretary of state, and everybody else in the room, agreed. The mission had been accomplished. Nobody disagreed. Scowcroft, ever cautious, had nagging doubts about what could happen, but kept them to himself and went along.[19]

"If that's the case," said the president, as he had been prepared to do even before the meeting started, "why not end it today?" Then, looking at the others down the U-shaped table, he said, "We're starting to pick up some undesirable public and political baggage with all those scenes of carnage. You say we've accomplished the mission? Why not end it?" He was ready, that evening, to make a public announcement.

Powell excused himself, went into the adjacent private study the president sometimes used, and made another call to Schwarzkopf.

"I don't have any problem," the commander said. "Our objective was to drive 'em out, and we've done it."

Bush heard about Schwarzkopf's reaction. He had thought about it for long, and wanted to say more. "We do not want to lose anything now with charges of brutalization, but we are also very concerned with the issue of prisoners. The issue is how to find a clean end." He had another thought: it was "not going to be like the battleship *Missouri*," he added, referring to General MacArthur's acceptance of the Japanese surrender in 1945.

The president looked around, glancing down the table, taking in the expressions on the faces of Powell, Sununu, Cheney, Quayle, Haass, Gates, Scowcroft, and Baker. "Why do I not feel elated?" He had been thinking that thought, worrying about it, really wondering why. "But we need to have an end," he finally said. "People want that. They are going to want to know we won and the kids can come home. We do not want to screw this up with a sloppy, muddled ending." His words, recorded by a note-taker in the room, were virtually duplicated when he later dictated for his diary.[20]

Powell noted that it was 5:57 P.M. when Bush said they should end the fighting.

John Sununu then had another thought about the "suspension of hostilities," the politic description for what was about to happen. Schwarzkopf could use more time anyway to get those Guard units. "Why not make it effective midnight our time?" suggested Bush's chief of staff. "That'll make it the Hundred Hour War."[21]

They all agreed, giving little thought to the five weeks of air war. Fighting would stop at 0800 hours February 28, Riyadh time.

Once more, Powell called Schwarzkopf, who passed the word to his commanders.

For the officers on the scene, such as Maj. Gen. Barry McCaffrey, the war was not over, the enemy not yet destroyed. McCaffrey, the youngest division commander, had prepared his Twenty-fourth Mechanized Division for the final battle. It was clear that neither McCaffrey, Lt. Gen. Calvin Waller, nor any other ranking officers on the scene thought the job was done. "The closer one got to the battlefield," Michael Gordon and Bernard Trainor have reported, "the more questionable the decision to end the war seemed." The enemy could still be cut off without an inordinate loss of life on either side.[22]

"You have to be shitting me. Why a cease-fire now?" Waller asked Schwarzkopf.

"One Hundred Hours has a nice ring," explained the commander.

"That's bullshit," Waller exclaimed.

"Then you go argue with them," said Schwarzkopf.[23]

Fighting had hardly begun, it seemed, before the president went on the air that Tuesday night to announce the liberation of Kuwait and the end of the war.[24] It was not, he told the world, "a time of euphoria"; nor, privately, did he feel euphoric.

Once it was all over, expectations shifted, as Bush had feared. There were many who, like former chairman of the Joint Chiefs of Staff, Adm. William Crowe, went from favoring continued reliance on sanctions to wanting the war continued until the total collapse of Iraq and the demise of Saddam. Schwarzkopf himself, in a televised interview with David Frost, suggested that ending the ground war after only one hundred hours was premature, which brought admonitions from the president, Cheney, and Powell, all of whom pointed out that the decision was made with his consent.[25]

Yet, there was a point. Contrary to Schwarzkopf's advisory at his briefing in Riyadh, the "gates" were not closed. "Spotty intelligence," as had been pointed out, "no doubt played a role in the decision. Only after the war, when spy plane and spy satellite imagery was fully analyzed, would it become clear that half the Republican Guard equipment had not been destroyed and that the vast majority of the fleeing Iraqi army was still south of Basra in the path of the army's planned advance when the war ended."[26] They had, at the same time, managed to evacuate with some of their best T-72 tanks. There were even strong doubts about the efficacy of the Patriot missiles. The numbers of Scuds actually intercepted and destroyed kept getting revised downward from the original 96 percent figure.[27]

Saddam was still alive, and very much in control, neither overthrown nor having fled, probably deep in his bunker below the Presidential Palace in the heart of Baghdad, unreachable by the air force's "get-Saddam" weapon. Those GBU-28s, as they were called, shipped down from the Watervliet Arsenal in upstate New York, were 4,200-pound laser-guided bombs with the ability to plow themselves shaftlike straight into the ground. Only two were yet available, and neither made a dent where it counted. Getting Saddam was a much harder proposition than getting that bastard Noriega. Nor, as they found out later, had the attacks destroyed his chemical warfare stocks or capacity for nuclear mischief. UN inspectors later reported that stocks of sarin nerve gas, mustard gas, and possibly biological agents remained unaccounted for. The Gulf War, alas, contributed its own kind of "syndrome," complaints by American veterans of a mysterious array of ailments. They did, however, secure the release of the American prisoners, five men and one woman. One hundred and forty-six of their comrades were killed.[28]

Seven Iraqi generals, but not Saddam, met for two hours with General Schwarzkopf on the desert at Safwan, an airfield just north of the border with Kuwait, to formally accept all of the coalition's conditions for a permanent cease-fire, while Baghdad radio announced acceptance of the UN resolutions.[29]

Subsequent debates over how far the military should have been allowed to continue suggest that, short of breaking with the UN mandate and taking over Iraq, the allied forces could not have gone far enough. As General Powell has drawn the perspective, such arguments became reminiscent of whether General Meade should have mopped up Robert E. Lee's army after the battle of Gettysburg, whether the Nazi underbelly during World War II should have been attacked through the Balkans, whether Eisenhower should have gone east in Germany to head off the advancing Russians instead of pursuing Hitler's remnants toward the south, or whether General MacArthur should have been given freedom to go after the Chinese Communists north of the Yalu River during the Korean War. Citing an argument by former undersecretary of defense for policy, Fred Ikle, he pointed out that "every war must end." More importantly, in Ikle's words, is whether the "outcome of the war, not the outcome of the campaigns within it," serve the nation's interest.[30]

Later, given an opportunity for further reflection, Bush reiterated much the same point: "If we continued the fighting another day, until the ring was completely closed, would we be accused of a slaughter of Iraqis who were simply trying to escape, not fight?"[31]

Alone with his thoughts after the months of Desert Shield and Desert Storm, Bush felt a strong letdown, the terrible anguish of a presidency for whom the cheering has suddenly stopped. The polls were crazy. Gallup had him at 89 percent, higher than even Harry Truman on the day the Nazis surrendered.[32]

The orgy of patriotism behind Desert Storm that placed little yellow ribbons on trees, posts, and collar lapels all over America had its play in Congress. As Democrats pinned them on their chests, Republicans, with bragging rights for having backed the president more fully on using force in the Gulf, countered with big yellow buttons. The Democrats, not to be outdone, stuck American flag lapel pins to their chests, which inspired the president's men to favor little red-white-and-blue flags that they could wave in their hands, and, more importantly, make a colorful display for television cameras. "Success," wrote Maureen Dowd, recalling a line from John F. Kennedy, "has many fathers, of course, and in the rush to claim paternity many Democrats were eager to forget their early skepticism about the war."[33] On Saturday night, March 10, Bush went to Ford's Theater for a country music gala. The actor

Morgan Freeman appeared on the stage and paid a tribute to what the sixteenth president did to keep the Union together and end slavery. He then saluted the box where Abraham Lincoln sat when was assassinated. With that, he stepped forward, faced the forty-first president, recalled the great victory in the Persian Gulf, and saluted again. "And thank you, Mr. President," he said. When Bush returned to the White House that night, he said that he "felt the tears rolling down my eyes again. The emotions are so powerful." And the country "music is just marvelous for these times. The flags, patriotism, and someone's praying." It was just fantastic, everything he hoped it would be. He was already looking forward to a trip down to Sumter, South Carolina, that next weekend, where he knew he would find so many more flags, and so much patriotism, that he would feel the glow even more.[34]

Already it was turning. It couldn't last, and he knew it couldn't last; maybe that's why he could not feel euphoric. The Democrats, he knew, were just waiting for the fall to come. "I feel the buildup now on the domestic side," he noted. "When will Bush stumble; what about the domestic agenda; can he handle it?" And he did not like it one bit. Worse, he thought, he lacked the visceral desire to slug it out with the Democrats, but he knew he would have to do it. He read, along with accounts of the effusion of patriotism, that the public was down on the economy, down on crime, especially drugs. He was sending forward a new crime bill, one that was essentially the same as last year's. He watched the scenes from Los Angeles, where policemen repeatedly clubbed a fallen motorist, Rodney King, and was appalled. Horrible. "We cannot condone that kind of behavior. No excuse whatsoever," but Police Chief Darryl Gates, whom he had met and had a good talk with during the 1988 campaign, was not necessarily the one to blame. Bush was still opposed to signing a bill mandating a seven-day waiting period to buy handguns. But, thinking about the economy, crime, and guns, he thought he'd be glad to sign that bill passed by the Senate in 1990 with restrictions on automatic weapons, "even though the National Rifle Association disapproves. We need to crack down a little bit on that."[35]

Reading the press now, you could see the letdown, that whole mood change. Saddam was still there, alive and in power, beating up the Shiites in the south, chasing the Kurds in the north and from helicopters. The attacks had to stop, Bush said publicly, but he couldn't do anything about it while the fight was going on, and, although some of the Saudis were pressing for at least covert help for the Shiites, he was not about to restart the war. And he certainly had no taste for putting into motion a process that could end with Iraq being chopped up into little pieces and God knows what kind of chaos in the Middle East.[36]

Even Dan Quayle got into the act, at the end of the month, saying that they should have gone further into Iraq, "a new right-wing theme," Bush noted. Sununu thought he saw the hand of Bill Kristol. Whatever the case, wrote the president, "It doesn't help Quayle with me and it doesn't help him at all."[37] Quayle, who had embarrassed Bush early on by comments about

Central America that appeared blatantly targeted to the right wing, had also been the victim of allegations by a convicted perjurer and drug dealer who claimed to have sold him marijuana in the 1970s. The charges, which were termed groundless by the Drug Enforcement Agency, nevertheless became the subject of a syndicated comic strip by Garry Trudeau. *Doonesbury*'s creator suggested that federal officials were covering up for him.[38] Quayle, who remained a chronic embarrassment, even fell out with elements of the religious right by saying he would stand by his daughter if she needed an abortion. "Quayle was his [Bush's] decision," a Republican consultant said, speaking off the record, and Bush, by dropping him, would "have to admit that he's made a monumental mistake, and he won't do that."[39]

The Quayle experience was one of many with the press, and now they were beginning to complain about "no democracy in Kuwait." His big hope, Bush decided, "is that the economy comes out of its downturn sooner than expected as a result of the end of the war."[40]

He met with his cabinet Tuesday evening, March 12. The presentations went around the room, each, in turn, talking about his own agenda. Carla Hills offered a bundle of problems about trade, and the president worried about that. Lou Sullivan talked about health care. Nick Brady's deputy, John F. Robson, talked about reforming the system for financial ratings. "They're good, strong, work together," with "only a few grandstanders."[41]

Kemp worried him. "He's so enthusiastic and really such a good guy, but he just can't contain himself." Kemp seemed discouraged and kept saying he was "a failure." He was always prodding other departments. He sent a letter to Jim Baker complaining we were going too easy on Gorbachev over Lithuania, and almost got into a fistfight with the secretary of state after insisting the U.S. should recognize the independence of the government in Vilnius. An enraged Baker, right there in the Oval Office, faced the secretary of HUD and shouted, "Fuck you, Kemp!" and turned down the corridor. Kemp "reacted like a quarterback who had just been victimized by unnecessary roughness" and charged him. Scowcroft finally got in the way and broke them up. "I wonder," contemplated the president, "how he would feel if Jim wrote him and said, 'Dear Secretary Kemp: We ought to change our policy on housing.' "[42]

Baker, like everybody else, had a run-in with Sununu, also in the Oval Office. The chief of staff drove the secretary of state "through the roof" because he was seeing ambassadors on his own, like the one from Kuwait, despite the president's warning that it was not his turf. Baker was hardly the only one upset about "the governor": Brady, Cheney, and Mosbacher were, too. "I hate these damn things," said the president.[43]

Still, how in the world could the Democrats do better, he wondered? How would they manage with domestic policy? Imagine *their* cabinet! How could they get anything done with a "Secretary" Ted Kennedy, a "Secretary" Dick Gephardt, a "Secretary" Paul Wellstone, a "Secretary" George Mitchell, or a "Secretary" Gary Hart?[44]

He could, Bush figured, use that kind of line in the elections, still a year away; he had time. But, at the moment, it was a cold March morning in Washington and he was just plain tired, worn out. Even last night's workout left him feeling no better. Maybe, he thought, it was because he had never really enjoyed the "flush of victory" even though he thrilled at "what's happened in the country" and looked forward like hell to seeing those folks in Sumter.[45]

"I don't know whether it's the anticlimax or that I'm too tired to enjoy anything, but I just seem to be losing my perspective." Maybe he was feeling the aftermath of the five A.M. calls to the Situation Room, "nudging things, worrying about things; phone calls to the foreign leaders; trying to keep things moving forward; managing a massive project." Maybe, he thought, "I don't seem to have the drive" or much taste left for "this political stuff anymore," like fund-raising. He never liked the money part, but he put up with it, especially when he chaired the RNC, and did it as vice president. He certainly did it, and did it effectively, for his own campaign, and drummed up cash for others during the last midterm elections. He didn't like the thought of having to do it again for '92.[46]

But it wasn't only that; it was the ugliness, especially from the press, with their "sniping, carping, bitching, predictable editorial complaints, the newsboys of the world." Most of all, the bottom line was "the cynical liberalism that comes down on any president," especially from such cartoonists as Herblock and Trudeau, "a little elitist who is spoiled, derisive, ugly, and nasty."[47]

His fantasies offered some exhilaration, but, as he went on, the picture clarified. It might turn out just like George Deukmejian told him the other day about how he felt after announcing that he was giving up the governorship of California. "I've never seen him more relaxed—never seen him more happy," Bush said into his tape. Imagine, if he, like Duke, had the pressure drained off him. They could get someone who was better "at all of this rough and tumble, and maybe who likes it better." No, he would not be able to say he had finished everything. He could, though, say he had done his best and that history "will say we made a contribution."

He could do a lot of things. He would be free to help Neil, whose problems he so blamed on himself and the office he held that the thought made him teary. Maybe even drive his own car, do all the things a private citizen can do. "Sometimes I really like the spotlight," he thought, "but I'm tired of it. I've been at the head table for many years, and now I wonder what else is out there. Well, I'm sure this is just a stage and I'll get through it, but this is what I'm feeling on March 13th."[48]

The next day, he flew to Martinique, where he met with François Mitterrand. They faced the press together. Bush was really happy to see the French president. He was genuinely very pleasant. He thought about the contrast between his visit with Mitterrand and the "way it was during the Reagan days." Mitterrand pointed that out, too.[49] Two days later, he was in Bermuda seeing John Major. He waded into the ocean, "and everyone thought I was nuts, but the water was far warmer than in Maine." It was great, also, walking into the Four Ways Restaurant. The tourists, a lot of them Americans, stood up, clapped, and cheered. He "felt the glowing inside."[50]

Then it was on to Sumter. It was just like he expected, a very emotional event in the South Carolina town. They came out by the thousands. War veterans, veterans of the Gulf War. "I mention[ed] Vietnam veterans, and the place stood up and cheered." A little kid, three or four, tugged at a vet still in his camouflage fatigues, saying, "That's my dad, that's my dad," and the crowd went wild. "It touched a chord," he noted. "There's a lot of Vietnam-era families who see that their sons, daughters, husbands, sisters, and brothers [were] walked down upon, so it worked out pretty well."[51]

Baker also checked in with him from Moscow. Gorbachev, the secretary reported, was determined to hang on. Baker wasn't sure he was going to make it. How to handle all this was one of the big problems. "My view is you dance with who is on the dance floor," said the president, and certainly not to do anything that could be described as blatant destabilization. Then, flying back to Washington, he had a couple of martinis. They must have depressed him, and he was sad when he got off the helicopter. As he stepped onto the White House lawn, Millie was there. The dog, Bush saw, kept looking back for Barbara, but the First Lady was in Houston.

He was, he kept thinking, dead tired, even after three pleasant days in Bermuda. He realized that he didn't "really care, and that's bad, that's bad." But he knew he had to get in there and try; at least they could go ahead with the issues now that the "Kuwait liberation war" was settled. But Saddam was still a problem, acting up. "I worry about it. I guess it's just a kind of mood downer now. For some reason, my whole body is dragging and I'm tired. I don't understand it."[52] He went to Bethesda on the twenty-seventh and came away with a clean bill of health.[53]

At the other side of town, at George Washington University Hospital two days later, Lee Atwater's life came to a bitterly painful end. He was only a month past forty. The president's physician, Burton Lee, had given him a year to live, and that's how it happened, almost to the day, after 165 days spent in various hospitals. Only a Dick Morris, perhaps, could match Atwater's combination of personal recklessness and brilliance as a political tactician, which had led to suggestions that he had, single-handedly, institutionalized political consultants in American politics. He had, as the newsman who knew him best wrote, become by the age of thirty-nine "the dark prince of politics, admired and perhaps feared by Republican colleagues, disliked and feared by many Democrats."[54]

Dan Quayle delivered a eulogy at the funeral in the Trinity Cathedral at Columbia, South Carolina. The president and Quayle went to a memorial service at the Washington National Cathedral, where rhythm-and-blues singer Chuck Jackson sang. When he heard "You'll Never Walk Alone," George Bush dabbed his eyes with a handkerchief.[55]

Meanwhile, the press, and especially Todd Brewster in *Life* magazine, seizing on Atwater's born-again sick-bed discovery of Jesus and an apology to Mike Dukakis for some of the mean things he had said in '88, had him recanting those Willie Horton ads. He hadn't; they were not his work to begin with, and he had nothing to be sorry about. His biographer has put it best: "Lee Atwater's most memorable creation was Lee Atwater."[56]

It was not, really, a good time for George Bush. Best, perhaps, was the big blowout New York City gave for veterans of the Gulf War, when, under a snowfall of spectacular ticker tape, 24,000 marched through Broadway's "canyon of heroes." Some 4.7 million, according to police estimates, lined the route from Battery Park to Worth Street. Triumph, even then, was diluted, Bush read, by a clash of antiwar protesters and police, which, to his real dismay, resulted in injuries to thirteen officers. At that point, nearly six weeks after the end of the fighting, those questioned along the parade route told reporters of their anxieties about recession, crime, race relations, and municipal finances.[57] George McGovern had the gall to claim that the president had "led the nation in an outpouring of self-congratulatory jingoism that would have been more appropriate in the days of Caesar."[58] But another liberal, Russell Baker, thought that Bush had achieved so high "a popularity and stature almost inconceivable for any president in his third year in office" that to defy "the second-term curse would take a reckless, impetuous personality alien to Mr. Bush's solid conservative figure."[59]

The thought of not running was not entirely confined to the Bush diaries. Dr. Lee noted that the president's sleep pattern was more erratic than usual, and he was also starting to lose some weight—ultimately fifteen pounds. It was in April that Patty Presock noted, and told the White House physician, that there were changes in Bush's handwriting.[60] George W. wondered aloud to his father about running again. "I haven't made up my mind," he replied.[61] Marlin Fitzwater remembered that "there was a point after the war it seemed to me that he had a real feeling that he didn't want to run." At Kennebunkport, Fitzwater went up to Andy Card, Sununu's deputy, and asked about what he was hearing. Card said he had the same feeling about Bush. Then, while walking down the long driveway at Walker's Point, just inside the security gate, he put the question to George W. The younger Bush, the press secretary recalled, was direct. "I don't know that he will run again. There's a good chance that he won't." If the news got out, they all knew, "if we told anybody else that, we were dead meat." Barbara, her attitude about a second term ambivalent at best, had swung to the negative.[62]

On Saturday, May 4, Bush had just reached Camp David and was out taking his usual jog with his Secret Service detail, when, at 4:20 P.M., he developed shortness of breath. He was examined by Dr. Michael Nash, who determined that he had suffered an atrial fibrillation, which manifests itself as a rapid, irregular heartbeat, but, finally, leaves no damage. He was airlifted the twenty minutes to Bethesda Naval Hospital. He walked without assistance from the helicopter to the car that took him to the entrance. While he was still hooked up to a cardiac monitor, there was, noticed some observers, "a subtle psychological shift" in Washington, with "old certainties not taken for granted." Speculation centered on the question of Quayle's competence to take over and whether Bush would run again. The stock market, too, felt the shock, with a quick forty-point drop.[63] At the hospital, however, the diagnosis was not at all alarming.

By the time he returned from Bethesda on Monday, still attached to a monitor and placed under Dr. Lee's care, the diagnosis was Graves' disease. That, at least, allayed rumors that he had lupus, the problem that beset their springer spaniel. The probability that George and Barbara would both have Graves', with Millie ill from lupus, could never be explained other than as a strange coincidence. Millie's condition was different, but it was also an autoimmune disease. Basically, however, the president had been bothered at least since March, when his personal complaints of weariness increased, by damage to his thyroid system. Graves' led to an overactive thyroid and the arrhythmia.[64]

The problem, of course, was to keep in motion the man Dr. Lee knew as one who "operates like a tornado." Disabling his thyroid and replenishing him with thyroid hormones risked a marked weight increase. Dr. Lee, after consultations at the National Institutes of Health, explained the option to the president. "I pushed his thyroid up to what I thought was the limit, trying to see if it could compensate in some way," thereby slowing Bush's heartbeat, he recalled. Presock, whose work as an administrative assistant brought her into close contact with the president almost daily, was also asked by the physician to watch for signs of anything unusual. When after nearly a month Bush seemed to be doing fine, he was placed on a normal dosage. Nevertheless, it was not without its effect.

"All I can say," Dr. Lee acknowledged as he reviewed the procedure, "is that our treatment for it did him some very, very, very minimal, unavoidable damage that he never quite recovered from. I think that in a normal person you'd never, never, never notice that; but in a person functioning in a presidential level, the teeniest little problem becomes noticeable."

In reflection, then, about the consequences, he concluded that "we paid a penalty for that thyroid disease." The Bush of 1992 was not the Bush of 1988. "That was for sure." For the remainder of the presidency, and especially as he campaigned for a second term, the doctor received reports "that people had noticed that the president didn't seem to have the same zest as he used to."[65]

The consequences of the illness and treatments had other effects. By mid 1991, Sununu "was simply shutting down any proposal or initiative before it reached the Oval Office."[66] Rich Bond thought that there was an outrageous "decision" that was "totally inspired by John Sununu, to disengage from active politics after the Gulf War." Many said that Sununu was the author of a "reign of terror" from which the White House staff "never really recovered their political instincts," and that the chief of staff, more than any single individual, was most liable for Bush's ultimate defeat.[67]

Once again, reminiscent of the earlier experience with Jennifer Fitzgerald, the gatekeeper was being blamed for the president's reactions. Lost was the obvious fact that Bush was the person who called the shots. "The president always gets what the president wants," Sununu later recalled. "This was not based on my determination." There was "no specific decision" to hold things off after Bush's illness, just a "stricter priority filter." Actions were determined on "constant reviews with the president on what we wanted to do in terms of workloads and . . . always on feedback from the president on whether he was getting too much or too little in terms of a given area and in total quantity."[68]

But Sununu had become the target of a community execution—death by slow leaks to the media. Nobody "knew" the leakers. They were just coming "out of the woodwork to tip off reporters" to every misstep, unique to him or not.[69] When he fell, not a person offered to help. Bush, in dealing with the problem of his chief of staff, felt powerless. "Everybody seemed to have a Sununu story."[70]

They may have sneered at him as "that fat little pirate," but Bush owed a powerful debt to the governor who grew up in New York City's working-class borough of Queens.[71] Without Sununu, Bush may well not have won the 1988 New Hampshire primary, and, without that, the nomination. He was also a vital link to Republican conservatives who had never learned to trust Bush. He took the fall for the president with business groups, mollifying their demands while Bush could, for example, work on his public relations image "as a friend of the environment."[72]

Sununu's downfall began with stories in the *Washington Post* and *U.S. News & World Report* and continued on that indispensable purveyor of modern information, television, with its immense national audience. Story after story reported Sununu abusing his transportation privileges by using air force jets for personal visits to his dentist in Boston and family ski vacations out West. He used his government chauffeur to drive to New York so he could pick up almost $5,000 worth of rare stamps at Christie's. He came under fire as anti-Israel, in articles carried by the *Post*, *The Wall Street Journal*, and *Newsweek*, which charged that Sununu, a Lebanese-American, was in cahoots with Arabs. He was the country's only governor, one reported, who had refused to condemn the UN resolution that equated Zionism with racism.[73] All in all, according to Pentagon records that showed seventy-seven trips on military aircraft, forty-nine were listed as official. His personal trips cost the government a half million dollars.[74]

His responses did not help matters. What, he once asked, was the difference between the Iraqi Air Force and Air Sununu. The answer: "Sununu makes a lot more flights." Asked why he took a limo instead of a train to New York, he explained that his twenty-four-hour-a-day job required constant accessibility by phone.[75]

"John Sununu, with his large family and small means, might be the least comfortable member of the Bush team," wrote Brit Hume in *The American*

Spectator, "but with his bay window and know-it-all manner, he fits the mold of a fat cat."[76]

With his health stabilized, Bush got cranked up again. Baker and his staff got the Russians to yield on the question of allowing dissidents to leave, especially Soviet Jews, while Washington granted MFN rights for Moscow, easing the way for Bush to do what was necessary. Gorbachev's position was becoming more tenuous daily. His prime minister, Valentin Pavlov, was trying to finagle his way to power through the parliament. In June, Boris Yeltsin was elected president of the Russian Republic, their first popularly elected leader ever.

In mid July, at a G-7 summit in London, Gorbachev also found tepid support from Western leaders less and less willing to bet on his political survival. Beset on one side by hard-line Communists, and on the other by populists fearful of unemployment and inflation resulting from free market reforms, he also faced Western democracies aware that his economy was in a state of free fall. The Kremlin's own latest figures revealed a 46 percent greater deficit than planned with a 37 percent drop in foreign trade. Gorbachev was lucky to leave London with a pledge of even limited aid, largely in the form of technical assistance. The sinking Soviet economy, they thought, needed stronger leadership toward a market-oriented system.[77]

Bush's trip to England, Athens, Crete, and Ankara, where he got together with President Ozal, was ample evidence of his physical revival. On July 29, after a week back in Washington, he took off for Moscow in the new Air Force One, a Boeing 747, with a much roomier section for the staff. There, he joined Gorbachev to sign the Strategic Arms treaty (START).[78] Nine years in the making, START, which was ratified by the Senate on October 1, provided for the mutual reduction of ICBMs and missile warheads. At the moment, before the addition of START II in 1992, which devolved upon four Soviet republics the responsibility for control of the nuclear missile arsenal, the accomplishment was more of a boost for Gorbachev than a new breakthrough.[79]

Back home for the first weekend in August, Bush assembled his senior political people at Camp David, largely in response to the whispers that he might not run for a second term. He told his three dozen guests quite clearly that, yes, he was planning on running again, but, no, this was not the time to start a campaign. "I wouldn't waste your time if I knew I wasn't running," he told them.[80]

What he did intend, he said, despite the urging of just about everybody there, was to hold off until January or February. He was president, and he thought he could be most effective as president. "I want to postpone politics 1992," was Bush's version of what he told them, essentially the words they heard and found dismaying.

Ron Kaufman reminded him that campaign finance laws were involved in the decision.

"The longer we wait," said Bush, "the more money we'll have in the end."

He would, he was told, have to bear the brunt of raising something like a $100 million—first $28 or $29 million to receive federal matching funds, followed by the "soft money" needed for the congressional campaigns and the RNC.

"My God," Bush thought, "isn't there any freebie that comes from being president—doesn't that mean we have to do a little bit less because of the name recognition and all that?"

Mosbacher was impatient. He wanted to get going. The earlier the announcement, the earlier the laws governing funds kicked in. His advice was echoed by Quayle and Bond. Nobody really spoke up *against* running or *for* delaying, except the president. And nobody thought he had made "a particularly telling observation" with his point about possibly needing less money because he already was so well known.

It was going to be harder, too, Mosbacher advised. Some of the Team 100* guys, especially from California, were grumbling. They were hurting, too, including the $100,000 real estate people who usually put up so much money. Values were falling, their businesses were in trouble. And the banks, Bush heard, were playing tight money for real estate loans. They were already overloaded. Bob Teeter pointed out that the 2.5 percent growth in the money supply was "the lowest by far for coming out of any recession," and that, which really worries people, was completely in the hands of the Fed.

Rich Bond and the others came away "very, very disquieted by the lack of speed and focus that he had on the reelection effort." What a contrast with the way the Reagan people got going! "Bush," said Bond, "really made the wrong call on getting ready for the presidential campaign."

He didn't want to give the Democrats any reasons for getting themselves together any sooner than necessary, Bush explained. Nor was he crazy about sending a signal that they were well organized, which would only help jump-start their response.[81]

Of course, as he had feared earlier when rejecting that loan request, any business with Gorbachev seemed to displease the Republican right. According to John O'Sullivan in the *National Review*, Bush "clung to his personal endorsement of the failing Gorbachev" and overlooked the repression of the republics. Bush's remarks during a side trip to Kiev were taken by American conservatives as complicity with Gorbachev in squelching lunges toward independence. Yeltsin, to such Bush critics, including Richard Nixon, was a better bet for true democracy. By toadying up to Gorbachev, Bush was helping him postpone hard choices and merely resuscitating the Soviet bureaucracy.[82]

In Seattle, where Democratic governors were meeting, the emphasis was on the economy. Their concerns, pressed by Governor Bill Clinton of Arkansas, culminated in a resolution that assailed the president for his "refusal to recognize that 8.5 million Americans out of work is a tragedy and

*People who contributed $100,000 or more.

an emergency." The next day, Clinton was far more subdued. "We ought to give the president a decent breathing space to find out what the facts are and make a statement on behalf of the United States," he told reporters. "Then the rest of us can decide what we think about it."[83]

Hurricane Bob churning up the Atlantic Coast had everybody's attention at Walker's Point. The Coast Guard thought eighty-mile-an-hour winds and damaging tidal waves were possible. The disastrous winter storm of 1977, in which the compound was torn apart by wind-driven ice ("the storm of the century"), was still very much part of modern memory. A different sort of storm, however, a coup in Moscow, threw off all timetables.[84]

The president heard it first from Scowcroft. The general, staying as usual at the Nonantum Hotel between the Point and Dock Square, rang Bush's phone at just about bedtime. CNN, he told his boss, was reporting that Gorbachev was out and the vice president, Gennadi Yanayev, was in.

"My God!" said Bush, who later, remembering the timing of Saddam's invasion the year before, asked rhetorically, "What is it about August?"[85] Yanayev, he remembered, was a very unlikely-looking adventurer.

He was right. The "putsch of fools," as one Russian later called it, had begun. Gorbachev, at work in his vacation home, a Crimean dacha, had pushed his trusted colleagues too far. The plotters finally reacted to his signing of a new union treaty that promised to devolve power to the republics. Gorbachev, defiant, fortunately had protective bodyguards. He and his family could only wait it out.

Bush and Scowcroft got back to Washington in a hurry, while the Secret Service evacuated Barbara, the president's ninety-year-old mother, and the ever-present assortment of other relatives at Walker's Point to the safety of the interior. The *Fidelity* was lifted right out of the ocean in advance of Hurricane Bob.

The tempest fell short of its potential, at least for that part of the shoreline. Waves, accompanied by heavy rain, smashed against the rocks. Ocean Avenue was littered with tree limbs, and some parts of town lost power. But it was only a glancing blow.

Meanwhile, in Moscow, the conspirators were inept, ill-supported and, at a crucial moment, intoxicated, no match for Boris Yeltsin's theatrical, and effective, defiance. Climbing atop a hostile tank, he rallied Muscovites, his burly figure producing memorable photos. As he held firm in support of Gorbachev and the government, and with only meager defections by the military, the KGB, and key members of Gorbachev's national security council, the plotters inevitably caved in. One took his own life. The whole upheaval lasted three days.

Bush, gambling on that failure, worked the phones and mobilized Gorbachev's Western colleagues. Unable after several attempts to make contact with the isolated Gorbachev, he reached Yeltsin with assurances of support. Then, expediting the dispatch to Moscow of the new U.S. ambassador,

Robert Strauss, only recently designated to replace the retiring Matlock, and getting Baker off to a foreign ministers meeting at Brussels, Bush orchestrated the isolation of the rebels.

"We're making very clear to the coup plotters that there will not be normal relations with the United States as long as this illegal coup remains in effect," Bush said publicly, careful about being both firm and moderate. Clearly, by intervening in Soviet internal politics, the president was risking falling on the wrong side of the outcome. He reached at least a dozen allies whose support for Gorbachev undercut what little backing the plotters did have.[86]

"GORBACHEV BACK AS COUP FAILS, BUT YELTSIN GAINS NEW POWER," announced the *Times*'s six-column banner headline on the twenty-second. "Welcome back, Gorby!" read a newly installed billboard in downtown Detroit. "Next Time Vacation in Michigan."[87] Back at Walker's Point, a smiling, relaxed, but tired president in an open-collar long-sleeved sports shirt stood outside the house with four broadly grinning aides, Scowcroft, Sununu, Card, and Baker.

Bush, graciously but prematurely, said that Gorbachev has "certainly not been diminished by this at all."[88] Two days later, the president of the USSR, trying to retain credibility as a political force in the face of the onrushing Mr. Yeltsin, resigned as head of the Communist Party and disbanded its leadership.[89] The force that had ruled the Soviet Union for over seven decades was no more. Everything else that followed was quite logical. Succumbing to pressure from the American president, Gorbachev recognized the independence of the Baltic states, a formality Bush had extended four days earlier. By the end of the year, the Union of Soviet Socialist Republics had gone out of business.[90]

Even before the coup nudged events toward that denouement, a *Wall Street Journal* poll showed that Bush's leadership had made its mark at home. Nearly three-quarters of those surveyed said they were confident in Bush's "dealing with national security and foreign policy."[91] But, by wide agreement, when it came to domestic policy, he was, as Kenneth T. Walsh observed early on, "strangely ill at ease and reluctant to act decisively."[92] What that meant was not always clear. Over time it became more apparent that it was often not so much doing "something" as reflecting a specific point of view. On the issue of abortion, for example, perhaps the most emotional hot button issue, Bush's belief that the procedure should be legal in cases involving rape or saving the life of the mother reflected the mainstream of American public opinion. Fifty-three percent of respondents agreed that abortion should be legal under "certain circumstances." This opinion, taken in various Gallup surveys, hardly differed over time. Bush represented neither those activists at one extreme who wanted the administration to propose a constitutional amendment criminalizing abortion, nor those who believed that the best policy was one of laissez-faire.[93]

The ongoing debate through the months preceding the presidential election involved improving the economy. When the Gallup poll of registered

Democrats, released on September 3, 1991, produced a list of eleven key issues for the 1992 campaign, the economy "in general" led the list with 62 percent.[94] More Americans, in subsequent surveys, rated themselves as worse off than before. By March, a narrow majority, 51 percent, thought they were being hurt.[95] Approval of Bush's presidency spiralled downward, from the Desert Storm high of 89 percent, into the seventies, sixties, fifties, forties, and thirties by mid 1992, even, in late July and early August, touching 29 percent.[96]

As early as May of 1990, pollster Lou Harris had warned that the declining state of America's relative economic power was jeopardizing Bush's reelection prospects. Heavy coverage of foreign investments in the U.S. by such countries as Japan implied that America was falling behind them economically. During that spring, by 62 to 35 percent, according to Harris, voters lacked confidence in Bush's management of the economy. Surprisingly large numbers of respondents said they were willing to pay higher taxes to reduce the deficit, and there was concern, too, over the relative plight of the poor. Their average income had declined by 9 percent over the past ten years while that of the wealthy, reported Harris, had "soared by nineteen percent."[97] Harris, a Democrat, was seconded several months later by a Republican analyst, Kevin Phillips, who warned that the slumping economy "is likely to be the more decisive in the long run" and that "the economic dominoes could be tumbling and unemployment deepening even into 1991."[98] As with Saddam's saber-rattling and arms buildup during the 1980s, the warnings were plain.

In response, Lloyd Bentsen, at the helm of the Senate Finance Committee, proposed $5.8 billion for the expansion of unemployment insurance benefits. The Senate also passed a $123 billion highway bill designed to create jobs, and the Democratic leadership proposed cutting middle-income taxes and other steps to energize the economy. Appearing before the Senate Budget Committee on July 17, 1991, Dick Darman, speaking for the administration, deflected such needs with the assurance that the economy "is turning up."[99] He and Sununu also urged the president to sit tight. They warned that any stimulus package they might send to the Democratic Congress would be converted into a Democratic bill. The president himself kept denying that there was a recession.[100] Jack Kemp was almost alone among Republicans in urging a more aggressive approach.

Meanwhile, Attorney General Dick Thornburgh had resigned to run for the Senate from Pennsylvania in a special election, and Bush had put his own stature on the line by campaigning for him. Thornburgh's defeat by Senator Harris Wofford, an interim appointee, by the stunning margin of 57 to 43 percent, marked a loss to a Kennedy-era liberal, and was viewed by many as a referendum on the economy. When Dick Darman appeared on CBS-TV's *Face the Nation,* in December, even he admitted, "The economy is flat and we've got to get it going." The middle class, he suggested, ought to be targeted with a package they can perceive as fair.[101]

Domestic policy, as Bush's successor and predecessors had discovered, could incapacitate presidents. As the 1992 campaign year progressed, Bush continued to urge that the American people try something that had not been done during his adult political life: give the Republican party control over both the presidency and Congress.[102] But with a divided government, he presided helplessly over an economy that moved upward only in fits and starts. When, in early August, his economic adviser, Michael Boskin, brought news that unemployment had dropped by just one-tenth of a percentage point, the president, desperate to wave something "good" and eager to show that he "cared," decided to hold a news conference.[103] Other markers indicated that the economy was even weaker than first reported. The stock market retreated as the Federal Reserve failed to act to cut interest rates.[104] When things did edge upward, as they did in the final quarter of the year, the improvement was too late to influence the voting.

Globally, at least, Bush could exert presidential leadership in powerful ways to affect international commerce. He launched what he called the "Enterprise for the Americas" in 1990, an initiative aimed at lowering trade barriers with Latin America. In Detroit, on September 10, 1992, he unveiled his "Agenda for the American Renewal," an incentive formula, as he explained it, to "open new markets, prepare our people to work, strengthen our families, save and invest so that we can win." International trade would bring economic growth, and based on "an entrepreneurial capitalism that grows from the bottom up, not the top down."[105] On December 17, 1992, he and Prime Minister Mulroney, whose country had entered into a free trade agreement with the United States in 1987, joined President Salinas of Mexico in signing the North American Free Trade Agreement (NAFTA), which the Democratic-led Congress failed to ratify before Bush left office. NAFTA also served as a precedent for the later creation of the World Trade Organization.[106] The Bush presidency, by its very conservatism, had created designs for long-term growth, none of them very useful to convince the public that help was on the way, at least before the election.

But at home there was controversy. In the summer of 1991 Bush named Judge Clarence Thomas to the Supreme Court to replace retiring Justice Thurgood Marshall. An African-American conservative, Thomas's race and ideology made him an ideal candidate. The recommendation raised questions about his competence from both professional and lay groups, but nothing prepared the administration for the allegations of a law professor from Oral Roberts University in Tulsa, Oklahoma. Anita Hill, who had worked for Thomas at the Department of Education and then moved on with him to the Equal Employment Opportunity Commission, charged that, ten years before, she had been a victim of his sexual harassment. The sensational televised hearings that followed brought the nation explicit revelations but unsubstantiated charges. Most people, at the time, were not convinced. But the questioning of the star witness at Thomas's confirmation hearings featured such sharp cross-examination of Hill by several senators that public opinion, which originally tended to believe the nominee, sympathized more and more with her, which was where it stood by the fall of 1992.[107] Whatever gender gap had opened during the Reagan years had widened.

Bush's simultaneous concern about a primary election in Louisiana, where an ex-Klansman, David Duke, ran a strong race after declaring himself a Republican, gave him little choice but to go along with a compromise civil rights bill, one hardly different from the one he had vetoed the year before. This time, Bush did most of the compromising. "Where did the quotas go?" one Democrat scoffed during the House debate. "They swam upstream, as red herrings often do."[108]

He was hardly less embarrassed on civil rights a few months later over the acquittal of the police officers who were tried for the beating of Rodney King, and the rioting that followed in Los Angeles. The King situation was the problem of local government, and the jurisdiction belonged to the Los Angeles Police Department and its chief, Darryl Gates. And yet, it was an outrage; revolted by the original beatings, Bush now deplored the riots in the city's South Central district. "You see blacks going after Asians," he noted. "What does that have to do with Rodney King? It has to do with the turmoil in the ghetto."[109] Finally, and after being chided for his absence by H. Ross Perot, he made a personal tour of the area on a prescheduled trip to the city. As though to balance his actions with his own political needs, he carefully attributed the disturbances to the failure of the social programs of the 1960s. Bush, a social liberal on matters of race, too often seemed representative of enlightenment that belonged to an even earlier decade.[110]

In handling foreign affairs, however, he could make progress. He decided that the containment of Saddam ought to be but a first step toward a more general settlement for the Middle East.

As Jim Baker later put it, without a quick follow-through, there was fear that "the window of opportunity created by Desert Storm would slam shut out of inertia. Peace would be the loser, but American credibility and prestige would also suffer." So, he wrote in an April 6 memorandum to the president, "we owe it to ourselves and everyone else to make the effort."[111]

The president, long dismayed by Israel's continued occupation of the West Bank, had, as president, become increasingly determined to take on the issue despite the obstructions. If he did not act soon, while the diplomatic wheels were in gear, then "the ball will shift back to the domestic front, and we will be back to the old political game of who's up and who's down," with all those "loud voices of the 'Capitol Gang.'" His old annoyance with Israel and Shamir had turned into outright anger. "Israel rolled us," he wrote in early March. "They are very, very difficult in spite of the fact that they've been restrained" by conditions in the Middle East. But "we kicked Saddam Hussein and solved their security problem in the area," so now "they're going to have to move on the peace process." Shamir, with his request for new loans, was making "unreasonable demands." Recalling Phil Gramm's caution that "Jewish money is essential" for political fund-raising, Bush waved that off. He, for one, would do what "no president has done since Ike." He would "stand up for what is fair and right. They are never going to get peace in the Middle East without solving the Palestinian question," wrote the president. "I know it; they know it; the Arabs know it; the French and Europeans know it; and we're standing alone against reason a lot of times." If it came down to it, Bush added, "I'm perfectly prepared to defend Israel."[112]

The Israelis, standing fast on the "no land for peace" principle, felt the pressure deeply. So it was, for Baker, another round of shuttle diplomacy, and largely between Syria's Assad and Shamir. Finally, on August 1, after being, as Baker put it, "genuinely shocked, almost thunderstruck, and quite suspicious" at Assad's acceptance, Shamir went along with the concept of a regional peace conference. Bush and Baker had, as Clyde Haberman reported, liberated the Israelis "from the stigma of being the chief naysayer[s] of the Middle East," thereby shifting that onus to the Palestinians. Bush, they suspected, had obtained his first objective, freeing two long-captive Western hostages, which followed a few days after the Israeli consent. Israel's largest paper, *Yediot Aharonot,* saw fit to comment that "it was predictable. It was the handwriting on the wall, and yet it is impossible not to be astonished: we have been the bad guys in the hostage affair."[113] Equally predictable to Bush was William Safire's comment that "there is no greater obstacle to peace in the Middle East than George Bush's obsession with forcing Israel out of the West Bank."[114] Not until the end of October, after Assad had found reasons for delay, did the conference open at the Royal Palace in Madrid. One Democratic congressman hailed the event, which was televised, as "the dawn of a new age of peace." The hosts were Bush and Gorbachev.[115] The denouement was no quick settlement, not even by Middle Eastern standards. Baker had, from the beginning, warned that the talks were but a first step. In getting them jump-started, the administration's achievement was substantial. Unable, finally, to budge Shamir from insisting on expanding West Bank settlements on land won by Israel during the Six Day War, Bush finally did agree with Labor party successor, Yitzhak Rabin, on terms for a five-year package of loan guarantees. The road led eventually to an accord signed by the most improbable of soul mates, Rabin and Yasir Arafat.

When the reelection effort finally did get under way it became the worst-run campaign in the memory of every key participant, lacking the skill of a Lee Atwater, the savvy of a Roger Ailes (whom Bush managed to consult surreptitiously, away from the eyes of the peeping press), and the smarts of a John Sununu, who had finally been dumped in December and replaced as chief of staff with the very nice but unprepared Sam Skinner. Most of all, the campaign, given a candidate for whom slugging it out was demeaning of his high office, lacked central direction, planning, and coordination. Bush, hesitant about placing himself out front to begin with, was a victim of poor coordination offered by the troika placed in charge, pollster Bob Teeter, money-raiser Bob Mosbacher, and Fred Malek, the ex-Nixon aide and wealthy former Marriott Hotel executive. A careful observer of Bush's fortunes, Brian Mulroney, lamented the president's failure to replace them. Bush's problem was "a big heart and a sense of loyalty." He had trouble "doing things a politician has to do." He was the perfect example of the problem of a "nice guy" in politics.[116] Lyn Nofziger, who never worried about letting "nice guys" get in the way of things, regretted the absence of Reagan people at the top level. "None of them knew what they were doing," said the consultant.[117]

It was, in short, a disaster; and it was a disaster that ran head-on into the efforts led by a skilled practitioner at the art of campaigning, the governor of Arkansas. Clinton relished the fight, thought of himself as "the comeback kid," and performed with zest uncharacteristic of the president. To make matters even worse, compounding the disorganization and the effects of the dragging economy, to say nothing of the opprobrium of having broken the tax pledge (although, in early 1992, he said that reneging had been a mistake, a comment some thought only worsened the situation), Ross Perot decided to run for president.

Perot, entering the race largely for his own ego and to fulfill his vendetta against Bush, appeared as a fresh alternative for those disillusioned by Democratic and Republican politics. He had no established party machinery behind him, just endless amounts of money and a self-engineered, grassroots reputation as a multibillionaire animated only by pure patriotism. Perot was a self-made tycoon who had built a company called Electronics Data Systems, sold it to General Motors for a neat profit, and had become one of the richest men in the country. His almost legendary derring-do was solidified after his attempt to rescue some of his employees held hostage by the Iranians. His ability to take charge contrasted sharply with Jimmy Carter's attempts to deal with Iran and Bush's with a hostile Congress and struggling economy. When, in February, Perot announced on Larry King's CNN interview program that he was ready to run if the people "wanted" him, the response was virtually unheard of for a third-party candidate in American history. Computer hackers sallied forth with their electronic horses along the Internet, "Perot is coming! Perot is coming!" the first modern-age candidate to rise from digitalized origins. His appeal cut into all the traditional remnants of the mid-American electorate, plus new-age professionals, ultimately taking, in the analysis of later experts, two voters from Bush for every one from Clinton, who, when the Democratic primaries finally ended, easily won the nomination to become Bush's principle opponent.

For three months, Perot's standing, fueled by his "volunteers" and genuine grassroots enthusiasts, gave him polling figures that put him alongside Clinton and Bush. Able to endlessly spend his own money, unrestricted by campaign financing regulations, his presence shocked the established order. He bought more experienced consultants. Ed Rollins (although his wife still worked for Bush) went over to him and had a short, unhappy experience, as did Carter's ex–chief of staff, Hamilton Jordan. Perot's eccentricity was confirmed when, confronted by skeptical and even jeering voters, he suddenly announced the withdrawal of his candidacy in July.

Clinton was the immediate beneficiary of a boost in the polls. Bush, running against ratings that reflected the economic ills—and, worst of all, his seeming inability as the wealthy, patriarchal establishment man to show, in the words of the governor of Arkansas, that he, too, could "feel their pain"— struggled to catch up.

His health, however, caused additional worries. Millions of TV viewers were shocked in January when they saw him collapse and throw up on the lap of the Japanese prime minister as he prepared to deliver a luncheon address during a trade trip to Tokyo. Dr. Lee's reassurances that the president was "the healthiest guy you could have" did not still whispers about his fitness.[118] Despite what Bush had said about doing "whatever it takes to win," many who saw him on television thought that he seemed weary, if not ill. His rhetoric began to betray his frustration. When the Democratic convention chose the ticket of Clinton and Senator Al Gore, a Tennessee moderate, Bush became more scornful.

Bush, once more the victim of rehashed unconfirmed allegations about Jennifer Fitzgerald in the tabloids, labored to pull back into the GOP-defecting white males, the heart of the Reaganite Democratic constituency. His open appeals to the religious right, which dated back to vice presidential days, as well as to the more traditional party base, well-to-do conservatives and small-town Protestants, who supported him in such matters as reducing federal regulations and lowering capital gains taxes, were generally successful. He had by then, however, broken faith. The budget agreement, with acceptance of additional taxes, more than weakened his credibility. It destroyed the respect he had worked so hard to develop with the very people he had had to spend much of his career cultivating, the vein of deep Republican economic conservatism.

He, like Clinton, worked at convincing the sidelined Perot to throw his support, along with his followers', in his direction. From a telephone at the Baker ranch in Wyoming, he futilely pleaded for backing from the man who was relishing cutting him down. Then, another surprise: Perot, just as abruptly as he had withdrawn, announced his reentry into the race.

The Bush forces went after Americans disillusioned not only with the economy but the state of modern morality. Societal values, traditional concepts of home and family, found expression in the vague phrase "family values," all the more readily because society was, indeed, undergoing a radical transformation. Dan Quayle got an enthusiastic response from conservatives when he hit upon the idea of excoriating the contributions to moral decline that many associated with the mass media. In his case, it was the TV sitcom *Murphy Brown,* which portrayed an unwed but professionally successful single mother.

Bush, in trying to mobilize that constituency, asked Craig Fuller, who had been his vice presidential chief of staff, to organize their nominating convention at Houston's Astrodome.[119] Fuller pitched the tone toward a celebration of traditional values blended with laissez-faire economics. He added a touch of populism by including right-wing columnist, TV personality, and former Nixon-era speechwriter Pat Buchanan. Buchanan's independent effort to counter Bush during the preconvention primaries had exposed a hard core of some 30 percent of Americans annoyed by what they regarded as Bush's indifference to the plight of ordinary Americans, to which his background made him particularly vulnerable. Buchanan openly played xenophobic themes, bashing gays, liberals, and radicals among the Democrats. He called their convention a "great masquerade ball" with the greatest "exhibition of cross-dressing in American history," and blasted past Democratic leadership under McGovern, Carter, Mondale, and Dukakis. The crowd loved it. "Buchanan Brigades" waved high their placards as he contrasted such "malcontents" with "one of the great statesmen of modern times, Ronald Reagan." Bill Clinton and Al Gore, he said, "represent the most progay and prolesbian ticket in history." Then, winding down his demagogic oratory, he declared, "There is a religious war going on in the country. It is a cultural war as critical to the kind of nation we shall be as the cold war itself. . . . Take back our country. God bless you, and God bless America." The thunderous ovation, chanting and jumping, filled the Astrodome. Buchanan had roused the heart of the Republican right, which had not enough votes to win the primaries but was sufficient to take over the party's core; this was the force Bush had been skirting and trying to hold at arm's length for most of his political career.

There was also no doubt that the Bush renomination convention was, alas, a Reagan affair. The delegates swooned when The Gipper spoke standing firm, strong, and looking ruddy, betraying nothing of the Alzheimer's disease that was already affecting his system. He had all the old touches, everything the crowd had loved and missed. "Tonight is a very special night for me," he said, using a familiar Reagan one-liner. "At my age, eighty-one, every night is a special night." Recalling the cold war triumph over the Russians, he said, "America is the moral force that defeated communism." Finally, as though he would never get there, as signs were waved with such messages as STOP THE LIBERAL MEDIA/LYNCH MOB, he declared a strong endorsement of the incumbent: "We need George Bush."

Bush, after a strongly hard-line speech by the vice presidential candidate's wife Marilyn, and a tempered, well-received one on family values by Barbara, gave his acceptance address. Introduced by Bob Dole, he immediately made a point to praise his running mate, a reaffirmation of Quayle's place on the ticket that he had made that afternoon. Tall and handsome in his black suit, using the TelePrompTer without glasses, he also addressed himself to rumors about his health. "I feel fine," he said firmly and convincingly.

He bragged a bit about his foreign policy accomplishments, especially the more recent Middle Eastern peace talks. The cheers were loudest when he reminded them that he had "locked a tyrant [Saddam Hussein] in the prison of his own country." Clinton, whom he had long since considered a "sleaze-ball," contemptuous of his having "dodged" the draft in the 1960s and teaming up with antiwar, anti-American demonstrators while a student in London, he called, "the leader of the Arkansas National Guard." (One delegate wore a button that said, "If Hillary Can't Trust Him, How Can We?") Evoking the stature of his high office, and reminding them of the dignity with which he had provided leadership, he vowed never to "let politics interfere with a foreign policy decision. I will do what is right for the national security of America, and that is a pledge from my heart."

The postconvention bounce was not enough, even with Jim Baker recalled to take over from Skinner as campaign director. He should, everybody thought, have been there from the start. In nearly mid October, the Gallup poll showed the Bush-Quayle ticket fully fifteen points behind Clinton-Gore, with Perot and his running mate, retired Adm. James Stockdale, trailing well to the rear.[120] Throughout, Bush remained convinced that the American people would, in the end, reward him for his patriotism, dedication, and spotless leadership.

He had trouble imagining it otherwise. He had, after all, decided to run again because, really, he had no choice. That was what you do for your country. You give it the best you have, serve it honorably, and, as in war, do not flinch from your duty. As he flew back to the White House on a Thursday in October, he realized how much he would, if he had to, miss the tranquility, peace, and joy of the retreat in the Catoctins. "I love my little office there," he said into his tape recorder, "and I love Aspen Lodge where I can sit and relax and enjoy life, and there are no press conferences anywhere near."[121]

He could see, from above, the city of Washington sparkling on a beautiful, clear, cool day. Visibility extended almost all the way to Andrews Air Force Base. The Washington Monument looked beautiful, and the Lincoln Memorial, even with the scaffolding around it, was "fantastic." Flags were flying, he saw from the air. One memorialized POWs, and Bush's mind went back "to that crazy Ross Perot." He watched, as though he had never seen before, perhaps conscious of the need to hold on to the vision, the sight of the decoy helicopters turning past the Washington Monument, and even saw people waving from the green below.

"It is a beautiful city, a city to which I probably won't return if I do not win this election." But, he thought, reconsidering, "that's all right—we'll just shift gears. I still have this quiet confidence of winning and I believe we're going to do it," although there was concern about Perot, "a real spoiler."[122]

In all, that October, three presidential debates were held, on the eleventh, fifteenth, and nineteenth. The second, a "town hall meeting" affair in Richmond, played right to Clinton's strength. He waded into the audience, microphone in hand, taking questions and conversing like "just plain folks." Bush, asked by a young woman about whether the national debt hurt him personally, looked puzzled, uncomprehending until he finally realized that she really meant "recession," so his response seemed tempered and lame. Later, while Perot was holding forth, Bush glanced at his wristwatch. One camera caught that, and the director put it on the air. The image seemed to confirm everything: he was impatient, bored, uninterested in the job. The debates did even less good than the convention.[123]

Bush, working up the juices that flowed against his better nature, finally called Clinton a "bozo." A couple of right-wing congressmen, Bob Dornan and Randy Cunningham, both from California, suggested trying to find out just what Clinton was doing when, as an Oxford student, he went to Moscow, implying he had contact with the KGB. The ugliness followed the desperation.

Bush's past activities, too, were being questioned. By dribs and drabs that fall, more information came out about the Iran-contra affair—that he had had a secret meeting with Aviram Nir, that he knew about the arms dealings. "Who *was* in the loop?" was asked once again. Word came that the special prosecutor, Lawrence Walsh, had completed his investigation.

Tracking polls were, at the same time, showing a pickup; maybe they were catching on about Clinton; maybe there was a scent of better times, with the economy gradually gaining. Maybe it wasn't too late. One point a day was not bad. "5 MORE DAYS TO GO!!!" said Barbara's diary entry, which also noted hearing about a CNN poll claiming that "we were within a point of Clinton."[124] Other surveys even had them in a dead heat, although CBS had Clinton still ten points ahead.[125]

Until then, the race was perceived as relatively close. All that changed quickly, however, when Lawrence E. Walsh, chose to drop his bombshell. A one-count indictment was entered against former Defense Secretary Caspar Weinberger, but the significance to Bush involved evidence of his presence in the secretary's office on January 7, 1986. Not only did this appear to confirm that the then-vice president supported the sale of antitank missiles to rescue the hostages, but as Robert Pear wrote somewhat hyperbolically in *The New York Times,* the information provided the "clearest indication yet that Mr. Bush was more familiar with the terms of the arms sale than he has acknowledged."[126]

Why wait until the Friday before the elections? Bush always thought it was politics pure and simple. The "more generous" view at the White House was that Walsh was trying to strengthen his legal position for use against Weinberger at a trial.[127] Bush didn't believe it, although he later found out through Griffin Bell that Walsh had not acted according to "some grand design."[128] It hardly mattered.

What he did know was that the special prosecutor had precipitously killed his momentum. As Fitzwater later put it, "We lost Friday night's news, Saturday night's news, and the Sunday talk shows," and that was it.[129] Bush, defying the flu and a cold, went right on campaigning, even doing a full ninety minutes on *Larry King Live.* Yet, in those closing days, one perceptive reporter got the impression that, in reality, Bush "wanted to spend his time the way most men do who are sixty-eight and have the money to indulge themselves after a long career." He was, wrote Russ Hodge, "tired of pretending he was happy to be with that governor or this congressional candidate and to have to listen to . . . the out-of-tune high school marching band. He wanted to play with his grandchildren, race his boat, and play golf, and enjoy himself." In short, Hodge added, "with the cold war ended and with the Gulf War behind him he felt his mission had been fulfilled. . . . He didn't feel comfortable in a world where an interview with MTV was smart tactics and particularly when the other dog fought back so well."[130]

He also, at that point, got a note from Richard Nixon. From his office in New Jersey, Nixon faxed the copy of a letter that he had received on Election Day from Thomas E. Dewey thirty-two years earlier. "If you are defeated," it advised, "pay no attention to the Monday morning quarterbacks. Everybody knows how to conduct a campaign better after the event. No one could have worked harder with higher fidelity to duty and integrity; no one could have done more for Party and Country. You have earned the best and the nation will always be in your debt."[131]

The final Gallup trial heat, released on the eve of the election, showed Clinton-Gore winning with 44 percent, Bush-Quayle with 36, and 14 percent for Perot-Stockdale.[132] Barbara, campaigning through Iowa, North Dakota, and Colorado with Marvin, sensed defeat but tried to shake it off. On election morning, back from New Jersey and home in Houston, Bush told her he thought he could still make it. By afternoon, however, their son George informed them that exit polls showed that it was all over.[133] Of some small solace, he took 50 percent of the three-way vote in Kennebunkport, which was better than another patrician, FDR, used to do in his native county.

On election eve, there was another poll, revealing the problem for which Bush afterward blamed himself.[134] Although the economy had been moving upward, with the last quarter showing a 3.5 percent growth rate, three-quarters of Americans thought the national economy was in bad shape.[135] Blame fell upon the media for its intense coverage of economic negatives. Subsequent analyses made at the Joan Shorenstein Barone Center on the Press, Politics, and Public Policy at Harvard University's Kennedy School of Government, the Center for Media and Public Affairs, and drawing from the Times-Mirror Center on the People and the Press, concurred that campaign reportage was markedly harder on Bush than on Clinton.[136] Examining the pattern of public responses to the economy, however, suggests that it was less Bush's failure to get credit for the economic upturn than the public's readiness to grant to Clinton and the Democrats the ability to improve *their* future prospects. For a recession that had lasted since mid 1990, the turnover in consumer confidence was remarkable. The outcome was hardly confirmed before a rush of consumer confidence developed. The lag between statistics and responses was unusually sharp. Report after report showed the same thing. The rebound, reported John Berry in the *Washington Post,* was "triggered by the end of the campaign."[137] Clinton had promised change. It had long since been axiomatic in American politics for the public to trust Republicans more on foreign policy and Democrats to handle pocketbook issues. It was no different in 1992. Bush's problem may well have been beyond the reach of his ability to fine-tune perceptions. His party had limited credibility when it came to economic optimism. As *Newsweek* put it, "Americans had grown weary of twelve years of Republican rule, symbolized by a president who seemed insensitive to their bread-and-butter concerns."[138] Bush's mission to strengthen the long-term health of the U.S. in a global economy was not their priority. As though to underscore that point, a *New York Times/CBS News* poll, released at year's end, showed that half of all respondents thought that the economy would improve under Clinton.

The final electoral vote count gave Clinton 357 to 168 for Bush and none for Perot. The distribution of the popular vote percentages was 43-38-19, arithmetic that suggests the possibly decisive presence of the third-party candidate in the final outcome. The Connecticut Yankee did best in the South and in the heartland of rural America, from the Appalachian high-lands through the Great Plains, winning most heavily in the most sparsely populated counties. In the Senate, after a special election in December, the party lineup remained unchanged for the 103rd Congress. Republicans picked up one seat and gained ten in the House, a modest score after their expectations and the scandals that cast so much popular disfavor on con-gressmen. Exit polls taken by the Voter Research Survey showed no evidence of a shift back toward liberalism.[139]

Little more than two weeks after the election, George flew to Greenwich with Doro to be with his mother at her home on Pheasant Lane. She had had a stroke and slipped into semiconsciousness. He sat and held her hand for several hours and told her that they loved her. "She knew," wrote Barbara.[140] As she lay on a pillow, he saw her as "tiny, with her mouth open, fighting, fighting hard for every breath, and then suddenly she would be quiet." She had with her, near her bed, her frayed Bible. As he sat sobbing, he saw close by notes he had written to her from Andover and a happy-birthday card sent when he was eighteen. Burton Lee said the prognosis was not good. She would, he said, be in heaven in a few hours. The president hugged her and told her he loved her, and so did Doro. Then he had to return to Washington to attend a credentials ceremony for new ambassadors. While he was there, she died in Greenwich at 5:05 P.M. at the age of ninety-one. He knew because, as he sat with an ambassador's wife and her two boys, Patty Presock walked over to whisper to Bar. Bush could read her lips and knew something had happened. He finished saying his good-bye to the lady, "and then Bar came and told me, 'Your mum has died.' " She was, he dictated, "the beacon in our family—the center, the candle around which all the moths fluttered—she was there, the strength, the center, the power but never arrogance, just love was her strength, kindness her main virtue. How many times she taught us to be kind to the other guy, never hurt feelings, love."[141] The funeral at Christ Church was private, and she was buried next to her husband at Putnam Cemetery in Greenwich.[142]

It hurt, and it hurt that much more coming right after his defeat. Colin Powell joined the Bushes, with his wife Alma, at Camp David the weekend right after the election. As the two men walked along the path ahead of the women, Bush said, softly, "It hurts. It really hurts to be rejected." How in the world could the American people have chosen Bill Clinton over him? He never could understand.[143] When Brian Mulroney joined him at Aspen Lodge before he gave way to his successor, Bush told him that he had been "outfoxed by a very shrewd politician, Clinton." He regretted not having put his campaign team in place earlier, and, most of all, his failure to respond more quickly and more dramatically to the downturn in the economy. He should have known, he should have known. He remembered that Quayle had told him, as early as June after a campaign trip to California, that people thought the administration did not care. How wrong that was! But he failed to soothe their cares. He was, however, pleased that he had led his country in the right direction. He had helped end the cold war, led the coalition in the Persian Gulf, and maintained solid relationships in Europe with the Soviet breakup and the reunification of Germany, which became official on October 3, 1990.[144]

He did tell Powell that he was upset at the way things were now moving. There was, after the election, the breaking scandal about Bush aides searching through the passport files at State to find negative material about Clinton and Perot. They wanted so much to confirm what those California right-wingers were hinting—that Clinton must have consorted with Soviet agents in Moscow during the Vietnam War—but they couldn't find a thing. They behaved stupidly, Lawrence Walsh said, but none broke the law. Jim Baker, upset and feeling responsible as secretary of state, offered his resignation to the president, which, of course, Bush refused. "Trying to link Jim Baker, the most honorable guy, to having done anything wrong," said Bush, "I think is absolutely absurd."[145]

He told Powell and all his senior advisers he did not want to leave president-elect Clinton with the ongoing mess in Somalia, where tribal warfare and individual gangsters were doing their best to destroy United Nations efforts to distribute desperately needed food and other supplies. UN Secretary General Boutros Boutros-Ghali came in on November 24 and read Bush a letter pleading for help. The authorities in that miserable African country were competing with ordinary people for anything of value, and the outcome was more often decided by armed threats and killings. "Looting and banditry are rife," it went on to say. "In essence, humanitarian supplies have become the basis of an otherwise nonexistent Somali economy," with delivery of food impossible. The Pakistanis were already there with 500 troops. The UN needed U.S. help.[146]

Bush sent Larry Eagleburger to follow through with Boutros-Ghali. He faced his NSC clearly determined that Americans had to do something about it. General Powell, confirming that there could be an "exit strategy" to keep that, too, from becoming another Vietnam, outlined a plan to send in 28,000 Americans.[147]

"Why can't the civilized world do something about it, you know?" Powell said later, after his retirement. "If these were not poor black folks in Africa," he remembered telling the NSC, "you guys would have done something by now." The State Department was sensitive, but the Pentagon, worried again about troop commitments, was holding back, the nature of the bureaucracy. We will, we had told the UN, lend our good offices, "use our aircraft, C-130 transports, to move food into Somalia from neighboring Kenya and we will dispatch a group of about fifteen or sixteen C-130 airplanes, and about 1,600 troops may also get involved." But the problem was not so easily avoided.[148]

Bush did not want to leave the decision to Clinton. He also wanted to leave office on the note of doing the right thing, in a noble cause, a mission of mercy, undertaken as an "act of idealism," as a student of the affair has concluded.[149] In early January, the outgoing president traveled to Somalia to see it for himself, just as he had done in Panama and Saudi Arabia.

Reporter Fred Barnes said on National Public Radio at the start of the new year that Bush's intervention in Somalia is the most likely postelection event to be remembered because it was the first such move for humanitarian purposes.[150] It all was working, Powell added privately, and "we were, within about a month, in the process of setting up security around the whole country" and planning on leaving and turning the whole thing over to the United Nations in the spring. "It was a functioning operation. The starvation was over," and the mission was accomplished. "It was at that point, though," Powell added with obvious disgust at what he recalled as a breakdown of discipline and policing, "that the Clinton administration decided that, 'Gee, we've never had a nice little colonial country like this one before. Let's frisk this one. Whee!' Multilateral assertiveness, and all kinds of fuzzy liberal ideas, and it was a disaster. And then, when it blew up in their face, they ran." Powell regretted that he had not been sufficiently persuasive in getting "what we were doing reversed and getting the hell out."[151]

Bush also found himself under increasing pressure to help bolster the UN position in Bosnia, where the situation at Sarajevo was deteriorating. That was, during the final days of his presidency, far too multifaceted, far more involved with multilateralism, and an even more daunting sinkhole with respect to risking American lives. He was, though, on the brink of intervening in Iraq during his final days. As Saddam, defying the terms of the armistice, moved missiles into areas patrolled by U.S. jets, Bush once again unleashed air strikes. The Iraqis backed down.

He had, by then, in a bold and defiant final move, pardoned Caspar Weinberger, Elliott Abrams, George Shultz, Bud McFarlane and two other ex-

CIA officials. It was, an adviser said, "a close call," a risky move, "not morally risky, but risky in the cosmic sense of his place in history." Nancy Reagan acknowledged that she had stopped her husband from doing the same for his people. Jeffrey Toobin, who had worked for Walsh as a prosecutor, understood why Reagan did not act. "He was unburdened by an ethic of sacrifice," the lawyer explained. "For all his surface good nature, he was fundamentally ungenerous to those around him." Bush was not that way. He believed, explained Fred Barnes, "in loyalty down, not just loyalty up."[152]

Bush also produced what few around him knew he had, excerpts from diary entries, specifically those related to Iran-contra. Turning them over to the independent counsel investigating the matter, Lawrence E. Walsh, the segments, which were also published in the *Washington Post* and *The New York Times*, confirmed his loyalty to Reagan.[153]

He took care of other final obligations. He spent his last weekend at Camp David hosting, over cocktails, the National Security Council, justices of the Supreme Court, and two of president-elect Clinton's people, Vernon Jordan and Warren Christopher, who were helping with the transition. Brian Mulroney, who was also there, noted a contrast with the way things were done in his own country. It would have been extraordinary, he remarked, for an outgoing prime minister to have included his successor's aides at that kind of a reception.[154] Also present was a country singer, George Strait of Texas, another good friend of George Bush.

He said his good-byes during that last morning in the White House, after a final walk around the grounds watching over his dogs, Ranger and Millie. He thanked his horseshoe team, "the guys to whom I feel so very, very close." It was especially hard to leave the staff, Patty Presock and all the gang. "I love her very much," he wrote. She exuded a love and goodness. He took one last took at the Washington Monument through the White House window. The day was crystal clear and he could see six of the many flags around it. He left a note in the desk for Bill Clinton. "I don't want it to be overly dramatic, but I did want him to know that I would be rooting for him." He felt, he thought, the "same sense of wonder and majesty about this office today as I did when I first walked in here. I've tried to keep it; I've tried to serve here with no taint or dishonor; no conflict of interest; nothing to sully this beautiful place and this job I've been privileged to hold." He also had, that morning, his last briefing from the CIA team.[155]

After President Clinton had taken the oath and delivered his address, George and Barbara Bush, joined by Dan and Marilyn Quayle, got onto the helicopter to Andrews Air Force Base; then, for the ex–First Family, it was on to Houston, where George Bush looked forward to working in his new office and living in a rented house until his home went up in the Tanglewood section, ironically on the very same small lot the press had been skeptical about for years.

He had, at least, the satisfaction of seeing how quickly his approval ratings rebounded, almost as though the public were saying that they, too, were sorry. The American people had, as political analyses then showed, not really rebelled against Republicans or the direction of government toward which Bush had tried to lead them. They just wanted someone with more obvious empathy, and Clinton had promised that. Gallup's new figures also showed George and Barbara Bush heading the new list of "most-admired" Americans. Bush, watching those postelection numbers, remained confident that history would be on his side.[156]

Notes

BGSU: Bowling Green State University, Ohio
BPMP: Bush Presidential Materials Project, Bush Presidential Library, College Station, Texas
GRFL: Gerald R. Ford Library, Ann Arbor, Michigan
LAT: Los Angeles Times
LBJL: Lyndon B. Johnson Library, Austin, Texas
NPMP: Nixon Presidential Materials Project, Library of Congress, College Park, Maryland
NYT: The New York Times
OGB: Office of George Bush, Houston
OIC: Office of the Independent Counsel
TGP: The Gallup Poll
WP: Washington Post
WSJ: The Wall Street Journal

PROLOGUE

[1]Polly Whittell, "On Board with George Bush," *Motorboat & Sailing*, March 1988, p. 122.
[2]Norman Baxter, *Houston Post*, October 4, 1981.
[3]John Yang, "Bush on Vacation," *WP,* August 16, 1991.
[4]George Bush, with Victor Gold, *Looking Forward: An Autobiography* (New York: Bantam Books, 1988), p. 27.
[5]Ibid., p. 29.

CHAPTER ONE

[1]Steve Lohr, *NYT,* July 5, 1988. Burke's Peerage, then run from London by a transplant from Baltimore, Maryland, enjoyed confirming the genetic superiority of royalty, a biological attribute that the genealogical enterprise also associated with the American presidency. The head of the enterprise, Harold Brooks-Baker, a self-appointed expert on the aristocracy, has traced the lineages of all American presidents and royal families from all over the world. Mr. Brooks-Baker claimed that "the genes or chromosomes for leaders come forward whether it's kings or presidents. You cannot hold back the genes." Asked about the possible royal antecedents of Michael Dukakis, George Bush's opponent in the 1988 presidential election, he replied, "The son of a Greek immigrant—the chance of getting very far with him is remote."
[2]Steve Lohr, *NYT,* July 5, 1988. Subsequent genealogical examinations done by Burke's about President Bill Clinton found similar origins. They may, in fact, be related, claimed Brooks-Baker in 1992, saying his researchers had established common ancestors for the two men in the English village of Gotham, about ninety miles north of London. Of course, Brooks-Baker explained, "in small towns in England several hundreds of years ago—we're talking about a hamlet, not a town—every person was related. They couldn't travel very far, so they had to marry among themselves." While he could offer no documentary evidence, his analysis was that the Bushes and Clintons were "prominent landowners. Bush had more relations in the minor aristocracy than Clinton. But they were both very, very similar—minor landed farmers with large families." Both could be traced back to Simon de Montford, one of King Henry III's soldier-statesmen who lived from 1208 to 1265 and married the king's sister Eleanor. "He tried to wrest power from the king to secure a more democratic government but after he was defeated and killed in battle, his body was cut into hundreds of pieces and sent around the country to show what happened to people who didn't agree with their sovereign." Bush and Clinton were, according to Burke's Peerage, related to Henry III and several other medieval monarchs, such as King Robert I of France. A linear genealogical progression could then be drawn through Davy Crockett and three American presidents, Andrew Jackson, William Henry Harrison, and Benjamin Harrison. "Beyond any shadow of doubt," proclaimed Brooks-Baker, "Governor Clinton is top of the genealogical pool. The leadership genes that have been submerged for years have at last come forward." (Associated Press, "Presidential Genealogy," October 1, 1992, and "Britain-Presidential Pedigrees," October 22, 1992)
[3]George Bush, with Victor Gold, *Looking Forward*, p. 28; Fitzhugh Green, *George Bush: An Intimate Portrait* (New York: Hippocrene Press, 1991), p. 19; interviews with Louis Walker, June 6, 1995, and Nancy Bush Ellis, November 12, 1992.
[4]Stevens Institute of Technology, PR Newswire, November 9, 1988; *NYT* obituary, February 9, 1948.
[5]Interview with Nancy Bush Ellis, September 16, 1993.
[6]Ibid.
[7]Stevens Institute of Technology, PR Newswire, November 9, 1988.
[8]Interview with Nancy Bush Ellis, September 16, 1993.
[9]Prescott S. Bush, Columbia Oral History Project, interviewed by John T. Mason Jr., 1966.
[10]Interview with Phillip K. Allen, January 16, 1992.
[11]Green, *Bush*, pp. 6–7; interview with Nancy Bush Ellis, November 12, 1992.
[12]Prescott S. Bush, Columbia Oral History Research Office, interviewed by John T. Mason Jr., 1966, at BPMP.
[13]Interview with Elliott Vose, December 2, 1992.

[14]Green, *Bush*, p. 2.
[15]Interviews with Prescott S. Bush by John T. Mason Jr. for the Eisenhower Project, Oral History Research Office, Columbia University, 1977, at BPMP.
[16]Nancy Bush Ellis to author, September 9, 1993, and Jonathan Bush to author, September 10, 1993.
[17]Prescott S. Bush, Columbia Oral History Research Office, interviewed by John T. Mason Jr., 1966.
[18]Interview with Nancy Bush Ellis, September 16, 1993.
[19]Prescott S. Bush, Columbia Oral History Research Office, interviewed by John T. Mason Jr., 1966.
[20]"Mrs. Bush's New Life," *Connecticut Life,* May 4, 1961.
[21]Barry Bearak, "Team Player Bush: A Yearning to Serve," *LAT,* November 22, 1987.
[22]Interview with Prescott Bush Jr., January 14, 1994.
[23]George Plimpton, "Congressman Born and Bred," *Sports Illustrated,* January 2, 1989, p. 144; George Bush quoted as recollecting the incident, in *Greenwich Time,* November 20, 1992; interview with Prescott Bush Jr., January 14, 1994.
[24]Green, *Bush,* p. 16.
[25]Ann Devroy, "Dorothy Walker Bush Dies at Age 91," *WP,* November 20, 1992.
[26]Interview with Nancy Bush Ellis, November 12, 1992.
[27]"Mrs. Bush's New Life," *Connecticut Life,* May 4, 1961.
[28]Joe Hyams, *Flight of the Avenger: George Bush at War* (New York: Berkeley Books, 1992), p. 17.
[29]George Bush, with Victor Gold, *Looking Forward* (New York: Bantam Books, 1988), pp. 28–29. Despite Bush's claim that the nickname belonged to his childhood, old acquaintances continued to use it long afterward, including former Yale classmates. See, for example, a letter from Lud Ashley to Bush, January 8, 1960, Thomas Ludlow Ashley Papers, MS-159, Center for Archival Collections. BGSU.
[30]Interview with Louis Walker, June 6, 1995.
[31]Prescott S. Bush, Columbia Oral History Research Office, interviewed by John T. Mason, Jr., 1966.
[32]Rudy Abramson, *Spanning the Century: The Life of Averell Harriman, 1891–1986* (New York: Morrow, 1992), p. 197.
[33]Walter Isaacson and Evan Thomas, *The Wise Men: Six Friends and the World They Made* (New York: A Touchstone Book, 1988), pp. 111–12.
[34]Ibid., p. 112.
[35]Prescott S. Bush, Columbia Oral History Research Office, interviewed by John T. Mason Jr., 1966, at BPMP.
[36]Press Release, December 26, 1952, Box 3, Prescott S. Bush Papers, University of Connecticut at Storrs.
[37]Darwin Payne, *Initiative in Energy: Dresser Industries, Inc., 1880–1978* (New York: Simon & Schuster, 1979), p. 10.
[38]Kevin Lahart, *Financial World,* May 17, 1988, p. 32.
[39]Prescott S. Bush, Columbia Oral History Research Office, interviewed by John T. Mason Jr., 1966, at BPMP.
[40]Payne, *Initiative in Energy,* p. 232.
[41]Roy Rowan, "Welcome to the Megalopolis, 1920–1989," in *Greenwich: An Illustrated History* (Greenwich, CT: The Historical Society of the Town of Greenwich, 1990), p. 79.
[42]John S. Sweeney, "George Bush Slept Here . . . And Here," *Greenwich Time,* March 13, 1988.
[43]Microfiche of 1938 map found in the Greenwich Public Library.
[44]John S. Sweeney, "George Bush Slept Here . . . And Here," *Greenwich Time,* March 13, 1988.
[45]Interview with Prescott Bush Jr., January 14, 1994.

CHAPTER TWO

[1]John Cheever, "The Swimmer," *The Stories of John Cheever* (Alfred A. Knopf: New York, 1978), p. 605.
[2]Interview with Nancy Bush Ellis, November 12, 1992.
[3]Ibid.
[4]Jonathan Bush, as quoted in Barry Bearak, *LAT,* November 22, 1987.
[5]Interview with George Upson Warren, January 29, 1992.
[6]Interviews with Nancy Bush Ellis, November 12, 1992, and Alexander Chodaczek Jr., October 4, 1993.
[7]Prescott S. Bush, Columbia Oral History Research Office, interviewed by John T. Mason Jr., 1966, at BPMP.
[8]Remarks of Moderator George Griswold, October 14, 1958, typescript in the Greenwich Public Library. Highlights of action taken by the Representative Town Meeting as listed in the preface of *Greenwich: An Illustrated History* (Greenwich, CT: The Historical Society of Greenwich, 1990).
[9]Timothy Noah, "Old Bland-Dad," *The New Republic,* April 3, 1989, p. 18.
[10]Interview with George Upson Warren, January 29, 1992.
[11]Confidential interview, June 21, 1993.
[12]Interview with Elliott Vose, December 2, 1992; Barbara Bush, *Barbara Bush: A Memoir* (New York: Scribner, 1994), p. 31.
[13]Interview with Mary Walker by Esther H. Smith, April 26, 1991, Greenwich Public Library Oral History Project.
[14]Suzy T. Kane, "What the Gulf War Reveals About George Bush's Childhood," *The Journal of Psychohistory,* Fall 1992, p. 154.
[15]Interview with George Upson Warren, January 29, 1992.
[16]Noah, "Old Bland-Dad," p. 18; Randall Rothenberg, *NYT,* March 6, 1988.
[17]Sidney Blumenthal, *Pledging Allegiance: The Last Campaign of the Cold War* (New York: HarperCollins, 1990), p. 56.

[18]Hyams, *Avenger,* p. 28; Roy Reed, "George Bush On the Move," *New York Times Magazine,* February 10, 1980, p. 54.

[19]Richard Cohen, *WP,* October 18, 1992.

[20]Interview with Nancy Bush Ellis, November 12, 1992.

[21]Barry Bearak, *LAT,* November 22, 1987.

[22]Bush, *Looking Forward,* p. 27.

[23]Interview with Frank DiClemente, January 22, 1992.

[24]Hyams, *Avenger,* p. 27.

[25]Ibid.

[26]Bush, *Looking Forward,* p. 27.

[27]Barry Bearak, *LAT,* November 22, 1987.

[28]Interview with Nancy Bush Ellis, November 12, 1992.

[29]As quoted by Barry Bearak, *LAT,* November 22, 1987.

[30]Susan E. Elia, Renee F. Seblatnigg, and Val P. Storms, *Greenwich Country Day School: A History, 1926–1986* (Canaan, NH: Phoenix Publishing Company, 1988), p. 3.

[31]Ibid., p. 5.

[32]Ibid., p. 20.

[33]Arthur E. Grant, interviewed by Cecie Munkenbeck for the Greenwich Public Library Project, 1978.

[34]Ibid.

[35]Interview with George Upson Warren, January 29, 1992.

[36]Interview with Arthur E. Grant by Cecie Munkenbeck, for the Greenwich Public Library Project, 1978.

[37]Elia, et al, *Greenwich Country Day,* p. 18.

[38]*Greenwich Time,* February 4, 1938.

[39]Interview with Frank DiClemente, January 22, 1992; Hyams, *Avenger,* p. 22; Mary Walker, interviewed by Esther H. Smith, Greenwich Oral History Project, April 26, 1991; interview with Prescott Bush Jr., January 14, 1994.

[40]Nicholas King, *George Bush: A Biography* (New York: Dodd Mease and Company, 1980), p. 17; Richard Ben Cramer, *What It Takes: The Way to the White House* (New York: Random House, 1992), p. 90.

[41]*Greenwich Time,* March 13, 1988.

[42]Arthur E. Grant, interviewed by Cecie Munkenbeck for the Greenwich Public Library Project, 1978.

[43]Barry Bearak, "Team Player Bush: A Yearning to Serve," *LAT,* November 22, 1987.

[44]Interview with Nancy Bush Ellis, November 12, 1992; King, *Bush,* p. 19; Bearak, *LAT,* November 22, 1987.

[45]Green, *Bush,* p. 13.

[46]" 'Rock Ledge,' The Summer Home of George H. Walker, Esq.," *American Homes and Gardens,* July 1905, pp. 27–30.

[47]Bush, *Looking Forward,* p. 26.

[48]Kane, "Childhood," p. 156.

[49]Green, *Bush,* p. 17.

[50]George Christian to Barefoot Sanders, March 6, 1968, WHCF, Bush Folder, Box 611, LBJL.

[51]Green, *Bush,* p. 12.

[52]Interview with George Upson Warren, January 29, 1992.

[53]Interview with Mary Walker by Esther H. Smith, Greenwich Public Library Oral History Project, April 26, 1991.

[54]John Yang, "Bush on Vacation," *Washington Post,* August 16, 1991.

[55]Mary Walker interviewed by Esther H. Smith, for the Greenwich Public Library Oral History Project, 1991.

[56]Elliott Vose to author, December 2, 1992.

[57]Ibid., December 11, 1992.

[58]Interview with Elliott Vose, December 2, 1992.

[59]Cramer, *What It Takes,* p. 89.

[60]Interview with Hart Day Leavitt, January 22, 1992, and confidential interview, June 21, 1993.

[61]Interview with Hart Day Leavitt, January 22, 1992.

[62]Ibid.; Kane, "Childhood," p. 160.

[63]Green, *Bush,* pp. 21–22.

[64]Kane, "Childhood," p. 159.

[65]Interview with Hart Day Leavitt, January 22, 1992.

[66]Interview with George Upson Warren, January 29, 1992.

[67]Ibid.

[68]Interview with Elliott Vose, December 2, 1992.

[69]Interview with Frank DiClemente, January 22, 1992.

[70]Ibid.

[71]Interview with Elliott Vose, December 2, 1992.

[72]Richard L. Berke, "Million-Dollar Team Keeping Bush Campaign in the Money," *NYT,* May 23, 1988.

[73]Interview with Prescott Bush Jr., January 14, 1994.

[74]Green, *Bush,* p. 22; Interviews with George Upson Warren, January 29 1992, and Hart Day Leavitt, January 22, 1992.

[75]Yearbook of Phillips Andover, *Pot Pouri,* 1942, pp. 80–81.

CHAPTER THREE

[1]John E. Yang, "Bush's Life Changed on School Walk," *WP,* December 8, 1991.
[2]Elting E. Morison, *Turmoil and Tradition: A Study of the Life and Times of Henry L. Stimson* (Boston: Houghton Mifflin Company, 1960), pp. 529–530; Godfrey Hodgson, *The Colonel: The Life and Wars of Henry Stimson, 1867–1950* (New York: Alfred A. Knopf, 1990), pp. 242–243; Henry L. Stimson and McGeorge Bundy, *On Active Service in Peace and War* (New York: Harper & Brothers, 1948), pp. 390–91.
[3]Richard R. Lingeman, *Don't You Know There's A War On?* (New York: G. P. Putnam's Sons, 1970), p. 27.
[4]John Morton Blum, *V Was for Victory* (New York: Harcourt Brace Jovanovich, 1976), p. 151.
[5]Peter Irons, *Justice at War* (New York: Oxford University Press, 1983), p. 27.
[6]Ibid., pp. 30–31; author's personal recollection.
[7]Green, *Bush,* p. 65.
[8]Interview with Nancy Bush Ellis, November 12, 1992.
[9]Barbara Bush, *Barbara Bush,* p. 16.
[10]Ibid., p. 5.
[11]Donna Radcliffe, *Simply Barbara Bush* (New York: Warner Books, 1989), pp. 74–75; Pamela Kilian, *Barbara Bush: A Biography* (New York: St. Martin's Press, 1992), pp. 21–22.
[12]Radcliffe, *Simply Barbara Bush,* p. 79.
[13]Ibid., p. 84.
[14]Marjorie Williams, "Barbara's Backlash," *Vanity Fair,* August 1992, p. 124.
[15]Radcliffe, *Simply Barbara Bush,* p. 91.
[16]Hodgson, *The Colonel,* pp. 213–14.
[17]Green, *Bush,* p. 28.
[18]Interview with Prescott Bush Jr., January 14, 1994, by John T. Mason Jr., Columbia University Oral History project, at BPMP.
[19]Michael Duffy and Dan Goodgame, *Marching in Place* (New York: Simon & Schuster, 1992), p. 99; interview with Nancy Bush Ellis, November 12, 1992.
[20]Joe Hyams, *Flight of the Avenger: George Bush at War* (New York: Berkeley Books, 1992), p. 43.
[21]Ibid., p. 39; David Frost, "George Bush on God, War and Ollie North," *U.S. News & World Report,* December 14, 1987, p. 47.
[22]Hyams, *Flight of the Avenger,* p. 41.
[23]Interview with Frank DiClemente, January 22, 1992.
[24]Bush, *Looking Forward,* p. 30.
[25]Hyams, *Flight of the Avenger,* p. 44.
[26]Interview with George Bush, January 25, 1995.
[27]Bush, *Looking Forward,* p. 30; Hyams, *Flight of the Avenger,* pp. 46–47.
[28]Eric Larrabee, *Commander in Chief* (New York: Harper & Row, 1987), p. 385.
[29]Ronald H. Spector, *Eagle Against the Sun* (New York: The Free Press, 1985), p. 177.
[30]Hyams, *Flight of the Avenger,* pp. 49–50.
[31]Ibid., p. 61.
[32]Ibid., p. 55.
[33]Kilian, *Barbara Bush,* p. 40; Hyams, *Flight of the Avenger,* p. 63.
[34]Hyams, *Flight of the Avenger,* p. 69.
[35]Bush, *Barbara Bush,* p. 19.
[36]Radcliffe, *Simply Barbara Bush,* p. 96.
[37]Kilian, *Barbara Bush,* pp. 40–41; Bush, *Looking Forward,* p. 31.
[38]*The New York Herald-Tribune,* December 12, 1943.
[39]Robert B. Stinnett, *George Bush: His World War II Years* (McLean, VA: Brassey's, U.S., Inc., 1992), p. 26; Spector, *Eagle Against the Sun,* pp. 457–58.
[40]Stinnett, *Bush,* p. 29.
[41]Ibid., p. 63.
[42]Morison, *Victory in the Pacific,* p. 41.
[43]Hyams, *Flight of the Avenger,* p. 72.
[44]Stinnett, *Bush,* p. 21.
[45]Ibid., p. 22.
[46]Bush, *Looking Forward,* p. 34.
[47]Stinnett, *Bush,* p. 17; Hyams, *Flight of the Avenger,* p. 81.
[48]Hyams, *Flight of the Avenger,* p. 104.
[49]Ibid., p. 108.
[50]Samuel Eliot Morison, *The Two-Ocean War* (Boston: Little, Brown, 1963), p. 343.
[51]Spector, *Eagle Against the Sun,* p. 310.
[52]Morison, *The Two-Ocean War,* p. 330.
[53]Ibid., p. 334.
[54]Hyams, *Flight of the Avenger,* pp. 104–5.
[55]Ibid., p. 103.
[56]Stinnett, *Bush,* pp. 51, 60, and 62.
[57]Ibid., p. 63; Spector, *Eagle Against the Sun,* p. 301.
[58]Morison, *The Two-Ocean War,* pp. 331 and 333.

[59]Stinnett, *Bush*, pp. 63 and 69; Morison, *The Two-Ocean War*, p. 336.

[60]Spector, *Eagle Against the Sun*, pp. 301–3.

[61]Stinnett, *Bush*, p. 73.

[62]Ibid., p. 79; Hyams, *Flight of the Avenger*, p. 113.

[63]Morison, *The Two-Ocean War*, p. 425.

[64]Hyams, *Flight of the Avenger*, pp. 131–32; Stinnett, *Bush*, p. 89.

[65]Stinnett, *Bush*, p. 103; Hyams, *Flight of the Avenger*, pp. 133–34.

[66]Morison, *Victory in the Pacific*, pp. 9–10; Richard Ben Cramer, *What It Takes: The Way to The White House* (New York: Random House, 1992), p. 80.

[67]Hyams, *Flight of the Avenger*, pp. 136–37; Morison, *Victory in the Pacific*, p. 6.

[68]Stinnett, *Bush*, pp. 119–25.

[69]Ibid.

[70]Cramer, *What It Takes*, p. 80.

[71]Hyams, *Flight of the Avenger*, pp. 141–42.

[72]Bush, *Looking Forward*, p. 35.

[73]Ibid.; Hyams, *Flight of the Avenger*, p. 143; Stinnett, *Bush*, pp. 119 and 125; Cramer, *What It Takes*, p. 82.

[74]Bush, *Looking Forward*, p. 36.

[75]Ibid.

[76]Stinnett, *Bush*, p. ix.

[77]Hyams, *Flight of the Avenger*, p. 152.

[78]Ibid., p. 147.

[79]Roy Reed, "George Bush On the Move," *New York Times Magazine*, February 10, 1980, pp. 24 and 54.

[80]Ibid., p. 54.

[81]Hyams, *Flight of the Avenger*, p. 147; Bush, *Looking Forward*, p. 38; Green, *Bush*, p. 34.

[82]Morison, *The Two-Ocean War*, p. 425.

[83]As quoted in Hyams, *Flight of the Avenger*, p. 161.

[84]Allan Wolper and Al Ellenberg, "The Day Bush Bailed Out," *New York Post*, August 12, 1988; Stinnett, *Bush*, p. 157; telephone interview with Chester Mierzejewski, December 13, 1993; Sidney Blumenthal, "War Story," *The New Republic*, October 12, 1992, pp. 17–20.

[85]Stinnett, *Bush*, pp. 157–161; Hyams, *Flight of the Avenger*, p. 152.

[86]Testimony of Maj. Sueo Matoba: Tokyo War Crimes trial transcript page 15,033 *passim*, as quoted in Stinnett, *Bush*, pp. 115 and 119.

[87]Interview with George Bush, January 25, 1995.

[88]Morison, *The Two-Ocean War*, p. 505; Morison, *Victory in the Pacific*, p. 10.

[89]Hyams, *Flight of the Avenger*, pp. 194–97.

[90]As quoted in Hyams, *Flight of the Avenger*, p. 193.

[91]Hyams, *Flight of the Avenger*, p. 168.

[92]As quoted in Hyams, *Flight of the Avenger*, pp. 193–94.

[93]Bush, *Looking Forward*, p. 41.

[94]Ibid.; Hyams, *Flight of the Avenger*, p. 201; Green, *Bush*, p. 40; Kilian, *Barbara Bush*, p. 44; Radcliffe, *Simply Barbara Bush*, pp. 98–99.

[95]Green, *Bush*, p. 41.

CHAPTER FOUR

[1]Marjorie Williams, "Barbara's Backlash," *Vanity Fair*, August 1992, pp. 176–77; Hyams, *Flight of the Avenger*, pp. 203–4.

[2]Radcliffe, *Simply Barbara Bush*, p. 100; Kilian, *Barbara Bush*, p. 45.

[3]Hyams, *Flight of the Avenger*, p. 205.

[4]Ibid., p. 206.

[5]Bush, *Looking Forward*, p. 41; Bush, *Barbara Bush*, p. 25.

[6]Hyams, *Flight of the Avenger*, p. 210.

[7]Bush, *Barbara Bush*, p. 27.

[8]Stimson and Bundy, *On Active Service*, p. xv.

[9]"Yale's Most Famous Graduate," *U.S. News & World Report*, October 16, 1989, p. 68.

[10]King, *Bush*, pp. 38–39.

[11]Confidential interview.

[12]Harry Hurt III, "George Bush, Plucky Lad," *Texas Monthly*, June 1983, p. 139; Owen Johnson, *Stover at Yale* (Boston: Little, Brown, 1912), pp. 15 and 209–11; Green, *Bush*, p. 49; Bob Woodward and Walter Pincus, "George Bush: Man and Politician," *WP*, August 7, 1988.

[13]Barry Bearak, "Team Player Bush: A Yearning to Serve," *LAT*, November 22, 1987; Walter Pincus and Bob Woodward, "George Bush: Man and Politician," *WP*, August 7, 1988.

[14]Richard L. Berke, "Million-Dollar Team Keeping Bush Campaign in the Money," *NYT*, May 23, 1988.

[15]Walter Pincus and Bob Woodward, "George Bush: Man and Politician," *WP*, August 7, 1988.

[16]Interview with Thomas Ludlow Ashley, December 29, 1992.

[17]Morton Kondracke, "Vice President Moonbeam," *The New Republic*, March 30, 1987; interviews with Hart Day Leavitt, January 22, 1992, and Robert Fuhrman, June 21, 1993.

[18]Jefferson Morley, "Bush and the Blacks: An Unknown Story," *The New York Review of Books*, January 16, 1992;

Green, *Bush*, p. 84; "Prescott Bush-biographical," Box 1, Manuscript & Archives Division, University of Connecticut at Storrs; Barry Bearak, *LAT*, November 22, 1987.

[19]Interview with Louis Walker, June 6, 1995.

[20]Telephone interview with Phillip K. Allen, January 16, 1992.

[21]Jack Cavanaugh, "Yale First Baseman Bush Once Caught Scouts' Eyes," *Sporting News*, November 7, 1988.

[22]Bush was inducted into the Maine Baseball Hall of Fame in 1994. Plimpton, "Sportsman Born and Bred," p. 144; *NYT*, July 11, 1994.

[23]Cavanaugh, *Sporting News*, November 7, 1988; Bush, *Looking Forward*, p. 45.

[24]Green, *Bush*, p. 47.

[25]Bush, *Barbara Bush*, p. 31.

[26]Interview with Prescott Bush Jr., January 14, 1994.

[27]Ibid.

[28]Ibid.

[29]Prescott S. Bush, Columbia Oral History Research Office, interviewed by John T. Mason Jr., 1966.

[30]Darwin Payne, *Initiative in Energy: Dresser Industries, 1890–1978* (New York: Simon & Schuster, 1979), pp. 113 and 171.

[31]Payne, *Initiative in Energy*, p. 187; Mallon obituary in the *NYT*, March 3, 1983.

[32]Bush, *Looking Forward*, p. 46.

[33]Bush, *Barbara Bush*, p. 30.

[34]Bush, *Looking Forward*, pp. 22–23.

[35]Peggy Noonan, *What I Saw at the Revolution: A Political Life in the Reagan Era* (New York: Random House, 1990), p. 303.

[36]King, *Bush*, p. 41.

[37]Interview with Prescott Bush Jr., January 14, 1994.

[38]Interview, Earle Craig Jr., January 23, 1992.

[39]Ibid.

[40]Seymour Freedgood, "Life in Midland," *Fortune*, April 1962.

[41]Neil R. Peirce and Jerry Hagstrom, *The Book of America: Inside 50 States Today* (New York: W. W. Norton & Company, 1983), p. 623.

[42]Robert H. Ryan, *Midland: The Economic Future of a Texas Oil Center* (Austin: University of Texas, 1959), p. 45.

[43]D. W. Meinig, *Imperial Texas* (Austin: University of Texas Press, 1969), p. 81.

[44]Ryan, *Midland*, p. 47.

[45]John Howard Griffin, *Land of the High Sky* (Midland, TX: First National Bank of Midland, 1959), pp. 170–73.

[46]Daniel Yergin, *The Prize* (New York: Simon & Schuster, 1991), p. 752.

[47]Velma Barrett and Hazel Oliver, *Odessa: City of Dreams* (San Antonio, TX: The Naylor Company, 1952), p. 9.

[48]Ibid., p. 107.

[49]Ibid., p. 109.

[50]Ryan, *Midland*, p. 49.

[51]Payne, *Initiative in Energy*, pp. 185, 219, and 229.

[52]Peirce and Hagstrom, *The Book of America*, p. 623.

CHAPTER FIVE

[1]George Bush to Jennifer L. Platen, August 10, 1989, courtesy of Ms. Platen.

[2]Barrett and Oliver, *Odessa*, p. 114; George N. Green, "The Far Right Wing in Texas Politics, 1930s–1960s," unpublished Ph.D. dissertation, Florida State University, 1966, pp. 8–9.

[3]Bush, *Looking Forward*, p. 48.

[4]Green, *Bush*, p. 56; Cramer, *What It Takes*, p. 145.

[5]Green, *Bush*, p. 56; King, *Bush*, p. 44.

[6]Interview with Clyde Heron, January 12, 1992.

[7]Alexander Cockburn and James Ridgeway, "He Ran the GOP for Nixon, he Ran the CIA for Ford," *Rolling Stone*, March 20, 1980.

[8]Green, *Bush*, p. 57.

[9]David Oshinsky, *A Conspiracy So Immense* (New York: The Free Press, 1983), p. 116; Sidney Hyman, *The Lives of William Benton* (Chicago: University of Chicago Press, 1969), *passim*; Thomas C. Reeves, *The Life and Times of Joe McCarthy* (New York: Stein & Day, 1982), pp. 377–78.

[10]Prescott S. Bush Sr., interview by John T. Mason Jr., Columbia Oral History Research Office, 1966, at BPMP.

[11]Reeves, *McCarthy*, p. 372.

[12]Oshinsky, *Conspiracy*, pp. 157–60 and 168–69.

[13]*Hartford Courant*, November 6, 1950.

[14]Hyman, *Benton*, pp. 440–41.

[15]Oshinsky, *Conspiracy*, p. 239.

[16]*Hartford Courant*, October 24 and October 29, 1950.

[17]Oshinsky, *Conspiracy*, p. 239.

[18]Hyman, *Benton*, p. 441.

[19]*Hartford Courant*, October 14, 1950.

[20]Chester Bowles, *Promises to Keep: My Years in Public Life, 1941–1969* (New York: Harper & Row, 1971), pp. 232–43.

[21]Dorothy Walker Bush in Prescott Bush Sr. interview by John T. Mason Jr., Columbia Oral History Research Office, 1966.

[22]Hyman, *Benton*, p. 443, identifies the broadcast as a Walter Winchell program, not Drew Pearson as Bush recalled it; interview with Prescott Bush Jr., January 14, 1994; David J. Garrow, *Liberty and Sexuality: The Right to Privacy and the Making of Roe* v. *Wade* (New York: Macmillan Publishing Company, 1994), p. 751 n. 62; George Bush introduction to Phyllis Tilson Piotrow, *World Population Crisis: The United States Response* (New York: Praeger Publishers, 1973), p. vii.

[23]Garrow, *Liberty and Sexuality*, p. 124.

[24]Woodward and Pincus, *WP*, August 8, 1988.

[25]Bush, *Looking Forward*, p. 56.

[26]Ibid., p. 58.

[27]John Bainbridge, *The Super-Americans* (New York: Signet Books, 1963), p. 45.

[28]Sally Helgesen, *Wildcatters: A Story of Texas* (Garden City, NY: Doubleday, 1981), p. 87.

[29]Bush, *Looking Forward*, p. 58.

[30]Green, *Bush*, p. 61.

[31]Interview with Earle Craig Jr., January 23, 1992.

[32]Bush, *Barbara Bush*, p. 38.

[33]Green, *Bush*, p. 61.

[34]Scott McCartney, *Houston Post*, June 26, 1988.

[35]Art Wiese, *The Houston Post*, September 12, 1974; Bush News Release, September 11, 1963, Texas Room, Houston Public Library.

[36]Telephone interview with Earle Craig Jr., January 23, 1992.

[37]Radcliffe, *Simply Barbara Bush*, pp. 6 and 112–17; Marjorie Williams, "Barbara's Backlash," *Vanity Fair*, August 1992, p. 177; Kilian, *Barbara Bush*, pp. 56–59.

[38]Radcliffe, *Barbara Bush*, p. 118.

[39]Bush, *Barbara Bush*, pp. 48–49.

[40]Harry Hurt III, "George Bush, Plucky Lad," *Texas Monthly*, June 1983, p. 193.

[41]Barry Bearak, *LAT*, November 22, 1987; Green, *Bush*, pp. 58 and 64; Cramer, *What It Takes*, pp. 235–236; Walter Pincus and Bob Woodward, *WP*, August 7 and 11, 1988.

[42]Barry Bearak, *LAT*, November 22, 1987.

[43]Hurt, "George Bush, Plucky Lad," p. 194.

[44]Ibid., pp. 192–93.

[45]Bush, *Looking Forward*, p. 67.

[46]King, *Bush*, p. 48; Thomas Petzinger Jr., *Oil & Honor: The Texaco-Pennzoil Wars* (New York: G. P. Putnam's Sons, 1987), p. 40; Scott McCartney, *Houston Post*, June 26, 1988.

[47]Clifford Pugh, *Houston Post*, August 16, 1992.

[48]*Midland Reporter-Telegram*, January 1 and 2, 1954.

[49]Ibid., January 1, 1956.

[50]Ibid.

[51]Press Releases, April 5, 21, and 27, 1953, Prescott S. Bush Papers, Box 3, University of Connecticut.

[52]King, *Bush*, p. 49.

[53]"Relationship Between Zapata Off-Shore Company and Zapata Petroleum Company and Pennzoil Company," Undated and unsigned typescript, Bush-Connally Folder, Yarborough Papers, Box ZR508, Barker Texas History Center, Austin; King, *Bush*, p. 54; "Bush Reportedly Formed Secret Link with Oil Group," *Houston Chronicle*, September 19, 1988.

[54]Hurt, "George Bush, Plucky Lad," p. 194.

[55]Ibid.; Bearak, *LAT*, November 22, 1987.

[56]Hurt, "George Bush, Plucky Lad," p. 194.

[57]Petzinger, *Oil & Honor*, pp. 61–63 and 449.

[58]Ibid., p. 136.

[59]Ibid., p. 243; Woodward and Pincus, *WP*, August 11, 1988; Tarpley and Chaitkin, *Bush*, p. 328.

[60]Interview with Earle Craig Jr., January 23, 1992; Kathy Lewis, *Houston Post*, July 15, 1990.

[61]Bush to Thomas Ludlow Ashley, February 13, 1963, Ashley Papers, MS-159, Center for Archival Collections, Bowling Green State University, Bowling Green, OH.

CHAPTER SIX

[1]Howard Fineman, "The Bush Family Franchise," *Newsweek*, July 4, 1994, p. 39.

[2]Interview with Peter Roussel, July 19, 1995.

[3]*Kingsville* (Texas) *Record*, September 16, 1964; *Houston Chronicle*, May 28, 1964.

[4]Kathy Lewis, *Houston Post*, May 1, 1983; Bush, *Looking Forward*, pp. 11–12.

[5]Ashley to George Bush, June 28, 1960, Thomas Ludlow Ashley papers, MS-159, Center for Archival Collections, BGSU.

[6]*NYT*, August 31, 1991.

[7]Bush to Ashley, July 3, 1961, Thomas Ludlow Ashley papers, MS-159, Center for Archival Collections, BGSU. Emphasis supplied.

[8]Interview with Thomas Ludlow Ashley, December 29, 1992.

[9]Press Release, April 5, 1957, Prescott S. Bush Papers, Box 5, University of Connecticut.

[10]Press Release, January 18, 1961, Prescott S. Bush Papers, Box 6, University of Connecticut; *Hartford Courant,* May 23, 1961.

[11]Press Release, Prescott S. Bush papers, Box 6, University of Connecticut.

[12]Press Release, June 9, 1961, Prescott S. Bush Papers, Box 6, University of Connecticut.

[13]Prescott S. Bush to Arthur Krock, November 9, 1962, and November 12, 1968, Krock Papers, Seeley G. Mudd Manuscript Library, Princeton.

[14]Willie Morris, "Houston's Superpatriots," *Harper's Magazine,* October 1961, p. 48.

[15]John R. Knaggs, *Two-Party Texas: The John Tower Era, 1961–1984* (Austin: Eakins Press, 1986), p. 7.

[16]Interview with Roy Goodearle, June 30, 1993.

[17]Havard, *Changing Politics of the South,* p. 209.

[18]Knaggs, *Two-Party Texas,* p. 1.

[19]Morris, "Houston's Superpatriots," p. 51.

[20]Green, *Establishment in Texas Politics,* p. 6.

[21]Green, "The Far Right in Texas Politics," p. 4.

[22]Theodore H. White, *America in Search of Itself* (New York: Harper & Row, 1982), p. 58.

[23]Green, *Establishment in Texas Politics,* pp. 56, 104, and 174; James Reston Jr., *The Lone Star: The Life of John Connally* (New York: Harper & Row, 1989), p. 178.

[24]Peirce and Hagstrom, *Book of America,* p. 625; Green, *Establishment in Texas Politics,* p. 52; *The Texas Observer,* November 3, 1961.

[25]Arnold Forster and Benjamin Epstein, *Danger on the Right* (New York: Random House, 1964), p. 40.

[26]Ibid., p. 18; Benjamin R. Epstein and Arnold Forster, *The Radical Right* (New York: Random House, 1966), p. 143.

[27]Willie Morris, "Houston's Superpatriots," p. 49; Don E. Carleton, *Red Scare!* (Austin: Texas Monthly Press, 1985), pp. 297–99; Chandler Davidson, *Race and Class in Texas Politics* (Princeton, NJ: Princeton University Press, 1990), p. 203.

[28]Olien, *From Token to Triumph,* p. 194.

[29]*Houston Chronicle,* February 21, 1963; Knaggs, *Two-Party Texas,* pp. 19–20 and 23; Webster Griffin Tarpley and Anton Chaitkin, *George Bush: The Unauthorized Biography* (Washington, D.C.: Executive Intelligence Review, 1992), p. 169.

[30]Hurt, "George Bush, Plucky Lad," p. 186.

[31]Bush, *Looking Forward,* pp. 84–85; Claudia Feldman, *Houston Chronicle,* December 13, 1992; interview with Roy Goodearle, June 30, 1993.

[32]Interview with Roy Goodearle, June 30, 1993.

[33]Tarpley and Chaitkin, *Bush,* p. 166.

[34]Bush, *Looking Forward,* p. 85.

[35]Green, *Bush,* pp. 81–82; Bush, *Looking Forward,* p. 85; Cramer, *What It Takes,* p. 413.

[36]Bush to Ashley, February 13, 1963, Thomas Ludlow Ashley Papers, MS-159, Center for Archival Collections, BGSU.

[37]*Houston Chronicle,* February 21, 1963.

[38]Cramer, *What It Takes,* p. 413; Green, *Bush,* pp. 81–82.

[39]Cramer, *What It Takes,* pp. 414–15; interview with Molly Ivins, January 7, 1992.

[40]Bush, *Looking Forward,* p. 86.

[41]Interview with Roy Goodearle, June 30, 1993.

[42]Tarpley and Chaitkin, *Bush,* p. 167; *Houston Chronicle,* July 3, 1963; Ronnie Dugger, "The Substance of the Senate Contest," *The Texas Observer,* September 18, 1964.

[43]Harold Deyo, "Coalition of Conservatives to Beat the Bushes," June 2, 1964, Yarborough Papers, Box ZR508, Barker Texas History Center, Austin.

[44]Interview with Ralph Yarborough, July 23, 1992.

[45]Bush to Ashley, March 18, 1963, and Ashley to Bush, March 19, 1963, Thomas Ludlow Ashley Papers, MS-159, Center for Archival Collections, BGSU.

[46]Knaggs, *Two-Party Texas,* p. 33.

CHAPTER SEVEN

[1]Bush Headquarters letter to Texas voters, August 21, 1964, Yarborough Papers, Bush Folder, Box ZR508, Barker Texas History Center, Austin.

[2]T. R. Fehrenbach, *Lone Star: A History of Texas and the Texans* (New York: Macmillan, 1968), p. 661.

[3]Reston, *Lone Star,* p. 171; Richard Severo, *NYT,* June 16, 1993.

[4]Knaggs, *Two-Party Texas,* p. 4.

[5]William Greider, *Who Will Tell the People?* (New York: Simon & Schuster, 1992), p. 87.

[6]Green, *Bush,* p. 85; Green, *Establishment in Texas Politics,* p. 202.

[7]Molly Ivins, "Inside the Austin Fun House," *The Atlantic,* May 1975, pp. 48–55.

[8]Peirce and Hagstrom, *Book of America,* p. 629n.

[9]Interview with Ralph Yarborough, June 1980.

[10]Green, *Establishment in Texas,* pp. 156 and 158–59.

[11]Phillips, *Yarborough,* p. 43.

[12]Garry Wills, "The Hostage," *The New York Review of Books,* August 13, 1992, p. 21; Phillips, *Yarborough,* p. 46.

[13]*The Texas Observer,* April 4, 1963, p. 15; *The Dallas Morning News,* September 12, 1963; *San Antonio Express,* September 12, 1963; *Houston Chronicle,* November 11, 1963.

[14]Ronnie Dugger, *The Texas Observer,* July 22, 1961.

[15]Peirce and Hagstrom, *Book of the States,* p. 625; William Manchester, *Death of a President* (New York: Harper & Row, 1967), p. 20.

[16]Richard Severo, *NYT,* June 16, 1993.

[17]Interview with John C. Connally, May 19, 1986.

[18]Herbert S. Parmet, *JFK: The Presidency of John F. Kennedy* (New York: The Dial Press, 1982), p. 337; Fehrenbach, *Lone Star,* p. 661.

[19]Reston, *Lone Star,* pp. 178–79.

[20]Knaggs, *Two-Party Texas,* p. 34.

[21]Ibid., p. 45.

[22]Ibid., p. 34; *The Dallas Morning News,* September 12, 1963.

[23]*San Antonio Express,* September 12, 1963.

[24]*Houston Post,* April 25, 1964.

[25]Deaver, *Behind the Scenes,* p. 127; Deyo, "Coalition of Conservatives to Beat the Bushes,"; Cramer, *What It Takes,* p. 580.

[26]Peirce and Hagstrom, *Book of the States,* p. 621.

[27]Lawrence I. Barrett, *Gambling with History: Reagan in the White House* (New York: Penguin Books, 1984), p. 375; Deaver, *With Reagan* pp. 128 and 132.

[28]Cannon, *President Reagan,* p. 70.

[29]Confidential interviews.

[30]Duffy and Goodgame, *Marching in Place,* p. 208; Jane Ely, *The Houston Chronicle,* November 15, 1988; Roy Bragg, *The Houston Chronicle,* December 10, 1989; Tarpley and Chaitkin, *Bush,* p. 248.

[31]Thomas Petzinger Jr., *WSJ,* July 20, 1992.

[32]Associated Press, "Mosbacher-Thumbnail," December 6, 1991; *NYT,* May 23, 1988; *Common Cause,* vol. 18, no. 2, April/May/June, 1992, p. 27; Jill Abramson and Thomas Petzinger Jr., *WSJ,* June 11, 1992; Thomas Petzinger Jr., *WSJ,* July 20, 1992; Green, *Bush,* p. 166.

[33]Barbara Bush, *C. Fred's Story* (New York: Doubleday, 1984), p. 2.

[34]Knaggs, *Two-Party Texas,* p. 35.

[35]Manchester, *Death of a President,* p. 44.

[36]Gerald Posner, *Case Closed: Lee Harvey Oswald and the Assassination of JFK* (New York: Random House, 1993), pp. 369–370.

[37]Manchester, *Death of a President,* pp. 21–22 and 132–34; Bruno, *Advance Man,* pp. 86–87; Reston, *Lone Star,* pp. 266–81; interview with Ralph Yarborough, June 1980.

[38]Report of Special Agent Graham W. Kitchell of the FBI, November 23, 1963, Houston File: 62-2115, "Assassination of President John F. Kennedy, November 22, 1963," and John Edgar Hoover to Director, Bureau of Intelligence and Research, Department of State, November 29, 1963, FBI files, obtained through Freedom of Information Act requests 354, 056, and 057, 1992; Joseph McBride, " 'George Bush,' C.I.A. Operative," *The Nation,* July 16/23, 1988, pp. 1 and 41–42.

[39]Bush, *Barbara Bush,* p. 60.

[40]Interview with Ronnie Dugger, November 18, 1992; *The Texas Observer,* April 17, 1964.

[41]*NYT,* May 4, 1964; Green, *Bush,* p. 83.

[42]Tarpley and Chaitkin, *Bush,* pp. 174–75; Knaggs, *Two-Party Texas,* p. 45; *Dallas Morning News,* April 9 and 10, 1964; *The Houston Chronicle,* April 9, 1964.

[43]Bush to Ashley, June 22, 1964, Thomas Ludlow Ashley Papers, MS-159, Center for Archival Collections, BGSU.

[44]Ashley to Bush, June 19, 1964, Thomas Ludlow Ashley Papers, MS-159, BGSU.

[45]Green, *Bush,* p. 84.

[46]*Houston Chronicle,* October 28, 1964.

[47]H. J. Yarborough to Ralph W. Yarborough, August 19, 1964, Bush Folder, Box ZR508, Yarborough Papers, Barker Texas History Center.

[48]Jefferson Morley, "Bush and the Blacks: An Unknown Story," *The New York Review of Books,* January 16, 1992; *San Benito* (Texas) *News,* September 14, 1964.

[49]*Lockney* (Texas) *Press,* September 17, 1964.

[50]Ronnie Dugger, "The Substance of the Senate Contest," *The Texas Observer,* September 18, 1964, pp. 2–7; Davidson, *Race and Class in Texas Politics,* p. 202.

[51]Kilian, *Barbara Bush,* p. 85.

[52]*Kingsville* (Texas) *Record,* September 16, 1964.

[53]Wills, "The Hostage," p. 22; Knaggs, *Two-Party Texas,* p. 53; Morley, "Bush and the Blacks."

[54]Quoted from Bush Bulletin, September 18, 1964, in Morley, "Bush and the Blacks," p. 21; *San Benito* (Texas) *News,* September 14, 1964.

[55]*NYT,* October 28, 1964.

[56]Duffy and Goodgame, *Marching in Place,* p. 203; Bush, *Barbara Bush,* p. 58.

[57]*The Texas Observer,* April 17, 1964.

[58]Green, *Bush,* p. 185.

[59]Leslie Carpenter to Walter Jenkins, August 14, 1964, White House Central Files, Bush Files, Box 611, LBJL.

[60]*Corpus Christi Times,* October 12, 1964.

[61]Richard Nixon to the author, November 16, 1992.

[62]Undated (c.1964) and unsigned typescript found in the Bush-Connally Folder, Yarborough Papers, Box ZR508, Barker Texas History Center.

[63]*Houston Chronicle,* September 16, 1964, and *Fort Worth Star-Telegram,* September 29, 1964.

[64]*Fort Worth Star-Telegram,* October 4, 1964.

[65]*NYT,* November 1, 1964.

[66]Interview with Robert A. Mosbacher, July 24, 1995.

[67]Interview with George Upson Warren, January 29, 1992.

[68]Knaggs, *Two-Party Texas,* p. 53.

[69]*Houston Chronicle,* November 4, 1964.

[70]Knaggs, *Two-Party Texas,* pp. 56 and 71.

[71]*National Review,* December 1, 1964, as quoted in Morley, "Bush and the Blacks," p. 21.

[72]Green, *Bush,* p. 91.

CHAPTER EIGHT

[1]*Houston Chronicle,* May 16, 1965.

[2]Morley, "Bush and the Blacks," p. 21.

[3]Ibid.

[4]David Frost, "George Bush on God, War and Ollie North," *U.S. News & World Report,* December 14, 1987, pp. 47–48.

[5]Interview with Ronnie Dugger, November 18, 1992.

[6]*The Texas Observer,* July 23, 1965, pp. 7–8 and 14; interview with Ronnie Dugger, November 18, 1992.

[7]Hugh Davis Graham, *The Civil Rights Era* (New York: Oxford University Press, 1990), pp. 171–73; Earl Black and Merle Black, *Politics and Society in the South* (Cambridge, MA: Harvard University Press, 1987), pp. 136–37.

[8]Michael Barone, Grant Ujifusa, and Douglas Matthews, *The Almanac of American Politics 1972* (Boston: Gambit Incorporated, 1972), pp. 792–93. In 1994, a panel of federal judges found that two of Houston's newer districts, the nineteenth and twenty-ninth, were invalid because they were the products of racial gerrymandering in order to provide "safe" seats in Congress for minority representatives. Terri Langford, Associated Press, August 17, 1994.

[9]Garry Wills, "The Hostage," *The New York Review of Books,* August 13, 1992, p. 22.

[10]Bush, *Looking Forward,* p. 88; Hurt, "George Bush, Plucky Lad," p. 196.

[11]Green, *Bush,* p. 93; Barone, et al., *Almanac . . . 1972,* p. 793.

[12]Green, *Bush,* p. 94.

[13]*Houston Press,* November 3, 1966, as quoted by Morley, "Bush and the Blacks," p. 22.

[14]Ibid.

[15]Bush Bulletin No. 2, July 12, 1966, Thomas Ludlow Ashley Papers, MS-159, Center for Archival Collections, BGSU.

[16]Joe McGinniss, *The Selling of the President* (New York: Trident Press, 1969), pp. 44–45.

[17]*WSJ,* June 30, 1966.

[18]Bush Bulletin No. 2, July 12, 1966, Thomas Ludlow Ashley Papers, MS-159, Center for Archival Collections, BGSU.

[19]Morley, "Bush and the Blacks," January 16, 1992, p. 22; Bush Bulletin No. 2, July 12, 1966, Thomas Ludlow Ashley Papers, MS-159, Center for Archival Collections, BGSU.

[20]*Houston Post,* November 8, 1966.

[21]*Houston Post,* November 8 and 9, 1966; Green, *Bush,* p. 95; *Houston Chronicle,* November 9, 1966; Marge Crumbaker, *Houston Post,* November 9, 1966.

[22]King, *Bush,* p. 55; Green, *Bush,* p. 102.

[23]Bush, *Barbara Bush,* p. 64

[24]Ibid., pp. 67–68.

CHAPTER NINE

[1]*Congressional Quarterly Almanac,* 90th Congress, 1st Session, 1967, p. 112.

[2]*Congressional Record,* August 11, 1967, pp. 818–20.

[3]Morley, "Bush and the Blacks," p. 22.

[4]*Report of the National Advisory Committee on Civil Disorders* (New York: E. P. Dutton and Co., Inc., 1968), p. 332.

[5]George Bush to Lyndon Johnson, April 9, 1968, White House Central File, Bush Folder, Box 611, Lyndon B. Johnson Library; Morley, "Bush and the Blacks," pp. 23–24.

[6]Interview with Barber Conable, July 8, 1993.

[7]William Crotty in Paul T. David and David H. Everson (eds.), *The Presidential Election and Transition, 1980–81* (Carbondale and Edwardville, IL: University of Southern Illinois Press, 1983), p. 5; Garry Wills, "The Hostage," *The New York Review of Books,* August 13, 1992, p. 22; Art Wiese, "Bush Remains 'Common as an Old Shoe' Despite Power, Fame," *Houston Post,* September 12, 1974.

[8]Interview with Barber Conable, July 8, 1993.

[9]Cramer, *What It Takes,* p. 591.

[10]Hedrick Smith, *The Power Game* (New York: Random House, 1988), p. 26.

[11]Bearak, *LAT,* November 22, 1987; Duffy and Goodgame, *Marching in Place,* p. 215; CNN Special Report, "The Battle to Lead: The Public Mind of George Bush," October 25, 1992; interview with Barber Conable, July 8, 1993; interview with Gerald R. Ford, July 14, 1995.

[12]Interview with Barber Conable, July 8, 1993.

[13]Prepared comments for George Bush's address before the New Haven Chamber of Commerce, April 13, 1978. Bush Prepresidential Speeches and Interviews, BPMP.

[14]CNN Special Report, "The Battle to Lead: The Public Mind of George Bush," October 25, 1992.

[15]Robert Sherrill, *The Oil Follies of 1970-1980* (New York: Anchor Press/Doubleday, 1983), p. 63.

[16]Ken Sheets, " 'Emotional' Attacks on Oil Have Bush Worried Sick," *Houston Chronicle,* July 3, 1969; *Houston Post,* July 8 and 19, 1969.

[17]Sherrill, *Oil Follies,* p. 64.

[18]Ibid., p. 65.

[19]*Fort Worth Press,* June 29, 1969.

[20]Yergin, *The Prize,* p. 754.

[21]H. R. Haldeman, *The Haldeman Diaries: Inside the Nixon White House* (New York: G. P. Putnam's Sons, 1994), pp. 114–15.

[22]Sherrill, *Oil Follies,* p. 65; *Congress and the Nation,* vol. 3, pp. 84 and 844–45.

[23]Claudia Townsend, *Ralph Nader Congress Project: George D. Aiken* (Washington, D.C.: Grossman Publishers, 1972), p. 2; Herbert S. Parmet, "George Aiken and the GOP," paper delivered at the University of Vermont, October 26, 1991. The comment was made a few days before Bush was elected to the House.

[24]Ken Sheets, *Houston Chronicle,* December 19, 1967.

[25]George Bush to Don Rhodes, January 2, 1968, Don Rhodes Collection, BPMP, Texas A&M, College Station, TX.

[26]Handwritten speech notes, Bush Personal Papers, Congressional File—Vietnam Trip, BPMP, College Station, TX.

[27]Reading text of Bush speech, January 11, 1968, Bush Personal Papers, Congressional File—Vietnam Trip, BPMP, Texas A&M, College Station, TX.

[28]*Houston Chronicle,* January 7 and 8, 1968; Bush prepared statement, January 11, 1968, Bush Personal Papers, Congressional File—Vietnam Trip, BPMP, Texas A&M, College Station, TX.

[29]Interview with Rose Zamaria, April 19, 1995.

[30]Reid Beveridge, *Houston Chronicle,* February 13, 1969.

[31]Ronald H. Spector, *After Tet: The Bloodiest Year in Vietnam* (New York: The Free Press, 1993), p. 5.

[32]Richard G. Mack to George Bush, March 27, 1968, BPMP, College Station, TX.

[33]George Bush to Richard G. Mack, April 14, 1968, and Mack to Bush, May 21, 1968, BPMP, College Station, TX.

[34]Morley, "Bush and the Blacks," p. 24; *Houston Post,* April 11, 1964.

[35]Bush, *Barbara Bush,* p. 71.

[36]Charles Culhane, "Local Congressmen Split on Rights Bill Vote," *Houston Post,* April 11, 1968.

[37]Ibid.; Jack Cleland, "Rights Bill Dilemma for Texans," *Houston Chronicle,* April 11, 1968.

[38]Culhane, "Local Congressmen Split on Rights Bill Vote," April 11, 1968.

[39]George Bush to Richard G. Mack, April 14, 1968, BPMP, College Station, TX.

[40]Randall Rothenberg, "In Search of George Bush," *NYT,* March 6, 1988, p. 46.

[41]Green, *Bush,* p. 107.

[42]Interview with Rose Zamaria, April 19, 1995.

[43]Ibid.

[44]As quoted in Rothenberg, "In Search of George Bush," *NYT,* March 6, 1988, p. 46.

[45]Morley, "Bush and the Blacks," January 16, 1992, p. 24.

[46]William F. Swindler, *Court and Constitution in the Twentieth Century: The New Legality, 1932–1968* (Indianapolis and New York: Bobbs-Merrill, 1968), p. 481; *Congress and the Nation,* vol. 2 (Washington, D.C.: Congressional Quarterly Services, 1969), p. 677.

[47]Garrow, *Liberty and Sexuality,* pp. 343–61.

[48]*Congress and the President,* vol. 2, pp. 676 and 683–85; *Public Papers of the Presidents—Richard Nixon, 1969* (Washington, D.C.: U.S. Government Printing House, 1971), pp. 467 and 529.

[49]Tarpley and Chaitkin, *Bush,* pp. 196 and 198.

[50]Garrow, *Liberty and Equality,* p. 471.

[51]*Congressional Record,* February 24, 1969, pp. 4 and 207–10, as quoted by Morley, "Bush and the Blacks," p. 24.

[52]Ibid., July 8, 1970, pp. 23 and 193, as quoted by Morley, "Bush and the Blacks," p. 25.

[53]Garrow, *Liberty and Sexuality,* pp. 471–72.

[54]Ibid., vol. 3, pp. 777–78; Tarpley and Chaitkin, *Bush,* p. 198.

[55]Bush, *Looking Forward,* p. 5.

[56]Richard Nixon to the author, November 16, 1992; *The New Yorker,* October 5, 1992, pp. 60–62.

[57]*NYT,* August 17, 1968.

[58]Stephen Ambrose, *Nixon: Triumph of a Politician, 1962–1972* (New York: Simon & Schuster, 1989), p. 138; McGinniss, *Selling of the President,* p. 41.

[59]*Houston Post,* January 3, 1969; James T. Wooten, *NYT,* October 27 and November 5, 1969.

CHAPTER TEN

[1]Interview with Prescott Bush, Columbia University Oral History Research Office, by John T. Mason Jr., 1966.

[2]Interview with Nancy Bush Ellis, November 12, 1992.

[3]Interview with Jack Steel, January 25, 1995.

[4]Green, *Bush*, pp. 110–11.

[5]Ibid.

[6]As quoted in Pincus and Woodward, *WP,* August 8, 1988.

[7]Ken Sheets, "Bush Believes LBJ Policy is Winning War," *Houston Chronicle,* January 12, 1968; *Houston Post,* January 15, 1969.

[8]Green, *Bush,* p. 108; Hurt, "George Bush, Plucky Lad," p. 198; Joe B. Frantz to Lyndon B. Johnson, January 23, 1969, and Johnson to Bush, January 31, 1969, Post-Presidential Name File, Bush Folder, Box 22, LBJL.

[9]Billy Graham to Lyndon B. Johnson, June 21, 1968, Post-Presidential Name File, Box 367, LBJL.

[10]Reston, *Lone Star,* p. 375; Haldeman, *Diaries,* p. 135.

[11]Ibid., pp. 376–77; Ambrose, *Nixon: Triumph of a Politician,* p. 395.

[12]Wills, "The Hostage," August 13, 1992.

[13]*Dallas Morning News,* December 19, 1969.

[14]Stephen Labaton, *NYT,* January 26, 1996.

[15]Tom Johnson to Lyndon B. Johnson, April 3, 1969, Bush to Lyndon Johnson, April 12, 1969, Tom Johnson to Lyndon Johnson, May 28, 1969, and Bush to Lyndon Johnson, May 29, 1969. Post-Presidential Name File, George Bush Folder, Box 22, LBJL; Green, *Bush,* p. 109.

[16]Jamie Anderson to Ralph Yarborough, February 27, 1969, Bush Folder, Yarborough Papers, Box ZR508, Barker Texas History Center, Austin.

[17]*Houston Chronicle,* December 29, 1969.

[18]Jill Abrams and Thomas Petzinger Jr., *WSJ,* June 11, 1992.

[19]Jack A. Gleason to Harry S. Dent, May 7, 1970, John Dean staff files, Box 109, Library of Congress.

[20]*Dallas Morning News,* July 8, 1969.

[21]Robert Sherrill, *Oil Follies,* pp. 61–65; *NYT,* September 27, 1969.

[22]*Houston Post,* September 27, 1969; *Houston Chronicle,* September 30, 1969.

[23]*San Antonio Express,* October 3, 1969.

[24]*Houston Chronicle,* December 14, 1969.

[25]Interview with Ralph Yarborough, July 23, 1992.

[26]*NYT,* May 4, 1970.

[27]Green, *Bush,* p. 112.

[28]Pete Brewton, *The Mafia, CIA & George Bush* (New York: S.P.I. Books, 1992), unnumbered page; Peirce, *Megastates of America,* p. 518.

[29]Pincus and Woodward, *WP,* August 8, 1988.

[30]Ambrose, *Triumph,* p. 534.

[31]Jack A. Gleason to Harry S. Dent, John Dean Staff Files, Box 109, Library of Congress.

[32]Hoff-Wilson (ed.), "The President's Meeting Files, 1969–1974," July 22, 1970, Nixon Papers, University Microfilms, NPMP.

[33]Pincus and Woodward, *WP,* August 8, 1988.

[34]Undated memorandum of telephone call from Robert Strauss to Tom Johnson, Post-Presidential Name File, Connally Folder, Box 31, LBJL.

[35]Olien, *From Token to Triumph,* p. 222.

[36]*The Texas Observer,* August 7, 1970, p. 24.

[37]Green, *Bush,* p. 113.

[38]*Public Papers of the Presidents: Richard Nixon, 1970,* p. 697.

[39]Green, *Bush,* pp. 113–14; Ehrlichman, *Witness,* p. 153; *Houston Post,* October 29, 1970.

[40]Pincus and Woodward, *WP,* August 8, 1988.

[41]Ibid.; Jack A. Gleason to Robert Mosbacher, October 16, 1970, John W. Dean III Staff Files, Box 109, Library of Congress; Nicholas M. Horrock, *NYT,* November 5, 1975.

[42]Molly Ivins, "Tubing with Lloyd/George," *The Texas Observer,* October 30, 1970, p. 3.

[43]Bruce Oudes (ed.), *From: The President—Richard Nixon's Secret Files* (New York: Harper & Row, 1989), p. 169; Reed, "George Bush On the Move," p. 58. During the 1992 campaign, President Bush similarly rejected pressures from within his staff for the use of allegations about Bill Clinton's private life. "Can you imagine other world leaders reading that before he's even inaugurated?" he was quoted as having said. Peter Goldman and Thomas M. D'Frank, "Dirt Patrol: Who Was 'Naomi'?" *Newsweek,* November 7, 1994, p. 39.

[44]Papers of Lawrence Higby, Haldeman Staff Files, Box 252, Library of Congress.

[45]Anonymous telegram, October 29, 1970, Post-Presidential Name File, Bush Folder, Box 22, LBJL; Olien, *From Token to Triumph,* p. 221.

[46]*Washington Post,* November 1, 1970, as quoted by Morley, "Bush and the Blacks," January 16, 1992, p. 26.

[47]*Houston Post,* November 3, 1970.

[48]Olien, *From Token to Triumph,* p. 225; Barry Lawes, "Bush Concedes, Wishes Bentsen 'Best of Luck,' " *Houston Chronicle,* November 4, 1970.

[49]Interview with Jack Steel, January 25, 1995.

[50]Reston, *Lone Star,* p. 380.

[51]Wills, "The Hostage," p. 25; Tarpley and Chaitkin, *Bush,* p. 215.

[52] H. R. Haldeman, *The Haldeman Diaries: Inside the Nixon White House* (New York: G. P. Putnam's Sons, 1994), pp. 212 and 215.

[53] Richard Nixon to author, November 16, 1992.

[54] Reston, *Lone Star,* p. 380.

[55] Haldeman, *Diaries,* pp. 215–16; interview with George H. W. Bush, January 25, 1995.

[56] Green, *Bush,* pp. 115–16; Bush, *Barbara Bush,* p. 81.

[57] Haldeman, *Diaries,* p. 181.

[58] Hoff-Wilson (ed.), "The President's Meeting Files, 1969–1974," Nixon Papers, University Microfilms; interview with George H. W. Bush, January 25, 1995.

[59] Richard Nixon to author, November 16, 1992.

[60] Interview with Thomas Ludlow Ashley, December 29, 1992; interview with Jack Steel, January 25, 1995.

[61] Cramer, *What It Takes,* p. 610; *The Texas Observer,* December 29, 1970, p. 8; interview with Molly Ivins, January 7, 1992; *NYT,* December 15, 1972.

[62] Bernard Gwertzman, *NYT,* July 29, 1972; interview with Seymour Maxwell Finger, March 15, 1995.

[63] Seymour Maxwell Finger, *Your Man at the UN: People, Politics, and Bureaucracy in Making Foreign Policy* (New York: New York University Press, 1980), p. 218.

[64] Interviews with George H. W. Bush, January 25, 1995, and Seymour Maxwell Finger, March 15, 1995.

[65] Ibid.

[66] *The Nation,* March 29, 1971.

[67] *NYT,* October 19, 1971.

[68] Ibid.

[69] Barry Bearak, *LAT,* November 22, 1987; interview with Seymour Maxwell Finger, March 15, 1995.

[70] *NYT,* October 19, 1971.

[71] *NYT,* February 28, 1971.

[72] *Time,* September 20, 1971; Finger, *Your Man at the UN,* pp. 216–19.

[73] Barry Bearak, *LAT,* November 22, 1987.

[74] *NYT,* June 22, 1971.

[75] Bush, *Barbara Bush,* pp. 81–82.

[76] *NYT,* February 28, 1971.

[77] *NYT,* December 1, 1994.

[78] Carol Jaffin memorandum to Ambassador Bush, October 18, 1972, Special Staff Files, Box 1, Library of Congress.

[79] *NYT,* October 13, 1971.

[80] James Reston, *NYT,* October 20, 1971.

[81] As quoted by Tarpley and Chaitkin, *Bush,* pp. 223–24.

[82] *NYT,* October 19, 1971.

[83] Wicker, *One of Us,* p. 594.

[84] Interview with Seymour Maxwell Finger, March 15, 1995.

[85] George Bush to Frank P. Stelling, May 27, 1971, Special Staff Files, Box 1, Library of Congress.

[86] *NYT,* October 19, 1971.

[87] *NYT,* October 26, 1971.

[88] Tom Lias to George Bush, October 26, 1971, Special Staff Files, Box 2, Library of Congress; Raymond L. Garthoff, *Detente and Confrontation: American-Soviet Relations from Nixon to Reagan,* rvd. ed. (Washington: The Brookings Institution, 1994), p. 235.

[89] Haldeman, *Diaries,* pp. 368–69.

[90] Cf., Richard Nixon, *Beyond Peace* (New York: Random House, 1994), *passim.*

[91] Garthoff, *Detente,* pp. 295 and 311; Seymour Hersh, *The Price of Power: Kissinger in the Nixon White House* (New York: Summit Books, 1983), pp. 451–57; Henry Kissinger, *The White House Years* (Boston: Little, Brown, 1979), pp. 913–18; Richard Nixon, *RN: Memoirs* (New York: Grosset & Dunlap, 1978), pp. 525–32.

[92] Haldeman, *Diaries,* p. 379; Kissinger, *White House Years,* p. 911.

[93] Green, *Bush,* p. 122–23; *NYT,* March 17 and 30, 1972; Dick Combs to Tom Lias, Special Staff Files, Box 2, Library of Congress; *NYT,* May 26, 1972.

[94] Interview with George H. W. Bush, January 25, 1995.

[95] Bush, *Barbara Bush,* p. 90.

[96] *The Nutmegger,* February 1989.

[97] Tribute by Dorothy Walker Bush in the possession of Nancy Bush Ellis made available to the author.

CHAPTER ELEVEN

[1] Theodore H. White, *Breach of Faith: The Fall of Richard Nixon* (New York: Atheneum Publishers, 1975), p. 179.

[2] Thomas Petzinger Jr., *Oil and Honor* (New York: Putnam, 1987), pp. 64–65; Jill Abramson and Thomas Petzinger Jr., *WSJ,* June 11, 1992; Hurt, "George Bush, Plucky Lad," p. 199; *NYT,* August 25 and September 13, 1972; Staff of *The New York Times, The Watergate Hearings, Break-in and Cover-up* (New York: The Viking Press, 1973), pp. 232–33.

[3] Haldeman, *Diaries,* pp. 469–70.

[4] Stephen E. Ambrose, *Nixon: Ruin and Recovery, 1973–1990* (New York: Simon & Schuster, 1991), pp. 12 and 15.

[5] Richard Nixon, *RN: Memoirs* p. 769.

[6]Interview with George Bush, July 6, 1995.

[7]Interview with Ray Price, February 22, 1995.

[8]Ehrlichman notes of meetings with the president, November 17, 1972, Fenn Gallery, Santa Fe.

[9]Ibid., November 20, 1972.

[10]Green, *Bush,* p. 129; interview with Dan Gilchrist, September 13, 1995.

[11]Bob Woodward and Walter Pincus, *WP,* August 9, 1988.

[12]Haldeman Action Memoranda, November 10 and 12, 1972, Subject File, Box 112, NPMP.

[13]Ehrlichman notes of meetings with the president, November 20, 1972, Fenn Gallery, Santa Fe.

[14]Ibid., November 28, 1972; Haldeman, *Diaries,* p. 534.

[15]Rothenberg, *New York Times Magazine,* March 6, 1988, p. 46; Haldeman, *Diaries,* pp. 534, 550, 551.

[16]Green, *Bush,* p. 129.

[17]Sidney Blumenthal, *Pledging Allegiance: The Last Campaign of the Cold War* (New York: HarperCollins, 1990), p. 62; Ehrlichman notes of meetings with the president, November 20, 1972, Fenn Gallery, Santa Fe.

[18]Green, *Bush,* pp. 125 and 129–30; Nixon to author, November 18, 1992.

[19]Hurt III, *Texas Monthly,* June 1983, p. 20; Bearak, *LAT,* November 22, 1987.

[20]Haldeman, *Diaries,* p. 545; Elizabeth Kolbert, *NYT,* June 21, 1996.

[21]Haldeman, *Diaries,* p. 553.

[22]Tom Wicker, *NYT,* December 12, 1972.

[23]White House News Summary, Bruce Kehrli reports, as quoted in Bruce Oudes (ed.), *From the President: Richard Nixon's Secret Files* (New York: Harper & Row, 1989), p. 576.

[24]"Notes on People," *NYT,* December 21, 1972; Robert Alden, *NYT,* December 23, 1972.

[25]George Bush, "Peking Diary." Courtesy of President Bush.

[26]*NYT,* January 7, 1973.

[27]Stanley Karnow, *Vietnam: A History* (New York: The Viking Press, 1983), p. 654; George C. Herring, *America's Longest War: The United States and Vietnam, 1950–1975,* 2d ed. (New York: Alfred A. Knopf, 1986), p. 256.

[28]Herring, *Longest War,* p. 256.

[29]Pincus and Woodward, *WP,* August 9, 1988.

[30]Cramer, *What It Takes,* p. 613.

[31]Ibid., pp. 612–13.

[32]*NYT,* March 30, 1973.

[33]Ibid., July 24 and 25, 1973; Lou Cannon, *WP,* July 19, 1973.

[34]Haldeman, *Diaries,* p. 651; Rothenberg, *New York Times Magazine,* March 6, 1988, p. 46; Bush, *Barbara Bush,* p. 103; Schaller, Scharff and Schulzinger, *Present Tense,* p. 429.

[35]Woodward and Pincus, *WP,* August 9, 1988.

[36]Cannon, *Time and Chance,* p. 211; Ambrose, *Ruin and Recovery,* p. 238.

[37]*NYT,* January 20 and February 20, 1974; Bush, *Barbara Bush,* p. 104.

[38]Interview with George Bush, July 6, 1995.

[39]Christopher Lydon, "Governor's Race Weighed by Bush," *NYT,* November 4, 1973.

[40]George Bush to James A. Baker III, Public Service Archives, Series IV, Box 7, Woodson Research Center, Rice University, TX.

[41]Knaggs, *Two-Party Texas,* p. 186.

[42]Ambrose, *Nixon: Ruin and Recovery,* p. 342.

[43]Cannon, *Time and Chance,* p. 262.

[44]Ibid., p. 314.

[45]Bush notes for August 5, 1974. Courtesy of President Bush.

[46]Bush notes for August 5, 1974. Courtesy of President Bush.

[47]Bush's notes for August 6, 1974. Courtesy of President Bush.

[48]Interview with George Bush, July 6, 1995.

[49]Ibid., pp. 316–18; interviews with William Simon, October 9, 1974, and Ben Stein, July 10, 1985; Henry Kissinger, *Years of Upheaval* (Boston: Little, Brown, 1982), p. 1202; Theodore H. White, *Breach of Faith—The Fall of Richard Nixon* (New York: Atheneum Publishers, 1975), pp. 23–24; Gerald R. Ford, *A Time to Heal* (New York: Harper & Row, 1979), p. 21; *NYT,* August 7, 1974; George Bush's notes for August 6, 1974. Courtesy of President Bush.

[50]Green, *Bush,* pp. 135–36.

[51]Staff of the *Washington Post, The Fall of a President* (New York: A Dell Book, 1974), pp. xvii–xxi.

[52]Ambrose, *Nixon: Ruin and Recovery,* p. 437.

[53]Greene, *Ford,* p. 5.

[54]*Newsweek,* August 19, 1974, p. 52; Cannon, *Time and Chance,* p. 368.

[55]Cannon, *Time and Chance,* p. 368.

[56]*Newsweek,* August 19, 1974, p. 32.

[57]Cannon, *Time and Chance,* pp. 423–25; Pat Buchanan to Gerald Ford, August 12, 1974, and Dean Burch to Gerald Ford, August 13, 1974, Robert Hartmann Papers, Box 19, GRFL.

[58]William Scranton to Gerald Ford, August 16, 1974, Philip Buchan Papers, GRFL.

[59]Green, *Bush,* p. 136.

[60]Kenneth Rush to Gerald Ford, August 17, 1974, Robert Hartmann Papers Box 19, GRFL.

[61]*NYT,* August 12, 1974.

[62]*Newsweek,* August 19, 1974, p. 52.

[63]*NYT,* August 8, 9, 10, 1974.
[64]Norman Baxter, *Houston Chronicle,* August 11, 1974.
[65]James A. Baker III to Jane Kinney and to Don Rhodes, August 15, 1974, Baker Papers, James A. Baker III Public Service Archive, Series IV, Box 7, Woodson Research Center, Rice University, TX.
[66]James A. Baker III, handwritten personal memorandum, August 16, 1974, Baker Papers, James A. Baker III Public Service Archive, Series IV, Box 7, Woodson Research Center, Rice University, TX.
[67]Art Wiese, *Houston Post,* August 21, 1974.
[68]*NYT,* August 15, 1974; *Newsweek,* August 26, 1974, p. 18; interview with Richard L. Herman, June 19, 1995.
[69]Pincus and Woodward, *WP,* August 9, 1988.
[70]*NYT,* August 14, 1974.
[71]Ibid., August 13, 1974.
[72]*Newsweek,* August 26, 1974, pp. 18–19; *NYT,* August 19, 1974.
[73]Nicholas M. Horrock, *NYT,* November 5, 1975; James A. Sterba, *NYT,* November 8, 1975; Walter Pincus and Bob Woodward, *WP,* August 9, 1988; interview with George Bush, July 6, 1995.
[74]Interview with Richard Cheney, April 21, 1995.
[75]Interview with Gerald R. Ford, July 14, 1995.
[76]Ibid.
[77]Interview with George Bush, July 6, 1995.
[78]George Bush to Thomas Ludlow Ashley, August 21, 1974, Thomas Ludlow Ashley Papers, MS-159, Center for Archival Collections, Bowling Green State University, Bowling Green, OH.
[79]George Bush, "Peking Diary," p. 254. Courtesy of President Bush.
[80]*NYT,* September 9, 1974.
[81]Woodward and Pincus, *WP,* August 9, 1988.
[82]Bush, *Barbara Bush,* pp. 107–8.
[83]Bush, "Peking Diary," p. 4.
[84]Bush, "Peking Diary," pp. 2–6.
[85]Don Oberdorfer, *WP,* December 2, 1974.
[86]Marquis Childs, *Baltimore Sun,* September 13, 1974.
[87]Bush, "Peking Diary," pp. 6–7.
[88]Bush, "Peking Diary," p. 74.
[89]*NYT,* November 5, 1995.
[90]Bush, "Peking Diary, pp. 17, 220, 224–25, 234.
[91]Ibid., p. 312.
[92]Ibid., "Peking Diary," p. 212.
[93]Ibid., "Peking Diary," pp. 220–21.
[94]Ibid., "Peking Diary," pp. 152, 169, and 178.
[95]Ibid., "Peking Diary," pp. 135, 177–78.
[96]Pearl S. Buck, *China, Past and Present* (New York: John Day, 1972).
[97]Bush, "Peking Diary," pp. 104, 135, 151–52, 169, 178, 291, 307.
[98]Ibid., p. 294.
[99]Ibid., pp. 157 and 311.
[100]Ibid., p. 26.
[101]Ibid., pp. 123 and 299.
[102]Ibid., pp. 22, 58–59 and 66.
[103]Ibid., p. 281.
[104]Ibid., p. 92.
[105]Green, *Bush,* p. 144.
[106]George Bush to Thomas Ludlow Ashley, February 18, 1975, Thomas Ludlow Ashley Papers, MS-159, Center for Archival Collections, BGSU.
[107]Bush, "Peking Diary," p. 3.
[108]Ibid., p. 141.
[109]Ibid., p. 122.
[110]Interview with George Bush, March 7, 1996.
[111]Green, *Bush,* p. 144; interview with Catherine Barr, November 19, 1991.
[112]Bush, "Peking Diary," pp. 88–325.
[113]Interview with George Bush, July 6, 1995.
[114]Ibid.; Gerald Ford to Bush, January 27, 1975, Bush Folder no. 2, GRFL; *NYT,* January 28, 1975; Dr. W. Tabb Moore to George Bush, February 25, 1975. Courtesy of President Bush.
[115]Bush, "Peking Diary," p. 129.
[116]Don Oberdorfer, *WP,* December 2, 1974.
[117]Ibid.
[118]Knaggs, *Two-Party Texas,* p. 181.
[119]Bush, "Peking Diary," pp. 170 and 245; George Bush to Thomas Ludlow Ashley, March 27, 1975, Thomas Ludlow Ashley Papers, MS-159, Center for Archival Collections, BGSU.
[120]Knaggs, *Two-Party Texas,* pp. 224 and 229.
[121]Russell Rourke to Jack Marsh, March 20, 1975, John Marsh Files, Box 6, GRFL.
[122]Bush, "Peking Diary," pp. 245 and 306.

[123]William Shawcross, *Sideshow: Kissinger, Nixon and the Destruction of Cambodia* (New York: Simon & Schuster, 1979), pp. 360–61.

[124]John Prados, *Keeper of the Keys: A History of the National Security Council From Truman to Bush* (New York: Morrow, 1991), p. 369; Ford, *A Time to Heal*, p. 276; Cannon, *Time and Chance*, pp. 396–99; Greene, *Ford*, pp. 143–151.

[125]Green, *Bush*, p. 153.

[126]Richard L. Berke, *NYT*, September 2, 1994; Bush, *Barbara Bush*, p. 104.

[127]Green, *Bush*, p. 153; interview with Barber Conable, July 8, 1993.

CHAPTER TWELVE

[1]Interview with William Colby, April 20, 1995.

[2]*Christian Science Monitor*, September 11, 1974; *Newsweek*, September 23, 1974.

[3]John Ranelagh, *The Agency: The Rise and Decline of the CIA, from Wild Bill Donovan to William Casey* (New York: Simon & Schuster, 1986), p. 593; *Newsweek*, September 30, 1994, p. 39; Green, *Bush*, p. 148.

[4]Seymour Hersh, "Huge CIA Operations Reported in U.S. Against Anti-War Forces, Other Dissidents in Nixon Years," *NYT*, December 22, 1974; Ranelagh, *The Agency*, pp. 571–75.

[5]Interview with William Colby, April 20, 1995.

[6]Interviews with William Rusher, June 16 and 20, 1995; William A. Rusher, *The Rise of the Right* (New York: William Morrow & Co., 1984), p. 265.

[7]David W. Reinhard, *The Republican Right Since 1945* (Lexington: The University Press of Kentucky, 1983), p. 229.

[8]R. Emmett Tyrrell Jr., *The Conservative Crack-Up* (New York: Simon & Schuster, 1992), p. 148.

[9]Rusher, *The Rise of the Right*, p. 265.

[10]Herbert S. Parmet, *Richard Nixon and His America* (Boston: Little, Brown, 1990), pp. 474–75; William A. Rusher, *The Rise of the Right*, *passim;* interviews with David Keene, May 26, 1993, and William Rusher, October 2, 1984.

[11]Rusher, *The Rise of the Right*, pp. 268, 275–76.

[12]James MacGregor Burns, *The Crosswinds of Freedom* (New York: Alfred A. Knopf, 1989), p. 637.

[13]Marlin Fitzwater, *Call the Briefing!* (New York: Times Books, 1995), p. 349.

[14]Ken Cole to Gerald Ford, January 22, 1975, Box 32, GRFL.

[15]Max L. Friedersdorf to Gerald Ford, July 14, 1975, Presidential Handwriting File, Box 32, GRFL.

[16]Interview with Richard Cheney, April 21, 1995; Eleanora W. Schoenebaum, *Profiles of an Era: The Nixon/Ford Years* (New York: Harcourt Brace Jovanovich, 1979), p. 553.

[17]Bearak, *LAT*, November 22, 1987.

[18]Donald Rumsfeld to President Ford, July 10, 1975, Richard Cheney Papers, Box 5, GRFL; interviews with Adm. Daniel J. Murphy, April 19, 1995, and Richard Cheney, April 21, 1995.

[19]Bush, *Looking Forward*, p. 153.

[20]Woodward and Pincus, *WP*, August 9, 1988.

[21]Interview with Hugh Liedtke, January 25, 1995.

[22]U.S. Senate, 94th Congress, 1st Session, *Hearings Before the Committee on Armed Services* (Washington, D.C.: U.S. Government Printing Office, 1975), p. 70.

[23]Green, *Bush*, p. 150.

[24]Interview with George Bush, January 25, 1995.

[25]*NYT*, November 5, 1975.

[26]William Roth to George Bush, November 20, 1975, John O. Marsh Files, Box 1, GRFL; James Sterba, *NYT*, November 8, 1973.

[27]U.S. Senate, 94th Congress, 1st Session, *Hearings Before the Committee on Armed Services United States Senate* (Washington, D.C.: U.S. Government Printing Office, 1975), p. 70.

[28]Ibid., p. 49.

[29]As quoted in Tarpley and Chaitkin, *Bush*, p. 293.

[30]Anderson, *Revolution*, pp. 165–66.

[31]Javits press release, November 28, 1975, Jacob K. Javits Papers, Special Collections, State University of New York Library at Stony Brook.

[32]George Bush to Max Friedersdorf, November 27, 1975, William T. Kendall Files, Box 7, GRFL.

[33]Jack Marsh to Max Friedersdorf, November 4, 1975, John O. Marsh Papers, Box 1, GRFL.

[34]Confidential source.

[35]Bush, *Barbara Bush*, p. 132.

[36]*U.S. News & World Report*, January 6, 1976, p. 51; U.S. Senate, 94th Congress, *Hearings Before the Committee on Armed Services* (Washington, D.C.: U.S. Government Printing Office, 1975), p. 70.

[37]Interview with Richard Cheney, April 21, 1995.

[38]Transcript of speech by Frank Church, November 11, 1975, Jacob K. Javits Papers, Department of Special Collections, SUNY at Stony Brook; Bush, *Barbara Bush*, p. 13; Bush cable to Jack Marsh, December 7, 1975, William T. Kendall Files, Box 7, GRFL.

[39]Barbara Earp to Bill Kozina, December 8, 1975, Bush Folder no. 2, GRFL.

[40]*Hearings*, p. 23.

[41]John Ranelagh, *The Agency: The Rise and Decline of the CIA, From Wild Bill Donovan to William Casey* (New York: Simon & Schuster, 1986), pp. 587 and 633.

[42]*Hearings,* pp. 30 and 38.

[43]*Hearings,* p. 85; U.S. Senate, 95th Congress, 1st Session, *Hearings Before the Select Committee on Intelligence,* April 27 and 28, 1977. (Washington, D.C.: U.S. Government Printing Office, 1977), p. 81.

[44]Gerald R. Ford to John Stennis, December 18, 1975, Robert K. Wolthius File, Box 1, GRFL.; Thomas J. Mcintyre, et al., to committee colleagues, January 19, 1976, Jacob K. Javits Papers, Special Collections, SUNY at Stony Brook.

[45]*Houston Chronicle,* January 28, 1976.

[46]*NYT,* January 28, 1976.

[47]Teresa Rosenberger to Gwen Anderson, January 28, 1976, David Gergen Papers, Box 2, GRFL.

[48]Interview with William Colby, April 20, 1995.

[49]Green, *Bush,* pp. 158 and 162.

[50]Bush, *Barbara Bush,* p. 135; Gail Sheehy, *New Passages* (New York: Random House, 1995), p. 200.

[51]Interview with William Colby, April 20, 1995.

[52]Green, *Bush,* p. 159.

[53]Interview with Adm. Daniel J. Murphy, April 19, 1995.

[54]Rhodri Jeffreys-Jones, *The CIA and American Democracy* (New Haven: Yale University Press, 1989), p. 210.

[55]George Bush to Gerald Ford, August 3, 1976, Presidential Handwriting file, FGCIA2, GRFL.

[56]U.S. Government Printing Office, *Public Papers of the Presidents: 1976, Gerald R. Ford,* pp. 348–49; John M. Crewdson, *NYT,* February 19, 1976; Nicholas M. Horrock, *NYT,* February 19, 1976.

[57]Persico, *Casey,* p. 41; memorandum by Leo Cherne, October 25, 1975, Leo Cherne Papers, Box 1, GRFL.

[58]Editorial, "Reforming the C.I.A.," *NYT,* February 20, 1976.

[59]Nicolas Horrock, *NYT,* February 21, 1976.

[60]*NYT,* February 23, 1976.

[61]George Bush to Gerald Ford, August 3, 1976, Presidential Handwriting file, FGCIA2, GRFL.

[62]Green, *Bush,* p. 160.

[63]W. John Moore, "In From the Cold," *National Journal,* October 8, 1994, p. 2328.

[64]Nicholas Horrock, *NYT,* February 19, 1976.

[65]Interviews with James Killian, June 12, 1980, and William Colby, April 20, 1995.

[66]Interviews with Richard Pipes, May 5, 1995, and William Colby, April 20, 1995; Richard Pipes, "Team B: The Reality Behind the Myth," *Commentary,* October 1986, p. 32.

[67]U.S. Senate, 94th Congress, 2nd Session, *Final Report of the Select Committee to Study Government Operations with Respect to Intelligence Operations* (Washington, D.C.: U.S. Government Printing Office, 1976), *passim.*

[68]Garthoff, *Detente,* p. 455.

[69]Garthoff, *Detente and Confrontation,* p. 595; Richard Pipes, "Team B: The Reality Behind the Myth," *Commentary,* October 1986, p. 29.

[70]Jeffreys-Jones, *CIA,* p. 213; Committee on Foreign Relations, United States Senate, January 18, 1977, declassified on November 28, 1995.

[71]Interview with William Colby, April 20, 1995.

[72]Interview with Richard Pipes, May 5, 1995; Bush testimony before the Senate Foreign Relations Committee, January 18, 1977.

[73]David Binder, *NYT,* December 26, 1976; Pipes, "Team B," p. 31; Garthoff, *Detente,* p. 607.

[74]Report of Team "B," Intelligence Community Experiment in Competitive Analysis: Soviet Strategic Objectives, an Alternative View. Central Intelligence Agency, 1976, pp. 41–42. Declassified October 1992 and obtained through the Freedom of Information Act.

[75]Ibid.

[76]U.S. Senate, 96th Congress, 1st Session, *Report to the Senate of the Select Committee on Intelligence* (Washington, D.C., U.S. Government Printing Office, 1979), p. 36; interview with Daniel J. Murphy, April 19, 1995.

[77]Interview with George Bush, July 6, 1995.

[78]Buckley, *Panama,* p. 21.

[79]Oliver L. North, with William Novak, *Under Fire: An American Story* (New York: HarperCollins, 1991), p. 226.

[80]John Dingnes, *Our Man in Havana,* rvd. and updated ed. (New York: Times Books), 1991, p. xi.

[81]Dinges, *Our Man in Panama,* p. 33; Michael L. Conniff, *Panama and the United States: The Forced Alliance* (Athens: The University of Georgia Press, 1992), p. 149.

[82]Asa Barber, "The President's Manhood," *Playboy,* August 1990, p. 39.

[83]Seymour H. Hersh, *NYT,* June 13, 1986; Dinges, *Our Man in Panama,* p. 89.

[84]Dinges, *Our Man in Panama,* pp. 69–71.

[85]Buckley, *Panama,* p. 21.

[86]R. M. Koster and Guillermo Sanchez, *In the Time of the Tyrants: Panama, 1968–1990* (New York: W. W. Norton & Company, 1990).

[87]Dinges, *Our Man in Panama,* p. 118; Andrew Cockburn, *WP,* July 7, 1991.

[88]Dinges, *Our Man in Panama,* p. 87.

[89]Ibid., pp. 83–84.

[90]Kempe, *Divorcing the Dictator,* p. 31.

[91]Dinges, *Our Man in Panama,* p. 80.

[92]Kempe, *Divorcing the Dictator,* p. 30.

[93]Colin Powell, with Joseph E. Persico, *My American Journey* (New York: Random House, 1995), p. 415.

[94]Interview with George Bush, March 7, 1996.

[95]Stephen Engelberg and Jeff Gerth, *NYT,* September 28, 1988; Dinges, *Our Man in Panama,* pp. 88–89; Buckley, *Panama,* p. 19.

[96]Dinges, *Our Man in Panama,* p. 90; Buckley, *Panama,* p. 19; Kempe, *Divorcing the Dictator,* pp. 31–32.

[97]Ibid.

[98]Anderson, *Revolution,* p. 46.

[99]*Houston Chronicle,* August 15, 1976.

[100]Interview with George Bush, January 25, 1995; *Houston Chronicle,* November 20, 1976.

[101]Bush, *Barbara Bush,* p. 137.

CHAPTER THIRTEEN

[1]George Bush to Thomas Ludlow Ashley, November 28, 1977, Thomas Ludlow Ashley Papers, MS-159, Center for Archival Collections, BGSU.

[2]Interview with George Bush, July 20, 1995.

[3]Interview with Chase Untermeyer, July 31, 1995.

[4]*The Texas Observer,* October 7, 1977.

[5]Walter Pincus and Bob Woodward, *WP,* August 11, 1988.

[6]*Houston Post,* June 16, 1979.

[7]*NYT,* February 26, 1978; George Bush response to written questions, August 9, 1995.

[8]Green, *Bush,* p. 168.

[9]Ibid.; Tarpley and Chaitkin, *Bush,* p. 327.

[10]Pincus and Woodward, *WP,* August 11, 1988; Bush to Ashley, April 14, 1977, Thomas Ludlow Ashley Papers, MS-159, Center for Archival Collections, BGSU.

[11]Pincus and Woodward, *WP,* August 11, 1988.

[12]Shelby Hodg, "Hussein, Rockefeller Meet, Dine with Bush," *Houston Post,* May 3, 1977; Bush, *Barbara Bush,* p. 137.

[13]Interviews with George Bush, January 25, 1995, and Dan Gilchrist, September 13, 1995.

[14]Harris Worcester, "Travels with Bush and Connally," *The Texas Observer,* September 22, 1978, pp. 18–19; Reed, "George Bush On the Move," p. 56; Cannon and Peterson, *Pursuit of the Presidency,* p. 130; interview with David Bates, July 17, 1996.

[15]Bush, *Barbara Bush,* pp. 138–40; interview with Chase Untermeyer, July 31, 1995.

[16]*NYT,* September 26, 1977; Bush, *Barbara Bush,* pp. 138–40; Petzinger Jr., *Oil and Honor,* p. 243; Woodward and Pincus, *WP,* August 11, 1988; interview with Chase Untermeyer, July 31, 1995.

[17]Claudia Feldman, *Houston Chronicle,* May 18, 1977.

[18]Leslie Loddeke, *Houston Post,* July 12, 1990.

[19]Interviews with J. Danforth Quayle, June 14, 1995, and David Bates, July 17, 1996.

[20]Transcripts of speeches at The Citadel, March 13, 1977, the University of Houston, August 13, 1977, Birmingham, Alabama, October 28, 1977, to the American Petroleum Institute at Houston, November 14, 1977, Georgetown University, Washington, D.C., January 25, 1978, Center for International Business, Houston, April 11, 1978, New Haven Chamber of Commerce, April 13, 1978, National Association of Manufacturers, Boston, Massachusetts, May 11, 1978, Phillips Academy at Andover, Massachusetts, June 2, 1978. Bush Prepresidential Speeches and Interviews, Bush Presidential Materials Project, Texas A&M University, College Station, TX.

[21]Interview with Lanny Griffith, July 31, 1996.

[22]Ibid.

[23]Draft statement, George Bush on Abortion, November 14, 1979, Baker Papers, Series VIII, Box 21, Rice University, TX.

[24]Interviews with Chase Untermeyer, July 31, 1995; George Warren Upson, January 29, 1992; Barbara Bush, July 6, 1995; and David Keene, May 26, 1993.

[25]Michael Schaller, *Reckoning with Reagan: America and Its President in the 1980s* (New York: Oxford University Press, 1992), p. 18.

[26]Jack W. Germond and Jules Witcover, *Blue Smoke and Mirrors: How Reagan Won and Why Carter Lost the Election of 1980* (New York: The Viking Press, 1980), pp. 100–1.

[27]*NYT,* May 3, 1978.

[28]Interviews with James W. Cicconi and Lyn Nofziger, October 17, 1995.

[29]Lloyd Grove, *WP,* July 31, 1992.

[30]Interview with David Bates, July 17, 1996.

[31]Interview with John Connally, May 19, 1986.

[32]*TGP 1980,* p. 83; Michael Barone, Grant Ujifusa, and Douglas Matthews, *The Almanac of American Politics 1980* (New York: E. P. Dutton, 1979), p. 265.

[33]Tom Wicker, "Republicans Try to Get Their Act Together," *New York Times Magazine,* February 12, 1978, pp. 13, 15, and 59.

[34]Germond and Witcover, *Blue Smoke and Mirrors,* pp. 117–18; *NYT,* February 7, 1980; Harris Worcester, "Travels with Bush and Connally," *The Texas Observer,* September 22, 1978, p. 18.

[35]*TGP 1980,* pp. 11 and 35.

[36]Germond and Witcover, *Blue Smoke and Mirrors,* p. 116.

[37]Interview with David Keene, May 26, 1993.

[38]*NYT,* February 8, 1980, and February 18, 1980; Alexander Cockburn and James Ridgeway, "He Ran the GOP for Nixon, he Ran the CIA for Ford," *Rolling Stone,* March 30, 1980; Kilian, *Barbara Bush,* p. 105.

[39]Interview with David Keene, May 26, 1993.

[40]Interview with Barbara Bush, July 6, 1995.

[41]Philip Nobile and Eric Nadler, *The Village Voice,* November 15, 1988; Marsha Kranes, *New York Post,* August 11, 1992.

[42]Cannon and Peterson in Broder, *Pursuit of the Presidency,* pp. 132–33 and 152.

[43]Adam Clymer, *NYT,* January 20, 1980.

[44]Roy Reed, "George Bush On the Move," p. 58.

[45]Cockburn and Ridgeway, "He Ran the GOP for Nixon, he Ran the CIA for Ford."

[46]Interview with David Keene, August 30, 1995.

[47]Ibid., May 26, 1993.

[48]E. J. Dionne Jr., *NYT,* February 26, 1980.

[49]Interview with David Keene, August 30, 1995; Brewton, *Bush,* pp. 165–67; Elizabeth Drew, "Letter From Washington," *The New Yorker,* July 21, 1983, pp. 132–33.

[50]Green, *Bush,* p. 171; interviews with William Colby, April 20, 1995, Daniel J. Murphy, April 19, 1995, and Mary Sheila Gall, February 24, 1992; Bill Peterson, *WP,* March 1, 1980; interview with Barber Conable, July 8, 1993.

[51]*WP,* January 16, 1993; Associated Press, January 16, 1993; interviews with Catherine Barr, November 19, 1991, and Mary Sheila Gall, February 24, 1992.

[52]*TGP 1980,* p. 104.

[53]Alan Crawford, *Thunder on the Right* (New York: Pantheon Books, 1980), pp. 159–63; William Greider in Broder, *Pursuit of the Presidency,* p. 165; *NYT,* August 20, 1980; Haynes Johnson, *Sleepwalking Through History: America in the Reagan Years* (New York: W. W. Norton & Co., 1991), p. 208; Paul T. David in David and Everson, *Presidential Election and Transition,* p. 161.

[54]"America and Religion: The Counterattack of God," *The Economist,* July 8, 1995, pp. 19–21; John B. Judis, "Crosses to Bear," *The New Republic,* September 12, 1994, p. 21.

[55]*NYT,* March 31, 1980.

[56]Interview with John B. Connally, May 19, 1986; Richard L. Berke, *NYT,* November 25, 1995.

[57]A. James Reichly notes of interview with Lyn Nofziger, January 5, 1978, A. James Reichly Papers, Box 3, GRFL.

[58]Cannon and Peterson in Broder, *Pursuit of the Presidency,* p. 132; Germond and Witcover, *Blue Smoke,* p. 104.

[59]Alphonse D'Amato, *Power, Pasta and Politics: The World According to Senator Al D'Amato* (New York: Hyperion, 1995), pp. 186–88; Germond and Witcover, *Blue Smoke,* p. 96.

[60]*Newsweek,* December 3, 1979, p. 44; interview with George Bush, January 25, 1995.

[61]Roy Reed, "George Bush On the Move," *New York Times Magazine,* February 10, 1980, pp. 23 and 58; Tom Wicker, *NYT,* February 23, 1979; Germond and Witcover, *Blue Smoke,* p. 119; Green, *Bush,* p. 174; Betty Beale, *Houston Chronicle,* May 6, 1979.

[62]Germond and Witcover, *Blue Smoke,* pp. 111 and 120.

[63]Cannon and Peterson in Broder, *Pursuit of the Presidency,* pp. 136–137; *NYT,* January 7, 1980.

[64]Cannon and Peterson in Broder, *Pursuit of the Presidency,* pp. 136–137.

[65]Germond and Witcover, *Blue Smoke,* pp. 114–15; *TGP 1980,* p. 2.

[66]*NYT,* January 6 and 12, 1980.

[67]Lou Cannon, *Reagan* (New York: G. P. Putnam's Sons, 1982), p. 247.

[68]Germond and Witcover, *Blue Smoke,* pp. 115 and 119.

[69]Ibid., p. 120.

[70]Bush to James A. Baker III, February 10, 1980, Baker Papers, Series VIII, Box 21, Rice University, TX.

[71]*NYT,* February 19, 1980.

[72]Amy Wilentz, "Bygones," *Time,* December 23, 1985, p. 24.

[73]A *New York Times/CBS News* poll published on February 20, 1980, for example, showed that many Bush supporters were uncertain of what he stood for, which enabled him to draw support from across the usual battle lines.

[74]Harris Worcester, *The Texas Observer,* September 22, 1978.

[75]Germond and Witcover, *Blue Smoke,* p. 119.

[76]Interview with David Keene, May 26, 1995.

[77]Cannon, *Reagan,* p. 251; Cannon and Peterson in Broder, *Pursuit of the Presidency,* p. 140; Germond and Witcover, *Blue Smoke,* p. 123.

[78]Interview with David Keene, May 26, 1995; Cannon and Peterson in Broder, *Pursuit of the Presidency,* p. 140; Cannon, *Reagan,* p. 251.

[79]Jon L. Breen to Hugh Gregg, February 11, 1980, Baker Papers, Series VIII, Box 21, Rice University, TX.

[80]Germond and Witcover, *Blue Smoke,* pp. 125–126; interview with David Keene, May 26, 1993.

[81]George Bush to Robert Dole, February 25, 1980, Baker Papers, Series VIII, Box 21, Rice University, TX.

[82]Interview with David Keene, May 26, 1993.

[83]Kitty Kelley, *Nancy Reagan: The Unauthorized Biography* (New York: Simon & Schuster, 1991), p. 261.

[84]Germond and Witcover, *Blue Smoke,* p. 127.

[85]Cannon and Peterson in Broder, *Pursuit of the Presidency,* p. 142.

[86]Interview with Peter Teeley, September 18, 1995.

[87]Germond and Witcover, *Blue Smoke*, p. 129.

[88]Ibid.

[89]Ibid., p. 131.

[90]*NYT,* February 27, 1980.

[91]Knaggs, *Texas,* p. 238.

[92]Hedrick Smith, *NYT,* February 28, 1980.

[93]For the Team B backgrounds of Reagan's advisers, cf., Hedrick Smith, *NYT,* May 25, 1980.

[94]Cannon and Peterson in Broder, *Pursuit of the Presidency,* p. 126.

[95]*NYT,* March 7, 1980; Adam Clymer, *NYT,* March 8, 1980.

[96]William Crotty in Paul T. David and David H. Everson (eds.), *The Presidential Election and Transition, 1980–81* (Carbondale and Edwardville, IL: University of Southern Illinois Press, 1983), p. 8.

[97]*NYT,* March 12, 13, and 16, 1980.

[98]As quoted in Chandler Davidson, *Race and Class in Texas Politics* (Princeton, NJ: Princeton University Press, 1990), p. 209.

[99]Howell Raines, *NYT,* March 8, 1980.

[100]Interview with Peter Teeley, September 18, 1995.

[101]Mary D. to David Keene, January 9, 1980, Baker Papers, Series VIII, Box 21, Rice University, TX; Douglas Kneeland, *NYT,* February 29, 1980; Francis X. Clines, *NYT,* March 7, 1980.

[102]Francis X. Clines, *NYT,* March 9, 1980; Barrett, *Gambling with History,* p. 377.

[103]Howell Raines, *NYT,* February 19, 1980; interview with George Bush, July 6, 1995.

[104]Hedrick Smith, *NYT,* May 5, 1980; *The Post and Courier* (Charleston, SC), March 3, 1980, and March 5, 1980.

[105]Interview with David Keene, May 26, 1993.

[106]Eric Alterman, "Playing Hardball," *New York Times Magazine,* April 30, 1989, pp. 31; Gerald M. Boyd, *NYT,* May 30, 1988; Sidney Blumenthal, *NYT,* April 22, 1991; *1989 Current Biography Yearbook,* pp. 25–29.

[107]Michael Oreskes, *NYT,* March 30, 1991; Gerald M. Boyd, *NYT,* May 30, 1988.

[108]*1989 Current Biography Yearbook,* pp. 25–29; *NYT,* March 8 and 9, 1980, and May 30, 1988; Haynes Johnson, *Sleepwalking Through History,* p. 394n; Gerald M. Boyd, *NYT,* May 30, 1988.

[109]*NYT,* April 24, 1980.

[110]William Crotty in David and Everson, *Presidential Election and Transition,* p. 6; *NYT,* May 23, 1980.

[111]*NYT,* May 26, 1980.

[112]Monica Reeves, *Houston Post,* May 25, 1980; confidential source.

[113]Interviews with Victor Gold, June 16, 1995, and David Keene, May 26, 1993; Green, *Bush,* pp. 178–79.

[114]Interview with Victor Gold, June 16, 1995.

[115]Interviews with David Keene, May 26, 1993, and Victor Gold, June 16, 1995; James A. Baker, III, with Thomas M. DeFrank, *The Politics of Diplomacy* (New York: G. P. Putnam's Sons, 1995), pp. 20–21.

[116]Green, *Bush,* pp. 178–179; Barbara Canetti, *Houston Post,* May 27, 1980; William Crotty in David and Everson, *Presidential Election and Transition,* p. 6.

[117]Jeb Bush to David Keene, August 1, 1980, Baker Papers, Series IX, Box 24, Rice University, TX; interview with Ron Kaufman, April 18, 1995; Ron Kaufman, interviewed by Michael L. Gillette, March 20, 1990, the Center for American History, the University of Texas at Austin.

CHAPTER FOURTEEN

[1]*WP,* August 16, 1992.

[2]Interview with Peter Teeley, September 18, 1995.

[3]Reading copies of Bush speeches at the National Press Club, May 1, 1979, and September 5, 1979, BPMP.

[4]Henry Hurt III, "George Bush, Plucky Lad," *Texas Monthly,* June 1983, p. 206.

[5]Interview with Dan Gilchrist, September 13, 1995.

[6]Interview with Mary Sheila Gall, September 14, 1995.

[7]Interview with David Keene, August 30, 1995.

[8]Interviews with Mary Sheila Gall, September 18, 1995, Ron Kaufman, April 18, 1995, and Craig Fuller, July 31, 1996.

[9]Duffy and Goodgame, *Marching in Place,* p. 110; Nobile and Nadler, *The Village Voice,* November 15, 1988.

[10]Nobile and Nadler, *The Village Voice,* November 15, 1988.

[11]*NYT,* April 6, 1978; Woodward and Pincus, *WP,* August 10, 1988.

[12]Marsha Kranes, *New York Post,* August 11, 1992.

[13]Nobile and Nadler, *The Village Voice,* November 15, 1988.

[14]Ibid.

[15]Interview with Catherine V. Barr, September 29, 1995.

[16]Duffy and Goodgame, *Marching in Place,* p. 110.

[17]Interview with Mary Sheila Gall, September 18, 1995.

[18]*WP,* July 1, 1987; interview with David Keene, August 30, 1995.

[19]Interview with Nancy Ellis Bush, November 12, 1992.

[20]Nobile and Nadler, *The Village Voice,* November 15, 1988.

[21]Interview with Catherine V. Barr, November 19, 1991.

[22]Nobile and Nadler, *The Village Voice,* November 15, 1988; Joe Conasan, *Spy,* July/August 1992, p. 35.

²³*NYT,* June 6 and 15, 1980.

²⁴Pomper in Pomper, *Election of 1980,* pp. 10–11; Joseph Persico, *Casey: From the OSS to the CIA* (New York: Viking, 1990), p. 185.

²⁵*TGP 1980,* p. 6.

²⁶Germond and Witcover, *Blue Smoke,* p. 309.

²⁷*NYT,* July 22, 1980.

²⁸King, *Bush,* p. 5.

²⁹Germond and Witcover, *Blue Smoke,* pp. 167 and 170; Bush, *Looking Forward,* p. 7; Cannon, *Reagan,* p. 266.

³⁰Confidential source.

³¹*NYT,* July 16, 1980; King, *Bush,* p. 2.

³²Bush, *Looking Forward,* pp. 9–10.

³³Johnson, *Sleepwalking Through History,* p. 209.

³⁴*NYT,* July 17, 1980; Germond and Witcover, *Blue Smoke,* p. 313.

³⁵Interview with Lyn Nofziger, October 17, 1995; Reagan, *My Turn,* p. 212.

³⁶Cannon, *Reagan,* p. 231; Associated Press release, August 14, 1992; interviews with Martin Anderson, July 7, 1993, and Lyn Nofziger, October 17, 1995; Reagan, *My Turn,* pp. 213 and 270–71.

³⁷Ibid.

³⁸Interviews with Nicholas F. Brady, November 7, 1995, and Ron Kaufman, April 18, 1995.

³⁹Bush, *Looking Forward,* p. 15.

⁴⁰*NYT,* July 17, 1980.

⁴¹Bill Peterson, *WP,* July 18, 1980, as quoted in Kelley, *Nancy Reagan,* p. 273.

⁴²Interviews with George Bush, July 6, 1995, and William Rusher, June 16, 1995; Cannon, *Reagan,* p. 216; Warren Weaver Jr., *NYT,* July 18, 1980; Robin Toner, *NYT,* February 25, 1996.

⁴³Interview with Dan Quayle, June 14, 1995.

⁴⁴Arthur Wiese, *Houston Post,* July 19, 1980.

⁴⁵*NYT,* July 18, 1980.

⁴⁶Cannon, *Reagan,* p. 340.

⁴⁷*NYT,* July 18, 1980.

⁴⁸Persico, *Casey,* p. 190.

⁴⁹*NYT,* August 10, 1980; Germond and Witcover, *Blue Smoke,* p. 197.

⁵⁰Germond and Witcover, *Blue Smoke,* p. 206.

⁵¹*TGP 1980,* pp. 169–70.

⁵²Arthur Wiese, *Houston Post,* July 19, 1980; *NYT,* July 26, 1980.

⁵³*NYT,* August 23 and 24, September 29, and October 16, 1980; Knaggs, *Texas,* p. 245.

⁵⁴Howell Raines, "Reagan Backs Evangelists In Their Political Activities," *NYT,* August 22, 1980; Rowland Evans and Robert Novak, *The Reagan Revolution* (New York: E. P. Dutton, 1981), p. 213.

⁵⁵Howell Raines, *NYT,* August 24, 1980.

⁵⁶*NYT,* August 22, 1980.

⁵⁷Ibid., August 25, 1980.

⁵⁸Ibid., September 13, 1980.

⁵⁹*Houston Post,* July 21, 1980.

⁶⁰*NYT,* October 19, 1980.

⁶¹Ibid., October 23, 1980, and November 3, 1980.

⁶²Jules Witcover, "Election of 1980," Arthur M. Schlesinger Jr., ed., *Running for President* (New York: Simon & Schuster, 1994) vol. 2, p. 391.

⁶³Gary Sick, *October Surprise* (New York: Times Books, 1991), p. 23.

⁶⁴Prescott Bush Jr. to James A. Baker III, September 2, 1980, Baker Papers, Series IX, Box 24, James A. Baker III Public Service Archive, Rice University, TX.

⁶⁵Stefan Halper to Ed Meese, October 19, 1980, "The Hostage Question." Courtesy of Sophia Casey.

⁶⁶Richard Harwood in Broder, *Pursuit of the Presidency,* p. 300.

⁶⁷Michael Schaller, *Reckoning with Reagan: America and Its President in the 1980s* (New York: Oxford University Press, 1992), p. 32.

⁶⁸Halper to Meese, October 19, 1980. Courtesy of Sophia Casey.

⁶⁹Germond and Witcover, *Blue Smoke,* p. 273.

⁷⁰Persico, *Casey,* p. 328.

⁷¹Ibid., p. 331.

⁷²Germond and Witcover, *Blue Smoke,* p. 272.

⁷³Ibid., p. 269.

⁷⁴Anderson, *Revolution,* pp. 339–41; Ronald Reagan, *An American Life* (New York: Simon & Schuster, 1990), p. 219.

⁷⁵Germond and Witcover, *Blue Smoke,* p. 281.

⁷⁶*NYT,* October 29, 1980.

⁷⁷Ibid., November 3, 1980.

⁷⁸Ibid.

⁷⁹Ibid.

CHAPTER FIFTEEN

[1]Smith, *Power Game*, p. 833.

[2]Barry Bearak, *LAT*, November 22, 1987.

[3]Interview with Chase Untermeyer, July 31, 1995.

[4]Arthur Wiese, *Houston Post*, December 9, 1980; interview with George Bush, July 6, 1995.

[5]Susan Warren, *Houston Chronicle*, August 16, 1992; John E. Yank, *WP*, December 30, 1991; *NYT*, August 14, 1992; Arthur Wiese, *Houston Post*, December 9, 1980; Bush, *Barbara Bush*, p. 163; Mark Carreau, *Houston Chronicle*, October 6, 1984.

[6]Interview with George Bush, July 6, 1995.

[7]Transcript of conversation between George Bush and A. James Reichley, Reichley Papers, Box 3, GRFL.

[8]Interview with James A. Baker, III, March 12, 1995.

[9]John W. Mashek, "George Bush: Number Two Man on the Spot," *U.S. News & World Report*, February 2, 1981, p. 26.

[10]Interview with Chase Untermeyer, October 5, 1995.

[11]Interview with Adm. Daniel Murphy, April 19, 1995.

[12]Interview with Ron Kaufman, April 18, 1995.

[13]Ibid.

[14]Cannon, *Reagan*, p. 340.

[15]Kelley, *Nancy Reagan*, p. 273; interview with Barbara Bush, July 6, 1995.

[16]Persico, *Casey*, p. 177.

[17]Alexander M. Haig Jr., *Caveat: Realism, Reagan, and Foreign Policy* (New York: Macmillan Publishing Company, 1984), p. 3.

[18]Bob Woodward, *Veil: The Secret World of the CIA 1981–1987* (New York: Simon & Schuster, 1987), p. 38.

[19]Kelley, *Nancy Reagan*, p. 364.

[20]David Stockman, *The Triumph of Politics: Why the Reagan Revolution Failed* (New York: Harper & Row, 1986), p. 82.

[21]Cannon, *Reagan*, p. 431; Barrett, *Gambling with History*, p. 375; Reagan, *My Turn*, p. 241.

[22]Interview with Lyn Nofziger, October 17, 1995.

[23]Ibid.

[24]Johnson, *Sleepwalking Through History*, p. 20.

[25]Lynn Rosellini, *NYT*, January 21, 1981.

[26]White, *America in Search of Itself*, p. 306.

[27]Cannon, *Reagan*, p. 18.

[28]David E. Rosenbaum, *NYT*, January 21, 1981.

[29]Bernard Gwertzman, *NYT*, January 21, 1981.

[30]Bush, *Barbara Bush*, p. 162.

[31]Cannon, *Reagan*, p 21; *NYT*, January 21, 1981.

[32]Lynn Rosellini, *NYT*, January 21, 1981.

[33]Randall Rothenberg, "In Search of George Bush," *New York Times Magazine*, March 6, 1988, p. 47.

[34]Interview with George Bush, March 8, 1996.

[35]Ibid.

[36]Interview with Nicholas F. Brady, November 7, 1995.

[37]Randall Rothenberg, "In Search of George Bush," *NYTM*, March 6, 1988, p. 48.

[38]Fred Barnes, "On the Supply Side: Bush Comes Down in the Corporate Camp," *Business Month*, September 1988.

[39]Meese, *With Reagan*, p. 75; Barrett, *Gambling with History*, p.88; Cannon, *Reagan*, p. 329.

[40]Anderson, *Revolution*, p. 260.

[41]*Business Week*, March 9, 1981.

[42]Green, *Bush*, pp. 195–96; Saul Friedman, *Houston Post*, March 27, 1981.

[43]Randall Rothenberg, "In Search of George Bush," *New York Times Magazine*, March 6, 1988, p. 48; William Greider, "When Big Business Needs a Favor, George Bush Gets the Call," *Rolling Stone*, April 12, 1984, p. 14; Green, *Bush*, pp. 194–95;

[44]Green, *Bush*, p. 196; *Houston Post*, April 2, 1984; William Greider, "When Big Business Needs a Favor, George Bush Gets the Call," Rolling Stone, April 12, 1984, p. 8; *The Economist*, September 24, 1988, p. 20.

[45]Randall Rothenberg, "In Search of George Bush," *NYTM*, March 6, 1988, p. 48; Jefferson Morely, "Crack in Black and White," *The Washington Post National Weekly Edition*, Dec. 4–10, 1995, pp. 21–22.

[46]Morton Kondracke, "Vice President Sunbeam: The Man Who Isn't There," *The New Republic*, March 30, 1987, pp. 20–23; Steven Emerson, "Bush's Toothless War Against Terrorism," *U.S. News & World Report*, October 31, 1988, p. 25.

[47]Tom Watson, *Boston Globe*, March 21, 1992; Rhonda Cook, *Atlanta Journal & Constitution*, October 9, 1994; Abiola Sinclair, *Amsterdam News*, January 27, 1990; Maria Odum, *Atlanta Journal & Constitution*, January 21, 1990; Gary Abramson, *Atlanta Journal & Constitution*, June 22, 1989; Saul Friedman, *Houston Post*, March 27, 1981; *Houston Chronicle*, August 9, 1981.

[48]Barrett, *Gambling with History*, p. 230; Cannon, *President Reagan*, p. 197; Saul Friedman, "Bush Skill As Team Player Scored in Battle With Haig," *Houston Post*, March 27, 1981; Smith, *Power Game*, p. 309.

[49]Green, *Bush*, p. 190; Herbert S. Abrams, *The President Has Been Shot* (New York: Norton, 1992), p. 28; Barrett, *Gambling with History*, p. 107.

[50]Haig, *Caveat*, p. 153.

[51]Bush, *Looking Forward*, p. 221.

[52]Fred Bonavita, *Houston Post*, March 31, 1981; Larry Speakes with Robert Pack, *Speaking Out* (New York: Charles Scribner's Sons, 1988), p. 6; Reagan, *An American Life*, p. 8.

[53]Bush, *Looking Forward*, pp. 215–22; Barrett, *Gambling with History*, pp. 109–11.

[54]Haig, *Caveat*, p. 153; Barrett, *Gambling with History*, pp. 113–114.

[55]Haig, *Caveat*, p. 157.

[56]Haig, *Caveat*, p. 158.

[57]Speakes, *Speaking Out*, pp. x and 11.

[58]Cannon, *Reagan*, p. 199.

[59]Haig, *Caveat*, p. 164.

[60]Haig, *Caveat*, p. 165.

[61]Cannon, *President Reagan*, p. 199; Haig, *Caveat*, p. 160.

[62]Barrett, *Gambling with History*, pp. 114–15.

[63]Bush, *Looking Forward*, p. 222.

[64]Barrett, *Gambling with History*, pp. 112 and 120.

[65]Speakes, *Speaking Out*, p. 10.

[66]Haig, *Caveat*, p. 162.

[67]Green, *Bush*, pp. 188–89; *OIC*, v. 1, p. 474.

[68]Polly Whittell, "On Board with George Bush," *Motorboard & Sailing*, March 1988, p. 122.

[69]*NYT*, January 5, 1983.

[70]Leslie H. Gelb, *NYT*, July 8, 1985.

[71]Interview with Prescott Bush Jr., January 14, 1994; George Bush diary entry, April 8, 1991, OGB.

[72]Michael Barone and Grant Ujifusa, *The Almanac of American Politics 1986* (Washington, D.C.: The National Journal, 1985), p. 235.

[73]Interview with Prescott S. Bush Jr., January 14, 1994.

[74]Woodward and Pincus, *WP*, August 7, 1988.

[75]Interview with H. R. (Bob) Haldeman, January 25, 1985.

[76]Michael Barone, *Our Country* (New York: The Free Press, 1990), p. 661.

[77]Cannon, *Reagan*, p. 157.

[78]Stockman, *Triumph of Politics*, p. 9.

[79]Stockman, *Triumph of Politics* pp. 4, 82, and 353; Edwin Meese III, *With Reagan: The Inside Story* (Washington, D.C.: Regnery Gateway, 1992), pp. 144–47 and 178; Donald Regan, *For the Record: From Wall Street to Washington* (San Diego and New York: Harcourt Brace Jovanovich, 1988), p. 184.

[80]Daniel J. Mitchell, "Bush's Rasputin," *The New Republic*, December 28, 1992.

[81]Anderson, *Revolution*, p. 240.

[82]Stockman, *Triumph of Politics*, p. 402.

[83]Alan Brinkley, *The Unfinished Nation* (New York: McGraw-Hill, 1993), p. 883.

[84]Stockman, *Triumph of Politics*, p. 407.

[85]Brinkley, *Unfinished Nation*, p. 833; Stockman, *Triumph of Politics*, p. 302.

[86]Stockman, *Triumph of Politics*, pp. 332–33.

[87]Newt Gingrich to James A. Baker III, Baker Papers, Series X, Box 28, Rice University, TX.

[88]Ibid.

[89]Newt Gingrich to James A. Baker III, March 2 and April 1, 1982, Baker Papers, Series X, Box 28, Rice University, TX.

[90]Michael L. Conniff, *Panama and the United States: The Forced Alliance* (Athens: The University of Georgia Press, 1992), p. 152; text of NSC paper on policing in Central America and Cuba, *NYT*, April 7, 1983.

[91]Clifford Kraus, *NYT*, November 9, 1993.

[92]Mark Danner, *The Massacre at El Mozote: A Parable of the Cold War* (New York: Vantage Books, 1994), *passim;* Shirley Christian, *NYT*, November 23, 1991; Clifford Kraus, *NYT*, July 16, 1993; Larry Rohter, *NYT*, February 12, 1996.

[93]Bob Woodward, *Veil*, pp. 112–13.

[94]Woodward, *Veil*, p. 113; Gilboa, "Panama Invasion," p. 539; Linda Robinson, *Intervention or Neglect* (New York: Council on Foreign Relations, 1991), p. 111.

[95]Johnson, *Sleepwalking Through History*, p. 258; Koster and Sanchez, *Time of Tyrants*, pp. 274–75; Bob Woodward, *Veil*, 167.

[96]Persico, *Casey*, pp. 274; Stephen Kinzer, *Blood Brothers: Life and War in Nicaragua* (New York: G. P. Putnam's Sons, 1991), p. 143; Leslie Cockburn, *Out of Control* (New York: The Atlantic Monthly Press, 1987), pp. 10–11.

[97]Michael Mayer, "The Iran-Contra Affairs and the Trial of Oliver North," in Michael R. Belknap (ed), *American Political Trials*, rvd. ed. (Westport, CT: Praeger, 1994), pp. 258–59; Woodward, *Veil*, p. 228; Draper, *A Very Thin Line*, pp. 18–19.

[98]Michael Mayer, "The Iran-Contra Affair and the Trial of Oliver North," in Michael R. Belknap (ed.), *American Political Trials* rvd. ed. (Westport, CT: Praeger, 1994), p. 259; Kinzer, *Blood Brothers*, p. 97; Robert Kagan, *A Twilight Struggle: American Power and Nicaragua, 1977–1990* (New York: The Free Press, 1996), pp. 466–67; *Tower Commission*, pp. 342–43.

[99]Persico, *Casey*, p. 273.

[100]*OIC*, vol. 2, p. 396.

[101]Ledeen, *Perilous Statecraft*, p. 288.

[102]Kagan, *A Twilight Struggle*, p. 466; interview with Elliott Abrams, May 26, 1993; Interview with George Bush, March 7, 1996; Richard Secord, with Jay Wurts, *Honored & Betrayed* (New York: John Wiley & Sons, 1992), p. 275.

[103]*OIC*, vol. 1, p. 487; Draper, *A Very Thin Line*, p. 575.

[104]*OIC*, vol. 1, pp. 493 and 500.

[105]Interview with George Bush, March 7, 1996; *NYT,* August 5, 1992.

[106]James LeMoyne, *NYT,* October 14, 1986; Howard Kohn and Vicki Monks, "The Dirty Secrets of George Bush," *Rolling Stone,* November 3, 1988, pp. 42 and 46–47; Lawrence Walsh, *Final Report of the Independent Counsel for Iran/Contra Matters* (3 vols; Washington, D.C.: United States Court of Appeals for the District of Columbia Circuit, 1993), vol. 2, p. 396, and vol. 1, pp. 247, 480, 485, and 503; Persico, *Casey*, pp. 275–76; Koster and Sanchez, *In the Time of Tyrants,* pp. 273–74; George Lardner and Walter Pincus, *WP,* September 20, 1991, August 27, 1992, and September 17, 1992; Draper, *A Very Thin Line,* p. 576. Gregg did testify before the Senate Foreign Relations Committee.

[107]John Lewis Gaddis, *The United States and the End of the Cold War* (New York: Oxford University Press, 1992), p. 19.

[108]Cannon, *Reagan*, pp. 446–47.

[109]Woodward, *Veil*, p. 289.

[110]Woodward, *Veil*, p. 290; Cannon, *Reagan*, p. 447.

[111]Buckley, *Panama*, p. 104; Stephen E. Ambrose, *Rise to Globalism* (New York: Penguin Books, 1993), p. 314.

[112]Stuart Taylor Jr., *NYT,* November 6, 1983.

[113]*The Gallup Poll 1983*, p. 262.

[114]James David Barber, *Washington Monthly*, October 1991, p. 25; Gerald Boyd, *NYT,* November 20, 1987; Randall Rothenberg, "In Search of George Bush," *New York Times Magazine*, March 6, 1988, p. 48.

[115]Michael Isikoff, *WP,* February 4, 1992.

[116]Stephen Engelberg and Jeff Garth, *NYT,* September 28, 1988; Buckley, *Panama*, p. 148; North, *Under Fire*, pp. 225–26; interview with Daniel Murphy, April 15, 1995.; Draper, *A Very Thin Line*, p. 574.

[117]North, *Under Fire*, pp. 227–28.

[118]Ibid., p. 226.

[119]Stephen Engelberg and Jeff Garth, *NYT,* September 28, 1988; interview with Daniel Murphy, April 19, 1995; Koster and Sanchez, *In the Time of Tyrants*, p. 301; Gilboa, "Panama Invasion," p. 543.

[120]Interview with George Bush, March 7, 1996.

[121]*Department of State Bulletin*, January 1982, pp. 12–14.

[122]George P. Shultz, *Turmoil and Triumph: My Years as Secretary of State* (New York: Charles Scribner's Sons, 1993), pp. 639 and 625–26.

[123]Interview with George Bush, March 7, 1996.

[124]Buckley, *Panama*, pp. 59–60.

[125]Eytan Gilboa, "The Panama Invasion Revisited: Lessons for the Use of Force in the Post–Cold War Era," *Political Science Quarterly*, vol. 110, no. 4, 1995–96, p. 547.

[126]Interview with Elliott Abrams, May 26, 1993.

[127]Lawrence Eagleburger, *The Case Against Panama's Noriega* (Washington, D.C.: U.S. Department of State, 1989), p. 2.

[128]Quoted in Warren Fiske, Knight-Ridder Tribune News Service, October 23, 1994; Derrick Z. Jackson, *Berkshire Eagle,* September15, 1996.

[129]Buckley, *Panama*, pp. 154–55; Hinckle and Turner, *The Fish Is Red*, pp. 118 and 175; interview with W. Robert Plumlee, June 20,1991; Gary Hart to John Kerry, February 14, 1991. Courtesy of Gus Russo; Buckley, *Panama*, pp. 154–55; U.S. Senate, Subcommittee on Terrorism, Narcotics, and International Operations of the Committee on Foreign Relations, *Drugs, Law Enforcement, and Foreign Policy: A Report* (Washington, D.C.: U.S. Government Printing Office, 1989), *passim;* Warren Fiske, "North's Notes Suggest He Knew of Drug-Running by Contras," Knight-Ridder Tribune News Service, October 23, 1994; Col. David Hackworth, "Is North Today's Benedict Arnold?" syndicated column, October 21, 1994; Michael Janofsky, *NYT,* October 25, 1994.

[130]Buckley, *Panama*, p. 104; Kempe, *Divorcing the Dictator,* p. 33.

CHAPTER SIXTEEN

[1]Murray Waas and Craig Unger, "In the Loop: Bush's Secret Mission," *The New Yorker,* November 2, 1992.

[2]Waas and Unger, "In the Loop," pp. 64 and 75.

[3]Alan Friedman, *Spider's Web* (New York: Bantam Books, 1993), p. 6.

[4]Hersh, *Samson Option*, p. 9; Friedman, *Spider's Web*, p. 4.

[5]Friedman, *Spider's Web*, p. 95.

[6]As quoted in Waas and Unger, "In the Loop," p. 70.

[7]Waas and Unger, "In the Loop," p. 70.

[8]Draper, *A Very Thin Line,* pp. 106–7; Dinges, *Our Man in Panama*, pp. 7–8.

[9]"Secret" Memorandum, Assistant Secretary of State Richard Murphy for circulation among State Department officials, January 14, 1984, in Waas and Unger, "In the Loop," p. 70.

[10]Waas and Unger, "In the Loop," p. 71.

[11]Ibid., p. 66.

[12]Steven R. Weisman, *NYT,* January 21, 1983.

[13]Peter Goldman and Tony Fuller, et al, *The Quest for the Presidency 1984* (New York: Bantam Books, 1995), p. 33.

[14]Richard B. Wirthlin to President Reagan, November 1, 1983, Baker Papers, Series X, Box 27, Rice University, TX.

[15]*NYT,* March 9, 1983; Reagan, *An American Life,* pp. 570–71; Cannon, *Reagan,* p. 316; Woodward, *Veil,* p. 236.

[16]Interview with Richard Nixon, June 4, 1984.

[17]Ibid.

[18]Rollins, *Bare Knuckles,* p. 169.

[19]Ibid., p. 172.

[20]"Studies Say Reagan Reverses Redistribution," *WSJ,* December 12, 1983.

[21]*The Gallup Poll 1983,* p. 272.

[22]Goldman and Fuller, *Quest,* p. 262.

[23]Jane Mayer and Doyle McManus, *Landslide: The Unmaking of a President* (Boston: Houghton Mifflin, 1988), p. 7.

[24]Germond and Witcover, *Wake Us When It's Over,* pp. 33–34 and 514.

[25]Charles Kolb, *White House Daze* (New York: The Free Press, 1994), p. 104.

[26]Goldman and Fuller, *Quest,* p. 265.

[27]"America's Problem: 'Trying to Do Everything for Everybody—A Conversation with Theodore H. White,' " *U.S. News & World Report,* July 5, 1982, p. 60.

[28]Robert Reno, *Berkshire Eagle,* January 21, 1996; interview with Arthur Link, February 22, 1996.

[29]Germond and Witcover, *Wake Us When It's Over,* pp. 504, 509–10, 513, 514, 528; Gerald Pomper, et al., *The Election of 1984: Reports and Interpretations* (New Jersey: Chatham House, Inc., 1985), p. 150; Goldman and Fuller, *Quest,* p. 437.

[30]Germond and Witcover, *Wake Us When It's Over,* pp. 532–33.

[31]Thomas E. Cronin, "The Presidential Election of 1984," in Ellis Sandoz and Cecil V. Crabb Jr., *Election of '84: Landslide Without a Mandate* (New York: New American Library, 1985), pp. 36 and 39.

[32]Noonan, *What I Saw at the Revolution,* p. 245.

[33]*The Gallup Poll 1984,* p. 182.

[34]Kurt Anderson, "Spotlight on the Seconds," *Time,* October 15, 1984.

[35]Interview with Ronald C. Kaufman, April 18, 1995.

[36]Geraldine A. Ferraro with Linda Bird Francke, *Ferraro: My Story* (New York: Bantam Books, 1985), p. 257.

[37]Richard B. Wirthlin to Ronald Reagan, November 1, 1983. Baker Papers, Series X, Box 28, Rice University, TX.

[38]Elizabeth Drew, *Campaign Journal: The Political Events of 1983–1984* (New York: Macmillan, 1985), p. 609.

[39]Joseph P. Shapiro with John Mashek, "Ahead for George Bush: Highers Profile as No. 2," *U.S. News & World Report,* November 12, 1984, p. 25.

[40]Cronin, "The Presidential Election of 1984," p. 44.

[41]Germond and Witcover, *Wake Us When It's Over,* p. 326.

[42]John Mashek, "The View from the Onstage Debate," *U.S. News & World Report,* October 22, 1984; William R. Doerner, *Time,* October 22, 1984; Sidney Blumenthal, "Spurious George," *The New Republic,* November 5, 1984; "TRB From Washington," *The New Republic,* October 15, 1984.

[43]Gerald Seib, *WSJ,* September 14, 1987.

[44]Goldman and Fuller, *Quest,* p. 437; as quoted in Thomas Byrne Edsall with Mary D. Edsall, *Chain Reaction* (New York: W. W. Norton & Company, 1991), pp. 221–22.

[45]Germond and Witcover, *Wake Us When It's Over,* p. 534.

[46]Ibid., p. 533.

[47]Goldman and Fuller, *Quest,* pp. 283–84, 331; Hedrick Smith, *NYT,* November 8, 1984, and Phil Gailey, *NYT,* November 8, 1984.

[48]*NYT,* October 4 and 5, 1984; *Houston Chronicle,* October 6, 1984; *Houston Post,* October 9, 1984; Bush, *Barbara Bush,* p. 195.

[49]John Maslek and J. Shapiro, "Ahead for George Bush: Higher Profile as No. 2," *U.S. News & World Report,* November 12, 1984; "Election Special," *Newsweek,* November/December 1984; Fred Barnes, "On the Supply Side: Bush Comes Down in the Corporate Camp," *Business Month,* September 1988.

[50]Victor Gold, "The Metamorphosis of Bush," *National Review,* December 14, 1984.

[51]Bush, *Barbara Bush,* p. 197.

[52]Ibid., p. 220.

[53]Interview with Ronald C. Kaufman, April 18, 1995.

[54]*NYT,* February 14 and 16, March 22, 1985; interviews with Ronald C. Kaufman, March 21, 1996, and David Bates, July 17, 1996; Gerald M. Boyd, "The Front-Runner," *New York Times Magazine,* February 23, 1986. p. 30; Gail Sheehy, "Beating Around," *Vanity Fair,* September 1988; interview with Nicholas Brady, November 7, 1995; *U.S. News & World Report,* February 8, 1988, pp. 58–60.

[55]Eric Alterman, "Playing Hardball," *New York Times Magazine,* April 30, 1989, p. 66.

[56]Ibid.; Janet Mullins, interviewed by Michael Gillette, in *Snapshots of the 1988 Presidential Campaign* (Austin: Lyndon B. Johnson School of Public Affairs, The University of Texas, 1992), p. 12.

[57]Interviews with David Bates, July 17, 1996, Ron Kaufman, March 19, 1996, and Craig Fuller, July 31, 1996; William Greider, "The Power of Negative Thinking," *Rolling Stone,* January 12, 1989, p. 52; Eric Alterman, "Playing Hardball," *New York Times Magazine,* April 30, 1989, pp. 66 and 68.

[58]Blumenthal, *Pledging Allegiance,* p. 69.

[59]Malcolm Gladwel, "Jerry Dumps George," *The New Republic,* November 24, 1986, p. 15; David Frost, "George Bush on God, War and Ollie North," *U.S. News & World Report,* December 14, 1987, p. 47.

[60]Amy Wilentz, "Bygones," *Time,* December 23, 1985, p. 24.

[61]Jack W. Germond and Jules Witcover, *Whose Broad Stripes and Bright Stars? The Trivial Pursuit of the Presidency 1988* (New York: Warner Books, 1989), p. 92.

[62]*NYT,* October 4, 1987.

[63]Germond and Witcover, *Whose Broad Stripes?,* p. 88.

[64]Ibid., pp. 98–99; *NYT,* January 23 1988.

[65]Janet Mullins in Gillette, *Snapshots,* p. 12; interviews with David Bates, July 17, 1996, and Ron Kaufman, March 19, 1996.

[66]*Department of State Bulletin,* May 1985, pp. 22–24.

[67]Ibid.; Bush, *Barbara Bush,* pp. 199–200.

[68]Michael R. Beschloss and Strobe Talbott, *At the Highest Levels* (Boston: Little, 1993), p. 7.

[69]Waas and Unger, "In the Loop," p. 72.

[70]Johnson, *Sleepwalking Through History,* p. 287; Waas and Unger, "In the Loop," p. 72; McFarlane, *Special Trust,* p. 99.

[71]Waas and Unger, "In the Loop," p. 72; John Prados, *Keeper of the Keys: A History of the National Security Council from Truman to Bush,* (New York: Morrow, 1991), p. 497.

[72]Draper, *A Very Fine Line,* pp. 121 and 135–36; North, *Under Fire,* p. 43.

[73]Waas and Unger, "In the Loop," p. 72.

[74]Bush, *Barbara Bush,* p. 201; Regan, *For the Record,* p. 9; Reagan, *An American Life,* pp. 499–502.

[75]Regan, *For the Record,* p. 18.

[76]McFarlane, *Special Trust,* p. 27.

[77]Ibid., p. 26; Persico, *Casey,* p. 451; Regan, *For the Record,* pp. 20–24.

[78]McFarlane, *Special Trust,* pp. 26–28.

[79]*OIC,* vol. 1, p. 481.

[80]McFarlane, *Special Trust,* p. 56.

[81]Draper, *A Very Thin Line,* p. 133.

[82]Cannon, *Reagan,* pp. 634–35; Anderson, *Revolution,* pp. 343 and 346; Morton Kondracke, "Vice President Moonbeam: The Man Who Wasn't There," *The New Republic,* March 30, 1987; McFarlane, *Special Trust,* pp. 31, 50, 54–62, and 66.

[83]McFarlane, *Special Trust,* p. 66; *The Tower Commission Report* (New York: Bantam Books and Times Books, 1987), p. 338.

[84]Walter Pincus and George Lardner Jr., *WP,* September 27, 1992; *Tower Commission,* pp. 350–51.

[85]Bush, *Barbara Bush,* pp. 202-3; Marvin Bush, "My Second Chance," *Ladies Home Journal,* March 1989, pp. 138 ff.

[86]Jack W. Germond and Jules Witcover, *Houston Post,* October 9, 1986.

[87]George Bush to Dr. William M. Watson, March 13, 1975, and Dr. Kenneth D. Burman to Dr. Burton Lee, May 11, 1991, Office of George Bush; Molly Ivins, "Texas George," *Ms.,* May 1988, p. 24; Kelley, *Nancy Reagan,* p. 506; George Will, *WP,* January 30, 1986; interview with Daniel Murphy, April 19, 1995, and George Bush, March 7, 1996.

CHAPTER SEVENTEEN

[1]Howard Kohn and Vicki Monks, "The Dirty Secrets of George Bush," *Rolling Stone,* November 3, 1988, p. 41.

[2]Robert D. Hershey Jr., *NYT,* April 2, 1986; *WSJ,* April 7, 1986; Lou Cannon and Paul Taylor, *WP,* April 9, 1986; David B. Ottaway, *WP,* April 10, 1986; interview with George Bush, March 7, 1996.

[3]Waas and Unger, "In the Loop," p. 76.

[4]Ibid.

[5]Walter Pincus and George Lardner, Jr., *WP,* September 27, 1992.

[6]Waas and Unger, "In the Loop," p. 75.

[7]Ibid.; Draper, *A Very Thin Line,* p. 169.

[8]Richard Secord with Jay Wurts, *Honored & Betrayed* (New York: John Wiley & Sons, 1992), p. 280.

[9]*Tower Commission,* pp. 385–89; Michael Ledeen, *Perilous Standoff: An Insider's Account of the Iran-Contra Affair* (New York: Charles Scribner's Sons, 1988), p. 289; Cannon, *Reagan,* p. 660; Walter Pincus and George Lardner Jr., *WP,* September 27, 1992; Brian Duffy, "Guess Who's in the Loop?" *U.S. News & World Report,* October 5, 1992, p. 45.

[10]Waas and Unger, "In the Loop," pp. 79–80; Friedman, *Spider's Web,* p. 104.

[11]Interview with Robert Plumlee, June 20, 1991.

[12]Michael S. Serrill, "Shot Out of the Sky," *Time,* October 20, 1986, pp. 44–46.

[13]Richard Halloran, *NYT,* October 8, 1986; James LeMoyne, *NYT,* October 8, 1986.

[14]Editorial, *NYT,* October 9, 1986; Richard Halloran, *NYT,* October 9, 1986.

[15]James LeMoyne, *NYT,* October 10, 1986.

[16]*OIC,* vol. 1, p. 499; *NYT,* October 12, 1986; Gerald M. Boyd, *NYT,* December 16, 1986.

[17]Regan, *For the Record*, pp. 28–29; Cannon, *Reagan*, pp. 674–75.
[18]Michael Schaller, *Reckoning with Reagan: America and Its President in the 1980s* (New York: Oxford University Press, 1992), p. 164.
[19]Cannon, *Reagan*, p. 711.
[20]Regan, *For the Record*, pp. 35–36; Christopher Hitchens, "Minority Report," *The Nation*, October 17, 1988.
[21]*TGP 1986*, pp. 253 and 256; Cannon, *Reagan*, p. 704.
[22]Theodore Draper, "The Iran-Contra Secrets," *New York Review of Books*, May 27, 1993, p. 44.
[23]Shultz, *Turmoil and Triumph*, p. 832.
[24]Draper, "The Iran-Contra Secrets," p. 44.
[25]Bush diary, *WP*, January 31, 1993.
[26]Bush diary, November 9, 1986, as quoted in *OIC*, vol. 1, p. 481; Shultz, *Turmoil and Triumph*, pp. 808–9.
[27]Ibid., November 14, 1986.
[28]Ibid., November 16, 1986.
[29]Ibid., November 18–20, 1986.
[30]Ibid., November 20, 1986.
[31]Ibid., November 21, 1986.
[32]Cannon, *Reagan*, p. 699.
[33]Ibid.
[34]Cannon, *Reagan*, p. 700; Regan, *For the Record*, pp. 38–39.
[35]Kenneth T. Walsh, "Iran Fiasco's Other Casualty," *U.S. News & World Report*, December 1, 1986.
[36]Bush diary, *WP*, January 31, 1993.
[37]Bush diary, January 1, 1987, Ibid., January 31, 1993.
[38]Bush diary, December 17, 1986, Ibid.
[39]Bush diary, December 4, 1986, Ibid.
[40]Gerald M. Boyd, *NYT*, December 4, 1986.
[41]*The Economist*, April 4, 1992, p. 24; Joan Hoff, *Nixon Reconsidered* (New York: Basic Books, 1994), p. 223; Posner, *Citizen Perot*, pp. 115ff. and p. 206; Bob Woodward and John Mintz, *WP*, June 21, 1992.
[42]Posner, *Citizen Perot*, p. 200; interview with George Bush, January 25, 1995.
[43]Woodward and Mintz, *WP*, June 21, 1992; Posner, *Citizen Perot*, pp. 214–15; interview with George Bush, January 25, 1995.
[44]Nene Foxhall, *Houston Chronicle*, October 13, 1987; Germond and Witcover, *Whose Broad Stripes?*, p. 141.
[45]Interview with George Bush, July 6, 1995.
[46]*CBS Evening News*, January 25, 1988.
[47]*NYT*, December 28, 1987.
[48]McFarlane, *Special Trust*, pp. 28 and 51.
[49]Regan, *For the Record*, p. 372.
[50]Cannon, *Reagan*, p. 629.
[51]Shultz, *Triumph and Turmoil*, p. 809.
[52]Cannon, *Reagan*, p. 629; Draper, "Iran-Contra Secrets," p. 43.
[53]David Broder, *WP*, August 6, 1987.
[54]Waas and Unger, "In the Loop," p. 73.
[55]*NYT*, January 8, 1988.
[56]Steven V. Roberts, *NYT*, January 18, 1988.
[57]Germond and Witcover, *Whose Broad Stripes?*, p. 108.
[58]Ibid., p. 102.
[59]Ibid., pp. 111–12.
[60]Michael Oreskes, *NYT*, January 9, 1988; E. J. Dionne Jr., *NYT*, January 11, 1988; *CBS Evening News*, January 26, 1988; Germond and Witcover, *Whose Broad Stripes?*, p. 113.
[61]Germond and Witcover, *Whose Broad Stripes?*, pp. 128 and 129; E. J. Dionne Jr., *NYT*, January 11, 1988.
[62]Germond and Witcover, *Whose Broad Stripes?*, p. 118.
[63]Cramer, *What It Takes*, p. 851; Blumenthal, *Pledging Allegiance*, p. 75; William Safire, *NYT*, January 27, 1988; Germond and Witcover, *Whose Broad Stripes?*, p. 119.
[64]Cramer, *What It Takes*, pp. 851–52.
[65]*CBS Evening News*, January 25, 1988; Draper, *A Very Thin Line*, p. 574.
[66]*CBS Evening News*, January 25, 1988.
[67]Blumenthal, *Pledging Allegiance*, p. 75.
[68]Peggy Noonan, *What I Saw at the Revolution* (New York: Random House, 1990), p. 297.
[69]Laurie Mifflin, *NYT*, March 11, 1996.
[70]*CBS Evening News*, January 26, 1988.
[71]Ibid.; William Safire, *NYT*, January 27, 1988.
[72]*NYT*, March 2, 1988.
[73]R. W. Apple Jr., *NYT*, February 16, 1988.
[74]E. J. Dionne Jr., *NYT*, March 17, 1988.
[75]R. W. Apple Jr., *NYT*, February 29, 1996.
[76]Interview with John Sununu, April 20, 1995.
[77]James M. Perry, *WSJ*, January 7, 1988.
[78]Interview with George Bush, January 15, 1995.

[79]Germond and Witcover, *Whose Broad Stripes?*, pp. 141–42; interview with Peter Teeley, June 7, 1996; Richard Stendel, "The Man Behind the Message: Ailes," *Time*, August 22, 1988, pp. 28–29.

[80]Interview with John Sununu, April 20, 1995.

[81]Gerald M. Boyd, *NYT*, February 10, 1988.

[82]Germond and Witcover, *Whose Broad Stripes?*, p. 109.

[83]Marlin Fitzwater, *Call the Briefing!* (New York: Times Books, 1995), p. 175.

[84]William Schneider, "The Republicans in '88," *The Atlantic*, July 1987; R. W. Apple Jr., *NYT*, February 16, 1988.

[85]E. J. Dionne Jr., *NYT*, February 17, 1988.

[86]*NYT*, April 3, 1988; interview with Ronald C. Kaufman, March 19, 1996.

[87]Ibid., April 27, 1988.

[88]Ibid., April 28, 1988.

[89]Ibid., April 25, 1988.

[90]*TGP 1988*, p. 69.

[91]E. J. Dionne Jr., *NYT*, April 28, 1988.

[92]Albert, *Case Against the General*, p. 57.

[93]Buckley, *Panama*, pp. 152–53.

[94]Interview with George Bush, March 7, 1988.

[95]Gilboa, "Panama Invasion," pp. 544–45 and 547; Albert, *Case Against the General*, p. 17.

[96]Buckley, *Panama*, pp. 131–33.

[97]Ibid., pp. 106–7.

[98]Ibid., p. 133.

[99] Ibid., p. 142.

[100]Ibid., pp. 143 and 155.

[101]Powell, *My American Journey*, p. 388; interview with Colin Powell, April 17, 1995.

[102]Buckley, *Panama*, p. 156.

[103]Powell, *My American Journey*, p. 387.

[104]Ibid., p. 387; interview with Colin Powell, April 17, 1995.

[105]Powell, *My American Journey*, p. 387; Buckley, *Panama*, p. 143.

[106]Gerald M. Boyd, *NYT*, May 31, 1988; Bush diaries, May 28, 1988, OGB.

[107]Bush diaries, May 28 and 30, 1988, OGB.

CHAPTER EIGHTEEN

[1]Bill Keller, *NYT*, June 1, 1988; Cannon, *Reagan*, p. 785.

[2]Cannon, *Reagan*, pp. 790–91.

[3]E. J. Dionne Jr., *NYT*, May 17, 1988.

[4]Michael Dukakis interviewed by Dan Rather, CBS-TV, July 18, 1988.

[5]Bush diaries, May 28, 1988, OGB.

[6]Donald Morrison (ed.), *The Winning of the White House 1988* (New York: A Times Book, 1988), p. 220.

[7]Interviews with Ronald C. Kaufman, March 19, 1996, James Pinkerton, June 25, 1996, and George Bush, March 8, 1996.

[8]Robert James Bidinetto, "Getting Away with Murder," *Reader's Digest*, July 1988, p. 57; Robin Toner, *NYT*, July 5, 1988.

[9]Duffy and Goodgame, *Marching in Place*, p. 76; Germond and Witcover, *Whose Broad Stripes?*, pp. 157–60; Johnson, *Sleepwalking Through History*, pp. 396–97.

[10]Jamieson, *Dirty Politics*, p. 25; Germond and Witcover, *Whose Broad Stripes?*, pp. 11–12; interviews with Ronald C. Kaufman, March 19, 1996, Kathleen Hall Jamieson, April 25, 1996, Peter Teeley, June 17, 1996, James Pinkerton, June 25, 1996, George Bush, March 8, 1996, and James Cicconi, June 22, 1996.

[11]Michael Orestes, *NYT*, March 30, 1991; Jack E. White, "Bush's Most Valuable Player, *Time*, November 14, 1988, p. 20.

[12]Michael L. Gillette interviews of Rich Bond, July 19, 1990, and David Bates, April 19, 1990, the Center for American History, the University of Texas at Austin; Bush diaries, May 28, 1988, OGB.

[13]Robert Mosbacher, interviewed by Michael L. Gillette, June 27, 1990, the Center for American History, the University of Texas at Austin.

[14]Interview with Marlin Fitzwater, July 30, 1996.

[15]Bush diary, June 12, 1988.

[16]Ibid., June 8, 1988.

[17]Ibid., June 7, 1988,

[18]Gerald M. Boyd, *NYT*, June 14, 1988; Bush diary, June 7, 1988.

[19]Ibid., June 2, 1988.

[20]Gerald M. Boyd, *NYT*, June 1, 1988.

[21]Germond and Witcover, *Whose Broad Stripes?*, p. 366; Bush diary, June 7, 1988.

[22]Interview with Craig Fuller, July 31, 1996.

[23]Ibid.

[24]Maureen Dowd, *NYT*, August 8, 1988.

[25]Fred Barnes, "Bush Rolls Right," *The New Republic*, February 6, 1989, p. 9.

[26]Kennebunkport Trip Materials, Thomas Collamore Trip Files/Schedule. BPMP, College State, TX.

[27]Janet Mullins, *Snapshots,* p. 30; Gerald M Boyd, *NYT,* June 17, 1988; Maureen Dowd, *NYT,* October 12, 1988; Morton Zuckerman, "When Will the Real George Bush Stand Up?" *U.S. News & World Report,* June 27, 1988; Garry Wills, "The Born-Again Republicans," *The New York Review of Books,* September 24, 1992, p. 22; Maureen Dowd, *NYT,* October 12, 1988.

[28]Bush diaries, May 30, 1988, OGB.

[29]Ibid., June 4, 1988.

[30]Richard A. Viguerie, *NYT,* June 3, 1988.

[31]Editorial, "Where's George?" *National Review,* September 2, 1988.

[32]Maureen Dowd, *NYT,* June 10, 1988; Cramer, *What It Takes,* pp. 1010–11; Robert K. Dornan, "My Pit Bull, George," *National Review,* November 6, 1987.

[33]Bush diary, June 9, 1988.

[34]Bush diaries, June 8, 1988.

[35]Cannon, *Reagan,* pp. 800–2.

[36]*TGP 1988,* p. 123.

[37]Germond and Witcover, *Whose Broad Stripes?,* pp. 368–69; Ken Bode, *NYT,* May 28, 1996; Michael L. Gillette's interviews with Rich Bond, July 19, 1990, Center for the Presidency, the University of Texas, and with Janet Mullins July 17, 1990, in *Snapshots,* pp. 35–36; interview with David Q. Bates, July 17, 1996.

[38]*TGP 1988,* p 133; Bush diaries, August 14, 1988, OGB.

[39]Michael L. Gillette interview with David Bates, April 19, 1990, the Center for the Presidency, the University of Texas at Austin; Janet Mullins, *Snapshots,* p. 34.

[40]Robert Teeter to George Bush, July 15, 1988, Vice Presidential Selection Folder, OGB.

[41]Interview with George Bush, January 25, 1995.

[42]*NYT,* August 6, 1988.

[43]Interview with J. Danforth Quayle Jr., June 14, 1995.

[44]Roger Ailes to Robert Teeter, July 20, 1988, Vice Presidential Selection Papers, OGB.

[45]Ibid.

[46]Ibid.

[47]Bob Woodward and David Broder, *Dan Quayle: The Man Who Would be President* (New York: Simon & Schuster, 1992), p. 24.

[48]Bob Woodward and David Broder, *WP,* January 5, 1992; Dan Quayle, *Standing Firm* (New York: Harper-Collins Publishers, 1994), p. 24.

[49]Gerald Boyd, *NYT,* August 18, 1988.

[50]Morrison, *Winning of the White House,* p. 204.

[51]Gerald Boyd, *NYT,* August 13, 1988.

[52]Interview with Kenneth Adelman, April 19, 1995; Woodward and Broder, *Quayle,* pp. 29–30.

[53]Quayle, *Standing Firm,* p. 5; Richard Brookhiser, *National Review,* November 7, 1988, p. 34.

[54]Rich Bond interviewed by Michael L. Gillette, July 19, 1990, the Center for American History, the University of Texas at Austin.

[55]Woodward and Broder, *Quayle,* p. 57.

[56]Morrison, *Winning of the White House,* p. 202.

[57]Ibid., pp. 197–204; Darman, *Who's in Control?* pp. 189–90; Woodward and Broder, *Quayle,* pp. 58–59; Quayle, *Standing Firm,* pp. 29–30; interview with Dan Quayle, June 14, 1995.

[58]Morrison, *Winning of the White House,* p. 204; Bush diaries, August 21, 1988, OGB.

[59]E. J. Dionne Jr., *NYT,* August 16, 1988.

[60]Peggy Noonan, *What I Saw at the Revolution,* pp. 296 and 314.

[61]Ibid., p. 313.

[62]Darman, *Who's In Control?,* p. 192.

[63]*NYT,* August 24, 1988.

[64]R. W. Apple Jr., *NYT,* August 19, 1988; Morrison, *Winning of the White House 1988,* p. 210; Noonan, *What I Saw at the Revolution,* p. 311.

[65]*TGP 1988,* p. 147; *NYT,* August 22 and 23, 1988; Germond and Witcover, *Whose Broad Stripes?,* pp. 393–94.

[66]Bush diaries, August 21, 1988.

[67]Morrison, *Winning of the White House,* p. 260.

[68]Germond and Witcover, *Whose Broad Stripes?,* pp. 406 and 411.

[69]Dennis Frankenberry, in Gillette, *Snapshots,* p. 58.

[70]Sig Rogich interviewed by Michael L. Gillette, April 27, 1990, the Center for American History, the University of Texas at Austin.

[71]Kathleen Hall Jamieson, *Dirty Politics: Deception, Distraction, and Democracy* (New York: Oxford University Press, 1992), p. 19.

[72]Martin Schram, "The Making of Willie Horton," *The New Republic,* May 28, 1990, pp. 17–18.

[73]Jamieson, *Dirty Politics,* pp. 20–21; Morrison, *Winning of the White House,* p. 261; Andy Plattner, "The Key Ingredient," *U.S. News & World Report,* pp. 54–55.

[74]Editorial, "The Strange Death of Liberal America," *The Economist,* September 24, 1988, p. 20.

[75]*NYT,* October 8, 1988.

[76]R. W. Apple Jr., *NYT,* September 18, 1988.

[77]Bush diaries, May 28, 1988, and June 4, 1988, OGB.

[78]Germond and Witcover, *Whose Broad Stripes?,* p. 408; *NYT,* August 26, 1988.

[79]Bush, *Barbara Bush*, p. 231.

[80]Fred Barnes, "Mr. Congeniality," *The New Republic*, October 3, 1988.

[81]Maureen Dowd, *NYT*, September 21, 1988; Germond and Witcover, *Whose Broad Stripes?*, p. 435.

[82]Maureen Dowd, *NYT*, September 21, 1988; *TGP 1988*, p. 184.

[83]Richard L. Berke, Michael Wines, and Stephen Engelberg, *NYT*, November 3, 1988; Joe Conason, *The New Republic*, May 28, 1990, p. 18; Charles R. Babcock, *WP*, January 16, 1992; Martin Schram, "The Making of Willie Horton," *The New Republic*, May 28, 1990, pp. 17–18; interview with James Pinkerton, June 25, 1996.

[84]Germond and Witcover, *Whose Broad Stripes?*, pp. 433–434.

[85]Ibid., p. 441.

[86]Ibid., pp. 440, 442, and 443n.

[87]Ibid., pp. 446–48; *NYT*, October 15, 1988, and October 18, 1988; Bush, *Barbara Bush*, p. 240.

[88]Dully and Goodgame, *Marching in Place*, p. 33.

[89]Kilian, *Barbara Bush*, p. 152; *NYT*, November 9 and 10, 1988; Alan Brinkley, *The Unfinished Nation* (New York: McGraw-Hill, 1993), p. 889; Duffy and Goodgame, *Marching in Place*, p. 33; George C. Edwards III in Campbell and Rockman, *Bush Presidency*, p. 130.

[90]Transcript of News Conference, *NYT*, November 10, 1988.

[91]As quoted by Charles O. Jones in Campbell and Rockman, *Bush Presidency*, p. 51.

[92]Bush, *Barbara Bush*, p. 254.

[93]Bob Woodward, *The Commanders* (New York: Simon & Schuster, 1991), pp. 54–55.

CHAPTER NINETEEN

[1]Michael Oreskes, *NYT*, January 22, 1989.

[2]George Plimpton, "Sportsman Born and Bred," *Sports Illustrated*, January 2, 1989; Michael Oreskes, *NYT*, January 22, 1989; James P. Pfiffner, *The Bush Transition: A Friendly Takeover*, (Richmond, VA: The Institute of Public Policy, George Mason University, 1995), pp. 2–3; Maureen Dowd, *NYT*, January 15, 1989.

[3]Fitzwater, *Call the Briefing!*, pp. 172–73; interview with Marlin Fitzwater, July 30, 1996.

[4]R. W. Apple Jr., *NYT*, November 20, 1988.

[5]Interview with Martin Anderson, July 7, 1993.

[6]Burt Solomon, "A Gathering of Friends," *National Journal*, June 10, 1989, p. 1403.

[7]Mervin, *Bush*, p. 130; R. W. Apple Jr., *NYT*, January 13, 1989.

[8]Susan F. Rasky, *NYT*, January 16, 1989; excerpts from Baker's testimony to the Foreign Relations Committee, *NYT*, January 16, 1989; Thomas L. Friedman, *NYT*, January 19, 1989.

[9]Interview with Martin Anderson, July 7, 1993.

[10]Burt Solomon, "A Gathering of Friends," *National Journal*, June 10, 1989, p. 1403.

[11]Interview with John Sununu, April 20, 1995.

[12]David Gergen, "George Bush's Balky Start," *U.S. News & World Report*, January 30, 1989, p. 34; Burt Solomon, "A Gathering of Friends," *National Journal*, June 10, 1989, p. 1403.

[13]R. W. Apple Jr., *NYT*, January 20, 1989; Michael Oreskes, *NYT*, January 20, 1989; Bernard Weinraub, *NYT*, January 24, 1989; Pfiffner, *Bush Transition*, p. 9; Burt Solomon, "A Gathering of Friends," *National Journal*, June 10, 1989, p. 1403.

[14]Interview with Kenneth Adelman, April 19, 1995.

[15]Interview with Martin Anderson, July 7, 1993.

[16]Interview with Lyn Nofziger, October 17, 1995.

[17]Pfiffner, *Bush Transition*, pp. 3–4.

[18]Interview with Martin Anderson, July 7, 1993.

[19]David E. Rosenbaum, *NYT*, February 28, 1989; Bob Woodward, *WP*, October 5, 1992.

[20]Interview with Robert Strauss, November 14, 1995.

[21]Interview with Kenneth Adelman, April 19, 1995; Quayle, *Standing Firm*, p. 192.

[22]*The Economist*, December 3, 1988, pp. 25–26; Gerald M. Boyd, *NYT*, January 13, 1989; Howard Fineman, *Newsweek*, December 5, 1988, p. 22; *NYT*, December 22, 1988; Bush diaries, January 18, 19, and 21, 1989, OGB.

[23]Text of News Conference, November 10, 1988; *Jet*, November 28, 1988, p. 4.

[24]*Houston Post*, January 17, 1989; Andrew Rosenthal, *NYT*, January 14, 1989; Maureen Dowd, *NYT*, January 17, 1989; Julie Johnson, *NYT*, January 19, 1989; R. W. Apple Jr., *NYT*, January 20, 1989.

[25]Maureen Dowd, *NYT*, January 15, 1989; R. W. Apple Jr., *NYT*, January 20, 1989.

[26]*Houston Chronicle*, January 20, 1989.

[27]Prescott S. Bush Jr., "Inauguration Exclusive," *The Nutmegger*, February 1989, at the Greenwich Public Library.

[28]Michael Oreskes, *NYT*, January 19, 1989.

[29]*Houston Chronicle*, January 20, 1989; Prescott Bush Jr., "Inauguration Exclusive," *The Nutmegger*, February 1989, at the Greenwich Public Library.

[30]Hendrick Hertzberg, "The Nice Age," *The New Republic*, February 13, 1989, p. 4.

[31]*Public Papers of the Presidents: George Bush, 1989*, pp. 1–4; R. W. Apple Jr., *NYT*, January 21, 1989.

[32]Hendrick Hertzberg, "The Nice Age," *The New Republic*, February 13, 1989, p. 4.

[33]Harrison Rainie, "His Moment Arrives," *U.S. News & World Report*, January 30, 1989, p. 18.

[34]Cannon, *Reagan*, p. 19; Bush, *Barbara Bush*, p. 260.

[35]Michael Oreskes, *NYT,* January 19, 1989; Maureen Dowd, *NYT,* January 22, 1989; Bush diaries, January 21, 1989.

[36]Gerald Boyd, *NYT,* January 22, 1989.

[37]Inventory of the Oval Office, Office of the Curator, the White House, June 22, 1989, BPMP, Texas A&M University, College Station, TX.

[38]Gerald Boyd, *NYT,* January 22, 1989; Cannon, *Reagan,* p. 16.

[39]Bush, *Barbara Bush,* p. 262.

[40]Bush diaries, January 21, 1989, OGB.

[41]Hendrick Hertzberg, "The Nice Age," *The New Republic,* February 13, 1989.

[42]*Congressional Quarterly Almanac, 101st Congress 1st Session . . . 1989,* p. 3.

[43]Daniel Patrick Moynihan, "Reagan's Inflate-the-Deficit Game," *NYT,* July 21, 1985.

[44]Sidney Blumenthal, "The Sorcerer's Apprentice," *The New Yorker,* July 19, 1993, pp. 30–31.

[45]Moynihan, *NYT,* July 21, 1985.

[46]Alan S. Blinder, "The Republican Riverboat Gamble," *NYT,* August 20, 1996; Morrison, *Winning of the White House,* p. 19; Schaller, *Reagan,* p. 46.

[47]Stephen Skowronek, *The Politics Presidents Make: Leadership from John Adams to George Bush* (Cambridge, MA: Harvard University Press, 1993), p. 427.

[48]Bush diaries, January 26, 1989, OGB.

[49]*PPP-Bush 1989,* vol. 1, pp. 19–20, and 22; R. W. Apple Jr., *NYT,* April 12, 1989.

[50]David R. Gergen, "Bush Marches to His Own Beat," *U.S. News & World Report,* February 20, 1989, p. 20; Bush diaries, February 15, 1989, OGB.

[51]Bush diaries, February 9 and 15, 1989; *PPP-Bush, 1989,* vol. 1, p. 65; Kevin Phillips, *LAT,* April 5, 1992; Jeff Gerth, "A Onetime Aid to Bush Shows a Lobbyist's Magic," *NYT,* July 15, 1990.

[52]*PPP: Bush, 1989,* vol. 1, p. 28.

[53]Ibid., p. 28.

[54]Ibid., p. 51.

[55]Ibid., vol. 1, p. 75; Kolb, *White House Daze,* p. 7; E. J. Dionne Jr., *NYT,* February 10, 1989; Bush diaries, February 11, 1989, OBG.

[56]Bush diaries, February 19, March 1, 1989, and October 1, 1992, OGB.

[57]Bush diaries, February 12, 1989, OGB; Michael R. Beschloss and Strobe Talbott, *At the Highest Levels* (Boston: Little, Brown, 1993), pp. 22–23.

[58]Bush diaries, February 2, 5, 11, and 12, 1989, OGB.

[59]Bush diaries, January 25, 26, 29, and February 2, 9, 1989, OGB.

[60]Bush diaries, February 9, 1989, OGB.

[61]Elizabeth Drew, "Letter From Washington," *The New Yorker,* March 20, 1989, pp. 97–106.

[62]Interview with Nicholas Brady, November 7, 1995; Drew, "Letter From Washington," March 20, 1989, p. 98.

[63]Interview with Richard Nixon, November 16, 1988; Bush diaries, February 9, 1989, OGB.

[64]Drew, "Letter From Washington," March 20, 1989, p. 98; John G. Tower, *Consequences: A Personal and Political Memoir* (New York: Little, Brown, 1991), pp. 119–21.

[65]John G. Tower, *Consequences: A Personal and Political Memoir* (New York: Little, Brown, 1991).

[66]Bush diaries, February 7, 1989, OGB.

[67]*PPP: Bush, 1989,* vol. 1, pp. 113–14.

[68]James A. Mallory, "All Rumors Against Tower 'Gunned Down' by FBI Report, Bush Says," *Atlanta Constitution,* February 22, 1989.

[69]Bush diaries, February 21, 1989, OBG.

[70]Ibid., February 25, 1989, OBG; *PPP: Bush,* vol. 1, p. 135.

[71]R. W. Apple Jr., *NYT,* February 27, 1989; Bush diaries, February 23 and 25, 1989, OGB.

[72]Maureen Dowd, *NYT,* February 26, 1989; R. W. Apple Jr., *NYT,* February 27, 1989.

[73]Gerald M. Boyd, *NYT,* February 26, 1989; Robert B. Semple Jr., *NYT,* March 1, 1989.

[74]Bush diaries, February 26, 1989, OBG.

[75]Gerald M. Boyd, *NYT,* February 26, 1989.

[76]*PPP: Bush, 1989,* vol. 1, p. 844; Bush diaries, February 26, 1989; Gerald M. Boyd, *NYT,* February 26. 1989.

[77]Pei Minxim, "As Mr. Bush Partied in Beijing . . . ," *NYT,* February 28, 1989.

[78]Bush diaries, February 26, 1989; *Department of State Bulletin,* August 1989, p. 26; *NYT,* April 9, 1990.

[79]Nicholas D. Kristof, *NYT,* February 27 and 28, 1989.

[80]Bush diaries, February 26, 1989, OGB.

[81]*PPP: Bush, 1989,* vol. 1, p. 189.

[82]Interview with Colin Powell, April 17, 1995.

[83]Susan F. Rasky, *NYT,* February 28, 1989; Maureen Dowd, *NYT,* March 10, 1989; Bernard Weinraub, *NYT,* March 13, 1989.

[84]Nene Foxhall, *Houston Chronicle,* October 13, 1987.

[85]Gerald M. Boyd, *NYT,* February 20, 1987; *The Economist,* January 21, 1989, p. 13; Blumenthal, *Pledging Allegiance,* p. 54; Fitzwater, *Call the Briefing!,* p. 245.

[86]David Gergen, "Bush Marching to His Own Beat," *U.S. News & World Report,* February 20, 1989, pp. 20–24; Sidney Blumenthal, "Bull Moose," *The New Republic,* January 7–14, 1991, pp. 11–16.

[87]Nelson Polsby, as quoted in Pfiffner, *Bush Transition,* p. 10.

[88]E. J. Dionne Jr., *NYT,* January 22, 1989; interview with Roger Porter, July 15, 1996.

[89]David Mervin, *George Bush and the Guardianship Presidency* (New York: St. Martin's Press, 1996), p. 32.

[90]Michael Mandelbaum, "The Bush Foreign Policy," *Foreign Affairs*, vol. 70, no. 1, p. 20; Henry Kissinger, *Diplomacy* (New York: Simon & Schuster, 1994), p. 53.

[91]*PPP: Bush, 1989*, vol. 1, p. 160.

[92]Ibid., pp. 55–56; Cf., Kissinger, *Diplomacy*, p. 806.

[93]Cf., Michael Mandelbaum, "The Bush Foreign Policy," *Foreign Affairs*, vol. 70, no. 1, p. 18.

[94]Editorial, "Reaganism with a Human Face," *The Progressive*, April 1989, pp. 7–8; *Congress and the Nation*, vol. 8, pp. 41–21; *PPP: Bush 1989*, vol. 1, pp. 424–26; R. W. Apple Jr., *NYT*, March 20 and April 16, 1989; Bernard Weinraub, *NYT*, July 2, 1989; Thomas DeFrank, Ann McDaniel, and Richard M. Smith, "An Interview with Bush," *Newsweek*, January 30, 1989, p. 32.

[95]R. W. Apple Jr., *NYT*, April 2, 1989; Steven V. Roberts, "The Dawning of the Bush Method," *U.S. News & World Report*, April 17, 1989, pp. 34–35; *Department of State Bulletin*, June 1989, vol. 89, p. 4; Baker, *Politics*, pp. 57–58.

[96]Kenneth T. Walsh, *U.S. News & World Report*, May 1, 1989, pp. 24–25; R. W. Apple Jr., *NYT*, April 26, 1989; Bernard Weinraub, *NYT*, April 1, 1989.

[97]"The Five Faces of George Bush," *The Economist*, April 15, 1989, p. 27; *TGP 1989*, p. 103.

[98]Editorial, "The Five Face of George Bush," *The Economist*, April 15, 1981, p. 27.

[99]*PPP: Bush, 1989*, vol. 1, pp. 504–7.

[100]Cf., Anatoly Dobrynin, *In Confidence: Moscow's Ambassador to America's Six Cold War Presidents* (New York: Times Books, 1995), p. 550.

[101]Paul Johnson, "Europe and the Reagan Years," *Foreign Affairs*, vol. 68, no. 1, p. 35.

[102]As quoted in Blumenthal, *Pledging Allegiance*, p. 329.

[103]Blumenthal, *Pledging Allegiance*, pp. 322–23.

[104]Richard Nixon, "The Bush Agenda," *Foreign Affairs*, vol. 68, no. 1, pp. 200, 204, 208.

[105]Blumenthal, *Pledging Allegiance*, p. 327. *PPP: Bush, 1989*, vol. 1, p. 23.

[106]Beschloss and Talbott, *Highest Levels*, p. 26.

[107]Ibid., p. 27; Blumenthal, *Pledging Allegiance*, pp. 323–24.

[108]Beschloss and Talbott, *Highest Levels*, p. 44.

[109]Dobrynin, *In Confidence*, p. 629.

[110]Interview with George Bush, March 7, 1996; Philip Zelikow and Condoleezza Rice, *Germany Unified and Europe Transformed: A Study in Statecraft* (Cambridge, MA: Harvard University Press, 1995), p. 29.

[111]William H. Mobley to George Bush, February 27, 1989, Speech Files, BPMP, College Station, TX.

[112]Zelikow and Rice, *Germany Unified*, p. 26; Condoleezza Rice draft, Speech Files for Texas A&M speech of May 12, 1989, BPMP, College Station, TX; interview with Condoleezza Rice, June 7, 1995.

[113]Kissinger, *Diplomacy*, pp. 765 and 770.

[114]Interview with Condoleezza Rice, June 7, 1995.

[115]*PPP: Bush, 1989*, vol 1, pp. 540–43; Bush diaries May 12, 1989; Zelikow and Rice, *Germany Unified*, p. 26.

[116]Zelikow and Rice, *Germany Unified*, p. 26; interview with Condoleezza Rice, June 7, 1995.

[117]Beschloss and Talbott, *Highest Levels*, pp. 24–25; Zelikow and Rice, *Germany Unified*, p. 25; Baker, *Politics of Diplomacy*, pp. 92–93.

[118]Thomas L. Friedman, *NYT*, June 4, 1989.

[119]Interview with Brent Scowcroft, April 18, 1995.

[120]Woodward, *The Commanders*, p. 51.

[121]Duffy and Goodgame, *Marching in Place*, pp. 138–39; interview with Condoleezza Rice, June 7, 1995.

[122]Zelikow and Rice, *Germany Unified*, pp. 23–24 and 154; interview with Condoleezza Rice, June 7, 1995.

[123]Interview with Condoleezza Rice, June 7, 1995.

[124]Interviews with Richard Cheney, April 21, 1995, and Condoleezza Rice, June 7, 1995.

[125]Michael R. Gordon, *NYT*, May 20, 1989; Bernard Weinraub, May 21, 1989; Zelikow and Rice, *Germany Unified*, p. 30; Baker, *Politics of Diplomacy*, pp. 93–94.

[126]*PPP: Bush, 1989*, vol. 1, pp. 582–85 and pp. 601–4.

[127]*Department of State Bulletin*, (Washington, D.C.: U.S. Government Printing Office, August 1989), pp. 11ff.

[128]*PPP: Bush, 1989*, vol. 1, pp. 650–54.

[129]*Department of State Bulletin*, August 1989, vol. 89; Michael Mandelbaum, "The Bush Foreign Policy," *Foreign Affairs*, vol. 70, no. 1, p. 8; Baker, *Politics*, pp. 159–60; Bernard Weinraub, *NYT*, June 2, 1989; James M. Markham, *NYT*, June 4, 1989; Thomas L. Friedman, *NYT*, June 4, 1989.

[130]*PPP: Bush, 1989*, vol. 1, pp. 650–54.

[131]Editorial, "Another New George Bush," *The Economist*, June 10, 1989, p. 23; R. W. Apple Jr., *NYT*, June 2, 1989; James M. Markham, *NYT*, June 4, 1989; interview with Condoleezza Rice, June 7, 1995.

[132]Zelikow and Rice, *Germany Unified*, p. 31.

[133]Maureen Dowd, *NYT*, June 27, 1989.

[134]*The Economist*, June 10, 1989, p. 23.

CHAPTER TWENTY

[1]*PPP: Bush, 1989*, vol. 1, p. 666.

[2]Nicholas D. Kristof, *NYT*, June 4, 1989.

[3]*WSJ*, June 5, 1989; *PPP: Bush, 1989*, vol. 1, pp. 669–70; Thomas L. Friedman, *NYT*, June 5, 1989; Bernard Weinraub, *NYT*, June 6, 1989; Tom Wicker, *NYT*, June 6, 1989.

⁴Stephen Engelberg, *NYT*, May 21, 1989; Nicholas D. Kristof, *NYT*, May 20 and 21, 1989; E. J. Dionne Jr., *NYT*, June 4, 1989.

⁵E. J. Dionne Jr., *NYT*, June 9, 1989.

⁶Ibid.

⁷Interview with Marlin Fitzwater, July 30, 1996.

⁸Maureen Dowd, *NYT*, June 15, 1989; David E. Rosenbaum, *NYT*, June 17, 1989; interview with George Bush, March 7, 1996.

⁹Linda Greenhouse, *NYT*, July 2, 1996; James Sterngold, *NYT*, December 8, 1996.

¹⁰Nathaniel C. Nash, *NYT*, July 6, 1989; *Congress and the Nation*, vol. 8, p. 120.

¹¹Steven Wilmsen, *Silverado: Neil Bush and the Savings & Loan Scandal* (Washington, D.C.: National Press Books, 1991), p. 47.

¹²Editorial, *NYT*, June 4, 1989.

¹³Wilmsen, *Silverado*, p. 59.

¹⁴Ibid., pp. 85 and 87; Thomas C. Hayes, *NYT*, January 19, 1990; Steven Wilmsen, "The Corruption of Neil Bush," *Playboy*, June 1981, p. 98.

¹⁵Thomas C. Hayes, *NYT*, January 19, 1990; Ann McDaniel, et al., "A Crisis in the First Family," *Newsweek*, July 23, 1990, p. 18; Stephen Hedges, "Inside the Silverado Scandal," *U.S. News & World Report*, August 13, 1990, pp. 28ff.

¹⁶Bush diaries, February 19, 1989, OGB.

¹⁷Sidney Blumenthal, "The Sensitive Son," *The New Republic*, October 8, 1990, pp. 21ff.

¹⁸Bush diaries, May 18, 1990, OGB.

¹⁹Marjorie Williams, "Barbara's Backlash," *Vanity Fair*, August 1992, p. 180; Ann McDaniel, et al., "A Crisis in the First Family," *Newsweek*, July 23, 1990, p. 18; Bush diaries, August 8, 1990, February 2, 1991, and March 3, 1991.

²⁰*NYT*, March 1, 1989.

²¹Marvin Bush, "My Second Chance," *Ladies Home Journal*, March 1989, pp. 138ff.

²²Bush, *Barbara Bush*, p. 283.

²³Lawrence Altman, *NYT*, January 4, 1990; Kilian, *Barbara Bush*, pp. 61–62.

²⁴Bush diary, May 8, 1989, OGB.

²⁵Robert Pear, *NYT*, June 16, 1989.

²⁶Henry Kissinger, *Diplomacy* (New York: Simon & Schuster, 1994), pp. 772 and 781; Baker, *Politics of Diplomacy*, p. 112.

²⁷C.f., Jacob Heilbrunn, "Yew Turn," *The New Republic*, December 9, 1996, pp. 20–21.

²⁸As quoted in Thomas L. Friedman, *NYT*, June 5, 1989.

²⁹Interview with Brent Scowcroft, April 18, 1995.

³⁰Ibid.; Stephen E. Ambrose, *Ruin and Recovery 1973–1990* (New York: Simon & Schuster, 1991), p. 568; Baker, *Politics of Diplomacy*, pp. 109–10.

³¹Baker, *Politics of Diplomacy*, p. 113; *Congress and the Nation*, vol. 8, pp. 755–56; Blumenthal, *Pledging Allegiance*, p. 345.

³²Blumenthal, *Pledging Allegiance*, p. 345; Ambrose, *Ruin and Recovery*, pp. 568–69.

³³Baker, *Politics of Diplomacy*, pp. 113–14; interview with Brent Scowcroft, April 18, 1995.

³⁴Bush diaries, May 29, 1990, OGB.

³⁵Jim Drinkard, AP, July 11, 1991, and July 23, 1991; Steve Gerstel, AP, July 20, 1991; Guy Gugliotta, *WP*, July 21, 1991; Kathy Wilhelm, AP, July 24, 1991, and January 15, 1994; interview with George Bush, March 6, 1996.

³⁶Amy Fried, Mary G. Dietz, and John L. Sullivan, "Patriotism, Politics, and the Presidential Election of 1988," *American Journal of Political Science*, February 1991, pp. 200–34.

³⁷Robin Toner, *NYT*, June 26, 1989; Bernard Weinraub, *NYT*, July 7, 1989; Editorial, *The Economist*, July 1, 1989, p. 19.

³⁸*PPP: Bush, 1989*, vol. 1, p. 805.

³⁹Ibid., p. 815.

⁴⁰Ed Rollins with Tom DeFrank, *Bare Knuckles and Back Rooms* (New York: Broadway Books, 1996), p. 196.

⁴¹Fred Barnes, "Caving In," *The New Republic*, July 17, 1989, pp. 8–10.

⁴²Ibid.

⁴³Bernard Weinraub, *NYT*, May 7, 1989.

⁴⁴Bush diaries, May 21, 1990, OGB.

⁴⁵Barnes, "Caving In," p. 11.

⁴⁶Robin Toner, *NYT*, July 24, 1989.

⁴⁷Maureen Dowd, *NYT*, July 1, 1989.

⁴⁸Robin Toner, *NYT*, July 2, 1989.

⁴⁹*Congress and the Nation*, vol. 8, p. 761.

⁵⁰Robin Toner, *NYT*, July 2, 1989.

⁵¹*TGP 1990*, p. 66.

⁵²Jack F. Matlock Jr., *Autopsy of an Empire* (New York: Random House, 1995), p. 226.

⁵³*PPP: Bush*, 1989, vol. 1, p. 1753.

⁵⁴Interview with Condoleezza Rice, June 7, 1995.

⁵⁵*Department of State Bulletin* (Washington, D.C.: U.S. Government Printing House, 1989), pp. 22ff.; *NYT*, July

11, 1989; R. W. Apple Jr., *NYT,* July 12, 1989; Speech File, State of the Union, Folder 3, BPMP; interview with Condoleezza Rice, June 7, 1995.

[56]*PPP: Bush, 1989,* vol. 2, p. 972.

[57]Interview with Marlin Fitzwater, July 30, 1996; *PPP: Bush, 1989,* vol. 2, p. 936.

[58]*Department of State Bulletin* (Washington, D.C.: U.S. Government Printing Office, 1989), vol. 89, number 2149, pp. 11ff.; Beschloss and Talbott, *Highest Levels,* pp. 92–93.

[59]*PPP: Bush, 1989,* vol. 2, pp. 969–76.

[60]Baker, *Politics of Diplomacy,* pp. 168–69; Beschloss and Talbott, *Highest Levels,* pp. 93–94; Janice Castro, "Grapevine," *Time,* October 5, 1992, p. 17; "White House Watch—Bush Penchant for Secrecy," *The New Republic,* February 26, 1990, pp. 13–14.

[61]Matlock, *Autopsy,* p. 236.

[62]Zelikow and Rice, *Germany Unified,* pp. 67–68.

[63]Ibid., p. 73.

[64]Ibid., pp. 93, 99–100, and 105.

[65]Matlock, *Autopsy,* p. 275.

[66]Elizabeth Drew, "Letter From Washington," *The New Yorker,* January 1, 1990, p. 80.

[67]Zelikow and Rice, *Germany Unified,* p. 107.

[68]Matlock, *Autopsy,* p. 282; interview with Condoleezza Rice, June 7, 1995.

[69]Matlock, *Autopsy,* pp. 253–54.

[70]Matlock, *Autopsy,* pp. 250–51; Elizabeth Drew, "Letter From Washington," *The New Yorker,* January 1, 1990, pp. 80–81.

[71]Baker, *Politics of Diplomacy,* p. 169.

[72]Interview with Condoleezza Rice, June 7, 1995; Kenneth T. Walsh, "Summit Meetings," *U.S. News & World Report,* December 4, 1989, p. 21; Drew, "Letter From Washington," January 1, 1990, p. 81.

[73]As quoted in Baker, *Politics of Diplomacy,* p. 170.

[74]Matlock, *Autopsy,* p. 272.

[75]Ibid., pp. 271–74; Baker, *Politics of Diplomacy,* p. 170.

[76]Powell, *American Journey,* pp. 416–17; Eytan Gilboa, "The Panama Invasion Revisited: Lessons for the Use of Force in the Post–Cold War Era," *Political Science Quarterly,* vol. 110, pp. 550–51.

[77]Buckley, *Panama,* pp. 181–82; Woodward, *Commanders,* p. 84.

[78]Woodward, *Commanders,* pp. 84–85, 90, and 92.

[79]Bush diaries, October 3, 1989, OGB.

[80]Buckley, *Panama,* p. 203.

[81]Bush diaries, October 4, 1989, OGB.

[82]Woodward, *Commanders,* p. 127; Buckley, *Panama,* pp. 203–4; Powell, *American Journey,* p. 420.

[83]Interviews with Colin Powell, April 17 and Dick Cheney, April 21, 1995; Bush diaries, October 29, 1989, OGB.

[84]Bush diaries, October 4, 1989, OGB.

[85]Interview with Dan Quayle, June 14, 1995; Bush diaries, October 6, 1989; *NYT,* October 6, 1989.

[86]Woodward, *Commanders,* p. 128.

[87]Bush diaries, December 18, 1989, OGB.

[88]Woodward, *Commanders,* p. 128; Baker, *Politics of Diplomacy,* p. 187.

[89]Woodward, *Commanders,* pp 139–40.

[90]Stephen Engerberg, *NYT,* October 23, 1989; Thomas L. Friedman, *NYT,* October 27, 1989.

[91]*PPP: Bush,* 1989, vol. 2, pp. 1408–4; Bush diaries, October 28, 1989, OGB.

[92]Kempe, *Divorcing the Dictator,* p. 8; Kostner and Sanchez, *Time of the Tyrants,* p. 371; Buckley, *Panama,* pp. 226 and 231.

[93]Buckley, *Panama,* p. 229; Woodward, *Commanders,* p. 159.

[94]Confidential interview.

[95]Woodward, *Commanders,* p. 158; Bush diaries, December 18, 1989, OGB.

[96]Prados, *Keepers of the Keys,* p. 556; Powell, *American Journey,* pp. 423–24.

[97]Powell, *American Journey,* p. 427.

[98]Woodward, *Commanders,* pp. 170–71.

[99]Bush, *Barbara Bush,* p. 321.

[100]Bush diaries, December 23, 1989, OGB; Powell, *American Journey,* p. 426.

[101]Powell, *American Journey,* pp. 424 and 429.

[102]*PPP: Bush,* 1989, vol. 2, p. 1,729.

[103]Powell, *American Journey,* p. 428.

[104]Ibid., p. 431.

[105]Buckley, *Panama,* p. 241.

[106]Ibid., pp. 247–54; Powell, *American Journey,* p. 433.

[107]Sidney Blumenthal, "All the President's Wars," *The New Yorker,* December 28–January 4, 1990, p. 67.

[108]Powell, *American Journey,* p. 434.

[109]*TGP 1990,* p. 18.

[110]Ann McDaniel and Thomas M. DeFrank, "Bush: The Secret Presidency," *Newsweek,* pp. 26–27; Jack W. Germond and Jules Witcover, *Boston Globe,* January 6, 1990.

CHAPTER TWENTY-ONE

[1]*Human Events,* October 14, 1989, p. 3, as quoted by Steve C. Ropp, "Panama: The United States Invasion and Its Aftermath," *Current History,* March 1991, p. 114.

[2]Richard J. Barnet, "Bush's Splendid Little War," *The Nation,* January 22, 1990, pp. 73ff; Alexander Cockburn, "The Conquest of Panama," *The Nation,* January 29, 1990, pp. 114–15; Robert Parry and Douglas Waller, "The Bush-Noriega Relationship," *Newsweek,* January 15, 1990, pp. 16–17.

[3]Interview with Marlin Fitzwater, July 30, 1996.

[4]Maureen Dowd, *NYT,* February 1, 1990.

[5]Interview with Marlin Fitzwater, July 30, 1990; Bush diaries, May 16, 1990.

[6]Owen Ullmann, *The State* (Columbia, SC), July 22, 1990.

[7]Interview with Brian Mulroney, February 6, 1997.

[8]William L. Eagle and Emily M. Mead to Jim Pinkerton, November 6, 1989, and Roger B. Porter to David Demarest, January 22, 1990, Office of Speechwriting, State of the Union 1990, Folder 2, BPMP, College Station, TX; Congressional Quarterly, *Almanac, 101st Congress, 1st Session . . . 1989* (Washington, D.C.: Congressional Quarterly Inc., 1989), pp. 3–9.

[9]*PPP: Bush, 1990,* vol. 1, pp. 129–34; R.W. Apple Jr., and Andrew Rosenthal, *NYT,* February 1, 1990.

[10]Office of Speechwriting, White House News Summary, Network Television Coverage, January 31, 1990, SOTUS, 1990, Folder 1, BPMP, College Station, TX.

[11]Ibid., Jim Cicconi to Mr. President, February 1, 1990.

[12]*TGP 1990,* p. 17.

[13]*NYT,* January 23, 1990; Ann McDaniel and Thomas J. DeFrank, "Bush Plays Macho Man," *Newsweek,* February 5, 1990, p. 20; *NYT,* February 6, 1990; Bush, *Barbara Bush,* p. 330; *PPP: Bush, 1990,* vol. 1, pp. 222–28.

[14]*Congressional Quarterly Almanac,* vol, 46, p. 20.

[15]George F. Will, "Bush: Read My Polls," *Newsweek,* May 7, 1990, p. 78.

[16]Mandlebaum, "The Bush Foreign Policy," *Foreign Affairs,* vol. 70, p. 9; Zelikow and Rice, *Germany Unified,* p. 197; interview with Condoleezza Rice, June 7, 1995.

[17]Interview with Roger Porter, July 15, 1996; *Congress and the Nation,* vol. 8, pp. 1181–82.

[18]Interview with George Bush, March 7, 1996; *Congress and the Nation,* vol. 8, pp. 743–52; Daniel J. Mitchell, "Bush's Rasputin," *National Review,* December 28, 1992, p 31; Duffy and Goodgame, *March in Place,* p. 79.

[19]Interview with Barbara Bush, July 6, 1995.

[20]Confidential interviews; interview with George Upson Warren, January 29, 1992.

[21]Bush, *Barbara Bush,* pp. 325 and 385.

[22]Kilian, *Barbara Bush,* p. 160.

[23]Kenneth T. Walsh, "The Hidden Life of Barbara Bush," *U.S. News & World Report,* May 28, 1990, pp. 24ff.; Judith Viorst, "It's Time to Bring Back the Family," *Redbook,* May 1991, pp. 40ff.; Goldman, et al, *Quest,* p. 379; interview with Martin Anderson, July 7, 1993; Reagan, *My Turn,* pp. 270–71; interview with Barbara Bush, July 6, 1995; Kilian, *Barbara Bush,* p. 160; Marjorie Williams, "Barbara's Backlash," *Vanity Fair,* August 1992, p. 179.

[24]*Houston Chronicle,* March 26, 1990; Quayle, *Standing Firm,* p. 79.

[25]Interview with Brian Mulroney, February 6, 1997.

[26]Maureen Dowd, *NYT,* May 1, 1990.

[27]Interviews with Dave Keene, May 26, 1993, and Marlin Fitzwater, July 30, 1995.

[28]Thomas C. Hayes, *NYT,* January 19, 1990; Bush, *Barbara Bush,* p. 325.

[29]*NYT,* May 24, 1990.

[30]Ann McDaniel, "A Crisis in the First Family," *Newsweek,* July 23, 1990, pp. 17–18; *Congressional Quarterly Almanac, 101st Congress, 2nd Session . . . 1990* (Washington, D.C.: Congressional Quarterly, Inc., 1990), vol. 46, p. 6.

[31]Kathleen Day, *WP,* July 27, 1991; Jerry Knight, *WP,* January 14, 1993; Kenneth T. Walsh, *U.S. News & World Report,* August 13, 1990, pp. 42–43; Martin Tolchin, *NYT,* July 19, 1991.

[32]Lee Bandy, *The State* (Columbia, SC), March 5, 1991.

[33]*NYT,* March 7, 1990; Lee Bandy, *The State* (Columbia, SC), March 5 and April 3, 4, 6, and 8, 1991; Mary Matalin and James Carville, with Peter Knobler, *All's Fair* (New York: Random House, 1994), p. 50; Michael Kelly, "Big Bad John," *Playboy,* November 1990, pp. 112ff.

[34]Anthony Kind and Giles Alston, "Good Government and the Politics of High Exposure," in Campbell and Rockman (eds.), *Bush Presidency,* p. 258; Bob Woodward, *WP,* October 4, 1992; Elizabeth Drew, "Letter From Washington," *The New Yorker,* June 4, 1990, p. 94.

[35]James Pfiffner, "The President's Chief of Staff: Lessons Learned," *Presidential Studies Quarterly,* Winter 1993, pp. 90–99; Mervin, *Bush,* p. 157.

[36]Interview with George Bush, January 25, 1995.

[37]Bush diaries, May 24, 1990.

[38]Confidential interview.

[39]Kelly, "Big Bad John," pp. 112ff.

[40]Drew, "Letter From Washington," *The New Yorker,* June 4, 1990, p. 96.

[41]Laurence Barrett, "1,000 Points of Spite," *Time* (International Edition), October 15, 1990, p. 24, as quoted in Mervin, *Bush,* p. 143.

[42]Confidential interviews; interview with Nicholas F. Brady, November 7, 1995; Michael Kelly, "Big Bad John," *Playboy,* November 1990, pp. 112ff.

[43]Interview with Nicholas F. Brady, November 7, 1995.

[44]Kolb, *White House Daze*, p. 95.

[45]Bob Woodward, *Washington Post*, October 6 and 7, 1992; interview with Andrew Card, January 13, 1997.

[46]Juan Williams, *Washington Post*, November 24, 1991, as quoted in Pfiffner, "The President's Chief of Staff," p. 95.

[47]Kolb, *White House Daze*, p. 13.

[48]*Congress and the Nation*, vol. 8, p. 712.

[49]Interview with Roger Porter, July 15, 1996.

[50]*TGP 1990*, p. 67; Bush diaries, March 6, 1991; *Congress and the Nation*, vol. 8, p. 712.

[51]Elizabeth Drew, "Letter From Washington," *The New Yorker*, November 12, 1990, pp. 113–14.

[52]Bush, *Barbara Bush*, p. 327; *PPP: Bush, 1990*, vol. 1, p. 913; Darman, *Who's in Control?*, p. 250.

[53]Darman, *Who's in Control?*, pp. 250–51; King and Alston, in Campbell and Rockman (ed.), *Bush Presidency*, pp. 258–59.

[54]Drew, "Letter From Washington," p. 96; Darman, *Who's in Control?*, p. 251.

[55]Elizabeth Drew, "Letter From Washington," *The New Yorker*, June 4, 1990, p. 98.

[56]Ibid., p. 97.

[57]Bush diary, May 12, 1990; *PPP: Bush, 1990*, vol. 1, p. 657.

[58]Bush diaries, May 15 and 16, 1990.

[59]Cannon, *Reagan*, pp. 185–86; Darman, *Who's in Control?*, pp. 72–73.

[60]*PPP: Bush, 1990*, vol. 1, p. 710.

[61]Drew, "Letter From Washington, *The New Yorker*, June 4, 1990, p. 95; Barbara Sinclair, in Campbell and Rockman (eds.), *Bush Presidency*, pp. 175–76.

[62]*PPP: Bush, 1990*, vol. 1, p. 868.

[63]Quayle, *Standing Firm*, pp. 192–93.

[64]Maureen Dowd, *NYT*, April 24 1989; interview with Gen. Brent Scowcroft, April 18, 1995.

[65]Lynn Ashby, *Houston Post*, June 29, 1990, as quoted in Barbara Sinclair, in Campbell and Rockman (eds.), *Bush Presidency*, p. 176.

[66]John W. Mashek, *Boston Globe*, July 1, 1990.

[67]Sidney Blumenthal, "The Drifter," *The New Republic*, November 4, 1991, p. 23; David Brock, *The Real Anita Hill: The Untold Story* (New York: The Free Press, 1993), p. 27.

[68]Bush diaries, July 24, 1990.

[69]Neil A. Lewis, *NYT*, July 31, 1990; Joan Biskupic, *WP*, November 13, 1994, and July 2, 1995.

[70]Interview with James Cicconi, June 23, 1996.

[71]C. Boyden Gray to George Bush, May 4, 1990, BPMP, College Station, TX; interview with C. Boyden Gray, July 30, 1996; *PPP: Bush, 1990*, vol. 2, p. 1438; *NYT*, May 25, 1991; *Congress and the Nation*, vol. 8, p. 758.

[72]*PPP: Bush, 1990*, vol. 1, pp. 746 and 753.

[73]Zelikow and Rice, *Germany Unified*, p. 276; Baker, *Politics of Diplomacy*, p. 254; *PPP: Bush, 1990*, vol. 1, p. 753; Beschloss and Talbott, *Highest Levels*, p. 224.

[74]*PPP: Bush, 1990*, vol. 1, p. 754.

[75]Bush, *Barbara Bush*, p. 348; Beschloss and Talbott, *Highest Levels*, p. 237; interview with Brian Mulroney, February 6, 1997.

[76]Sarah Bartlett, *NYT*, June 10, 1990.

[77]Nathaniel C. Nash, *NYT*, June 29, 1990.

[78]Jeff Gerth, *NYT*, July 3, 1990.

[79]Nathaniel C. Nash, *NYT*, July 11 and 12, 1990.

[80]Jeff Gerth, *NYT*, July 15 and July 22, 1990; Nathaniel C. Nash, *NYT*, August 1, 1990.

[81]Martin Tolchin, *NYT*, July 12, 1990.

[82]Andrew Rosenthal, *NYT*, July 23, 1990.

[83]Ann McDaniel, "A Crisis in the First Family," *Newsweek*, July 23, 1990, p. 17.

[84]*NYT*, July 15, 1990.

[85]Susan F. Rasky, *NYT*, July 3, 1990, and July 18, 1990.

[86]Nathaniel C. Nash, *NYT*, August 26, 1990.

[87]Bush diaries, July 24 and 31, and August 11, 1990, OGB.

[88]105th Congress, 1st Session, House of Representatives, *Report of The Committee on Standards of Official Conduct: In the Matter of Representative Newt Gingrich* (Washington, D.C.: U.S. Government Printing Office, January 17, 1997), paragraph C(1); Katharine Q. Seelye, *NYT*, January 18, 1997.

[89]Elizabeth Drew, "Letter From Washington," *The New Yorker*, November 12, 1990, p. 114.

[90]Nathaniel C. Nash, *NYT*, August 1, 1990.

[91]Bush diaries, July 31, 1990, and August 2, 1990, OGB; Susan F. Rasky, *NYT*, July 31, 1990.

CHAPTER TWENTY-TWO

[1]Bush diaries, July 31 and August 1, 1990, OGB; Susan F. Rasky, *NYT*, July 31, 1990.

[2]Bush diaries, August 3, 1990, OGB.

[3]Elizabeth Drew, "Letter From Washington," *The New Yorker*, February 18, 1991, p. 72.

[4]Murray Waas, "Who Lost Kuwait?" *The Village Voice*, January 22, 1991, and *The Berkshire Eagle*, March 1, 1991.

[5]Christopher Hitchens, "Why We Are Stuck in the Sand," *Harper's Magazine*, January 1991, pp. 70–78.

⁶Staff of *U.S. News & World Report, Triumph Without Victory* (New York: A Times Book, 1993), p. 98; Jean Edward Smith, *George Bush's War* (New York: Henry Holt and Company, 1992), p. 8.

⁷Arthur Schlesinger Jr., "Iraq, War and the Constitution," *WSJ,* November 12, 1990.

⁸*TGP 1990,* pp. 55–56 and 75; Nathaniel C. Nash, *NYT,* August 26, 1990.

⁹Woodward, *Commanders,* p. 315.

¹⁰Staff of *U.S. News, Triumph Without Tragedy,* p. 105; Fred Barnes, "Hour of Power," *The New Republic,* September 3, 1990, p. 14.

¹¹Lawrence Freedman and Efraim Karsh, *The Gulf Conflict, 1990–1991* (Princeton, NJ: Princeton University Press, 1993), p. 74; *U.S. News,* p. 63.

¹²Freedman and Karsh, *Gulf Conflict,* p. 16.

¹³Baker, *Politics of Diplomacy,* pp. 118–19.

¹⁴Cannon, *Reagan,* p. 396; Baker, *Politics of Diplomacy,* p. 118.

¹⁵Baker, *Politics of Diplomacy,* p. 118; Freedman and Karsh, *Gulf Conflict,* p. 16.

¹⁶"Talk of the Town," *The New Yorker,* August 27, 1990, p. 28.

¹⁷David Majovsky, Kenneth T. Walsh, and Louise Lief, "Bush's Big Blunder," *U.S. News & World Report,* March 26, 1990, pp. 32–33; Bush diaries, May 23, 1990, OGB; Baker, *Politics of Diplomacy,* p. 116.

¹⁸John Kifner, *NYT,* August 8, 1990.

¹⁹Dennis Hevesi, *NYT,* August 5, 1990.

²⁰Staff of *U.S. News, Triumph Without Victory,* p. 96.

²¹Michael Wines, *NYT,* August 13, 1990; Freedman and Karsh, *Gulf Conflict,* pp. 26–27 and 37; Smith, *Bush's War,* p. 45; Waas and Unger, "In the Loop," *The New Yorker,* November 2, 1992, p. 83; Anthony Lewis, *NYT,* October 5, 1990; Jane E. Allen, AP, June 19, 1991.

²²Murray Waas and Craig Unger, "In the Loop," *The New Yorker,* November 2, 1992, pp. 82–83; Anthony Lewis, *NYT,* October 5, 1990; George Bush, *Larry King Live,* CNN, October 4, 1992.

²³Woodward, *Commanders,* p. 218.

²⁴Elizabeth Drew, "Letter From Washington," *The New Yorker,* September 24, 1990, p. 105.

²⁵Freedman and Karsh, *Gulf Conflict,* pp. 57, 60, and 448.

²⁶Ibid., p. 60.

²⁷Michael Wines, *NYT,* January 24, 1991; Michael R. Gordon and General Bernard E. Trainor, *The Generals' War: The Inside Story of the Conflict in the Gulf* (Boston: Little, Brown, 1995), p. 5.

²⁸Gordon and Trainor, *Generals' War,* p. 6.

²⁹Freedman and Karsh, *Gulf Conflict,* p. 57.

³⁰H. Norman Schwarzkopf, with Peter Petre, *The Autobiography: It Doesn't Take a Hero* (New York: A Bantam Book, 1992), p. 294; Powell, *American Journey,* p. 461.

³¹Schwarzkopf, *Autobiography,* p. 295.

³²Smith, *Bush's War,* pp. 52–53.

³³Baker, *Politics of Diplomacy,* p. 4.

³⁴Powell, *American Journey,* p. 461; Schwarzkopf, *Autobiography,* pp. 294–95.

³⁵Powell, *American Journey,* p. 462.

³⁶Staff of *U.S. News, Triumph Without Victory,* pp. 27–28.

³⁷Ibid., p. 36.

³⁸Woodward, *Commanders,* p. 224; Bush diaries, August 2, 1990, OGB.

³⁹Fred Barnes, "Hour of Power," *The New Republic.* September 3, 1990, p. 14.

⁴⁰Freedman and Karsh, *Gulf Crisis,* pp. 67 and 73; Smith, *Bush's War,* pp. 13–14.

⁴¹Bush diaries, August 2, 1990, OGB.

⁴²Robert D. McFadden, *NYT,* August 4, 1990; Freedman and Karsh, *Gulf Conflict,* p. 141.

⁴³Bush diaries, August 15, 1990, OGB.

⁴⁴Smith, *Bush's War,* p. 17; Elizabeth Drew, "Letter From Washington," *The New Yorker,* September 24, 1990, p. 106.

⁴⁵Cf., Smith, *Bush's War,* p. 17.

⁴⁶*PPP: Bush, 1990,* vol. 2, pp. 1083.

⁴⁷Bush diary, August 2, 1990, OGB.

⁴⁸C.f., Smith, *Bush's War,* p. 17.

⁴⁹Interview with Dick Cheney, April 21, 1995.

⁵⁰*NYT,* August 3, 1990.

⁵¹Freedman and Karsh, *Gulf War,* p. 74; Maureen Dowd, *NYT,* August 9, 1990; interview with Dick Cheney, April 21, 1995.

⁵²Freedman and Karsh, *Gulf Conflict,* p. 75; Smith, *Bush's War,* p. 64; Staff of *U.S. News, Triumph Without Victory,* p. 62; George Bush to James McCall, March 7, 1996, and Bush diaries, August 2 and 3, 1990, OGB.

⁵³Bush diaries, August 2 and 3, 1990, OGB; Joel Brinkley, *NYT,* August 3, 1990; R. W. Apple Jr., *NYT,* August 4, 1990.

⁵⁴Margaret Thatcher, *The Downing Street Years* (New York: HarperCollins, 1993), pp. 753, 768, and 783–84.

⁵⁵Interview with Brian Mulroney, February 6, 1997.

⁵⁶Thatcher, *Downing Street Years,* p. 828; Baker, *Politics of Diplomacy,* p. 279.

⁵⁷*Time,* January 28, 1991, p. 33, as quoted in Smith, *Bush's War,* p. 66.

⁵⁸Bush diaries, August 2 and 3, 1990; Joel Brinkley, *NYT,* August 3, 1990.

[59]Bush diaries, August 2, 1990, OGB.

[60]Ibid.; Maureen Dowd, *NYT,* August 3, 1990.

[61]Thatcher, *Downing Street Years,* p. 824.

[62]Ibid., p. 818.

[63]*PPP: Bush, 1990,* vol. 2, p. 1087; Smith, *Bush's War,* p. 7; Freedman and Karsh, *Gulf Conflict,* pp. 74–75; Staff of *U.S. News, Triumph Without Victory,* pp. 62–63; Fred Barnes, "Hour of Power," *The New Republic,* September 3, 1990, p. 14; Anthony Lewis, *NYT,* August 7, 1990; Bush diaries, August 2 and 3, 1990; confidential interview.

[64]John Kifner, *NYT,* August 4, 1990.

[65]Bush diary, August 3, 1990, OGB; Thatcher, *Downing Street Years,* p. 817.

[66]Interview with Brian Mulroney, February 6, 1997.

[67]Thomas L. Friedman, *NYT,* August 4, 1990.

[68]Interview with Brian Mulroney, February 6, 1997.

[69]Robert D. Hershey Jr., *NYT,* August 4, 1990.

[70]Dennis Hevesi, *NYT,* August 5, 1990.

[71]Bush diaries, August 3, 1990.

[72]Powell, *American Journey,* p. 463.

[73]Interview with Gen. Colin Powell, April 17, 1995.

[74]Powell, *American Journey,* p. 463.

[75]John Kifner, *NYT,* August 5, 1990.

[76]Freedman and Karsh, *Gulf Conflict,* p. 88.

[77]Powell, *American Journey,* p. 465.

[78]Gordon and Trainor, *Generals' War,* p. 48.

[79]Interview with Dick Cheney, April 21, 1995; Freedman and Karsh, *Gulf Conflict,* p. 89.

[80]Staff of *U.S. News, Triumph Without Victory,* pp. 68–69; Powell, *American Journey,* p. 466; Elizabeth Drew, "Letter From Washington," *The New Yorker,* August 20, 1990, pp. 25–26.

[81]Powell, *American Journey,* pp. 465–66.

[82]Ibid., p. 466.

[83]Bush diaries, August 2, 1990, OGB; Staff of *U.S. News, Triumph Without Victory,* p. 75.

[84]Interview with Dick Cheney, April 21, 1990; Woodward, *Commanders,* p. 263.

[85]Powell, *American Journey,* p. 466; interview with Colin Powell, April 17, 1995; Freedman and Karsh, *Gulf Conflict,* p. 90.

[86]Woodward, *Commanders,* p. 260.

[87]Smith, *Bush's War,* p. 90.

[88]Gordon and Trainor, *Generals' War,* p. 49.

[89]Elizabeth Drew, "Letter From Washington," *The New Yorker,* February 4, 1991, p. 82.

[90]Powell, *American Journey,* p. 467.

[91]Interview with Marlin Fitzwater, July 31, 1996.

[92]Freedman and Karsh, *Gulf Conflict,* pp. 92–93; interview with Dick Cheney, April 21, 1990; excerpts from News Conference by Cheney and Powell, *NYT,* August 9, 1990; Smith, *Bush's War,* p. 93; Elizabeth Drew, "Letter From Washington," *The New Yorker,* February 4, 1991, p. 82; Fred Barnes, "Hour of Power," *The New Republic,* September 3, 1990, p. 15.

[93]John Brady, *Bad Boy: The Life and Politics of Lee Atwater* (New York: Addison Wesley Publishing Company, 1997), p. 309.

[94]Bush diaries, August 7, 1990, OGB.

[95]Interview with Brian Mulroney, February 6, 1997.

[96]Ibid.; Baker, *Politics of Diplomacy,* pp. 42–43.

[97]Gordon and Trainor, *Generals' War,* p. 37.

[98]Ibid.

[99]As quoted in Freedman and Karsh, *Gulf Conflict,* p. 115.

[100]Bush diaries, August 6, 1990, OGB.

[101]Ibid., August 7, 1990, OGB.

[102]Interview with Dick Cheney, April 21, 1995.

[103]Ibid.

[104]*PPP: Bush, 1990,* vol. 2, p. 1108.

[105]Cf., Duffy and Goodgame, *Marching in Place,* p. 147.

[106]Michael Wines, *NYT,* August 9, 1990.

[107]*PPP: Bush, 1990,* vol. 2, pp. 1109–14; Bush diaries, August 8, 1990.

[108]Bush diaries, August 8, 1990, OGB.

[109]Fred Barnes, "Hour of Power," *The New Republic,* September 3, 1990, p. 13.

[110]*NYT,* August 11, 1990.

[111]Mueller, *Policy and Opinion,* p. 180.

[112]*NYT,* August 9, 1990.

[113]Cf., Brigette Lebens Nacos, "Presidential Leadership During the Persian Gulf Conflict," *Presidential Studies Quarterly,* (vol. XXIV, no. 3), Summer 1994, p. 558.

[114]Freedman and Karsh, *Gulf Conflict,* p. 222.

[115]Bush, *Barbara Bush,* p. 354.

[116]Freedman and Karsh, *Gulf Conflict,* p. 139.
[117]Bush diaries, August 17, 1990, OGB.
[118]Evan Thomas, "Bush's Hostage Dilemma," *Newsweek,* August 27, 1990, p. 23; Woodward, *Commanders,* p. 316.
[119]Freedman and Karsh, *Gulf Conflict,* p. 201.
[120]Staff of *U.S. News, Triumph Without Victory,* p. 129.
[121]Duffy and Goodgame, *Marching in Place,* p. 151; Freedman and Karsh, *Gulf Conflict,* p. 222.
[122]Freedman and Karsh, *Gulf Conflict,* p. 240; U.S. Department of State Dispatch, *The Gulf: A World United Against Aggression* (Washington, D.C.: U.S. Government Printing Office, 1990), pp. 295–96.
[123]Freedman and Karsh, *Gulf Conflict,* p. 135.
[124]Ibid., p. 192.
[125]Ibid., pp. 223-24; Woodward, *Commanders,* p. 317.
[126]Freedman and Karsh, *Gulf Conflict,* p. 161; Bush, *Barbara Bush,* pp. 355–56.
[127]Bush, *Barbara Bush,* p. 355; Bush diaries, August 17, 1990, OGB.
[128]Woodward, *Commanders,* pp. 282 and 285.
[129]Staff of *U.S. News, Triumph Without Victory,* p. 139.
[130]C.f., Archie Brown, *The Gorbachev Factor* (New York: Oxford University Press, 1996), pp. 240–41.
[131]Freeman and Karsh, *Gulf Conflict,* p. 163.
[132]Kenneth T. Walsh, "Bush's Split Personality," *U.S. News & World Report,* September 17, 1990, p. 26.
[133]*PPP: Bush, 1990,* vol. 2, p. 1206.
[134]Baker, *Politics of Diplomacy,* p. 472.
[135]*PPP: Bush, 1990,* vol. 2, p. 1219.
[136]"Talk of the Town," *The New Yorker,* August 27, 1990, p. 28.
[137]Interview with Brian Mulroney, February 6, 1997.
[138]*PPP: Bush, 1990,* vol. 2, pp. 1326–27.
[139]Mervin, *Bush,* p. 133.
[140]*PPP: Bush, 1990,* vol. 2, pp. 1349–50.
[141]Mervin, *Bush,* p. 145.
[142]Andrew Rosenthal, *NYT,* October 3, 1990.
[143]Barbara Sinclair, in Campbell and Rockman, *Bush Presidency,* pp. 178–79; Charles O. Jones, in Ibid., pp. 179–254; Howard E. Shuman, *Politics and the Budget: The Struggle Between the President and the Congress* (Englewood Cliffs, NJ: Prentice Hall, 1992), pp. 324–25; Mervin, *Bush,* p. 155.
[144]Shuman, *Politics and the Budget,* p. 325.
[145]*WP,* October 11, 1990; Shuman, *Politics and the Budget,* p. 326; *National Review,* November 5, 1990, pp. 18–19.
[146]Ed Rollins to Republican Members of Congress, October 15, 1990, BPMP, College Station, TX.
[147]Interviews with Marlin Fitzwater, July 30, 1996, and Guy Vander Jagt, January 8, 1997.
[148]Rollins, *Bare Knuckles,* p. 207.
[149]Confidential interviews; Rollins, *Bare Knuckles,* p. 222.
[150]*The Economist,* October 27, 1990, p. 34.
[151]Shuman, *Politics and the Budget,* p. 329.
[152]Barbara Sinclair, in Campbell and Rockman, *Bush Presidency,* p. 179; *The Economist,* October 27, 1990, p. 34; Mueller, *Policy and Opinion,* p. 180.
[153]Michael Duffy, *Time,* November 5, 1990.
[154]Jack W. Germond and Jules Witcover, "Bush Takes a Hit," *National Journal,* November 10, 1990, p. 2732.
[155]James P. Pfiffner, "The President and the Postreform Congress," in Roger H. Davidson, *The Postreform Congress* (New York: St. Martin's Press, 1992), p. 218; Rollins, *Bare Knuckles,* p. 207.
[156]William Safire, *NYT,* October 1, 1990; Elizabeth Drew, "Letter From Washington," *The New Yorker,* December 31, 1990, p. 87.
[157]Woodward, *Commanders,* p. 317.
[158]As quoted in Jennifer Grossman to Mark Lange, January 13, 1991, Speech File, State of the Union 1991 folder, BPMP, College Station, TX.
[159]Interviews with Brent Scowcroft, January 22 and February 3, 1997.
[160]Elizabeth Drew, "Letter From Washington," *The New Yorker,* December 31, 1990, p. 87.
[161]Matlock, *Autopsy of an Empire,* p. 524.
[162]George Bush to James McCall, March 7, 1996, OGB.
[163]Confidential interview.
[164]*PPP: Bush, 1990,* vol. 2, p. 1582.
[165]"Talk of the Town," *The New Yorker,* November 19, 1990,
[166]*NYT,* November 20, 1990; C.f., Dan Rather, *CBS Reports: The Gulf War + 5,* January 18, 1996.
[167]Chronology, *Current History,* January 1991, p. 44; *Congress and the Nation,* vol. 8, p. 305; Drew, "Letter From Washington," December 31, 1990, p. 88.
[168]*PPP: Bush, 1990,* vol. 1, p. 1720.
[169]*Congress and the Nation,* vol. 8, p. 308.
[170]Ibid.
[171]Ibid., p. 309.
[172]*PPP: Bush, 1991,* vol. p. 40.

[173]Ibid., pp. 28–40.
[174]Bush diaries, January 15, 1991, OGB; Bush, *Barbara Bush,* p. 388.
[175]Bush diaries, January 16, 1991, and Bush to James McCall, March 7, 1996, OGB.
[176]*PPP: Bush, 1991,* vol. 1, p. 43.

CHAPTER TWENTY-THREE

[1]Kenneth T. Walsh, "Bush's Split Personality," *U.S. News & World Report,* September 17, 1990, p. 26.
[2]Jason DeParle, *NYT,* May 5, 1991; Edwin Diamond, "Who Won the Media War," *New York,* March 18, 1991, pp. 26–29; John Corry, "TV News and the Neutrality Principle," *Commentary,* May 1991, pp. 24–27.
[3]Andrew Rosenthal, *NYT,* January 22, 1991.
[4]*PPP: Bush. 1991,* vol. 1, p. 170.
[5]Ibid., pp. 168–70.
[6]Bush diaries, February 26, 1991, OGB.
[7]Ibid.
[8]Flora Lewis, *NYT,* January 22, 1991.
[9]Bush diaries, February 23, 1991, OGB, interview with Dick Cheney, April 21, 1995.
[10]Bush, *Barbara Bush,* p. 400.
[11]Interview with Dick Cheney, April 21, 1995; Bush diaries, February 23 and 24, 1991, OGB.
[12]Neil MacFarquhar, *NYT,* September 9, 1996.
[13]Televised documentary, *Frontline,* and the BBC, "The Gulf War," WGBH Educational Foundation, 1996, two parts.
[14]Gordon and Trainor, *Generals' War,* p. 415.
[15]Ibid., p. 417.
[16]Interview with Norman Schwarzkopf, "The Gulf War"; Powell, *American Journey,* pp. 519–20.
[17]Bush diaries, February 26, 1991, OGB.
[18]Televised interview with Colin Powell, Frontline, and BBC, "The Gulf War."
[19]Confidential interview; Scowcroft interview on *Frontline,* "The Gulf War."
[20]Gordon and Trainor, *Generals' War,* p. 416.
[21]Powell, *American Journey,* p. 523,
[22]Gordon and Trainor, *Generals' War,* p. 425.
[23]Ibid., p. 423.
[24]*PPP: Bush. 1991,* vol. 1, p. 187.
[25]Patrick E. Tyler, *NYT,* March 28, 1991.
[26]Gordon and Trainor, *Generals' War,* p. 424.
[27]Philip J. Hilts, *NYT,* February 24, 1996.
[28]Gordon and Trainor, *Generals' War,* p. 410; Neil MacFarquhar, *NYT,* September 9, 1996; Daniel S. Greenberg, *WP,* January 25, 1997.
[29]Steve Coll and Guy Gugliotta, *WP,* March 4, 1991.
[30]Powell, *American Journey,* p. 519.
[31]Gordon and Trainor, *Generals' War,* p. 416.
[32]*TGP 1991,* pp. 67–68; Everett Carll Ladd, "The 1992 Vote for President Clinton: Another Brittle Mandate?" *Political Science Quarterly,* Spring 1993, p. 25.
[33]Maureen Dowd, *NYT,* March 8, 1991.
[34]Bush diaries, March 10, 11, 13, 16, 17, 1991, OGB.
[35]Ibid., March 13, 1991, OGB.
[36]Gordon and Trainor, *Generals' War,* p. 455.
[37]Bush diaries, March 29, 1991, OGB.
[38]Tom Raum, AP, November 21, 1991; Michael Fleeman, AP, November 8, 1991; Michael Isikoff, *WP,* November 19, 1991.
[39]Bush diaries, March 29, 1991, and July 24, 1992, OGB; Elizabeth Drew, "Letter from Washington," *The New Yorker,* May 27, 1991, p. 86.
[40]Maureen Dowd, *NYT,* March 8, 1991; Bush diaries, March 5 and 8, 12, 1991, OGB.
[41]Bush diaries, March 13, 1991, OGB.
[42]Fitzwater, *Call the Briefing!,* p. 351; Bush diaries, March 13, 1991, OGB.
[43]Bush diaries, March 27, 1991, OGB.
[44]Ibid., March 13, 1991.
[45]Ibid.
[46]Ibid., March 18, 1991.
[47]Ibid., March 13, 1991.
[48]Bush diaries, OGB; Peter Goldman and Thomas DeFrank, *Quest for the Presidency 1992* (College Station: Texas A&M Press, 1994), p. 367; Bush, *Barbara Bush,* p. 327.
[49]Bush diaries, March 14, 1991, OGB.
[50]Ibid., March 16, 1991.
[51]Ibid., March 17, 1991.
[52]Ibid., March 18, 1991.
[53]Ibid., March 28, 1991, OGB; Patrick E. Tyler, *NYT,* March 28, 1991.
[54]Lee Bandy, *The State* (Columbia, S.C.), March 30, 1991.

[55]Ibid., April 5, 1991.
[56]Brady, *Bad Boy*, pp. 321–22; Matalin and Carville, *All's Fair*, pp. 53–54.
[57]*NYT,* June 11, 1991.
[58]Ibid., September 8, 1991.
[59]Russell Baker, *NYT,* August 13, 1991.
[60]Interview with Dr. Burton Lee III, March 20, 1996.
[61]Goldman and DeFrank, *Quest* (College Statio: Texas A&M Press, 1994), p. 4.
[62]Interview with Marlin Fitzwater, July 30, 1996; Goldman and DeFrank, *Quest*, pp. 299 and 367; Bush, *Barbara Bush*, p. 327.
[63]Maureen Dowd, *NYT,* May 5, 1991, May 6, 1991; Elizabeth Drew, "Letter from Washington," *The New Yorker,* May 27, 1991, p. 88.
[64]Interview with Dr. Burton Lee III, March 20, 1996.
[65]Ibid.; Ann Devroy and David Brown, *WP,* July 21, 1992.
[66]Duffy and Goodgame, *Marching in Place*, p. 123.
[67]Interview with Rich Bond, July 25, 1996; Matalin, *All's Fair,* pp. 50–51, and p. 163; Kolb, *White House Daze,* p. xviii.
[68]Interview with John Sununu, February 25, 1997.
[69]Duffy and Goodgame, *Marching in Place*, p. 125.
[70]Fitzwater, *Call the Briefing!,* pp. 179–90; interview with David Bates, January 8, 1997.
[71]Duffy and Goodgame, *Marching in Place*, p. 113.
[72]Ibid., p. 115.
[73]Larry Martz, et. al, "Sununu and the Jews," *Newsweek,* July 8, 1991, p. 27.
[74]Fitzwater, *Call the Briefing!,* p. 177.
[75]Brit Hume, "The Grounding of Air Sununu," *The American Spectator,* p. 15.
[76]Ibid., p. 14.
[77]Michael Dobbs, *WP,* July 19, 1991; Maureen Johnson, AP, July 19, 1991.
[78]Baker, *Politics of Diplomacy*, pp. 471–72; Matlock, *Autopsy of an Empire*, pp. 563–66.
[79]Duffy and Goodgame, *Marching in Place*, p. 179.
[80]Goldman and DeFrank, *Quest*, p. 301.
[81]Ibid.; Bush diaries, August 3, 1991, OGB; interviews with Ron Kaufman, March 19, 1996, Rich Bond, July 25, 1996, and Dan Quayle, June 14, 1995; *NYT,* August 3, 1991.
[82]Editorial, *National Review,* August 26, 1991, pp. 12–15; "American Survey," *The Economist,* August 24, 1991.
[83]Robin Toner, *NYT,* August 20, 1991.
[84]Tom Raum, AP, August 19, 1991; *Houston Chronicle,* October 4, 1981; Bush, *Barbara Bush,* p. 430; Beschloss and Talbott, *Highest Levels,* pp. 421–22.
[85]Beschloss and Scowcroft, *Highest Levels*, p. 422, c.f., Chapter 21 for a detailed account; "American Survey," *The Economist,* August 24, 1991, p. 23.
[86]Beschloss and Talbott, *Highest Levels*, p. 427; R. W. Apple Jr., *NYT,* August 21, 1991; Bill Keller, *NYT,* August 25, 1991.
[87]*NYT,* August 24, 1991.
[88]Andrew Rosenthal, *NYT,* August 23, 1991.
[89]Serge Schmemann, *NYT,* August 25, 1991.
[90]Beschloss and Talbott, *Highest Levels*, pp. 444 and 458.
[91]David Shribman, *WSJ,* August 20, 1991.
[92]Kenneth T. Walsh, "Bush's Split Personality," *U.S. News & World Report,* September 17, 1990, p. 26.
[93]*TGP 1991,* pp. 188–89; *TGP 1992,* pp. 7–8.
[94]Ibid., p. 187.
[95]Ibid., pp. 219 and 249; *TGP 1992,* p. 75.
[96]Mueller, *Policy and Opinion*, pp. 180–82.
[97]Lou Harris, *NYT,* May 23, 1990.
[98]Kevin Phillips, *NYT,* October 10, 1990.
[99]*NYT,* July 22, 1991.
[100]*CBS Evening News,* program n29, November 8, 1991.
[101]Steven Mufson, *WP,* December 9, 1991.
[102]George Bush interviewed by Harry Smith and Paula Zahn, *Today,* CBS-TV, July 1, 1992.
[103]Ruth Marcus, *WP,* August 8, 1992.
[104]Robert D. Hershey, Jr., *NYT,* October 3, 1992.
[105]*PPP: Bush, 1992–93,* vol. 2, p. 1526.
[106]Baker, *Politics of Diplomacy*, pp. 42–43; interview with Brian Mulroney, February 6, 1997.
[107]David Brock, *The Real Anita Hill: The Untold Story* (New York: The Free Press, 1993), p. 17.
[108]*Congress and the Nation,* vol. 8, p. 780.
[109]Bush diaries, May 4, 1992, OGB.
[110]Ibid., May 11, 1992, OGB.
[111]Baker, *Politics of Diplomacy*, p. 443.
[112]Bush diaries, February 27, March 5, and March 9, 1991, OGB.
[113]As quoted in *NYT,* August 13, 1991.
[114]William Safire, *NYT,* September 9, 1991.

[115]Baker, *Politics of Diplomacy,* pp. 501–13; *Congress and the Nation,* vol. 8, p. 277.

[116]Interview with Brian Mulroney, February 6, 1997.

[117]Interview with Lyn Nofziger, October 17, 1995.

[118]Ann Devroy and David Brown, *WP,* July 21, 1992.

[119]Interview with Craig Fuller, July 31, 1996.

[120]*TGP 1992,* p. 179.

[121]Bush diaries, October 1, 1992, OGB.

[122]Ibid.

[123]"Face to Face in Prime Time," *Newsweek,* November/December 1992, pp. 88–91.

[124]Bush, *Barbara Bush,* p. 496.

[125]AP, October 30, 1992; R. W. Apple Jr., *NYT,* October 30, 1992.

[126]Robert Pear, *NYT,* October 31, 1992.

[127]Fred Barnes, "Pardon Me," *The New Republic,* December 21, 1992, p. 11.

[128]Bush diaries, OGB.

[129]Fred Barnes, "Pardon Me," *The New Republic,* December 21, 1992, p. 11.

[130]Russ Hodge, "White Men Can't Jump," *New York,* November 30, 1992, p. 47.

[131]Thomas E. Dewey to Richard Nixon, November 2, 1992, provided to the author with the courtesy of Mr. Nixon, November 13, 1992.

[132]*TGP 1992,* p. 192.

[133]Bush, *Barbara Bush,* p. 497.

[134]Interview with Brian Mulroney, February 6, 1997.

[135]Everett Carll Ladd, "The 1992 Vote for President Clinton: Another Brittle Mandate?" *Political Science Quarterly,* Spring 1993, pp. 20–21.

[136]Howard Kurtz, *WP,* November 15, 1992; Elizabeth Kolbert, *NYT,* November 22, 1992.

[137]John Berry, *WP,* December 12, 1992.

[138]Howard Fineman, "The Torch Passes," *Newsweek,* November/December 1992, p. 6.

[139]Everett Carll Ladd, "The 1992 Vote for President Clinton: Another Brittle Mandate?" *Political Science Quarterly,* Spring 1993, pp. 1–28.

[140]Bush, *Barbara Bush,* pp. 502–3.

[141]Bush diaries, November 20, 1992, OGB.

[142]*Greenwich Time,* November 20, 1992.

[143]Interview with Colin Powell, April 17, 1995.

[144]Interview with Brian Mulroney, February 6, 1997.

[145]Bush diaries, November 20, 1992, OGB.

[146]Fred Barnes, "Last Call," *The New Republic,* December 28, 1992, p. 11; Stephen F. Burgess, "Operation Restore Hope: Somalia and Frontiers of the New World Order," paper presented at the George Bush Presidential Conference, Hofstra University, April 19, 1997.

[147]Ibid.

[148]Interview with Colin Powell, April 17, 1995.

[149]Michael Wines, *NYT,* December 6, 1992; Burgess, "Operation Restore Hope," paper presented at Hofstra University, April 19, 1997.

[150]Interview with Fred Barnes on National Public Radio, January 3, 1993.

[151]Interview with Colin Powell, April 17, 1995.

[152]Fred Barnes, "Pardon Them," *The New Republic,* January 18, 1993, p. 11.

[153]Michael Wines, *NYT,* January 16, 1993.

[154]Interview with Brian Mulroney, February 6, 1997.

[155]Bush diaries, January 20, 1997, OBG.

[156]Lydia Saad, "George and Barbara Back Again to 'Most Admired' Lists," *Gallup Poll Monthly,* December 1992, pp. 30–31; CNN, "Inside Politics," January 14, 1993; James A. Barnes, "Changing the Guard," *National Journal,* January 16, 1993, p. 141; *NYT*/CBS Survey, *NYT,* January 19, 1993.

Index